San Francisco
Bay Area
Restaurants
2008

LOCAL EDITOR
Meesha Halm
STAFF EDITOR
Randi Gollin

Published and distributed by
Zagat Survey, LLC
4 Columbus Circle
New York, NY 10019
T: 212.977.6000
E: sanfran@zagat.com
www.zagat.com

ACKNOWLEDGMENTS

We thank Jon, Olive and Jude
Fox, Amanda Berne and Steven
Shukow, as well as the following
members of our staff: Josh
Rogers (assistant editor),
Christina Livadiotis (editorial
assistant), Sean Beachell,
Maryanne Bertollo, Sandy Cheng,
Reni Chin, Larry Cohn, Bill
Corsello, Deirdre Donovan,
Alison Flick, Jeff Freier, Caroline
Hatchett, Roy Jacob, Natalie
Lebert, Mike Liao, Allison Lynn,
Dave Makulec, Andre Pilette,
Becky Ruthenburg, Carla Spartos,
Kilolo Strobert, Liz Borod Wright,
Sharon Yates and Kyle Zolner.

Contents

Ratings & Symbols

Zagat Top Spot	Name	Symbols	Cuisine	Zagat Ratings			
				FOOD	DECOR	SERVICE	COST

Area, Address & Contact

Ø **Tim & Nina's** ◐ *Seafood* ▽ 23 | 9 | 13 | $15

Embarcadero | 999 Mission St. (The Embarcadero) | 415-555-7233 | www.zagat.com

Review, surveyor comments in quotes

Open "more or less when they feel like it", this bit of un-embellished Embarcadero ectoplasm excels at seafood with Asian-Argentinean-Albanian accents; the staff seems "fresh off the boat", and while the view of the garbage barges is "a drag", no one balks at the bottom-feeder prices.

Ratings   **Food, Decor** and **Service** are rated on a scale of 0 to 30.

0	-	9	poor to fair
10	-	15	fair to good
16	-	19	good to very good
20	-	25	very good to excellent
26	-	30	extraordinary to perfection

▽   low response | less reliable

Cost reflects our surveyors' average estimate of the price of a dinner with one drink and tip and is a benchmark only. Lunch is usually 25% less.

For **newcomers** or survey **write-ins** listed without ratings, the price range is indicated as follows:

I $25 and below
M $26 to $40
E $41 to $65
VE $66 or more

Symbols

Ø   Zagat Top Spot (highest ratings, popularity and importance)
◐   serves after 11 PM
Ⓢ   closed on Sunday
Ⓜ   closed on Monday
⇗   no credit cards accepted

Maps   Index maps show restaurants with the highest Food ratings in those areas.

About This Survey

Here are the results of our **2008 San Francisco Bay Area Restaurants Survey,** covering 1,153 establishments in the greater San Francisco Bay Area, including Wine Country and Lake Tahoe. Like all our guides, it's based on the collective opinions of thousands of avid local consumers who have been there before you.

WHO PARTICIPATED: Input from 8,161 frequent diners forms the basis for the ratings and reviews in this guide (their comments are shown in quotation marks within the reviews). Of these surveyors, 47% are women, 53% men; the breakdown by age is 8% in their 20s; 26%, 30s; 20%, 40s; 22%, 50s; and 24%, 60s or above. Collectively they bring roughly 1.3 million annual meals worth of experience to this Survey. We sincerely thank each of these participants – this book is really "theirs."

HELPFUL LISTS: Whether you're looking for a celebratory meal, a hot scene or a bargain bite, our lists can help you find exactly the right place. See our overall lists – Key Newcomers (page 9), Most Popular (page 10), Top Ratings (pages 11–17), Best Buys (page 18) and Prix Fixe Bargains (page 19) – as well as the Top Ratings lists at the front of each section. We've also provided 44 handy indexes.

OUR EDITOR: Special thanks go to our longtime local editor, Meesha Halm, who is both a Bay Area restaurant critic and a cookbook author.

ABOUT ZAGAT: This marks our 28th year reporting on the shared experiences of consumers like you. What started in 1979 as a hobby involving 200 of our friends has come a long way. Today we have over 300,000 surveyors and now cover dining, entertaining, golf, hotels, movies, music, nightlife, resorts, shopping, spas, theater and tourist attractions worldwide.

SHARE YOUR OPINION: We invite you to join any of our upcoming surveys – just register at **zagat.com,** where you can rate and review establishments year-round. Each participant will receive a free copy of the resulting guide when published.

AVAILABILITY: Zagat guides are available in all major bookstores, by subscription at **zagat.com** and for use on a wide range of mobile devices via **Zagat To Go** or **zagat.mobi.**

FEEDBACK: There is always room for improvement, thus we invite your comments and suggestions about any aspect of our performance. Just contact us at sanfran@zagat.com.

New York, NY
September 21, 2007

Nina and Tim

Nina and Tim Zagat

What's New

Seasonal, local and organic ingredients are almost a given in this green-centric part of the country, but this year the Bay Area raised the bar even higher in terms of responsible eating practices. The City of San Francisco outlawed the restaurant use of non-biodegradable plastic foam take-out containers and began phasing out large markets' petroleum-based plastic shopping bags. And new and established restaurateurs took even more initiative to do the right thing.

 THE YEAR OF LIVING CONSCIOUSLY: Sustainable agriculture advocate Alice Waters created a literal watershed moment when she ceased selling bottled water at her Berkeley legend Chez Panisse due to environmental concerns about plastic bottles and the fuel spent transporting them. The historic oceanfront Cliff House became the first SF restaurant to go carbon neutral, partnering with a local environmental organization that uses the 1,000-tons-per-year of carbon dioxide emitted by Cliff House operations to help revive ecosystems. And Wolfgang Puck (who recently closed his Palo Alto branch of Spago) banished foie gras and factory-farmed animals from Postrio and his other kitchens. Expensive practices? Maybe, but 67% of our surveyors say they're willing to pay more for sustainably raised ingredients. That bodes well for eco-innovators like the newly sprouted Spruce, which plans to convert its used cooking oil into biodiesel, which will also fuel the trucks that deliver its farm-fresh larder.

FAST FOOD WITH FLAIR: Our respondents say they eat out or take out nearly 48% of their meals – and often those meals are downed on the fly or in casual quarters. But even when they turn to guilty-pleasure quick eats, a PC patina is a plus, as evidenced by the organic frankfurters served by newcomer Underdog and the fresh ingredients that top the pies at Gialina, an upscale pizzeria arrival. And though Downtown is still the most coveted zip code for fine dining, it will also soon be home to a herd of new patty purveyors dishing up fancy (and usually hormone-free) chopped beef: Best-O-Burger; Hubert Keller's luxe Burger Bar (an offshoot of his Vegas place known for its $65 Rossini Kobe Beef Burger laced with foie gras and Perigord truffles); and Custom Burger Lounge. North of SF, old-school burger joint Taylor's Automatic Refresher is slated to open a second branch in Napa's new Oxbow Public Market, while Thomas Keller, who turned his once-temporary bistro, ad hoc, into a permanent affair, continues to seek a venue for his Burgers and Half Bottles concept.

GRAZE AND GUZZLE: Chez Nous, the Mediterranean that unleashed the small-plates craze in 2000 and forever changed the dining habits of San Franciscans, closed in 2007 (SPQR, a Roman osteria from the A16 team, plans to open in the space this fall), but the trend lives on. An influx of new nibbling-and-tippling destinations (with the emphasis often on the latter) offers Californian riffs on the concept, including Spanish tapas bar Laïola; the

Italian- and European-inspired Bar Bambino, District, Nua and Rouge et Blanc; and San Fran interpretations of gastropubs like The Alembic and Salt House. With so many opportunities to imbibe, it's no wonder that 43% of surveyors say they'd rather sip wine by the glass than the bottle (39%) – a turnaround compared to just a few years ago.

EYES ON IZAKAYA: While newcomers like Perbacco and Le P'tit Laurent satisfy surveyors' passion for Italian and French fare, voted the two most popular cuisines, an uptick in izakayas – or Japanese-style taverns – points to a rising demand for options beyond sushi from the Land of the Rising Sun. Joining old-timer Oyaji are such stylish ingénues as Hime, Sudachi and Umami, all doling out small plates and sake drinks.

ALL TOGETHER NOW: Forty-eight percent of surveyors say they're happy to eat at the bar – if there's no other option. Enter the communal table, which increasingly serves as a refuge for the young and the reservationless. These oversized social networking hubs not only provide another alternative to bar seating, they also make it easy to break the ice while breaking bread with strangers. Hence they're becoming a de rigueur design element in new restaurants, as at Mexico DF, Pres a Vi, the Presidio Social Club and Terzo.

MONEY MATTERS: The cost of an average meal in SF rose 3.1% from last year to $37.08, a few bucks higher than the U.S. norm of $33.39. The city's 20 most expensive places averaged $103.25, up 5% from last year's $98.30.

BLOCK PARTY: Even though San Francisco spans just a modest seven square miles, several micro-neighborhoods are emerging, many poised to make an imprint on the culinary landscape starting in fall 2007. First up is Rincon Park along the Embarcadero waterfront, where restaurateur Pat Kuleto is readying two highly anticipated places: the fish house Water Bar and Epic Roasthouse, a bilevel steakhouse. Soon after, Mint Plaza, a newly constructed, European-style pedestrian piazza south of Market, is slated to welcome offshoots of Blue Bottle Café, Chez Papa and Sushi Groove. Over in Dogpatch, Piccino Café will be joined by a yet-to-be-named sibling of the Slow Club. Across town, the Fillmore Jazz Preservation District will shepherd in a slew of supper clubs including a new flagship venue for Yoshi's. And a reenergized Japantown will welcome O Izakaya Lounge, named after the legendary baseball star Sadaharu Oh, in the renovated Hotel Kabuki, as well as the American bistro Kabuki Kitchen, set to debut in conjunction with the new Sundance Cinema, which in turn is replacing the former Kabuki Theater.

San Francisco, CA
September 21, 2007

Meesha Halm

KEY NEWCOMERS

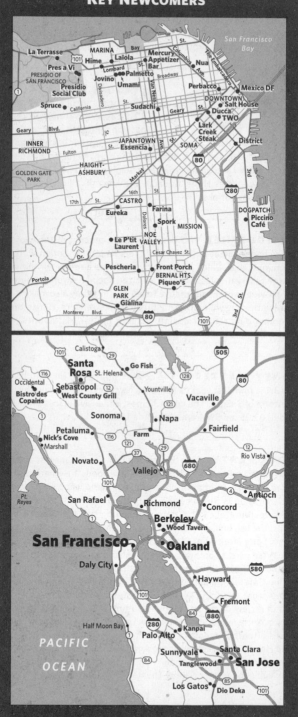

San Francisco Bay

La Terrasse

MARINA

Laïola

Hime

Mercury
Appetizer
Bar

Nua

Pres a Vi

PRESIDIO OF
SAN FRANCISCO

Palmetto

Lombard St.

Jovino

Presidio
Social Club

Umami

Broadway

Perbacco

Mexico DF

DOWNTOWN

Spruce

California St.

Sudachi

Geary St.

Salt House

Ducca

TWO

Lark
Creek
Steak

District

Geary Blvd.

INNER
RICHMOND

Fulton

JAPANTOWN

Essencia

SOMA

GOLDEN GATE
PARK

HAIGHT-
ASHBURY

16th St.

CASTRO

Farina

DOGPATCH

Piccino
Café

Eureka

Spork

Le P'tit
Laurent

NOE
VALLEY

MISSION

Cesar Chavez St.

Pescheria

Front Porch

Dr.

BERNAL HTS.

Piqueo's

Portola

GLEN
PARK

Gialina

Monterey Blvd.

Calistoga

Santa
Rosa

St. Helena

Go Fish

Occidental

Sebastopol

Bistro des
Copains

West County Grill

Yountville

Vacaville

Sonoma

Napa

Petaluma

Farm

Fairfield

Nick's Cove

Marshall

Novato

Rio Vista

Pt.
Reyes

Vallejo

San Rafael

Richmond

Concord

Antioch

Berkeley

Wood Tavern

San Francisco

Oakland

Daly City

Hayward

PACIFIC

Half Moon Bay

Kanpai

OCEAN

Palo Alto

Fremont

Sunnyvale

Santa Clara

Tanglewood

San Jose

Los Gatos

Dio Deka

Key Newcomers

Our take on the most notable new arrivals of the past year. For a full list, see the Noteworthy Newcomers index on page 295. Places outside of San Francisco are marked as: E=East of SF; N=North; and S=South. When a restaurant has locations both inside and out of the city limits, we include the notation SF as well.

Bistro des Copains	Mexico DF
Dio Deka/S	Nick's Cove/N
District	Nua Restaurant
Ducca	Palmetto
Essencia	Perbacco
Eureka Restaurant	Pescheria
Farina	Piccino Café
Farm/N	Piqueo's
Front Porch	Pres a Vi
Gialina	Presidio Social Club
Go Fish/N	Salt House
Hime	Spork
Jovino	Spruce
Kanpai/S	Sudachi
Laïola	Tanglewood/S
Lark Creek Steak	TWO
La Terrasse	Umami
Le P'tit Laurent	West County Grill/N
Mercury Appetizer Bar	Wood Tavern/E

Newcomers sprouted up in established neighborhoods – and once-overlooked areas – and more are on the way. Glen Park, which recently welcomed the pizzeria **Gialina** and French bistro **Le P'tit Laurent,** will soon be home to the Asian fusion ingénue **Sangha**; Lombard Street, a gritty Marina stretch that's in transition, became the stomping ground for hot spots like **Hime** and **Mercury Appetizer Bar** while The Presidio opened its doors to **Pres a Vi** and the **Presidio Social Club.** Later this fall, the restaurateurs behind Pizza Antica, **Spruce** and Village Pub will reopen **Brasserie Vache** in the former Prego space in Cow Hollow, *bien sûr*. And in the year ahead, Loretta Keller of Coco500 and Charles Phan of Slanted Door fame plan to open a new child-friendly restaurant/cafe with a healthy, multicultural bent in the new Academy of Sciences in SF's Golden Gate Park.

Most Popular

Each surveyor has been asked to name his or her five favorite places. This list shows their choices, as plotted on the map in the back of this book.

1. Gary Danko
2. Boulevard
3. Slanted Door
4. French Laundry/N
5. Michael Mina
6. Aqua
7. Delfina
8. Cyrus/N
9. Chez Panisse Café/E
10. Kokkari Estiatorio
11. Myth
12. Zuni Café
13. Farallon
14. Yank Sing
15. Jardinière
16. Chez Panisse/E
17. Quince
18. A 16
19. Fleur de Lys
20. Chapeau!
21. Bistro Jeanty/N
22. Bouchon/N
23. Rivoli/E
24. Manresa/S
25. Masa's
26. Evvia/S
27. Ame
28. Tamarine*/S
29. Ritz-Carlton Din. Rm.
30. Range
31. Chow/Park Chow/E/SF
32. Il Fornaio/E/N/S/SF
33. Tadich Grill*
34. Firefly
35. BIX
36. Piperade
37. Postrio
38. Redd Restaurant/N
39. Bay Wolf/E
40. La Folie
41. Acquerello
42. Auberge du Soleil*/N
43. Town Hall
44. Zachary's Pizza/E
45. Campton Place
46. Va de Vi/E
47. Buckeye Roadhse./N
48. Betelnut Pejiu Wu
49. Sushi Ran/N
50. Mustards Grill/N

It's obvious that many of the above restaurants are among the San Francisco Bay Area's most expensive, but if popularity were calibrated to price, we suspect that a number of other restaurants would join their ranks. Given the fact that both our surveyors and readers love to discover dining bargains, we have added a list of 80 Best Buys and restaurants offering prix fixe bargains on pages 18-19. These are restaurants that give real quality at extremely reasonable prices.

---

* Indicates a tie with restaurant above

Top Food Ratings Overall

Ratings are to the left of names. Lists exclude places with low votes.

__29__ Gary Danko
French Laundry/N

__28__ Cyrus/N
Erna's Elderberry/E
Fleur de Lys
Sushi Ran/N
Kaygetsu/S
Michael Mina

__27__ Chez Panisse/E
Le Papillon/S
Ritz-Carlton Din. Rm.
Manresa/S
Chez Panisse Café/E
La Folie
Acquerello
Chapeau!
Masa's
Rivoli/E
Boulevard
Farmhouse Inn/N

L'Auberge Carmel/S

__26__ Aqua
Quince
Tartine Bakery
Marinus/S
Sierra Mar/S
Redd Restaurant/N
ad hoc/N
House, The
Terra/N
Jardinière
Cafe La Haye/N
Marché/S
Navio/S
Delfina
La Toque*/N
Ame
Mirepoix/N
Frascati
Range

BY CUISINE

AMERICAN (NEW)

__29__ Gary Danko
French Laundry/N
__28__ Michael Mina
__27__ Manresa/S
Boulevard

AMERICAN (TRAD.)

__26__ ad hoc/N
__25__ Mama's Wash. Sq.
__23__ Lark Creek Inn/N
BIX
__22__ Maverick

ASIAN FUSION

__26__ House, The
__24__ Silks
Bushi-tei
__23__ SUMI
Eos Rest./Wine Bar

BAKERIES

__26__ Tartine Bakery
__25__ Gayle's Bakery/S
__24__ Downtown Bakery/N
__22__ Alexis Baking Co./N
Boulange/N/SF

BARBECUE

__23__ Bo's Barbecue/E
Buckeye Roadhse./N
__20__ Memphis Minnie's
Q
Everett & Jones/E

CAJUN/CREOLE/SOUL

__22__ Chenery Park
Kate's Kitchen
__20__ Everett & Jones/E
__19__ PJ's Oyster Bed
Elite Cafe

CALIFORNIAN

__28__ Erna's Elderberry/E
__27__ Chez Panisse/E
Farmhouse Inn/N
L'Auberge Carmel/S
__26__ Jardinière

CHINESE

__26__ O'mei/S
__25__ Yank Sing
Ton Kiang
__24__ Tommy Toy's
__23__ Koi Palace/S

CONTINENTAL

24 Fresh Cream/S
23 Anton & Michel/S
22 Bella Vista/S
21 Ecco/S
   Maddalena's/S

DIM SUM

25 Yank Sing
   Ton Kiang
23 Koi Palace/S
22 Great Eastern
   Good Luck Dim Sum

ECLECTIC

26 Sierra Mar/S
25 Willow Wood Mkt./N
   Firefly
24 Willi's Wine Bar/N
   Va de Vi/E

FRENCH

27 La Folie
26 La Toque/N
   Cafe Jacqueline
25 Madrona Manor/N
   Auberge du Soleil/N

FRENCH (BISTRO)

27 Chapeau!
26 Mirepoix/N
25 Syrah/N
   Jojo/E
   Bistro Jeanty/N

FRENCH (NEW)

28 Cyrus/N
   Fleur de Lys
27 Le Papillon/S
   Ritz-Carlton Din. Rm.
   Masa's

HAMBURGERS

24 Joe's Cable Car
22 In-N-Out Burger/E/N/S/SF
21 Taylor's Automatic/N/SF
20 Mo's
19 Balboa Cafe

INDIAN

25 Amber India/S
24 Ajanta/E
23 Vik's Chaat Corner/E
   Roti Indian Bistro/S/SF
   Indian Oven

ITALIAN

27 Acquerello
26 Quince
   Delfina
25 Dopo/E
   Oliveto Restaurant/E

JAPANESE

28 Sushi Ran/N
   Kaygetsu/S
26 Zushi Puzzle
25 Hana Japanese/N
   Kirala/E

KOREAN

23 San Tung
22 Brother's Korean
21 Koryo BBQ/E
20 My Tofu House

LATIN AMERICAN

24 Fonda Solana/E
22 Limón
   Destino
   Fresca
21 El Raigon

MED./GREEK

27 Chez Panisse/E
   Chez Panisse Café/E
   Rivoli/E
26 Frascati
   Evvia/S

MEXICAN

24 Tamarindo Antojeria/E
   La Taqueria/S/SF
   Doña Tomás/E
22 Tacubaya/E
   Mamacita

MIDDLE EASTERN

23 Truly Mediterranean
   Dish Dash/S
22 Kabul Afghan/S
20 A La Turca
   Yumma's

PIZZA

25 Little Star Pizza
   Pizzeria Picco/N
   Tommaso's
   Pizzetta 211
24 Pizzeria Delfina

SEAFOOD

- **26** Aqua
- Swan Oyster Depot
- **25** Passionfish/S
- Hog Island Oyster
- Bar Crudo

SPANISH/BASQUE

- **25** Piperade
- **24** Fringale
- Zuzu/N
- **22** Bocadillos
- Zarzuela

STEAKHOUSES

- **25** Alexander's Steak/S
- Cole's Chop House/N
- Harris'
- **24** House of Prime Rib
- Ruth's Chris Steak

TAPAS (LATIN)

- **24** Zuzu/N
- **22** Bocadillos

- Zarzuela
- César/E
- **21** Iberia/S

THAI

- **24** Thep Phanom Thai
- **23** Manora's Thai
- Krung Thai/S
- Soi Four/E
- Khan Toke

VEGETARIAN

- **24** Greens
- Millennium
- Cha-Ya Vegetarian/E/SF
- **20** Udupi Palace/E/S
- **19** Café Gratitude/E/N/SF

VIETNAMESE

- **26** Tamarine/S
- Slanted Door
- **24** Pho 84/E
- Thanh Long
- **23** Crustacean

BY SPECIAL FEATURE

BREAKFAST

- **25** Campton Place
- Mama's Wash. Sq.
- Dottie's True Blue
- **22** La Note/E
- Zazie

BRUNCH

- **26** Navio/S
- **25** Zuni Café
- **24** Ritz-Carlton Terrace
- Greens
- **23** Universal Cafe

CHILD-FRIENDLY

- **24** Zachary's Pizza
- **21** Picante Cocina/E
- Taylor's Automatic/N/SF
- **18** Rigolo
- **16** Pasta Pomodoro/E/S/SF

HOTEL DINING

- **28** Cyrus/N
- (Les Mars Hotel)
- Erna's Elderberry/E
- (Château du Sureau)
- Michael Mina
- (Westin St. Francis)

- **27** Ritz-Carlton Din. Rm.
- Masa's
- (Hotel Vintage Ct.)

NEWCOMERS (RATED)

- **24** Perbacco
- **23** Farm/N
- **22** Hime
- Lark Creek Steak

OPEN LATE

- **25** Zuni Café
- Bouchon/N
- **24** Fonda Solana/E
- **23** NoPa
- **22** Scala's Bistro

PEOPLE-WATCHING

- **27** Boulevard
- **26** Jardinière
- Myth
- **25** Zuni Café
- **23** Town Hall

SMALL PLATES

- **26** Tamarine/S
- **25** rnm restaurant
- **24** Willi's Wine Bar/N
- À Côté/E
- Va de Vi/E

TASTING MENUS

29	Gary Danko
	French Laundry/N
28	Cyrus/N
	Michael Mina
27	Ritz-Carlton Din. Rm.

TRENDY

26	Tamarine/S
23	NoPa
21	Salt House
20	Frisson
	Sino/S

WINE BARS

23	A 16
	Eos Rest./Wine Bar
22	bacar
	Cav Wine Bar
20	Ottimista Enoteca

WINNING WINE LISTS

29	Gary Danko
28	Michael Mina
26	Terra/N
24	Rubicon
22	bacar

WORTH A TRIP

29	French Laundry/N
	Yountville
28	Cyrus/N
	Healdsburg
	Kaygetsu/S
	Menlo Park
27	Chez Panisse/E
	Berkeley
	Manresa/S
	Los Gatos

Top Decor Ratings Overall

Ratings are to the left of names.

__28]__ Pacific's Edge/S
Ahwahnee Din. Rm./E
Garden Court

__27]__ Shadowbrook/S
Navio/S
Farm/N
Cyrus/N
Marinus/S
Sierra Mar/S
Farallon
Fleur de Lys
Madrona Manor/N
Auberge du Soleil/N

__26]__ Gary Danko
French Laundry/N
Ana Mandara
Ritz-Carlton Din. Rm.
Erna's Elderberry/E
BIX
Postino/E

Étoile/N
Jardinière

__25]__ Carnelian Room
Coi
John Ash & Co./N
El Paseo/N
Press/N
Lark Creek Inn/N
Aqua
Ame
Martini House/N
Big 4
Silks
Myth
Wente Vineyards/E
Boulevard
Sutro's at Cliff Hse.
Roy's/S
Kokkari Estiatorio
Sunnyside Resort/E

OUTDOORS

Angèle/N
Anton & Michel/S
Auberge du Soleil/N
B44
Bistro Aix
Chez Spencer
Doña Tomás/E
Ducca
Foreign Cinema
Isa
MarketBar

Martini House/N
Medjool
Park Chalet Garden
Pres a Vi
Ritz-Carlton Terrace
Sam's Chowder Hse./S
Sociale
Townhouse B&G/E
Va de Vi/E
Wente Vineyards/E
Zazie

ROMANCE

Aziza
Bistro Elan/S
Cafe Beaujolais/N
Cafe Jacqueline
Chez Spencer
Chez TJ/S
Coi
El Paseo/N
Farmhouse Inn/N
Fleur de Lys
Jardinière

La Forêt/S
Lalime's/E
Les Amis
Madrona Manor/N
Michael Mina
Pianeta/E
Ritz-Carlton Din. Rm.
Sierra Mar/S
supperclub
Venticello
Woodward's Garden

ROOMS

Adagia/E
Ahwahnee Din. Rm./E
Ana Mandara
Big Four
Boulevard
Ducca
Farallon
Farina
Fleur de Lys
Frisson
Garden Court
Grand Cafe
Jardinière
Kokkari Estiatorio
Martini House/N
Michael Mina
Nick's Cove/N
Pearl Oyster Bar/E
Sino/S
Sutro's at Cliff Hse.
Umami
West County Grill/N

VIEWS

Ahwahnee Din. Rm./E
Albion River Inn/N
Auberge du Soleil/N
Beach Chalet
Bella Vista/S
Carnelian Room
Christy Hill/E
Étoile/N
Greens
Guaymas/N
Julius Castle
Navio/S
Nepenthe/S
Pacific's Edge/S
Roy's/S
Salute/E
Shadowbrook/S
Sierra Mar/S
Slanted Door
Sutro's at Cliff Hse.
Waterfront Restaurant
Wolfdale's/E

Top Service Ratings Overall

Ratings are to the left of names.

__28__ Erna's Elderberry/E
Cyrus/N
Gary Danko
French Laundry/N
Ritz-Carlton Din. Rm.

__27__ Marinus/S
Acquerello
Le Papillon/S
Michael Mina

__26__ Navio/S
Masa's
Fleur de Lys
Campton Place
Chez Panisse/E
Chapeau!
La Toque/N
La Folie
Sierra Mar/S
Albona Rist.
Silks

Mirepoix/N

__25__ Manresa/S
Chez TJ/S
Ritz-Carlton Terrace
Rivoli/E
Quince
Farmhouse Inn/N
Boulevard
Coi
Marché/S
Auberge du Soleil/N
Ame
Seasons
L'Auberge Carmel/S
Fifth Floor
Madrona Manor/N
Étoile/N
Aqua
Terra/N
Chez Panisse Café/E

Best Buys Overall

In order of Bang for the Buck rating.

1. In-N-Out Burger/E/N/S/SF
2. Saigon Sandwiches
3. Caspers Hot Dogs/E
4. Rosamunde Grill
5. Arinell Pizza/E/SF
6. Gioia Pizzeria/E
7. Taqueria Can-Cun
8. Papalote Mexican
9. Truly Mediterranean
10. Yumma's
11. La Cumbre Taqueria/S/SF
12. El Balazo
13. Cactus Taqueria/E
14. Mixt Greens
15. La Taqueria/S/SF
16. Taqueria 3 Amigos/S
17. Downtown Bakery/N
18. Kate's Kitchen
19. Good Luck Dim Sum
20. Burger Joint/S/SF
21. Pancho Villa/S/SF
22. Jay's Cheesesteak
23. Tartine Bakery
24. Boulange/N/SF
25. Nick's Crispy Tacos
26. Pluto's Fresh Food
27. Mama's Royal Cafe/E
28. Tacubaya/E
29. Picante Cocina/E
30. Gayle's Bakery/S
31. Vik's Chaat Corner/E
32. Pork Store Café
33. Dottie's True Blue
34. Fentons Creamery/E
35. Boogaloos
36. Sol Food/N
37. Chloe's Cafe
38. Bette's Oceanview/E
39. Joe's Cable Car
40. King of Thai

OTHER GOOD VALUES

Alembic, The
Asqew Grill/E/S/SF
Bar Bambino
Boonfly Café/N
Bovolo/N
B Star Bar
Burma Superstar
Chapeau!
Cha-Ya Vegetarian/E/SF
Chow/Park Chow/E/SF
Cindy's Backstreet/N
Dopo/E
fig cafe & winebar/N
Firefly
Flying Fish Grill/S
Frjtz Fries
Front Porch
Gator's Neo-Soul/S
Gialina
Goood Frikin' Chicken
Jovino
Le Charm Bistro
Le Cheval/E
Little Star Pizza
Market/N
Oliveto Cafe/E
Osha Thai Noodles
Out the Door
Passionfish/S
Pauline's Pizza
Piccino Café
Pizzaiolo/E
Pizzeria Delfina
Spork
Tajine
Tamarindo Antojeria/E
Underdog Hot Dog
Willi's Wine Bar/N
Wood Tavern/E
Xyclo/E

PRIX FIXE BARGAINS

DINNER ($30 & UNDER)

Ajanta/E	15.50	Kitchen 868 Grant/N	29.00
Alamo Square	14.50	Lark Creek/E	27.95
Axum Cafe	14.00	Lark Creek Steak	29.00
Baker St. Bistro	14.50	Le Charm Bistro	30.00
Basque Cultural Ctr./S	18.95	Ledford House/N	25.00
Bistro des Copains/N	30.00	Manzanita/N	25.00
Bistro Liaison/E	30.00	Mecca	30.00
Bodega Bistro	20.00	Mezze/E	28.00
Boonville Hotel/N	30.00	Moosse Café/N	20.00
Bovolo/N	27.00	One Market	29.00
Bridges/E	25.00	Passage to India/S	13.95
Cafe Gibraltar/S	20.00	rnm restaurant	28.00
Caffe Delle Stelle	25.95	Sanraku	19.00
Chez Panisse Café/E	28.00	Sonoma Meritage/N	24.00
Christophe/N	24.00	Stokes/S	29.00
Côté Sud	27.50	SUMI	30.00
Cuvée/N	30.00	Tao Cafe	16.50
1550 Hyde Café	29.95	Town's End	15.95
Gayle's Bakery/S	12.50	Tratt. La Siciliana/E	25.00
girl & the fig/N	30.00	Yankee Pier/N	19.95
Hayes St. Grill	29.00	Zazie	21.50
K&L Bistro/N	23.95		

LUNCH ($25 & UNDER)

Ajanta/E	11.50	Lark Creek/E	17.95
Alfred's Steakhouse	21.95	Lark Creek Inn/N	21.00
Ana Mandara	21.95	Lark Creek Steak	19.00
Anjou	16.00	Les Amis	25.00
bacar	21.95	Manzanita/N	16.00
B44	21.95	Market/N	17.95
Bistro Liaison/E	15.95	Maya	20.00
BIX	21.95	Oak City B&G/S	12.00
Brother's Korean	7.95	Pakwan/E	10.99
Café Marcella/S	21.00	Passage to India/S	10.95
Chez Panisse Café/E	24.00	Piperade	25.00
Citron/E	15.00	Rubicon	25.00
Destino	21.95	Sanraku	9.95
Ephesus Kebab/E	18.95	Scoma's	21.95
Espetus Churrascaria	18.95	Shanghai 1930	15.95
Hunan Home/Garden	5.00	Straits Cafe/S	20.00
Hurley's/N	17.00	231 Ellsworth/S	20.00
Junnoon/S	18.00	Vik's Chaat Corner/E	6.50
K&L Bistro/N	23.95	Yankee Pier/N	11.95

CITY OF SAN FRANCISCO

Top Food Ratings

Ratings are to the left of names. Lists exclude places with low votes.

29 Gary Danko	Ame
28 Fleur de Lys	Frascati
Michael Mina	Range
	Zushi Puzzle
27 Ritz-Carlton Din. Rm.	Cafe Jacqueline
La Folie	Slanted Door
Acquerello	Myth
Chapeau!	Swan Oyster Depot
Masa's	Kokkari Estiatorio
Boulevard	
	25 Coi
26 Aqua	Kabuto
Quince	Campton Place
Tartine Bakery	Yank Sing
House, The	Canteen
Jardinière	Zuni Café
Delfina	

BY CUISINE

AMERICAN (NEW)

29 Gary Danko
28 Michael Mina
27 Boulevard
26 Ame
Range

AMERICAN (TRAD.)

25 Mama's Wash. Sq.
23 BIX
22 Maverick
Liberty Cafe
21 Chloe's Cafe

ASIAN FUSION

26 House, The
24 Silks
Bushi-tei
23 SUMI
Eos Rest./Wine Bar

BAKERIES

26 Tartine Bakery
25 Mama's Wash. Sq.
22 Liberty Cafe
Boulange
20 Citizen Cake

CALIFORNIAN

26 Jardinière
25 Coi
Canteen
Woodward's Garden
24 Rubicon

CHINESE

25 Yank Sing
Ton Kiang
24 Tommy Toy's
23 San Tung
R & G Lounge

FRENCH

27 La Folie
26 Cafe Jacqueline
24 Chez Spencer
Isa
22 Boulange

FRENCH (BISTRO)

27 Chapeau!
24 Fringale
Clémentine
23 Chez Papa Bistrot
Jeanty at Jack's

FRENCH (NEW)

28 Fleur de Lys
27 Ritz-Carlton Din. Rm.
Masa's
25 Fifth Floor
22 Les Amis

HAMBURGERS

24 Joe's Cable Car
22 In-N-Out Burger
21 Taylor's Automatic
20 Mo's
19 Balboa Cafe

subscribe to zagat.com

INDIAN/PAKISTANI

23 Roti Indian Bistro
   Indian Oven
22 Shalimar
21 Pakwan
20 Dosa

ITALIAN

27 Acquerello
26 Quince
   Delfina
25 Tommaso's
24 Albona Rist.

JAPANESE

26 Zushi Puzzle
25 Kabuto
24 Bushi-tei
   Koo
   Ozumo

LATIN AMERICAN

22 Limón
   Destino
   Fresca
21 El Raigon
   Espetus Churrascaria

MED./GREEK

26 Frascati
   Kokkari Estiatorio
25 Zuni Café
24 Ritz-Carlton Terrace
   PlumpJack Cafe

MEXICAN

24 La Taqueria
22 Mamacita
   La Cumbre Taqueria
   Maya
21 Taqueria Can-Cun

MIDDLE EASTERN

23 Truly Mediterranean
20 A La Turca
   Yumma's
19 Goood Frikin' Chicken
   La Méditerranée

NOODLES

23 San Tung
22 Osha Thai Noodles
20 Citizen Thai
19 Citrus Club
18 Mifune

PIZZA

25 Little Star Pizza
   Tommaso's
   Pizzetta 211
24 Pizzeria Delfina
   Postrio

SEAFOOD

26 Aqua
   Swan Oyster Depot
25 Hog Island Oyster
   Bar Crudo
24 Farallon

SPANISH/BASQUE

25 Piperade
24 Fringale
22 Bocadillos
   Zarzuela
21 B44

STEAKHOUSES

25 Harris'
24 House of Prime Rib
   Ruth's Chris Steak
   Seasons
23 Morton's

TAPAS (LATIN)

22 Bocadillos
   Zarzuela
21 Esperpento
20 Ramblas
   Alegrias

VIETNAMESE

26 Slanted Door
24 Thanh Long
23 Crustacean
   Three Seasons
   Ana Mandara

BY SPECIAL FEATURE

BREAKFAST

25 Campton Place
   Mama's Wash. Sq.
   Boulette's Larder
   Dottie's True Blue
22 Zazie

BRUNCH

25 Canteen
24 Ritz-Carlton Terrace
   Greens
23 Universal Cafe
22 Liberty Cafe

CHILD-FRIENDLY

- 21 Taylor's Automatic
- 18 Asqew Grill
  - Rigolo
- 16 Pasta Pomodoro
- 13 Mel's Drive-In

NEWCOMERS (RATED)

- 24 Perbacco
- 22 Hime
  - Lark Creek Steak
- 21 Pescheria
  - Pres a Vi

OPEN LATE

- 25 Zuni Café
- 23 NoPa
- 22 Scala's Bistro
- 21 Globe
- 20 Absinthe

OUTDOOR SEATING

- 24 Chez Spencer
  - Isa
- 23 Blue Plate
  - Sociale
- 21 Foreign Cinema

PEOPLE-WATCHING

- 27 Boulevard
- 26 Jardinière
  - Myth
- 25 Zuni Café
- 23 BIX

POWER SCENES

- 26 Aqua
  - Jardinière

- 24 Rubicon
- 23 Jeanty at Jack's
- 22 One Market

ROMANCE

- 28 Fleur de Lys
- 26 Cafe Jacqueline
- 24 Chez Spencer
- 23 Venticello
- 22 Les Amis

SMALL PLATES

- 25 rnm restaurant
- 24 Isa
- 23 Eos Rest./Wine Bar
  - Cortez
  - Betelnut Pejiu Wu

TASTING MENUS

- 29 Gary Danko
- 28 Michael Mina
- 27 Ritz-Carlton Din. Rm.
  - La Folie
  - Masa's

TRENDY

- 23 NoPa
- 22 Poleng Lounge
  - Coco 500
  - Hime
- 21 Salt House

WINNING WINE LISTS

- 29 Gary Danko
- 28 Michael Mina
- 27 Acquerello
- 24 Rubicon
- 22 bacar

BY LOCATION

CASTRO/NOE VALLEY

- 25 Firefly
- 24 Incanto
- 23 SUMI
  - Anchor Oyster Bar
  - Rist. Bacco

CHINATOWN

- 23 R & G Lounge
- 22 Great Eastern
  - Hunan Home
  - Oriental Pearl
- 21 House of Nanking

COW HOLLOW/MARINA

- 26 Zushi Puzzle
- 24 Isa

- Greens
- PlumpJack Cafe
- 23 A 16

DOWNTOWN

- 28 Michael Mina
- 27 Masa's
- 26 Aqua
  - Myth
  - Kokkari Estiatorio

EMBARCADERO

- 27 Boulevard
- 26 Slanted Door
- 25 Boulette's Larder
  - Hog Island Oyster
- 24 Ozumo

FISHERMAN'S WHARF

- 29 Gary Danko
- 23 Grandeho Kamekyo
  - Ana Mandara
- 22 In-N-Out Burger
- 21 Scoma's

HAIGHT-ASHBURY/ COLE VALLEY

- 23 Eos Rest./Wine Bar
  - Grandeho Kamekyo
- 22 Boulange
  - Zazie
- 21 Pork Store Café

HAYES VALLEY

- 26 Jardinière
- 25 Zuni Café
- 22 Hayes St. Grill
  - Cav Wine Bar
- 21 paul k

LOWER HAIGHT

- 25 rnm restaurant
  - Rosamunde Grill
- 24 Thep Phanom Thai
- 23 Indian Oven
- 22 Kate's Kitchen

MISSION

- 26 Tartine Bakery
  - Delfina
  - Range
- 25 Little Star Pizza
  - Woodward's Garden

NOB HILL/RUSSIAN HILL

- 28 Fleur de Lys
- 27 Ritz-Carlton Din. Rm.
  - La Folie
- 26 Frascati
- 24 Ritz-Carlton Terrace

NORTH BEACH

- 26 House, The
  - Cafe Jacqueline
- 25 Coi
  - Mama's Wash. Sq.
  - Tommaso's

PACIFIC HEIGHTS/ JAPANTOWN

- 26 Quince
- 24 Bushi-tei
- 23 Maki
  - Vivande Porta Via
  - CAFÉ KATi

RICHMOND

- 27 Chapeau!
- 25 Kabuto
  - Pizzetta 211
  - Ton Kiang
- 24 Aziza

SOMA

- 26 Ame
- 25 Yank Sing
  - Fifth Floor
- 24 Fringale
- 23 Manora's Thai

SUNSET/W. PORTAL

- 24 Koo
  - Thanh Long
- 23 San Tung
  - Roti Indian Bistro
  - Ebisu

Top Decor Ratings

Ratings are to the left of names.

<u>28</u> Garden Court

<u>27</u> Farallon
     Fleur de Lys

<u>26</u> Gary Danko
     Ana Mandara
     Ritz-Carlton Din. Rm.
     BIX
     Jardinière

<u>25</u> Carnelian Room
     Coi

Aqua
Ame
Big 4
Silks
Myth
Boulevard
Sutro's at Cliff Hse.
Kokkari Estiatorio
Frisson
Grand Cafe

Top Service Ratings

Ratings are to the left of names.

<u>28</u> Gary Danko
     Ritz-Carlton Din. Rm.

<u>27</u> Acquerello
     Michael Mina

<u>26</u> Masa's
     Fleur de Lys
     Campton Place
     Chapeau!
     La Folie
     Albona Rist.

Silks

<u>25</u> Ritz-Carlton Terrace
     Quince
     Boulevard
     Coi
     Ame
     Seasons
     Fifth Floor
     Aqua
     Jardinière

Best Buys

In order of Bang for the Buck rating.

1. In-N-Out Burger
2. Saigon Sandwiches
3. Rosamunde Grill
4. Arinell Pizza
5. Taqueria Can-Cun
6. Papalote Mexican
7. Truly Mediterranean
8. Yumma's
9. La Cumbre Taqueria
10. El Balazo
11. Mixt Greens
12. La Taqueria
13. Kate's Kitchen
14. Good Luck Dim Sum
15. Burger Joint
16. Pancho Villa
17. Jay's Cheesesteak
18. Tartine Bakery
19. Boulange
20. Nick's Crispy Tacos

OTHER GOOD VALUES

A La Turca
Bar Bambino
B Star Bar
Burma Superstar
Front Porch
Gialina
Goood Frikin' Chicken
Osha Thai Noodles
Out the Door
Pacific Catch
Shanghai Dumpling
Tajine
Underdog Hot Dog
Zadin

City of San Francisco

	FOOD	DECOR	SERVICE	COST

Absinthe ⬤Ⓜ *French/Mediterranean* | 20 | 22 | 20 | $44 |
Hayes Valley | 398 Hayes St. (Gough St.) | 415-551-1590 |
www.absinthe.com

Few places "so aptly capture" the feel of a "cool Parisian-type hang" like this *"très jolie"* "Francophile's dream" of a French-Med brasserie with a "Toulouse-Lautrec flair" on a Hayes Valley corner; early-risers insist the "hearty brunch" is the "highlight", while culture vultures coo it's "perfect" pre-symphony or for a "late-night bite and quaff" (try the "fabulous cocktails" or the "legal version of absinthe"); N.B. ex Levende chef Jamie Lauren is now at the reins, which may impact the Food score.

Ace Wasabi's *Japanese* | 20 | 14 | 16 | $33 |
Marina | 3339 Steiner St. (bet. Chestnut & Lombard Sts.) | 415-567-4903

It may be more "pickup joint than sushi bar", nonetheless this "crazy loud" "rock 'n' roll" Japanese hangout, the "Marina sister to the Mission's Tokyo Go Go" serves up "inventive" fin fare that's "better than you'd expect"; it's "still an 'Ace' among" the "fraternity boy crowds" who "kick off the night" with bingo, "scope out" the "hot waitresses", suck down sake bombs and "scream over their California rolls" – in fact, "go with caution if you're over 35."

Acme Chophouse Ⓜ *Steak* | 19 | 19 | 18 | $48 |
South Beach | AT&T Park | 24 Willie Mays Plaza (bet. King & 3rd Sts.) | 415-644-0240 | www.acmechophouse.com

Traci Des Jardins' "strategically located", "solid" chophouse boasting "top-quality ingredients", a "clubby atmosphere", "manly drinks" and a "crazy" "pre-game party" scene may be your "best bet" on the AT&T Park grounds for a "gourmet meal"; but while fans go to bat for the "tender, tasty" grass-fed beef and "primo side dishes" (a "must"), it runs afoul for critics who feel it "doesn't wow", citing "inattentive service" and "high prices"; P.S. "unless you like it super noisy, go when the Giants are out of town."

Ⓩ Acquerello ⓈⓂ *Italian* | 27 | 24 | 27 | $74 |
Polk Gulch | 1722 Sacramento St. (bet. Polk St. & Van Ness Ave.) | 415-567-5432 | www.acquerello.com

One of SF's "rare quiet", "formal" Italian restaurants with "old-world sophistication", this "intimate" Polk Gulch "foodie delight" ("no noisy young 'uns here") set in a converted church is "the absolutely perfect setting" for a "fantastic celebratory experience"; "raid your piggy bank", order the chef's "sublime" wine-inclusive tasting menu ("each table gets their own decanter") and "ride it all the way", letting the "remarkable staff cater to your every need"; N.B. a recent remodel may not be reflected in the Decor score.

Alamo Square *French/Seafood* | 21 | 16 | 18 | $30 |
Western Addition | 803 Fillmore St. (Grove St.) | 415-440-2828 |
www.alamosquareseafoodgrill.com

"If you get the right combo, it can be magic" – yes, seafood lovers always remember the Alamo, a "darling little" "romantic" French bistro in the Western Addition noted for its "straightforward" "fresh" fish, "prepared in one of three ways, with a choice of sauces" ("perfect for the 'Sally' in the crowd") and "wonderful" vin de pays; the "no corkage on Wednesdays is a steal", plus there's a nightly $14.50 prix fixe menu and free parking to boot.

A La Turca *Turkish*   20 | 8 | 18 | $19

Tenderloin | 869 Geary St. (Larkin St.) | 415-345-1011 | www.alaturcasf.com
"No one else in the city comes this close to the real thing" avow well-traveled diners who "make a beeline" for "satisfying" lamb kebabs, meat pies and other "tasty" Istanbul vittles executed "a lot better than your standard gyro joint" at this "friendly" "cheap eats" outpost in the Tenderloin; it's as "authentic" as it gets, from the "bare-bones" "diner setting" "down to the Turkish soccer on the TV."

Albona Ristorante Istriano ⑤Ⓜ *Italian*   24 | 17 | 26 | $43

North Beach | 545 Francisco St. (bet. Mason & Taylor Sts.) | 415-441-1040 | www.albonarestaurant.com
With its "seriously inconspicuous" side-street entrance and "congenial host" Bruno Viscovi who "seduces you into loving" his "interesting", "reasonably priced" Venetian fare – and who's "always one second away from joining you at your table" – this "cozy", "old-world charmer" in North Beach is unlike anything "you've ever experienced before"; the "Austrian-Hungarian edge" appeals to the jaded "anti-Tuscan" crowd, still, the "slightly somber" digs may not be for those "looking for a lively, trendy" spot; N.B. free valet parking.

Alegrias, Food From Spain *Spanish*   20 | 16 | 17 | $33

Marina | 2018 Lombard St. (Webster St.) | 415-929-8888
"One of those 'go-to' places" "that could be in Madrid", this "undiscovered" Spaniard on Lombard Street serves up "very authentic", "tasty" tapas and paella with a "caring attitude"; if the less-impressed shrug that the fare is "not particularly inspiring" and feel the "nondescript" digs "lack atmosphere", defenders retort it's "not chichi, but it's a lot quieter than most of the hot spots" and "their sangria is tough to beat"; N.B. closed Tuesdays.

ⓃⒺⓌ Alembic, The ❶ *Eclectic*   ▽ 22 | 21 | 21 | $28

Haight-Ashbury | 1725 Haight St. (bet. Cole & Shrader Sts.) | 415-666-0822 | www.alembicbar.com
For a "perfect date", catch a "movie at the Red Vic" then pop into this "wonderful" gastropub, an "oasis" with an "old-time feel" that's "tiny" and "crowded" enough to make you "feel special about getting a table", yet "doesn't attract the usual Haight Street kids"; the "limited" Eclectic small-plates menu of "original treats" shows "imagination", but for most the "main attractions" are the "classic cocktails", artisanal spirits ("unique bourbons and whiskeys") and the "super beer selection from sister brewpub Magnolia."

Alfred's Steakhouse *Steak*   21 | 18 | 20 | $48

Downtown | 659 Merchant St. (bet. Kearny & Montgomery Sts.) | 415-781-7058 | www.alfredssteakhouse.com
"About as old-fashioned as any restaurant left", this Downtown "Rat Pack"–era "classic San Francisco steakhouse" with its "plush" "red velvet" "bordello ambiance", "perfect martinis" and "tuxedoed waiters" can still "run with all the big boys without the price tag"; the "excellent hunks of beef" are "beautifully aged and reasonably priced – and you

FOOD DECOR SERVICE COST

don't have to look at mummified samples and listen" to descriptions delivered by "rote before ordering one"; still, others scoff it's "tired", adding the "Caesar salad is no longer prepared tableside."

Alice's *Chinese*
19 | 14 | 17 | $19

Noe Valley | 1599 Sanchez St. (29th St.) | 415-282-8999
"In a town not lacking for Chinese food", this "go-to" Noe Valley haunt hawking "wonderful, healthy" "economical" Sino fare "with a California spin" "performs equally well" as its "copycat" "competition" "without the wait and the noise"; despite its "pretty interior" decorated with "lovely hand-blown glass" and "beautiful orchids", regulars just as often opt for takeout, noting if they delivered, Alice's owners "would take over all" of the neighborhood.

Alioto's *Italian*
19 | 17 | 18 | $40

Fisherman's Wharf | 8 Fisherman's Wharf (Taylor St.) | 415-673-0183 | www.aliotos.com
When it comes to "amazing out-of-town guests", "you can't beat" the dockside location of this Fisherman's Wharf "tourist trap" overlooking "remnants of the fishing fleet and the Golden Gate"; diehards adore the "excellent chowder" served in a sourdough bowl and "savory" Sicilian seafood specialties like cioppino; still, nitpickers pout it's "worn out" and "coasting on its famous name" so just "take your picture and skedaddle."

☑ Ame *American*
26 | 25 | 25 | $69

SoMa | St. Regis Hotel | 689 Mission St. (3rd St.) | 415-284-4040 | www.amerestaurant.com
"Hiro is my hero!" exclaim "real foodies" who "feel fortunate to sample" "genius" chef Sone's wildly "unexpected", "sublime" "exotic" New American creations "with subtle Asian and Euro accents" at Terra's "serene", "sophisticated" "big-city" SoMa outpost, a "real looker" set in the "luxe" St. Regis Hotel; the "tasting menu truly showcases his talents and the wine pairings are not to be missed", plus the "sake sommelier is invaluable"; P.S. for a "refreshing" change try the "adventurous" crudo at the custom-made marble sushi bar.

Americano *Californian*
17 | 22 | 18 | $41

Embarcadero | Hotel Vitale | 8 Mission St. (The Embarcadero) | 415-278-3777 | www.americanorestaurant.com
Located in the "chic boutique Hotel Vitale", this "sensationally popular" "very LA-esque" cafe with a "great outdoor patio" overlooking the Embarcadero "can't be beat" for "power breakfasts" or the "solid" Cal-American "brunch before hitting up the farmer's market"; but after work it turns into a "way-crowded" watering hole – "single" "yuppie" "eye-candy" come for the "insane" happy hour, not to eat (and odds of "flagging down a waiter" are "nonexistent").

Amici's East Coast Pizzeria *Pizza*
20 | 12 | 16 | $19

AT&T Park | 216 King St. (3rd St.) | 415-546-6666
Marina | 2200 Lombard St. (Steiner St.) | 415-885-4500
www.amicis.com
No "it ain't New Yawk", but when East Coast "transplants" are "craving" "crispy" "wood-oven-fired" thin-crust pies "burnt to perfection", this local chain offers a "great substitute for the real thing", served in typical "busy" "family-friendly" "pizza shop" digs or for home delivery;

still, considering "there are no slices" and "soy mozzarella" renditions reflect "pricey" Left Coast "'za sensibilities", purists posit "shouldn't it be called NorCal Pizzeria?"

☑ Ana Mandara *Vietnamese* 23 | 26 | 20 | $49
Fisherman's Wharf | Ghirardelli Sq. | 891 Beach St. (Polk St.) | 415-771-6800 | www.anamandara.com
"A 'beautiful refuge' (as the eponym implies)" in "touristy" Fisherman's Wharf, this "swanky" Franco-Vietnamese "whisks you off" to colonial Saigon with "poetically titled" dishes ('dreams of sea and fire', 'storm clouds brewing'); the "gorgeous" "Hollywood-style" dining room provides a "visual feast to go with what's on the table", while the "lavish" upstairs bar, populated with "playboys" and "MySpace people" lounging on "cozy couches" listening to "live jazz" and DJs, is a "scene"; the only buzzkills: "painfully slow" service and "expense-account" tabs.

Anchor Oyster Bar *Seafood* 23 | 14 | 20 | $32
Castro | 579 Castro St. (bet. 18th & 19th Sts.) | 415-431-3990
"More under the radar than the 'other famous oyster bar', but just as good", this "unassuming" "seafood joint" with "great local flavor" and "responsive service" in the "quieter part of the Castro" is "smaller than a matchbox", so "expect a wait"; it "feels like home" to regulars who drop anchor for a "limited menu" of "straightforward", "just-caught" shellfish and "awesome daily specials"; still, squawkers cry it's "cramped" and find the "layout inefficient."

Andalu *Eclectic* 20 | 18 | 17 | $35
Mission | 3198 16th St. (Guerrero St.) | 415-621-2211 | www.andalusf.com
"Everyone talks about the Tuesday $2 tacos" ("quite the draw") but "hipsters" also "pack" this "loud", "trendy Mission hot spot" for the preponderance of "scintillating", "nontraditional" Eclectic small plates; the "buzzing", feel-"good vibe" makes it a "favorite" place to "spend the night with friends" "or make new" over tapas and "incredible white sangria" or sipping "surprisingly good wine flights"; still, a handful feel the menu is "growing long-in-the-tooth", while the "aloof service" is just growing old.

Angkor Borei *Cambodian* ▽ 20 | 12 | 22 | $21
Mission | 3471 Mission St. (bet. Cortland Ave. & Kingston St.) | 415-550-8417 | www.cambodiankitchen.com
With its "traditional" (albeit "shabby") decor and "affordable" "fresh" "authentic" fare ("better than most places I've tried in Cambodia"), this "family-run" "local favorite" in the Outer Mission "transcends" thrifty armchair travelers to the birthplace of Maddox Jolie-Pitt, but what's truly "phnom-inal" is the "warm", "welcoming" staff that "makes you feel like you are part of the family" (they even "happily adjust dishes for vegans").

Anjou ☑Ⓜ *French* 23 | 19 | 21 | $43
Downtown | 44 Campton Pl. (bet. Grant Ave. & Stockton St.) | 415-392-5373 | www.anjou-sf.com
Francophiles "make the effort to find" this "tiny jewel box" "tucked away" in a Downtown alley off Union Square that "tastes and feels like Paris" – down to the "charming accents" – but *sans* the "snooty" 'tude or prices; sit "cheek by jowl" with "theatergoers", shoppers and "romantic"

couples ("I so enjoyed the conversation at the next table") and "you'll be rewarded with an "exquisite" "bargain" $16 two-course lunch or a *"très intime* dinner" revealing a "light touch on" Gallic standards.

Antica Trattoria Ⓜ *Italian*

| 23 | 19 | 21 | $40 |

Russian Hill | 2400 Polk St. (Union St.) | 415-928-5797 | www.anticasf.com
"Still crazy (or tasty) after all these years"; this "welcoming" trattoria is where Russian Hill habitués go when they "don't feel like climbing over" to North Beach for "traditional rustic" Northern Italian *cucina* "without the pretension" or "glitz"; it's almost "like we were invited to sit down to a large family dinner" exclaim enthusiasts who sit "shoulder-to-shoulder" with other "lucky" locals in the "cheerful, extremely noisy" room – this is the "way Italians like to eat it."

ANZU *Japanese*

| 21 | 19 | 19 | $51 |

Downtown | Hotel Nikko | 222 Mason St. (O'Farrell St.) | 415-394-1100 | www.restaurantanzu.com
Touting "excellent quality" beef and "super-fresh" flown-in raw fish, Hotel Nikko's "high-end", "soothing" Japanese steak spot with a "cozy sushi bar" draws visiting salarymen, theatergoers and Downtown diners; "what more could you ask for?" – how about a "wonderful" Sunday Jazz brunch and "sake martinis at happy hour"; still, quibblers squawk that that the "outdated" dining room feels too much like the "stuffy" lobby restaurant that it is; N.B. ex Betelnut chef Barney Brown recently came onboard, which may outdate the Food score.

Aperto *Italian*

| 20 | 15 | 19 | $31 |

Potrero Hill | 1434 18th St. (Connecticut St.) | 415-252-1625 | www.apertosf.com
The "dependable" standards and "creative specials" "keep me and my pocketbook well-fed and happy" while the "free fresh-from-the-oven muffins" make it a "wonderful brunch option" proclaim "Protrero-ites who continue to patron" this "everyday Italian eatery" that manages to "stand up to flashier newcomers"; a "friendly" crew and "homey", "laid-back" atmosphere help "outweigh the irritating 'no-reservations' policy", prompting visitors to sigh "wish it was in my 'hood."

Ⓩ Aqua *Californian/Seafood*

| 26 | 25 | 25 | $72 |

Downtown | 252 California St. (bet. Battery & Front Sts.) | 415-956-9662 | www.aqua-sf.com
"Posh", "packed" to the gills and "still swimming strong" under chef Laurent Manrique's stewardship, this Downtown "power-lunch institution" remains a "shrine to seafood", wowing fans with "fantastic" Cal-French "flavor combinations" (and "terrestrial options" like foie gras); "wine and dine your client or stuffy in-laws" with "inventive, unexpected" fare and "incredible wines" "artfully presented" by a "superlative" staff in a "chic" setting accented with "gorgeous flower arrangements fit for the glamorous" VIP crowd; there are "no à la carte options" but "if you have to look at the prices . . . well you know the rest."

Ariake Japanese Ⓩ *Japanese*

| ▽ 26 | 15 | 23 | $34 |

Outer Richmond | 5041 Geary Blvd. (bet. 14th & 15th Aves.) | 415-221-6210 | www.sfariake.com
"Sprung from the training ground" of "longtime favorite" Ebisu, this understated Japanese joint is worth "crossing the park" to the Outer

Richmond declare devotees who exult in "pristine fish" that's "as fresh as it gets" – and it's served "without attitude"; "sit at the bar and make friends" with "head chef wizard" Jin Kim, who "fawns over his regular customers", preparing "distinctive" "less common treats" "not on the menu" (when he's not at Kabuto, which he took over in 2006).

Arinell Pizza Pizza | 22 | 4 | 11 | $7 |
Mission | 509 Valencia St. (16th St.) | 415-255-1303
See review in East of San Francisco Directory.

A. Sabella's Seafood | 18 | 16 | 19 | $41 |
Fisherman's Wharf | 2766 Taylor St., 3rd fl. (Jefferson St.) | 415-771-6775 | www.asabellas.com

This Cal-seafood "standout among a sea of fish joints" "down by the docks" is not only a "great place to unwind after a tour of Fisherman's Wharf", it's also "just about the only place locals go" for "fresh crab" and "hard to find abalone"; sure, the *Jetsons*-era light fixtures" and "tired" decor needs an "update" but it's "part of the charm" – and besides, "you spend the meal looking out the floor-to-ceiling windows" from your third-floor perch.

Asia de Cuba Asian/Cuban | 21 | 24 | 20 | $56 |
Downtown | Clift Hotel | 495 Geary St. (Taylor St.) | 415-929-2300 | www.chinagrillmanagement.com

When you've "got money to blow", trot over to the Downtown outpost of Ian Schrager's Asian fusion–Cuban in the "ultrachic" Clift Hotel and experience the "global empire that's poised to take over the world, one mojito (or caipirinha) at a time!"; "fight your way past" the "meat market" that spills over from the adjacent Redwood Bar, join the "tourists" and "young, half-dressed" "*SATC*" "wannabes" noshing on "super-delicious" dishes served family-style by a "flirty" staff and "delight" in Philippe Starck's "dark, sexy" decor that's "off the charts."

AsiaSF Californian/Asian | 17 | 18 | 20 | $39 |
SoMa | 201 Ninth St. (Howard St.) | 415-255-2742 | www.asiasf.com

"Not for the faint of heart – or Republicans", this SoMa drag club gets as "crowded as Gold's Gym on January 2nd" with "large squealing bachelorette parties" and "open-minded out-of-towners" "laughing and drinking" "generous" cocktails and nibbling "overpriced" "above-average" Cal-Asian tapas; "drink orders get forgotten and meals get confused" when the "hot" waitrons break to "parade on the bar" and "belt out Tina Turner songs", nonetheless, this "very *Crying Game*" venue is a "riot."

⦿ A 16 Italian | 23 | 19 | 20 | $43 |
Marina | 2355 Chestnut St. (bet. Divisadero & Scott Sts.) | 415-771-2216 | www.a16sf.com

"*Veni, vici, vino!*" roar the "yuppie" crowds who "elbow their way into the fray" at this "always a-buzz" Neapolitan enoteca in the Marina; the "hustling staff aims to please" uncorking a "fascinating list" of Southern Boot wines that "pairs beautifully" with the "rustic", "*molto delizioso*" "soul food", from "house-cured salumis" to wood-fired "pizzas so light and crispy you could use them as Frisbees"; it "gets as loud as the Italian highway it's named after", but hey, it's a "happening scene."

	FOOD	DECOR	SERVICE	COST

Asqew Grill *Californian* | 18 | 11 | 15 | $15 |

Castro | 3583 16th St. (Market St.) | 415-626-3040
NEW **Downtown** | San Francisco Shopping Centre | 865 Market St. (bet. Cyril Magnin & Ellis Sts.) | 415-227-0306
Haight-Ashbury | 1607 Haight St. (Clayton St.) | 415-701-9301
NEW **Laurel Heights** | 3415 California St. (bet. Laurel & Locust Sts.) | 415-386-5608
Marina | 3348 Steiner St. (Chestnut St.) | 415-931-9201
www.asqewgrill.com

"Ask who? if you ask me", this oh-so-Californian "cheap", "healthy fast-food chain (if there's such a thing)" is the "next to go national" thanks to its "creative", self-serve "make-it-my-way meals" concept where "nearly everything comes on a skewer" (including a "grilled brownie sundae") complemented by a "wide range" of starches; the "low-frills" digs win "no awards for atmosphere", but the "tasty tidbits" can't be beat for a weekday meal or a "quick snack."

Axum Cafe *Ethiopian* | ▽ 20 | 9 | 18 | $15 |

Lower Haight | 698 Haight St. (Pierce St.) | 415-252-7912 | www.axumcafe.com

For some of the "best and cheapest Ethiopian food" around, head to this Lower Haight haunt serving groaning platters of "spicy" "warming" meat and vegetarian stews and sop it up with "authentic injera" "so good you want to eat too much"; true, "you don't go here for atmosphere", but prices range from "dirt-cheap to merely cheap", and it does the trick "when you're sick of the usual" ("try the honey wine") or want "to eat without utensils."

Azie 🛯 *Asian Fusion* | 19 | 21 | 18 | $45 |

SoMa | 826 Folsom St. (bet. 4th & 5th Sts.) | 415-538-0918 | www.restaurantlulu.com

"Still hip and interesting, despite chef changes", this SoMa sister of LuLu set in a converted warehouse emanates a "great" "romantic vibe" in the downstairs cocktail bar as well as upstairs where "comfy booths with curtains" set the stage for "making out with your date" – and "an intimate" Asian fusion dinner "served family-style"; still, cynics sputter this "East meets mess" is "way past its prime" – it needs to "reinvent itself" again.

Aziza *Moroccan* | 24 | 23 | 21 | $44 |

Outer Richmond | 5800 Geary Blvd. (22nd Ave.) | 415-752-2222 | www.aziza-sf.com

"Dark corners, candlelight and heavy brocade bring to mind Casablanca in the 1930s" at this "oasis in the Outer Richmond" where a "splash of rose water starts the evening" and "mint tea ends" it; still, this "white-tablecloth" "nouveau North African" manages to transcend the "fez-tastic fantasia", proffering "exotic", seasonal, modern Moroccan *sans* "cheesy" "distractions such as belly dancers or loud music"; P.S. "rock" the Kasbah with "innovative muddled drinks" at the tiled bar.

bacar *Californian/Mediterranean* | 22 | 23 | 21 | $51 |

SoMa | 448 Brannan St. (bet. 3rd & 4th Sts.) | 415-904-4100 | www.bacarsf.com

Even under new management, the "buzz is still on" at this "too-cool-for-words" tri-level brick warehouse in SoMa, an "oenophiles para-

FOOD　DECOR　SERVICE　COST

dise" "where wine is king" and the "excellent" Cal-Med menu from new chef Robbie Lewis (ex Jardiniere) is full of "culinary surprises"; the open kitchen is now enclosed, the "high-tech" "library" of vino is so "visually exciting" you want to "climb the walls to explore" it and it's no longer "noisy" – you can now "strut your stuff down the stairs" to enjoy the "terrific" nightly live jazz below.

Baker Street Bistro   French
20 | 16 | 20 | $31

Marina | 2953 Baker St. (bet. Greenwich & Lombard Sts.) | 415-931-1475
"Am I in Montmartre" or the Marina? – *oui*, "we feel like we should be talking French in this lovely little" "no-nonsense bistro" staffed with "convivial" *garçons* who "know your name" agree *amis*; "it's not trendy or flashy" and quarters are "tight", but the "tried-and-true" fare is "excellent" while the weeknight prix fixe dinner ($14.50) is a "steal", and if you "go at twilight" or for brunch, you can sit on the sidewalk and "enjoy the weather."

Balboa Cafe   American
19 | 18 | 18 | $34

Cow Hollow | 3199 Fillmore St. (Greenwich St.) | 415-921-3944 | www.plumpjack.com
"If you want a burger", a "wonderful" Bloody "or a new beau", "you can't beat" Cow Hollow's "classic old-school–style bar and grill"; midweek, it doubles as the "clubhouse for the Mayor, the Gettys" and other lunching "bigwigs", while on weekends it morphs into the triangle area's "cougar den"; yes, this "'in' place" "brings it all together" – but what also sets it apart is the "great California-centric wine list" with minimal mark-ups; N.B. the Squaw Valley outpost is closed and plans to relocate.

Baraka   French/Mediterranean
21 | 19 | 19 | $39

Potrero Hill | 288 Connecticut St. (18th St.) | 415-255-0387 | www.barakasf.net
It may take a bit of *baraka* (French for luck) to squeeze into this "crowded" Potrero Hill "date place" from the Chez Papa folks that's "charming in every respect", from the "tasty" Gallic-inflected Mediterranean small plates to the "cute" accented staff; "love the Kasbah feel" and the "moody color scheme" – "everyone looks good" "under dusky red lighting"; if a few bark about "slow service", other parties opine the "atmosphere makes the experience worth it."

NEW Bar Bambino   Ⓜ Italian
- | - | - | ⎦

Mission | 2931 16th St. (Mission St.) | 415-701-8466 | www.barbambino.com
This new all-Italian wine bar and late-night cafe in the Mission showcases Italy's obsession with bread – crostini, panini, bruschetta – along with a short list of pasta, contorni, cured meats and cheeses; the small plates are meant to be washed down with one of many vinos (or a shot of specialty coffee) at the long white marble bar or on the backyard patio.

Bar Crudo   🅂 Seafood
25 | 17 | 22 | $41

Downtown | 603 Bush St. (Stockton St.) | 415-956-0396 | www.barcrudo.com
"Really, really good-o" quip fin-atics who savor every "delicious bite" of "jewellike crudo" "from around the world" "prepared to perfection" along with other "amazingly tasty seafood" at this "cool hangout" Downtown above the Stockton tunnel; true, the "minimalist" zinc bar serving a "unique" selection of Belgian ales is "cramped" and the up-

stairs is "tiny" (you "feel like you're in a homey attic with the cutest decor") but "just ignore the claustrophobia and dig in – you won't regret it."

Barney's Gourmet Hamburgers *Hamburgers* | 19 | 12 | 14 | $15 |

Marina | 3344 Steiner St. (bet. Chestnut & Lombard Sts.) | 415-563-0307
Noe Valley | 4138 24th St. (Castro St.) | 415-282-7770
www.barneyshamburgers.com

"Families, soccer teams" and "college students" hankering for a "protein fix" go in 'n' out of these "creative","California-style" "hamburger joints" that let you "build a burger in a million ways"; critics beef "better" meat abounds and "rude" service astounds, but "zillions of toppings" plus an array of "mean" fries, salads and "excellent thick milkshakes" "still excite" carnivores and vegans alike; "weather permitting", skip the "coffee-shop" digs and "chill" on the "sweet outdoor patio."

Barracuda *Brazilian/Japanese* | ▽ 17 | 18 | 17 | $36 |

NEW **Castro** | 2251 Market St. (bet. 15th & 16th Sts.) | 415-558-8567 |
www.barracudasushi.com

It's almost as if the "owners couldn't decide if they wanted to open a sushi bar or a churrascaria" muse admirers who join the "attractive" Castro crowd gobbling up "surprisingly good" ceviche, "innovative rolls" and "creative" Brazilian entrees at this "upbeat" hybrid Japa-zilian "boystown" newcomer (and its recently opened Burlingame and Daly City branches); still, snarky sorts snort that the "odd mishmash" of cuisines don't "fuse well together" and deem the staff "clueless."

Bar Tartine Ⓜ *Mediterranean* | 22 | 20 | 19 | $37 |

Mission | 561 Valencia St. (bet. 16th & 17th Sts.) | 415-487-1600 |
www.tartinebakery.com

If it wasn't for the "line out the door", "you could almost miss" this sign-free, "industrial chic–meets-rustic" bistro/wine bar in the Mission; it's a sea of "sharp elbows" inside with "hip" habitués sharing "adventurous" Spanish-accented Mediterranean dishes offset by an "impressive" global selection of vinos, plus "yeasty loaves" and "outstanding desserts" that "do the Tartine name proud"; but given the revolving door of chefs and "inexperienced service" sourpusses suggest this "fabled bakery" sibling is "still finding its legs."

Basil Thai Restaurant & Bar *Thai* | 22 | 17 | 18 | $25 |

SoMa | 1175 Folsom St. (bet. 7th & 8th Sts.) | 415-552-8999 |
www.basilthai.com

Boasting a "stylish", "modern Asian Zen decor" and "uncommon dishes" "smartly turned into something that mainstream Americans can enjoy", this "SoMa stalwart" is "different than your neighborhood Thai restaurant"; the "healthy" "California sensibility" ("everything is not laden with coconut") and "reasonable" prices "hit the mark" – it's "perfect for groups and that evening when you want to go out but don't want to get dressed up."

Beach Chalet Brewery *American* | 13 | 19 | 13 | $30 |

Outer Sunset | 1000 Great Hwy. (bet. Fulton St. & Lincoln Way) |
415-386-8439 | www.beachchalet.com

This Outer Sunset "sports bar by the sea" racks up "ridiculous" lines of "out-of-towners" who "love dining next to the beach", but unlike other "tourist traps", this one is saved by "spectacular ocean views" and "tasty" "housemade brews" (and WPA murals downstairs that are "worth the trip"); still, others advise go for brunch or at twilight, "when you can see the surf and tanners", because the "overpriced" American pub grub is "nothing to write home about."

Belden Taverna ⊠ *Mediterranean*   20 | 19 | 19 | $39

Downtown | 52 Belden Pl. (bet. Bush & Pine Sts.) | 415-986-8887 | www.cafetiramisu.com

"After overhauling the menu (bye-bye Morocco)", this "real urban find" "nestled" on a "very European-style alley" Downtown near Union Square has "settled on a more traditional" New American–meets-Mediterranean menu with French accents; it's a "surprisingly pleasant dining experience in a touristy area" chime in cohorts – the fare's "enjoyable", "drinks are generous" and "on a warm evening" it feels "magical"; still, a few shrug "nice effort", but the "food's just so-so."

Bella Trattoria *Italian*   21 | 17 | 22 | $34

Inner Richmond | 3854 Geary Blvd. (3rd Ave.) | 415-221-0305 | www.bellatrattoria.com

"Forget North Beach" – you can "get a bit of Italy on Geary" reveal admirers who fall for the "authentic" Southern Italian "classics" including "creative pastas" and "pillows of heaven gnocchi" at this "softly candlelit" Inner Richmond trattoria; the "intimate", "romantic" atmosphere transports you a "million miles away", while the "super-friendly waiters" "treat you as if you're long-lost cousins from the old country"; still, a handful lament it's "*bella* mediocre."

Betelnut Pejiu Wu *Pan-Asian*   23 | 21 | 18 | $36

Cow Hollow | 2030 Union St. (bet. Buchanan & Webster Sts.) | 415-929-8855 | www.betelnutrestaurant.com

You almost "expect Tokyo Rose to amble in at any moment" at this Cow Hollow beer house with a "fun 1930s" "Shanghainese pulp decor" serving "freakin' delicious" Pan-Asian "street foods" – but "frat boys" and "one helluva 'floorshow' of lovelies" "cooling" off on "fruity drinks" "bring you back to SF reality"; despite "frosty" service and long waits ("even with reservations") it's "still raging after all these years" because "no one does fusion better" or at better prices.

B44 *Spanish*   21 | 17 | 18 | $39

Downtown | 44 Belden Pl. (bet. Bush & Pine Sts.) | 415-986-6287 | www.b44sf.com

"Festive as a Spanish restaurant should be", this "boisterous" Barcelona "favorite" specializing in seafood, sangria, "sunshine" and "beyond-the-classics" Catalan creations served in a "quaint" "Euro-style" pedestrian alleyway off Union Square ranks at "the 'tapa' of the list" for "business lunches" or "sublime" alfresco dinners "on warm nights"; the "crowded" room gets as "noisy" as a bull fight and service can be "slow", but fans would "suffer through anything for squid ink paella", one of nine variations available.

Big 4 ☽ *American*   22 | 25 | 24 | $55

Nob Hill | Huntington Hotel | 1075 California St. (Taylor St.) | 415-771-1140 | www.big4restaurant.com

"Wear your fur" and pretend you're dining in your "private rail car" at this "atmospheric" "class joint" in Nob Hill's Huntington Hotel that

FOOD DECOR SERVICE COST

"pampers" "big shots" ("old money or not") with "excellent" New American fare, including "wild stuff" (the "yearly game menu is the best"); it's "not for "food groupies wanting the latest", indeed, the "gents' club" ambiance exudes "retro elegance", "down to the dark-wood" paneling, "shining brass" and "deep leather chairs" made for "long lunches"; P.S. have a cheaper, "civilized meal in the bar" accompanied by live piano.

Bistro Aix *Californian/French* 22 | 17 | 21 | $37

Marina | 3340 Steiner St. (bet. Chestnut & Lombard Sts.) | 415-202-0100 | www.bistroaix.com

More "like a neighborhood restaurant in Paris" than what you'd expect in the "dreadfully sceney Marina", this "quaint" "fall-back favorite" with Gallic "flair", "welcoming" "American service" and a "wonderful", "ingredient-driven" Cal-French menu feels like "home away from home"; enjoy a "relaxed yet romantic" meal in the "busy interior" or "snag a seat" on the "delightful" heated back patio and sip "a glass of Côtes du Rhône" – either way, it's Aix-cellent.

Bistro Boudin *Californian* 20 | 17 | 16 | $25

Fisherman's Wharf | 160 Jefferson St. (near Pier 43½) | 415-928-1849 | www.boudinbakery.com

"When visiting the Wharf", this flagship of the famed sourdough outfit is "almost a required stop" concur carboloaders who peer into the "working bakery" and "fun" museum, then hotfoot it up to the second-floor bistro for "great views" of "tourist central" below and "fresh-baked" yeasty bread bowls "filled with anything from crab to clam chowder"; harried service "brings you in and shoves you out", but the "classic" Californian nosh, including newly added international dishes, is "better than expected."

Bistro Clovis Ⓜ *French* 19 | 16 | 18 | $38

Hayes Valley | 1596 Market St. (Franklin St.) | 415-864-0231 | www.bistroclovis.com

"Ooh-la-la!", this long-running yet "too-oft-forgotten" Gallic "pre-theater spot" with a "delightful" atmosphere "brings us back to those wonderful moments" abroad – it feels more like the "Left Bank" than Hayes Valley enthuse "Francophiles"; the Parisian owner is there "nightly", cooking up "satisfying", "old-school classics", the staff is "attentive" and it's especially handy if you're "going to the Orpheum" theater; still, a handful deem the fare "uninspired."

Ⓩ BIX *American/French* 23 | 26 | 22 | $51

Downtown | 56 Gold St. (bet. Montgomery & Sansome Sts.) | 415-433-6300 | www.bixrestaurant.com

"Wander down" a Downtown back alley and slip into the "fanciest speakeasy you've ever seen"– you half "expect to see Nick and Nora" "getting loaded" on "killer martinis" while listening to "terrific" jazz; the "excitement" of the "bar scene extraordinaire", brimming with "old-time money and high-paid newbie professionals", "spills over into the restaurant": so if you want to "escape the maddening noise", join the "little-black-dress" brigade and their "trust fund" dates in "ro-mantic booths" upstairs where a "solicitous tuxedo-clad staff" serves "lovely" seasonal American-French classics.

FOOD | DECOR | SERVICE | COST

Blowfish Sushi To Die For *Japanese* 21 | 20 | 16 | $41

Mission | 2170 Bryant St. (20th St.) | 415-285-3848 |
www.blowfishsushi.com

Flashing "more visual and aural stimulation than MTV", this "trendy", "postmodern" Japanese "discotheque" in the Mission (and Silicon Valley) rollicks with "video-gamers, G4TVfans" and "NY wannabes" who "fight their way" past the bar for "awesome drinks and "edgy" "eye-candy sushi" amid "roaring" "techno music" and "R-rated anime"; "the no-reservations policy blows" and "too-hip-for-you" service isn't "to die for", nonetheless clubbers concur the "party atmosphere" is just right to "start a wild night out."

Blue Jay Cafe *Southern* 15 | 12 | 13 | $21

Western Addition | 919 Divisadero St. (McAllister St.) | 415-447-6066

For "satisfying", "stick-to-your-ribs Southern comfort food" "with a Western Addition hipster vibe", locals and folks who want to "feel like one" home in on this "funky" roosting spot, hunkering down over a "mellow dinner" with occasional live jazz at the U-shaped counter or brunching on the "cute patio"; still, its "amazing inconsistency" can be a buzzkill – some say that this former songbird "went from great to fair when the ownership changed", adding service is "not so great."

Blue Plate, The ⊠ *American* 23 | 18 | 21 | $35

Mission | 3218 Mission St. (bet. 29th & Valencia Sts.) | 415-282-6777 |
www.blueplatesf.com

With its "friendly, neighborhood vibe", "$2 cans of Olympia" and blue-plate specials, this "laid-back, upscale diner" in the Mission may feel "homey", but "home was never as dark" or "hip" and the "swoonable", "seasonal New American comfort food" is "better than your mother ever made"; no, it ain't cheap, but "where else can you eat mashed potatoes with Napa Charbono?" ask dressed-down denizens who crowd the counter or lose themselves in the "enchanting" backyard garden.

⊉ Bocadillos ⊠ *Spanish* 22 | 17 | 18 | $34

North Beach | 710 Montgomery St. (bet. Jackson & Washington Sts.) |
415-982-2622 | www.bocasf.com

Piperade's Gerald Hirigoyen's "chic", "Euro-modern" walk-in tapas bar on the edge of North Beach and Fidi "succeeds admirably" in re-creating San Sebastian in SF; "old and young" "socialize and graze" on "whimsical", "bold" Basque- and Spanish-inspired small plates and "tiny sandwiches that give the restaurant its name", all "graciously served with Cava by the glass" or other "value Spanish wines"; "go early or else there won't even be a seat at the bar", let alone the communal table.

Bodega Bistro *Vietnamese* 23 | 12 | 17 | $24

Tenderloin | 607 Larkin St. (Eddy St.) | 415-921-1218

Oft described as "Slanted Door on a budget", this "absurdly cheap" Vietnamese with a "clean", mauve-colored interior prepares "remarkable" "traditional" "Hanoi street dishes" that are far "better than your typical" "gritty" Tenderloin "Southeast Asian storefront"; while the "very good pho" and other "standards" are "delicious", once the "great chef ("and even better person") "Jimmy realizes that you're there to eat, he pulls special French-flaired dishes out of his sleeve", all ferried out with the utmost "hospitality."

	FOOD	DECOR	SERVICE	COST

Bong Su Restaurant and Lounge M _Vietnamese_

22 | 24 | 21 | $46

SoMa | 311 Third St. (Folsom St.) | 415-536-5800 | www.bongsu.com
"Why beg to get into" "other trendy Vietnamese restaurants" now that Tamarine's "sleek, snazzy" younger SoMa sibling is in the picture; the "flavorful", "freshly prepared" "contemporary" regional cuisine fare is served in a "soothing" "beautifully lit", "bamboo-adorned" dining room that's conducive to a "quiet" lunch or dinner near the convention center, but after work, the "signature cocktails" and an "extensive wine list" lure a "beautiful crowd" into a lounge that's as "sexy" as the "hot hostess outfits."

Boogaloos _Southwestern_

17 | 13 | 16 | $15

Mission | 3296 22nd St. (Valencia St.) | 415-824-4088 | www.boogaloossf.com
The de facto "hipster brunch destination", this "greasy spoon" known for its "quirky artwork" and "heavily tattooed" staff hustles "hearty" helpings of Southwestern-inspired morning fare with "enough of a twist to make it interesting" ("biscuits and vegetable gravy is a health food, right?"); on weekends, "hellish" crowds of Missionites looking for a "hangover cure" and families with "small kids" descend – but why anyone would endure the "atrocious wait" when "you can get your groove on midweek" "boogalos the mind."

Boulange de Cole M _Bakery_

22 | 15 | 16 | $15

Cole Valley | 1000 Cole St. (Parnassus St.) | 415-242-2442
Boulange de Polk M _Bakery_
Russian Hill | 2310 Polk St. (Green St.) | 415-345-1107
La Boulange at Columbus _Bakery_
North Beach | 543 Columbus Ave. (bet. Green & Union Sts.) | 415-399-0714
La Boulange at Fillmore _Bakery_
Pacific Heights | 2043 Fillmore St. (bet. California & Pine Sts.) | 415-928-1300
La Boulange at Union _Bakery_
Cow Hollow | 1909 Union St. (bet. Charlton Ct. & Laguna St.) | 415-440-4450
www.baybread.com
"Who needs Paris?" when you can have "nice big bowls of latte", "buttery bliss" in the form of "out-of-this-world" French toast, "tasty tartines" or "luscious", "worth-the-calories" chocolate ganache cake at this "growing enterprise" of "terrific French-style boulangeries"; if you don't feel like fighting the "baby stroller brigade" for one of the "awkward" tables or sidewalk seats, just grab a "delicious" baguette to go.

Boulette's Larder _American_

25 | 17 | 19 | $36

Embarcadero | 1 Ferry Bldg. (Market St.) | 415-399-1155 | www.bouletteslarder.com
Boasting the "Bay, the buzz – and the beignets", this "tiny" "high-end take-out" shop in the Embarcadero's Ferry Building is "chock-full of hard-to-find delectables" "for your larder at home"; still, "foodie and wine snobs" prefer to "break bread" at the communal table (with the "huge namesake Hungarian sheepdog Boulette" underfoot) over "astronomically pricey" yet "absolutely scrumptious" New American lunch and Sunday brunch, "surrounded by bubbling stocks and herbaceous scents"; N.B. dinner for private parties only.

☑ Boulevard *American* — 27 | 25 | 25 | $64

Embarcadero | Audiffred Bldg. | 1 Mission St. (Steuart St.) | 415-543-6084 | www.boulevardrestaurant.com

This "sizzling" belle epoque brasserie on the Embarcadero with "breathtaking views of the Bay" may be a "wallet flattener", but remains the "consummate" "go-as-you-are" San Francisco hot spot delivering "unforgettable food" "without the 'tude"; "suits", "tourists and locals" "sit elbow to elbow" soaking up the "party" vibe and Nancy Oakes' French-influenced New American fare that's "inventive without being fussy", while the "sensational" staff "goes above and beyond the call of duty" and "never fails to provide the perfect" wine match.

Bow Hon 4 *Chinese* — ▽ 22 | 7 | 15 | $18

Chinatown | 850 Grant Ave. (bet. Clay & Washington Sts.) | 415-362-0601

Cantonese families and English-speaking diners at lunch and dinner descend on this two-story Chinatown storefront with "minimal decor" and service for "Chinese comfort food"; skip the usual suspects and stick to the "really good" signature clay pots bubbling over with meats, vegetables and dumplings – it's the ultimate "cheap" chow considering "at the end of the meal you send it back to the kitchen and the cook turns it into rice soup" for you.

Brandy Ho's *Chinese* — 20 | 11 | 16 | $24

NEW **Castro** | 4068 18th St. (bet. Castro & Hartford Sts.) | 415-252-8000
Chinatown | 217 Columbus Ave. (bet. Broadway St. & Pacific Ave.) | 415-788-7527
www.brandyhos.com

For "burn-your-mouth-good eating" and "smoky meats", heatseekers head to this "semi-Americanized" incendiary Hunan "institution" on the edge of Chinatown or its new Castro sibling; don't order it hot "unless you're dining with a fireman" but do cop a "seat at the counter to watch" the "cooks crank out dishes in giant woks" – that's "half the fun", plus it blocks out the "horrible decor and "marginal service."

Brazen Head, The ●⊖⇗ *American* — 20 | 20 | 20 | $36

Cow Hollow | 3166 Buchanan St. (Greenwich St.) | 415-921-7600 | www.brazenheadsf.com

It's "tough to find" – there's "no sign on the door to distinguish it" – but that just adds to the "low-key", "classy" allure of Cow Hollow's "darkly lit" "locals' secret" with an "old-timey" "speakeasy" vibe and a staff that "takes good care of you"; "drop in" with "special friends" for American "comfort food" – the late-night kitchen is the "savior of many" – and sip a "great cocktail" ("they're not afraid to pour liberal drinks") while waiting "for a table to open up" at 1 AM.

Brick ● *American* — 20 | 20 | 18 | $39

Tenderloin | 1085 Sutter St. (Larkin St.) | 415-441-4232 | www.brickrestaurant.com

"Everything's delicious, including the atmosphere" and the "young, fabulous crowd" at this "trendy looking" brick-walled "find" that's equal parts cocktail bar, art gallery and restaurant; the New American fare "takes risks", with "whimsical" small plates combining "familiar and inventive" ingredients – it's a "a great late-night option if you can deal" with the "rough-around-the-edges" Tenderloin neighborhood "at

FOOD   DECOR   SERVICE   COST

that hour"; still, some scoff that the staff is "inexperienced" and what's more, "tapas = me hungry."

Brindisi Cucina di Mare 🔒 *Italian/Seafood*   18   15   16 $38
Downtown | 88 Belden Pl. (Pine St.) | 415-593-8000 |
www.brindisicucina.com

"Pretend" you're in Southern Italy at this "lively" Downtown cafe serving "unusual" "Puglia-inspired" seafood, not the least because "getting 'hawked' in Belden Alley makes you feel like you're in Rome"; "outdoor seating is the attraction", and best "appreciated" in the day and on "warm nights", as the "intimate" frescoed interior can be "loud, crowded and warm", rendering the otherwise "tasty" food, utterly "forgettable."

Brother's Korean Restaurant *Korean*   22   5   13 $25
Inner Richmond | 4014 Geary Blvd. (bet. 4th & 5th Aves.) | 415-668-2028
Inner Richmond | 4128 Geary Blvd. (bet. 5th & 6th Aves.) | 415-387-7991 ◐

It sure "ain't my brother's Korean restaurant", nonetheless you "feel like you're eating at home", that is, if your abode is a DIY "authentic wooden charcoal barbecue" joint in the Richmond declare Seoul sisters and expats who hole up at the "granddaddy" and nearby sibling, digging into "delicious" kimchi and "freebies" doled out by the "attentive" staff while "manning the grill"; but "don't make" post-dinner plans – you may be "in a food stupor or attract too many hungry dogs."

NEW B Star Bar *Pan-Asian*   -   -   -   I
Inner Richmond | 127 Clement St. (bet. 2nd & 3rd Aves.) | 415-387-2147 |

This hip offshoot of the Inner Richmond's Burma Superstar, the legendary dive up the street, attracts a Generation Next crowd that knocks back mango mojitos before grazing on Pan-Asian tapas; diners craving the original locale's famous tea-leaf salad can get it here (albeit pre-mixed) without the two-hour wait, but the true draw is the tropical-style heated patio boasting Buddha sculptures and lush foliage.

Buca di Beppo *Italian*   14   15   16 $25
SoMa | 855 Howard St. (bet. 4th & 5th Sts.) | 415-543-7673 |
www.bucadibeppo.com

See review in South of San Francisco Directory.

Burger Joint *Hamburgers*   18   12   14 $13
Lower Haight | 700 Haight St. (Pierce St.) | 415-864-3833
Mission | 807 Valencia St. (19th St.) | 415-824-3494 ⊟

"Why go to a fast-food chain when you can" steer over to this "friendly", "only-in-SF" "interpretation of a classic hamburger joint" serving "guilt-free" Niman Ranch beef, free-range chicken and "crisp fries" in a "well-lit", "retro-hip" 1950s-style diner; if a few beef the "no-frills" patties are "bland" (they "don't offer a billion toppings"), countless carnivores contend they're "the best" in the Haight, the Mission or "wherever the take-out bag may carry you"; N.B. new branches are slated to open in South Beach and Burlingame.

Burma Superstar *Burmese*   24   14   18 $23
Inner Richmond | 309 Clement St. (4th Ave.) | 415-387-2147 |
www.burmasuperstar.com

"In a city of spoiled foodies who've seen it all", the "highly original", "delectable fusion of Indian, Chinese and Southeast flavors" at this

Inner Richmonder "lives up to its name", drawing "crowds large enough to rally for Burmese independence"; endure the "excruciating waits" ("leave your cell phone number" and "have a drink down the street") and you'll be "rewarded with exotic" "cheap eats" and a "friendly" staff that "helps decipher" the menu ("samosa soup and tea leaf salad: absolute perfection").

Bursa Kebab *Mideastern*   19 | 16 | 19 | $28

West Portal | 60 W. Portal Ave. (bet. Ulloa & Vicente Sts.) | 415-564-4006
Hawking Mediterranean cuisine in the heart of West Portal, this "friendly", "cozy" Turkish "treat" is a "step up from your average kebab-and-rice joint"; the skewered specialty comes in "big portions" and is "authentic and affordable", but there are also "interesting" "variations on the usual" suspects to get you "out of the regular Middle Eastern rut."

Bushi-tei ⓜ *Pan-Asian*   24 | 24 | 23 | $61

Japantown | 1638 Post St. (bet. Laguna & Webster Sts.) | 415-440-4959 | www.bushi-tei.com
Wood panels dating to 1863 rescued from a demolished house in Nagano accent a "sleek", glass-enclosed bi-level dining room, creating "clever decor" at this "beautiful Zen-like" "J-town gem"; add in chef Seiji ('Waka') Wakabayashi's "quirky" yet "sublime" Pan-Asian omakase menu and "inventive" à la carte offerings, incorporating "haute" French techniques, California ingredients and "Japanese sensibilities" and you've got a "feast for all five senses"; if quibblers feel it doesn't "live up to the hype", most retort the "hits are very, very impressive."

Butler & The Chef Bistro, The ⓜ *French*   20 | 18 | 15 | $20

SoMa | 155A South Park St. (bet. 2nd & 3rd Sts.) | 415-896-2075 | www.thebutlerandthechefbistro.com
"Parisian longings can be satisfied for a couple of hours" at this "adorable", "kitsch", "petite" sidewalk cafe in a "charming South Park" setting that's "perfect for an afternoon snack", a "divine lunch" or a "tasty brunch", all "cooked by a real Frenchman"; if a few find the "cramped tables" a "little 'too bistro' for comfort" and the staff sometimes "harried", even they admit all's "forgiven when you taste the crusty bread."

Butterfly *Asian/Californian*   19 | 21 | 19 | $42

Embarcadero | Pier 33 (Bay St.) | 415-864-8999 | www.butterflysf.com
With "gorgeous views of the Bay" through floor-to-ceiling windows and a "young, vibrant atmosphere" fueled by a "great bar" and "excellent" weekend DJs, this "stylish" spot ensures a "fun time out on the Embarcadero"; the "imaginative" Cal-Asian eats keep packs of "pretty people" and tourists "fluttering back", nonetheless some feel it's a "better lunch choice", as the music gets "deafening" "as the night progresses" and drinks become the "star"; N.B. there's a new branch in San Bruno.

Cafe Bastille Ⓢ *French*   18 | 16 | 17 | $33

Downtown | 22 Belden Pl. (bet. Bush & Pine Sts.) | 415-986-5673 | www.cafebastille.com
For a "true bistro meal", check out this "charming" "French hangout" on Downtown's "very-European Belden Place", where "office lunchers" and foreign "students wearing black and smoking cigarettes" fill

the "postage-stamp-sized tables" outside and the mood is *très* "lively"; the "straightforward", "dependable" fare conveyed by an "efficient if not friendly staff" further make diners feel like they're in Paree's "Latin Quarter."

Café Claude *French*

20 | 19 | 18 | $32

Downtown | 7 Claude Ln. (Sutter St.) | 415-392-3515 | www.cafeclaude.com

"Cheaper than a trip to Paris" and "nearly as gratifying", this "quaint", "out-of-the-way" French bistro Downtown serves steak tartare "the old-fashioned way" ("hand-chopped"), "tasty croque monsieur" and other "typical" yet "well-made" dishes, complemented by an "interesting wine list"; *oui*, it feels "authentic", right down to the sometimes "snotty", "accented" waiters – good thing they're so "cute"; P.S. live jazz Thursday–Saturday creates "romantic" evenings.

Café de la Presse *French*

16 | 18 | 15 | $33

Downtown | 352 Grant Ave. (bet. Bush & Sutter Sts.) | 415-249-0900 | www.aqua-sf.com/cdlp/

"*Parlez-vous français?*" – then grab a copy of *Le Monde* from the "selection of international publications", order an "authentic pain au chocolat" and soak up the "French atmosphere" at this "handsomely" remodeled bistro/coffeehouse "*avec* attitude"; indeed, the "infuriating" staffers "range from incredulous to arrogant", but its proximity to Union Square makes it "perfect for a light lunch" of "garlicky escargot", frisée salad and the like "after a day of shopping Downtown."

Café Gratitude *Vegan*

19 | 16 | 18 | $21

Inner Sunset | 1336 Ninth Ave. (bet. Irving & Judah Sts.) | 415-824-4652
Mission | 2400 Harrison St. (20th St.) | 415-824-4652
www.cafegratitude.com

"If you can stomach" the "over-the-top" "mother-earth" vibe of ordering "via hippie affirmations" ('I Am Abundant', 'I Am Flourishing', etc.), it's "hard to resist feeling grateful" for these "crunchy" Bay Area cafes where "starry-eyed idealists" "feed their souls" with "mostly raw and all vegan" foodstuffs that are "pricey" but "surprisingly flavorful"; better be "eternally patient" though, because for "food that isn't cooked, it sure takes a long time to get to your table."

Cafe Jacqueline   *French*

26 | 18 | 20 | $48

North Beach | 1454 Grant Ave. (bet. Green & Union Sts.) | 415-981-5565

This "unique" French old-timer only "does one thing", but it "does it superbly", whipping up "ethereal", "perfectly baked" "soufflés with soul" – both "savory and sweet" and "big enough" "to share with your honey" (it's one of the "most romantic spots in North Beach", so make reservations "now for next Valentine's Day"); the "adorable" Madame Jacqueline "personally works on each one" (check out her "bowl of 2,000 eggs"), so "be patient" and "thou shalt be rewarded" with the "ultimate indulgence."

CAFÉ KATi   *Asian Fusion*

23 | 16 | 20 | $44

Japantown | 1963 Sutter St. (bet. Fillmore & Webster Sts.) | 415-775-7313 | www.cafekati.com

For folks living near Japantown, this "informal", "cozy" longtime haunt is a "treat to have in the neighborhood", for not only is its "cre-

FOOD | DECOR | SERVICE | COST

ative, colorful" Asian fusion fare "served in such a beautiful and artistic manner that you almost don't want to eat it", but it tastes "dynamite" to boot; if the catty cry it's getting a bit "tired", admirers retort it's "worth the parking travails and the walk."

Café Majestic *Californian/French*

| - | - | - | E |

Pacific Heights | Hotel Majestic | 1500 Sutter St. (Gough St.) | 415-441-1280 | www.thehotelmajestic.com

Pacific Heights' recently remodeled and reopened historic Hotel Majestic is once again a stately setting for an elegant dinner, and breakfast too; the 58-seat turn-of-the-century dining room, resplendent with well-spaced tufted cream-colored banquettes and deco chairs, sets the stage for newly appointed chef Ian Begg's refined, seasonal-driven Californian-French menu; guests can repose over a cocktail at the hotel's 20-seat mahogany-and-slate-topped 'Butterfly Bar' named such for the collection of rare, framed winged-insects on the walls.

Café Tiramisu ⊠ *Italian*

| 21 | 17 | 18 | $37 |

Downtown | 28 Belden Pl. (bet. Bush & Pine Sts.) | 415-421-7044 | www.cafetiramisu.com

"Forget the diet" and "try the ravioli, no matter what's in it" (or be good and order an "excellent grilled-seafood" plate) at this Italian "treasure" in the "midst of a French-dominated alley" Downtown; it can get "crowded" and "noisy" inside the "quaint" quarters, so try to snag a table outside where "heat lamps allow for year-round alfresco dining" and soak up that "European street-cafe atmosphere."

Caffe Delle Stelle *Italian*

| 16 | 14 | 18 | $30 |

Hayes Valley | 395 Hayes St. (Gough St.) | 415-252-1110

"Nothing fancy", just "good down-home Italian cookery" at "bargain-basement prices" and "free sparkling water" applaud fans of this Hayes Valley trattoria; its "convenient" location near the opera and symphony ensures it's "always chaotic" pre-show but "they know how to get you out in time" for the curtain; still, others bow out citing "predictable" eats and a "less-than-stellar" wine list.

Caffè Macaroni ⊠⇄ *Italian*

| 20 | 14 | 19 | $28 |

North Beach | 59 Columbus Ave. (Jackson St.) | 415-956-9737 | www.caffemacaroni.com

"The genuine article in a sea of poseurs", this "quirky, kitschy" North Beach trattoria is "the closest you'll come to being in a street cafe" in Naples thanks to "cheap", "simple", "solid" Southern Italian standards doled out by "playful", "joke"-telling staffers ("be careful, they might pinch your cheeks"); the "cramped quarters" lend the feeling of "eating in a family member's kitchen" – if said family member festooned his ceiling with dried macaroni.

Caffè Museo *Italian/Mediterranean*

| 16 | 14 | 10 | $20 |

SoMa | San Francisco Museum of Modern Art | 151 Third St. (bet. Howard & Mission Sts.) | 415-357-4500 | www.caffemuseo.com

Grab "a quick salad or sandwich" "before wandering the halls" of SoMa's SFMoMA or "discuss the exhibition" afterward over a leisurely lunch at this "cafeteria-style" cafe, which serves "better-than-usual museum fare" of the Italian-Med variety; on warm days, "Moscone convention crowds" can often be found commandeering the outdoor tables because they're "already in the neighborhood" – however, it's "not a destination spot"; N.B. closed Wednesday, open for dinner Thursday.

Campton Place *American/Mediterranean* | 25 | 24 | 26 | $72 |

Downtown | Campton Place Hotel | 340 Stockton St. (bet. Post & Sutter Sts.) | 415-955-5555 | www.camptonplace.com

"So you want to be pampered?" – then make a res at this "old-school" hotel "hideaway" near Union Square Downtown, "where the well-dressed turn up for rich-tasting (and -priced)" New American–Med meals and service "fit for royalty"; the "genteel", "elegant" interior is conducive to "a quiet meeting" over "awesome breakfasts", "pre-shopping" lunches or "long, leisurely" "romantic dinners", while "even the most jaded palates" find "surprises" in the "innovative" wine-paired tasting menus; N.B. jacket suggested.

Canteen *Californian* | 25 | 14 | 20 | $44 |

Downtown | Commodore Hotel | 817 Sutter St. (Jones St.) | 415-928-8870 | www.sfcanteen.com

Dennis Leary's "micro restaurant" Downtown offers a "one-of-a-kind" experience: patrons "wait in the dreary lobby" of the Commodore Hotel for set seating times only to be "rushed" by a "perfunctory" staff in and out of the "cramped", "drab" "old" "luncheonette"; luckily, the "cuisine does not match the decor", as the "master" prepares "absolutely remarkable" Californian fare that "never fails" to "astound"; P.S. the "short but well-structured menu" "changes daily", but "the vanilla soufflé is always served, and you'd be insane not to have it."

Carnelian Room *Californian* | 17 | 25 | 21 | $61 |

Downtown | Bank of America Ctr. | 555 California St., 52nd fl. (bet. Kearny & Montgomery Sts.) | 415-433-7500 | www.carnelianroom.com

Whether you "bring a date or a visiting dignitary" to this "elegant", "iconic" Downtown "sky room" atop the Bank of America tower for "well-prepared" Californian fare, it's a sure bet they'll be "impressed" with the "extraordinary views of the City and the Bay Area"; even detractors who deride the chow as an "overpriced" "afterthought" advise "dine elsewhere – but don't miss cocktails at sunset."

Catch *Seafood* | 19 | 20 | 18 | $37 |

Castro | 2362 Market St. (bet. Castro & 16th Sts.) | 415-431-5000 | www.catchsf.com

"The Castro needs more places like this" "bit of class", an "attractive" seafooder filled with slightly industrial fixtures, exposed brick and "great live piano music"; in the front, an "awesome open-air dining space" anchored by a "circular fireplace" is a "see-and-be-seen scene", as a crowd primarily made up of "lots of cute gay boys" "watches the passing parade on the street"; as for the fish itself, a few feel it's "hit-or-miss", and too "pricey" at that.

Cav Wine Bar & Kitchen ⊠ *Mediterranean* | 22 | 21 | 22 | $34 |

Hayes Valley | 1666 Market St. (bet. Franklin & Goss Sts.) | 415-437-1770 | www.cavwinebar.com

Although this Hayes Valley haunt "bills itself foremost as a wine bar", the Mediterranean "small and large plates that complement the featured" vini are also "top-notch", as is the "knowledgeable, friendly" staff; after-theater, the "modern-industrial" digs fill up with

FOOD DECOR SERVICE COST

"raucous" crowds that get "happily lubricated" from the "quirky", "exhaustive list", much of which can be "enjoyed by the taste, so you can cover more ground."

Cha Am Thai *Thai*

| 19 | 14 | 16 | $20 |

SoMa | Museum Parc | 701 Folsom St. (3rd St.) | 415-546-9711 | www.chaamthaisf.com

"One of the first" Thai restaurants in Berkeley's gourmet ghetto, this "tree house" (a "giant palm grows through the middle" of the "sunny" dining room) has "remained at the top of the heap" for over two decades, offering "fresh ingredients, beautiful presentations" and "artifacts to look at"; much like its younger, separately owned "solid" SoMa cousin, it's a "favorite" for "quick", "affordable" meals – though a handful huff it's "less than breathtaking" "now that there's competition" "practically on every corner."

Cha Cha Cha *Caribbean*

| 19 | 17 | 14 | $26 |

Haight-Ashbury | 1801 Haight St. (Shrader St.) | 415-386-5758
Mission | 2327 Mission St. (bet. 19th & 20th Sts.) | 415-648-0504
www.cha3.com

Hungry "hipsters" "don't care" about the "insane waits" they have to endure to get into these "funky" Caribbean tapas meccas on Haight Street and in the Mission – they're "worth every minute" for the "endless" selection of "reasonably priced", "sinful", "spicy" small plates served; as to the "slow", "lackluster service" and "noisy nightclub atmosphere", well, pitchers of "awesome", "knockout" sangria eventually "black out" any aggravation.

☑ Chapeau! Ⓜ *French*

| 27 | 18 | 26 | $47 |

Outer Richmond | 1408 Clement St. (15th Ave.) | 415-750-9787

"Budget-minded foodies" "make the trek" to this "quaint" – alright, "cramped" – bistro so "religiously", they "should move" to the Outer Richmond, because the "extraordinary" French cuisine is "better than restaurants [that charge] twice the price" (the "early-bird prix fixe is a steal"); the pièce de résistance is Philippe Gardelle, the "charming" chef-owner who "personally greets everyone" as well as "seats, cuts meats and pecks cheeks", transforming every meal into "a special experience"; N.B. an ongoing renovation may impact the Decor score.

Charanga ⓏⓂ *Pan-Latin*

| ▽ 21 | 15 | 20 | $28 |

Mission | 2351 Mission St. (bet. 19th & 20th Sts.) | 415-282-1813 | www.charangasf.com

Caribbean, Cuban and Costa Rican flavors provide the "tasty spin" on the tapas served at this "cozy and courteous" Pan-Latin spot where "spicy" small plates delight Missionaries "interested in taking a walk on the wild side without falling off the edge" (or into debt); even though it often lacks the "mobs of loud drunks" that plague similar joints in the area, service "can be slow" – but the "must-try" sangria and mojitos are "worth the wait."

Chaya Brasserie *French/Japanese*

| 21 | 21 | 19 | $49 |

Embarcadero | 132 The Embarcadero (bet. Howard & Mission Sts.) | 415-777-8688 | www.thechaya.com

"East meets West on the Embarcadero" at this "posh", "happening" French-Japanese spot where "high-end tourists", "Financial District types" and "hip and trendy" people who "can't decide between steak and sushi" spend "fun happy hours", "business lunches" and "special-occasion" dinners; while some feel it "suffers from being overambitious" and "overpriced", they're usually overwhelmed by the "killer Bay views" beyond the oversized windows.

Cha-Ya Vegetarian Japanese Restaurant ✍ Japanese/Vegan

24 | 12 | 18 | $21

NEW Mission | 762 Valencia St. (bet. 18th & 19th Sts.) | 415-252-7825
See review in East of San Francisco Directory.

Cheesecake Factory, The American

16 | 16 | 16 | $28

Downtown | Macy's | 251 Geary Blvd., 8th fl. (bet. Powell & Stockton Sts.) | 415-391-4444 | www.thecheesecakefactory.com
Ingest a "full day's calories" in one meal at these "predictable" yet "dependable" American chain links where "gargantuan portions" of "light-on-the-pocketbook" eats are listed on a menu that, even if you "cut in half, still takes 20 minutes" to peruse; it's so "popular" with "tourists and families with kids" that the "horrendous waits" can run "well over an hour" – no wonder the "staff often seems harried and exhausted"; P.S. the "cheesecakes are, of course, wonderful."

ⓩ Chenery Park Ⓜ American

22 | 18 | 22 | $37

Glen Park | 683 Chenery St. (Diamond St.) | 415-337-8537 |
www.chenerypark.com
The "type of neighborhood restaurant everyone wants" nearby, this "upscale" yet "homey" storefront in the "local village" of Glen Park serves up "delicious", "down-to-earth" New American (with Cajun touches) "comfort food at comfort prices" matched with a "deep" California-centric wine list; the "cheerful ambiance" and "jolly" staff that "treats you like family" make it the "go-to" choice for "every occasion" but it particularly appeals to parents who "miss the fancy restaurants Downtown"; P.S. "avoid Tuesday's kids' night if you don't have them."

Chez Maman French

21 | 14 | 19 | $28

Cow Hollow | 2223 Union St. (bet. Fillmore & Steiner Sts.) | 415-771-7771
Potrero Hill | 1453 18th St. (bet. Connecticut & Missouri Sts.) | 415-824-7166
www.chezmamansf.com
"*Mon Dieu!*", what a "charmer" weep Francophiles who insist it's "worth the wait" to "pull up a counter seat" at this all-day, "teensy weany" Potrero Hill Chez Papa sibling (or the larger Cow Hollow branch); it's "always exactly what I want" – a "glass of Châteauneuf du Pape" with "fussy-free" yet "*magnifique*" "bistro staples" prepared short-order style *à la* "French diner" yet far better than "our *mamans* made for us" – plus it's "tough to say what is hotter: the oven . . . or the staff."

Chez Papa Bistrot French

23 | 17 | 21 | $39

Potrero Hill | 1401 18th St. (Missouri St.) | 415-824-8210 |
www.chezpapasf.com
Oui, the "Left Bank has nothing" on this "magical" "bistro on top of Potrero Hill" say the "Francophiles" who find "comfort" in the "substantial portions" of "hearty" French "classics" served here; for some, the "tiny" quarters are "too cramped", thus leading to "noise levels" that can "border on unbearable", but most just happily "get to know their

neighbors", perhaps by sharing something from the "superb wine list"; N.B. a new branch is slated to open in the Mint Plaza fall 2007.

Chez Spencer ⊠ *French*

24 | 20 | 22 | $55

Mission | 82 14th St. (bet. Folsom & Harrison Sts.) | 415-864-2191 | www.chezspencer.net

"'*Chez* Romantic' should be the name" of this "adorable", "secluded" French bistro "off the beaten gentrified track" of the Mission offering a "congregation of foodies" and first-daters dressed in everything "from leather to sweaters and pearls" a "bit of extravagance"; indulge in "*très cher* but *très bon*" fare, including "sensually flavored", "adventurous" "meats roasted in the brick oven" with "fabulous cocktails" in the "lovely" "vine-covered garden" or the "noisy", "vaulted-loft", "funky" "industrial warehouse" – what a "satisfying experience."

NEW Chiaroscuro ⊠ *Italian*

- | - | - | M

Downtown | 550 Washington St. (bet. Hotaling Pl. & Sansome St.) | 415-362-6012 | www.chiaroscurosf.com

Located Downtown by the Transamerica Pyramid, this midpriced Italian channels the glamour of 1940s and '50s black-and-white cinema in its stylized dining room; slip into a poured-concrete bench beneath oversized street lanterns, order a plate of gnocchi and you'll feel transported to a streetside cafe in Rome; N.B. beer and wine only.

Chloe's Cafe ⊅ *American*

21 | 12 | 17 | $16

Noe Valley | 1399 Church St. (26th St.) | 415-648-4116

The "people of Noe" "brave long lines", packing into this "tiny", "popular corner" sidewalk cafe for "splendid" scrambles, pancakes and other Traditional American breakfast and lunch chow served with a "smile"; the "homey", "cramped quarters", "reminiscent of a B&B" are "part of the charm", plus you can also "sit outside on a sunny morning with a dog in tow"; still, snarky sorts snort the "comfort food" is "only a revelation to those who have never cracked an egg."

Chouchou *French*

21 | 17 | 20 | $36

Forest Hills | 400 Dewey Blvd. (Laguna Honda Blvd.) | 415-242-0960 | www.chouchousf.com

This "darling" storefront bistro may be in Forest Hills, but given the "excellent country cooking", "Frenchie" waiters (all "hugs and air kisses") and "elbow-to-elbow seating", it's feels so much like a "slice of Paris" "you expect to see the Eiffel Tower reflected in the windows"; the "fantastic" signature cassoulets and "sublime" "fruit tarts are as good as any" in France – and "no wonder: the owner is from the City of Light and owns a pastry shop in Montmartre."

∄ Chow/Park Chow *American*

20 | 15 | 18 | $23

Castro | 215 Church St. (bet. 15th & Market Sts.) | 415-552-2469
Inner Sunset | 1240 Ninth Ave. (bet. Irving & Lincoln Sts.) | 415-665-9912

When you "don't know what you feel like eating", these Inner Sunset and Castro "workhorses" are a "top choice" for "diverse" yet "failsafe" Californian-style New American "comfort food" whose Asian, French and Italian influences provide "something for everyone in the family", from "carnivores to vegetarians", from folks in their "20s" to the "80s set"; no reservations are taken, but there's an "advance callin" system; N.B. there's also a branch in Lafayette, East of San Francisco.

NEW Circa *American*

18 | 19 | 16 | $40

Marina | 2001 Chestnut St. (Fillmore St.) | 415-351-0175 |
www.circasf.com

At this "swankier" successor to the Marina's previously "doomed" tenant, Cozmo's, "striking" crystal chandeliers set the stage for the "updated" New American small-plates menu featuring the "unique, satisfying" likes of PB&J foie gras sandwich and "to-die-for lobster macaroni"; however, the "servers are still trying to figure it out" and you still need to be "beautiful and cool to get in" to the adjoining bar area that "turns into a nightclub-ish scene after hours."

Circolo ⧉ *Asian/Nuevo Latino*

19 | 21 | 16 | $43

Mission | 500 Florida St. (Mariposa St.) | 415-553-8560 | www.circolosf.com

The "vibe is like a trendier city" at this "cool, contemporary", multi-level "supper club–meets-discotheque" "find" in a "transitional" part of the Mission serving "unexpectedly generous" portions of "interesting", "well-executed" Nuevo-Latino–Asian fare; night owls hoot it's a "good venue to hold a party – you can linger over food and cocktails" like "t-d-f mango mojitos" "without moving to another bar"; still, a few shrug "not my scene" and deem the staff "inept."

Citizen Cake/Cupcake *Bakery/Californian*

20 | 16 | 17 | $30

Downtown | Virgin Megastore | 2 Stockton St., 3rd fl. (Market St.) |
415-399-1565 | www.citizencupcake.com

Hayes Valley | 399 Grove St. (Gough St.) | 415-861-2228 |
www.citizencake.com Ⓜ

There are two camps at this "hip", "minimal" Hayes Valley bakery/restaurant: "sweet-tooth" loyalists are "ready to sign up for citizenship" just to taste Elizabeth Falkner's "orgasmic pastry delights", while square-meal types counter it's "not just" baked goods – the "innovative" Californian fare is "wonderful" too; head to the "delightful" Union Square cafe above Virgin Megastore for a "quick lunch", cocktails and, of course, "delicious cupcakes"; N.B. diners may no longer have to sit "cheek" by "jowl" at the Grove Street locale thanks to a recent remodel.

Citizen Thai and The Monkey *Thai*

20 | 21 | 19 | $30

North Beach | 1268 Grant Ave. (Vallejo St.) | 415-364-0008

A "neighborhood place with pizzazz" and a respite from North Beach's "glut of mediocre Italian, this downstairs Thai/upstairs noodle twosome with a bar to boot boasts a "beautiful" setting, "fun" atmosphere, "truly mouthwatering", "surprisingly inexpensive" dishes and, yes, "inventive cocktails"; curry served in a "real carved pumpkin is a must-get" – it's the kind of food that's sure to "make Buddha happier" – or make an impression on a "first date."

Citrus Club *Pan-Asian*

19 | 12 | 15 | $17

Haight-Ashbury | 1790 Haight St. (Shrader St.) | 415-387-6366

Never mind the "no-frills" setting on Haight and the "ridiculously long waits" – just follow the "enticing smells that pull you in from the side-walk" advise admirers who come to this "fun and funky" Pan-Asian "joint" for a "quick noodle fix"; "you can't go wrong" with the "super-cheap, very filling" "big ol'" bowls of "mind-blowing" soups and "flavorful" stir-fries that "satisfy your belly without straining your wallet"; still, the less-impressed shrug it's "kinda bland."

Clémentine 🗷 *French*

24 | 21 | 23 | $43

Inner Richmond | 126 Clement St. (bet. 2nd & 3rd Aves.) | 415-387-0408

"Everyone actually speaks French" at this "charming" piece of "Paris in the Richmond" that "whisks you" abroad with its "heavenly" bistro fare, luring an "older crowd" that comes for the "excellent value" "prix fixe locals' menu" and early-bird specials and a younger set that "rendezvous" with their main squeeze later on; the "lovely" staff "makes everyone feel special", and the fare is "always better than you remembered" – what a "class act."

Cliff House Bistro *Californian*

18 | 24 | 19 | $38

Outer Richmond | 1090 Point Lobos Ave. (Geary St.) | 415-386-3330 | www.cliffhouse.com

What a "big step forward" – even Sutro's more casual sibling in the Outer Richmond feels "swankier" following its $18 million renovation in 2004; sure, the "unmatched view" of the Pacific, "surfers and sea otters" makes it a "tourist" "favorite", but the "wonderful aura" makes it a "must for nostalgia" fans and "old locals"; "go at sunset" and grab one of the "best burgers", a drink or "surprisingly good" Californian fare, or for optimal observation, try the "sumptuous" Sunday brunch – you "feel like you're on vacation."

Coco 500 🗷 *Californian/Mediterranean*

22 | 20 | 20 | $43

SoMa | 500 Brannan St. (4th St.) | 415-543-2222 | www.coco500.com

Truly an "incredibly successful transformation" coo acolytes cuckoo for Coco, a "hipper", "swankier", "darker" SoMa den than Loretta Keller's former bistro, Bizou, that's made for "tête-à-tête" conversations; servers with "ESP" serve "novel", "frequently changing" Cal-Med small plates and those "justifiably famous flatbreads" and tempura green beans "foodies" would "walk a mile for" while a "trendy", "under-35 crowd" "bellies up to the bar" for the latest "inventive" whiskey drink – despite a "din" akin to "dining at a NASCAR event."

Coi 🗷 Ⓜ *Californian/French*

25 | 25 | 25 | $94

North Beach | 373 Broadway (Montgomery St.) | 415-393-9000 | www.coirestaurant.com

"This bloke is seriously talented" marvel "adventurous" eaters agog over "rogue chef" Daniel Patterson's "esoteric", "cutting-edge" "El Bulli-style" Californian-French four-course prix fixe and "11 bites" tasting menus; although the scent-illating meals "theatrically" presented with a "dab of perfume alongside" in this minuscule, "minimalist" "tranquil sanctuary amid the strip clubs on Broadway" are "not for everyone", the less formal, late-night lounge offering an additional à la carte menu sans the "big league" prices is a "real boon."

Colibrí Mexican Bistro *Mexican*

20 | 19 | 18 | $35

Downtown | 438 Geary St. (bet. Mason & Taylor Sts.) | 415-440-2737 | www.colibrimexicanbistro.com

"Not your neighborhood taco joint" "by a long shot", this "festive" "theater-district misfit" Downtown is "the real deal: a modern Mexican" "find" that's "great for pre-matinee" meals serving "fabulous muddled margaritas" and a tapas-style menu of "well-prepared", "inventive" dishes; "trust me – order the guacamole made fresh at your table and seasoned to taste" – "it's so good I want to bathe in it" and it comes with "piping hot tortillas"; still, a handful shrug "don't know what the fuss is about."

Cortez *Mediterranean*

23 | 22 | 20 | $46

Downtown | Adagio Hotel | 550 Geary St. (Taylor St.) | 415-292-6360 | www.cortezrestaurant.com

A "hoppin', hip place for the younger crowd" and an "excellent date" spot, this "swanky eatery" in the Adagio Hotel serves up "imaginative" Mediterranean small plates boasting "exquisite pairings of tastes"; the "upbeat" "bar scene is kind of crazy" ("go later to miss the pre-theater crowd"), the staff "cheerful" and, if you "sit in the back of the long, narrow" space, you can "watch the ballet" of "confident" chefs in the open kitchen; N.B. there are now larger entrees for bigger appetites.

Cosmopolitan, The Ⓢ *American*

20 | 20 | 20 | $44

SoMa | Rincon Ctr. | 121 Spear St. (bet. Howard & Mission Sts.) | 415-543-4001 | www.thecosmopolitancafe.com

"Sit, relax and watch everyone else hurry by" at SoMa's "touch of New York tucked into the waterfront scene" near the Embarcadero where "lively piano music" "adds to the atmosphere" and there's "nice stuff coming out of the kitchen"; it's a "comfortable" spot to sip "wonderful cocktails" ("love the Cosmos") and nibble bar food "done right" or "solid all-around" New American fare; still, the less-jazzed shrug it's a "safe bet, but no wows to be had here."

Côté Sud Ⓢ *French*

20 | 17 | 19 | $37

Castro | 4238 18th St. (bet. Collingwood & Diamond Sts.) | 415-255-6565 | www.cotesudsf.com

It's "well worth the walk up" the stairs to this "charming yet modest" "*classique*" French bistro that brings a "touch of Provence" to this sunny Victorian in the Castro; sit on the "small" terrace with "your significant other" and order the "prix fixe dinner that's impossible to beat" – just budget *beaucoup* of time as the "charming" accented *garçons* ("authentic or not") can be "really slow."

Couleur Café *French*

16 | 14 | 16 | $25

Potrero Hill | 300 De Haro St. (16th St.) | 415-255-1021 | www.couleurcafesf.com

"Just like Chez Maman without the cramped atmosphere", this *couleur*-ful all-day Potrero Hill cafe with "Gallic charm to spare" is just "right" for "sharing Brie" and wine "in the sun when the rest of the city is shrouded in fog"; on Sunday nights "relax" with a French flick while dining on "very tasty" French-Med fare with an Arabic accent or "simple" burgers; still, others sing the blues, grumbling "it's not up to par" with its siblings.

Crustacean *Vietnamese*

23 | 17 | 19 | $51

Polk Gulch | 1475 Polk St. (California St.) | 415-776-2722 | www.anfamily.com

"Rising high above Polk Street" (look for the "crustacean in the sky"), this "marvelous", "kitschy" Vietnamese seafooder, like its sibling Thanh Long, is the "absolute king of crab"; sip an "exotic drink" and "stuff yourself happily with garlic noodles" drenched in a "closely guarded secret sauce" and "giant", "succulent" whole-roasted Dungeness you'll "dream about" – and "don't forget the crazy dress code."

Daimaru *Japanese*   ▽ 24 | 10 | 23 | $33

Castro | 290 Sanchez St. (16th St.) | 415-863-9128

A Castro "standby" in spite of its "off-the-beaten-path" location and plain white, bright decor, this "favorite" "bargain" spot lures locals with its "surprising and delicious" Japanese fare, "frequently orgasmically fabulous" sushi and "innovative" specialty rolls; "sit at the bar and get to know the chef" or put yourself in the hands of the "attentive staff" – it "aims to know and please customers."

Deep Sushi ⑤ *Japanese*   21 | 18 | 15 | $35

Noe Valley | 1740 Church St. (bet. 29th & 30th Sts.) | 415-970-3337 | www.deepsushi-sf.com

Despite being "soo deep in Noe Valley", this "raucous" "disco sushi" joint for a "younger 20s crowd" has a "minimalist", "NY-ish feel"; the vibe is "groovy", the "sake drinks potent" and the "hot" chefs crank out "inventive but not wacky" maki like the "'G-roll' (that definitely hits the spot")"; if a few make waves about "too hip to care" service and "barstools tantamount to torture", even they admit "takeout is a great option."

Delancey Street Ⓜ *Eclectic*   18 | 15 | 21 | $27

Embarcadero | 600 The Embarcadero (Brannan St.) | 415-512-5179

"Feed your stomach" with "solid" Eclectic fare "like your bubbe might have cooked" – and "your soul" – by supporting the "humanitarian, socially conscious mission" of helping ex-cons and substance abusers "turn their lives around" at this nonprofit, "worthy culinary stop" near the Embarcadero; the digs are "comfortable", the "patio is a perfect sanctuary" for brunch or an "impromptu lunch", plus service is "personable"; N.B. a recent renovation may outdate the Decor score.

☑ Delfina *Italian*   26 | 19 | 23 | $45

Mission | 3621 18th St. (bet. Dolores & Guerrero Sts.) | 415-552-4055 | www.delfinasf.com

"You won't find tomato sauce" at this "go-to" "Mission treasure" with a "cool, comfy neighborhood vibe", but you will find "exquisitely prepared", "tasty modern" Northern Italian dishes "bursting with flavor" accompanied by an "approachable wine list", all delivered by a "scantily dressed" staff; the "divine", "deceptively simple menu" is so in demand that "it's brutal getting a reservation", so "try waiting for a seat at the bar" – it's even worth enduring the "ridiculous noise factor."

Destino *Nuevo Latino*   22 | 18 | 19 | $35

Castro | 1815 Market St. (bet. Guerrero & Valencia Sts.) | 415-552-4451 | www.destinosf.com

"Good luck getting a table on weekends" at this "romantic" "little sliver of Latin America" on a deserted stretch of Market Street near the Castro serving up "colorful", "contemporary" Peruvian-influenced "small plates that go down easy"; knock back some "potent sangria" or "pisco sours made the right way" while waiting for your "cozy" booth, then indulge in "delicious" fare that "titillates the appetite and dreams long after."

NEW District ◐Ⓜ *Eclectic*   ▽ 17 | 24 | 20 | $35

SoMa | 216 Townsend St. (bet. Ritch & 3rd Sts.) | 415-896-2120 | www.districtsf.com

"Go early to get a seat" and "watch the show" – the servers are "cute", and "good-looking" "bankers and cougars abound" at this "bustling",

FOOD DECOR SERVICE COST

"welcome addition to the SoMa scene" set in a converted "exposed-brick warehouse"; the U-shaped bar boasting an Arc de Triomphe–style wine tower in the center is "amazing" and the vino selection is "fabulous" – and it's matched by a "thoughtful" variety of Eclectic small plates "designed to go with" the vintages (not the other way around).

Dosa Ⓜ Indian
| 20 | 18 | 18 | $28 |

Mission | 995 Valencia St. (21st St.) | 415-642-3672 | www.dosasf.com
"Upscale" "South Indian street food trumped up with a fusiony flash" curries favor at this "hectic" "hipster-tested, Indian-approved" Mission hot spot specializing in "tantalizing dosas" that "give French crêpes a run for their money"; it's costlier than your typical "Formica-table" curry joint and the wait can be "insane" (there's no reserving for parties smaller than five), but "excellent" cocktails from the "unbearably loud" yet "beautiful bar" help numb the pain.

Dottie's True Blue Cafe Diner
| 25 | 12 | 18 | $17 |

Tenderloin | 522 Jones St. (bet. Geary & O'Farrell Sts.) | 415-885-2767
"Gird your loins" and hit the "gritty" Tenderloin for "hearty", "hangover"-curing American breakfasts, brunches and lunches (served till 3 PM closing) at this "cheap" "hole-in-the-wall" '60s-style diner – "the grandfather of all" daytime "joints"; it's "well worth" the "epic" wait to grab a "great cup of joe" and "sit at the counter" where the "friendly" crew "never rushes you", but "better start walking those SF hills right afterwards to burn the calories."

Dragon Well Chinese
| 20 | 16 | 19 | $24 |

Marina | 2142 Chestnut St. (bet. Pierce & Steiner Sts.) | 415-474-6888 | www.dragonwell.com
"Flavorful and well prepared with a minimum of 'bad stuff'", the "reliable" chow at this "clean, modern" Marina mainstay offers "a healthier take" on Chinese chow that's "much better than your typical takeout"; stop in for a "quick no-frills lunch" or for dinner when a "hip dimmed-light ambiance" prevails; if a few fire-breathers fume it's "ersatz" Sino, most maintain that the "differences are for the better", and what's more, the "staff really cares."

NEW Ducca Italian
| - | - | - | M |

SoMa | Westin San Francisco | 50 Third St. (Market St.) | 415-977-0271 | www.duccasf.com
Kitted out with enough hand-blown glass chandeliers and brocade booths to be worthy of a ducca, this sweeping Venetian-inspired Northern Italian in the remodeled Westin San Francisco Market Street is one of SoMa's swankiest new dining spots, complete with a frescoed alfresco terrace and fire pit; the menu focuses on seafood as well as cicchetti (bar snacks), which are laid out on a 12-ft.-long, marble-topped bar in the center of the main dining room.

E&O Trading Company SE Asian
| 19 | 20 | 18 | $36 |

Downtown | 314 Sutter St. (bet. Grant Ave. & Stockton St.) | 415-693-0303 | www.eotrading.com
With a "wild colonial decor" straight out of an "*Indiana Jones* set" that's "dark, a bit forbidding" and "transporting", a "lively bar scene" and an "interesting" menu that "takes the best of every" Southeast Asian "culture and presents it like a gift", this trio (Downtown and

in San Jose and Larkspur) is "wonderful in all ways"; "order an assortment" of "tasty small plates" and "eat family-style" with a "large group" and "experience different flavors" – and "don't forget" the "delightful corn fritters."

E'Angelo ⊠⇪ *Italian*

20 | 10 | 19 | $28

Marina | 2234 Chestnut St. (bet. Pierce & Scott Sts.) | 415-567-6164
It's worth enduring the "hideous lines" to chow down with "real, actual San Francisco Italians" at this "longtime" Marina eatery where they "squeeze you" into a "tiny, tight" "narrow space"; the decor may not be fancy, but the "hearty, old-style" "red-gravy" dishes are "dependably good" and "in tune with the ambiance", and the servers are reminiscent of "my godfathers"; still, a few feel its "charm is fading."

Ebisu *Japanese*

23 | 13 | 17 | $34

Inner Sunset | 1283 Ninth Ave. (Irving St.) | 415-566-1770 | www.ebisusushi.com
Even "in a town with so many options" this "time-honored" Inner Sunset Japanese "blows them out of the water" insist "sushi-seekers" who claim that the "awesome rolls" are "well worth" the "long" "wait in the cold and fog"; once inside, sit "traditional-style, on the floor, with shoes off" or "at the bar and order super-fresh (or even live) seafood" "without the Downtown markup" – you'll "walk away happy"; still, cynics retort that it "doesn't live up to the hype"; N.B. renovation plans are underway.

El Balazo *Mexican*

18 | 14 | 14 | $12

Haight-Ashbury | 1654 Haight St. (Clayton St.) | 415-864-2140 | www.elbalazo.net
"You'll be stuffed beyond recognition" after inhaling "hearty burritos made with unusual ingredients" at this "colorful", "cool-looking", "hollowed-out Victorian"-turned-Mexican-taqueria on Upper Haight that's "survived years of patchouli damage with nary an ill effect"; "watch the parade of characters stroll by" while enjoying the "excellent" veggie variation named after The Dead or "tasty" tacos – there's "no skimping on the shrimp or fish"; still, a handful huff "go to the Mission if you want the real" deal.

Elite Cafe *Cajun/Creole*

19 | 19 | 19 | $43

Upper Fillmore | 2049 Fillmore St. (bet. California & Pine Sts.) | 415-673-5483 | www.theelitecafe.com
"Bring your earplugs and be ready to wait" for the "spicy" Cajun-Creole food that's "better with the new chef" at this "venerable" Upper Fillmore haunt with a "good buzz" and "New Orleans" feel; still, some members of the Elite fleet opt for the "delicious brunch" offering "buttery, flaky" biscuits,"unique takes on standard fare" and "beguiling Bloody Marys" rather than the "less-impressive" dinner, declaring "it just did not float my boat."

Eliza's *Chinese*

22 | 16 | 15 | $23

Pacific Heights | 2877 California St. (bet. Broderick & Divisadero Sts.) | 415-621-4819
Potrero Hill | 1457 18th St. (bet. Connecticut & Missouri Sts.) | 415-648-9999
The "Matisse-esque" decor and "pretty glass-globe" ceiling fixtures may "break the mold", but the "California-ized Chinese" vittles at this

	FOOD	DECOR	SERVICE	COST

Pac Heights/Potrero Hill pair are "uniformly delicious"; even "food snobs" "forget Chinatown" and fulfill their "inexpensive Asian cravin'" here, scarfing down "memorable meals" in portions that would please "Goldilocks" as they're "not too much, not too little – but just right"; still, nitpickers pout service is "rude" and "rushed" – they make you feel like a "burden."

Ella's American

20	13	18	$22

Presidio Heights | 500 Presidio Ave. (California St.) | 415-441-5669 | www.ellassanfrancisco.com

Join the "long line every weekend morning" to get into this daytime Presidio Heights "brunch godmother", dishing out "generous portions" of "really homey" American "comfort food"; yeah, it "looks like a hotel coffee shop", but it's "entertaining to sit at the counter watching" the staff make "freshly baked bread", chicken hash that "shines" and "pancakes the size of your head"; but it doesn't egg-ree with detractors who tut it's "tired."

El Metate Mexican

▽ 23	13	17	$9

Mission | 2406 Bryant St. (22nd St.) | 415-641-7209

"Off the beaten path" in the Mission, this "cheerful", "cutesy taqueria" with a "cantina" feel and "sidewalk seating to boot" delivers "authentic, tasty" Baja-style fish tacos "made from scratch" and "homestyle" dishes "without charging any more than the sketchy place on the corner"; "another plus" is the "friendly and accommodating owner" who oversees everything like a "Mexican auntie", including a new on-site market and a recent expansion.

El Raigon ⊠ Argentinean

21	18	19	$48

North Beach | 510 Union St. (Grant Ave.) | 415-291-0927 | www.elraigon.com

Decorated with "cow-print paintings", this "stable"-like "beef eater's delight" serving "every variety", from the "unreal *asado de tira* to the more common" "rib-eye and New York strip" may not be the "place to take your vegetarian friends", but when you want a "meat-night-out in North Beach" it's one of the "best" options "this side of Buenos Aires"; make like a "gaucho" and gobble up the "tender, mouth-wateringly flavorful" steaks, but take heed: the "steep" prices "appear to exceed Argentina's GNP."

Emmy's Spaghetti Shack Italian

19	16	16	$22

Bernal Heights | 18 Virginia Ave. (Mission St.) | 415-206-2086

The "classic spaghetti and gia-normous meatballs" "can't be beat" at Bernal Heights' "darling", "divey" "hipster hangout for night owls" and "hot, young chefs", where you can also "belly up" to the bar for "gourmet cocktail concoctions"; "some folks might ding" the "kitschy" decor and scoff that the "staff lets you know if you're not cool enough", but for most it's "everything you could hope for" in a "funky" "favorite."

Emporio Rulli Dessert

20	20	15	$23

Downtown | Union Square Pavilion | 225 Stockton St. (bet. Geary & Post Sts.) | 415-433-1122
Marina | 2300 Chestnut St. (Scott St.) | 415-923-6464
www.rulli.com

See review in North of San Francisco Directory.

FOOD | DECOR | SERVICE | COST

Enrico's Sidewalk Cafe 🕙Ⓜ *American/Mediterranean*

– | – | – | M

North Beach | 504 Broadway (Kearny St.) | 415-982-6223

The beat goes on once again at this legendary North Beach sidewalk cafe that's reopened under the direction of a new team of restaurant vets (also behind Venticello, Bambudda and others); while the view of Broadway from the massive heated front patio and the nightly live jazz in the recently spiffed-up, now Parisian-style digs (featuring the original mural of the Howl posse) remain the lure, the New American-Med menu offering sliders, pizza and pasta also reels 'em in.

Eos Restaurant & Wine Bar *Asian/Californian*

23 | 19 | 20 | $41

Cole Valley | 901 Cole St. (Carl St.) | 415-566-3063 | www.eossf.com

This "swanky" "gem" in "parking-nonexistent" Cole Valley retains the "perfect balance of buzz and energy" and still delivers "inventive" Cal-Asian fare "in bite-size increments"; is it a "scaled-up neighborhood joint, a not-quite destination restaurant" or a "romantic" "date night place"? – whichever, the "wine list is from heaven" both in the restaurant and the attached "hip yet unassuming" vino bar, and the "all-knowing staff" helps "pair them up" with the "unique" small plates.

Eric's *Chinese*

20 | 14 | 16 | $20

Noe Valley | 1500 Church St. (27th St.) | 415-282-0919

Noe Valleyites profess a "deep, abiding love" for this "popular" "neighborhood reliable" serving up "healthier" Chinese food with a "twist" in a "lovely", "high-ceilinged" Victorian flat; the vegetables are "pristine", the "inventive" dishes "several cuts above typical Asian" fare and "you can't beat" the "great-value lunch" – "if you know what to order, you know its secret" charms; still, don't expect to "linger" as the "super-fast service is designed to get you fed and out the door."

Esperpento *Spanish*

21 | 16 | 16 | $26

Mission | 3295 22nd St. (Valencia St.) | 415-282-8867

"Bring lots of friends", order the "interesting array" of "super tapas" "dripping with olive oil" and "redolent of garlic" that's certain to be a "crowd-pleaser" – and "don't forget the sangria" advise admirers of this "funky" Missionite; the "vibrant ambiance" is occasionally enhanced by visits from a "random mariachi band" and on weekends you can graze all day long; still, a handful hiss that service is "tricky" and cry it's "way too loud."

Espetus Churrascaria *Brazilian*

21 | 16 | 21 | $46

Hayes Valley | 1686 Market St. (bet. Brady & Haight Sts.) | 415-552-8792 | www.espetus.com

A "real Brazilian experience" in Hayes Valley, this "carnivore's dream" "convenient to the symphony and opera" elicits "occasional bursts of 'wow'" – and no wonder: the "veritable meat parade of marching gauchos carrying skewers" of "superbly grilled chicken hearts", filet mignon and other "fun, all-you-can-eat" barbecued "treats" on "extremely long sticks" is "irresistible"; when the "relentless assault" brings on a protein "coma", "turn over the sign on your table" that tells the "staff to stop stuffing you."

	FOOD	DECOR	SERVICE	COST

NEW Essencia 🗷 *Peruvian* | - | - | - | M

Hayes Valley | 401 Gough St. (Hayes St.) | 415-552-8485 |
www.essenciarestaurant.com

Occupying a prime corner in Hayes Valley, this midpriced Nuevo
Peruvian with a Californian-organic edge heralds the eagerly awaited
return of chef Anne Gingrass Paik (formerly of Desiree Café and
Hawthorne Lane); the earth-toned dining room is outfitted with red
acacia tabletops and an oversized triptych canvas depicting the three
natural elements of Peru – mountain, ocean and jungle.

NEW Eureka Restaurant & | ▽ 21 | 20 | 22 | $41
Lounge Ⓜ *American*

Castro | 4063 18th St. (bet. Castro & Hartford Sts.) | 415-431-6000 |
www.eurekarestaurant.com

Eureka! – this "worthy spin-off of Chenery Park" "brings high style" to the
"cuisine-challenged Castro", wooing "comfort-food" fans with "excellent" "nouvelle" American fare delivered by "attentive yet unobtrusive" staffers; "grab a window seat upstairs" in the "stylish", "intimate
bar" and sip "foo-foo" cocktails while watching the nightly parade of
"hipsters pass by"; but spoilers suggest "the downtown prices" are "a
bit rich" for what's really a "fancied-up" "neighborhood place."

Ⓩ Farallon *Seafood* | 24 | 27 | 24 | $63

Downtown | 450 Post St. (bet. Mason & Powell Sts.) | 415-956-6969 |
www.farallonrestaurant.com

"Where's my *Little Mermaid*?" quip acolytes who drop anchor at the
"new raw bar" then "dive" headlong into the "aquatic fantasy" of this
"whimsical" Downtown "temple to seafood" that pumps up the "visual
drama" with an "under-the-sea" decor "oozing maritime decadence";
the "huge jellyfishlike lamps adorning" the "gorgeous mosaic ceiling"
and "conch-shell booths" add to the "great escapist dining experience" sure to "impress" visitors while the "fin-ominally good", "delec-
tably" prepared fish "concoctions are more intricate than they let on",
and it's all delivered by "well-schooled" servers.

NEW Farina *Italian* | - | - | - | M

Mission | 3560 18th St. (Guerrero St.) | 415-565-0360

Elbowing its way into the 18th Street gourmet ghetto, this airy Italian that
just swung open its casement windows is already attracting a Mission
crowd as good-looking as its modern decor (dark woods, marble tabletops, designer light fixtures); authentic Genovese-style focaccia reigns
here, but the all-day menu also includes housemade gnocchi, pastas,
cured meats and seafood; N.B. a full bar is in the works.

farmerbrown *Soul Food* | 19 | 19 | 17 | $30

Tenderloin | 25 Mason St. (bet. Eddy & Turk Sts.) | 415-409-3276 |
www.farmerbrownsf.com

"Dressed-up soul food (not like mama used to make)", "tasty cocktails"
served in "darling Mason jars" and "cool beats from the DJ" lure an "interesting mix of tourists" and regulars to this "nouveau industrial-chic"
standby in a "seedy" area of the Tenderloin; the "satisfying" "riffs on
comfort classics" made with "feel-good" organic, biodynamic and/or
sustainable ingredients sourced from local and African-American
farmers "never disappoint" – they "get better with every visit."

	FOOD	DECOR	SERVICE	COST

1550 Hyde Café & Wine Bar Ⓜ *Californian/Mediterranean*

| 22 | 17 | 20 | $43 |

Russian Hill | 1550 Hyde St. (bet. Jackson & Pacific Aves.) | 415-775-1550 | www.1550hyde.com

Touting "a wine list with five times as many choices as there are seats in the place" and a "sommelier who knows his stuff", this "unassuming" Russian Hill "neighborhood haunt" "with a cable car going by every now and then" "packs so much creative culinary talent" and "passion" into "such a small", "minimalist" space; despite the "din" and "impossible parking", the "reasonably priced", seasonal organic Cal-Med fare (don't miss the midweek prix fixe) and "charming" staff make it "worth the trek up."

Fifth Floor Ⓩ *Californian/French*

| 25 | 24 | 25 | $87 |

SoMa | Hotel Palomar | 12 Fourth St., 5th fl. (Market St.) | 415-348-1555 | www.fifthfloorrestaurant.com

"Low lit" and "oh-so-hip" with "zebra-striped carpets" and an art deco "supper-club" vibe, this "dot-com" survivor in SoMa's Hotel Palomar remains the "haunt of businessmen and couples celebrating events"; the "discreetly dressed, expert staff" dotes on diners, delivering "sophisticated" "splurge"-worthy Californian–New French fare along with a 1,400-bin wine list that's still its "shining virtue"; but the less-floored feel the fare "depends on who's the chef du jour" – and indeed the top toque is soon expected to change again.

Fior d'Italia *Italian*

| 19 | 18 | 20 | $46 |

North Beach | San Remo Hotel | 2237 Mason St. (Chestnut St.) | 415-986-1886 | www.fior.com

The "less-formal" ambiance with "better lighting" makes this "North Beach staple" "sing like Caruso" chorus fans of America's oldest Italian restaurant, a "food lover's delight" that relocated to this San Remo Hotel location in 2005 and "still delivers" "flavorful", "traditional" Northern Boot fare; but the wistful whistle another tune sighing it's "not what it once was despite – or on account of – the massive tourist trade."

Firecracker Ⓜ *Californian/Chinese*

| 19 | 17 | 18 | $29 |

Mission | 1007½ Valencia St. (21st St.) | 415-642-3470

"Way better than you would think it would be" applaud "consistently pleased" admirers who commend the "clean, inventive" Cal-Chinese fare and "out-of-the-ordinary sauces" at this "solid" Missionite; but detractors explode that it has "so much potential" but it's "lost its way" (and its "fizzle") – "some dishes are divine", other offerings just have "no verve"; P.S. "bring your own lighting if you want to read the menu."

Ⓩ Firefly *Eclectic*

| 25 | 20 | 23 | $40 |

Noe Valley | 4288 24th St. (Douglass St.) | 415-821-7652 | www.fireflyrestaurant.com

A "real powerhouse" boasting "extraordinary charm" and seasonal, "soulful, flavorful" "Eclectic gourmet" fare, this "unpretentious", "cozy nook" "perfect" for an "intimate weeknight dinner with friends" or a "romantic" interlude with a "loved one" attracts "Noe Valley natives in-the-know", but it's "definitely worth the trip" "for folks from other neighborhoods"; the "homey atmosphere welcomes you", and once the "gracious staff" delivers the "just plain delicious" "treats" and "healthy wine list", the place "starts buzzing" and everyone seems to "glow."

⊠ Fleur de Lys ⊠ *Californian/French*   28 | 27 | 26 | $94

Nob Hill | 777 Sutter St. (bet. Jones & Taylor Sts.) | 415-673-7779 | www.fleurdelyssf.com

"Can you improve on fabulous?" ask the starstruck who spend a "magical evening of luxury" at Nob Hill's "ultraromantic" Cal–New French "oasis of calm and civility" where "even the menu is pretty", the decor is *très* "Moulin Rouge" and the "bright servers suggest, deliver and describe" the "culinary delights"; longtime chef Hubert Keller keeps everything "fresh and exciting", crafting "decadent" prix fixe options (including an "exquisite" vegetarian choice) with "whimsical touches"; *oui*, prices are "princely", but the "outstanding" wine list alone "seduces you back."

Florio *French/Italian*   19 | 18 | 18 | $41

Pacific Heights | 1915 Fillmore St. (bet. Bush & Pine Sts.) | 415-775-4300 | www.floriosf.com

What a "grand neighborhood classic" laud loyalists of this "sophisticated, but unpretentious" Pac Heights "trattoria-cum-bistro", the "kind of place" where the "dark", "lively" "atmosphere makes dinner special" and the "French-Italian home cooking" is "up to snuff", right "down to the last hot frites"; it's "small", so forget "super-secretive conversations", but they don't "rush you to make way for the next group", so you can count on "a nice evening out"; N.B. a recent chef change may impact the Food score.

Fog City Diner *American*   19 | 19 | 18 | $35

Embarcadero | 1300 Battery St. (Greenwich St.) | 415-982-2000 | www.fogcitydiner.com

The original "San Francisco treat" – "toot, toot" – set in a "classy", "totally retro" converted railroad car "just a short trolley jaunt away" from The Wharf along the Embarcadero, this "aptly named" "local institution" is "not a diner like they make 'em back East"; it's not the 1980s "hot spot" "you've seen in the VISA commercial" either, but it still attracts a "convivial" mix of tourists, celebrities and "characters as good" as the "eccentric" New American fare.

Foreign Cinema *Californian/Mediterranean*   21 | 24 | 20 | $44

Mission | 2534 Mission St. (bet. 21st & 22nd Sts.) | 415-648-7600 | www.foreigncinema.com

"Have a little Fellini with your frites" at the Mission's "novel", "arty" "repeat venue" where "hipsters" sip "killer mojitos" and sup on "excellent" Cal-Med fare in the "chic loft-style" dining room; "on a starry night", "escape to another world" outside on the courtyard amid heat lamps and "old-time drive-in speaker boxes" where "foreign flicks are projected on a wall", "candlelight glows on your partner's face" – and servers exude the "cheeriness of an Ingmar Bergman" film.

Fournou's Ovens *Californian/Mediterranean*   22 | 21 | 22 | $59

Nob Hill | Renaissance Stanford Ct. | 905 California St. (Powell St.) | 415-989-1910 | www.fournousovens.com

"Sit near the ovens" to view "theater in progress" at the Renaissance Stanford Court's "pleasant carnivorous surprise" boasting an

	FOOD	DECOR	SERVICE	COST

"expense-account setting" with a "cool, old-time atmosphere" in "historic" Nob Hill; an "extremely helpful" staff delivers Cal-Med "standards" such as "crisp duck, hot out of the oven" "prepared to your liking" – it's "added entertainment if your date isn't interesting"; but hotheads huff this "once-favored spot" emanates a "faded glory" that just feels "tired."

☑ Frascati *Californian/Mediterranean* | 26 | 20 | 24 | $45 |
Russian Hill | 1901 Hyde St. (Green St.) | 415-928-1406 | www.frascatisf.com

Though "still a neighborhood classic", this "beguiling Russian Hill boîte" with a "romantic-in-a-rustic-sort-of-way" atmosphere and a "cable car rambling by" has also "graduated to a destination" spot; it's "consistently wonderful in every way", from the "stunning" Cal-Med fare and "definite buzz" factor to the staff that "treats you like you're part of the family"; yes, the owner has changed, but the "charm and warmth" "remain intact" – it's always a "sure thing for a first date or an evening of celebration."

Fresca *Peruvian* | 22 | 18 | 17 | $33 |
West Portal | 24 W. Portal Ave. (Ulloa St.) | 415-759-8087
Noe Valley | 3945 24th St. (bet. Noe & Sanchez Sts.) | 415-695-0549
Upper Fillmore | 2114 Fillmore St. (California St.) | 415-447-2668
www.frescasf.com

"Who needs Machu Pichu" when this "wildly popular" "Inca-meets-Noe"/Upper Fillmore/West Portal outfit stirs up such a "lively scene", replete with "fine Peruvian fare", a "damn good" selection of "delicious" ceviche, "amazing sangria" and "margaritas that make almost everything else go down nicely"; still, kvetchers carp that the "distracted but well-meaning" staff "needs to get its act together."

☑ Fringale *French* | 24 | 18 | 21 | $46 |
SoMa | 570 Fourth St. (bet. Brannan & Bryant Sts.) | 415-543-0573 | www.fringalesf.com

SoMa's long-running "great imitation of a French bistro" remains a "reliable standby" for "tasty" "Basque-hearty" fare with Mediterranean touches and a "compact wine list" that "doesn't gouge" customers' wallets; a "true Gallic experience" right down to the "cramped, noisy" setting and heavily accented, "witty" garçons, the spot's "lively patrons" include both business-lunchers and "starry-eyed dates", all of whom agree that it's "aging nicely" "even with the change in chef and ownership."

Frisson ☒ *American* | 20 | 25 | 20 | $52 |
Downtown | 244 Jackson St. (bet. Battery & Front Sts.) | 415-956-3004 | www.frissonsf.com

"It isn't Justin Timberlake that's bringing sexy back" – so is this Downtown "Kingdom of Cool" with its "funky" '70s-style "lounge setting" and "hip DJ music" where "hotties" "pose" over "experimental cocktails" at the "bumpin'" bar, over platefuls of "sophisticated" New American eats that reveal "occasional flashes of brilliance" and in the "unisex bathrooms"; still, detractors cavil that the fare "doesn't quite come up to par" or justify the "steep tabs" and chafe at "cheeky" service that's "as ephemeral as the name."

Frjtz Fries *Belgian*
19 | 14 | 13 | $15

Hayes Valley | 579 Hayes St. (Laguna St.) | 415-864-7654
NEW Mission | 590 Valencia St. (17th St.) | 415-863-8272
www.frjtzfries.com

"So many dips and not enough" frites "to eat them all" weep fanatics who frjeak over the "addicting" "fat" "Belgian frjes" and "harder-to-find" selections of "Trappist beer" at Hayes Valley's "bohemian" "art cafe" that also serves "ok" crêpes and "decent" salads; "stay for the down-tempo music and cushy seating" or retreat to the "pleasant" patio area outside; N.B. the new black-and-white Mission perch boasts window seats and a bigger menu selection.

NEW Front Porch, The *Caribbean*
20 | 17 | 17 | $27

Mission | 65A 29th St. (Tiffany Ave.) | 415-695-7800 |
www.thefrontporchsf.com

Juxtaposing a "homey" "kitschy" vibe "complete with old tin ceilings" and rocking chairs with "hip" "head-ringingly loud music", this affordable, Caribbean-inspired gastropub "feels more like you're in the East Village" than the Outer Mission where it's "a neighborhood hit"; hipster habitués cool their jets on the, you guessed it, front porch, before sharing a "popcorn bucket" of "out-of-this-world" fried chicken and "a box of wine"; alas, service can be as "slow" as molasses.

Z Garden Court *Californian*
19 | 28 | 21 | $52

Downtown | Palace Hotel | 2 New Montgomery St. (Market St.) |
415-546-5010 | www.gardencourt-restaurant.com

"Without a doubt the grandest room in San Francisco", this "spectacular" "historic landmark" in the Downtown Palace Hotel – originally the hotel's "carriage court" – is "reminiscent of Victorian aristocracy" promising a "postcard-perfect ambiance" and Californian cuisine, including afternoon tea that's "fit for a queen" and a "wonderful" Sunday jazz brunch; even grumps who groan that the "pricey" spreads are "more of a feast for the eyes than the tummies" admit that the "beautiful" stained-glass atrium is worth a "peek in to admire"; N.B. daytime-only – no dinner is served.

Garibaldis *Californian/Mediterranean*
21 | 20 | 21 | $45

Presidio Heights | 347 Presidio Ave. (bet. Clay & Sacramento Sts.) |
415-563-8841 | www.garibaldisrestaurant.com

"You can't go wrong" at this "lovely", "welcoming" Presidio Heights "standby" (and its East Bay sibling, "perhaps the closest thing to Manhattan in Oakland") serving "delicious", "satisfying" Cal-Med fare that "never disappoints"; the "caring" staff, "charming" digs and "reliable" fare make it a "place you'd be proud to take your parents" – and it's also a "favorite" for "real-life events" like "engagements, anniversaries and occasions where everything must be" "memorable."

Z Gary Danko *American*
29 | 26 | 28 | $104

Fisherman's Wharf | 800 N. Point St. (Hyde St.) | 415-749-2060 |
www.garydanko.com

"Gary Swanko" "fully merits its superb reputation" gush "flush" "foodies" who vote the "celebrity" chef-owner's "sleek" New American "temple of gastronomy" in Fisherman's Wharf No. 1 in the SF Survey for Food and Popularity; it's an "epicurean extravaganza" from

	FOOD	DECOR	SERVICE	COST

the glass of champagne when you sit down to the "impeccable" "build-your-own" "haute" tasting menus and "perfect wine pairings" you'll "talk about for weeks, months and years" to the "simply amazing cheese course"; add in a "surprisingly unstuffy", "synchronized" staff that "treats customers like VIPs" and it's little wonder devotees declare it's the "epitome of fine dining, San Francisco–style."

Gaylord India *Indian*

18	17	18	$36

Downtown | 1 Embarcadero Ctr. | 275 Battery St. (Sacramento St.) | 415-397-7775 | www.gaylords1.com

Part of a global chain, this Sausalito subcontinental with "knockout City views" serves "tasty" Northern Indian fare that keeps loyalists "going back" in an "elaborate" setting that's "better looking than many in the 'Tandoori'-loin; on weekdays it's "geared toward the business crowd" but on weekends, live sitar music makes it a "real treat"; still, spice-seekers shrug it's "not distinctive"; P.S. the separately owned SF branch near the Embarcadero theater is "convenient" before catching a "flick."

NEW Gialina *Pizza*

∇ 24	16	21	$24

Glen Park | 2842 Diamond St. (Kern St.) | 415-239-8500 | www.gialina.com

"Things are stepping up in Glen Park" say devotees of this Chianti-colored newcomer where "neighbors" and "industry foodies" munch on "fantastic" Neopolitan-style "thin-crust" pizzas topped with the "freshest" "creative" ingredients (including a "worth-the-drive", "kid-friendly" dessert pie); don't be cowed by the no-reservations policy – the "sweet" staff "turns tables quickly" and, once in, the "nicely chosen" list of Italian vinos soothes spirits.

Giordano Bros. *Sandwiches*

∇ 21	13	19	$15

North Beach | 303 Columbus Ave. (Broadway St.) | 415-397-2767

"Who knew I wanted french fries, coleslaw and meat in the same sandwich?" – even "homesick" Pittsburgh folk are "impressed" with the "all-in-one" cheese steaks served up by "friendly owners" at this North Beach "joint" that's so "small" "economy of movement is required for eating"; "wash down that delicious grease" with a "Stella in a bucket" and "listen to really loud" free "local music", which is either "intense" or "chill", depending on your threshold; N.B. open till 1 AM on weekends.

Giorgio's Pizzeria *Pizza*

20	11	17	$18

Inner Richmond | 151 Clement St. (3rd Ave.) | 415-668-1266 | www.giorgiospizza.com

"Every neighborhood should have one" of these "1960s-style" "non-pretentious" pizzerias, complete with "classic" red-and-white checked tablecloths, "artificial" grapevines and Chianti bottles, all of which give the "dark" and "dated" Inner Richmond dining room a "small town, East Coast feel"; just don't go to this prime "pie and a pitcher with friends" spot "too early" in the eve, or "you'll be overrun by the toddler set."

Globe ● *Californian/Italian*

21	17	20	$40

Downtown | 290 Pacific Ave. (bet. Battery & Front Sts.) | 415-391-4132

"After all these years", this "funky lil' Downtowner" is still one of the "classiest late-night restaurants in town", "jammed" after dark with "restaurant folks" and "under-30" night owls dining on "rustic" Cal-Italian eats (like steak for two) served "with a smile" in a "hip", "down-tempo" "NYC-like atmosphere"; earlier eaters rave that it's also "ideal" for weekday lunches, and the "Sunday Market Menu nights are the most fun of all."

Goat Hill Pizza *Pizza* | 19 | 9 | 15 | $17 |

Potrero Hill | 300 Connecticut St. (18th St.) | 415-641-1440
SoMa | 715 Harrison St. (3rd St.) | 415-974-1303
www.goathill.com

"Bring the kids" – they're always "welcomed" at Potrero Hill's "historic" pizzeria (and its take-out-only SoMa offshoot), serving "quintessential" sourdough "crispy" crusts laced with "incredibly fresh" and "abundant" toppings, including vegetarian "favorites"; "deep neighborhood roots", local Anchor Steam on tap and all-you-can-eat Monday nights that feel like a "middle school pizza party that never ends" ratchet up the "homey, friendly" vibe – it's a "keeper."

Godzila Sushi *Japanese* | 17 | 8 | 15 | $25 |

Pacific Heights | 1800 Divisadero St. (Bush St.) | 415-931-1773

The sushi "comes in Godzilla-size pieces" at this little Pac Heights Japanese joint where "wannabe hipster yuppies" and "rich old men" gather for a "casual night out after work or on weekends"; be ready for decor that some find "entertainingly humorous" and others label head-scratchingly "strange", as well as a "stressed-out" staff – they may not be "attentive", but at least they're "quick."

Gold Mountain *Chinese* | 20 | 10 | 12 | $22 |

Chinatown | 644 Broadway (bet. Columbus Ave. & Stockton St.) | 415-296-7733

When it comes to "old-fashioned", "authentic" dim sum that is "really fresh" and "comes quickly out of the kitchen", go for the gold at this "cavernous", "busy" Chinatown banquet hall serving "consistently first-rate seafood" and Chinese specialties that are especially "good if you can bring nine friends"; on the downside, the decor is "dated" and unless you "understand a little Cantonese", the "service is nonexistent."

Good Luck Dim Sum ⊅ *Chinese* | 22 | 4 | 10 | $10 |

Inner Richmond | 736 Clement St. (bet. 8th & 9th Aves.) | 415-386-3388

"Hands down the best" "among a menagerie of dim sum joints on Clement", this dumpling dive steams up "amazing fresh har gow and pork buns" that are the "steal of a century" given that "you could feed an army with $5 worth"; there's no need to speak "Chinese to get by", just "line up with the locals" and "point to what you want" – and do takeout "unless you're into decor masochism" and "unfriendly service."

Goood Frikin' Chicken *Mideastern* | 19 | 9 | 14 | $15 |

Mission | 10 29th St. (Mission St.) | 415-970-2428 | www.gfcsf.com

"The name is truth in advertising" at this Middle Eastern chicken joint near the Outer Mission that "sets a new standard for takeout" with two styles of birds, "the best hummus ever" and other "frikin' tasty" choices; the recently added dining room "makes eating here possible", and even though service "can be spotty", most contend that the staff is "very accommodating of young kids."

	FOOD	DECOR	SERVICE	COST

Grand Cafe *French*

| 20 | 25 | 20 | $46 |

Downtown | Hotel Monaco | 501 Geary St. (Taylor St.) | 415-292-0101 | www.grandcafe-sf.com

This "big", "beautiful", "bold" Downtown pre-theater "favorite" makes you feel like you're "really dining out" thanks to the "cozy" booths and "grand" art nouveau decor reminiscent of "La Coupole in Montparnasse"; the "well-presented" French fare is a "surprising treat" (even if the "chefs keep changing"), especially if you "stick to the standards, nothing esoteric"; still, the less-impressed feel the "food and service don't measure up" to the "gorgeous", "stylish setting."

Grandeho's Kamekyo *Japanese*

| 23 | 14 | 20 | $33 |

Fisherman's Wharf | 2721 Hyde St. (bet. Beach & N. Point Sts.) | 415-673-6828

Cole Valley | 943 Cole St. (bet. Carl St. & Parnassus Ave.) | 415-759-8428

For "sushi in the 'hood", "we don't go anywhere else" confess regulars of this tiny, "top-notch" Japanese joint "tucked into Cole Valley's soul" (with a "handy" outpost "if you are stuck at the Wharf") serving up "stupendous sashimi" in "fine, fat fresh" portions; locals laud the "convivial" atmosphere and "familylike service", and advise putting yourself in "the sushi chefs' hands" since they are "more creative than the menu leads you to believe."

Great Eastern ● *Chinese*

| 22 | 12 | 14 | $27 |

Chinatown | 649 Jackson St. (bet. Grant Ave. & Kearny St.) | 415-986-2500

While it "looks like a tourist trap", this "leader" of the Chinatown pack is "where locals go" for "some of the tastiest", "freshest" Chinese food around, namely "mouthwatering" seafood (picked while it is "still swimming in the tanks" and "prepared any way you like") and "delicious" dim sum ("no carts!"); just disregard the "simple surroundings" and staffers who at times "act annoyed to be serving you."

Green Chile Kitchen & Market *Mexican*

| ∇ 19 | 16 | 20 | $16 |

Western Addition | 601 Baker St. (Fulton St.) | 415-614-9411 | www.greenchilekitchen.com

It may be a long way from from Santa Fe, but this Western Addition spot feels "very close" thanks to this "environmentally conscious" rotisserie-chicken and "burrito shop" that dishes out "cheap" "organic" "New Mexican standards" featuring "refreshing" spins on its namesake peppers and hormone-free meats – and "on groovy plates to boot"; while the kitchen "tempts the neighborhood with lovely smells", dialed-in dine-at-home folks confide you can also call for curbside delivery.

⊠ Greens *Vegetarian*

| 24 | 23 | 22 | $40 |

Marina | Bldg. A, Fort Mason Ctr. (Buchanan St.) | 415-771-6222 | www.greensrestaurant.com

"Even nonvegetarians find plenty to love" at Annie Somerville's "grande old dame" of "haute Zen cuisine", a veritable "Garden of Eden" that presents "amazingly fresh", "artfully prepared" fare made from "ingredients grown on its own farm" and complemented by "fabulous" biodynamic wines; to top it all off, the "overwhelming" views of the Marina, Bay and Golden Gate make the "simple" "warehouse" setting "sublime" – just brace yourself for "wallet shock."

Hamano Sushi *Japanese*

<u>20</u> <u>13</u> <u>17</u> <u>$30</u>

Noe Valley | 1332 Castro St. (24th St.) | 415-826-0825 |
www.hamanosushi.com

When Noe Valleyites with a yen for Japanese "want to stay in the 'hood", they head to this "safe bet", a "solid, middle-of-the-road" sushi joint serving up "huge slabs" of "fresh fish" "*sans* frills"; the dining room's "harsh lighting" and "mighty boring decor" "leave a lot to be desired", so "eat at the bar" (that's "where you get the good stuff" anyway).

Hard Rock Cafe *American*

<u>13</u> <u>21</u> <u>15</u> <u>$25</u>

Fisherman's Wharf | Pier 39 | Bldg. Q1 (Beach St.) | 415-956-2013 |
www.hardrock.com

"The specter of fading fame" – which some say is "fading fast" – haunts this Fisherman's Wharf iteration of the national chain; though it has "lots of great rock memorabilia" (making it a "fun place to go if you have kids in tow" or are a "die-hard groupie"), with the exception of a "reliable burger", the "predictable" American eats are definitely "not for food aficionados" – so "buy a shirt", but "save your appetite."

Harris' *Steak*

<u>25</u> <u>22</u> <u>23</u> <u>$59</u>

Polk Gulch | 2100 Van Ness Ave. (Pacific Ave.) | 415-673-1888 |
www.harrisrestaurant.com

A "classic" "piece of old-school San Francisco", this "excellent" Polk Gulch steakhouse "transports you back to the '50s" with "big", "succulent", "wonderfully aged" chops "prepared perfectly and without fuss"; "tall ceilings", "deep leather booths and thick velvet curtains" (not to mention "pampering" service) further the "gentlemen's club" feel – just make sure you bring a "billfold as thick as the beef"; P.S. "try eating in the bar" for "great live jazz" Thursday–Saturday.

Hayes Street Grill *Seafood*

<u>22</u> <u>16</u> <u>22</u> <u>$46</u>

Hayes Valley | 320 Hayes St. (bet. Franklin & Gough Sts.) | 415-863-5545 |
www.hayesstreetgrill.com

"What a way to begin an evening at the theater", opera or symphony applaud the pre-curtain crowds who "depend" on this Hayes Valley "institution" for "wonderful", "simple preparations" of grilled seafood ("that was swimming a short while before being cooked") served alongside "to-die-for fries"; the "small" space itself may suffer from a "lack of pizzazz", but the "pleasant" staff performs like a "well-oiled machine."

Henry's Hunan ⧈ *Chinese*

<u>21</u> <u>7</u> <u>15</u> <u>$19</u>

Downtown | 674 Sacramento St. (bet. Kearny & Montgomery Sts.) |
415-788-2234
SoMa | 1016 Bryant St. (bet. 8th & 9th Sts.) | 415-861-5808
SoMa | 110 Natoma St. (2nd St.) | 415-546-4999
Hunan *Chinese*
Chinatown | 924 Sansome St. (Broadway) | 415-956-7727
www.henryshunanrestaurant.com

"Make sure you have plenty of water on hand" – or better yet, "bring a fire hose" – because "atomic-spicy dishes are the trademark" of these "not-for-the-faint-of-heart" Hunan "hole-in-the-wall" haunts; though many "can't wait to head back" for the "cheap" "indulgences", some wonder "what the fuss is" as "everything tastes the same" and "can be really greasy."

	FOOD	DECOR	SERVICE	COST

Herbivore *Vegan* | 17 | 13 | 15 | $19 |

Mission | 983 Valencia St. (21st St.) | 415-826-5657
Western Addition | 531 Divisadero St. (bet. Fell & Hayes Sts.) |
415-885-7133
www.herbivorerestaurant.com

An "inexpensive" "variety" of "healthy", "uncomplicated" "vegan comfort food", including "plenty of sandwiches", noodle dishes and even desserts, draws "bustling brunch", lunch and dinner crowds to these Mission and Western Addition cafes; but veggies who "really want to like" this duo are still "disappointed" by the "bland" offerings (conveyed by "apathetic" staffers – "eventually") while grinches groan it should be called "Herbi-bore."

NEW Hime M *Japanese* | 22 | 23 | 18 | $49 |

Marina | 2353 Lombard St. (bet. Pierce & Scott Sts.) | 415-931-7900 |
www.himerestaurant.com

A "sleek addition to the Marina" (despite its "deadish spot on Lombard"), this izakaya-style sushi spot turns out a "refreshing" array of traditional and "modern riffs on Japanese cuisine" using "fresh seafood" in "fancy rolls" "stacked high and wide" – and "interesting" Kobe beef dishes too; sporting a "knock-you-out design" of glowing bamboo and dark wood, it's "sexy" enough "for singles at the bar" or "dates at tables."

Hog Island Oyster Co. & Bar *Seafood* | 25 | 17 | 19 | $33 |

Embarcadero | 1 Ferry Bldg. (Market St.) | 415-391-7117 |
www.hogislandoysters.com

Bivalves that seemingly "jumped out of the water and onto your plate" are the special of every day at this Embarcadero mollusk mecca where an "all-shuck, no-jive" crew ferries "oysters so fresh they quiver on the shell", "chowder that leaves you clam-oring for more" and "stew so rich", "you'll require a couple of glasses of Sancerre to wash it down"; its "sparse" Ferry Building digs are "saved" by the "terrific views" of the Bay.

Home *American* | 18 | 16 | 18 | $28 |

Castro | 2100 Market St. (Church St.) | 415-503-0333 |
www.home-sf.com

Castro residents make this American comfort-food haven their "second home on Sunday mornings" thanks to a "hit" brunch starring a "cheap, fun" "make-your-own Bloody Mary bar" and settle in for "unpretentious", "ample" chow and "creative" "signature cocktails" at "fantastic prices" the rest of the week too; but house-wreckers blast "bland" flavors and a setting so "noisy" it sometimes "sounds like a war zone", adding "if this were my" abode, "I'd run away."

Hotei *Japanese* | 18 | 15 | 17 | $20 |

Inner Sunset | 1290 Ninth Ave. (Irving St.) | 415-753-6045 |
www.hoteisf.com

"What could be more comforting than slurping" "oodles" of udon "on a cold, foggy night?" ask fans of this "friendly" Inner Sunset Japanese "noodle house" where frigid folks "warm up" over "steaming bowls" of "fresh and flavorful broths"; insiders also know that this "cozier and cheaper alternative to big sis Ebisu across the street" is also the "best way" to get the legendary sushi "without the wait."

☒ House, The *Asian Fusion* 26 | 16 | 21 | $41

North Beach | 1230 Grant Ave. (bet. Columbus Ave. & Vallejo St.) |
415-986-8612 | www.thehse.com

"In the maze of North Beach Italian restaurants", this "trendy" "jewel
box" creates "superlative", "drop-dead-delicious" yet "reasonably
priced" Asian fusion fare in which "delicate balancing acts of flavors"
are "done with skill" and presented as "works of art"; "fighting" the
"exciting dining experience" are the waits for tables ("regardless of
your reservation") in the "jam-packed", "minimally" decorated dining
room – still, most "will suffer the conditions to go back."

House of Nanking *Chinese* 21 | 6 | 12 | $20

Chinatown | 919 Kearny St. (bet. Columbus Ave. & Jackson St.) |
415-421-1429

"It may be a hole-in-the-wall and the service brisk", but that doesn't
deter "natives and tourists" from queuing up on the "massive, never-
ending line" at this "must-stop" in Chinatown because the "heavenly"
Chinese fare "is all it's hyped to be"; "don't bother with a menu" – let
"funny owner" Peter "order the perfect amount for your group" and
bring you "hot, delicious" "food until you cry 'uncle!'"; just remember
to "sit, eat and leave quickly."

House of Prime Rib *Steak* 24 | 18 | 20 | $47

Polk Gulch | 1906 Van Ness Ave. (Washington St.) | 415-885-4605
"You'll never leave hungry" at this "over-the-top beef experience" in
Polk Gulch that "does things the old-fashioned way": "generous" cuts
of "juicy", "tender" prime rib "carved tableside" and served with "traditional sides" like "baked potatoes with the works", Yorkshire pudding and creamed spinach; the "worn" decor may be "cheesy", but
that's one reason why folks who've "been eating here for 40 years"
"love it" – plus, it's "inexpensive for what you get."

Hunan Home's Restaurant *Chinese* 22 | 11 | 18 | $24

Chinatown | 622 Jackson St. (bet. Grant Ave. & Kearny St.) |
415-982-2844

Both "Westernized" and "spicy" "real-deal" dishes comprise the
"large" menu proffered at this Hunan haunt in Chinatown (with
branches in Los Altos and Palo Alto) where "intergenerational families
(and not just Chinese)", "tourists" and "students" congregate over
"moderately priced", "generously portioned" meals; the "dilapidated"
decor is "typical of good food dives", but the service is "far more
pleasant than is the norm", so don't be afraid to ask the staffers "about
what to order" – "they make excellent suggestions."

Hyde Street Bistro *French* 21 | 18 | 19 | $42

Russian Hill | 1521 Hyde St. (bet. Jackson St. & Pacific Ave.) | 415-292-4415 |
www.hydestreetbistrosf.com

"If you miss" your favorite "Paris bistro", head up to this "super-
cute" "charmer" on Russian Hill for the kind of "textbook-traditional
French fare", "good wines" and "crowded tables" that you remember from your last trip to the City of Lights; the service can seem a
bit "haphazard", but the staff "works hard to please", so be patient
if your "wait's longer than expected" and you'll be rewarded with
a "romantic treat."

	FOOD	DECOR	SERVICE	COST

⚁ Il Fornaio *Italian*   `19` `20` `18` `$37`

Downtown | Levi's Plaza | 1265 Battery St. (bet. Greenwich & Union Sts.) |
415-986-0100 | www.ilfornaio.com

Regional Italian menus that change monthly keep this "dependable"
Bay Area outfit "fresh and interesting", luring "every type of diner,
from romancing couples to families to large groups"; "you can't go
wrong", whether you go for a "power breakfast" (watch "Silicon
Valley's best job-interview scene"), a "leisurely" brunch or lunch on the
"peaceful patio" (no outdoor seating in San Jose) or a "divine" dinner;
if chain-phobics "avoid at all costs", fans retort "can't get enough" of
its "brick-oven bliss."

Iluna Basque *Spanish*   `17` `17` `16` `$35`

North Beach | 701 Union St. (Powell St.) | 415-402-0011 |
www.ilunabasque.com

"Snack and cruise" jibe grazers who settle into the communal table at
this "cool, trendy" North Beach bastion, nibbling on small Basque
dishes that add a "new flare to the traditional tapas fare" conjured up
by a "cute" "golden-boy chef"; you could "return many times without
being bored with the menu", plus prices are "super reasonable" and
drinks are "good and strong"; but not everyone's over the moon – gripers grumble "spent too much and left hungry."

Imperial Tea Court Ⓜ *Tearoom*   `17` `22` `18` `$19`

Embarcadero | 1 Ferry Bldg. (Market St.) | 415-544-9830 |
www.imperialtea.com

"Transcendental" tea "is the driver", taking the proverbial cup "to new
heights" with "remarkable" selections at these salon offshoots of the
Chinatown importer in the Embarcadero's Ferry Building (and an
Epicurious Garden outpost), both "lovely resting spots" for "quiet con-
templation"; "learn how to make and buy real" brews, but "don't miss"
the "tasty" organic Northern Chinese "treats" that also hold court;
N.B. the Berkeley Teahouse branch stays open for dinner.

Incanto *Italian*   `24` `22` `23` `$44`

Noe Valley | 1550 Church St. (Duncan St.) | 415-641-4500 | www.incanto.biz

"Weary foodie palates" welcome the "challenges" presented at this
"elegant" Northern Italian "slow-food" "destination" in Noe Valley
with a "Tuscan villa" feel where chef Chris Cosentino "coaxes" "rustic", "off-the-beaten-path flavors" to "intriguing" "peaks"; the "indul-
gent" staff is not only "ready to explain the unusual menu" (much of
which "centers" around "interesting" offal), but also suggests "amazing wines" from the all-Boot cellar; still, a few fume "what's up" with
the "irritating" "extra tip" that goes to the kitchen staff?

Indian Oven *Indian*   `23` `14` `17` `$27`

Lower Haight | 233 Fillmore St. (bet. Haight & Waller Sts.) | 415-626-1628 |
www.indianovensf.

Lower Haightians "drool just thinking about" the "addictively" "tasty",
"rich" cuisine at this Indian spot where "you can chose your spice level"
(they "take you at your word when you say 'very spicy'!"); true, "you have
to put up with a lot to enjoy" it – namely "long waits", a "loud", "crowded"
interior and "absent-minded" staffers who sometimes dish "an extra
helping of attitude" – regardless, most "can't wait to go back."

	FOOD	DECOR	SERVICE	COST

Indigo ⓜ American
20 | 18 | 21 | $42

Civic Center | 687 McAllister St. (Gough St.) | 415-673-9353 |
www.indigorestaurant.com

"Opera crowds" that "don't want to pay Jardinière prices" "mob" this
"hip", cobalt-colored Civic Center New American where owner Greg
Medow, "the host with the most", presents "consistently good" "pre-
performance dinners with aplomb"; if you're not going to a show, come
after 8 PM for "the bargain of the century": "$49 for three courses and all
the wine you can drink" from a specified list – "yes, you read that right."

☑ In-N-Out Burger ⦿ Hamburgers
22 | 10 | 17 | $8

Fisherman's Wharf | 333 Jefferson St. (bet. Jones & Leavenworth Sts.) |
800-786-1000 | www.in-n-out.com

"One of the great guilty pleasures of modern life", this "classic" West
Coast chain may "lube your arteries", but many consider it a "step
above" other "fast-food joints" – and it's rated the Survey's No. 1 Bang
for the Buck – with its "juicy", "made-to-order burgers" "slathered with
sauce and topped with lettuce and tomato", "fresh-cut fries" ("ask for
double-dipped" to make them crispier) and "fantastic" "milkshakes
made from real ice cream" – and "where do they find such friendly
teenagers" to serve them?; N.B. customize your meal by studying the
'secret menu' on the Web site.

Isa ☒ French
24 | 18 | 20 | $44

Marina | 3324 Steiner St. (bet. Chestnut & Lombard Sts.) | 415-567-9588 |
www.isarestaurant.com

Dining at unsung chef Luke Sung's "fun, festive" "family-style" small-
plater in the Marina is an "event" where "you just can't wait to see and
taste" what "gorgeous French tapas" the "well-choreographed" staff
brings out next; go with "a group" to "try everything", or better yet,
grab "someone special" to "sit under the twinkling lights" on the "pic-
turesque" "covered patio" – just know that the "stellar samplings" can
add up to "big prices."

Isobune Japanese
17 | 14 | 16 | $26

Japantown | Kintetsu Mall | 1737 Post St. (bet. Laguna & Webster Sts.) |
415-563-1030

"Don't miss the boat" jest fin fans who lunge for the "bargain"-priced
sushi as it "swishes by" on a moat at this Japan Center "experience"
where "prices are calculated by the number and types of plates you
select" – what a "blast" for "beginners"; but not all hands are on deck –
detractors decry that some dishes "tend to go around the table too
many times" and huff "management prefers that you don't linger."

Izzy's Steaks & Chops Steak
19 | 16 | 18 | $40

Marina | 3345 Steiner St. (bet. Chestnut & Lombard Sts.) | 415-563-0487

"Death to the diet!" – "why count calories" when "strapping on the
feed bag" at this "old-style" Marina steakhouse (with branches in
Corte Madera and San Carlos) when you can just submit to "huge",
"no-frills" "slabs of beef" accompanied by "excessively rich",
"delicious" sides like creamed spinach and "Izzy's special potatoes"
au gratin, all at "reasonable prices"?; because it's an "unfailingly mediocre" experience retort naysayers, adding, "it may be an institution", but we'd "rather escape."

	FOOD	DECOR	SERVICE	COST

Jack Falstaff ⚠ *Californian*

| | 20 | 21 | 19 | $50 |

SoMa | 598 Second St. (Brannan St.) | 415-836-9239 | www.plumpjack.com
Wend your way through the "ballpark crowd" "on game days" to get to this "quiet", "elegantly modern" Californian in SoMa that looks "like a Pottery Barn showroom"; Jacks and Jills enjoy "delightfully delicious" dishes "showcasing the season's best" "organic" ingredients coupled with an "exceptionally priced wine list" (as "can be expected at all Plumpjack" places) that makes the "hearty" "food taste that much better"; still, the disappointed "don't really get the appeal", citing "bland" fare and "slow" service.

Jackson Fillmore 🅼 *Italian*

| | 21 | 13 | 18 | $35 |

Upper Fillmore | 2506 Fillmore St. (Jackson St.) | 415-346-5288
"Damn good" "down-home" "Italian classics" keep Upper Fillmore folks "lined up at the door" (reservations only for parties of three or more) of this "small and popular" trattoria – it's "worth the wait" for the "excellent free bruschetta alone"; still, the atmosphere "teeters" between "'neighborhood joint' and 'dive'", and the servers can sometimes be "unsmiling" and "gruff."

Jai Yun 🚫 *Chinese*

| | ▽ 23 | 6 | 15 | $50 |

Chinatown | 923 Pacific Ave. (Mason St.) | 415-981-7438
"If decor and service are critically important to you", "pick a different Chinatown restaurant", otherwisde, join the "true connoisseurs" hungry to experience "genuine" "gourmet banquet food rarely found outside China", "bring friends", "big bucks", "your favorite wine" and "leave yourself in Chef Nei's expert hands"; don't fret about the "limited English" spoken, just "choose the price" and "he chooses the food", which always includes an "amazing", "idiosyncratic" array of "sophisticated" "delicacies."

Jake's Steaks *Cheese Steaks*

| | ▽ 20 | 10 | 16 | $17 |

Cow Hollow | 3301 Buchanan St. (bet. Chestnut & Lombard Sts.) | 415-922-2211 | www.jakessteaks.net
"You want a real Philly cheese steak?" – well, "don't be fooled by imitators", pop into Cow Hollow's "real-deal" sub stop where "belly-filling" meat and Whiz are piled high on "real Amoroso rolls flown in" from the City of Brotherly Love; it also "doubles as a sports hangout", as the "flat screen TV" is usually tuned to either the Giants or the Eagles.

🆉 Jardinière *Californian/French*

| | 26 | 26 | 25 | $69 |

Hayes Valley | 300 Grove St. (Franklin St.) | 415-861-5555 | www.jardiniere.com
Even "when the opera is having a bad night, you know" that Traci Des Jardins' "posh", "pricey", pre- and post-performance "enchanter" in Hayes Valley "will still be hitting all the right notes", belting out "exceptional" Cal-French fare in a "sexy" setting; *oui,* the "pitch-perfect service" gets the "well-heeled" habitués to their "limos" on time, but what a "waste" to be in haste when the "gorgeous bar" below is such a "sparkling" spot "to engage in a cocktail or get engaged" or just hang out, especially following a recent revamp.

Jay's Cheesesteak *Cheese Steaks*

| | 17 | 7 | 13 | $11 |

Mission | 3285 21st St. (bet. Mission & Valencia Sts.) | 415-285-5200 🚫

FOOD | DECOR | SERVICE | COST

(continued)

Jay's Cheesesteak
Western Addition | 553 Divisadero St. (bet. Fell & Hayes Sts.) |
415-771-5104

Grilling up "a little bit of South Philly in San Fran", this duo of "cardiol-ogist delights" in the Mission and the Western Addition is "a dangerous habit" for "high schoolers" and "cheap eat"–loving snackers looking to "satisfy" their "cheese-steak cravings"; while Eagle eyes "acquainted with the real" deal balk they're "not quite authentic", NorCal devotees retort they're "better", citing "quality Niman Ranch beef" and "veggie" and "seitan" renditions – "who'd a thunk it?"

Jeanty at Jack's *French*
23 | 21 | 21 | $51
Downtown | 615 Sacramento St. (bet. Kearny & Montgomery Sts.) |
415-693-0941 | www.jeantyatjacks.com

Phillipe Jeanty's "brassy" Downtown "temple to French bistro food" delivers "pitch-perfect", "hearty" and *"très français"* dishes and a *carte du vins* that's "almost as good as" P.J. Steak, his "Yountville classic" (fans 'fess to have "followed him just for" the "puff-pastry-covered tomato soup!"); every level of the "beautifully restored" multifloor Victorian edifice "offers a different ambiance", but each presents "old-world charm" and "professional service", making it a *"toujours magnifique"* destination for "business lunches" and "romantic dinners."

Joe DiMaggio's
20 | 24 | 22 | $51
Italian Chophouse *Italian/Steak*
North Beach | 601 Union St. (Stockton St.) | 415-421-5633 |
www.joedimaggiosrestaurant.com

"If you like Marilyn, Joe, big juicy steaks" and "delightful" lasagna "like mama made", head to this "baseball lover's dream" of an Italian chop-house in North Beach where DiMaggio's "legacy lives" on; slip into an "old-world booth" and enjoy "extremely generous" portions with one of the "coldest martinis in town" as "Sinatra tunes play in the back-ground", but while the "1950s atmosphere" and "amazing photos" of the famous couple are a "home run", a few sluggers shrug the "medi-ocre" food needs "more attention."

⧫ Joe's Cable Car *Hamburgers*
24 | 14 | 16 | $18
Excelsior | 4320 Mission St. (Silver Ave.) | 415-334-6699 |
www.joescablecar.com

"Don't let the less-than-desirable" Excelsior location, "blindingly bright neon signs" and "reusable cutlery" reminiscent of a "seven-year-old's birthday party" "put you off" – the "juicy, tender, perfectly grilled burgers" made with "famous fresh-ground chuck" are "worth the "side trip" – and "every dime" – concur carnivores who canter over to this "kitschy" cable car; wash it down with "thick shakes" and "root beer floats (brother, they do not skimp on the ice cream)" and "pre-pare to leave stuffed."

NEW Jones Restaurant ☾ *American*
‒ | ‒ | ‒ | M
Marina | 2400 Lombard St. (Scott St.) | 415-440-2000 | www.jones-sf.com

Marina-ites jonsesing for good ol' American grub and grog head to this wood-paneled, modern day roadhouse with a vintagey feel serv-ing comfort food with a twist, from sliders and nibbles to prime dry-aged steaks; when the evening's done, or before it's begun, sidle up to the bar, order something refreshing from the extensive martini and wine-by-the-glass list and kick out the jams with the quirky soundtrack that mixes country, blues and Sinatra standards.

NEW Jovino *Coffeehouse/Eclectic*

— | — | — | I

Cow Hollow | 2184 Union St. (Fillmore St.) | 415-563-1853
Promising everything from joe to vino, this country-chic, counter-service coffeehouse/wine bar hybrid in Cow Hollow is luring a diverse crowd of ladies who lunch, starving students and the laptop brigade (free WiFi); former Meetinghouse chef Joanna Karlinsky, who oversees the extensive menu, bakes her legendary buttery biscuits on the weekends only.

Juban *Japanese*

17 | 15 | 16 | $33

Japantown | Kinokuniya Bldg. | 1581 Webster St. (bet. Fillmore & Webster Sts., enter on Post St.) | 415-776-5822 | www.jubanrestaurant.com
See review in South of San Francisco Directory.

Julius Castle *Italian*

— | — | — | M

Telegraph Hill | 1541 Montgomery St. (Union St.) | 415-392-2222 | www.juliuscastle.com
Perched just below Coit Tower on Telegraph Hill, this recently remodeled 1922 landmark castle has reopened under new owners who've brought in a chef from Scott's Seafood to oversee the midpriced, French-accented Italian dinner menu, which revives old-school classics like lobster Thermidor; the famed terrace, affording sweeping views of the Bay, Alcatraz, Treasure Island and beyond, is open for cocktails and Sunday brunch.

Kabuto *Japanese*

25 | 13 | 17 | $40

Outer Richmond | 5121 Geary Blvd. (bet. 15th & 16th Aves.) | 415-752-5652 | www.kabutosushi.com
The "sushi Nazi is gone", but the fin fare at this "famously busy", "minuscule" "mandatory stop" in the Outer Richmond "still tastes like it was just fished from the ocean"; the chef, like the owner, is also of Ariake, and seems to "do a bit of freestylin'", crafting "crazy strange" but "artful" rolls and "incredibly inventive Japanese cooking"; "if you appreciate plated presentation" and "delicious food", it's "worth every yen" – just remember there's "not much atmosphere" and "lines can be tedious"; N.B. no reservations on weekends

Kan Zaman *Mideastern*

17 | 19 | 15 | $21

Haight-Ashbury | 1793 Haight St. (Shrader St.) | 415-751-9656
"Low tables where you can lounge on pillows", "tasty hookahs", "inexpensive" meze and a "lively belly dancer" some nights lure loyalists to this "funky" Middle Eastern standby that's "tons of fun" for groups; still, neat-freaks feel it "needs a pick me up and good dusting", and find the "walk through the stoned beggars" on Haight Street somewhat "dreary."

Z Kate's Kitchen ⊅ *Southern*

22 | 13 | 16 | $14

Lower Haight | 471 Haight St. (bet. Fillmore & Webster Sts.) | 415-626-3984
They could change the name to "Grandma's Kitchen" – what with the "plentiful portions" of Southern cooking and "utilitarian decor" this daytime Lower Haight "hole-in-the-wall" "reminds me of" her house – except for the "line that's always out the door" and "coffee like rocket

fuel"; "go with an appetite" (you "may go back to sleep" afterwards) and devour an "amazing" morning meal; "you won't be disappointed" – It's "everything a good breakfast joint should be."

Katia's Russian Tea Room Ⓜ Russian ▽ 19 | 14 | 21 | $29

Inner Richmond | 600 Fifth Ave. (Balboa St.) | 415-668-9292 | www.katias.com

Perhaps the "best of very slim pickings for Russian restaurants in San Francisco", this "interesting", "intimate" Inner Richmond corner cafe concocts dishes that are "lighter but no less tasty" than the old-school versions; Muscovites commend "charming owner-hostess" Katia and her staff who offer "warm" "personal service" and find the "live music very soothing and relaxing"; still a few rude-skis snipe "scotch the accordion player" and deem the delicacies "disappointing."

Khan Toke Thai House Thai 23 | 24 | 21 | $28

Outer Richmond | 5937 Geary Blvd. (bet. 23rd & 24th Aves.) | 415-668-6654

"Shoeless in San Francisco – and happy for it" quip patrons who get their kicks at this "lovely" Thai "winner" in the Outer Richmond where the "ornate wood carvings" of "village scenes" "teleport" you through "space and time" out of the fog bank and "into imperial Siam"; slip off the sneakers, slink into the "tricky" sunken tables and "sit cross-legged" as you enjoy the "excellent, creative" regional food served by a "gracious staff" – little wonder regulars "return again and again."

Kiji Sushi Bar & Cuisine Ⓜ Japanese ▽ 24 | 19 | 18 | $35

Mission | 1009 Guerrero St. (22nd St.) | 415-282-0400 | www.kijirestaurant.com

Tucked in a Victorian on a "quieter street" of the Mission, this "classy, hip" izakaya raises the red lantern (outside) and the culinary bar (inside) in green-tea–tinted digs accented by beaded lamps; the Sushi Groove alum/chef-owner whips up a "wider variety" of "excellent" fin fare and cooked items "than your average" Japanese "joint" (housemade gyoza, yakitori, "unique appetizers"), plus over 30 premium sakes – perhaps another reason why it's become a new "favorite."

King of Thai ⊄ Thai 19 | 7 | 14 | $13

Downtown | 184 O'Farrell St. (Powell St.) | 415-677-9991 ◐
Downtown | 420 Geary St. (bet. Mason & Taylor Sts.) | 415-346-3121 ◐
Inner Richmond | 346 Clement St. (bet. 4th & 5th Aves.) | 415-831-9953 ◐
Inner Richmond | 639 Clement St. (bet. 7th & 8th Aves.) | 415-752-5198 ◐
Outer Sunset | 1507 Sloat Blvd. (Everglade Dr.) | 415-566-9921
Outer Sunset | 1541 Taraval St. (26th Ave.) | 415-682-9958 ◐
www.kingofthainoodle.com

"Better the later it is" nod night owls who fly over to this "bare-bones" Thai outfit for a "post-bar diversion" that "satisfies" when "you need calories with flavor" delivered "quick to the table"; slurp "saucy, tasty noodles" and other "delicious, accessible" dishes for "under $10" doused with "fishy, spicy or 'help, I'm on fire'" sauces – what an "unbelievable feast" for "tight budgets"; N.B. the Sloat Boulevard site closes earlier.

Kiss Sushi ⊠Ⓜ Japanese ▽ 27 | 14 | 23 | $61

Japantown | 1700 Laguna St. (Sutter St.) | 415-474-2866

"Despite 12 seats and zero decor", this reservations-essential cult Japanese standby adds up to one of the most touted destinations for "pure decadence" on the Japantown circuit according to devotees who shower it with kisses; it's "so small and understated you literally walk right by, but once inside, give yourself over to the genius of the chef", who "makes you feel like a guest in his home", crafting "creative" omakase dinners and "melt-in-the-mouth" sushi.

Koh Samui & The Monkey *Thai* | 21 | 19 | 18 | $27 |

SoMa | 415 Brannan St. (bet. 3rd & 4th Sts.) | 415-369-0007 | www.kohsamuiandthemonkey.com

The "crave-able" curries at this "classy" SoMa "gem" "have a slant you don't find" at the "average" Siamese stop – it's such a "refreshing change" you may "rethink your impression of Thai food" assert admirers who've evolved into the "biggest junkies"; add in "gracious" service (what "wonderful costumes" the servers wear), a "laid-back ambiance" and a "cozy" feel and it's easy to see why fur-vent fans consider it a "favorite."

☒ Kokkari Estiatorio ☒ *Greek* | 26 | 25 | 24 | $53 |

Downtown | 200 Jackson St. (Front St.) | 415-981-0983 | www.kokkari.com

"If you can't wrangle a trip to Greece", head to this "really special enclave Downtown" for a bit of Hellenic "heaven"; it's "cozy for such a cavernous place" with a "fire blazing in the fireplace, the bar calling with super cocktails", those "outta-this-world" lamb chops and "absolutely divine" "specials from the spit (food for the gods)"; the "happy" "staff goes out of its way to make the guests feel welcome" and the people-watching is "super" – no wonder loyalists proclaim "you will come back" "again and again."

Koo ☒ *Asian Fusion* | 24 | 19 | 19 | $38 |

Inner Sunset | 408 Irving St. (bet. 5th & 6th Aves.) | 415-731-7077 | www.sushikoo.com

With "soothing" "background jazz music" and "mod" lamps throughout, this "undiscovered treasure" with "half the crowds of the better-known" Inner Sunset spots "offers a Koo-l atmosphere" for savoring "delicious, very satisfying" Asian fusion–Japanese tapas and "creative" rolls; "request a seat at the sushi bar" "where you're treated like royalty" and you can chat up the "devoted regulars" about the "can't-miss" specialties, then "let the chef do his thing"

Kuleto's *Italian* | 20 | 19 | 19 | $42 |

Downtown | Villa Florence Hotel | 221 Powell St. (bet. Geary & O'Farrell Sts.) | 415-397-7720 | www.kuletos.com

Founding chef Robert Helstrom is back at the reins of this "bustling" "old-time" "favorite" that still brings a "bit of Italy to Union Square", even under new management; tourists, "pre-theater and post-shopping" folk "socialize" and feast on "fresh", "inventive" Northern Italian fare and when seeking more "entertainment", sit by the open kitchen and "watch the action"; still, others shrug there's "nothing groundbreaking here"; P.S. the separately owned Burlingame branch "works in a pinch."

Kyo-Ya ☒ *Japanese* | 23 | 20 | 22 | $57 |

Downtown | Palace Hotel | 2 New Montgomery St. (Market St.) | 415-546-5090 | www.kyo-ya-restaurant.com

"Stop dawdling – just go now" urge devotees of this "stylish", straight-out-of-Osaka Dowtowner in the Palace Hotel that "caters to Japanese businessmen"; true, the "must-try" gold leaf sushi and "delicious" dishes are "best enjoyed on an expense account" but "little touches like real wasabi" and "tiny rooms" "suited to intimate conversations" (an "unexpected treasure of peace") make it "super in every way"; but not everyone's onboard the Ya-Ya brotherhood – cynics deem the "highly touted *kaiseki* " menu "disappointing."

La Ciccia ⓜ *Italian*   22 | 13 | 23 | $39

Noe Valley | 291 30th St. (Church St.) | 415-550-8114 | www.laciccia.com
Anchoring Noe Valley's Restaurant Row, this "welcoming", "off-the-beaten-path" Sardinian trattoria makes you feel like you're "leaving the country and going to" the Bel Paese "without the language worry"; "spank the palate with the botarga" and "linger over" "soulful" dishes that "deserve the spotlight", like "simply cooked seafood" and "deeply flavored pasta", accompanied by "rare wine finds"; sure it's "cramped" and the decor seems "DIY", but that just adds to the "happy Italian family" ambiance.

La Cumbre Taqueria *Mexican*   22 | 8 | 15 | $11

Mission | 515 Valencia St. (bet. 16th & 17th Sts.) | 415-863-8205
"Not just a legend" – this "classic taqueria" is part of the "burrito van-guard in the Mission" rave admirers who "wait in line" to devour "fla-vorful", "filling" Mexican eats; never mind the "barren" digs – just focus on the "juicy" carne aseda soft tacos topped with "hot salsa and a cold beer" – it's "still the king" for a "cheap", "quick bite"; N.B. the "rustic"-looking San Mateo sibling also serves "really fresh stuff."

ⓩ La Folie Ⓢ *French*   27 | 23 | 26 | $87

Russian Hill | 2316 Polk St. (bet. Green & Union Sts.) | 415-776-5577 | www.lafolie.com
Oui, "'twould be a folly to miss" this "haute French" "culinary experience" on Russian Hill where "masterful chef" "Monsieur Passot cooks his heart out" crafting "perfection on a plate" à la carte dishes and "artfully dis-played" prix fixe menus "well worth the special-occasion prices"; it's *magnifique* in every way", from the "amazing wine" list and "grand", "in-timate environment" to the "dazzling" staff that exudes a "touch of Gallic humor"; P.S. if the "elbow-to-elbow seating" in the main room "crimps your privacy", the back room provides "an elegant alternative."

NEW Laïola *Spanish*   - | - | - | M

Marina | 2031 Chestnut St. (bet. Fillmore St. & Mallorca Way) | 415-346-5641 | www.laiola.com
At this stylish Spanish joint from the Frisson folks, Mark Denham, a chef with a Chez Panisse pedigree, conjures up small- and full-size plates including housemade charcuterie; the seductive yet rustic-looking space is dominated by an L-shaped, copper-clad bar and floor-to-ceiling windows for maximum people-watching; N.B. soon, oenophiles will also be able to choose from a 100-label, all-Iberian wine list.

La Méditerranée *Mediterranean/Mideastern*   19 | 14 | 17 | $22

Castro | 288 Noe St. (Market St.) | 415-431-7210
Upper Fillmore | 2210 Fillmore St. (Sacramento St.) | 415-921-2956
www.cafelamed.com
"Wow-sers" – for a "light, just right, quick bite" "you can't beat the in-expensive" Middle Eastern–Med fare at this "no-frills", "always packed"

trio with "funky decor" in the Castro, Upper Fillmore and Berkeley; you get "relatively large portions" of "earthy", "simply done" dishes "for the price" (you "never walk away hungry"), plus the "staff creates a hospitable", "homey" "atmosphere for such a very busy place."

La Provence Restaurant 🅼 French ▽ | 18 | 18 | 18 | $37

Mission | 1001 Guerrero St. (22nd St.) | 415-643-4333 | www.laprovencerestaurant.net

This "unassuming" French cafe lures locals with a "cozy atmosphere not usually found in the brash, trendy spots or hole-in-the-wall places common to the Mission" and "interesting Provencal" dishes (pissaladière, bouillabaisse) "like you would get in Nice"; it's an Aix-cellent "change from heavy classic" fare, plus "the owner is often on hand" to offer a "warm" *bienvenue,* "answer questions and chat."

NEW Lark Creek Steak Steak | 22 | 22 | 21 | $49

Downtown | Westfield San Francisco Ctr. | 845 Market St., 4th fl. (bet. 4th & 5th Sts.) | 415-593-4100 | www.larkcreeksteak.com

More than a "respite from shopping", Bradley Ogden's "new generation steakhouse" with a "wonderful contemporary feel", 30-ft. illuminated glass-and-steel sculpture and a large open kitchen is fast becoming a "destination" in Downtown's "humongous" Westfield Centre; the chef "really steps up" the traditional American chop "concept several notches" with a farm-to-table sensibility, offering "flavorful" beef, plus "elegant" sides and fish dishes and "not-to-be-missed" desserts ("just don't expect" typical offerings like "cheesecake the size of your head").

La Scene Café | 17 | 17 | 18 | $41
& Bar *Californian/Mediterranean*

Downtown | Warwick Regis | 490 Geary St. (Taylor St.) | 415-292-6430 | www.warwicksf.com

"Reminiscent of a Manhattan theater restaurant" – and "handy" to the Curran and Geary nearby, this "serene oasis" serves up "solid" Cal-Med fare in a "cozy, romantic atmosphere"; it's a "dependable standby" – the "price is right", the "dozens of photos" of "old Hollywood royalty" lend a "fun touch" – and the "pleasant" staff "gets you to the show on time"; still, those who fail to make the Scene sigh it's "lost its luster."

Last Supper Club, The *Italian* | 19 | 18 | 18 | $32

Mission | 1199 Valencia St. (23rd St.) | 415-695-1199 | www.lastsupperclubsf.com

"I wouldn't have my last supper" here but "it's a lot fun" concede Missionaries who flock to this "gimmicky" but "cool" "haunt" for an immaculate collection of "unique" cocktails and stay to *ciao* down, family-style, at "long tables" on Southern Italian specialties; it's "awesome" "for a night out with a group" (the "loud" "hipster" crowd goes "crazy for the down-home cooking") but don't expect a "romantic" meal by "candlelight"; P.S. go for brunch – the "pace is slow" and "relaxed."

☑ La Taqueria ⌀ *Mexican* | 24 | 7 | 12 | $11

Mission | 2889 Mission St. (25th St.) | 415-285-7117

Mere "mention" of this "hole-in-the-wall Mexican" in the Mission (and its San Jose sibling) "provokes Pavlovian drooling"; crowds "circle for parking" and "clamor" for the "carnitas nothing short of heaven", "most fabu-licious tacos in the whole damn town" and "filler"-free burritos ("cylinders of happiness") washed down with agua frescas; the "taq-shop" decor and "factory" service are "no *problemo*" 'cuz it's among the "best places" to "eat yourself silly on not that much money."

NEW La Terrasse *French*

19 18 16 $52

Presidio | 215 Lincoln Blvd. (bet. Graham St. & Keyes Ave.) | 415-922-3463 | www.laterrassepresidio.com

You "can't beat the view" of the Golden Gate or the "special location" in The Presidio that "makes you feel like you've left the city" agree early adopters who tout this "promising" all-day French newcomer, a Chez Spencer spin-off with "interesting" decor and now, an à la carte menu too, boasting brasserie standards; sit "under the umbrellas on a sunny day" or prearrange a "delicious" prix fixe dinner; still, grinches gripe that "service needs a bit of seasoning."

Le Central Bistro ⑤ *French*

19 16 19 $41

Downtown | 453 Bush St. (bet. Grant Ave. & Kearny St.) | 415-391-2233 | www.lecentralbistro.com

This centrally located, "venerable" French "classic", once "the bistro pioneer" in Downtown's "Little Paris", "conjures up memories" of "Willie (Brown), Wilkes (Bashford) and Herb (Caen)", "local heroes" who transformed it into *the* "power"-lunch hangout; while it'll "never be the same without that trio", the "very attentive service" and "*ancienne* cuisine" (including "hearty rainy day dishes" like "cassoulet that's "been cooking forever") continues to draw today's "politicos" and business brass looking for a Gallic "fix."

Le Charm French Bistro Ⓜ *French*

21 17 21 $37

SoMa | 315 Fifth St. (bet. Folsom & Shipley Sts.) | 415 546 6128 | www.lecharm.com

Although this "aptly named" "romantic" little French joint "seems out of place in the SoMa loft zone", it "delivers" the "well-prepared" "somewhat old-fashioned bistro food" it "promises", at "fire-sale prices", including a "wonderful" prix fixe that's a "steal"; the "charming" "low-key" digs boast "lots of atmosphere" ("even better with the new remodel") and a "quaint outdoor garden", making it a "favorite lunch spot" on a "sunny day", while service couldn't be "sweeter."

Le Colonial *French/Vietnamese*

21 24 19 $47

Downtown | 20 Cosmo Pl. (bet. Post & Taylor Sts.) | 415-931-3600 | www.lecolonialsf.com

A "world away from Union Square", this "exotic", "romantic" retreat with an "amazing", "lush", "dreamlike atmosphere" and "pampering" staff "whisks" you back to Vietnam's French colonial era and "envelopes" you in the "mists of Saigon"; settle in downstairs for "alluring", "wonderfully spiced" fusion fare "mixed to perfection" and "don't forget" the "cool", "festively themed bar upstairs" or the outdoor patio where you can "enjoy" "delicious drinks" with "street food snacks" and listen to "fun" DJs on Fridays and Saturdays.

Le Petit Robert *French*

19 18 18 $35

Russian Hill | 2300 Polk St. (Green St.) | 415-922-8100 | www.lepetitrobert.com

Check out the "hip city yuppies" and "young families" in the "airy", "high-ceilinged" interior or sit "outside in the sunshine" and "watch

FOOD | DECOR | SERVICE | COST

the street traffic" on Russian Hill "while nibbling" brunch – either way, this "delightfully packed" "*très bon* bistro" "never disappoints", delivering "flavorful "fussy-free" French fare; but while Francophiles advise "every chance you get, come here", the less *ami*-able sigh service ranges from "attentive" to "snooty"; N.B. a recent chef change may outdate the Food score.

NEW Le P'tit Laurent *French*

| - | - | - | M |

Glen Park | 699 Chenery St. (Diamond St.) | 415-334-3235

This little French bistro is the latest installment in what's fast become Glen Park's Restaurant Row; much like his previous venture, Clementine, owner Laurent Legendre presents an affordable slate of classic Gallic dinner standards plus a weekly changing three-course prix fixe ($19.99) and weekend brunch, all served in a charming, get-to-know-your-neighbors dining room that's already filled nightly with families, some *avec bébés*.

Les Amis ⊠ *French*

| 22 | 21 | 23 | $52 |

Downtown | 568 Sacramento St. (Montgomery St.) | 415-291-9145 | www.lesamissf.com

For a "leisurely", "pricey" "fine-dining meal Downtown", expense-accounters leave the Downtown "hustle and bustle" behind and embrace "serenity" at this "very cozy (in a good way)", "itty-bitty" "converted old firehouse" in a "badass location"; the "professional", wine-"knowledgeable" staff and "delicious" French prix fixe and à la carte menus "foster good conversation" – it's "definitely a FiDi go-to for business lunches" – while the "romantic" red decor "reminiscent of a French bordello" makes it a "sleeper" "special-occasion spot."

Le Soleil *Vietnamese*

| 20 | 14 | 17 | $24 |

Inner Richmond | 133 Clement St. (bet. 2nd & 3rd Aves.) | 415-668-4848

Though a "little more exotic" following a remodel, this "hidden gem" in the Inner Richmond retains its very "homey", "neighborly feel", serving up a "refreshing menu" of "delicious", "inventive" Vietnamese cuisine at "the right price"; the staff is "almost intuitive" and "you can hear your own conversation" – what a "pleasant surprise"; P.S. the "new look is a huge improvement" and may not be reflected in the Decor score.

Lettus: Cafe Organic *Health Food*

| 20 | 14 | 13 | $18 |

Marina | 3352 Steiner St. (bet. Chestnut & Lombard Sts.) | 415-931-2777 | www.lettusorganic.com

You feel like you're "doing the right thing for the body" at this all-day health food cafe, a "delicious escape" with an "environmental slant" that provides the "Marina mommy crowd" with "greens for little greens"; "considering you line up at the counter, hoping upon hope for a table, brunch is awesome", while the "inventive", organic dishes are "perfect" for a "quick lunch"; still, leaf-it-aloners quip "I'd rather eat dirt" – "maybe I'm not hippie enough."

Levende ⊠ *Eclectic*

| 20 | 20 | 18 | $38 |

Mission | 1710 Mission St. (Duboce Ave.) | 415-864-5585 | www.levendesf.com

Enjoy "dinner, then stay around" for "music, mojitos and more" at this "sexy, dark" Missionite that accomplishes the "hard task of combining restaurant, bar and late-night lounge"; the "cool ambiance", "beautiful

FOOD | DECOR | SERVICE | COST

people", "awesome DJs" and "innovative" Eclectic small plates make for an "unusual" meal; still, "go early if you're over 23 or want to preserve what's left of your hearing"; N.B. there's a new branch called Levende East in Oakland.

Le Zinc *French*　　　　　　18 | 19 | 16 | $33
Noe Valley | 4063 24th St. (bet. Castro & Noe Sts.) | 415-647-9400 | www.lezinc.com

"Step off of 24th Street and into Paris" at this "tastefully decorated", "quaint little" "Frenchy" bistro that makes you "feel as though you're in the City of Lights" not Noe Valley; from the "pups on the patio" and "zinc-topped bar" to the "crusty bread", "well-executed classics", sinful" brunches and *carte des vins,* it's "just what a neighborhood" place "should be"; *oui,* service can be "aloof" and "slow", but that "adds to the authenticity."

Liberty Cafe & Bakery Ⓜ *American*　　22 | 17 | 20 | $29
Bernal Heights | 410 Cortland Ave. (Bennington St.) | 415-695-8777 | www.thelibertycafe.com

It may not "look that exciting" but this "homey" Bernal Victorian with a "welcoming", "New Englandy atmosphere" is "full of pleasant surprises", from the "satisfying" Traditional American dishes as "tasty" as "mom's cooking" and "perfect for a chilly winter dinner" to the "rightly famous pies" ("chicken, veggie, banana cream" – "basically anything with a crust" is a "winner") to the "fun wine bar"; "on warm days", libertarians "skip the front" altogether and make a "beeline for the backyard."

Lime ⦿ *Eclectic*　　　　　　18 | 21 | 17 | $31
Castro | 2247 Market St. (bet. Noe & Sanchez Sts.) | 415-621-5256 | www.lime-sf.com

Perhaps it's "more disco than restaurant", but this Castro spot "has it all": a "trippy", "retro-chic" decor with "white leather booths" and Eclectic small-plate "munchies"; "what a scene" – "young", "hip" party animals graze on "precious" "progressive takes" on "classics" like deviled eggs and sliders, washed down with "sassy cocktails" "while groovin'" to DJs and "drink endless mimosas" at Sunday's "lush brunch"; still, a few scoff "it's like eating overpriced finger food in an iPod."

Ⓩ Limòn *Peruvian*　　　　　22 | 18 | 19 | $40
Mission | 524 Valencia St. (16th St.) | 415-252-0918 | www.limon-sf.com

"Modern, cool" and teeming with "hipsters", the Mission's "perky" Peruvian with a "buzzy atmosphere" will "change the way you think about" South American fare; "we'd climb the Andes" for the "addictive", "terrific ceviche" concur acolytes who also flip for the "fancied-up", "flavor-packed" specialties and "lively" sauces; sip selections from the "interesting wine list" or "even better sangria" – it helps mitigate the "interminably long waits for everything (food, service, seating)."

Little Nepal Ⓜ *Nepalese*　　　21 | 18 | 20 | $23
Bernal Heights | 925 Cortland Ave. (Folsom St.) | 415-643-3881 | www.littlenepalsf.com

"*Namaste* indeed!" declare devotees who bow to this "peaceful", "calming" "worthy destination" with "blond-wood decor" "off the beaten" Bernal Heights path serving up a "taste of the Himalayas"; the menu is "conveniently concise" while the "delightful", "nicely spiced"

Nepalese fare is comparable to "Indian food except with a deeper richness of flavor" – and it's all served by a "warm staff" whose "hospitality flows effortlessly and joyously."

☑ Little Star Pizza Ⓜ⌷ *Pizza*

25 | 15 | 16 | $22

NEW **Mission** | 400 Valencia St. (15th St.) | 415-551-7827
Western Addition | 846 Divisadero St. (bet. Fulton & McAllistar Sts.) |
415-441-1118
www.littlestarpizza.com

"Finally, a pizzeria that knows how" to create "mind-blowing" pies – makes you feel like you're "living in Chicago" chime in transplants and "hipsters" who groove to the "awesome jukebox" while chowing down at this "urban", cash-only "king of the deep dish" in the Mission and Western Addition; even the thin-crust versions "tear you up" – they're "ridiculously good" – especially when "paired with PBR" – and "worth the wait" (but "be patient" – "Rome wasn't built in a day").

L'Osteria del Forno ⌷ *Italian*

24 | 13 | 18 | $29

North Beach | 519 Columbus Ave. (bet. Green & Union Sts.) | 415-982-1124 |
www.losteriadelforno.com

"Step out of neon-lighted North Beach into the warmth of grandma's kitchen" at this "postage stamp–size" "hole-in-the-wall", a "local's hangout", that, despite no stovetop, "no hip chefs, no reservations" and no credit cards, serves "superb" oven-baked pizza and "astounding" daily specials; "bring a coat" as "there's always a line" (day and night), "but once you're through the Dutch door", the Northern Italian cooking is "memorable" and the staff "never rushes you"; "mamma mia!" now "that's an osteria!"

Lovejoy's Tea Room Ⓜ *Tearoom*

20 | 22 | 21 | $23

Noe Valley | 1351 Church St. (Clipper St.) | 415-648-5895 |
www.lovejoystearoom.com

"Doilies, dolls" and "double Devon cream" reign at Noe Valley's "cutesy-charming" English "twee" tearoom "swarming with bachelorette parties, girlfriends gossiping and the occasional 10-year-old in her party dress"; make a reservation, then "pop in" for a cuppa and "sinful" "finger foods" served on "mismatched china" in a "kitschy" antiques-filled setting reminiscent of "grandmother's parlor"; it's "not formal like" the "Ritz" – but it's sure "perfect" for a "delightful afternoon diversion."

Luella *Californian/Mediterranean*

22 | 20 | 21 | $43

Russian Hill | 1896 Hyde St. (Green St.) | 415-674-4343 | www.luellasf.com

"Eat here . . . now" urge devotees of this "outstanding", "plenty comfortable" Russian Hill locals' "favorite" with "sweet service" that doubles as a "celeb hideout" (ahem, "there's always the potential of a Gavin sighting"); the "short menu" of "excellent" Cal-Med fare, including the "amazingly tender Coca-Cola–braised pork shoulder", "hits all the right notes" – even "mundane-sounding" items "impress" – plus the chef-owner sometimes steps out of the open kitchen to check "how things are" and help "pick out wines."

Luna Park *American/French*

19 | 16 | 17 | $32

Mission | 694 Valencia St. (18th St.) | 415-553-8584 | www.lunaparksf.com

It's "quite a scene" at this "kitschy", "cavernous" spot "hidden in the hip Mission", especially "once the masses arrive", so just grab a "stand-

	FOOD	DECOR	SERVICE	COST

out" cocktail and wait to sup on the "relatively simple", but "well-executed" French–New American fare while "getting cozy in the little booths"; what "fresh, seasonal goodness" – this is what "solid" "home cooking should taste like"; still, it can get "deafeningly" "loud", so bring "someone you'd rather look at than talk to" – or call for delivery.

Maki 🅜 _Japanese_
23 | **16** | **20** | **$35**

Japantown | Japan Ctr. | 1825 Post St., 2nd fl. (bet. Fillmore & Webster Sts.) | 415-921-5215

"Authentic" Japanese specialties like "divine wappa meshi" (bowls of steamed rice, vegetables and meats), chawan mushi (savory custards) and soothing sukiyaki draw crowds to this "sweet", tobiko-size "oasis" in Japantown's otherwise "sterile Japan Center"; it's like visiting Tokyo "without needing to fly 13 hours", and the "friendly servers will gladly explain any dish" and help navigate the "large sake selection."

Mamacita ● _Mexican_
22 | **19** | **16** | **$34**

Marina | 2317 Chestnut St. (Scott St.) | 415-346-8494 | www.mamacitasf.com

By most accounts, this "stylish", "lively" Marina cantina's "upscale nouveau" Mexican fare, including "ridonculous" tacos and "not-to-be-missed" margaritas, "makes up for" any drawbacks associated with its "hip" and "trendy" status, i.e. "attitude" at the door, "uneven" service, "exorbitantly long" waits at the singles scene bar and "off-the-charts" noise – "learn sign language" and it's "well worth a try."

🅩 Mama's on Washington Square 🅜🕱 _American_
25 | **13** | **17** | **$20**

North Beach | 1701 Stockton St. (Filbert St.) | 415-362-6421 | www.mamas-sf.com

Wake "really early" or expect a "long, long line" at this "cozy" North Beach American where locals and tourists alike "belly up to the counter" to order what many call "the best brunch" and breakfast in town (no dinner); fans consider it the "ultimate comfort food" and "well worth" the crazy waits – just bring "reading material and a dose of patience."

Mandalay _Burmese_
21 | **15** | **20** | **$21**

Inner Richmond | 4348 California St. (6th Ave.) | 415-386-3895 | www.mandalaysf.com

"Go with a big party, so you can try everything and not look like a pig" advise fans of this Inner Richmond Burmese where "India, Thailand and China collide" in "mouth-gasmic", "extremely consistent" dishes; "rock-bottom prices", "attentive" servers, "little to no waiting" for a table and "super-cute" digs make it a "welcome" alternative in a "town overloaded with Asian restaurants."

Mangarosa 🅜 _Brazilian/Italian_
19 | **18** | **18** | **$40**

North Beach | 1548 Stockton St. (bet. Green & Union Sts.) | 415-956-3211 | www.mangarosasf.com

An "oddly brilliant fusion" of Brazilian and Italian (including "delicious" steak rechaud, finished tableside on a grill) sets this "hip" joint a "step up from the normal North Beach tourist trap"; "large portions", "funky yet classy" decor and a "happening crowd" that, in true Buenos Aires style, ramps up "around 9:30" don't hurt either; don't be shocked if "almost naked women" "dance around your table" on Thursday samba nights.

Mangosteen ⊉ *Vietnamese* ▽ 18 | 14 | 15 | $22

Tenderloin | 601 Larkin St. (Eddy St.) | 415-776-3999

"One of the nicer holes-in-the-wall" in the Tenderloin with design details like "cool vinyl menus", ceiling fans and paintings of the namesake mangosteen, this cash-only, no-reserving Little Saigon storefront offers "cheap, healthy" Vietnamese "street food" and "tasty beers"; the eats more than "make up for" service that can be "less than competent" at peak times when it gets "overcrowded and hectic."

☑ Manora's Thai Cuisine *Thai* 23 | 14 | 19 | $25

SoMa | 1600 Folsom St. (12th St.) | 415-861-6224 | www.manorathai.com

This "authentic", "colorful" SoMa Thai has "been around forever" and customers who line up for its "super-fast, super-fresh, super-tasty" dishes "hope it stays that way"; even its few detractors are mostly gentle ("once great, now good"), and no one is complaining about the "sinfully cheap" tabs.

Mario's Bohemian Cigar Store Cafe *Italian* 18 | 15 | 15 | $17

North Beach | 566 Columbus Ave. (Union St.) | 415-362-0536 | www.mariosbohemiancigarstore.com

"Watch North Beach walk by" as you enjoy "wonderful, warm" Italian sandwiches on focaccia (including "the planet's best" meatball version) at this "no-frills", "crowded" corner "hangout" on the edge of Washington Square Park, beloved for its "classic" interior and "old SF vibe"; "don't be discouraged" if the staff "takes a few minutes to get to you" – it's "not fast food", but rather a "perfect place to relax with a panini and beer."

MarketBar *Mediterranean* 17 | 17 | 16 | $36

Embarcadero | 1 Ferry Bldg. (Market St.) | 415-434-1100 | www.marketbar.com

"It's all about sitting outside" on the "huge outdoor patio" at this "festive", all-day Med brasserie in a "primo" Ferry Building location; whether you go to "people-watch" during happy hour, or for a "creative" farmer's market meal "while the sun is still up", it's "always so satisfying"; but others pout if the service wasn't "wildly inconsistent" and the fare wasn't a "little boring" "it'd be a runaway success."

Marnee Thai *Thai* 22 | 13 | 17 | $22

Inner Sunset | 1243 Ninth Ave. (bet. Irving St. & Lincoln Way) | 415-731-9999
Outer Sunset | 2225 Irving St. (bet. 23rd & 24th Aves.) | 415-665-9500
www.marneethaisf.com

Go on "an adventure with proprietress" Marnee, who "is sometimes in her own universe" reading palms and telling fortunes at this "very noisy, very tiny" "cramped" Sunset duo; expect "gratuitous advice on" which Thai dish to eat ("don't take it personally if she yells at you") but rest assured the "excellent" food "never fails to deliver" – you're "likely to stuff yourself silly."

☑ Masa's *French* 27 | 24 | 26 | $93

Downtown | Hotel Vintage Ct. | 648 Bush St. (bet. Powell & Stockton Sts.) | 415-989-7154 | www.masasrestaurant.com

Bring "your quiet voice" and "a few credit cards" to Downtown's "high-end bastion" of "old-boy network" fine dining that's "settled into a rhythm" since chef "Gregory Short was poached from French Laundry" to oversee the "haute" New French tasting menus; the "taupe everything" digs are "understated", but the *gastronomique* "theatrics" are definitely not "for a simple steak-and-potatoes eater", while the "wine list is thicker than the Bible"; in short, it's "worth" donning a "loaner blazer" and the "Brobdingnagian prices."

Massawa African   ▽ 21 | 12 | 18 | $20

Haight-Ashbury | 1538 Haight St. (bet. Ashbury & Clayton Sts.) | 415-621-4129

The "exotic flavors" "excite my taste buds" – they "keep you coming back for more" maintain spice-seekers who descend on this East African–Ethiopian standby in the Upper Haight for a "fork-less eating" adventure; tuck into the "tasty dishes that you can eat family-style" with spongy bread as your utensil washed down with honey wine, all at "reasonable" prices.

Matterhorn Swiss Restaurant Ⓜ Swiss   21 | 18 | 19 | $40

Russian Hill | 2323 Van Ness Ave. (bet. Green & Vallejo Sts.) | 415-885-6116 | www.matterhorn.citysearch.com

Vant a "little kitsch" with your schnitzel, "dahlink?" then trek up Russian Hill to this "Swiss-chalet–style" stomping ground where the "fondue festival never ends" and the "welcoming" owner "pairs wines well with the cheesy goodness"; what a "riot" – "you'll swear you're in Switzerland from the moment" you enter the "*Heidi* fantasy setting" and dip your fork into the "vats" "until you roll out, stuffed to the gills"; still, a few yodel, like the "tired banner", it seems "stuck on the Matterhorn."

Maverick American   22 | 19 | 22 | $39

Mission | 3316 17th St. (bet. Mission & Valencia Sts.) | 415-863-3061 | www.sfmaverick.com

"Why not call it 'cutie pie'?" muse admirers of this "adorable", "smaller-than-my-apartment" Mission maverick illuminated by a map of the U.S. that still "delights" "thirtysomethings" with "some visiting parents thrown in"; the "consistently excellent renditions" of "classic American" "comfort food" and "scrumptious brunch" are served by "genuinely friendly" folks, plus you "can't beat Monday's 40 percent off wine deal!"; still, the noise-sensitive squawk it's still "freaking loud", despite the new soundproofing.

Max's Deli   16 | 14 | 16 | $25

Downtown | The Maxwell Hotel | 398 Geary St. (Mason St.) | 415-646-8600

Downtown | Bank of America Ctr. | 555 California St., concourse level (bet. Kearny & Montgomery Sts.) | 415-788-6297 Ⓢ

Civic Center | Opera Plaza | 601 Van Ness Ave. (Golden Gate Ave.) | 415-771-7301

www.maxsworld.com

"Leave the diet at the door" and indulge in "massive", "stuffed"-to-the-max "New York deli-style" sandwiches at this Bay Area chain; loyalists not only "come back again and again" for an "East Coast fix" – they also applaud the "huge, unending menu" filled with "old-fashioned", "tasty comfort food" (don't miss the "eye-popping desserts"), the "partylike atmosphere" and at some locations, "classically trained" servers who "take breaks" to sing opera or "musical theater standards."

	FOOD	DECOR	SERVICE	COST

Maya *Mexican* — 22 | 21 | 19 | $39

SoMa | 303 Second St. (Folsom St.) | 415-543-2928 | www.mayasf.com
It's "not a slam-down-tequila-shot kind" of cantina and it's "miles away" from taqueria turf too – yes, this "serene" "beautifully appointed" SoMa hacienda is not only "ideal for a date", it also offers a "truly mouthwatering experience", proving that "Mexican cuisine can be as gourmet as any"; this is what "they serve in heaven" sigh amigos who praise the "wonderful and imaginative" dishes, "delicious guac", and "incredible margaritas", adding "another trip is clearly in order!"

Mayflower *Chinese* — 22 | 12 | 14 | $27

Outer Richmond | 6255 Geary Blvd. (27th Ave.) | 415-387-8338
Expect "all the classics" at this "lively" Hong Kong–style seafooder in the Richmond where the "kitschy decor" and "hustle bustle add to the fun", but don't overlook the "wildly interesting dim sum" "not regularly found elsewhere"; "it isn't your average Chinese" chime madams and misters who sail over for "delicious" dishes "prepared expertly" and crustaceans plucked "straight out of their fish tanks", declaring we'd "certainly come back."

Maykadeh *Persian* — ∇ 23 | 17 | 20 | $31

North Beach | 470 Green St. (bet. Grant Ave. & Kearny St.) | 415-362-8286 | www.maykadehrestaurant.com
When you're craving "something different in North Beach" trek over to this "Persian paradise" with an "old-school feel" and "treat" yourself to an "outstanding selection of traditional stews and kebabs" complemented by "warm pita" and "awesome" hummus; it's the "real" deal and a "value" for the buck too – chances are you'll "go home" with leftovers.

McCormick & Kuleto's *Seafood* — 19 | 22 | 19 | $44

Fisherman's Wharf | 900 N. Point St. (Larkin St.) | 415-929-1730 | www.mccormickandkuletos.com
You can't "beat" the "knockout" views of Alcatraz at this "nautical-themed" Fisherman's Wharf chain link that's "lovely for lunch on a clear day"; the "solid" lineup of "well-prepared seafood" hooks fin fans, plus "lots of tourists" make for "interesting people-watching", and you can rely on the "old-time servers" who "really know their stuff" to steer you toward the "best dishes"; still, the put-off opine it's "past its prime."

Mecca Ⓜ *American* — 20 | 22 | 19 | $46

Castro | 2029 Market St. (bet. Church & Delores Sts.) | 415-621-7000 | www.sfmecca.com
"Fads come and go", but this "chic", "cabaretlike" "dark cave of warmth" in the Castro, expected to reopen following a light refurb in late-September 2007, "continues to reinvent itself"; the New American menu is a "cut above" its neighbors, offering "something for every taste", while the "terrific drinks" shaken and poured by "attentive" bartenders are well "worth the trip" (and "happy hour is not to be missed"); N.B. live jazz on weekends.

Medicine Eatstation Ⓔ *Japanese/Vegetarian* — 18 | 20 | 16 | $30

Downtown | Crocker Galleria | 161 Sutter St. (bet. Kearny & Montgomery Sts.) | 415-677-4405 | www.medicinerestaurant.com
"Om your way" over to this weekday lunch-only "treat" near Crocker Galleria, a "spartan", "pseudo-Zen vegetarian" that now

also serves seafood; share a bench and slurp "healthy" Japanese noodle and rice "mountain monk" dishes that "may appear small and simple, but are large in taste" or grab a to-go bento box; N.B. come fall 2007, the main dining room is slated to reopen as Medicine-Ryori, a formal dinner house presenting refined Kyoto-inspired, organic kaiseki-style menus.

Medjool *Mediterranean*   18 | 21 | 16 | $33

Mission | 2522 Mission St. (bet. 21st & 22nd Sts.) | 415-550-9055 | www.medjoolsf.com

"Go straight" to the "incredible" rooftop patio of this multifloor Mission "hot spot" and mingle with "hipsters, politicos" and "twentysomethings" before descending to the main restaurant; "it's hard to tell what's sexier, the decor" – it "truly is a Med jewel" – or the "attractive", "tasty small plates" from "all over the region"; grazers agree the "unique environment creates a lust for tasting" "interesting flavors" – and most "leave satisfied with the experience"; P.S. it's a "big party zoo" on weekends.

Mel's Drive-In ● *Diner*   13 | 15 | 15 | $17

Civic Center | 1050 Van Ness Ave. (Geary St.) | 415-292-6358
Inner Richmond | 3355 Geary Blvd. (bet. Beaumont & Parker Aves.) | 415-387-2255
Marina | 2165 Lombard St. (Steiner St.) | 415-921-2867
SoMa | 801 Mission St. (4th St.) | 415-227-0793
www.melsdrive-in.com

"Journey back in time" to *American Graffiti* land" at this "old-fashioned greasy spoon" diner chainlet that's a "step up from fast food" where the "spirit of the '50s" "still lives"; the "juicy burgers" and "soda fountain treats" (try the "addictive milkshakes") "make you wish you were 13 again and not watching calories"; whether you satisfy that "craving" "in the wee hours" "after a concert" or have "kids to entertain", there's "no place better for grabbing grub."

Memphis Minnie's BBQ Joint Ⓜ *BBQ*   20 | 11 | 14 | $18

Lower Haight | 576 Haight St. (bet. Fillmore & Steiner Sts.) | 415-864-7675 | www.memphisminnies.com

"Piggy never tasted so good" and the "portions are humongous" – the "fall-apart tender" "brisket rocks your socks off" – yup, this Lower Haight's "authentic roadside BBQ joint" "takes the art of slow cooking meat to new heights"; down-home denizens fill up on "finger lickin'" greens and "all the right sides", adding the "temptation to take out (so you can have more later) shouldn't be resisted"; still, 'cue-critics kvetch the meat is "just not juicy enough."

NEW Mercury Appetizer Bar ● *Pan-Asian*   - | - | - | M

Marina | 1434 Lombard St. (Van Ness Ave.) | 415-922-1434 | www.mercurysf.com

The mercury is definitely rising on an otherwise dreary stretch in the Marina since the arrival of this "fabulous", fashionable cocktail lounge where well-heeled revelers stop by as much for the chill tunes and "strong, creative" libations (say, a Thai basil gimlet) as for the midpriced Pan-Asian–inspired small plates; the brunch bunch also touches down on weekends for Spam delicacies as well as good ol' American-style eggs and hash browns.

FOOD | DECOR | SERVICE | COST

Mescolanza *Italian*

22 | 17 | 21 | $30

Outer Richmond | 2221 Clement St. (bet. 23rd & 24th Aves.) | 415-668-2221 | www.mescolanza.net

A "true find in the Outer Richmond" for "excellent", "totally affordable" Italian proclaim locals who "go out their way to visit" this "beautifully lit", "delightful neighborhood favorite" for "tasty salads", "phenomenal pasta" and "creative" dishes made with "authentic, fresh ingredients"; it's "charming" on a "cold and foggy night" – or any other – and the "intimate" digs "fill up quickly", so arrive "early" or be prepared to wait.

NEW Mexico DF ● *Mexican*

- | - | - | M

Embarcadero | 139 Steuart St. (Mission St.) | 415-808-1048

Felipe Sandoval (Maya) has teamed up with David Rosales (ex Fonda Solana) to bring this festive cantina to the Embarcadero, with high-quality fare typical of what you'd find in Mexico City (DF stands for Distrito Federal), including carnitas by the pound; stop by for *botanas* (street snacks) from 4 to 6 PM or stay for a full menu (and DJ) until 1 AM; N.B. a 16-seat communal table in the dining room welcomes walk-ins.

☑ Michael Mina *American*

28 | 24 | 27 | $108

Downtown | Westin St. Francis | 335 Powell St. (bet. Geary & Post Sts.) | 415-397-9222 | www.michaelmina.net

"Mmmmichael Mmmmmina's" Downtown "hi-style, hi-concept, hi-priced" temple to "food wizardry" (where "everything comes in three different preparations") is a "triple treat" attest "foodies" who enjoy the "sublime experience of being coveted, cosseted and pampered"; the "delectable" New American tasting menus and "mind-boggling" wine list are served in a "stunning" setting, plus you can order "classics" à la carte at the bar – what a "marvelous" way to "spend all your money"; if some shout "you need a semaphore to talk" over the Westin lobby din, others retort "there's a lovely energy, but it's never raucous."

Mifune *Japanese*

18 | 12 | 13 | $18

Japantown | Kintetsu Mall | 1737 Post St. (bet. Laguna & Webster Sts.) | 415-922-0337

"Don't go" for the "no-nonsense" atmosphere – instead, follow in the footsteps of "weary walkers" and "nearby business" folk and head to "slurp city" in Japantown to "soothe your soul" with a "reliable bowl" of all "different and wonderful kinds" of udon or soba noodles; cold or hot, the "cheap eats" are "perfectly prepared and rapidly served" by a "perpetually brusque" staff; add in "lovely plum wine" and you'll be "over the moon."

Mijita *Mexican*

20 | 12 | 12 | $16

Embarcadero | 1 Ferry Bldg. (Market St.) | 415-399-0814 | www.mijitasf.com

Soak up the "million-dollar view of the Bay Bridge from the outdoor patio" while enjoying a "quick bite" brimming with "bright, fresh, robust flavors" at Traci des Jardins' "quasi-self service" "upscale taqueria" in a "cool" Ferry Building location; but while the "savory" "Mexican *comida*" made with sustainable ingredients and "outstanding agua frescas" "transport you to the streets of Mexico" "seating may be more abundant south of the border", especially on Saturdays when the "farmer's market is going on."

	FOOD	DECOR	SERVICE	COST

⚡ Millennium *Vegan*   24 | 21 | 22 | $44

Downtown | Hotel California | 580 Geary St. (Jones St.) | 415-345-3900 |
www.millenniumrestaurant.com

After "making do" elsewhere, "gourmet" garden groupies "delight" in
dining at the "center of the vegan universe" at this "sophisticated"
"restaurant with a conscience" in the "quaint" Hotel California
Downtown; the "delicate, complex, refined" dishes reveal "ingenious
flavors at every turn", proving that "you don't have to lose excitement
by leaving out the meat" – and that even "devout carnivores" find what
they do with "veggies amazing", especially with the added bonus of a
"heavily" biodynamic wine list.

Mixt Greens ⑤ *Health Food*   22 | 13 | 16 | $14

Downtown | 114 Sansome St., Suite 120 (bet. Bush & Pine Sts.) |
415-433-6498

🆕 **Downtown** | 475 Sansome St. (Commercial St.) | 415-296-9292
www.mixtgreens.com

Whether you choose a "delicious", premade "signature salad" or endure "awful queues" that "move quicker than you might think" to "design your own" greens tossed to "perfection" by a "mixologist", you
can't help but feel "energetic and cleansed" after chowing down at this
"crazy busy" "eco-friendly" health food lunch spot Downtown and its
new sibling; it's a "tad expensive" but the "variety of ingredients are
incredible", plus it goes the "extra mile to support sustainability."

Mochica *Peruvian*   ∇ 23 | 19 | 19 | $35

SoMa | 937 Harrison St. (bet. 5th & 6th Sts.) | 415-278-0480 |
www.mochicasf.com

Although the "friendly" owners have opened the contemporary Piqueo's
across town, this "cozy", "colorful, intimate" storefront "on a dusty,
crusty stretch of SoMa" just gets "better and better", delivering "generous portions" of "excellent", "real-deal" "traditional Peruvian cuisine"; "do the small-plates thing and taste lots of different dishes" and
sample the "delicious" ceviche too – every "burst of flavor leaves you
wanting more" – especially when accompanied by some sangria.

Modern Tea Ⓜ *Californian/Tearoom*   20 | 19 | 20 | $23

Hayes Valley | 602 Hayes St. (Laguna St.) | 415-626-5406 |
www.moderntea.com

Yes, this "delightful" "hip" Hayes Valley corner cafe is a "bright, relaxed" retreat for a "spot o' tea", but habitués hail it as "so much more",
praising the "petite portions" of organic Californian "comfort food"
"done healthy" and the "friendly" servers that help you "decipher" the
"overwhelming" menu of "Chinese, green" and/or herbal brews and
and "match" them with your "tasty nibbles"; still, a few hotheads hiss
the fare's "too pure and plain" and the service "very slow."

Moishe's Pippic ⑤🍴 *Deli*   ∇ 19 | 9 | 15 | $14

Hayes Valley | 425-A Hayes St. (bet. Gough & Octavia Sts.) | 415-431-2440

"Worth going just so you can tell your bubbe or *zayde*" that you ate
here declare denizens who delight in this "kitschy" daytime deli in
Hayes Valley kitted out with "sports posters and junk on the walls";
the owner is "on hand to give you a pickle", and the "really sweet guys"
behind the counter serving up chopped liver, "classic, Chicago-style

Reubens" and "excellent" Windy City dogs are "great characters" – "just don't ask for anything special."

Moki's Sushi & Pacific Grill *Japanese*   21 | 17 | 17 | $28

Bernal Heights | 615 Cortland Ave. (bet. Anderson & Moultrie Sts.) | 415-970-9336 | www.mokisushi.com

Now settled in "more contemporary", "fancy digs" down the street, this "neighborhood gem" in Bernal Heights "buzzes with excitement almost every night", serving up Japanese fare with a "Hawaiian touch"; fin fans rave about the "incredible, unique" house rolls while "those who insist on their meal cooked" choose from lots of "tasty selections"; still, a handful "miss the South Pacific vibe" of the original site and sigh service can be "iffy."

MoMo's *American*   17 | 19 | 17 | $37

South Beach | 760 Second St. (King St.) | 415-227-8660 | www.sfmomos.com

The "place to be before and after Giants games" cheer fans of this "comfortable", "convivial" South Beach spot located a "stone's throw" from AT&T Park; "nothing beats" chowing down on "American classics" with "martinis the size of swimming pools" on the outdoor patio on "sunny days", especially when it's "hopping" with "stadium activity"; but while "you could conceivably catch a foul ball" between bites hecklers huff "unfortunately" the fare is "nothing to write home about."

Moose's *American*   20 | 21 | 20 | $47

North Beach | 1652 Stockton St. (bet. Filbert & Union Sts.) | 415-989-7800 | www.mooses.com

Yup, "the buzz has died down a bit" now that Ed Moose no longer "holds forth", but the "bonhomie lingers" at this "venerable", "cosmopolitan", always "crowded" stomping ground in North Beach near Washington Square Park; "politicos" and "movers and shakers" maintain that the "soul-warming" New American fare, "well-poured" drinks and "wonderful" live jazz music still add up to a "happening" "night on the town"; but other hunters shoot it down, declaring "it ain't the same."

Morton's, The Steakhouse *Steak*   23 | 21 | 22 | $67

Downtown | 400 Post St. (bet. Mason & Powell Sts.) | 415-986-5830 | www.mortons.com

If it's a "good hunk of beef" that you "crave", you "can't go wrong" at these "upscale chain" links with a "gentleman's club" feel Downtown (and in San Jose); the "dependable", "ample" portions and "welcoming" vibe make it the "perfect staple for biz travelers" and "single diners" alike; add in "large, juicy and flavorful" steaks you can "inspect" before they're cooked and you've got a "carnivore's delight" for all.

Mo's *American*   20 | 9 | 14 | $16

North Beach | 1322 Grant Ave. (bet. Green & Vallejo Sts.) | 415-788-3779
SoMa | Yerba Buena Gardens | 772 Folsom St. (bet. 3rd & 4th Sts.) | 415-957-3779
www.mosgrill.com

"You will not leave hungry" vow loyalists who laud the "juicy, sloppy" "ginormous" flame-broiled burgers "prepared the old-fashioned way" with "all the fixin's", "reliable" American fare and "thick milkshakes" at this "no-attitude" diner duo in North Beach and SoMa; there's "not much ambiance", and "service is sometimes off" since the servers "answer the phones", "run the food" and "take orders" simultaneously, but the "excellent value" chow "more than makes up" for it.

☑ Myth ⓈⓂ *American* | 26 | 25 | 24 | $57 |

Downtown | 470 Pacific Ave. (bet. Montgomery & Sansome Sts.) | 415-677-8986 | www.mythsf.com

"Believe the hype": this "sexy", "sophisticated" "'in' place" Downtown packed with "pretty people" provides an "unforgettable experience" that "never fails to dazzle" – and that's "no myth"; "Gary Danko grad" Sean O'Brien "hits it out of the park", conjuring up "divine" New American "creations" that "shine" ("love the half-portion alternative") accompanied by a "stellar" wine list, all served by an "attentive" staff ("without the jaded" attitude); "go, go, go", even if it's for a "wonderful drink" at the bar; P.S. Cafe Myth next door purveys "elegant bag lunches at bargain prices."

My Tofu House *Korean* | 20 | 9 | 15 | $18 |

Inner Richmond | 4627 Geary Blvd. (bet. 10th & 11th Aves.) | 415-570-1818

"Sample an endless parade of kimchi appetizers", "delicious" beef and "home-cooked soft tofu soup" that's the "next best thing" to "*umma*'s" "on a cold foggy night in the Richmond" at this "crowded", "bare-bones" Korean BBQ joint; you may "cower in fear as the molten, frothing, cast-iron pot" of "comfort-food" stew "bubbles onto your table", but you'll "walk away entertained and satiated – all for less than the cost of a haircut."

Naan 'n Curry *Indian/Pakistani* | 18 | 6 | 10 | $14 |

Downtown | 336 O'Farrell St. (bet. Mason & Taylor Sts.) | 415-346-1443 ☽
Inner Sunset | 642 Irving St. (bet. 7th & 8th Aves.) | 415-664-7225 ☽
North Beach | 533 Jackson St. (Columbus Ave.) | 415-693-0499 ☽
Tenderloin | 398 Eddy St. (bet. Jones & Leavenworth Sts.) | 415-775-1349

"Gorge yourself for the price of one grande latte" – "who needs decor" when the Indian food is this "reasonable", "fresh and perfectly spiced" rejoice admirers who congregate for a "quick bite" at this "simple", "no-frills" chainlet with branches in San Francisco and Berkeley; as the name implies though, it's best to "stick" to the "soft naan" and "plentiful" portions of "full-flavored" curries; P.S. it's also "excellent for takeout."

Nectar Wine Lounge *Californian* | 19 | 23 | 20 | $35 |

Marina | 3330 Steiner St. (bet. Chestnut & Lombard Sts.) | 415-345-1377 | www.nectarwinelounge.com

"Interesting", even "spectacular" wines are the "focus" at this "happening" enoteca/retail shop in the Marina, but oenophiles also praise the "savory" Californian small and large plates; order a "pleasing" pour from a staff that "knows its stuff", "chat up" your bar mates or "share intimate moments" in the "sexy" digs and "treat" yourself to "creative" pairings "any day of the week"; P.S. the newer, "way-hip-for-the-Peninsula" branch in Burlingame offers an expanded menu.

New Asia *Chinese* | ▽ 18 | 11 | 13 | $24 |

Chinatown | 772 Pacific Ave. (bet. Grant Ave. & Stockton St.) | 415-391-6666

"For a cheap trip" to Hong Kong, head to this "barnlike", bi-level "frill"-free banquet hall in Chinatown "crowded with large parties" where servers "rush from table to table" wheeling cartloads of "authentic dim sum" for the "adventurous" diner, sure, it's so "loud and raucous"

	FOOD	DECOR	SERVICE	COST

"you can't hear yourself eat" but you will "feel like you lived a little" after the experience.

Nick's Crispy Tacos ⊅ *Mexican*

| 20 | 9 | 13 | $12 |

Russian Hill | 2101 Polk St. (Broadway) | 415-409-8226

Never mind the "departure" of the namesake tortilla titan, you still "gotta get" your "cheap, cheap" fish taco 'Nick's way': "crispy, juicy" with "salsa and guac" at this "charmingly tacky" makeshift taqueria inside Russian Hill's Rouge nightclub; the Baja-style Mexican "quick bites" make for a "surefire hangover cure" – and set this "kitschy" "joint" "apart from the others", though imbibers confide that the "real thing" margaritas may be the "best-kept secret" around.

Nihon ◐🆇 *Japanese*

| ▽ 21 | 23 | 20 | $42 |

Mission | 1779 Folsom St. (14th St.) | 415-552-4400 | www.nihon-sf.com

You "have to be in-the-know" to "come across" this izakaya-style Japanese Missionite in the "middle of the nowhere" that "feels like a secret spot" – and, of course, "you pay for all this hipness"; the "fresh, tasty" small plates and "awesome sushi" are indeed "unique" and the staff "attractive and engaging", but for many the real lure is the "incomparable whiskey bar" upstairs stocked with "obscure, delicious" selections (hint: "stay for a nightcap").

Nob Hill Café *Italian*

| 20 | 15 | 19 | $31 |

Nob Hill | 1152 Taylor St. (bet. Clay & Sacramento Sts.) | 415-776-6500 | www.nobhillcafe.com

"Intimate", "super-quaint" and "bustling every night", this "true neighborhood cafe" "nestled in Nob Hill" "always delivers" "good-size portions" of "insanely satisfying" Northern Italian food made with "fresh, seasonal ingredients"; it's "nothing special, nothing fancy", just "classic everyday" fare served by a "personable" crew; whether you sit outside on a "misty night" and "watch the buzz" or join the locals in what "feels like a friend's dining room" it's "always a pleasure."

NoPa ◑ *Californian*

| 23 | 21 | 21 | $41 |

Western Addition | 560 Divisadero St. (bet. Fell & Hayes Sts.) | 415-864-8643 | www.nopasf.com

So "hot" it single-handedly "redefined an entire neighborhood" declare denizens who descend on the Western Addition's "crazy loud" "food lovers' mecca" "of the moment", a "huge but still cozy" "former Laundromat" boasting "funky wall murals", an open kitchen and a communal table that "totally works"; ex Chow and Chez Nous chef Laurence Jessel "does his magic" "conjuring up" "heavenly" "rustic" Cal "comfort food" "brilliantly matched" with a "well-chosen" wine list, and it's all served by a staff that thankfully lacks "SUV-size egos"; P.S. the "lively" bar serves "sublime" drinks.

North Beach Lobster Shack *Seafood*

| 21 | 11 | 14 | $28 |

North Beach | 532 Green St. (Grant Ave.) | 415-829-3634 | www.lobshack.com

See Old Port Lobster Shack review in South of San Francisco Directory.

North Beach Pizza *Pizza*

| 18 | 9 | 14 | $16 |

Excelsior | 4787 Mission St. (bet. Persia & Russia Aves.) | 415-586-1400 ◑

(continued)

North Beach Pizza

Fisherman's Wharf | Pier 39 (bet. Grant Ave. & Stockton Sts., off The Embarcadero) | 415-433-0400
Haight-Ashbury | 3054 Taraval St. (41st Ave.) | 415-242-9100 🌓
Haight-Ashbury | 800 Stanyan St. (Haight St.) | 415-751-2300 🌓
North Beach | 1310 Grant Ave. (Vallejo St.) | 415-433-2444
North Beach | 1499 Grant Ave. (Union St.) | 415-433-2444 🌓
www.northbeachpizza.com

"It's not much to look at", and it may not be for "pizza snobs", but this North Beach "institution" with Bay-wide branches sure "satisfies a craving" opine pie-eyed fans who praise the "zesty sauce", "big hearty toppings from a laundry list of options" and "attentive" service; but the underwhelmed decry "bland doughy" crusts "inundated with tons of cheese", adding it's "lost its edge."

North Beach Restaurant ● *Italian* | 21 | 19 | 21 | $44 |

North Beach | 1512 Stockton St. (bet. Green & Union Sts.) | 415-392-1700 | www.northbeachrestaurant.com

Experience "old school at its finest" at this "bustling" "Tuscan classic" in North Beach where "attentive" servers don "black suits with white napkins on their wrists" and the "wonderful" Italian fare is "authentic in every way"; "sit downstairs in the curing room for a true rustic experience" – the housemade "prosciutto to die for" and the vibe is straight out of "Parma"; still, a handful harrumph it's "packed with tourists" and the fare "won't knock you over."

NEW Nua Restaurant & Wine Bar Ⓜ *Mediterranean* | - | - | - | M |

North Beach | 550 Green St. (Jasper Pl.) | 415-433-4000 | www.nuasf.com

A "nice addition to North Beach" agree grazers who've discovered this modern wine bar Nua-comer boasting accordion-style windows, exotic wood accents and "lots" of "wonderful" seasonal Med small and large plates inspired by Andalucia, Provence and regional Italy; the "very interesting" list of global vinos includes a rotating roster by the glass, to further enhance the "pairing and sharing" experience.

One Market Ⓩ *American* | 22 | 20 | 21 | $53 |

Embarcadero | 1 Market St. (Steuart St.) | 415-777-5577 | www.onemarket.com

"Woo clients over a business lunch, woo" a date over dinner or just "de-stress after work over a glass of wine" at Bradley Ogden's "timeless" "definite go-back" spot, a "bustling", "big open space" "at the foot of Market Street" that's been humming with "electric" energy since the "dot-com boom"; the "delectable" New American chow makes "your taste buds sing", plus it's "lovely to look at the Embarcadero" between bites; still, detractors lament it's "lost its luster."

Oola Restaurant & Bar ● *Californian* | 20 | 19 | 18 | $42 |

SoMa | 860 Folsom St. (bet. 4th & 5th Sts.) | 415-995-2061 | www.oola-sf.com

"Quite the trendy hangout" for "young" "post-dot-com crowds" and "restaurant industry folk", this "borderline clublike" SoMa "hot spot" "satiates all those late-night hankerin's"; it's an "enjoyable scene", from the "hearty portions" of Californian dishes offering "clever spins

FOOD | DECOR | SERVICE | COST

on the classics" to the "freshly made cocktails" to the "modern, simple" decor; but a few grumble the "only downside" is that it's "too dark and too loud" "to be comfortable."

O'Reilly's Holy Grail *Continental/Seafood* ▽ 18 | 23 | 20 | $37

Polk Gulch | 1233 Polk St. (Bush St.) | 415-928-1233 | www.oreillysholygrail.com

"Love" the "unique" "semi-cathedral" medieval setting complete with "wonderful imported Irish-stained glass windows", a "fun ambiance" and live music on weekends avow worshipers of this "beautiful" Polk Gulch haunt; the "wonderful oysters" and "interesting", "modern" Continental-seafood offerings "go beyond pub food", and it's served by a "charming" staff; but the less-entranced quest on, kvetching that the "mediocre" fare "reads a lot better than it actually is" and just isn't "equal to the decor."

Oriental Pearl *Chinese* 22 | 14 | 17 | $28

Chinatown | 760 Clay St. (Walter U. Lum Pl.) | 415-433-1817 | www.orientalpearlsf.com

"Chinese food for discerning palates" opine patrons who "dream of returning soon" to this "festive", "family-friendly" two-level "favorite" in Chinatown; the "atmosphere is nothing to write home about", but the "wonderful", "well-priced dim sum" and "heavenly" dishes "make you forget all about the decor"; still, the less-bedazzled shrug "not sure what sets this apart."

Original Joe's *American/Italian* 18 | 14 | 18 | $29
(aka Joe's, OJ's)

Tenderloin | 144 Taylor St. (bet. Eddy & Turk Sts.) | 415-775-4877 | www.originaljoessf.com

When you're craving freshly ground "giant burgers", "red-sauce Italian" and a "taste of old Frisco", "venture" into this 1930s "throwback" in the "seedy" Tenderloin, boasting "red-vinyl banquettes", "tuxedo-clad" servers "crustier than the bread", a "gum-chewing hostess of a certain age" and crowds of "judges, cops and brokers"; nostalgists also "take a step back in time" at the unaffiliated "1950s-retro" San Jose "favorite" serving similarly "big portions"; N.B. a recent remodeling of the SF location may impact the Decor score.

Osha Thai Noodles *Thai* 22 | 18 | 17 | $23

NEW **Cow Hollow** | 2033 Union St. (Webster St.) | 415-567-6742 ◐
NEW **Downtown** | 4 Embarcadero Ctr. (Clay St.) | 415-788-6742
Mission | 819 Valencia St. (19th St.) | 415-826-7738 ◐
SoMa | 149 Second St. (bet. Howard & Mission Sts.) | 415-278-9991
Tenderloin | 696 Geary St. (Leavenworth St.) | 415-673-2368 ◐
www.oshathai.com

"You'll swear that your Thai grandmother is cooking in the back", well, maybe your "hip" grandma since this "stylish" chainlet traffics in "trendsetting reinventions of old-school" Siamese chow including "distinctively flavored" curries and dishes made with "beautiful fresh ingredients"; "nightlife lovers" laud the "casual" original on Geary for a "noodle pick-me-up" while seekers of the "next level" commend the other "loungey" branches, particularly the Embarcadero Center site, but all bow to the "swift, courteous" staff.

	FOOD	DECOR	SERVICE	COST

Ottimista Enoteca-Café ⓜ *Italian/Mediterranean*

| 20 | 21 | 20 | $31 |

Cow Hollow | 1838 Union St. (Octavia St.) | 415-674-8400 | www.ottimistasf.com

Boasting a "perfect wine bar atmosphere" that's "inviting for girls' night, double-dates or afterwork drinks", this "convivial" enoteca with a "delicious" Italian-Med small-plates menu adds a "much-needed touch of class to Cow Hollow"; "snag a table outside" and watch the "hustle-bustle" or inside the "lively" digs – either way, you may be tempted to "drink your meal" since the "extensive" list is so "interesting"; still, the less-optimista crack it can "sound like a cackling hen house."

Out the Door *Vietnamese*

| 22 | 14 | 17 | $22 |

NEW **Downtown** | Westfield San Francisco Ctr. | 845 Market St. (bet. 4th & 5th Sts.) | 415-541-9913

Embarcadero | Ferry Plaza | 1 Ferry Bldg. (bet. Mission & Washington Sts.) | 415-321-3740 ⓢ

The Slanted Door's "casual" offsprings crank out "quick", "tasty" Vietnamese "worth its weight in green papaya salad", and remain free of the lines that stretch literally "out the door" at the original; the "convenient" take-out-only Ferry Building location is great for a "shopping break", while the Westfield Centre spot, complete with eat-in service and "honeycomb wall" decor, is a "little oasis" beyond the "insanity of the food court."

Oyaji ⓜ *Japanese*

| ▽ 23 | 14 | 18 | $33 |

Outer Richmond | 3123 Clement St. (bet. 32nd & 33rd Sts.) | 415-379-3604

Japanese expats hit this "zero atmosphere" joint in the Outer Richmond "for excellent sushi" and an "authentic izakaya experience" (featuring "traditional" Japanese "tavern cuisine" like yakitori), all at a "reasonable" price; adding to the "homey" vibe, diners "rub shoulders" with each other at the bar and "drink sake" with the "playful" owner ("oyaji means old man").

Ozumo *Japanese*

| 24 | 23 | 19 | $52 |

Embarcadero | 161 Steuart St. (bet. Howard & Mission Sts.) | 415-882-1333 | www.ozumo.com

"Hipsters" "guzzle sake and slurp sushi" at the "dark", "mobbed bar", while "Japanese food lovers" take in "breathtaking views of the Bay Bridge" to the rear and consume "killer", "crazy expensive" "traditional dishes" composed like "contemporary art" at this "cool" spot on the Embarcadero; aesthetes agree that the digs are "luxurious" and the servers as "hot as the wasabi" – though a few mutter they're "mind-numbingly slow"; N.B. a new branch is slated to open in Lake Merritt (East of SF) in spring 2008.

Pacific Café *Seafood*

| 22 | 16 | 22 | $32 |

Outer Richmond | 7000 Geary Blvd. (34th Ave.) | 415-387-7091

"Only the prices have changed" since 1974, when this "unpretentious" seafooder in the Outer Richmond began serving its menu of "fresh", "old-fashioned" basics; the prices are still "decent", the slightly "worn" decor retains a "funky 1970s style" and the crowds still line up for tables, lapping up the "free wine while you wait in line."

Pacific Catch *Seafood*

| 21 | 12 | 16 | $20 |

Marina | 2027 Chestnut St. (bet. Fillmore & Steiner Sts.) | 415-440-1950 | www.pacificcatch.com

"Satisfy your fish tooth without breaking the bank" at this "family-friendly" Pacific Rim seafooder in the Marina (with a bigger branch in Corte Madera and soon, Inner Sunset) where you can watch staffers prepare "inventive" fare like "delicious" tacos and sweet potato fries (they're an"addiction") "before your very eyes"; P.S. the "tiny" Chestnut Street spot can be a "zoo" – but it's "worth the wait."

Pakwan *Pakistani*

| 21 | 5 | 9 | $13 |

Mission | 3182 16th St. (bet. Guerrero & Valencia Sts.) | 415-255-2440 ☞
Tenderloin | 501 O'Farrell St. (Jones St.) | 415-776-0160 ☽

"Spot-on spicing", "the juiciest Tandoori on the planet" and curry sauce so "delicious" "you should drink it" raise this "no-frills" trio in the Mission, Tenderloin and Hayward above the Pak; with "no decor to speak of" and a "bus your own table" policy, it's "not the most pleasant place to dine", but it's hard to beat the "really cheap prices."

Palio d'Asti ☒ *Italian*

| 19 | 19 | 20 | $42 |

Downtown | 640 Sacramento St. (bet. Kearny & Montgomery Sts.) | 415-395-9800 | www.paliodasti.com

An "established fixture of the Financial District" this Northern Italian "attracts power-lunch crowds" with "solid, modern" nosh ("particularly good during truffle season") served in a "festive" albeit "loud" setting by a "professional" staff; the tempo really gallops during "happy hour" thanks to a "free" "thin-crust pizza" with every two drinks ordered, but just an hour later, at dinnertime, the normally "zoolike" spot turns into a "quiet oasis"; N.B. closed weekends.

🆕 Palmetto *Mediterranean*

| - | - | - | M |

Cow Hollow | 2032 Union St. (Buchanan St.) | 415-931-5006 | www.palmetto-sf.com

This swanky Cow Hollow boîte, which replaces Home restaurant, sports a handsome, glassed-in patiolike front dining room with an elevated see-and-be-seen lounge area; the twentysomething swells who gather at cocktail hour would do well to stay for the midpriced Mediterranean cuisine prepared by fine-dining veteran Andy Kitko (ex Aqua, Tartine and Gary Danko).

Pancho Villa Taqueria *Mexican*

| 20 | 8 | 13 | $12 |

Embarcadero | Pier 1, The Embarcadero (Washington St.) | 415-982-2182
Mission | 3071 16th St. (bet. Mission & Valencia Sts.) | 415-864-8840 ☽

Amigos from "all walks of life" gather at this trio of "classics" for "super-fresh" Mexican "served quickly" and "with a smile", even when the "assembly line service is rushed"; expect to pay very "little for such good food" and opt for an agua fresca to "wash down" burritos "the size of your arm"; P.S. mavens maintain the Mission locale is "far superior" to the Embarcadero and San Mateo branches.

Pane e Vino *Italian*

| 22 | 17 | 20 | $37 |

Cow Hollow | 1715 Union St. (Gough St.) | 415-346-2111 | www.paneevinotrattoria.com

"It's like visiting an Italian family" when you *ciao* down at this "quaint" Cow Hollow "neighborhood fallback" with a "down-home feeling" where "comely" servers tote to table "awesome thin-crust pizza" and "delicious" fresh pasta that's "always a treat"; if a noise-sensitive few sound off that the "decibel level" "gives you tinnitis" and find the digs "not as intimate as its original location", the majority maintains it's "still *bueno* after all these years."

Papalote Mexican Grill   *Mexican*   21 | 12 | 14 | $11

Mission | 3409 24th St. (Valencia St.) | 415-970-8815
Western Addition | 1777 Fulton St. (Masonic Ave.) | 415-776-0106
www.papalote-sf.com

"*This* is fresh Mex" holler hipsters and UCSF gringos who "get their grub on" at these upscale taquerias in the Mission and the "non-burritoville" Western Addition; although "pricier" than their "'hard-core greasy" brethren, these twins "slug it out" for "the best" category thanks to "vegan friendly" varieties ("marinated tofu" and "soyrizo") plus "addictive salsa"; despite the "order-at-the-counter and seat-yourself atmosphere", "expect a wait just about any day"

Park Chalet Garden Restaurant   *American*   15 | 21 | 15 | $27

Outer Sunset | 1000 Great Hwy. (bet. Fulton St. & Lincoln Way) | 415-386-8439 | www.beachchalet.com

"Sit outside on the lounge chairs" at this "greenhouselike" parkside restaurant near Ocean Beach in the Outer Sunset and drink in the "fantastic" views "on a sunny day"; the "informal" and "affordable" New American food is no "match" for the "beautiful setting", but the "refreshing array of brews" and "mellow" atmosphere still compensate, making this a prime spot for "people-watching" with the kids and dogs in tow.

Park Grill   *American*   20 | 19 | 22 | $50

Downtown | Park Hyatt Hotel | 333 Battery St. (Clay St.) | 415-296-2933 | www.hyatt.com

It feels like "half of the financial community" holds court at this "natural meeting place" for a "business breakfast" or lunch – and no wonder, since the Park Hyatt digs Downtown are "quiet" and "subdued" enough for "confidential conversation" and service is "excellent"; still, a few rake the "rather 1980s"-looking decor over the grill and grouch that the "pricey" American fare "fancies itself a bit more gourmet than it really is"; N.B. no dinner served.

Pasta Pomodoro   *Italian*   16 | 13 | 16 | $20

Castro | 2304 Market St. (16th St.) | 415-558-8123
Cow Hollow | 1875 Union St. (Laguna St.) | 415-771-7900
Laurel Heights | 3611 California St. (Spruce St.) | 415-831-0900
Noe Valley | 4000 24th St. (Noe St.) | 415-920-9904
North Beach | 655 Union St. (Columbus Ave.) | 415-399-0300
Outer Sunset | 816 Irving St. (9th Ave.) | 415-566-0900
www.pastapomodoro.com

"As quick as fast food, but with much better quality", this "super-casual" Italian chain with "pleasant decor" and an "outdoor area to boot" caters to families and groups dining "on the fly", doling out "reliable" pasta dishes and seasonal specials at "reasonable prices"; still, starchy sorts sputter that the spaghets are "bland" and "predictable" adding, "frankly my dear, I'd rather eat at home."

	FOOD	DECOR	SERVICE	COST

Patxi's Chicago Pizza Ⓜ *Pizza*

20 | 12 | 16 | $20

Hayes Valley | 511 Hayes St. (Octavia St.) | 415-558-9991 |
www.patxispizza.com
See review in South of San Francisco Directory.

Pauline's Pizza ⓈⓂ *Pizza*

22 | 13 | 17 | $23

Mission | 260 Valencia St. (bet. Duboce Ave. & 14th St.) | 415-552-2050 |
www.paulinespizza.com
The "consistently unique" pizzas at this "Mission classic" "elevate" the humble thin-crust pie "to high art", thanks to "self-sourced organic ingredients" including the "best pesto ever" – and the salads, too, are "garden (their own) fresh"; the "slightly upscale-ish locale" (with matching prices) is "crowded" with "hipsters in-the-know", but the "unpretentious staff tries to alleviate the long waits by playing bartender at the door."

paul k Ⓜ *Mediterranean*

21 | 17 | 21 | $42

Hayes Valley | 199 Gough St. (Oak St.) | 415-552-7132 |
www.paulkrestaurant.com
There's "no fusion confusion" at this "modern, minimalist" Hayes Valley "neighborhood standby", a "t-i-n-y" "underrated" Med "gem" that's "perfect before the symphony"; the effusive staffers "alone are worth the dinner price", regaling customers with a "choreographed set of gesticulations and intonations" while describing the "tasty" dishes in "intimate detail"; still, a few shrug it's "nothing to write home about."

Pazzia Ⓢ *Italian*

22 | 14 | 20 | $30

SoMa | 337 Third St. (bet. Folsom & Harrison Sts.) | 415-512-1693
"*Viva Italia*" cheer cohorts of this "delightful", "always hopping" "favorite" with a "really authentic trattoria feel" and a "charming" owner; never mind that "it looks like a take-out place" from the street – the dishes are "delicious", the "vino is excellent" and you get "attentive, involved" service with an accent – "what could be better?" – especially when you're "visiting SoMa museums and the Yerba Buena Center."

🆕 Perbacco Ⓢ *Italian*

24 | 21 | 21 | $50

Downtown | 230 California St. (bet. Battery & Front Sts.) | 415-955-0663 |
www.perbaccosf.com
Downtown's year-old "power-lunch spot" and "showy date place" lures in "young trendies, old lawyers" and "celebs" with chef Staffan Terje's (ex Scala's Bistro) "incredibly good" Piedmonte and Ligurian specialties including "scrumtious pasta" and "salumi made on-site"; the "split-level", "modern"-Milan-meets–"old Gold Coast" decor is a refreshing (if "noisy") "alternative" to "seafood row", so though the staff seems overwhelmed "with the popularity", concensus is that it's "one of the best newcomers of the year."

Pesce *Italian/Seafood*

22 | 18 | 20 | $39

Russian Hill | 2227 Polk St. (bet. Green & Vallejo Sts.) | 415-928-8025
It's "always a blast to sit at the bar" or "on your neighbor's lap" and "share food with friends" at this "aptly named", sardine-size, "dark", no-reservations Russian Hill "hangout" that reels in locals with "incredibly fresh, inspired Venetian" seafood including small plates and "inventive entrees"; if a few carp that the joint is "floundering in its old age", most maintain it's still going "strong."

	FOOD	DECOR	SERVICE	COST

NEW Pescheria *Seafood*

21 | 17 | 21 | $42

Noe Valley | 1708 Church St. (29th St.) | 415-647-3200

This latest catch from restaurateur Joseph Manzare (Globe, Zuppa, Tres Agaves) is "packed" with Noe Valley locals who appreciate having a "wonderful", "reasonably priced" "seafood restaurant in a non-touristy part of the city"; the "delectable" Boot-inspired fish is complemented by "great wine choices" and "casual but efficient" service, so no wonder it's "difficult to get a table" in the aquamarine tiled digs; P.S. "walk-ins" can "eat at the bar" or the "patio out back in the warmer months."

NEW Piccino Café *Californian/Italian*

▽ 19 | 18 | 17 | $21

Dogpatch | 801 22nd St. (Tennessee St.) | 415-824-4224 | www.piccinocafe.com

Although this "lively", "cute" corner sidewalk cafe in Dogpatch just "got off the ground", it's fast become the "new neighborhood haunt" for a "quick coffee break" (the Blue Bottle java is "bliss") complete with "homemade pastries"; it may be "tiny", but it's "big on lovely food", from "delicious pizza" served at lunch to Cal-Ital dinner fare, served Thursday–Saturday; still, a few nitpiccinos natter that the staff is still working some "kinks out."

Z Piperade S *Spanish*

25 | 21 | 22 | $48

Downtown | 1015 Battery St. (Green St.) | 415-391-2555 | www.piperade.com

"Doting" chef-owner Gerald Hirigoyen "takes great care to see that everyone is happy" at his "lively" Downtown "Basque heaven", a "rustic" "exposed-brick" haunt boasting "old-country charm" and "accommodating" servers; the "distinctive", "savory" "regional specialties" and "marvelous flavor combinations" provide "intrigue", offering a "wonderful escape" from the expected, especially when paired with "unusual wines"; if some see red over "spotty" service and environs so "chaotic" "you feel like one of the bulls in Pamplona" most retort it's a "delightful experience."

NEW Piqueo's *Peruvian*

– | – | – | M

Bernal Heights | 830 Cortland Ave. (Gates St.) | 415-282-8812 | www.piqueos.com

Nestled high above the city in the hills of Bernal Heights, this newcomer from Carlos Altamirano (Mochica) offers mostly small plates – hence the name – of authentic Peruvian fare like fried stuffed yuca balls and ceviche, as well as larger entrees; the warren of little brick-red rooms connected by a series of archways makes you feel as if you're in the chef's home, particularly when you park yourself in the front room by the open kitchen

Pizzeria Delfina *Pizza*

24 | 15 | 19 | $24

Mission | 3621 18th St. (Guerrero St.) | 415-437-6800 | www.delfinasf.com

The "*fantastico*", "authentic Neapolitan"–style thin-crust pizza" "just like you remember from Italy" is "one hell of a consolation prize for not getting in next door" quip patrons who revere this "relaxed" sibling from the "masters of Delfina"; the pies are laced with "imaginative" "straight-out-of-the-garden" ingredients, plus the "salads and starters are divine" and the "affordable" wine list "excellent"; still, it "requires patience" as the wait for a table can be "interminable."

Pizzetta 211 ⊘ *Pizza*
| 25 | 13 | 13 | $25 |

Outer Richmond | 211 23rd Ave. (California St.) | 415-379-9880
"For thin-crusters", this "four-table charmer" in the Outer Richmond "deserves its reputation" serving the "best" artisanal "pizza west of Arguello" (particularly the fried egg special – "I kid you not") accompanied by "killer" salads and desserts; this local "institution" is a "labor of love", but there's little coming from staffers that "blow hot and cold" and "prices are by no means neighborly"; still it's worth "going early before they run out of dough" and it's "nice to sit outside."

PJ's Oyster Bed Ⓜ *Creole/Seafood*
| 19 | 15 | 17 | $31 |

Inner Sunset | 737 Irving St. (9th Ave.) | 415-566-7775 |
www.pjsoysterbed.com
The Creole-seafood "preparations are both light and deft" at this Inner Sunset "institution" declare diehards who particularly dig the "wonderful oysters" and New Orleans–style offerings that are oftentimes "hard to find in this town", all served by a "well-trained" staff; but a few mutter that it "doesn't deliver" on the Big Easy "thing" and sometimes mistakes "overly spicy for tasty."

Plouf Ⓩ *French*
| 22 | 16 | 18 | $38 |

Downtown | 40 Belden Pl. (bet. Bush & Pine Sts.) | 415-986-6491 |
www.ploufsf.com
Every day is like "Bastille Day" at this "frantic" French bistro in Downtown's "Euro" "pedestrian alley" filled "wall to wall" with "girls ogling" the "studly waiters'" "muscles in their sailor gear" and "business district" guys noshing some of the "best" moules and "crispy" frites this "side of the pond" "washed down with a great bottle of Sancerre"; just "grab a seat outside" "on a lovely SF night" or "warm, sunny day" – and avoid the "cramp factor" and "dungeon"-like digs.

PlumpJack Cafe *Californian/Mediterranean*
| 24 | 21 | 23 | $55 |

Cow Hollow | 3127 Fillmore St. (bet. Filbert & Greenwich Sts.) |
415-563-4755 | www.plumpjackcafe.com
Boasting a "blow your socks off" wine list priced "near retail cost", an "intriguing", "constantly changing" Med menu showcasing the "freshest ingredients" and a "knowledgeable staff" that makes "spot-on" pairing suggestions, this "dimly lit" "refuge from Cow Hollow mania" is "as California as can be" – "in the very best way"; natch, there are "beautiful people all around" ("like the mayor" who [once] owned it), but there's "depth beyond the hype"; P.S. shussh to the "super-sexy" Squaw Valley branch on your "ski rendezvous."

Pluto's Fresh Food for a Hungry Universe *American*
| 19 | 12 | 14 | $13 |

Inner Sunset | 627 Irving St. (bet. 7th & 8th Aves.) | 415-753-8867
Marina | 3258 Scott St. (bet. Chestnut & Lombard Sts.) | 415-775-8867
www.plutosfreshfood.com
"Just the basics . . . elevated" – and "dirt-cheap prices" too declare loyalists over the moon about the "hearty", "straightforward" American chow, "delicious side dishes" and "solid sandwiches" at this "counter-type" Marina/Inner Sunset duo; but it's the "made-to-order"

salads that really send fans into orbit – they're "incredible" "because you tell them what you want" tossed in; what a "satisfying" "healthy alternative" to fast food – and all at a "moment's notice."

Poleng Lounge Ⓜ *Pan-Asian*
22 | 20 | 20 | $33

Western Addition | 1751 Fulton St. (bet. Central & Masonic Aves.) | 415-441-1751 | www.polenglounge.com

"Ridiculously delicious" declare Poleng-amists who vault over to the Western Addition's "stylish" Bali-inspired hangout for the "biggest small plates on this side of the Bay" boasting "sparkling" Pan-Asian flavors (try the "addictive adobo chicken wings"); listen to "DJs while you dine" and sip "exotic cocktails", a "soothing accompaniment to the spicy food"; still, polemics find the multiple "identities problematic", pouting "are you a club" restaurant or teahouse? – "you can't have it both ways."

Pomelo *Eclectic*
22 | 14 | 19 | $22

Inner Sunset | 92 Judah St. (6th Ave.) | 415-731-6175
Noe Valley | 1793 Church St. (30th St.) | 415-285-2257
www.pomelosf.com

"Come with your nearest and dearest" as "you'll practically be sitting in one another's laps" at this "cozy", "bright" "secret" in the Inner Sunset and slightly "bigger" Noe Valley sibling (look for the giant pomelo out front) serving up an "inventive", "constantly changing" Eclectic menu meshing French, Californian and Asian cuisines; overlook the "lack of elbow room" – the "healthy grains" and noodle dishes are "comforting" ("carbs are the stars"), and packed with "flavors to savor."

Ponzu *Pan-Asian*
21 | 20 | 19 | $41

Downtown | Serrano Hotel | 401 Taylor St. (bet. Geary & O'Farrell Sts.) | 415-775-7979

An "ideal pre-theater stop" that's "perfect" for "afterwork drinks" too, this "romantic choice" alongside Downtown's Serrano Hotel seduces ticket-holders, colleagues and canoodlers with "lush", "sexy intimate banquettes", "dark" lighting, a "cool vibe" and "unique" Pan-Asian fare; the "inventive" "small plates are the way to go" – what better way to "try and share different things"; still, a few feel the fare is "too complicated" and "overdone" sighing "style over substance."

Pork Store Café *American*
21 | 11 | 17 | $15

Haight-Ashbury | 1451 Haight St. (bet. Ashbury St. & Masonic Ave.) | 415-864-6981
Mission | 3122 16th St. (bet. Guerrero & Valencia Sts.) | 415-626-5523

"Get your grub on" – and "eat until you squeal" oink tickled-pink patrons who endure "long lines" to pig out at this "true Haight experience" and more "spacious" 16th Street sidekick slinging "old-fashioned all-American breakfasts" – the kind of "hearty" fare "your daddy was raised on"; the "hole-in-the-wall" original may not be the "place to linger" but it's certainly where "hipsters" "nurse hangovers" and satisfy "bacon cravings"; N.B. the Mission branch serves alcohol.

Ⓩ Postrio *American*
24 | 23 | 23 | $62

Downtown | Prescott Hotel | 545 Post St. (bet. Mason & Taylor Sts.) | 415-776-7825 | www.postrio.com

"Yes, it's touristy", but you'll also find "luminaries everywhere" assert admirers of this Downtown "wonderland" serving "distinctive" New

American fare and those "famous" "gourmet pizzas"; few menus are as "intriguing and inviting" as Wolfgang Puck's, plus you feel like you're grabbing your own "15 minutes of fame" as you "descend the grand staircase" to the "theatrical dining room"; still, the put-off posit that the "tired" menu needs a "makeover."

Powell's Place Southern   ▽ 18 | 13 | 14 | $21

Western Addition | Fillmore Jazz Preservation Ctr. | 1521 Eddy St. (Fillmore St.) | 415-409-1388

When that urge for "no-frills" "down-home" vittles hits, hightail it to this "sweet", "soulful" Southern belle in the Fillmore Jazz Preservation district; "there's no better" "good-time-spot for gatherings" "west of Harlem" – especially on Sunday Gospel nights; yes, service can be "spotty", but the "heavenly fried chicken", cornbread and greens "make up for it" (plus there's a take-out counter too).

NEW Pres a Vi Eclectic   21 | 25 | 18 | $49

Presidio | 1 Letterman Dr. (Lombard St.) | 415-409-3000 | www.presavi.com

"Tucked" in the Presidio's Letterman Digital Arts Center, this "knock-out" sibling of Walnut Creek's Va de Vi bistro generates "buzz" aplenty with an "outstanding" vino selection, "intriguing" Eclectic small plates and "stunning" interior that's like a "cross between a wine cellar and a wine barrel"; soak up the "exquisite" views of the Palace of Fine Arts from the "lovely patio" or watch the "chefs in action" from the communal table – either way, the space is "awesome"; still, the less-impressed pout about "over-tweaked" dishes and "chaotic" service.

NEW Presidio Social Club American   18 | 20 | 19 | $37

Presidio | 563 Ruger St. (Lombard St.) | 415-885-1888 | www.presidiosocialclub.com

Eating in the "old army barracks" "inside the Presidio sets the vibe for a cool evening" agree enlistees who promote this "new 'in' place" to "instant classic" status; the ambiance "invokes the spirit" of a "1940s country club" with a "sleek, modern" edge while the "super drinks" and "diverse", "hearty" New American menu also "harks back to an-other era"; still, a few break rank whining about food that needs a "bit more punch" and staff attitude that needs more "polish."

Public, The ⊠Ⓜ American   ▽ 18 | 18 | 16 | $34

SoMa | 1489 Folsom St. (11th St.) | 415-552-3065 | www.thepublicsf.com

The "tasty" New American "food will surprise you" assert Public speak-ers who congregate at this "very industrial", "funky converted ware-house" in a "quirky" SoMa setting; the "scene is very cool", providing a "good social" forum, plus service is "really friendly" and "attentive"; if more private types whisper that the fare is "not super special", even they allow that it's "better than" many "other choices in the vicinity."

Puerto Alegre Mexican   18 | 11 | 15 | $17

Mission | 546 Valencia St. (bet. 16th & 17th Sts.) | 415-255-8201

"Kick back" with "killer margaritas" and "simple" Mexican fare that's "definitely a step up" from "local taquerias" at this "happy", "lively" Mission standby replete with "roving mariachi bands"; if few deem the chow "just so-so" and consider drinks the "sole attraction" ("what wouldn't taste good" after sipping pitchersful of the "strong stuff?), most "keep returning" because it's "cheap" and "somehow charming."

Q *American* | 20 | 16 | 17 | $24 |

Inner Richmond | 225 Clement St. (bet. 3rd & 4th Aves.) | 415-752-2298

Get yer "generous" portions of "satisfying" BBQ, and "straight-up American comfort classics, done right" at this "unique hybrid", a "really groovy", "funky-cozy" space in the Inner Richmond where "young and old feel comfortable mixing"; "who can resist macaroni and cheese with Tater Tots" matched with an "extensive", "well-chosen" wine list?; apparently a few questers quibble it's "more about" the "homey" "mood than the food", noting it "doesn't quite live up to its billing."

Ⓩ Quince *French/Italian* | 26 | 23 | 25 | $68 |

Pacific Heights | 1701 Octavia St. (bet. Bush & Pine Sts.) | 415-775-8500 | www.quincerestaurant.com

A "definite 'must' on the foodie circuit" when you want a "dining extravaganza" but don't "want to eat in a theater" this "quinti-sensual", "fancy with a curlicue 'f'" Pac Heights "delight" is "like being in a fine home with a private waiter and chef"; the "dazzling", "one-of-a-kind" New French–Italian creations are fashioned from "pure", "pedigreed ingredients" ("handmade" "luscious pastas" "should be mandatory") while the "excellent" staff is "beyond reproach"; if a few wince it's "a bit prissy", for most it's "lovely in all respects."

Ramblas *Spanish* | 20 | 18 | 17 | $29 |

Mission | 557 Valencia St. (bet. 16th & 17th Sts.) | 415-565-0207 | www.ramblastapas.com

Named for one of Barcelona's most happening neighborhoods, this "lively" Spanish "tapas stop" aptly situated in a "very scene-y section of the Mission" "transports you right" to Spain; bring "friends" and sample the "painfully good", "delicious" nibbles and "creative libations" and ask the "hip" but "down-to-earth staff" to "keep the sangria pouring"; still, a few ramblers grumble the fare's "solid, but not extraordinary."

R & G Lounge *Chinese* | 23 | 12 | 14 | $29 |

Chinatown | 631 Kearny St. (bet. Clay & Sacramento Sts.) | 415-982-7877 | www.rnglounge.com

Although it's often "overrun by tourists", this "Hong Kong–style" eatery is one of the few Chinatown joints "any self-respecting Chinese person would go to when yearning" for "authentic Cantonese" chow that's "isn't dumbed-down" for "Western palates"; "if you prefer food over decor", "skip the funky bar" and "white tablecloths" upstairs and "join local Asian families" in the "dingy downstairs" to feast on "flapping"-fresh seafood specialties fished out of the tanks minutes earlier.

Ⓩ Range *American* | 26 | 20 | 23 | $46 |

Mission | 842 Valencia St. (20th St.) | 415-282-8283 | www.rangesf.com

"I want to be home on this Range nightly" agree urban cowboys who cool their heels at this "awesome-all-around" stomping ground that's bringing "sexy" – and "tasty" – "back to the Mission"; yeah, "parking is impossible" and the "cool" bar "gets very crowded, but nothing can take away from the inventive and often brilliant" New American fare that's "priced right"; add in "super-friendly" staffers and a "hip environment" and it's plain to see it "deserves the buzz."

	FOOD	DECOR	SERVICE	COST

Red Door Café ⊘ *Eclectic* — ▽ 20 | 17 | 18 | $17

Nob Hill | 1494 California St. (Larkin St.) | 415-447-4102

"What a find!" remark admi(red)ers of this "wonderful neighborhood" Nob Hill corner cafe that's "only open until after the lunch rush" and staffed by "friendly counter" folk; there's "always a line on weekends, and rightfully so" as the "tiny kitchen" produces "really fresh, tasty sandwiches", egg dishes and Eclectic midday fare, and the "cozy" tag sale interior "feels like a little bit of France"; still, "nothing's better than watching the cable cars pass from a cute" sidewalk table.

Red's Java House *Hamburgers* — 14 | 10 | 12 | $12

Embarcadero | Pier 30 (Bryant St., off The Embarcadero) | 415-777-5626

Once a longshoreman's restaurant and now a "darn good" American "burger shack", this "slice of old San Francisco" on the Embarcadero gives you a "real feel of the waterfront"; to call it "unpretentious is an understatement" – it's a "classic" "blue-collar" "dive" offering "grease on the cheap" that's "perfect for a sunny afternoon lunch", especially if you "find a spot outside"; N.B. closes at 6 PM weekdays, earlier on weekends.

NEW Restaurant Cassis Ⓜ *French* — - | - | - | M

Pacific Heights | 2101 Sutter St. (Steiner St.) | 415-440-4500 | www.Restaurantcassis.com

Two chef-owner brothers bring their native South of France cuisine to this casual new bistro in Pacific Heights, set in the former Winterland space; the moderately priced menu features Niçoise's greatest hits (pissaladière, duck confit, tarte Tatin) along with Italian-inspired pastas and pizzas.

Restaurant LuLu *French/Mediterranean* — 20 | 18 | 19 | $39

SoMa | 816 Folsom St. (bet. 4th & 5th Sts.) | 415-495-5775

LuLu Petite *Sandwiches*

Embarcadero | 1 Ferry Bldg. (Market St.) | 415-362-7019 www.restaurantlulu.com

Although the "dot-coms and their constantly ringing cell phones are gone", SoMa's "cavernous", "buzzing" French-Med brasserie with an "inviting" open kitchen has reemerged "Internet 2.0" style; "expect to see young, swaggering bucks" mixing with "wine lovers" at the "lively bar" or sharing "toasty" "treats" like "tasty" pizza from the wood-burning ovens and "wonderful" rotisserie dishes; still, "bring texting devices" because when it's "noisy", "it's the only way to have a proper conversation"; N.B. the Ferry Building's LuLu Petite offers takeout.

Richmond Restaurant and Wine Bar, The Ⓢ *Californian* — 22 | 17 | 21 | $39

Inner Richmond | 615 Balboa St. (bet. 7th & 8th Aves.) | 415-379-8988 | www.therichmondsf.com

"Take people you want to impress with your level of being in-the-know" to this "winning little" "locals' gem" in the Inner Richmond serving "amazing-for-the-price" Californian fare; the "friendly" owners "want to succeed by making your visit a joy" confide insiders who sing the praises of the "limited" but "excellently executed" organic selections, "well-crafted wine list" and "attentive service", vowing "I'll go back again and again any day."

	FOOD	DECOR	SERVICE	COST

Rigolo *French*

18 | 12 | 13 | $20

Presidio Heights | Laurel Village Shopping Center | 3465 California St. (Laurel St.) | 415-876-7777 | www.rigolocafe.com

Pascal Rigo's "civilized" cafe presenting "simple fare with French flair", "sinfully flaky pizzas" and mac 'n' cheese oozing "gooey goodness" has "taken Laurel Village by storm"; grab a "quick breakfast", a "casual" lunch or "take the kids" but still "relax" over a "simple" "adult" dinner; just note that during a "portion of the afternoon" it can become a "major parking spot" for the "perambulating" "mommy and me" crew, and service can be "scatterbrained."

Ristorante Bacco *Italian*

23 | 20 | 22 | $36

Noe Valley | 737 Diamond St. (bet. Elizabeth & 24th Sts.) | 415-282-4969 | www.baccosf.com

"Mama mia" now that's Italian, "without the airfare", "jug wine" or "hordes in North Beach" air-kiss devotees "who love coming back" to this "longtime" "gem" in the western end of Noe Valley; everyone from "twentysomethings on their first date" to "older couples toting sleeping babies" receive a "warm welcome", dining on made-to-order "killer" risottos, "scrumptious homemade pasta" and other "genuinely authentic" "unprepossessing" Tuscan fare and Boot bottlings in the "cozy" arched dining room.

Ristorante Ideale *Italian*

24 | 17 | 21 | $40

North Beach | 1309 Grant Ave. (Vallejo St.) | 415-391-4129

"In an area dedicated to high-priced tourist traps", this "boisterous", "festive" trattoria with "raffish style" just "off the hectic Columbus Avenue corridor" offers a slice of modern day" Italy, as "opposed to old North Beach"; *amici* chow down on vino-friendly "uncomplicated" "*vera cucina Italiana*" and "delicious thin-crusted Roman pizzas" that are "as fresh as" the "fun" staffers with "real" accents – and always leave you "sated and pleased."

Ristorante Milano *Italian*

24 | 16 | 23 | $39

Russian Hill | 1448 Pacific Ave. (bet. Hyde & Larkin Sts.) | 415-673-2961 | www.milanosf.com

"Break away from the tourists and the expense-account crowd" at this "cozy", recently refurbished storefront "neighborhood gem high up on Russian Hill", a "real trattoria run by a real Roman" "for two decades"; it's a "favorite" for "romantic evenings" or a "neighborly night out", and the "welcoming" staff makes you feel like "like family", plying "solid", "well-priced" Northern Italian *cucina* "like I wish mama could make" ("anything gnocchi-related is a must").

Ristorante Parma   *Italian*

22 | 16 | 20 | $30

Marina | 3314 Steiner St. (bet. Chestnut & Lombard Sts.) | 415-567-0500

The "walls are painted to appear like the ancient ruins" of Rome and the "hearty dishes" are "just like your old Italian grandmother would make", nevertheless you'll find this "old San Francisco favorite" in the Marina; it's "noisy" and "crowded" and "everyone is happy – and no wonder" what with "warm, friendly service", "very 'Parma' feeling" and "cheap house Chianti" – what a "cozy" place for your "pasta fix."

	FOOD	DECOR	SERVICE	COST

Ristorante Umbria ⊠ *Italian* | 20 | 17 | 19 | $36 |

SoMa | 198 Second St. (Howard St.) | 415-546-6985 | www.ristoranteumbria.com

There's no "friendlier place" than this "convivial" corner SoMa trattoria where "you'll keep the smile on your face after you leave, even if you do eat too much" Umbrian fare; the "charming" owner is "worth getting to know, as he'll mysteriously find a table for you" during lunch "rush hour" when it's "packed with businesspeople" and "conventioneers" "grabbing a bite" on the sidewalk; P.S. stop by for a "quiet" dinner before a Yerba Buena event.

☑ Ritz-Carlton Dining Room ⊠Ⓜ *French* | 27 | 26 | 28 | $96 |

Nob Hill | Ritz-Carlton Hotel | 600 Stockton St. (bet. California & Pine Sts.) | 415-773-6198 | www.ritzcarltondiningroom.com

"For that special occasion when a little formality (some would call stuffiness) is called for" ("tux optional"), Ritz it up at this "pampering" Nob Hill dining room; you can almost "hear an orchestra warming up" before embarking on chef Ron Siegel's prix fixe or tasting menu and wine pairings showcasing "unimaginable", "untraditional" New French creations "with Japanese touches"; it's akin to an operatic "performance", "from the first amuse"-bouche down to the "candy cart", with "lots of 'eye-closing' moments" in between.

☑ Ritz-Carlton Terrace *Mediterranean* | 24 | 24 | 25 | $59 |

Nob Hill | Ritz-Carlton Hotel | 600 Stockton St. (bet. California & Pine Sts.) | 415-773-6198 | www.ritzcarlton.com

Most "certainly not a hotel 'coffee shop'" in terms of "menu or price", this "casual" Ritz-Carlton "backup" is a "pleasant", "relaxed" perch to "soak up some Nob Hill ambiance"; enjoy a "wonderful breakfast", a Mediterranean lunch "your way, any way you want it prepared" or for a "real treat", "impress friends, relatives and out-of-town guests" with Sunday brunch on the gardenlike terrace complete with jazz, champagne and a caviar bar; N.B. dinner served Monday and Sunday only.

rnm restaurant ⊠Ⓜ *American/French* | 25 | 22 | 23 | $40 |

Lower Haight | 598 Haight St. (Steiner St.) | 415-551-7900 | www.rnmrestaurant.com

Thirtysomething chef-owner Justine Miner mines "magic in her kitchen" cooking up "gutsy" American-French large and "small plates done right" for a "young", "trendy" crowd; the chain mail curtains "filter out the grunge" of the "less than impressive" "sketchy" Lower Haight – behold: a "sweet staff" and an "unexpectedly fabulous", "swanky" "urban setting" that doubles as an "ideal date" destination and an "easy local" "gourmet delight" with a "cool lounge area upstairs" serving "exotic" drinks.

NEW Roadside Barbecue *BBQ* | ▽ 19 | 13 | 16 | $17 |

Inner Richmond | 3751 Geary Blvd. (bet. Arguello Blvd. & 2nd Ave.) | 415-221-7427 | www.roadside-bbq.com

"Yee-haw", "finally, tasty BBQ in the City" hoot 'n' holler Roadies who rejoice over the "juicy" wood-smoked babyback ribs", "brisket so tender that it cuts itself" and "sides of surprising quality" at this Inner Richmond American 'cue house that's "better than its curb appeal would suggest"; it's also a "good place to bring the kids as it's cafeteria-style", right down to the "paper towel rolls on the table" and the "friendly smile behind the counter."

RoHan Lounge *Pan-Asian*
▽ 18 | 20 | 17 | $23

Inner Richmond | 3809 Geary Blvd. (bet. 2nd & 3rd Aves.) | 415-221-5095 | www.rohanlounge.com

The "cool" racy red "lounge vibe", "fantastic soju cocktails" and "DJs spinning deep cuts" "trick you into thinking" that this "fun", "hip" haunt is just a watering hole in the "relatively style-free Inner Richmond" – "who would have guessed" that it also serves "killer Korean BBQ" and "inventive" Pan-Asian fusion small plates?; stick around till after 11 and you may also be "pleasantly surprised" by the "nouveau bar snacks."

Rosamunde Sausage Grill ⊖ *German*
25 | 8 | 18 | $9

Lower Haight | 545 Haight St. (bet. Fillmore & Steiner Sts.) | 415-437-6851

"Two words: sausage fest!" *ja*, "amid the grunge and hipsters" of the Lower Haight is "one fantastic" "hole-in-the-wall" counter-service German "haus" of wurst and "with so many choices" ("e.g. wild boar, pheasant, tofu, beef, pork, rabbit"), "grilled to order" and topped "with the works", it's "hard to go wrong"; grab a stool and "satisfy a quick food craving" or take it to Toronado, the bar next door, for a "good beer pairing" since no suds are available on-site.

Rose Pistola *Italian*
21 | 20 | 19 | $44

North Beach | 532 Columbus Ave. (bet. Green & Union Sts.) | 415-399-0499 | www.rosepistola.com

"If you can bear the sidewalk crush", it's "worth the effort" to dine at this "cosmopolitan" North Beach standby serving "sparkling fresh seafood" cooked Ligurian-style, pizza from the wood-burning oven/grill, "delectable" fresh pasta and "delicious fried anythings" that "still beguile"; nab a seat by the "front windows" and "watch the world go by" – the "bustling" "atmosphere makes you want to linger all evening", especially when the "live music is on."

Rose's Cafe *Italian*
21 | 17 | 18 | $31

Cow Hollow | 2298 Union St. (Steiner St.) | 415-775-2200 | www.rosescafesf.com

There's "nothing complicated" about this "sweet" Cow Hollow "sidekick to Rose Pistola" and Terzo too with "lovely service" and a "bohemian", "European atmosphere" that's "perfect for neighborhood Italian" (the "food never misses the mark"); it's also a "charming place" to "please a foodie" at lunchtime and a "brunch favorite" ("breakfast pizzas = amazing") – just "plan to wait in line" especially for the "very popular outdoor tables" that provide plenty of "dog-watching" opportunities.

Rotee *Indian/Pakistani*
▽ 18 | 13 | 14 | $15

Lower Haight | 400 Haight St. (Webster St.) | 415-552-8309 | www.roteesf.com

For "some of cheapest, tastiest" Indian-Pakistani chow in the Lower Haight take thee to the Rotee; the "simple" dishes "rise above the pun-filled menu" and the "brightly lit" orange-and-yellow "Ikea"-style decor – and almost make you "forget" the sketchy scene outside; naan the less, it's "best to do takeout" as parking is "nightmarish" and service can "range from openly rude to spacey."

	FOOD	DECOR	SERVICE	COST

Roti Indian Bistro *Indian*

23 | 19 | 19 | $32

West Portal | 53 W. Portal Ave. (bet. Ulloa & Vicente Sts.) |
www.rotibistro.com
See review in South of San Francisco Directory.

Rotunda *American*

20 | 24 | 20 | $38

Downtown | Neiman Marcus | 150 Stockton St. (bet. Geary & O'Farrell Sts.) |
415-362-4777 | www.neimanmarcus.com

When you want to "remember what it must have been like when women wouldn't be seen out without a proper hat", circle back to the "land of the ladies" "who lunch" atop Neiman Marcus; "shop till you drop, then drop in" for a "pampering" New American menu (the "lobster club is the bomb") or "wet your whistle" with "great martinis" or "afternoon tea" and popovers – "there's no better" "pit stop" than "underneath the cupola" overlooking the "Union Square bustle."

NEW Rouge et Blanc *French*

- | - | - | I

Downtown | 334 Grant St. (bet. Bush & Sutter Sts.) | 415-391-0207

Boasting a loungey ambiance complete with vinelike lighting fixtures and cozy couches, this newly incarnated Downtown wine bar, the latest installation from the Aqua folks, works for day and night, no matter your vino preference; join the Union Square tourists and FiDi suits for cafe fare at lunchtime or kick back after work and quaff selections from a well-priced list with Franco-oriented small plates and charcuterie.

Roy's *Hawaiian*

22 | 21 | 21 | $47

SoMa | 575 Mission St. (bet. 1st & 2nd Sts.) | 415-777-0277 |
www.roysrestaurant.com

Yamaguchi fan's are "never disappointed with anything on the menu" at this SoMa branch of the "upscale chain", the "Rolls-Roy's of Hawaiian fusion" renowned for its "mouthwatering seafood"; "chocoholics plan dinner around the chocolate soufflé", while "the less adventurous" "convention" crowd opts for the "prix fixe that gives a little of everything"; but even with the staff's "aloha spirit", a handful carp that the "mainland" version feels "too Trader Vic's" harrumphing it's filled with "people who are not paying out of their own pocket."

Rubicon ⧉ *Californian*

24 | 21 | 23 | $64

Downtown | 558 Sacramento St. (bet. Montgomery & Sansome Sts.) |
415-434-4100 | www.sfrubicon.com

"Forget the superstar owners", "you-know-who's" Downtown power spot, "where everyone is a big shot, or trying to look like one" is "still going strong after all these years"; chef Stuart Brioza's "full throated" Californian cuisine "complements" the "encyclopedic" wine list ("or vice versa"), plus the "staff helps you navigate" both "with ease"; the spartan "red-brick and white-tablecloth" digs may "lack glitz", but they're well suited to "close those important deals" or "impress a date", "especially if you sit upstairs"; N.B. open for lunch Wednesdays only.

Ruth's Chris Steak House *Steak*

24 | 19 | 22 | $62

Polk Gulch | 1601 Van Ness Ave. (California St.) | 415-673-0557 |
www.ruthschris.com

Sure it's a steakhouse "chain, but who cares if they're doing it right!" assert admirers who bring their "piggy banks" and stampede this "friendly" Polk Gulch link for "excellent", "buttery" rib-eye, filet mi-

	FOOD	DECOR	SERVICE	COST

gnon and more; "it's the sizzle" that makes you want to "indulge yourself early and often", plus the "tender", "prime cuts" and "excellent sides" like the "amazing" creamed spinach are "ideal for the people who might be afraid of trendy, fancy food."

Ryoko's ● Japanese
▽ 23 | 14 | 21 | $36

Tenderloin | 619 Taylor St. (bet. Post & Sutter Sts.) | 415-775-1028

"There's something strangely alluring" about this "recently discovered 'undiscovered Japanese gem'" that's as "down-home as can be" – as in it's a "basement" – and "feels more like Tokyo" than the Tenderloin; "needless to say, there's no view here" but "spectacular sushi" is "what locals come for", plus the "drinking" "party goes on" till 2 AM, with DJs spinning on weekends, and co-owner Ryoko donning the "biggest glasses this side of the Mississippi."

Saha Arabic Fusion Ⓜ Mideastern
▽ 24 | 20 | 23 | $36

Tenderloin | Carlton Hotel | 1075 Sutter St. (bet. Hyde & Larkin Sts.) | 415-345-9547 | www.sahasf.com

"Mohamed is the man", Mohamed Aboghanem, that is, the "gracious Yemen host" and chef of this intimate "date" "oasis"; it may be "hidden away from much of the Tenderloin" crowd, but besotted "locals know it's the place to go for the best Arabic food in the City"; the menu's elevated by a Californian vegetarian-oriented sensibility and a "wine list that's outstanding" for its genre, and "despite price increases, it's still a bargain" – especially the prix fixe.

Saigon Sandwiches ⊄ Sandwiches/Vietnamese
23 | 2 | 13 | $6

Tenderloin | 560 Larkin St. (Turk St.) | 415-474-5698

"The Tenderloin has its moments and Saigon is one of the good ones" wax "budget-conscious" diners who squeeze into the "teensy, crowded", "like-you're-on-the-subway" "hole-in-the-wall" for *bahn mi,* "overstuffed" with "spicy veggies" and meat; never mind that it's a "dump and in a bad neighborhood", these "traditional Vietnamese sandwiches" are the "most satisfying thing one can buy for less than $3", and the "ladies hustle" to make them to order; N.B. closes at 5:30 PM.

NEW Salt House ● American
21 | 20 | 20 | $46

SoMa | 545 Mission St. (bet. 2nd St. & Shaw Alley) | 415-543-8900 | www.salthousesf.com

SoMa's new "upbeat", late-night "gastropub" and oyster bar delivering "delicious riffs" on New American cuisine in a "converted printer warehouse" looks "dot-com-ish", but it still "feels like a visit to a friend's for a dinner" party, "with an 'in' place kind of vibe"; "JP Morgan" suits and "hip" locals "fight for a pre-dinner drink", then stay for fare so "innovative" it'll "catch you off guard"; if old salts prefer to "stick with" "sibling Town Hall", seasoned sorts predict "once they get their tricks down, it'll be a keeper."

Sam's Grill & Seafood Restaurant ☒ Seafood
20 | 16 | 19 | $40

Downtown | 374 Bush St. (bet. Kearny & Montgomery Sts.) | 415-421-0594

"Even minus the filched" bird, this Downtown "throwback to the days of the Maltese Falcon" – "one of the few remaining old SF grills" – is "still worth an occasional visit down memory lane" for the "classic, straightforward seafood" "best washed down by a Manhattan" while ensconced in a "curtained booth"; "except for the prices, nothing

FOOD DECOR SERVICE COST

has changed" in "over 50 years", including the "100-year-old" career waiters "wearing white coats", just "slightly less crusty than the wonderful sourdough bread."

Sanraku Four Seasons *Japanese* `23` `14` `20` `$37`
Downtown | 704 Sutter St. (Taylor St.) | 415-771-0803
SoMa | Sony Metreon Ctr. | 101 Fourth St. (Mission St.) | 415-369-6166
www.sanraku.com

For "high-quality sushi in an unpretentious environment" head to the "surprising little gem hidden in the belly of the Metreon" Center and its larger Downtown sidekick; the Japanese fare is "delectable" – you can see it in the "look on the out-of-towners' faces" and "judging by the regulars" who stop in for "varieties in season that you don't find anywhere else", plus the vibe is "welcoming" – just remember the decor is "very simple."

San Tung *Chinese/Korean* `23` `8` `13` `$18`
Outer Sunset | 1031 Irving St. (bet. 11th & 12th Aves.) | 415-242-0828

"Long waits outside and the loud, happy Cantonese and Mandarin chatter vibrating through" this "no-frills, cheap", "cramped" "fluorescent"-lit Chinese-Korean haunt confirms that the "last secret of the Outer Sunset has been revealed"; "ignore the menu" (and the "gruff" staff) – "just point at what other tables are ordering" – and remember, "house-made noodles and dumplings", all "amazing", are simply "side dishes to the dried fried chicken wings that give you daydreams, night-dreams and everyday fantasies."

Sauce ◐ *American* `18` `15` `20` `$37`
Hayes Valley | 131 Gough St. (Oak St.) | 415-252-1369 | www.saucesf.com

A "treat for the price" opine saucy sorts who pour into this "cozy", "cute" and "unassuming" Hayes Valley neighborhood nook for "after-show drinks" and American "comfort food" with a "modern spin"; "homestyle" offerings like "upgraded mac 'n' cheese", an "extensive bar" selection and "friendly" service make it a "favorite" for "groups or intimate gatherings"; but it's not everyone's gravy boat – a few feel "dessert outshines dinner", adding "it would be tops" if they "varied the menu."

Savor *Mediterranean* `18` `16` `17` `$21`
Noe Valley | 3913 24th St. (bet. Noe & Sanchez Sts.) | 415-282-0344

"Comforting, copious" Mediterranean breakfasts and "fantastic crêpes" served "from dessert to dinner" at this "quintessential" "neighborhood place" "give even the most depressed Noe Valley resident reason to get out of bed" on weekends and wait on line; "cozy" "fireplace tables are great on those (unfortunately frequent) cold SF nights" but the "patio seating in an enclosed courtyard" is "lovely" in warm weather – just be prepared to "eat with every child in the city" stroller-parked here.

Scala's Bistro ◐ *French* `22` `21` `21` `$44`
Downtown | Sir Francis Drake Hotel | 432 Powell St. (bet. Post & Sutter Sts.) | 415-395-8555 | www.scalasbistro.com

"Year after year", this "bustling" bistro next to the Sir Francis Drake Hotel "does a remarkably good job" delivering a "real Downtown SF experience" to "hordes of Union Square shoppers and theatergoers who crowd in" for "delectable" French entrees with an Italian accent; from the "linens and silver place settings" to the "visually interesting",

	FOOD	DECOR	SERVICE	COST

renovated room, it seems to "drip in money" but prices "won't break the bank"; N.B. the bar serves full meals till midnight.

Scoma's *Seafood* | 21 | 17 | 20 | $43 |

Fisherman's Wharf | Pier 47 | 1 Al Scoma Way (bet. Jefferson & Jones Sts.) | 415-771-4383 | www.scomas.com

"More intimate than most Fisherman's Wharf places", and one of the few "worth its salt", this "classic" Victorian "hideaway" and its "sister across the Bay in Sausalito" "definitely have charm" maintain habitués hooked on the "wonderful Italian-style seafood"; everything is "fresh off the boat and professionally served" by a "super staff"; still, others scoff it's "targeted to tourists" – certainly not "food aficionados" – "too bad" the chow "doesn't parallel" the "stunning view."

Scott Howard ⊠ *Californian/French* | 23 | 22 | 21 | $57 |

Downtown | 500 Jackson St. (Montgomery St.) | 415-956-7040 | www.scotthowardsf.com

"Great Scott!" this "dark house" for "expense-account" dining removed "from the hectic pace of Downtown" "looks like it's transplanted from Manhattan", but the "relaxed vibe" and seasonally driven French-influenced menu reflects a "quirky" Californian sensibility; chef "Scott Howard 'does the 'wild thing' well", and devotees "rave" that his re-vamped à la carte and prix fixe options are a "bargain" "for a chef of his repute"; however, while service is "improving", impatient sorts scoff "you'll need to bring a sleeping bag."

Sears Fine Food *Diner* | 18 | 11 | 16 | $20 |

Downtown | 439 Powell St. (Sutter St.) | 415-986-0700 | www.searsfinefood.com

"Bring on" the Swedish pancakes – they're like a "little slice of heaven" sigh fans who join the "line snaking out the door" at this "packed-to-the-gills" Downtowner where "breakfast rules" and lunch is "satisfying"; "sit at the counter where the surly-kitsch waitresses give you amusing attitude" – it feels like a "local" American "diner in a Midwestern town", but with SF "charm and nostalgia"; still, the less-retro-inclined quip "I still don't like Jell-O."

Seasons Steak and Seafood *Seafood/Steak* | 24 | 24 | 25 | $66 |

Downtown | Four Seasons Hotel | 757 Market St., 5th Fl. (bet. 3rd & 4th Sts.) | 415-633-3838 | www.fourseasons.com

Downtown's other "hidden gem on the fifth floor" feels like a "respite from the modern world" – and no wonder, since it's tucked into the Four Seasons and staffed with servers who "bend over" backwards to ensure "everything's to your liking"; since recently jettisoning the formal white tablecloths and transforming into a more casual fish- and chophouse, it's not just the "carriage trade" that turns up – you'll also find diners "dressed in jeans" chilling in the "sophisticated" room with "a view of the City."

Sebo ⊠Ⓜ *Japanese* | ▽ 25 | 20 | 21 | $52 |

Hayes Valley | 517 Hayes St. (Octavia St.) | 415-864-2122

"There isn't even a sign out front", which should tip you off that this "low-key", "posh" Hayes Valley Japanese joint with "no Godzilla or Philly rolls" "tarnishing the menu" is for "purists" – pretty "surprising from a couple" of American-born chefs; "sit at the sushi bar", order

FOOD | DECOR | SERVICE | COST

the "amazing omakase" and "let them" "do their magic"; sure, it'll "break your wallet" but "you won't be disappointed" especially if you top it off with "excellent sake" from the True Sake shop nearby.

Shabu-Sen *Japanese*   ▽ 18 | 13 | 17 | $27

Japantown | 1726 Buchanan St. (bet. Post & Sutter Sts.) | 415-440-0466

Despite a "pretty no-frills" interior and long waits on weekends, this "steamy, cozy", "cheap" Japantown "hot pot" spot "where you cook your own meal with a bowl right in front of you" is a "good place to go with non-sushi eaters" and vegetarians alike; "every spoonful" of the "very tasty shabu-shabu and sukiyaki" is "worth the wait" and effort "on a cold foggy day", plus "you can always snag a spot at the bar top."

Shalimar ●≢ *Indian/Pakistani*   22 | 3 | 9 | $15

Polk Gulch | 1409 Polk St. (Pine St.) | 415-776-4642
Tenderloin | 532 Jones St. (Geary St.) | 415-928-0333
www.shalimarsf.com

For "fiery, lusty", "extremely cheap" Indian and Pakistani "street food" and "real chai – not the New Age crap at Starbucks" – head to this Bay Area chainlet of BYO curry couriers; it's worth "wading through the swarms of homeless addicts" outside, and the "throngs of Southeast Asians" and late-night "hordes" inside to "spend that last dollar" on such "spicy goodness"; P.S. avoid the "truly Third World" "chaos" and "nonexistent service" and "send the least squeamish" for takeout.

Shanghai Dumpling King *Chinese*   22 | 5 | 12 | $15

Outer Richmond | 3319 Balboa St. (34th Ave.) | 415-387-2088

The "drab" "linoleum"-decorated digs at this "tiny mom-and-pop" "hole-in-the-wall" in the Outer Richmond are as "uncreative as its name", but the "incredibly authentic mainland Chinese" chow at "rock-bottom prices" are "as good as you'll find in Hong Kong"; "you may or may not get utensils", nonetheless "those darn" "utterly fresh, utterly delicate, utterly delicious" "soup-filled dumplings" keep you "coming back"; still, white-glove types suggest "get takeout."

Shanghai 1930 ⊠ *Chinese*   20 | 22 | 19 | $43

Embarcadero | 133 Steuart St. (bet. Howard & Mission Sts.) | 415-896-5600 | www.shanghai1930.com

With a "swanky" "period setting" reminiscent of long-ago Shanghai, a "hot bar and music scene" and the "feel of an exotic underground lair", this Embarcadero "crowd-pleaser" transforms "dinner with business associates" into a "party"; "descend into the slightly mysterious basement location" and order "spicy, savory" regional Chinese fare "enhanced by an after-dinner drink and smoke in the private cigar club" – it's a "true" SF "experience"; still, a handful note the jazz "seems more memorable" than the "uneven food."

⊠ Silks *Pacific Rim*   24 | 25 | 26 | $70

Downtown | Mandarin Oriental Hotel | 222 Sansome St. (bet. California & Pine Sts.) | 415-986-2020 | www.mandarinoriental.com

Though often "overlooked", Downtown's "dark horse" "gem" in the "elegant" Mandarin Oriental serves "delicious" Pacific Rim fare that will "blow you away" coupled with an "exquisite wine list"; "prepare to be pampered" – "everything is serene and smooth" from the "beautiful, hushed room" that's just right for a "quiet romantic evening or business dinner" to the "efficient" staff to the "flawless preparations."

☑ Slanted Door, The *Vietnamese* | 26 | 22 | 21 | $46 |

Embarcadero | 1 Ferry Bldg. (Market St.) | 415-861-8032 | www.slanteddoor.com

"Local celebs", "adventurous" tourists and Missionites who visited the old site "back in the day" all "fight for a table" at Charles Phan's "straight-up" "phantastic" Vietnamese "empire", a "jam-packed" waterfront-wonder deemed the "crown jewel" of the Embarcadero's Ferry Building; the "industrial" digs are as "noisy as a Hanoi street corner" and not everyone's cup of "blossoming tea" but the "high-end" Saigon specialties served "speedily" and enhanced by "insightful" wine pairings "shine brighter than the Bay Bridge" outside the "expansive windows"; N.B. for takeout pop into Out the Door next door.

Slow Club *American* | 22 | 18 | 19 | $33 |

Mission | 2501 Mariposa St. (Hampshire St.) | 415-241-9390 | www.slowclub.com

The "wonderful" New American menu is "comfort-plus" – and the "blissful antidote to fast food" – at this "out-of-the-way", "sexy little den" in the Mission that embodies "what a neighborhood restaurant should aspire to" be; the "industrial-chic setting" works for "dinner dates" and for brunch – with "no lines of hipsters stretching around the block" – just remember that "no reservations" can make it "true to it's name"; N.B. a new Dogpatch sibling is slated to open fall 2007.

So Ⓜ *Korean/Noodle Shop* | ▽ 21 | 11 | 13 | $15 |

Outer Sunset | 2240 Irving St. (bet. 23rd & 24th Aves.) | 415-731-3143

"Get your cheap grub on at this little Korean joint in the Outer Sunset" that serves the same "addictive" "signature spicy chicken wings", "juicy potstickers" and "giant bowls" of "saucy" "comforting" noodles as mother ship San Tung; the more "contemporary" setting may have created a "buzz when it first opened", but lately there seems to be just "one" "grumpy" server for the "whole restaurant" and some snipe the food is just "so-so."

Sociale 🄂 *Italian* | 23 | 21 | 22 | $43 |

Presidio Heights | 3665 Sacramento St. (bet. Locust & Spruce Sts.) | 415-921-3200 | www.caffesociale.com

We "always look forward to returning" to Presidio Heights' "secret garden restaurant", a "comfy but sophisticated" Northern Italian "treasure" that "feels like Europe" "tucked away in an alley off Sacramento Street"; the pace is "relaxed", the "outdoor heated patio is darling" and the "divine" food offers a "unique modern take" on the type of dishes that "mama used to make" matched with "wonderful wines" – what an "excellent experience."

South Park Cafe 🄂 *French* | 22 | 18 | 20 | $38 |

SoMa | 108 South Park St. (bet. 2nd & 3rd Sts.) | 415-495-7275 | www.southparkcafesf.com

"Locals rule" at this "quaint French bistro", a "hidden gem" overlooking "cute" South Park in SoMa "where location, pace", "tasty food and ambiance intersect"; what a "gratifying" confluence – it's "like finding" a bit of Paris "on this side of the pond" and it's "worth the hunt"; the "authentic" fare is "delicious", the prix fixe menu a "bargain", the staff "friendly" and the feel "very European" – *mais oui,* it's "an all-time favorite."

Sparrow *Asian/French* ▽ 20 | 18 | 21 | $49

Nob Hill | 1177 California St. (bet. Jones & Taylor Sts.) | 415-474-2000
This "hard-to-find, unheralded gem" may be "secluded on the ground floor of a Nob Hill condominium building" "across from Grace Cathedral", but birders still whistle about the "wonderful" Asian-French feed, noting "you can't beat the attentive", "well-versed" staff; but feather-rufflers chirp that this "bird" doesn't quite "fly", spotting "high-priced", "strange" combinations that "try too hard to be unique, but fall short."

NEW Spork 🖼 *American* - | - | - | M

Mission | 1058 Valencia St. (bet. 21st & 22nd Sts.) | 415-643-5000 | www.sporksf.com
Paying tongue-in-cheek homage to its KFC predecessor, this no-reservations Mission newcomer occasionally serves its affordable New American fare to neighborhood hipsters with one utensil, a spork, of course; the once-iconic red-tiled roof is now cloaked in gunmetal gray, while the candlelit dining room with an industrial feel re-purposes the vinyl booths and particleboard tables.

NEW Spruce ● *American* - | - | - | M

Presidio Heights | 3640 Sacramento St. (Spruce St.) | 415-931-5100 | www.sprucesf.com
Presidio Heights' newcomer strives to be the ultimate local-vore's gathering spot presenting sustainable New American fare sourced directly from its own five-acre Santa Cruz Mountains farm; eco-politics may be in the background, but it's the converted 1930s auto barn setting that takes center stage, with a library, white-marble–topped bar (choose from 70 wines by the glass) and dining room creating an inviting space; the adjoining cafe offers pastries, panini and housemade charcuterie to-go.

Stacks *American* - | - | - | I

NEW Hayes Valley | 501 Hayes St. (Octavia St.) | 415-241-9011 | www.stacksrestaurant.com
See review in South of San Francisco Directory.

St. Francis Fountain *Diner* ▽ 19 | 21 | 18 | $16

Mission | 2801 24th St. (York St.) | 415-826-4200
"One of the last true soda fountains" "left in the city", this "throwback" with "old-school booths" earns "extra points for the counter full of obsolete candy and mid-'80s trading cards" and "super-hip waitresses"; the "sundaes made with Mitchell's ice cream" make it a kid-magnet, but it's also become the "perfect Sunday brunch locale" where "hungover" "indie, arty Mission types" "ride the carbohydrate carousel", filling up on "piles" of "classic diner food" with "healthy twists."

Straits Cafe *Singaporean* 20 | 19 | 17 | $37

NEW Downtown | Westfield San Francisco Ctr. | 845 Market St., 4th fl. (bet. 4th & 5th Sts.) | 415-668-1783 | www.straitsrestaurants.com
For a post-Prada priandial, Downtown shoppers sashay over to the Westfield Centre's "fancier" new outpost of Chris Yeo's "creative"

"Sing-Malay" "local empire"; the "sleek" "Southeast Asian–Zen-like decor" and "exotic cocktails" "transport you" to, if not Singapore, perhaps "Vegas", plus it's "less of a tortured singles scene than its brethren" South of SF, still, straight-shooters fret what's "dire about these Straits" is they need to "turn down the music and turn up the service."

Street Restaurant ☒ American | 21 | 18 | 19 | $35 |
Russian Hill | 2141 Polk St. (bet. Broadway & Vallejo Sts.) | 415-775-1055 | www.streetrestaurant.com

"There's something about" the "dark", "cozy" Russian Hill environs that "make me want to keep coming back"; add in "excellent" "takes on nouveau" American "comfort food", "killer" "infused vodkas that'll knock your socks off" and a "welcoming" staff that makes you "feel like part of the family" and it's a "winning combo"; you "could dine here five times every week without growing tired", nevertheless the Streetwise suggest "go on Sundays for fried chicken."

NEW Sudachi Asian Fusion | - | - | - | M |
Polk Gulch | 1217 Sutter St. (bet. Polk St. & Van Ness Ave.) | 415-931-6951 | www.sudachisushi.com

Chef-owner Ming Hwang (ex Tokyo Go Go) has transformed a one-time teppan joint in Polk Gulch into this green-tea–tinted Japanese izakaya serving an array of Asian fusion tapas, specialty rolls and traditional sushi; the large, rustic-chic space includes a cocktail bar with house-infused soju, a fancier dining area with lantern-lit tatami tables, a more casual front lounge projecting silent nature movies on the wall and live jazz and blues performances on weekends.

SUMI French | 23 | 20 | 24 | $37 |
(fka Ma Tante Sumi)
Castro | 4243 18th St. (bet. Castro & Diamond Sts.) | 415-626-7864 | www.suminthecastro.com

"A quiet island amid the Castro's mayhem", this "tiny" "tucked-away" spot with "stylish", "minimalist" decor showcasing "superb" "architectural" Asian-inspired French fare is "still as good as ever", and perhaps "one of the better (if not the best) restaurants" in the 'hood to take "visiting relatives" for a "quiet" "conservative" dinner without the "queeny" vibe; it "isn't cheap", but if you "get there before 7 PM", the "fixed-priced 'neighborhood special'" is "an amazing bargain."

Suppenküche German | 21 | 16 | 17 | $29 |
Hayes Valley | 601 Hayes St. (Laguna St.) | 415-252-9289 | www.suppenkuche.com

"Bring your thirst" and "*gutten* appetite" to Hayes Valley's "zuper-cool" "rathskeller" resembling a "Deutschland" "beer hall", only "smaller" and "crowded" with the "beautiful set" "eating schnitzel" and downing "fabulous" Belgium suds "out of novelty steins"; the "delicious" "German comfort food" is "not for the carb conscious" – or the "picnic"-table adverse, but if you can withstand the lines and the "overworked waitresses", "it's impossible not to have a good time."

supperclub ☒ Eclectic | 17 | 24 | 19 | $73 |
SoMa | 657 Harrison St. (3rd St.) | 415-348-0900 | www.supperclub.com

SoMa's "edgy Euro-tainment" supper club "doesn't fit in, and neither will you" – that's what makes this Eclectic "dinner theater experience" "fantastic" report reclining guests who muse the "last days of the Roman Empire must have been" as much "naughty fun"; what with servers "hanging upside down from the rafters" to take orders and "swingers" slithering on "gigantic white pillows", food is "beside the point" concur conceptualists; still, the less-amused compare the "crazy four-hour" Eclectic prix fixe menus to a "shaky" "dress rehearsal."

Suriya Thai ⓜ *Thai* ▽ 23 | 15 | 20 | $23

Mission | 1432 Valencia St. (bet. 25th & 26th Sts.) | 415-824-6655

It's "well worth crossing town" to experience the "stimulating variety of tastes" on offer at this Mission Thai that "truly stands out from the crowd" in part because of "genius" owner Suriya who's a "character and delightful too"; Siam-seekers insist you'll find a "very unusual array of authentic dishes not seen elsewhere in the SF area", adding you "could live on the pumpkin curry alone."

Sushi Groove *Japanese* 23 | 19 | 17 | $38

Russian Hill | 1916 Hyde St. (bet. Green & Union Sts.) | 415-440-1905

SoMa | 1516 Folsom St. (bet. 11th & 12th Sts.) | 415-503-1950 Ⓢ

"Get your groove and your sushi on" at this "dark, trendy" trio with branches in Russian Hill, SoMa and Walnut Creek serving up "'tudes, tunes and tuna" to a "young, stylish crowd"; yeah, the "bartender rocks" and the "awesome DJ" "adds a 'club' feel" but "surprise", the "supremely fresh" fish and "nice fat, juicy rolls" are "utterly delicious"; you'll "wait forever" for the "ditzy", "hot" servers but "it's all groovy, baby" – just gives you time to "watch the sweet mamas saunter by"; N.B. a new branch is slated to open in Mint Plaza fall 2007.

Sushi Zone Ⓢ *Japanese* ▽ 26 | 14 | 17 | $28

Castro | 1815 Market St., Suite 5 (Pearl St.) | 415-621-1114

Perhaps it's the "size of a bento box", but this "tiny" Upper Market "hole-in-the-wall" has a "huge" following who "know the secret handshake"; "pray that the folks in front" of the line "abandon ship" so you can move your "party up" and in the door for "jumping fresh sushi", Hawaiian-inspired "inventive rolls" and cooked "appetizers that rival" the fin fare; the "two-plus hour wait" gets "pretty gnarly" but "that's what the liquor store" nearby is for.

🆕 Sutra Ⓢⓜ *Asian Fusion* ▽ 19 | 23 | 17 | $42

SoMa | 100 Brannan St. (bet. Delancey St. & The Embarcadero) | 415-593-9000 | www.sutrasf.com

This "spruced-up", "swanky" Pan-Asian "relaunch" of the "Chez Papa team's" "Frencho" "predecessor, La Suite", exudes a real "hot nightspot" "vibe" thanks to "fashion-conscious bar-goers", "trance music" and a "plush lounge decor" that "makes for a cool evening" out in SoMa; but some who venture into the Buddha-lined back dining room deem the Asian fusion fare "not bad but not memorable either" and fret that this karma chameleon's ambiance is "too clubby" for a restaurant.

Sutro's at the Cliff House *Californian* 19 | 25 | 18 | $48

Outer Richmond | 1090 Point Lobos Ave. (Great Hwy.) | 415-386-3330 | www.cliffhouse.com

A "total treat for all the senses", the "reinvented Cliff House" in the Outer Richmond serving "tasty" Californian fare has taken a "big step forward" confirm acolytes; "on a clear day", soak up "spectacular views" of the Pacific Ocean in the "grand space" while enjoying a "sumptuous brunch" or "sip champagne" at sunset while "waiting for dinner to arrive" – the vista is so "stunning" "you feel like you're at sea"; still, a handful confide the "sleeper here is the bar menu downstairs."

☑ Swan Oyster Depot ☒⇴ *Seafood*   26 | 11 | 21 | $28

Polk Gulch | 1517 Polk St. (bet. California & Sacramento Sts.) | 415-673-1101
Expect to see "cops, movie stars", "tourists" and other "card-carrying members of the Swan Oyster Cult" sitting "bumper to bumper" on "wobbly" "counter stools" at this "family-owned" Polk Gulch "seafood chuckwagon", a "unique" "pearl" with a "lack of decor" that's "part of it's charm"; the "cowboy servers" "entertain you" while shucking the straight-"from-the-docks" bivalves and serving "nothing fancy" fin fare that "blows away anything in Fisherman's Wharf" – it's an "experience to be shared"; N.B. closes at 5:30 PM.

Tablespoon *Californian*   22 | 18 | 22 | $42

Russian Hill | 2209 Polk St. (Vallejo St.) | 415-268-0140 |
www.tablespoonsf.com
The original chef cut out, but this "fine", "hectic" Russian Hill "neighborhood bistro" with a "local feel" still ladles out "way more than a tablespoon" of "ambitious", "but not pretentious" "creative" Cal-New American "comfort food" with "well-priced wines" and "friendly service" for "good" measure; the quarters may be "cramped", but never mind, "you'll walk away fat and happy" after eating the "tasty" mac 'n' cheese; P.S. the recently expanded bar area is "perfect" for drinks.

☑ Tadich Grill ☒ *Seafood*   22 | 19 | 19 | $41

Downtown | 240 California St. (bet. Battery & Front Sts.) | 415-391-1849
"Old as the hills and still a treat", Downtown's "ancient" fish house "still packs them in", serving "not-to-be-missed" sand dabs and some of the "best cioppino" around in "atmospheric", "old-school digs"; whether you sit at the long "bar with the company of a Bloody Mary" and the "power-lunch" crowd or in a "secluded booth with your heart's desire", expect "no-nonsense service" from the "crusty waiters"; P.S. arrive "early or brave the lines" as there are no reservations.

Tajine ⇴ *Moroccan*   ▽ 23 | 12 | 20 | $20

Polk Gulch | 1338 Polk St. (Austin St.) | 415-440-1718 |
www.tajinerestaurant.com
Former cab driver turned kebab slinger Mohammed Ghaleb's original "inexpensive", "tiny" Moroccan "hole-in-the-wall" was "worth bracing the 'loin for", and though it's relocated to larger Polk Gulch digs, it remains one of the "best deals in town"; it's still BYO, cash only and bare-bones, despite new tin lamps and the "superb" Marrakech dishes like chicken b'steeya, priced at less than taxi fare, and are served by the same "caring service" – but alas, it's "no longer a "secret."

Takara ☒ *Japanese*   22 | 14 | 18 | $31

Japantown | 22 Peace Plaza (bet. Laguna & Webster Sts.) | 415-921-2000
"Am I in Kyoto?" or Japantown quip patrons who dine side-by-side with "Japanese executives" on "homestyle dishes you rarely see" as well as "very fresh sushi" at this "peaceful" Peace Plaza "jewel"; the "everyday cooking" comes in an equally "simple package" – it's "authentic in look, fragrance, and taste" – and the meal ends with "savory

egg custard"; still, a few feel it "used to be much better" before the recent ownership change.

Tao Cafe *Vietnamese*   ▽ 18 | 16 | 16 | $28

Mission | 1000 Guerrero St. (22nd St.) | 415-641-9955 | www.taocafe.com

A "charming, low-key" "hangout" for some of the "most authentic" French-inflected "Vietnamese cuisine you will find this side of Saigon", or at least, on the Mission–Noe Valley border declare devotees; the "delightful" proprietress who lived in France and the 1930s-inspired colonial decor make it more "lovely"; still, the put-off pooh-pooh "I'll save my foodie dollars for elsewhere."

Taqueria Can-Cun ●◑⊟ *Mexican*   21 | 8 | 13 | $9

Downtown | 1003 Market St. (6th St.) | 415-864-6773
Mission | 2288 Mission St. (19th St.) | 415-252-9560
Mission | 3211 Mission St. (Valencia St.) | 415-550-1414

"Service is quick, business is bustling and finding a table is tough" at this "perfect late-night Mexican" trio that's a "must-stop" "during an evening out" touring the bars; the food is "simple and phenomenal", from the "mean veggie burrito" ("grilled tortillas are especially appreciated") to the "excellent" carne asada – "you'll be in heaven" as long as you "pardon the cheesy", "mariachi-themed decor" and jukebox that's a "shock to your senses"; N.B. no alcohol served at the Downtown location.

⚡ Tartine Bakery *Bakery*   26 | 13 | 13 | $15

Mission | 600 Guerrero St. (18th St.) | 415-487-2600 | www.tartinebakery.com

You can "gain 10 pounds" just "drooling" at the "otherworldly Parisian pastries" and "hot-pressed sandwiches" on "fresh baked breads" (available after 5 PM) best "washed down" with "large bowls of lattes" or hot chocolate at this cult Mission "boulangerie" and wine bar; despite being the "DMV of bakeries" with "out-of-control lines" and "snotty", "glacial service", "sugar"-happy hounds happily submit to "death by croissant" and "jostle" for their piece of "to-die-for pie."

Taylor's Automatic Refresher *Diner*   21 | 12 | 14 | $17

Embarcadero | 1 Ferry Bldg. (Market St.) | 866-328-3663 | www.taylorsrefresher.com

See review in North of San Francisco Directory.

Ten-Ichi *Japanese*   21 | 14 | 19 | $31

Upper Fillmore | 2235 Fillmore St. (bet. Clay & Sacramento Sts.) | 415-346-3477 | www.tenichisf.com

Devotees "keep coming back" to this "very welcoming", "dependable" Upper Filmore Japanese serving up "supremely fresh and well-executed sushi"; "it's my favorite place for a drop-in, informal" meal" – though "nothing fancy", it's "comfortable" and the "rolls are wonderful"; still, a few find dinner much more "delicious and peaceful", carping that the staff seems "harried" at lunchtime.

Terzo *Mediterranean*   22 | 21 | 19 | $46

Cow Hollow | 3011 Steiner St. (Union St.) | 415-441-3200 | www.terzosf.com

Even diners "so over small plates" concede that this "comfortably chic" Cow Hollow "hangout" from the Rose Pistola and Rose's Cafe folks "pulls off" the "mélange of Mediterranean" "morsels" menu with "real aplomb"; the "unpretentious" "combinations challenge your senses and win you over", the staff delivers "only smiles", "not attitude" and the "variety of seating options" including communal tables "make for a great night out"; however, the still-"hungry" huff that the portions are too "teeny" for the price.

Thai House Express *Thai*

20 | 12 | 16 | $19

Castro | 599 Castro St. (bet. 18th & 19th Sts.) | 415-864-5000
Tenderloin | 901 Larkin St. (Geary St.) | 415-441-2248 ◑

These Siamese brothers have "authentic cuisine Thai'd down to a T"; the "late-night" "Tenderloin freak-show clientele tempts you to dawdle, but the speedy servers keep" it "true to the 'Express' part of the name", while the Castro branch is "always an eyeful", with a "young hip gay scene and minimalist interior" that belies "how little money" you'll spend; P.S. "tell them you've been to Thailand" and you may need more than a Singha "to extinguish the fires."

Thanh Long Ⓜ *Vietnamese*

24 | 15 | 17 | $43

Outer Sunset | 4101 Judah St. (46th Ave.) | 415-665-1146 | www.anfamily.com

"There's no need to look at a menu" at "Crustacean's older", cheaper, "laid-back" Outer Sunset sibling where "almost every table has the same two" "famous offerings": "finger-licking good" Vietnamese-style "whole-roasted crab and garlic noodles" (and perhaps "seasonal vegetables to clean up the butter"); if some say the "dated decor" falls short and carp that the "outrageous" prices "set you spinning", diehards declare "where else" can you "have a plastic bib tied on for you" while sipping "infused vodka"?

ⓩ Thep Phanom Thai Cuisine *Thai*

24 | 16 | 18 | $27

Lower Haight | 400 Waller St. (Fillmore St.) | 415-431-2526 | www.thepphanom.com

"Everything you order" is a "Thai masterpiece" maintain mavens who consider this "phanom-enal" Lower Haight haunt the "apex of traditional" Siamese cooking; expect "memorable flavors both bold and subtle", all "creatively" executed and "beautifully" presented – just remember that you may have to queue up on a line that wraps "around the block at rush hour" or "sit on your neighbor's lap"; little wonder some "like it more for takeout."

Three Seasons *Vietnamese*

23 | 20 | 18 | $35

Marina | 3317 Steiner St. (bet. Chestnut & Lombard Sts.) | 415-567-9989 | www.threeseasonsrestaurant.com

Go "beyond the pho" – and take a "large group" – to this "upscale Vietnamese" duo serving a "huge variety" of "clever", "exotic" small plates, starring "amazing satays" and "rolls that rule" – all "tangy" "treats for the taste buds" – plus "well-mixed cocktails"; the Marina incarnation is "a little fancier than the usual", while the "funky" lunch-only Palo Alto "hidden gem" is an "excellent transormation of a 'barny' space" – with "tropical decor" to boot.

Ti Couz *French*

22 | 16 | 16 | $20

Mission | 3108 16th St. (bet. Guerrero & Valencia Sts.) | 415-252-7373

"Many have tried to copy" this "popular" French bistro's formula of "sweet and savory" buckwheat crêpes in the "thick, seriously stuffed"

"Breton-style", but this "cozy", "airy" spot still "puts all others to shame"; order hard "cider in a ceramic bowl for the full effect", add in "wonderful salads" and you "feel like you're in a beachside cafe in Dinard", Brittany – until the "tattooed" staff and "Mission hipsters" jolt you back to reality.

NEW Toast *American*   18 | 14 | 17 | $16
Noe Valley | 1748 Church St. (Day St.) | 415-282-4328 | www.toasteatery.com

"Solid breakfasts" served all day, with "dessert, salads and burgers thrown in" constitute the "21st-century" American "diner food" at this outer Noe Valley newcomer; the brown-tile counter and busboys' mechanic shirts add "retro" touches, but the prices (compared to the "greasy spoon" it replaced) are thoroughly modern (er, a "few bucks more per plate"); crusty sorts concur the staff "grinds without any love", adding waits are "interminable for basic food."

Tokyo Go Go *Japanese*   22 | 19 | 18 | $34
Mission | 3174 16th St. (bet. Guerrero & Valencia Sts.) | 415-864-2288 | www.tokyogogo.com

Though many find the Japanese fare "innovative", "beautiful" and "super-fresh", the "lively social scene" and "unbeatable" "hand-roll happy hours" are what really "keep this Mission sushi joint packed"; the "glitzy", "futuristic" izakaya surroundings may feel a little "nuevo riche" "for 16th Street", but the "blasting techno", "entertaining chef" and "great sake selection" make it "fun for a group dinner."

Tommaso's Ⓜ *Italian*   25 | 15 | 20 | $27
North Beach | 1042 Kearny St. (bet. Broadway St. & Pacific Ave.) | 415-398-9696 | www.tommasosnorthbeach.com

Truly a "shining light among all the strip clubs", this 70-year-old "real-deal" Southern Italian joint is "the place to take tourists wanting to experience the true flavor of old North Beach"; indeed, descending into the "kitschy" basement is like "stepping back in time", where a family of owners encourages diners to "eat, eat, eat" "excellent spaghetti and meatballs" and "perfect pizzas", which come from the "oldest wood-fired oven in town" – just "be prepared to wait" ("no reservations").

Tommy Toy's Cuisine Chinoise *Chinese*   24 | 24 | 24 | $60
Downtown | 655 Montgomery St. (bet. Clay & Washington Sts.) | 415-397-4888 | www.tommytoys.com

Tommy's "quintessential" "throwback" of "Oriental glitz" straddling Downtown and Chinatown "never fails to please" "business travelers" and "special-occasion" celebrants who expect to be "transported" to a "palace", "treated like an emperor" and "pampered" by a "retinue of servants" as they feast on "exquisite", "decadent" Chinese cuisine presented with French "flair" and served "Western-style (not family-style)"; just "bring your jacket" and your "expense account", because "Tommy doesn't toy with pricing."

Tonga Room *Pan-Asian/Pacific Rim*   13 | 24 | 16 | $40
Nob Hill | Fairmont Hotel | 950 Mason St. (bet. California & Sacramento Sts.) | 415-772-5278 | www.fairmont.com

"A perfect example of a place so 'out', it's 'in'", this "campy" Pan-Asian/Pacific Rim "throwback to '50s' tiki" "silliness" in Nob Hill's Fairmont

	FOOD	DECOR	SERVICE	COST

Hotel "has to be seen to be believed": amid "kitschy" "South Seas decor", a "cheesy cover band plays on a boat" on a "lake in the center of the room", above which a "storm" ("complete with rainfall and thunder") erupts every half hour; try "brain-numbing" mai tais for "liquid dinners", because "if you want great food, the Tonga is just wronga!"

◪ Ton Kiang *Chinese*   25 | 13 | 17 | $28
Outer Richmond | 5821 Geary Blvd. (bet. 22nd & 23rd Aves.) | 415-387-8273 | www.tonkiang.net

"Out-of-the-way" Outer Richmond "meets out-of-this-world dim sum" at this "landmark" Chinese "experience" that "deserves its reputation" for serving "always fresh", "terrific" and "piping hot" "familiar and wildly-outside-the-(steamer)-box" dumplings and other delicacies "all day" (Hakka-style dishes are also available à la carte); "throngs of hungry eaters" sometimes make the waits "absurd" (especially on Sunday mornings) and the "furnishings have seen better days", but its "worth it."

Town Hall *American*   23 | 20 | 21 | $50
SoMa | 342 Howard St. (Fremont St.) | 415-908-3900 | www.townhallsf.com

This "labor of love" from the Salt House boys is the "quintessential" "cool" "San Francisco eatery", dishing up "lively vibes" but "not a lot of attitude" along with "super", "midpriced" New American "comfort food for grown-ups" (including "un-freaking-believable" desserts) in a "trendy" but "not-over-the-top" SoMa "warehouse" "that screams 'I've arrived!'"; unfortunately, so will you, because it's "so noisy, you'll think you're in Grand Central Station."

Town's End Restaurant &   19 | 14 | 17 | $28
Bakery ☑ *American/Bakery*
Embarcadero | South Beach Marina Apts. | 2 Townsend St. (The Embarcadero) | 415-512-0749

A "divinely fresh" bread basket gets "heavenly" morning meals off to a "lavish" start at this "chef-owned" New American cafe and bakery on the Embarcadero ("there's always a line", so "arrive early"), but the "quiet, leisurely" pace at night, featuring "extremely reasonable three-course prix fixe" menus, makes it a "delightful" place for "casual" dinners as well; service can be "lukewarm", but "great views of the Bay Bridge" help alleviate the annoyance.

Trader Vic's *Polynesian*   16 | 21 | 18 | $45
Downtown | 555 Golden Gate Ave. (bet. Polk St. & Van Ness Ave.) | 415-775-6300 | www.tradervics.com
See review in East of San Francisco Directory.

Trattoria Contadina *Italian*   23 | 17 | 21 | $35
North Beach | 1800 Mason St. (Union St.) | 415-982-5728

For "real-deal", "old-style North Beach Italian", "hop on the cable car" to this "off-the-beaten-tourist-track" neighborhood trattoria cranking out "large portions" of "red-sauce" classics that "won't surprise you" but will fill you up "without the markup"; although the "small", "simply decorated" digs "can be noisy and crowded", the "energy" feels like a big "family" "party" with "grandmother in the kitchen."

Tres Agaves ● *Mexican*   18 | 18 | 17 | $33

South Beach | 130 Townsend St. (bet. 2nd & 3rd Sts.) | 415-227-0500 | www.tresagaves.com

Take a "crash course in tequila education" at this "trendy" South Beach "warehouse" near AT&T Park where a "knowledgeable" staff "guides you" (sometimes with "snob" "attitude") in selecting from an "exceptional" inventory of the gold stuff; beyond that, there's "overpriced" "haute taco cuisine" inspired by the Mexican village of Jalisco, which "baseball fans" and "grown frat boys" down while "drinking heavily" enough "to not notice" how "unbelievably noisy" it is "on game days" and during "happy hours."

Troya *Turkish*   ∇ 22 | 17 | 21 | $27

Inner Richmond | 349 Clement St. (bet. 4th & 5th Aves.) | 415-379-6000 | www.troyasf.com

"Go with friends" and "order a bunch" of "sampler platters", because the "mezes are the big draw" at this Turkish delight, "another fabulous ethnic restaurant on Clement Street" in the Inner Richmond; though they're "not quite gourmet", the "larger plates" of "standards" ("kebabs, casseroles", "falafel" etc.) "are hits too", as is the "pleasant and friendly" staff.

☑ Truly Mediterranean   *Mediterranean*   23 | 6 | 15 | $11

Mission | 3109 16th St. (Valencia St.) | 415-252-7482 | www.trulymedsf.com

"Slice me some meat off that spit" request regulars who insist this "schwarma heaven" "hole-in-the-wall" is "truly the best place" for "fast, filling" and "cheap" Mediterranean meals in the Mission; counter stools aside, "there's nowhere to sit", so take your "slammin' falafel" and "lovely baklava treats" to go – "luckily, Dolores Park is nearby."

Tsar Nicoulai Caviar Café   *Caviar/Seafood*   22 | 11 | 17 | $47

Embarcadero | 1 Ferry Bldg. #12 (Market St.) | 415-288-8630 | www.tsarnicoulai.com

"After a day" of "snacking here and there" in the Ferry Building, well-heeled shoppers "save room" for the "decadence" of a "little caviar" and "champers" at this "gourmet" roe bar/retail shop; although the "alcove" "makes an average Starbucks look fancy", it's "worth the wait for a seat" at the "small" U-shaped counter for "decadent", "sexy" lunches featuring blini and seafood sandwiches (it closes at 7 PM weekdays, earlier on weekends).

Tsunami Sushi & Sake Bar ●☑ *Japanese*   ∇ 23 | 22 | 18 | $42

Western Addition | 1306 Fulton St. (Divisadero St.) | 415-567-7664 | www.tsunami-sf.com

"Fancy" and "innovative rolls abound" at this "dark, sensual" late-night Western Addition Japanese joint, in which "NoPa hipsters" sample "awesome flights" from the "tremendous sake selection" while sprawled out on "low lounge-style seating"; there's no doubt that you're "paying for" the "chic" atmosphere (possibly "way too" "much"), but scene-makers say it's "well worth the sticker shock."

Tu Lan ☑⇤ *Vietnamese*   20 | 1 | 9 | $11

SoMa | 8 Sixth St. (Market St.) | 415-626-0927

"Intrepid" "foodies" "unable to resist the siren song" of the "cheap", "delicious" Vietnamese food" at this "cult-status" spot on one of the "creepiest", "skid-row" blocks in SoMa "step over" the homeless and "dodge" the "sketchy" sorts outside, then "gamely ignore the dingy floors" and "sticky coating of grease" on the walls inside; just don't take too close a "look at the kitchen" or you may be "turned off" enough to demand who cares if "Julia Child loved it"? – "I'm leaving the cult!"

2223 Restaurant *Californian*   21 | 19 | 20 | $39

Castro | 2223 Market St. (bet. Noe & Sanchez Sts.) | 415-431-0692 | www.2223restaurant.com

"Alive and kicking" since 1995, this "lively" "favorite" in the "gourmet-deprived" Castro "still shines", offering a "stylish" perch to "people-watch through the big windows onto Market Street" while "drinking and eating too much" "excellent" Californian–New American "comfort food"; the "bar is a hub for a well-heeled", "mostly gay local crowd" to "dish the dirt" while the "delightful" dining room boasts "compelling art" and "jovial" servers, both of which "provide incredible eye candy"; P.S. you "can't beat it for brunch."

NEW TWO *Californian*   21 | 19 | 21 | $43

SoMa | 22 Hawthorne St. (bet. Folsom & Howard Sts.) | 415-777-9779 | www.two-sf.com

The Hawthorne Lane folks present this "more casual" "reincarnation", featuring a "quirkier" Californian–New American menu of "inventive" small plates served family-style offset by a "pleasing '50 under 50' wine list"; indeed, while most maintain the "price-to-quality ratio" surpasses its predecessor, the "why-fix-what-ain't-broken" crowd contends the formerly "handsome" place is now a "garishly decorated" "fun house for those in their 20s" and beg "bring back the elegance!"

NEW Umami Ⓜ *Japanese*   ▽ 20 | 23 | 18 | $39

Cow Hollow | 2909 Webster St. (Union St.) | 415-346-3431 | www.umamisf.com

Head to "the newest hot spot" from the folks behind Mamacita, a Cow Hollow send-up of a Japanese izakaya that "combines the best that disparate Asian cuisines have to offer" in bi-level, rustic-Osaka-tavern-meets-Tokyo-"new-wave" digs (check out the "hopping bar" frequented by a "party"-ready crowd); "'umami' means most delicious taste", and while some feel "it lives up to its name", others think there are some "kinks to be worked out" in what they deem the "confusion fare."

NEW Underdog Hot Dog & Sausage ⌦ *Hot Dogs*   – | – | – | I

Inner Sunset | 1634 Irving St. (bet. 17th & 18th Aves.) | 415-665-8881

"Only in San Francisco" would you find this Inner Sunset "organic hot-dog place" run by "true believers" who "pour their hearts and souls" into the "hip, ecologically aware" fare, including vegan and veggie versions and fresh-baked pies, served in "closet"-size digs with just a couple of tables (there's additional seating on the neighbor's stoop); "hot, crispy Tater Tots", a BYO policy and green touches like biodegradable take-out containers also make chowhounds come running.

Universal Cafe Ⓜ *American*   23 | 16 | 19 | $34

Mission | 2814 19th St. (bet. Bryant & Florida Sts.) | 415-821-4608 | www.universalcafe.net

If you're not a Missionary, you'll probably "wish" this "hip" Multimedia Gulch New American "was in your neighborhood" once you sample its

	FOOD	DECOR	SERVICE	COST

ever-changing roster of "economical", "simple" yet "well-prepared" "organic" "fare with flair"; though it's "better known" for "creative breakfasts" and "inspiring brunches" (hence the often "excruciating waits on weekends"), "dinner is not to be missed", as it's not as "crowded" and "deafeningly loud"; P.S. "sit outside when it's warm."

Venticello *Italian*   23 | 22 | 21 | $44

Nob Hill | 1257 Taylor St. (Washington St.) | 415-922-2545 | www.venticello.com

"Arrive via cable car at sunset" to begin a "memorable" evening at this "lovely, comfortable" Nob Hill "Italian charmer", "one of the most romantic restaurants in the city"; indeed, the "cozy", bi-level space (which is "built around a brick oven") is "where people go to get engaged", to "celebrate a special occasion" or to "close the deal with a girlfriend" (or "in-laws") – and the "solid Tuscan cuisine" is "sensational" to boot.

NEW Vitrine *American*   – | – | – | M

SoMa | St. Regis | 125 Third St., 4th fl. (Mission St.) | 415-284-4049 | www.stregis.com/sanfrancisco

Tucked away on the fourth floor of SoMa's St. Regis, this spalike dining room, accented by sage-green upholstered chairs, well-spaced tables and curtains that filter in soft light, is a semi-secret safe haven for hotel guests and ladies who lunch – and breakfast; the New American morning menu features organic eggs Benedict and brioche French toast, while the midday offerings include corned beef (cured in house) on rye and fish flown in from Japan's Tsukiji Market; N.B. no dinner served.

Vivande Porta Via *Italian*   23 | 14 | 19 | $36

Pacific Heights | 2125 Fillmore St. (bet. California & Sacramento Sts.) | 415-346-4430 | www.vivande.com

"Charming" cookbook author Carlo Middione's Pac Heights Sicilian trattoria "might look like just a take-out" joint, but "sit down" and you'll be rewarded with "some of the freshest, tastiest Italian in town" ("especially the housemade pastas") and loads of "offbeat" wines; although "prices seem high" just to be "squashed next to a deli case", fans find it "fun to sit at the counter and watch the food being prepared."

Walzwerk *German*   20 | 18 | 20 | $27

Mission | 381 S. Van Ness Ave. (bet. 14th & 15th Sts.) | 415-551-7181 | www.walzwerk.com

"Like eating on the set of *Good Bye Lenin!*", this "quirky", "diminutive" East German Küche in the Mission is where "Eastern Bloc" "nostalgics" "hang out" to "channel the good old days" of "Trotsky and Stalin" while chowing down on "enormous plates" of "hearty-to-last-all-week" schnitzel, spaetzle, sausages, wurst and "beer thicker than the servers' accents"; of course, it all begs the question who knew the "Communist Era" could ever be so "kitschy"?

Washington Square   19 | 19 | 20 | $39
Bar & Grill *American/Italian*

North Beach | 1707 Powell St. (bet. Columbus Ave. & Union St.) | 415-982-8123

This "North Beach institution", aka the "good ol' dependable 'Washbag'", is "the place that would not die", thankfully, even with management changes: it "continues to draw a faithful older crowd" sopping up "nostalgic vibes" along with "solid" Italian–New American "pub grub" that "satisfies a wide range of appetites"; "old San Francisco" is further invoked in the interior, which manages to be "stately" "without feeling stuffy", and it has "live piano music" nightly.

Waterfront Restaurant *Californian/Seafood* | 18 | 22 | 18 | $43 |

Embarcadero | Pier 7, The Embarcadero (Broadway) | 415-391-2696 | www.waterfrontsf.com

"Soak up the beauty of San Francisco Bay" at this Embarcadero Californian-seafooder where you feel like you're dining "directly over the water", either on the "gorgeous" glass-"protected patio" or in the picture-window-laden dining room; unfortunately, the "outrageously high-priced" food only "sometimes matches the view" say locals who are further put off by sometimes "goofy" staff members that "treat customers as though they won't be returning" (read: "tourists").

NEW Weird Fish *Seafood* | ▽ 18 | 17 | 20 | $19 |

Mission | 2193 Mission St. (18th St.) | 415-863-4744

This "quirky", "hip" new Mission chippy and seafooder from the folks behind St. Francis Fountain is a "weird place" indeed – "where else can you get clam chowder for breakfast" – and "deep-fried pickles" – "and like it"?; the "cozy", old-timey crib is a "welcome change from the trendy lounges and taquerias" while the "wonderful sustainable policy" feels "heartfelt", plus there are "vegan options for your high-maintenance friends"; N.B. no reservations.

'wichcraft *Sandwiches* | 17 | 14 | 13 | $16 |

NEW Downtown | Bloomingdale's, Westfield San Francisco Ctr. | 868 Mission St., ground fl. (bet. 4th & 5th Sts.) | 866-942-4272 | www.wichcraftsf.com

"You don't have to go to NYC anymore" to sample Tom Colicchio's "clever" gourmet 'wiches muse the spellbound who "grab a healthy" midday meal or early dinner at his "urban lunch-eteria" after "shopping it up" at Bloomies in Downtown's Westfield Centre; the "fresh, interesting ingredients" make for "killer" choices, plus the "peanut butter–cream sandwich cookies are seriously better than sex"; still, snarky sorts snort it's "overpriced" "yuppified" fare, adding "he should stick to *Top Chef*."

Woodhouse Fish Company *New England/Seafood* | 19 | 14 | 17 | $25 |

Castro | 2073 Market St. (bet. 14 & Dolores Sts.) | 415-437-2722 | www.woodhousefish.com

For an "East Coast fix" head to this "bare-bones" "joint" that brings "a little bit of New England to 14th and Market" in the Castro, with a "corner" location for "watching the street scene"; an "energetic" crew serves "solid if basic chowderhouse fare" along with "Shipyard beer and lobster rolls", but Boston Brahmin carp the "faux Maine seafood" is "uninspiring and overpriced", "just like a [real] Cape Cod" fish 'n' chipster.

Woodward's Garden Ⓢ Ⓜ *American/Californian* | 25 | 18 | 22 | $43 |

Mission | 1700 Mission St. (Duboce St.) | 415-621-7122 | www.woodwardsgarden.com

True, this stealth Mission haunt serving "delightful food" and "fantastic" wine "under an expressway" may not be your garden-variety "date place", nevertheless it's a "cozy" nook for a "romantic" "tête-à-tête" ("perfection comes when you least expect it"); "half of the fun is watching the chef assemble" "just plain wonderful" New American–Cal creations in the "rough/elegant" digs, and staffers also strike a "balance between formal and relaxed", prompting would-be regulars to "wish it were in my neighborhood instead of under the freeway."

XYZ *American/Californian*　　　| 20 | 22 | 19 | $49 |

SoMa | W Hotel | 181 Third St. (Howard St.) | 415-817-7836 |
www.xyz-sf.com

"Just walking in" to this "sexy, dimly lit" SoMa "oasis" in the "midst" of the "hustle and bustle" "makes you feel farther ahead in the century"; most "don't come to the W for the food" or the "wine list that goes on forever", but you "leave feeling" that the "passion put into" the Californian–New American dishes and food "comes through"; still, it's not letter-perfect for others who pout it's "nothing to write home about."

Yabbies Coastal Kitchen *Seafood*　| 22 | 18 | 20 | $41 |

Russian Hill | 2237 Polk St. (bet. Green & Vallejo Sts.) | 415-474-4088 |
www.yabbiesrestaurant.com

A "hidden star" in Russian Hill, this seafooder named after an Australian crayfish remains a "popular locals'" spot that's perfect "for dates, for friends or an impromptu bite" of "outrageously fresh fish"; a few yabber-mouths yak that "sometimes you need a martini to go with oysters" instead of beer and wine, and carp the check can get "pricey", but the "Thursday clam bakes" help compensate.

Z Yank Sing *Chinese*　　　　　| 25 | 16 | 19 | $35 |

Downtown | 49 Stevenson St. (bet. 1st & 2nd Sts.) | 415-541-4949
SoMa | Rincon Ctr. | 101 Spear St. (bet. Howard & Mission Sts.) |
415-957-9300
www.yanksing.com

For the real, "wheeled" "San Francisco treat", join "everyone and their Chinese cousin" lining up at these "chichi" "reigning" dumpling "monarchs" and "brunch legends" Downtown and in SoMa; "circulating carts" "laden" with a "vast", "dimsummiest" selection of "Hong Kong–style" and "nouveau" small plates "tempt" lunching "corporate-accounters" and "trepidatious tourists" to "yank all the cash" out of their wallets; sure, the bill "stacks up faster than the tiny baskets", but these dishes "normally reserved for banquets" "make you sing"; N.B. no dinner.

Yuet Lee ☽ *Chinese*　　　　　| 21 | 5 | 13 | $21 |

Chinatown | 1300 Stockton St. (Broadway St.) | 415-982-6020

Could Chinatown's "least attractive hole-in-the-wall" with "putrid green walls" and "harsh fluorescent lighting" harbor "some of the best Chinese" chow in the City? – well, it wouldn't be the "crowded" "cop"-stop and "noted late-night chefs' hangout" otherwise; "service is abrupt", but for "amazing" bait-cheap seafood "to soak up beer" "after clubbing", this "greasy-spoon favorite" "is there when you need it" (till 3 AM).

Yumma's *Mediterranean/Mideastern*　| 20 | 9 | 18 | $12 |

Inner Sunset | 721 Irving St. (bet. 8th & 9th Aves.) | 415-682-0762

"Don't be fooled" into thinking it's a "cruddy little take-out joint" – just "say schwarma" and watch this Inner Sunset shack spit out "out-of-this-world", "cheap" Eastern Mediterranean fare and "plenty of it";

	FOOD	DECOR	SERVICE	COST

connoisseurs lavish praise on the "super-friendly owner's" "use of la-vash", organic "Niman Ranch meats" and "fresh" ingredients, and if a few whine that the atmosphere "could be a little less cafeterialike", Yumma-mites retort there's a "lovely patio out back."

Yuzu Ⓜ *Japanese* ▽ 19 | 21 | 19 | $36

Marina | 3347 Fillmore St. (bet. Chestnut & Lombard Sts.) | 415-775-1873 | www.yuzusf.com

"We like it so much we are almost a fixture" rejoice admirers who deem this "real deal" Japanese with "attentive service" a Marina "fa-vorite" for "creative sushi"; the "fish is outstanding and fresh" – it "seems like they were just swimming minutes before they're on the ta-ble" and the "Nippon-style" presentation is "beautiful", plus the digs are "swankier" than most; still, a few feel the fare "doesn't quite match up with the interior."

NEW Zadin Ⓜ *Vietnamese* - | - | - | I

Castro | 4039 18th St. (Hartford St.) | 415-626-2260 | www.zadinsf.com

The Castro's first Vietnamese restaurant, this wallet-friendly new-comer is not your father's pho house, but rather a West Elm–style chic storefront featuring a small menu of authentic standards prepared with a healthy twist; there's an emphasis on gluten-free ingredients – even the tamari is wheat-free.

Zante Pizza & Indian Cuisine *Indian/Pizza* 18 | 5 | 11 | $16

Bernal Heights | 3489 Mission St. (Cortland St.) | 415-821-3949 | www.zantespizza.com

Like a "full buffet in every bite" marvel admirers who relish the "cravable Indian curry pizzas" with "spicy toppings" – it's enough of a "novelty" to "lure" "adventurous" eaters to this Bernal Heights dive-"delight"; "if you can ignore" the "weird ambiance" and "tacky decor", keep your eyes on the pies and "don't bother with the traditional" fare, it's "definitely worth a try", especially if "you are adventurous"; N.B. they deliver too.

Zao Noodle Bar *Pan-Asian* 14 | 12 | 14 | $17

Upper Fillmore | 2406 California St. (Fillmore St.) | 415-345-8088 | www.zao.com

"Simple", "healthy", "filling noodles you can grab on the run" – "what more could you ask for, especially on a budget!" bellow boosters who "stop in" to this "no-frills" Pan-Asian Bay Area chainlet to slurp "piping hot" bowls of "tasty udon"; there's "lots of variety" to suit any "mood", and though it's "nothing fancy", it's "convenient" before the movies; but carbo-crashers blast the dishes are "bastardized" versions of the "real thing."

Zarzuela Ⓢ Ⓜ *Spanish* 22 | 17 | 21 | $35

Russian Hill | 2000 Hyde St. (Union St.) | 415-346-0800

This "welcoming" "little" Iberian at the "'tapa the world" in Russian Hill was "one of the first" around to offer "authentic Spanish tapas" – and it still has "staying power in this city of foodies"; the small plates prepared with "much care and skill" "rock" – and the "mains" are "de-licious" too, plus the staffers treat you like old "Spanish friends" and the "homey" room "echoes with collective conversation"; still, some noshers "wish they took reservations – it gets cold waiting outside."

	FOOD	DECOR	SERVICE	COST

Zazie *French* — 22 | 18 | 20 | $25

Cole Valley | 941 Cole St. (bet. Carl St. & Parnassus Ave.) | 415-564-5332 | www.zaziesf.com

"All the characteristics of a charming" "neighborhood bistro" are in evidence at this "Frenchy" "favorite" with a "super-friendly staff" in "upwardly mobile" Cole Valley; brunch on the "quaint" back patio (with heat lamps) is the "perfect way to spend a sunny Sunday" – "start the morning off right" with a "mimosa or latte" followed by "creative eggs Benedict options" ("can't get enough" of the *français* variations"); still, the ex-Zazie-perated whine about "crazy long waits" alongside the "yuppie/stroller" set.

NEW Zazil Coastal — 19 | 16 | 18 | $37
Mexico Cuisine *Mexican*

Downtown | Westfield San Francisco Ctr. | 845 Market St., 4th fl. (bet. 4th & 5th Sts.) | 415-495-6379 | www.zazilrestaurant.com

Much like its sister, Colibrí, this new, casual yet "upmarket" cantina is "not your typical" "chips and salsa" joint, but a showcase for "unusual", "delicious" regional "coastal" Mexican seafood with "fresh guacamole" prepared tableside and a "tequila list to compete with Tommy's"; the open floor plan, anchored by giant banyanlike trees that double as pillars, "transports you from the mall" and offers a "relaxing" retreat "after a long day of shopping" in Downtown's Westfield San Francisco Centre.

Zeitgeist ●⋻ *BBQ* — 16 | 14 | 9 | $13

Mission | 199 Valencia St. (Duboce Ave.) | 415-255-7505

"Cram" yourself "between bikers, art students" and party people who "haven't been home since Friday" at a picnic table at this "beer garden"– "cum-feed lot" and sip a "spicy Bloody Mary" in the "Mission sunshine"; that'll "hold you" till you hear the "gruff sound of your name" being "bellowed" for your BBQed burger – "listen carefully or they'll give your food away!" P.S. on "lucky" occasions, the Tamale Lady "appears like a goddess" and hands out "golden gifts of joy."

Z Zuni Café ●Ⓜ *Mediterranean* — 25 | 20 | 21 | $47

Hayes Valley | 1658 Market St. (bet. Franklin & Gough Sts.) | 415-552-2522 | www.zunicafe.com

"Before the fame, before the cookbooks" and before "Hayes Valley was invaded by hipsters", Judy Rodgers "worked her magic" – and continues to – "drawing crowds" of opera buffs and the "hoi polloi", "rain or shine", "day or night" to her "delicious, de-lovely" "iconic" "triangular" corner cafe/oyster bar; the "champagne flows and so does the evening", with devotees feasting on "heavenly", "deceptively simple" Mediterranean "comfort food" and "late-night burgers"; "even the 'attitudinal' service" and "one-hour wait" for "custom-roasted chicken" are "part of the charm."

Zuppa *Italian* — 19 | 17 | 17 | $40

SoMa | 564 Fourth St. (bet. Brannan and Bryant Sts.) | 415-777-5900 | www.zuppa-sf.com

For "nicely updated Southern Italian classics in a chic, industrial setting", trot over to Globe owners' Joseph and Mary Manzare's "hip SoMa joint"; join the "30-plus crowd" at the community table, on the

FOOD | DECOR | SERVICE | COST

balcony or perched on "kitchen counter stools" and enjoy "crisp pizzas", "awesome salumi" and "deliciously hearty" dishes that "celebrate the season's best ingredients" along with Boot bottlings; but nitpickers pout the fare's "not zuppa duppa", and whine about "extremely long waits" between courses.

Zushi Puzzle *Japanese*   26 | 9 | 18 | $37

Marina | 1910 Lombard St. (Buchanan St.) | 415-931-9319 | www.zushipuzzle.com

"Holy Neptune!", it's "no puzzle" why this Marina "hole-in-the-wall" is "now overcrowded" with "picky sushi-holics" and "really lucky tourists" – roger, it's Roger, the "wisecracking" host-chef who "spoils you with his remarkably" "FedEx"-"fresh fish and original 'remix'" rolls "not found anywhere else"; locals cry "if you're just ordering tempura and California rolls, go somewhere else" "so we can get a freakin' seat at the bar", as service at the "shabby" tables is "frustrating enough."

EAST OF SAN FRANCISCO

Top Food Ratings

Ratings are to the left of names. Lists exclude places with low votes, unless indicated by a ▽.

28 Erna's Elderberry

27 Chez Panisse
   Chez Panisse Café
   Rivoli

26 Lalime's

25 Wolfdale's
   Kirala
   Bay Wolf
   Jojo
   Dopo

Cafe Esin
Oliveto Restaurant

24 Ajanta
   Zachary's Pizza
   À Côté
   Va de Vi
   Gioia Pizzeria
   Citron
   Pearl Oyster Bar
   PlumpJack Cafe

BY CUISINE

AMERICAN
25 Cafe Esin
23 Forbes Mill Steak
22 Lark Creek
21 Bette's Oceanview
   Rick & Ann's

CALIFORNIAN
28 Erna's Elderberry
27 Chez Panisse
   Chez Panisse Café
   Rivoli
23 Wente Vineyards

CHINESE
23 Great China
20 Shen Hua
   Rest. Peony
17 Jade Villa
   Berkeley Tea

FRENCH
25 Jojo
24 À Côté
   Citron
   Gregoire
23 Olivia

INDIAN
24 Ajanta
23 Vik's Chaat Corner
22 Shalimar
21 Breads of India
20 Udupi Palace

ITALIAN
25 Dopo
   Oliveto Restaurant
24 Postino
   Prima
23 Tratt. La Siciliana

JAPANESE
25 Kirala
24 O Chamé
   Cha-Ya Vegetarian
   Uzen
23 Sushi Groove

MEDITERRANEAN
27 Chez Panisse
   Chez Panisse Café
   Rivoli
26 Lalime's
25 Bay Wolf

MEXICAN/PAN-LATIN
24 Tamarindo Antojeria
   Fonda Solana
   Doña Tomás
22 Tacubaya
21 Picante Cocina

SOUTHEAST ASIAN
24 Pho 84
23 Soi Four
21 Le Cheval
19 Cha Am Thai
   Plearn Thai

BY SPECIAL FEATURE

BREAKFAST/BRUNCH

23 Oliveto Café
22 Café Fanny
   La Note
21 Bette's Oceanview
   Rick & Ann's

CHILD-FRIENDLY

24 Zachary's Pizza
23 Great China
21 Pizza Antica
   Picante Cocina
20 Cactus Taqueria

MEET FOR A DRINK

24 Fonda Solana
   Prima
23 Oliveto Cafe
22 César
21 Townhouse B&G

OPEN LATE

24 Fonda Solana
21 Koryo BBQ
20 Everett & Jones
18 Caspers Hot Dogs
   Lanesplitter

OUTDOOR SEATING

25 Dopo
24 Va de Vi
   O Chamé
   Doña Tomás
23 Wente Vineyards

PEOPLE-WATCHING

27 Chez Panisse Café
24 Postino

23 Oliveto Cafe
22 César
20 downtown

ROMANCE

28 Erna's Elderberry
27 Chez Panisse
26 Lalime's
24 Citron
23 Wente Vineyards

SMALL PLATES

24 À Côté
   Va de Vi
   Pearl Oyster Bar
   Fonda Solana
22 César

TRENDY

24 À Côté
   Pearl Oyster Bar
   Doña Tomás
22 César
21 Café Rouge

VIEWS

25 Wolfdale's
23 Wente Vineyards
19 Ahwahnee Din. Rm.
   Blackhawk Grille
   Gar Woods Grill

WINNING WINE LISTS

28 Erna's Elderberry
27 Chez Panisse
   Rivoli
24 À Côté
   Va de Vi

BY LOCATION

BERKELEY

27 Chez Panisse
   Chez Panisse Café
   Rivoli
26 Lalime's
25 Kirala

LAKE TAHOE AREA

25 Wolfdale's
   Christy Hill∇

   Moody's Bistro∇
23 Dragonfly∇
   Soule Domain∇

OAKLAND

25 Bay Wolf
   Jojo
   Dopo
   Oliveto Restaurant
24 À Côté

Top Decor Ratings

Ratings are to the left of names.

28 Ahwahnee Din. Rm.

26 Erna's Elderberry
    Postino

25 Wente Vineyards
    Sunnyside Resort

24 Bing Crosby's

23 Chez Panisse
    Rivoli
    Wolfdale's
    Gar Woods Grill

22 Chez Panisse Café
    Adagia
    O Chamé
    Imperial/Berkeley Tea
    Blackhawk Grille
    Bridges
    Oliveto Restaurant

21 Pearl Oyster Bar
    Mezze
    Fonda Solana

Top Service Ratings

Ratings are to the left of names.

28 Erna's Elderberry

26 Chez Panisse

25 Rivoli
    Chez Panisse Café
    Wolfdale's

24 Bay Wolf
    Lalime's

23 Jojo
    Wente Vineyards
    Prima

    Citron
    Postino
    PlumpJack Cafe
    Oliveto Restaurant
    Cafe Esin

22 Mezze
    Ajanta

21 Forbes Mill Steak
    Ahwahnee Din. Rm.
    Olivia

Best Buys

In order of Bang for the Buck rating.

1. In-N-Out Burger
2. Caspers Hot Dogs
3. Arinell Pizza
4. Gioia Pizzeria
5. Cactus Taqueria
6. Mama's Royal Cafe
7. Tacubaya
8. Picante Cocina
9. Vik's Chaat Corner
10. Fentons Creamery
11. Bette's Oceanview
12. Udupi Palace
13. Imperial/Berkeley Tea
14. Barney's
15. Asqew Grill
16. Jimmy Bean's
17. Lanesplitter
18. Café Fanny
19. Zachary's Pizza
20. Juan's Place

OTHER GOOD VALUES

Blackberry Bistro
Cha-Ya Vegetarian
Chow
Everett & Jones
FatApple's
La Méditerranée

Lo Coco's
Pho 84
Shen Hua
Spettro
Uzen
Xyclo

East of San Francisco

	FOOD	DECOR	SERVICE	COST

À Côté *French/Mediterranean* 24 | 21 | 20 | $40

Oakland | 5478 College Ave. (Taft Ave.) | 510-655-6469 | www.acoterestaurant.com

Perhaps one of "the best small-plates restaurants in the East Bay", this "dark, glamorous" "rare late-night" neighborhood wine bar near the BART feels "like a private party" and "never fails to please" "regulars, just-off-the-train suited workers" and "Rockridge yuppies"; a "passionate" staff delivers "delectable" French-Med tapas, "killer cocktails" and wine for the "adventurous", which helps "mitigate the long waits" for seats inside (including communal tables) or on the "lovely patio"; N.B. open till midnight on weekends.

Adagia Restaurant *Californian* 19 | 22 | 18 | $34

Berkeley | Westminster House | 2700 Bancroft Way (College Ave.) | 510-647-2300 | www.adagiarestaurant.com

Flocks of coeds and professors dine on "tasty", mostly organic Californian "'grown-up food'" "in a bohemian environment" at this former religious student center near UC Berkeley that now "ministers to the need for sophisticated dining"; it's a "delight to sit by the fire" in the oft-"noisy" yet "charmingly" restored "Ivy League–like dining hall" interior, while the "beautiful courtyard" is a "lovely sheltered spot" in warm weather; the only sour note: "inexperienced (yet friendly) service."

☑ Ahwahnee Dining Room, The *American/Californian* 19 | 28 | 21 | $56

Yosemite | Ahwahnee Hotel | 1 Ahwahnee Rd. | Yosemite National Park | 209-372-1489 | www.yosemitepark.com

"After a gritty day outdoors", nothing's more "civilized" than dinner ("before it gets dark") or a Sunday buffet brunch at this "spectacular, timber-beamed" Yosemite restaurant famous for its "soaring ceilings and magical setting at the base of the Royal Arches" that's "almost as grand as the Valley" itself; sure, the "ordinary", "assembly-line" Cal-American fare served by an "earnest" but "unprofessional" staff "doesn't match its price or setting", but the "grand old" Ahwahnee Hotel still delivers an "unforgettable experience."

☑ Ajanta *Indian* 24 | 20 | 22 | $28

Berkeley | 1888 Solano Ave. (bet. The Alameda & Colusa Ave.) | 510-526-4373 | www.ajantarestaurant.com

"Dine like a rajah and rani" at this "elegant" Berkeleyite known for its "inventive" monthly regional and seasonal "green-conscious" fare that's not your "run-of-the-mill Indian", but rather a subcontinental banquet" replete with respectable wines and "solicitous service"; sure you might be able to book a "five-star hotel in Madras for the same cost", nonetheless it remains an "all-time favorite" for "business meetings, romantic dinners" and "university students who bring their parents to pay."

Amber Bistro ☒ *Californian* ▽ 20 | 19 | 21 | $42

Danville | 500 Hartz Ave. (Church St.) | 925-552-5238 | www.amberbistro.com

"Pretty good" Californian fare with Southeast Asian touches and fanciful drinks like "chocolate martinis" presented in a "zinging" "contemporary atmosphere" make this Danville destination a refreshingly "trendy" night out "for the 'burbs"; however, nostalgists sigh it's "no longer fabulous" like it was under its previous chef while the noise-sensitive huff it's hard to hear "over the din" ("I could have a quieter meal standing on a runway behind a jet").

Amici's East Coast Pizzeria *Pizza* | 20 | 12 | 16 | $19 |

Dublin | 4640 Tassajara Rd. (bet. Central Pkwy. & Dublin Blvd.) | 925-875-1600 | www.amicis.com
See review in City of San Francisco Directory.

Arinell Pizza ⊅ *Pizza* | 22 | 4 | 11 | $7 |

Berkeley | 2119 Shattuck Ave. (bet. Addison & Center Sts.) | 510-841-4035
Hawking "cheap" but "frickin' good" "greasy and oh-so-delicious", "foldable East Coast–style" "thin-crust delights" ("no tofu BBQ chicken nonsense"), these "gritty" "hole-in-the-wall" by-the-slice pizza "institutions" are "just the way they're supposed to be"; "don't come expecting good decor or service" (rather, "Missionista" and "hippie-ish" Berkeley counter boys) "or to even eat on the premises" (there are just a "few stools") – "just take it with you" and enter "New York heaven."

Asqew Grill *Californian* | 18 | 11 | 15 | $15 |

Emeryville | Bay Street Mall | 5614 Bay St. (Shellmound St.) | 510-595-7471 | www.asqewgrill.com
See review in City of San Francisco Directory.

Barney's Gourmet Hamburgers *Hamburgers* | 19 | 12 | 14 | $15 |

Berkeley | 1591 Solano Ave. (Ordway St.) | 510-526-8185
Berkeley | 1600 Shattuck Ave. (Cedar St.) | 510-849-2827
Oakland | 4162 Piedmont Ave. (Linda Ave.) | 510-655-7180
Oakland | 5819 College Ave. (Chabot Rd.) | 510-601-0444
www.barneyshamburgers.com
See review in City of San Francisco Directory.

Battambang 🅢 *Cambodian* | ▽ 22 | 11 | 19 | $19 |

Oakland | 850 Broadway (9th St.) | 510-839-8815
Named after the second largest city in Cambodia, this "quiet, unpretentious" "white-tablecloth" Southeast Asian eatery brings "a little slice of Phnom Penh to Downtown Oakland"; despite a recent change of ownership, the affordable, "awesome" traditional fare remains "fresh and spiced just right" and the service is "friendly", making it a refreshingly "different" alternative for "veggies and non-veggies alike."

🅩 Bay Wolf *Californian/Mediterranean* | 25 | 21 | 24 | $49 |

Oakland | 3853 Piedmont Ave. (Rio Vista Ave.) | 510-655-6004 | www.baywolf.com
Though surrounded by a "sea of changing restaurants", Michael Wild's "legendary" Piedmont Avenue "perennial" remains "steady as she goes", and, after 27 years, still "retains its luster"; the "always superb", "simple, seasonal" Cal-Med cuisine is imbued with "incredible flavors" (diners go quackers over the "lovingly prepared duck dishes") while the wine list offers selections that won't "break the bank", and it's all served with "sterling hospitality" in a "quiet" "homelike setting" capped with a heated veranda.

	FOOD	DECOR	SERVICE	COST

Berkeley Teahouse *Tearoom*   17 | 22 | 18 | $19

Berkeley | Epicurious Garden | 1511 Shattuck Ave. (bet. Cedar & Vine Sts.) | 510-540-8888 | www.imperialtea.com

See Imperial Tea Court review in City of San Francisco Directory.

Bette's Oceanview Diner *Diner*   21 | 15 | 18 | $18

Berkeley | 1807 Fourth St. (bet. Hearst Ave. & Virginia St.) | 510-644-3230 | www.bettesdiner.com

This "1950s-style diner" cranking out "delicious" "down-home" breakfast and lunch with a "Berkeley gourmet ghetto" spin boasts "an oceanless view" and "lines to the sidewalk" – but that's the only thing "amiss", so "put your name in and go shopping" (or head to the "take-out side"); once seated, fuel up on "Bette's divine" "soufflé pancakes" and "scrapple like they make in Philly" washed down with "coffee that'll grow hair on your chest"; N.B. no dinner.

Bing Crosby's *American*   18 | 24 | 19 | $50

Walnut Creek | 1342 Broadway Plaza (S. Main St.) | 925-939-2464 | www.bingcrosbysrestaurant.com

"Bubba-bubba-boo" – this Walnut Creek "supper club" boasting "luxurious velvet-covered 'shell' banquettes", live cabaret music and movie "memorabilia" "takes you back to the days when Bing was crooning"; the jive is always "jumping" with "an odd combination" of "cougars", "blue hairs" and "suburban" kids not "old enough to remember when 'White Christmas' was first recorded" "socializing at the bar"; still, some ratfinks pout that the "country club" American food (with Pan-Asian touches) is "iffy" and service "indifferent."

Bistro Liaison *French*   22 | 19 | 21 | $35

Berkeley | 1849 Shattuck Ave. (Hearst Ave.) | 510-849-2155 | www.liaisonbistro.com

Perhaps the "best evening-in-Paris experience you can get in Berkeley", this "lively" bistro on "the fringe of the gourmet ghetto" gets "jammed" with regulars "speaking French" and filling up on *plats* of "hearty" fare, "nice affordable wines" and "divine desserts" (the daily offerings are rubberstamped "right on" your paper tablecloth) "without breaking the bank"; if a few feel it's "good, not sublime", *amis* retort it's an "excellent choice" for brunch, lunch or a "romantic" liaison in ze hood.

Blackberry Bistro *Southern*   21 | 13 | 16 | $18

Oakland | 4240 Park Blvd. (Wellington St.) | 510-336-1088

"The Glenview could use more places like this" "fun" daytime hang with a "cool vibe" believe boosters who join the "insane" "Oakland crowds" gobbling down "gourmet omelets", "down-home brunch" and "Southern-comfort" lunches; weekends are "a booger bear trying to be seated" and the staff gets "frazzled" (you "could starve before" the "amazing French toast with berries" and "divine" shrimp and grits arrive) but hopefully the recent change of ownership will "improve" things.

Blackhawk Grille *Californian*   19 | 22 | 20 | $46

Danville | The Shops at Blackhawk | 3540 Blackhawk Plaza Circle (Camino Tassajara) | 925-736-4295 | www.blackhawkgrille.com

A San Ramon Valley "oasis", this "chic" Californian grill "overlooking the ponds" and "beautiful Blackhawk surroundings" is a "great food adventure" anytime, but it's "perfect for lunch" or a "peaceful", "alfresco" dinner "when shopping at the exclusive" namesake center; the "classy environment" and "suburbanite" clientele make it the kind of place "you can take both sweetheart and mother to"; still, squawkers squeal service "ranges from neglectful to respectful" and the fare is "erratic, depending on the chef at the moment."

⚡ Bo's Barbecue ⧄ *BBQ*   23 | 11 | 14 | $22

Lafayette | 3422 Mt. Diablo Blvd. (Brown Ave.) | 925-283-7133

"Bo knows 'Q'" brag "converted" 'cue-lovers who "grab Wet Naps" and "venture through the tunnel" for "passionate owner" McSwine's "lip-smacking" ribs at this "smokin'" Lafayette smokehouse; a few cry "bo-hoo" over steep prices for "cafeteria-style" service, but most maintain it's "worth the extra money" for "Niman Ranch beef, Acme bread" and a beer and "wine selection that would make Thomas Keller blush"; P.S. on weekends "enjoy the live jazz" and blues and "buzzing picnic atmosphere on the huge deck."

Breads of India & Gourmet Curries *Indian*   21 | 13 | 17 | $21

Berkeley | 2448 Sacramento St. (Dwight Way) | 510-848-7684 ⊟
Oakland | 948 Clay St. (bet. 9th & 10th Sts.) | 510-834-7684 ⧄
Walnut Creek | 1358 N. Main St. (bet. Duncan & Cypress Sts.) | 925-256-7684 Ⓜ
www.breadsofindia.com

"There's always something new to try" at the "stark" Berkeley original, "much plusher" Walnut Creek branch and "lively Oakland location" serving up an "interesting" "short menu" of "refined Indian" dishes from different regions made with the "freshest, organic ingredients"; the "real deal" fare makes your "taste buds dance", especially when paired with the "fantastic breads" ("you'll miss out on a treat if you skip" the carbs); N.B. renovations are underway at the Sacramento Street site.

Bridges Restaurant *Californian/Asian*   20 | 22 | 21 | $52

Danville | 44 Church St. (Hartz Ave.) | 925-820-7200 | www.bridgesdanville.com

"Looking for *Mrs. Doubtfire*?" then come to the "class choice of Danville" where the movie was filmed; it's "strong in the service department", the outside patio is "beautiful" on a "warm spring evening" and the "creative" Cal-Asian fare and "desserts to die for" show "moments of brilliance" – especially following the change of hands a few years ago; however, a few doubting Thomases fire back it's "tired" and portions can be "small", quipping "arrive rich, leave hungry."

Bridgetender Tavern *Pub Food*   ▽ 16 | 15 | 18 | $21

Tahoe City | 30 W. Lake Blvd. (Rte. 89) | 530-583-3342

The "great Bloody Marys" and "the best burgers in Tahoe Basin" are a "tradition" at this "popular pub" with a "hard-working staff"; whether you "go in summer and relax" on the "great outdoor patio" "as the Truckee river rushes by – fantastic!" or soak up the après-ski "studenty vibe" in the winter time, it's "exactly what you want in a tavern."

Bucci's ⧄ *Californian/Italian*   20 | 18 | 19 | $33

Emeryville | 6121 Hollis St. (bet. 59th & 61st Sts.) | 510-547-4725 | www.buccis.com

"Artists, execs and everyone in between feels taken care of" at this "old Emeryville standby", one of the few non-chain independents in "the bio-tech district" where you can "catch up" while chowing down "just plain tasty" Cal-Italian *cucina* and "made-from-scratch" pizzas; "mama Bucci is everywhere at once" in the "relaxing" "industrial" "warehouse", "presiding over the front of the house and the kitchen" "making sure it all goes well"; it all "adds up to a nice scene."

Cactus Taqueria *Mexican*

20 | 12 | 14 | $12

Berkeley | 1881 Solano Ave. (bet. The Alameda & Fresno Ave.) | 510-528-1881
Oakland | 5642 College Ave. (bet. Keith Ave. & Ocean View Dr.) | 510-658-6180
www.cactustaqueria.com

"Yeah, they're yuppie burritos" and tacos, but they "always satisfy" insist "addicted" "families and commuters from the nearby BART station" who line up at these "bustling" California-style Mexican taquerias in Berkeley and Oakland; the queue "moves faster than you'd think", while the "fresh", "surprisingly good" "cheap eats" fashioned from "sustainable meats and organic veggie", "quality ingredients" "never disappoint"; P.S. if the "din" and "day-care" vibe is "too much", opt for takeout.

Café Cacao *Californian/Coffeehouse*

20 | 17 | 17 | $24

Berkeley | Scharffen Berger Chocolate Maker Factory | 914 Heinz Ave. (7th St.) | 510-843-6000 | www.cafecacao.biz

After the factory tour, "follow your nose to this heaven-scented" Californian coffeehouse in Berkeley's Scharffen Berger HQ where the aroma "overwhelms you" (even in the "divine-smelling bathrooms") and the "inventive" breakfast and lunch dishes are laced with chocolate in "ways that you won't expect"; still, they're "secondary to the main attraction" – the "unbelievable" desserts and hot cocoa ("resistance is futile"); P.S. those who find the "plastic wicker seating" lacking may want to revisit following recent renovations.

Cafe Esin ⧄Ⓜ *American*

25 | 18 | 23 | $40

San Ramon | 2416 San Ramon Valley Blvd. (Crow Canyon Rd.) | 925-314-0974 | www.cafeesin.com

"Foodies" and "urban sophisticates" proclaim it's "worth the drive" to the suburbs to experience this "charming cafe" whose chef-owners create "innovative", "always-changing" New American meals with Mediterranean flair (be sure to "leave room" for Esin's "fabulous" "homestyle" desserts too); a move from its San Ramon strip-mall locale to snazzier digs in Danville's Rose Garden shopping center is slated for early 2008, which will most likely outdate the above Decor score.

Café Fanny *French*

22 | 12 | 13 | $17

Berkeley | 1603 San Pablo Ave. (Cedar St.) | 510-524-5447 | www.cafefanny.com

"You haven't experienced Berkeley until you've been" to Alice Waters' French cafe for "*petit déjeuner magnifique*", featuring "superior café au lait" served "in the traditional bowl", and "delicious" organic lunches ("who knew you could crave egg salad?"); sure, the staff can be "slow and smug", the location is "uninviting" (there's "nowhere to sit" besides "a few tables in the parking lot") and the prices are "exorbitant", but "if you can endure, you'll be rewarded" with "first-rate grub."

FOOD | DECOR | SERVICE | COST

Café Fiore *Italian*

▽ 24 | 16 | 23 | $41

South Lake Tahoe | 1169 Ski Run Blvd. (Tamarack Ave.) | 530-541-2908 | www.cafefiore.com

Looking every bit the "quaint", candlelit, wood-beamed "chalet" that it is, this "romantic" South Lake Tahoe retreat plies patrons with "great variations on Northern Italian classics" along with a "fantastic wine list, including many half bottles", all proffered by a "charming" staff that makes guests "feel very welcome"; reservations are a must during ski season, as there are only seven tables inside, but come summer, there's alfresco dining as well.

Café Gratitude *Vegan*

19 | 16 | 18 | $21

Berkeley | 1730 Shattuck Ave. (bet. Francisco & Virginia Sts.) | 415-824-4652 | www.cafegratitude.com

See review in City of San Francisco Directory.

Café Rouge *French/Mediterranean*

21 | 19 | 19 | $37

Berkeley | Market Plaza | 1782 Fourth St. (bet. Hearst Ave. & Virginia St.) | 510-525-1440 | www.caferouge.net

"Scrumptious burgers", "great steak frites" and "wonderful house-made charcuterie", all culled from humanely raised animals, are the stars of the French-Med menu at "Berkeley's red-meat haven", which includes a "bustling", "barnlike" dining room, a "treat" of a patio and an on-site butcher shop; although many appreciate that the menu, which changes biweekly, is "always interesting", a few have beefs with what they feel are "ridiculously small portions" that are "not worth the price, even with the free attitude."

Caffè Verbena Ⓢ *Californian/Italian*

▽ 19 | 18 | 18 | $35

Oakland | Walter Shorenstein Bldg. | 1111 Broadway (bet. 11th & 12th Sts.) | 510-465-9300 | www.caffeverbena.com

A beacon in the "vast wasteland of restaurant geography in Downtown Oakland", this "solid" Cal-Italian "power scene" is one of the "only places" local suits feel they "can take clients" for lunch (and its "surprising location" keeps it a "well-kept secret" for "tasty" dinners); an "elegant" setting, featuring cherry-wood paneling, banquettes and an enclosed Zen garden, along with an "enthusiastic" staff and "no corkage" fees have "loyal customers" bemoaning the place is "underappreciated."

Casa Orinda *Italian*

17 | 16 | 19 | $35

Orinda | 20 Bryant Way (Moraga Way) | 925-254-2981

"If you're into the spaghetti-western look", "mosey on down" to this "time-warp-wacky" Orinda "roadhouse" where both the decor ("animal heads", branding irons, huge "gun collection") and "patrons hark back to the '50s"; from the American-steakhouse side of the menu, the "famous fried chicken" still makes "mouths water", but some are leery of the "old-fashioned" Italian eats, as they can "resemble wedding food."

Caspers Hot Dogs ⊘ *Hot Dogs*

18 | 6 | 14 | $7

Albany | 545 San Pablo Ave. (bet. Brighton Ave. & Garfield St.) | 510-527-6611
Dublin | 6998 Village Pkwy. (Dublin Blvd.) | 925-828-2224
Hayward | 21670 Foothill Blvd. (Grove Way) | 510-581-9064 ◗
Hayward | 951 C St. (bet. Main St. & Mission Blvd.) | 510-537-7300
Oakland | 5440 Telegraph Ave. (55th St.) | 510-652-1668

(continued)

Caspers Hot Dogs

Pleasant Hill | 6 Vivian Dr. (Contra Costa Blvd.) | 925-687-6030 🌙
Richmond | 2530 MacDonald Ave. (Civic Center St.) | 510-235-6492
Walnut Creek | 1280 Newell Hill Pl. (San Miguel Dr.) | 925-930-9154
www.caspershotdogs.com

"Haute cuisine, it ain't", but these "old-fashioned" East Bay "wiener winners" – famed for "tasty" steamed franks that go "snap when you bite into them" – are so "dang good", no wonder "they've been around for many years" (since 1934); there's "orange and yellow Formica galore" and "somewhat surly" crews, but no matter – when you need a "quick hot-dog fix", they do the trick.

César *Spanish*
22 | **20** | **19** | **$34**

Berkeley | 1515 Shattuck Ave. (bet. Cedar & Vine Sts.) | 510-883-0222
Oakland | 4039 Piedmont Ave. (bet. 40th & 41st Sts.) |
510-883-0222
www.barcesar.com

"Tapa-rific!" tout the "electric crowds" of "mature hipsters" who "pack" "both the original" Berkeley locale and the new, "roomier" Oakland incarnation of these Spaniards where "outstanding cocktails" and an "eclectic wine list" complement the "addictive" dishes ("don't miss" the "irresistible shoestring fries"); some find the servers "efficient and good humored", others complain they're "lacking in sophistication or knowledge", but everyone agrees on one thing: "those small plates add up quickly."

Cha Am Thai *Thai*
19 | **14** | **16** | **$20**

Berkeley | 1543 Shattuck Ave. (Cedar St.) | 510-848-9664
See review in City of San Francisco Directory.

Cha-Ya Vegetarian
24 | **12** | **18** | **$21**
Japanese Restaurant *Japanese/Vegan*

Berkeley | 1686 Shattuck Ave. (bet. Cedar & Virginia Sts.) | 510-981-1213

"A succulent pillar in the increasingly robust vegan side of the gourmet ghetto", this Berkeley "Japanese gem" "could triple its size and still be crowded", as the "shockingly" "zesty", "inventive" and "artfully presented" tempura and "faux sushi" not only "satisfies", but leaves vegetarians "feeling virtuous"; the Mission locale may "lack the charm" of its sibling (lose the "atrocious cafeteria lighting" please), but it's larger and often lacks the "interminable waits" of the elder while serving the same "stellar food."

ⓩ Chez Panisse ⓢ *Californian/Mediterranean*
27 | **23** | **26** | **$80**

Berkeley | 1517 Shattuck Ave. (bet. Cedar & Vine Sts.) | 510-548-5525 |
www.chezpanisse.com

"Don't know whether to dine or bow" quip "those lucky enough" to savor the "sublime simplicity" of Berkeley "pioneer" Alice Waters' Cal-Med "culinary delights" that "celebrate what's at the peak of the season"; expect "no frills" at this "modest" Craftsman-style "mother ship", "just thrills, naturally" – "every foodie must go to complete their Bingo card" and "partake" of the "divine" daily prix fixe menu that spotlights the "clear, crisp" "essence" of local ingredients; the "combinations make you sigh with delight", the staff is "enthusiastic" and the wine list is a "knockout" – it's "all it's cracked up to be."

FOOD | DECOR | SERVICE | COST

☑ Chez Panisse
Café ⊠ *Californian/Mediterranean* | 27 | 22 | 25 | $50 |

Berkeley | 1517 Shattuck Ave. (bet. Cedar & Vine Sts.) | 510-548-5049 | www.chezpanisse.com

A "near mystical experience" – yes, "upstairs is the place for me" exclaim budget-conscious Berkeleyites who sample the "pure flavors" of "Alice Waters' culinary frontier" "without spending half the month's rent" at this "wonderfully relaxed" "Paradise Lite" cafe above the "legendary" original staffed with "attentive", not "smothering" servers; she may be "the Queen" but the organic, sustainable ingredients are "king", resulting in "dreamy pizzas" and "truly delectable", "straightforward" à la carte Cal-Med dishes that "reflect both the seasons and the incredible abundance" of local purveyors.

☑ Chow/Park Chow   *American* | 20 | 15 | 18 | $23 |

Lafayette | La Fiesta Sq. | 53 Lafayette Circle (Mt. Diablo Blvd.) | 925-962-2469
See review in City of San Francisco Directory.

Christy Hill Ⓜ *Californian* | ▽ 25 | 24 | 24 | $56 |

Tahoe City | 115 Grove St. (Lake Blvd.) | 530-583-8551 | www.christyhill.com
It's a Tahoe City "must" insist insiders who head up the 100-ft. elevated embankment to enjoy "terrific outdoor dining" in a "magnificent setting" at this waterside veteran; sit on the deck overlooking the "beautiful" Lake and dig into "contemporary" Californian cuisine accompanied by a "very good wine list", all served by a "highly professional staff" (a "hard-to-find combo" in these parts); if a handful find the fare "uninspired", even they shrug "with a view like that, who notices" anything else?

Citron   *Californian/French* | 24 | 20 | 23 | $49 |

Oakland | 5484 College Ave. (bet. Lawton & Taft Aves.) | 510-653-5484 | www.citronrestaurant.biz

Whether you order à la carte or from the "wonderfully flexible" prix fixe menu that will have you "stretching out your belt", the "serious", "interesting" Cal–New French food is "worth every penny" at this "very memorable" "special evening place" in Oakland; add in servers that "aim to please", an "extensive" yet "comfortable" wine list and an "elegant" setting and it's no wonder that even those who rarely cross the bridge deem it a "destination worth the trip from anywhere."

Cottonwood   *Eclectic* | ▽ 20 | 21 | 20 | $43 |

Truckee | Hilltop Lodge | State Hwy. 267 (Brockway Rd.) | 530-587-5711 | www.cottonwoodrestaurant.com

The "funky", "old-school" longboard memorabilia and "festive" vibe "fits the Truckee scene" to a tee attest admirers of the Hilltop Lodge's "casual" stomping ground; the staff is "cheerful" and the Eclectic "food delivers" – especially the "Caesar's salad, a garlic lover's dream"; "you can't beat" sitting on the porch "on a summer's night" listening to music, and in the winter the fireplace is "charming."

Doña Tomás ⊠Ⓜ *Mexican* | 24 | 18 | 18 | $33 |

Oakland | 5004 Telegraph Ave. (bet. 49th & 51st Sts.) | 510-450-0522 | www.donatomas.com

"Fresh, seasonal ingredients and unusual combinations" make this "*muy delicioso*", "hip" "haute Mexican" cantina in Oakland "an adventure measured in tequila and masa"; "it's a bit expensive" (hello, "it ain't no

	FOOD	DECOR	SERVICE	COST

taco truck"), and "quite noisy" and "crowded" by the bar, but "killer" margaritas "make it manageable" to "pass time" before scoring a seat on the "cute" courtyard – that's "the place to be" on "warm evenings."

Dopo ☒ *Italian* | 25 | 17 | 20 | $32 |

Oakland | 4293 Piedmont Ave. (Echo St.) | 510-652-3676
"Red-check tablecloth fanciers" should move on – but that would be dopey – they'd miss out on this "authentic, relaxed" neighborhood "treasure" exuding a "real Tuscan trattoria feel in Oakland"; it's "even better" following the expansion, and the "small but well-built menu anchored by pasta" and "seasonal renditions" of thin-crust pizza is a bit bigger too, plus the "superlative salumi", "adventurous fish dishes" and "novel wines", all toted to table by a "passionate staff" that "works their cute buns off", are "worth the wait."

downtown Ⓜ *Californian/Mediterranean* | 20 | 19 | 19 | $41 |

Berkeley | 2102 Shattuck Ave. (Addison St.) | 510-649-3810 | www.downtownrestaurant.com
This "bustling" Cal-Med bistro in Downtown Berkeley pleases most with its "excellent fresh" fare (kudos for the seafood), "remarkable wines", "wild" cocktails and weekend jazz, and theatergoers also applaud its "ideal" location ("a brisk walk" from the arts district) and staff that "gets you out on time"; if a few grumble about "San Fran prices", more appreciate finding "sophistication" "smack in college town."

Dragonfly *Asian/Californian* | ▽ 23 | 20 | 21 | $37 |

Truckee | Porter Simmon Bldg. | 10118 Donner Pass Rd. (Spring St.) | 530-587-0557 | www.dragonflycuisine.com
"Innovative" Cal-Asian fare is served by an "attentive, gracious staff" at this second-floor "hidden gem" in Downtown Truckee; though somewhat pricey, it "would give restaurants in SF a run for their money" according to fans, and ski bums will be happy to know that it recently "doubled in size and added a sushi bar", so "you can easily get a table", even one with a "great view" overlooking the historic train depot.

Duck Club, The *American* | 20 | 21 | 20 | $48 |

Lafayette | Lafayette Park Hotel & Spa | 3287 Mt. Diablo Blvd. (Pleasant Hill Rd.) | 925-283-3700 | www.lafayetteparkhotel.com
See review in South of San Francisco Directory.

Eccolo *Italian* | 20 | 20 | 19 | $43 |

Berkeley | 1820 Fourth St. (bet. Hearst Ave. & Virginia St.) | 510-644-0444 | www.eccolo.com
"Yet another nice Italian run by yet another Chez Panisse alum", this Berkeley osteria "transports you to Italy and back" with "satisfying" fare revealing "creative" touches; if a handful huff that the "wine list could use filling out" and find "service variable", there are compensations aplenty, including a "great bar", the "bonus of watching the Fourth Street shoppers buzz by" and "best of all", a "wonderful brunch" you can reserve.

Ephesus Kebab Lounge *Mideastern* | ▽ 21 | 17 | 22 | $35 |

Walnut Creek | 1321 Locust St. (bet. Cypress St. & Mt. Diablo Blvd.) | 925-945-8082 | www.ephesuslounge.com
"Bring on the lamb" bellow boosters torn between *kofte* and skewers of "awesome" meat at this "upscale, hipster" Turkish "gem" in Walnut

Creek; the "small-plates service fits right into that 21st century vibe", the ambiance is all "cool elegance" and the service is "always friendly without being smothering"; still, a close-fisted few quibble that's "some expensive" shish-kebab.

☑ Erna's Elderberry House *Californian/French*

| 28 | 26 | 28 | $84 |

Oakhurst | Château du Sureau | 48688 Victoria Ln. (Hwy. 41) | 559-683-6800 | www.elderberryhouse.com

Yosemite-bound adventurers "strike gourmet gold just south of the Gold Country" at this "quaint Europe-in-America setting" on the grounds of the Château du Sureau hotel in Oakhurst, basically the "middle of nowhere"; "what an amazing" "symphony" of flavors – every "breathtakingly beautiful" Californian-French dish on the prix fixe menus is "different and unexpected" – and coupled with "fine" wine pairings and "attentive service" that's rated No. 1 in this Survey, it's a "delightful dining experience" that will "put you in a high state."

Evan's American Gourmet Cafe *American*

| ▽ 27 | 19 | 24 | $55 |

South Lake Tahoe | 536 Emerald Bay Rd. (Lukins Way) | 530-542-1990 | www.evanstahoe.com

"A must if you get up" to South Lake Tahoe agree vacationers who vaunt this "romantic", "delicious gourmet", "special-occasion" affair with "wonderful service" "nestled in the pine trees" and set in what "looks like a charming house"; "hats off" to the husband-and-wife team and the "chef with a really nice touch" who conjures up "impeccable preparations" of seasonal New American fare, particularly the "fantastic game dishes" – and don't forget to "save room for scrumptious desserts"

Everett & Jones Barbeque *BBQ*

| 20 | 11 | 12 | $19 |

Hayward | 296 A St. (Filbert St.) | 510-581-3222 ☻
Oakland | Jack London Sq. | 126 Broadway (bet. Embarcadero W. & 2nd St.) | 510-663-2350
Oakland | 2676 Fruitvale Ave. (bet. Davis & E. 27th Sts.) | 510-533-0900 www.eandjbbq.com

"Bring me a pitcher of Saucey Sistah, a Wet-Nap", "savory", "smoky ribs just about falling off the bone and tender brisket" – this is "real deal" Southern 'cue "with all the fixin's"; each East Bay location has its "own flavor, vibe" and "barbecuing-in-your-backyard" look, but you "always come out" of all three "smelling like BBQ – and that's not a bad thing"; but while fans "love" the "prickly" staffers – they seem "forbidding but they're pussycats" – others moan they're "painfully slow."

FatApple's *Diner*

| 17 | 13 | 16 | $17 |

Berkeley | 1346 Martin Luther King Jr. Way (bet. Berryman & Rose Sts.) | 510-526-2260
El Cerrito | 7525 Fairmount Ave. (bet. Carmel & Ramona Aves.) | 510-528-3433

"Berkeley's version of a local greasy spoon" and its "cheerful" El Cerrito sibling are "the only places to go for olallieberry shakes", pumpkin pancakes, "juicy cheeseburgers" and "wonderfully chock-full" chicken pot pies; the "honest, American-style" diner food that "always hits the spot", "kid-friendly" atmosphere, "sunny" dining room and "pleasant servers" add to the "mom's kitchen" feel; P.S. the bakery goods are "off the hook" – and "hard to pass up on your way out."

	FOOD	DECOR	SERVICE	COST

Fentons Creamery *Ice Cream* | 18 | 14 | 15 | $15 |

Oakland | 4226 Piedmont Ave. (bet. Entrada & Glenwood Aves.) | 510-658-7000 | www.fentonscreamery.com

"Ever had a sundae bigger than your head?" – "don't pretend you want anything else" – just "forget food and your diet" because "it's all about the dripping goblets" of "delicious", "homemade, old-fashioned ice cream" at "Oakland's oldest and best" soda fountain where it's "worth the battle to get a table"; if you must eat before the "frivolity" of dessert ("one taste and you feel like you won the lottery"), try the "diner-style choices" like the "delightful" "fat, fresh crab sandwiches."

☑ Fonda Solana ◑ *Latin American* | 24 | 21 | 21 | $35 |

Albany | 1501A Solano Ave. (Curtis St.) | 510-559-9006 | www.fondasolana.com

Bringing a "touch of urban chic" to "otherwise sleepy" Albany, this "always bustling", "trendy neighborhood spot" lures the "'in' crowd" "Fonda eatin'" an "excellent variety" of "mouthwatering" Latin American small plates and sipping "out-of-this-world cocktails" that go down "super easy"; the hours are a "boon for late-night foodies", the "staff is rockin'" and the "setting absolutely adorable" – "what more do you want?"; still, "beware: you can drop a lot of ducats" and it can get "deafeningly loud."

Forbes Mill Steakhouse *Steak* | 23 | 21 | 21 | $60 |

Danville | 200 Sycamore Valley Road W. (San Ramon Valley Blvd.) | 925-552-0505 | www.forbesmillsteakhouse.com
See review in South of San Francisco Directory.

Fresh Ketch Restaurant *Seafood* | ▽ 18 | 19 | 21 | $39 |

South Lake Tahoe | 2435 Venice Dr. (off Tahoe Keys Blvd.) | 530-541-5683 | www.thefreshketch.com

The "outstanding" Sierra sunsets from the upstairs dining room of this "favorite" South Lake Tahoe seafooder right on Tahoe Keys Marina are off the hook, making it a "great place for a drink and dinner"; après skiers also feast on "darn good" fare by the fireside in the Koa wood bar, pairing sushi, oysters or "excellent" fish with a side of live music; but wherever you sit, whatever the season, "save room for hula pie."

Garibaldis *Californian/Mediterranean* | 21 | 20 | 21 | $45 |

Oakland | 5356 College Ave. (Manila Ave.) | 510-595-4000 | www.garibaldis-eastbay.com
See review in City of San Francisco Directory.

Gar Woods | 19 | 23 | 19 | $39 |
Grill & Pier *American/Mediterranean*

Carnelian Bay | Carnelian Bay | 5000 N. Lake Blvd. (California St.) | 530-546-3366 | www.garwoods.com

Sierra weekend warriors know to "dock your boat (or park your car)" at this "perfect" Carnelian Bay year-round lakeside hangout whose "fantastic" "location, location, location" ensures "killer views" of all "the action" on the mighty Blue "from anywhere in the restaurant"; the casual New American–Med eats are "nothing special", but "the stunning scenery and great drinks" ("start with their signature Wet Woody") served on "the deck in warm weather" by "waiters who give 100 percent" keep the summer stock "happy."

	FOOD	DECOR	SERVICE	COST

Gioia Pizzeria *Pizza*

`24` `10` `16` `$10`

Berkeley | 1586 Hopkins St. (bet. McGee & Monterey Aves.) | 510-528-4692
With "out-of-this-world" thin-crust pizzas and an ideal "sauce to cheese ratio", Berkeley locals and transplants decry that this New York–style pizzeria is "really like going back to Brooklyn", with traditional and "gourmet" pies, including a "love at first sight" pomodoro version; the "loud music", "brusque service", "hole-in-the-wall" decor and "packed counter" only add to the New York vibe.

Great China *Chinese*

`23` `10` `13` `$21`

Berkeley | 2115 Kittredge St. (bet. Oxford St. & Shattuck Ave.) | 510-843-7996
"Exotic" "delicacies", some of which are "not found elsewhere", keep "legions of repeat diners" vying for space at this "cramped" Berkeley Chinese spot that's so "cheap" and "delicious", it's "worth the trip from any part of town"; in fact, there's such a "cornucopia of flavors and spices" (the "famous" double-skin salad is a "must-have"), not even the "long lines", "minimal" decor and "unsmiling", "abrupt" servers detract.

Gregoire *French*

`24` `9` `16` `$20`

Berkeley | 2109 Cedar St. (Shattuck Ave.) | 510-883-1893
Oakland | 4001B Piedmont Ave. (40th St.) | 510-547-3444
www.gregoirerestaurant.com
"French takeout" is "no longer an oxymoron" thanks to these "awesome gems" where, though the "gourmet fast-food" "menu changes every month" (with the exception of some fundamentals like the "famously" "addictive" potato puffs), the offerings are always "fresh" and "intensely delicious"; the Berkeley original is "really just a glorified food stand", while the Oakland newbie "has a bit more seating", but both are "so small" you can barely "get your wallet out."

Home of Chicken and Waffles ● *Southern*

`15` `8` `13` `$16`

Oakland | 444 Embarcadero W. (Broadway) | 510-836-4446 | www.hcwchickenandwaffles.com
It "seems like an unlikely combo", but it's a "guilty pleasure" "ya gotta try to believe" crow devotees who "get their fill" of "sweet, sweet" "dreamy waffles" and "down-home deep-fried chicken" at Oakland's Southern soul food stomping ground that's open till the wee hours; there's "not much point in getting anything else", even if you're one of those "die-hard breakfast" people (and it "tastes especially great after a night of drinking").

☑ Il Fornaio *Italian*

`19` `20` `18` `$37`

Walnut Creek | 1430 Mt. Diablo Blvd. (Broadway) | 925-296-0100 | www.ilfornaio.com
See review in City of San Francisco Directory.

☑ In-N-Out Burger ● *Hamburgers*

`22` `10` `17` `$8`

Oakland | 8300 Oakport St. (Edgewater Dr.) | 800-786-1000 | www.in-n-out.com
See review in City of San Francisco Directory.

Jade Villa *Chinese*

`17` `9` `12` `$20`

Oakland | 800 Broadway (bet. 8th & 9th Sts.) | 510-839-1688
Look, the "decor is not the reason" to come to this Oakland Chinese "institution", the "dim sum is the draw" – just ask the "crowds" that

FOOD | DECOR | SERVICE | COST

"hang out on the sidewalk" on "Sunday mornings" "waiting for their numbers to be called" (it's served for lunch other days too); "other meals" may "lack distinction" and the service can be "inattentive and surly", but it's "cheap for what you get" and fun "for people-watching" to boot.

Jake's on the Lake *Californian* 16 | 20 | 16 | $34

Tahoe City | 780 N. Lake Blvd. (Jackpine St.) | 530-583-0188 | www.jakestahoe.com

"After a long day", enjoy the "relaxing atmosphere" and "lovely views of Lake Tahoe" from the deck "before the sun goes down" at this "reliable" TC "staple", a "pleasant surprise" serving "no-frills Californian cuisine that consistently delivers"; the setting is "ideal for lunch" "in the summertime with the family" or "perfect for a get-together" with drinks and appetizers; still, a handful huff the "predictable" fare is "not for the culinary" crowd.

Jimmy Bean's *Diner* 20 | 10 | 14 | $16

Berkeley | 1290 Sixth St. (Gilman St.) | 510-528-3435 | www.jimmybeans.com

Berkeley brunchers "never say 'no' when someone suggests" this "bargain" Californian diner, which also does "mean breakfasts" featuring silver-dollar pancakes that "melt in your mouth" and "delicious" lunches ("dinners are ok" too, but the place can seem "cold and dreary at night"); it's "semi-cafeteria-style", meaning you "place your order at the counter, try to find a table" ("it's deservedly popular") and the "brisk", sometimes-"testy" servers bring you your order.

Jodie's Restaurant ⓜ⌗ *American/Eclectic* ▽ 20 | 12 | 20 | $14

Albany | 902 Masonic Ave. (Solano Ave.) | 510-526-1109 | www.djovida.com/jodie

"Half the draw" of this six-stool Albany "hole-in-the-wall" where you "order off the wall" is "charming" proprietor Jodie – the other being his Eclectic–New American breakfasts and lunches featuring "burgers, sandwiches" and other "yummy food topped with luscious sauces" that are "great for the soul, if not the body"; if what you're craving isn't on the menu, ask – "he'll fix you almost anything you want."

Jojo ⓩⓜ *Californian/French* 25 | 19 | 23 | $44

Oakland | 3859 Piedmont Ave. (bet. 40th St. & Macarthur Blvd.) | 510-985-3003 | www.jojorestaurant.com

The "beautifully prepared", "simple yet delicious French country fare", "charming", "solicitous" staff and owners who seem "happy to see you" "make you realize quickly" that this "lovely, intimate" Oakland "gem" is "something special"; *amis* agree that the seasonal, "ever-changing menu is wonderful", and the "steak frites can't be beat", especially when accompanied by the "fine", "reasonably priced wine list"; P.S. the "cozy" room is "tiny, so reservations are a must."

Jordan's *French* ▽ 18 | 23 | 19 | $53

Berkeley | Claremont Resort & Spa | 41 Tunnel Rd. (Claremont Ave.) | 510-549-8510 | www.claremontresort.com

Always a "treat" attest admirers who drink in the "classy" ambiance and "awesome view" of the Bay while savoring "interesting" Cal-French fare with Moroccan touches at Berkeley's Claremont Resort; try it for a "lovely lunch after a day at the spa" or for the Sunday brunch – you "won't be disappointed"; but bashers balk at the "big fanfare", citing service that "needs tender loving care" and deeming the vistas its "only saving grace."

Juan's Place *Mexican*   16 | 11 | 17 | $16

Berkeley | 941 Carleton St. (9th St.) | 510-845-6904

This "no-nonsense", family-owned Mexican restaurant in Berkeley "hasn't changed in years" – it's "still going strong", serving "cheap, plentiful, completely authentic" "guilty pleasures" (a "full order is more like two plates") to "students and locals"; the setting is "festive", er, "funky", boasting "banquet-style seats" and bullfighter posters, but "the fried tortillas make up for absolutely everything" and it's all delivered by "crusty" servers who "move at lightning speed.

Kirala *Japanese*   25 | 15 | 16 | $34

Berkeley | 2100 Ward St. (Shattuck Ave.) | 510-549-3486

Kirala 2 *Japanese*

Berkeley | Epicurious Garden | 1511-D Shattuck Ave. (bet. Cedar & Vine Sts.) | 510-649-1384
www.kiralaberkeley.com

For "serious sushi-eteers", this "agonizingly popular" Japanese joint that's "mobbed even before it opens" is an East Bay "favorite" – "so long as you're willing to wait (for your seat, for your food, for your bill)"; the "pristine fish" (not camouflaged in "crazy designer rolls") "gets a thumbs-up", but the real "draw here" are the "savor-worthy grilled items from the robata"; "down a few sakes at the bar" while you kill time or grab takeout from Kirala 2.

Koryo Wooden Charcoal BBQ ● *Korean*   21 | 9 | 11 | $22

Oakland | 4390 Telegraph Ave. (Shattuck Ave.) | 510-652-6007

The Korean barbecue "tastes as good as it smells" at this "hole-in-the-wall" Oaklander, a "top contender for tabletop" cooking where meat-mongers "satisfy carnivorous" urges with "delicious" charcoal-grilled ribs and things; fill your plate with the "excellent" *panchan*, the side dishes and pickles and "you're in for a fiery treat" – it's a "real experience for the uninitiated"; still, quibblers quip "bring your own water and napkins" as the "service really, really needs work."

Lalime's *Californian/Mediterranean*   26 | 21 | 24 | $47

Berkeley | 1329 Gilman St. (bet. Neilson St. & Peralta Ave.) | 510-527-9838 | www.lalimes.com

"Like an elder statesman who ages gracefully" this "fabulous neighborhood treasure" in a "funky" former residence in Berkeley is a "comfortable" "class act" you want to "visit time and again"; the "rustic", "amazingly delectable" Cal-Med fare "prepared to absolute perfection" showcases "fresh, locally grown, mostly organic veggies" and "robust flavors" and it's all served in a "lovely, unassuming atmosphere" by an "engaging staff" – what a "treat"; P.S. "single diners at the bar are treated like gold."

La Méditerranée *Mediterranean/Mideastern*   19 | 14 | 17 | $22

Berkeley | 2936 College Ave. (Ashby Ave.) | 510-540-7773 | www.cafelamed.com

See review in City of San Francisco Directory.

	FOOD	DECOR	SERVICE	COST

Lanesplitter Pub & Pizza *Pizza* | 18 | 12 | 13 | $15 |

Berkeley | 1051 San Pablo Ave. (Monroe St.) | 510-527-8375
Berkeley | 2033 San Pablo Ave. (University Ave.) | 510-845-1652 ◑
Oakland | 4799 Telegraph Ave. (48th St.) | 510-653-5350 ◑
www.lanesplitterpizza.com

A "kid-friendly haven for parents looking to babysit over beers", this "no-frills" East Bay trio with "a biker bar" vibe offers the "if-it's-not-tattooed-pierce-it" crowd "relief from ridiculous California 'gourmet' pizzas" and the chance to get down to the "nitty gritty" of pie eating; motorcycle mamas and papas rave about "rock solid" versions, "variety of toppings" and "awesome beer selection", noting there's "quirky art to view while you wait"; N.B. the 1051 San Pablo site is takeout only.

La Note *French* | 22 | 20 | 17 | $24 |

Berkeley | 2377 Shattuck Ave. (bet. Channing Way & Durant Ave.) |
510-843-1535 | www.lanoterestaurant.com

You'll think "you've di(n)ed and gone to Provence" at this "charming country French bistro" in Downtown Berkeley where vintage posters, a "dreamy" *jardins* and "giant bowls of latte" "set the mood"; *oui*, they've "mastered the art of brunch", from the "divine" *pain perdu* bathed in lavender honey" to the "original, tasty" eggs ("you'll be so happy that you waited") but dinner, served Thursday–Saturday, is also "outstanding" – and on Friday nights you can "enjoy the accordion player" too; *alors*, "the service is often authentically inattentive."

Lark Creek *American* | 22 | 19 | 21 | $42 |

Walnut Creek | 1360 Locust St. (bet. Civic Dr. & Mt. Diablo Blvd.) |
925-256-1234 | www.larkcreek.com

Natch, there's "no creek in sight – not even the Walnut one", but Bradley Ogden's "all-day" American cafe showcasing "modern gourmet and comfort food" made in the wood-burning oven is "no lark, nor is the all-Yankee-only "wine list (that's even better in July when all the bottles are half off)"; this suburban sib may lack the charm or the panache of "the mother ship", but the bygone food "evokes the best memories" and "the butterscotch pudding, now, that's something to write home to mommy about!"

Le Cheval *Vietnamese* | 21 | 14 | 16 | $22 |

Oakland | 1007 Clay St. (10th St.) | 510-763-8495 | www.lecheval.com
Le Petit Cheval ⊠⇄ *Vietnamese*
Berkeley | 2600 Bancroft Way (Bowditch St.) | 510-704-8018

When "you're tired of hole-in-the-wall Asians, but don't want to spend Slanted Door money", queue up with "yuppies, foodies, families and cops on the beat" at Oakland's "bustling" "factory"; it's like "dining in a train station", what with the "noise" and "speedy" staff delivering "bargain" "Viet-yum" specialties (and your check) "to the table by the time you're done ordering"; P.S. the UC Berkeley crowd trots to Le Petit for "super-fast" "cafeteria-style" lunches; N.B. a new Walnut Creek branch is in the works.

Left Bank *French* | 18 | 20 | 17 | $38 |

Pleasant Hill | 60 Crescent Dr. (Monument Blvd.) | 925-288-1222 |
www.leftbank.com
See review in North of San Francisco Directory.

	FOOD	DECOR	SERVICE	COST

Levende East *Eclectic* | 20 | 20 | 18 | $38 |

NEW **Oakland** | 827 Washington St. (9th St.) | 510-835-5585 | www.levendeeast.com

See Levende review in City of San Francisco Directory.

Lo Coco's Restaurant & Pizzeria Ⓜ *Italian* | 21 | 14 | 20 | $23 |

Berkeley | 1400 Shattuck Ave. (Rose St.) | 510-843-3745
Oakland | 4270 Piedmont Ave. (Echo Ave.) | 510-652-6222
www.lococospizzeria.com

For a "real touch of old Sicily", head to this "homey" Berkeley-Oakland duo with a "sweet staff"; the setting is "so cozy you should come prepared to spend the evening" while the "flavorful and filling" fare and "distinctively fresh pizza" ("not thick, not thin, but just right") are reminiscent of the "dependable Italian" specialties you "remember from your childhood neighborhood" trattoria; P.S. it's "worth the crazy wait."

Luka's Taproom & Lounge *Californian/French* | 20 | 16 | 17 | $27 |

Oakland | 2221 Broadway (Grand Ave.) | 510-451-4677 | www.lukasoakland.com

Come to this "bright spot in Downtown Oakland" for the "terrific" European beers on tap, and "stay for the music, the colorful crowd", the "rocking atmosphere" and the "interesting" Californian-French brasserie fare ("including some of the tastiest fries around"); "weekends are one big party" – the "bar activity" "can be innervating or aggravating, depending on your mood" – so go for lunch "if you want to hear yourself think"; P.S. there's also an "amazing jazz brunch."

Mama's Royal Cafe ⇅ *American* | 20 | 13 | 16 | $15 |

Oakland | 4012 Broadway (40th St.) | 510-547-7600 | www.mamasroyalcafeoakland.com

Like "stepping into a '70s time machine", this Oakland "breakfast classic" (serving lunch too) "never changes", dishing up "solid" American "hangover-killer" food to "aging hipsters" and other fans of its "funky" setting and "punk-rock" vibe; expect "long weekend lines", but you can always "count the piercings" on the "feisty waitresses" to pass the time.

Marica *Seafood* | 22 | 18 | 20 | $37 |

Oakland | 5301 College Ave. (Broadway) | 510-985-8388 | www.maricaseafood.com

This "cool", "tiny", "under-the-radar" Oakland storefront caters to "those in-the-know" who appreciate its "ambitiously conceived" piscine cuisine that fans label some of "the best seafood in the East Bay"; the "prix fixe menu is a great deal" and the setting is "fancy but not pretentious", which helps make up for service that can be "excruciatingly slow."

Max's Ⓢ *Deli* | 16 | 14 | 16 | $25 |

Oakland | Oakland City Ctr. | 500 12th St. (bet. Broadway & Clay St.) | 510-451-6297 | www.maxsworld.com

See review in City of San Francisco Directory.

Mezze *Californian/Mediterranean* | 23 | 21 | 22 | $41 |

Oakland | 3407 Lakeshore Ave. (bet. Mandana Blvd. & Trestle Glen Rd.) | 510-663-2500 | www.mezze.com

"No longer just a neighborhood spot" – or a "secret" – this "local jewel" in Oakland is a real "treat" attest admirers who tout the "outstanding quality" of the Cal-Med small dishes and "creative" entrees and "stunning cocktails"; the chef is a "master" at "delivering innovative" fare while the "owners greet you like a long lost friend" and the servers are "very informed" – little wonder most consider it "my home away from home."

Moody's Bistro & Lounge *Californian*   ▽ 25 | 19 | 22 | $46

Truckee | Truckee Hotel | 10007 Bridge St. (off I-80) | 530-587-8688 | www.moodysbistro.com

After a "day in the Sierras", truck on over to the "rustic", "woodsy" Truckee Hotel and "hang out for a bite" of "super" Californian fare suggest admirers; the 1950s-style "wood bar and club setting" is "perfect" for "long talks over drinks" and listening to "wonderful" jazz in the lounge while the "hearty" "comfort food and gourmet" selections are "fresh and original" and delivered by an "experienced" crew.

Naan 'n Curry *Indian/Pakistani*   18 | 6 | 10 | $14

Berkeley | 2366 Telegraph Ave. (bet. Channing Way & Durant Ave.) | 510-841-6226

See review in City of San Francisco Directory.

Naked Fish, The *Japanese*   ▽ 22 | 14 | 18 | $34

South Lake Tahoe | 3940 Lake Tahoe Blvd. (bet. Hwy. 50 & Pioneer Trail) | 530-541-3474

Go for the "amazing selection" of cold sakes (the "sampler is also a winner"), "stay for the innovative, tasty" sushi advise finatics who revel in the raw selection at this South Lake Tahoe "favorite"; sip and sample the "creative rolls" done up "Hawaiian-style" and soak up the ambiance enhanced with an "interesting" nautical decor, squid-and-mermaid mural and a kitschy "'60s lounge" feel.

Nan Yang Rockridge Ⓜ *Burmese*   22 | 14 | 19 | $22

Oakland | 6048 College Ave. (Claremont Ave.) | 510-655-3298

This "cute little" Burmese spot is such a "welcome stop" in Rockridge agree "college and grad students on a budget" who tout the "wonderful mix" of options, "sublime, almost otherworldly" flavors and "plentiful portions"; even dishes that "sound so basic", like the "garlic noodle concoctions" are a "taste treat", plus service is "friendly and enthusiastic"; still, a few shrug "it's no holy grail" – and "not that unique."

Nizza La Bella *French/Italian*   19 | 17 | 18 | $30

Albany | 825 San Pablo Ave. (bet. Solano & Washington Aves.) | 510-526-2552 | www.nizzalabella.com

"It's hard to believe you're not in France" at this "lovely" "little neighborhood spot" in Albany that's "perfect on a cold, foggy" night; but while the "relaxed" setting says "cozy" 'bistro', the "delicious" fare "bridges the French-Italian gap" with a "Provençal take" on mussels and "creative" thin-crust pizzas baked in the wood-burning oven, all bolstered by an "interesting" wine list and "foofy drinks"; still, a few "put-off" pouters decry the "uninformed" staff.

North Beach Pizza ◗ *Pizza*   18 | 9 | 14 | $16

Berkeley | 1598 University Ave. (California St.) | 510-849-9800 | www.northbeachpizza.com

See review in City of San Francisco Directory.

O Chamé 🖼 *Japanese* · 24 | 22 | 21 | $34

Berkeley | 1830 Fourth St. (Hearst Ave.) | 510-841-8783

"Not your father's sushi bar" quip patrons – in fact no sushi is served at this "tranquil" "special treasure" that feels like a Japanese "oasis" amid Berkeley's "Fourth Street bustle"; you "feel so virtuous eating" the "satisfying, pristinely prepared", "simple, light dishes" – the flavors are "tremendous" and the "portions aren't too small" – plus the "spare", "enchanting" "Zen-like decor matches the food perfectly"; still, a few unenlightened yelp it's a lot of yen "for a bowl of udon."

Oliveto Cafe *Italian* · 23 | 19 | 20 | $31

Oakland | 5655 College Ave. (Keith St.) | 510-547-5356 | www.oliveto.com

"When we miss Europe" we head to this "cozy" all-day Italian cafe in Oakland where "fresh ingredients take front and center" and the vibe is more "approachable" than the upstairs restaurant; enjoy "breakfast with *The New York Times*", "recuperate" from "browsing the nearby shops" with a "relaxing wine-and-espresso lunch" complete with "addictive pizza" or "treat" yourself at dinnertime to "pasta al forno made with whatever's in season" – it's the "perfect antidote to a hectic day."

Oliveto Restaurant *Italian* · 25 | 22 | 23 | $56

Oakland | 5655 College Ave. (Keith St.) | 510-547-5356 | www.oliveto.com

Oakland's "serene" "mecca for Italian food" on "fashionable College Avenue" "continues to shine" assert "epicureans", Europhiles and the area's "upper crust" who "splurge" on "memorable", "superbly cooked" "exquisitely luxurious" meals boasting "artisanal" "favorites" like "wonderful housemade charcuterie" and rotisserie meats delivered by an "unobtrusive" staff; "nothing beats" "incredible" theme nights like February's Whole Hog dinner that spotlight chef Paul Canales's "signature rustic yet refined style", plus the "dishes you dream about" even "trickle out of the everyday menus" making us "squeal with delight!"

Olivia 🖼🅜 *French* · 23 | 19 | 21 | $38

Berkeley | 1453 Dwight Way (Sacramento St.) | 510-548-2322 | www.oliviaeats.com

"Intimate is the word to describe" this "tastefully appointed" neighborhood spot with a fireplace that "makes you feel like you're dining in the chef's home"; it's especially "cozy" on a "rainy Berkeley night", plus the "wonderful", "imaginative" French fare, "well-priced wine list" from Kermit Lynch, "pleasant atmosphere" and "attentive staff" amount to a "winning combination."

Pakwan 🍴 *Pakistani* · 21 | 5 | 9 | $13

Hayward | 26617 Mission Blvd. (Sorenson Rd.) | 510-538-2401

See review in City of San Francisco Directory.

Pappo 🅜 *Californian/Mediterranean* · ▽ 23 | 18 | 17 | $36

Alameda | 2320 Central Ave. (bet. Oak & Park Sts.) | 510-337-9100 | www.papporestaurant.com

A "real restaurant" with "fine dining", this intimate bistro has Alameda locals atwitter as they munch happily on its "regularly rotating" menu of Cal-Med eats that "linger in the memory for a couple of days"; though there's "never a misstep in the food" and the "decor is lovely", the tabs are "pricey" for the area and the "fun staff" can be a "little slow."

	FOOD	DECOR	SERVICE	COST

Pasta Pomodoro *Italian*

| | 16 | 13 | 16 | $20 |

Emeryville | 5614 Shellmound St. (Powell St.) | 510-923-1173
Oakland | 5500 College Ave. (Lawton Ave.) | 510-923-0900
www.pastapomodoro.com
See review in City of San Francisco Directory.

Pearl Oyster Bar & Restaurant *Seafood*

| | 24 | 21 | 19 | $41 |

Oakland | 5634 College Ave. (bet. Keith Ave. & Ocean View Dr.) |
510-654-5426 | www.pearloncollege.com
Small dishes make a big splash at this "cutting-edge" Rockridge tapas-style joint, "a hidden treasure" where diners "feel like hip mermaids under the sophisticated sea"; enjoy drinks at the glowing bar and munch "tasty" fin fare and "land-based meals" that "would make a gourmand weep"; still, some snackers whimper over "pricey", "skimpy portions", adding "service could be snappier" in the "crowded" room.

Pho 84 *Vietnamese*

| | 24 | 11 | 17 | $19 |

Oakland | 354 17th St. (Franklin St.) | 510-832-1338
"The waiters are running past so quickly, you'll have to trip them to get their attention" at this Oakland Vietnamese institution serving "rich and flavorful" pho (in servings so big that "each looks like it could serve several tables"), "exquisite" spring rolls and other "not too spicy" fare; "nothing here is noteworthy except the food" and the "bargain basement prices", so "slurp" away, but ignore the "chintzy decor."

Pianeta *Italian*

| | ▽ 23 | 22 | 20 | $38 |

Truckee | 10096 Donner Pass Rd. (off I-80) | 530-587-4694
This "hearty" *cucina* on the Downtown Truckee drag is a "great place to eat after a day of skiing" with "upscale", "crowd-pleasing" chow that, say some, is the "best Italian food in the Sierras"; the "warm", "comfortable" atmosphere comes complete with stone and exposed brick, and the "staff is helpful and friendly."

Piatti *Italian*

| | 19 | 19 | 19 | $36 |

Danville | 100 Sycamore Valley Rd. W. (San Ramon Valley Blvd.) |
925-838-2082 | www.piatti.com
A "class up from predictable chains" these "dependably delicious" Bay Area Italians use "fresh, local ingredients", serving "heaping plates" of pasta; though a few feel there's "no pizzazz to the food", most find that the "professional service" and "relaxed atmosphere" (including patio seating and, in Mill Valley, "great views") help to compensate.

Picante Cocina Mexicana *Mexican*

| | 21 | 13 | 14 | $15 |

Berkeley | 1328 Sixth St. (bet. Camelia & Gilman Sts.) | 510-525-3121
It's always a "fiesta" of "all ages and ethnicities" at this Berkeley Mexican cranking out *"muy sabroso"* "yuppified" *cocina* in a "colorful setting" that's as "loud as a school cafeteria, and with just as many kids"; you'll "pay more than you would at the usual burrito joint" for "fresh ingredients especially corn tortillas, made by hand next to the cash registers" ("no machina here"), but the "zooish" crowds "certainly don't notice."

Pizza Antica *Pizza*

| | 21 | 16 | 17 | $25 |

Lafayette | 3600 Mt. Diablo Blvd. (Dewing Ave.) | 925-299-0500 |
www.pizzaantica.com
See review in South of San Francisco Directory.

FOOD | DECOR | SERVICE | COST

Pizzaiolo 🗷 *Pizza*

24 | 18 | 19 | $32

Oakland | 5008 Telegraph Ave. (51st St.) | 510-652-4888 | www.pizzaiolo.us

Chez Panisse grad Charlie Hallowell's "East Bay gem" is not only "part of the new pizza revolution" – it "changed Temescal forever" rave "foodies" who withstand "ridiculous lines" to obtain "orgasmic" "bliss"; the "paper-thin, blistery" crusts with "just the right chew and crunch", "sophisticated combinations" and sustainable ingredients create "scrumptious" pies while the "perfectly composed mains", "compelling salumi, perfect contorni" and "superb wine" list "can't be beat"; still, a handful huff it's "noisy and frantic", plus service is "lax."

Pizza Rustica *Pizza*

19 | 11 | 14 | $18

Oakland | 5422 College Ave. (bet. Kales & Manila Aves.) | 510-654-1601
Oakland | 6106 La Salle Ave. (Moraga Ave.) | 510-339-7878
www.caferustica.com

"Tasty", "fun and cheap is almost always a winning combination" cheer cohorts of Oakland's "favorite" self-serve "pizza joint" and its College Avenue sidekick (with the "tiki-mecca" Conga Lounge, upstairs); the "wide variety of toppings", "huge" salads and "pretty nice" rotisserie chicken "satisfy every taste bud", making this "reliable" duo the "perfect weeknight dinner spot" – and "best of all, they deliver."

Plearn Thai Cuisine *Thai*

19 | 13 | 16 | $20

Berkeley | 2050 University Ave. (bet. Milvia St. & Shattuck Ave.) | 510-841-2148

Plearn Thai Palace *Thai*

Walnut Creek | 1510 N. Main St. (Lincoln Ave.) | 925-937-7999

"Students love this place", at least the "non-assuming" "mainstay" in Berkeley, and so do Walnut Creek folks, who also applaud the "nuanced" Thai food at "reasonable prices"; there's "no skimping on the spice" – the "authentic dishes" are "complex and flavorful", plus the "service is just right"; but aesthetes agree that the "shabby", "tired" University Avenue setting "needs to be redecorated after all these years."

PlumpJack Cafe *Californian/Mediterranean*

24 | 21 | 23 | $55

Olympic Valley | PlumpJack Squaw Valley Inn | 1920 Squaw Valley Rd. (Hwy. 89) | 530-583-1576 | www.plumpjackcafe.com

See review in City of San Francisco Directory.

🗷 Postino *Italian*

24 | 26 | 23 | $46

Lafayette | 3565 Mt. Diablo Blvd. (Oak Hill Rd.) | 925-299-8700 | www.postinorestaurant.com

"Go postal" on "date night" or for a "special celebration" when you're "feeling flush" – it's "not like any other post office" opine scribes who give this "atmospheric" Italian "find" in Lafayette their stamp of approval; the "cozy-but-alive" ambiance replete with "beautiful glasswork", brick walls, an atrium and "rustic European charm" is a "treat for the eye" while the "energetic bar" and "outstanding" fare (served in "generous portions" for "sharing and passing") "never disappoints."

Prima *Italian*

24 | 21 | 23 | $50

Walnut Creek | 1522 N. Main St. (bet. Bonanza St. & Lincoln Ave.) | 925-935-7780 | www.primaristorante.com

For "delicate", "beautifully presented" Northern Italian fare, "save your upgrades to Italy" and wing over to this "classy" "Walnut Creek classic" with a "relaxed" setting; it may be "a bit pricey", but the menu "constantly changes based on seasonality and availability of ingredients", the "endless wine list" is one of the "biggest and deepest" around (the owners own the vino shop next door) and it's all served by a staff that "knows" its stuff.

Red Hut Café ♥ American
▽ | 25 | 11 | 20 | $12

South Lake Tahoe | 2749 Lake Tahoe Blvd. (Al Tahoe Blvd.) | 530-541-9024

Nevada Red Hut Café ♥ American
Stateline | 227 Kingsbury Grade (Deer Run Ct.), NV | 775-588-7488

For the "best breakfast in Lake Tahoe", make like a local and head downhill to these "small", "wonderful", "always crowded" twin Sierra diner "fixtures" "expertly run by a cast" of mountain mamas; both locations "can't be beat" for "pre-hike blueberry pancakes" or a "good" lunch that'll "leave you so full you may just not be able to ski", but partisans point out "the view from the Stateline place is really nice."

Restaurant Peony Chinese
20 | 13 | 12 | $24

Oakland | Pacific Renaissance Plaza | 388 Ninth St. (bet. Franklin & Webster Sts.) | 510-286-8866 | www.restaurantpeony.com

Head to this "cavernous", "noisy", "hopping" Oaklander for dim sum and "experience a small piece of Chinese culture"; it's "packed at lunch" and "fills up on weekends" with everyone from "grandparents to babies", so "go early" and "choose your items from the many carts that whiz by your table"; if detractors sigh "don't expect to be treated with any kind of courtesy" – you may be "ignored", others opine "I'll take my chances."

Rick & Ann's American
21 | 14 | 17 | $21

Berkeley | 2922 Domingo Ave. (bet. Ashby & Claremont Aves.) | 510-649-8538 | www.rickandanns.com

"Always a wait and always worth it", this Berkeley "classic" that's "popular with the Spandex biking set" and families alike serves up "homemade" American chow that's "better than mom's"; "every item is wonderful" – it's "easy to try something new each time" and leave with a "full belly" – but what it's really known for is the "delightful breakfast"; still, a few scoff "service can be problematic"; N.B. dinner served Wednesday–Sunday only.

River Ranch Lodge & Restaurant Californian
▽ | 17 | 21 | 17 | $33

Tahoe City | 2285 River Rd. (Alpine Meadows Rd.) | 530-583-4264 | www.riverranchlodge.com

"Lovable and dependable", this "scenic" "landmark restaurant"/bar with an "Old Tahoe" lodge atmosphere cantilevered over the water in Tahoe City is a "family" favorite for "friendly" àpres-ski dining by the stone fireplace; "on a summer day, there's no better place than" the "large deck" where you can "watch river rafters" float by while supping on "simple beers, wings" and Californian fare; still, some lodgers shrug the "festive environment" "makes the so-so" chow more "tolerable."

☑ Rivoli Californian/Mediterranean
27 | 23 | 25 | $47

Berkeley | 1539 Solano Ave. (bet. Neilson St. & Peralta Ave.) | 510-526-2542 | www.rivolirestaurant.com

We "can't stop ooohing and ahing" about Wendy and Roscoe's "lovely, tranquil" Berkeley "treasure" exclaim hometown "foodies" and "even the fussiest oenophiles"; the "imaginative" and "soul-satisfying" California-Mediterranean cuisine is "comparable to anyplace in the City", plus it's all ferried to table by a staff that "seems to have PhDs in the art of making a meal enjoyable"; yes, you can expect "snug quarters", nevertheless it's still a "real treat" to look out at the "illuminated garden" filled with "a wildlife menagerie snacking" on their own food.

Salute E Ristorante at Marina Bay *Italian* ▽ 19 | 23 | 21 | $35

Richmond | 1900 Esplanade Dr. (Schooner Dr.) | 510-215-0803 | www.salutemarinabay.com

With a "lovely Marina setting", "tasty" Northern Italian fare and "wonderful views" of the San Francisco Bay, this "solid price performer" feels like the "Riviera in taste and style" – so much so that "you won't believe you are in the Richmond"; the "beautiful" vistas make it a "romantic" "destination" "for that first date or 10th anniversary", nonetheless a few carp the "decor beats the food" lamenting there's "lots of missed potential."

Saul's Restaurant & Delicatessen *Deli* 18 | 14 | 16 | $18

Berkeley | 1475 Shattuck Ave. (bet. Rose & Vine Sts.) | 510-848-3354 | www.saulsdeli.com

"The Stage this ain't", and you probably won't find "Woody Allen here", but "homesick ex-New Yorkers" can still "satisfy a pastrami" and "matzo ball soup" "deficiency" without the "opera singers" at this "ersatz" "kosher-style deli" in Berkeley's gourmet ghetto that does a "pretty good job of faking it"; from "the dish of pickles" "slapped down" by "old-time waitresses" to the "frantic atmosphere", it's as "heartwarming as eating" at "bubbe's" – though some say "it's a shonder" the nosh is "overpriced."

Scott's Seafood *Seafood* 19 | 18 | 18 | $40

Oakland | 2 Broadway (Water St.) | 510-444-5969 | www.scottsrestaurants.com
Walnut Creek | 1333 N. California Blvd. (Mt. Diablo Blvd.) | 925-934-1300 | www.scottsseafood.com

"They got me hook, line and sinker" – it's a "classic all around" assert admirers of this American seafooder in Oakland and Walnut Creek (and Palo Alto and San Jose too) with "gracious service" and "lovely decor"; some locales offer "beautiful views of the Bay" and an "outstanding" weekend jazz brunch that's a "gourmet feast", and all can be "counted on" for "delicious, fresh" fish; but a handful huff it's "unremarkable" and needs "pepping up."

Sea Salt *Seafood* 22 | 18 | 20 | $36

Berkeley | 2512 San Pablo Ave. (Dwight Way) | 510-883-1720 | www.seasaltrestaurant.com

The "Lalime's crew's" "kitschy" American "sea shack" is sailing "more smoothly" since taking reservations and "expanding" its "somewhat awkward dining room with a quieter, more refined space" report Berkeleyites; the "innovative" and "traditional" "sustainably caught" fin fare and "high-end deep-fried seafood" are "worth their weight in salt" but "land-lovers beware" – the menu is "almost exclusively fish"; still, "you can't beat $1 happy hour" and the newly opened garden patio; N.B. now serving weekend brunch.

Shalimar ⊋ *Indian/Pakistani*

| 22 | 3 | 9 | $15 |

Fremont | 3325 Walnut Ave. (Paseo Padre Pkwy.) | 510-494-1919 | www.shalimarsf.com

See review in City of San Francisco Directory.

Shen Hua *Chinese*

| 20 | 16 | 17 | $23 |

Berkeley | 2914 College Ave. (bet. Ashby Ave. & Russell St.) | 510-883-1777
When the craving for "upscale Chinese vittles" strikes, head to this "bustling" Berkeley "hangout" serving up "tasty renditions of the classics"; though perhaps "not terribly inventive", the fare is "fresh, hot and flavorful" and it "arrives quickly, once you're seated" in the "well-decorated" digs; still, detractors shout that the "experience is marred by insane", "off-the-charts noise" levels – it's "almost as loud as Downtown Beijing."

Soi Four 🄑 *Thai*

| 23 | 19 | 19 | $31 |

Oakland | 5421 College Ave. (bet. Kales & Manila Aves.) | 510-655-0889 | www.soifour.com
The "menu may say 'Bangkok street food', but you can expect some of the most refined", "delicious upmarket Thai food" around at this "sleek", "cool" Rockridge "knockout" with a "friendly neighborhood feel"; it's "best to go with a group and share" – the appetizers are downright "cravable", the "nicely presented" dishes are "colorful and flavorful" and the prices "won't break the bank"

Soizic 🄑🄜 *Californian/French*

| 22 | 18 | 21 | $43 |

Oakland | 300 Broadway (3rd St.) | 510-251-8100 | www.soizicbistro.com
It's "like going back to see a friend" declare devotees of this "comfortable" two-story Cal-French bistro set in an "unlikely" Jack London locale in the "middle" of Oakland's "produce district"; the "lovely" loftlike space may be "out of the way, but it's worth the hunt" to dine on fare that's "distinctive yet accessible and so tasty" served by "professional" staffers; an added bonus: there's "plenty of space between tables, which keeps the noise level down and the intimacy up."

Sol y Lago *Nuevo Latino*

| ▽ 17 | 21 | 17 | $39 |

Tahoe City | Boatworks Mall | 760 N. Lake Blvd. (Red Cedar St.) | 530-583-0358 | www.solylago.com
"Sit by the window" at this "lovely", bi-level waterside spot on the second floor of Tahoe City's Boatworks Mall and drink in the "fabulous view" of the "lake and the mountains" while sampling "inventive" Nuevo Latino mixed grill plates and "creative tapas"; if a handful harrumph it "hasn't found its footing yet", others assert "there's potential", adding it's the "perfect spot for lunch" on the weekends and during the week too, come winter.

Somerset *American*

| - | - | - | I |

Oakland | 5912 College Ave. (Chabot Rd.) | 510-428-1823
Noe Valley's long-running Miss Millie's closed, relocated and recently reopened as this new incarnation, a "homey" "comfort haven" in Rockridge serving "lots of dressed up", "familiar", "inexpensive" Traditional American classics such as chicken pot pie in a "beautiful wood-paneled dining room"; during the weekdays it's "quiet" but come the weekend, crowds congregate for one of the "best brunches ever."

	FOOD	DECOR	SERVICE	COST

Soule Domain 🅱 *American* ▽ 23 | 26 | 25 | $45

Kings Beach | 9983 Cove St. (Stateline Rd.) | 530-546-7529 |
www.souledomain.com

"Sitting cheek-by-jowl with its glitzy", "crowded Tahoe" "casino neighbors, this quaint log cabin of a restaurant" in Kings Beach owned by the Soule brothers feels "more like eating at someone's house"; one sibling "serves to please" guests while the other "carefully prepares" "rich", "guilty pleasure" New American fare perfect for "cold mountain nights"; "reservations are a must" at this "cozy little secret" where "romantics" "cuddle up with a drink" (needed to "ease the shock of the final bill").

Spettro *Californian/Italian* ▽ 20 | 16 | 20 | $22

Oakland | 3355 Lakeshore Ave. (Trestle Glen Rd.) | 510-451-7738

Perhaps the "coolest cat in town", this "favorite" on "Lake Merritt's main strip" specializes in "creative gourmet pizzas with decadent topping choices" (like "peanut butter") that may be a "little too interesting" for some, "but there's plenty of variety" on the Cal-Italian menu to appease "everyone in the family"; "experimentation is a good thing" – "you really can create what you want" – plus the "lights overhead are so charming", you almost forget how "cramped" the digs are.

Sunnyside Resort *Seafood/Steak* 18 | 25 | 20 | $39

Tahoe City | 1850 W. Lake Blvd. (bet. Pineland Dr. & Tahoe Park Ave.) |
530-583-7200 | www.sunnysideresort.com

It's "all about the cute snow bunnies and macho lifeguards" who create "quite a scene" at this "long-established, feel-good, post-skiing"/ "tie-up-your-boat" "Tahoe tradition" boasting an "unbelievable setting" "right on the lake with snow-capped mountains in the background"; the ambiance is "nothing special" and the steaks and seafood are "pricey" and "predictable", but service is "accommodating", and "it's hard to beat" drinks on the deck "on a sunny" summer day – or the "great bar action" year-round.

Sushi Groove 🅼 *Japanese* 23 | 19 | 17 | $38

Walnut Creek | 1523 Giammona Dr. (bet. Locust & N. Main Sts.) |
925-945-1400 | www.sushigroovewc.com

See review in City of San Francisco Directory.

Tacubaya *Mexican* 22 | 14 | 14 | $15

Berkeley | 1788 Fourth St. (bet. Hearst Ave. & Virginia St.) | 510-525-5160

"Doña Tomàs' little sister", a "haute" taqueria with "smaller prices" and "speedy service", offers peckish Berkeley shoppers a "satisfying in-and-out" "gourmet Mexican" meal "rarely found in local" joints; the "inventive" offerings are "not necessarily traditional", nevertheless the "homemade tortillas", "inimitable tacos" and organic breakfast, lunch and dinner fare is "worth crawling on your hands and knees to get to" and best "savored alfresco" while "enjoying the pulse of Fourth Street."

🆉 Tamarindo Antojeria Mexicana 🅱 *Mexican* 24 | 20 | 20 | $33

Oakland | 468 Eighth St. (bet. Broadway & Washington St.) | 510-444-1944 |
www.tamarindoantojeria.com

"Small plates go Mexican" at this "sweet, family-run" Downtown Oakland "favorite" where the "fresh", "assertive" "homemade everything" ("from tortillas to chunky guacamole") "pairs perfectly" with the "bright art" and "warm" staff; the "only thing lacking is a bigger dining room" and a reservation policy, still, to say the "excellent" regional fare and sangria are "worth the wait would be a tragic understatement."

Thai Buddhist Temple Mongkolratanaram Ⓜ *Thai* ▽ 20 | 11 | 12 | $11

Berkeley | 1911 Russell St. (bet. Martin Luther King Way & Otis St.) | 510-849-3419

"Where else but Berkeley" would you find the "hottest brunch spot" in the "backyard of a single family house that serves as a Thai temple"; pay for your "outdoor picnic" meal with tokens that "benefit the benevolent" Buddhists and "feast" on "home-cooked" Siamese fare for a "pittance" – it's "my favorite" weekend "ritual"; it's hard" to "find a seat at the plastic tables – you may end up joining" "crowds of hippies, students" and "eccentrics" on the lawn; N.B. open Sundays only.

Townhouse Bar & Grill Ⓢ *Californian* 21 | 19 | 21 | $32

Emeryville | 5862 Doyle St. (bet. 59th & Powell Sts.) | 510-652-6151 | www.townhousebarandgrill.com

"Don't be put off by the outside" of this "old bootlegger roadhouse" in Emeryville, because today, it's a "white-tablecloth", "something-for-everyone" Californian where "on-the-case" staffers cater to "business-lunchers" "on the company dime" and "cool folks" "at the bar"; the "lively" digs are also "pleasant" for dinner "celebrations without having to dress up", but it's "best on the deck" when it's warm, as the "noise level can be high inside"; P.S. Wednesday's "live jazz" is a "nice touch."

Trader Vic's *Polynesian* 16 | 21 | 18 | $45

Emeryville | 9 Anchor Dr. (Powell St.) | 510-653-3400 | www.tradervics.com

"Been there, done that, but probably would do it again" concede nostalgics of this "'50s tiki-bar's" Emeryville flagship (and its Downtown and Palo Alto sibs), which is "almost as original as Rice-a-Roni, and still a San Francisco treat"; the "island-fantasy" decor is "kitschy, but that's its hallmark", and the "delicious mai tais" and other "tropical-themed cocktails" are "still fun" – it's only the "cliche 'Polynesian' cuisine" that's a "disappointing" "throwback to a time when Americans were less discriminating."

Trattoria La Siciliana Ⓕ *Italian* 23 | 15 | 15 | $30

Berkeley | 2993 College Ave. (Ashby Ave.) | 510-704-1474 | www.trattorialasiciliana.com

"By the end of the night" – after you've "eaten everything on your plate" and "mopped up the sauce" – "everyone" at this "cramped", "crowded" Italian trattoria in Berkeley "is your friend, and you're ready to marry the cooks" (although maybe not the "slow", "inattentive" servers); if you're a party of three or more, you're allowed to "make reservations", but the "staff encourages" groups to order "family-style" (at least you'll avoid reported "hour-long waits"); P.S. "bring cash."

T Rex Barbecue *BBQ* 17 | 19 | 17 | $29

Berkeley | 1300 10th St. (Gilman St.) | 510-527-0099 | www.t-rex-bbq.com

"Great" "smells drive you into" (and linger "when you walk out" of) this "high-class" "loftlike" Berkeley BBQ joint, where "T-riffic" "smoked meats", "comfort-food sides", an "incredible selection of quality beers, wines and spirits" and "over-the-top brunches" keep

FOOD | DECOR | SERVICE | COST

many "coming back"("inconsistent service" notwithstanding); how-ever, connoisseurs feel the fare "lacks regional identity" and dismiss it as "overpriced barbecue for rich white people."

Udupi Palace ∅ *Indian/Vegetarian*

20 | 8 | 12 | $13

Berkeley | 1901-1903 University Ave. (Martin Luther King Jr. Way) | 510-843-6600 | www.udupipalace.net

"Budget" "food good enough for non-students" is the hallmark of this Berkeley "hole-in-the-wall", which serves "authentic" South Indian vegetarian fare such as "massive dosas" "stuffed with full-bodied curry" that "spills off the plate"; over at its Sunnyvale sibling, "follow-ing a slump in the post-dot-com era", surveyors report that the eats are "impressive" once again – which "makes up for" the "inattention to decor" and "spare" service.

Uzen ☒ *Japanese*

24 | 15 | 17 | $34

Oakland | 5415 College Ave. (bet. Hudson St. & Kales Ave.) | 510-654-7753

Get "full for a steal" at this "neighborhood" Japanese spot that offers "none of the fanfare of sake bombs and rolls galore", just "clean-tasting", "quality" nigiri augmented by "delicious tempura" and some "unusual and interesting choices"; the walls "need to be painted" and service can "run hot and cold", "but if you love your sushi simple and fresh, this is the place to go" in Oakland.

Va de Vi *Eclectic*

24 | 21 | 20 | $44

Walnut Creek | 1511 Mt. Diablo Blvd. (Main St.) | 925-979-0100 | www.vadevibistro.com

Walnut Creek's "va-va-voom" "hangout for the hip" "tempts" with "cutting-edge" Eclectic tapas in "fabulous flavor combinations" and "delightful" "wine flights of fancy", all of which is "great for sharing" (the tables in the "narrow" space are "so close together, you might end up sampling your neighbor's too"); factor in a "stunning patio" set around a "big oak tree", and CoCo County connoisseurs cheer they "love everything – except the bill."

Venezia *Italian*

20 | 21 | 21 | $30

Berkeley | 1799 University Ave. (Grant St.) | 510-849-4681 | www.caffevenezia.com

"Eating in a faux outdoor Italian piazza", replete with "trompe l'oeil murals" and "watchful pigeons (fake)" "above your head", is "the main attraction" at this "hugely popular" "touch of Venice" in Berkeley; the "dependable Italian fare with flair", which "changes as often" as the "laundry hanging overhead", makes it "particularly nice for group" "gatherings", while "paper tablecloths, crayons, noise" and "excellent value" make it easy to "bring the kids."

Venus *Californian*

19 | 15 | 18 | $27

Berkeley | 2327 Shattuck Ave. (Durant Ave.) | 510-540-5950 | www.venusrestaurant.net

"All organic", "fresh local ingredients" whipped into "inventive", "con-stantly changing" combinations keep this "delightfully Berkeley" Californian "hole-in-the-wall" "healthy and delicious"; a "solid" choice for "weekday breakfasts" and "before-theater" or "after-movie" victuals, it's also known for serving a "heavenly brunch" (starring "ethereal pan-cakes") that may "seem pricey" to some but is "so worth it" to most.

Vic Stewart's *Steak*

21 | 20 | 20 | $58

Walnut Creek | 850 S. Broadway (bet. Mt. Diablo Blvd. & Newell Ave.) |
925-943-5666 | www.vicstewarts.com

"All aboard" this "place to meet for meat" in Walnut Creek, an "old-school steakhouse" housed in a former train depot with an attached "converted railroad car" boasting "different rooms and themes" ("book well in advance" to get the "special" "private" space "for a secluded dinner for two"); the "men's-club decor" accounts for the "Republican ambiance", as do prices that warrant a "corporate Amex" – the high tabs may not, however, justify beef that many deem "good", "not superb."

Vik's Chaat Corner Ⓜ *Indian*

23 | 4 | 10 | $12

Berkeley | 724 Allston Way (bet. 4th & 5th Sts.) | 510-644-4412 |
www.vikdistributors.com

Considered a "cult favorite" among "students and locals", this Indian "sensation" corners the Berkeley market on "jaw-dropping", "incredibly cheap" "roadside snacks"; indeed, "it's the food" – not the "school-lunch-counter" decor, "plastic sporks", "paper plates" or "hustle-hustle" service – that "brings 'em back" to this "crowded and noisy" "madhouse", which offers "extra specials on weekends" and closes at 6 PM nightly; N.B. a post-Survey refresh was planned.

Wente Vineyards *Californian/Mediterranean*

23 | 25 | 23 | $53

Livermore | 5050 Arroyo Rd. (Wetmore Rd.) | 925-456-2450 |
www.wentevineyards.com

You "feel like Baron Phillipe" dining among the grapes at this "upscale, up-priced" "gourmet" "experience" out in the "fields of Livermore", where the vino is the "focus of the "excellent" "seasonal" Cal-Med meals; dress "elegant or wear shorts, it doesn't matter" – either way this "romantic getaway" offers the "perfect" "wine country setting", "especially in warm weather" when you can kick back with a "relaxing" lunch or dinner before their concert series in the vineyard – "you'll wish you" "'wente' sooner."

Wolfdale's *Californian*

25 | 23 | 25 | $54

Tahoe City | 640 N. Lake Blvd. (Grove St.) | 530-583-5700 |
www.wolfdales.com

A "favorite at the lake" since 1978, this "high-class" "foodies' heaven" overlooking the North Side may be the "very best the Tahoe region has to offer", showcasing "very inventive", "expensive" Asian-influenced Californian cuisine, and "interesting wines" in a "beautiful" waterfront setting; true, "there's not much competition in the mountains", but this "old standby" is "still top of the heap", with an enchanting outdoor deck and garden in summer and a "popular" locals' bar year-round.

🆕 Wood Tavern *Californian*

▽ 23 | 22 | 22 | $39

Oakland | 6317 College Ave. (bet. Alcatraz Ave. & 63rd St.) |
510-654-6607

The former owners of SF's Frascati "have done it again" declare Rockridge diners "hungry for an honest midrange spot", who "welcome to the 'hood" this "instantly popular" "perfect neighborhood" tavern where staffers who understand that "life is too short not to enjoy your wine" deliver "delicious" Californian eats all day; the revamped "warm" decor ("replacing the former Grasshopper, which got too old too soon") features "new everything, including wood" beams, plus there's also a "lively", "noisy" bar to boot.

NEW **Xyclo** *Vietnamese* ▽ 19 | 17 | 19 | $29

Oakland | 4218 Piedmont Ave. (bet. John St. & Ridgeway Ave.) | 510-654-2681 | www.xyclorestaurant.com

Although it's named for the cheap pedi-cabs of Saigon, this "nouvelle Vietnamese" newcomer presenting "distinctive", "more vertical-than-thou" modernized Mekong-inspired meals in minimalist digs decorated with origamilike chandeliers is not your typical pho house; the "helpful" staff and kitchen are still "finding their footing", but it's a "nice addition to Oakland's Piedmont Avenue", plus the "cute lounge in back" specializes in soju "cocktails you don't find everywhere."

Yoshi's at Jack London Square *Japanese* 18 | 20 | 18 | $39

Oakland | Jack London Sq. | 510 Embarcadero W. (bet. Clay & Washington Sts.) | 510-238-9200 | www.yoshis.com

Ticket-holders "who land" at Oakland's "legendary" nightclub for "world-class jazz" are "surprised" it's worth "staying for the tempura" to score "priority seating" for the performance; hep cats mew over the "revamped", "vastly improved" Japanese fare and "wide selection of sake" ushered in by new chef Shotaro Kamio (ex-Ozumo) but howl the amateur-hour service is "out of tune" when it "goes from empty to packed"; N.B. a much-anticipated branch at SF's Fillmore Heritage Center is slated to debut fall 2007.

Zachary's Chicago Pizza *Pizza* 24 | 11 | 15 | $18

Berkeley | 1853 Solano Ave. (The Alameda) | 510-525-5950
Oakland | 5801 College Ave. (Oak Grove Ave.) | 510-655-6385
NEW **San Ramon** | 3110 Crow Canyon Pl. (Hwy. 680) | 925-244-1215
www.zacharys.com

"Swooning East Bay fans" and "Midwest transplants" "high on the garlicky sauce" and "stuffed" on the "gut-busting" "deep-dish" pies (try the "'Pride & Joy'") consider this "legendary" outfit the "mother of all" "Chicago-style pizzerias" ("better climate", natch); it's "worth braving the bridge traffic" – "or the busy signal" – to reach "cheesy heaven", but "you could almost fly" to the Windy City by the time the "rowdy college" kids "vacate" your table – so consider getting it to "take and bake."

Zao Noodle Bar *Pan-Asian* 14 | 12 | 14 | $17

Emeryville | 5614 Bay St. (Shellmound St.) | 510-595-2888 | www.zao.com
See review in City of San Francisco Directory.

Zatar 🗵 🗏 ⇄ *Mediterranean* ▽ 21 | 19 | 19 | $35

Berkeley | 1981 Shattuck Ave. (University Ave.) | 510-841-1981 | www.zatarrestaurant.com

"Close to Cal campus" in Berkeley, this "funky" Mediterranean with Moorish decor is on the Zatar screen of both "value"-seekers and foodies with a "fond attachment" to "exotic" fare; the "lovingly prepared" meals made with "local, organic produce and free-range meats" "never fails to captivate my palate" – and they're "served by the owners themselves"; still, a few fail to zing its praises citing "so-so food" and service that's "ok – if you're a regular."

NORTH OF SAN FRANCISCO

Top Food Ratings

Ratings are to the left of names. Lists exclude places with low votes, unless indicated by a ▽.

29 French Laundry	**25** Madrona Manor
28 Cyrus	Hana Japanese
Sushi Ran	Auberge du Soleil
27 Farmhouse Inn	Martini House
26 Redd Restaurant	Syrah
ad hoc	Bistro Jeanty
Terra	K&L Bistro
Cafe La Haye	Willow Wood Mkt.*
La Toque	Cole's Chop House
Mirepoix	Étoile

BY CUISINE

AMERICAN

29 French Laundry
26 ad hoc
Terra
Cafe La Haye
25 Madrona Manor

CALIFORNIAN

27 Farmhouse Inn
26 Redd Restaurant
25 Auberge du Soleil
Syrah
Étoile

ECLECTIC

25 Willow Wood Mkt.
24 Willi's Wine Bar
Go Fish
23 Ravenous Cafe
Celadon

FRENCH

28 Cyrus
26 La Toque
Mirepoix
25 Madrona Manor
Bistro Jeanty

ITALIAN

25 zazu
24 Cucina Restaurant
Cook St. Helena
Picco
23 Bistro Don Giovanni

JAPANESE

28 Sushi Ran
25 Hana Japanese
22 Osake/Sake 'O
20 Robata Grill

MED./SPANISH

24 Insalata's
Zuzu
23 El Dorado Kitchen
22 Underwood Bar
20 Hurley's

SEAFOOD/STEAKS

25 Cole's Chop House
24 Fish
Go Fish
23 Press
Willi's Seafood

BY SPECIAL FEATURE

BREAKFAST/BRUNCH

25 Willow Wood Mkt.
24 Seaweed Café
Downtown Bakery
23 Lark Creek Inn
fig cafe & winebar

CHILD-FRIENDLY

22 In-N-Out Burger
21 Pacific Catch
Pizzeria Tra Vigne
Taylor's Automatic
17 Yankee Pier

NEWCOMERS

27	Bistro des Copains▽
24	Go Fish
23	Farm
-	AVA
-	West County Grill

OUTDOOR SEATING

25	Auberge du Soleil
	Martini House
	Cole's Chop House
	Étoile
23	John Ash & Co.

PEOPLE-WATCHING

26	Redd Restaurant
25	Martini House
	Bouchon
24	Mustards Grill
23	Bistro Don Giovanni

ROMANCE

28	Cyrus
27	Farmhouse Inn
26	La Toque
25	Madrona Manor
23	El Paseo

SMALL PLATES

24	Willi's Wine Bar
23	Willi's Seafood
22	Underwood Bar
21	Ora
18	Barndiva

TASTING MENUS

29	French Laundry
28	Cyrus
26	Redd Restaurant
	La Toque
25	Madrona Manor

WINE BARS

25	Martini House
24	Willi's Wine Bar
23	Willi's Seafood
	fig cafe & winebar
17	Bounty Hunter

WINNING WINE LISTS

29	French Laundry
28	Cyrus
26	Terra
	La Toque
25	Martini House

BY LOCATION

MARIN COUNTY

28	Sushi Ran
25	Pizzeria Picco
	Marché aux Fleurs
24	Cucina Restaurant
	Insalata's

MENDOCINO COUNTY

25	Mendo Bistro
	Cafe Beaujolais
24	MacCallum House
	Albion River Inn
23	Moosse Café

NAPA COUNTY

29	French Laundry
26	Redd Restaurant
	ad hoc
	Terra
	La Toque

SONOMA COUNTY

28	Cyrus
27	Farmhouse Inn
26	Cafe La Haye
	Mirepoix
25	Madrona Manor

Top Decor Ratings

Ratings are to the left of names.

27 Farm
Cyrus
Madrona Manor
Auberge du Soleil

26 French Laundry
Étoile

25 John Ash & Co.
El Paseo
Press
Lark Creek Inn

Martini House
Farmhouse Inn

24 Tra Vigne
Dry Creek Kitchen
Albion River Inn
Terra

23 MacCallum House
Wine Spectator
La Toque
Napa Wine Train

Top Service Ratings

Ratings are to the left of names.

28 Cyrus
French Laundry

26 La Toque
Mirepoix

25 Farmhouse Inn
Auberge du Soleil
Madrona Manor
Étoile
Terra
Pilar

24 Cafe La Haye
ad hoc

23 Albion River Inn
Mendo Bistro*
Redd Restaurant
Martini House
Cafe Beaujolais
El Paseo
Syrah
Cole's Chop House

Best Buys

In order of Bang for the Buck rating.

1. In-N-Out Burger
2. Downtown Bakery
3. Boulange
4. Sol Food
5. Barney's
6. Joe's Taco
7. Taylor's Automatic
8. Alexis Baking Co.
9. Jimtown Store
10. Pizzeria Picco
11. Café Gratitude
12. Emporio Rulli
13. Amici's Pizzeria
14. Pacific Catch
15. Dipsea Cafe
16. Lotus of India
17. Royal Thai
18. Pizza Antica
19. Las Camelias
20. Gary Chu's

OTHER GOOD VALUES

Betty's Fish & Chips
Bovolo
Cafe Citti
fig cafe & winebar
Fish
Flavor

Monti's Rotisserie
Pizzeria Tra Vigne
Rist. Fabrizio
Table Café
Willi's Wine Bar
Willow Wood Mkt.

North of San Francisco

	FOOD	DECOR	SERVICE	COST

☑ ad hoc *American*   26 | 19 | 24 | $58
Yountville | 6476 Washington St. (bet. California Dr. & Oak Circle) |
707-944-2487
Thomas Keller's now-permanent "version of a family-style home
cookin' eatery" is "the yang to the French Laundry's yin", presenting
"superb" four-course prix fixe traditional "Americana" dinners in a
Yountville diner "without the muss or fuss" of a "two month waiting
list" and at prices that "won't take you to the cleaners"; "you're s.o.l."
if you don't fancy the nightly selection, but "rest assured", the "generously portioned" chow is "always magnificent", as are the "spot-on
wine pairings" made by the "friendly, friendly" staff clothed in gear
reminiscent of "old-fashioned service-station" uniforms.

Albion River Inn *Californian*   24 | 24 | 23 | $49
Albion | 3790 North Hwy. 1 (Spring Grove Rd.) | 707-937-1919 |
www.albionriverinn.com
"Set atop a cliff overlooking the Pacific", this "special-occasion" Albion
"favorite" serves seasonal Californian cuisine that's "original without being too foo-foo"; the "terrific" fare "almost lives up" to the "spectacular
setting", but it's the "dramatic sunsets", piano player and "cozy" fireplace that really "elevate the experience to an absolute pleasure"; what
also "keeps you happy": the "unmatched wine list" and the "extensive"
single-malt scotch selection and "neighborhoody bar scene."

Alexis Baking Company *Bakery*   22 | 11 | 14 | $17
(aka ABC)
Napa | 1517 Third St. (bet. Church & School Sts.) | 707-258-1827 |
www.alexisbakingcompany.com
Considered "the breakfast place in the city of Napa", this "cute-as-a-
button", serve-yourself "neighborhood hangout" storefront serving
"oversized lattes", "energy-for-a-day scrumptious buns" and "killer
brunch" fare is the perfect "yuppified" spot to "prepare for a day of
wine-tasting"; "haphazard service is the norm" when it gets "full with
locals and some lucky visitors", but carboloaders insist the "wait is
worth it for their creative take on *chilaquiles,* huevos rancheros" and
those "amazing pastries."

All Season's Cafe & Wine Shop *Californian*   21 | 14 | 21 | $39
Calistoga | 1400 Lincoln Ave. (Washington St.) | 707-942-9111 |
www.allseasonsnapavalley.net
"Where else can you get mid-'80s Cabs at retail price – and eat
simple, well-prepared" seasonal Californian fare marvel "wine
geeks" who "love the idea of walking around" the on-site "wine shop
and picking your own bottle" (plus an "affordable $15 corkage") at
this "casual cafe" on "Calistoga's main drag"; still, the digs are
"nothin' fancy", which may explain "why after all these years", it still
remains a bit of a "secret."

Amici's East Coast Pizzeria *Pizza*   20 | 12 | 16 | $19
San Rafael | 1242 Fourth St. (bet. B & C Sts.) | 415-455-9777 |
www.amicis.com
See review in City of San Francisco Directory.

Angèle *French*

22	21	21	$46

Napa | 540 Main St. (3rd St.) | 707-252-8115 | www.angelerestaurant.com

"It's easy to imagine you're dining along the banks of the Seine" when "sitting on the terrace" at this converted boathouse bistro with a "lovely view of the Napa River" enjoying "rustic" French country fare and the "occasional cult find" wine; the "*magnifique*" location and "first-rate service" "make you feel that all is right with the world for now"; ditto the "cozy" bar, boasting "local hangout atmosphere" that's "often crowded late into the evening" with vintners and other regulars.

Annalien 🖼️Ⓜ️ *Vietnamese*

∇ 24	19	21	$30

Napa | 1142 Main St. (bet. 1st & Pearl Sts.) | 707-224-8319

"Charming owner" Annalien "greets you personally" at her "gem tucked away in Downtown Napa" serving "exceptional" "upscale" "colonial-era Vietnamese fare" and "terrific wines by the glass" in a 1930s period setting; forget "bargain $4 pho here – this is upscale stuff" and it's so "exceptional" you want to "keep it to yourself"; still, word is out about this "welcome addition to the challenged ethnic scene" – it's "quickly become popular with locals, so get there early."

Applewood Inn & Restaurant 🖼️Ⓜ️ *Californian*

24	21	21	$46

Guerneville | 13555 Hwy. 116 (River Rd.) | 707-869-9093 | www.applewoodinn.com

This "rustic Tuscan-style" "romantic bed and breakfast inn" with a restaurant and a rock fireplace "tucked in the redwoods" near Guerneville "doesn't get the hype of the Healdsburg stars, but it is worth going out of the way for"; "all the elements are right", from the "breathtaking setting" and "individualized attention each diner receives" to the "carefully" crafted regional Californian fare and "terrific local wine list" – what a "delightful" "getaway spot for foodies."

🅩 Auberge du Soleil *Californian/French*

25	27	25	$82

Rutherford | Auberge du Soleil | 180 Rutherford Hill Rd. (Silverado Trail) | 707-967-3111 | www.aubergedusoleil.com

Perched "up high" on a "lavender hillside" with "heartbreakingly beautiful views" of the vineyards below, this "romantic" Rutherford "oasis" provides flush foodies with the "ultimate" dining "fantasy" replete with "doting" waiters who lavish "foodgasm"-worthy Cal-French tasting menus and an "exceptional" "phonebook"-sized wine list; it's "one of the top meals in Napa Valley you can actually get a reservation for" but if you lack "truckloads of money", go for a "wonderful lunch on the terrace" or "sunset cocktails and hors d'ouevres."

ⓃⒺⓌ AVA 🖼️Ⓜ️ *American*

-	-	-	M

San Anselmo | 636 San Anselmo Ave. (Magnolia Ave.) | 415-453-3407 | www.avamarin.com

Just as a wine's AVA (American Viticultural Area) reflects its grape-growing designation, this cozy Downtown San Anselmo newcomer from the husband-and-wife duo behind Marché aux Fleurs tethers its identity to the Marin terrior, crafting Cal-New American fare from ingredients supplied by farmers, ranchers and fishermen within 100 miles; the California vino list also hews to the local credo, boasting a wide array of appellations from only family-owned wineries.

	FOOD	DECOR	SERVICE	COST

Avatars ⊠ *Eclectic* ▽ 22 | 11 | 23 | $26

Sausalito | 2656 Bridgeway (Coloma St.) | 415-332-8083

Although this "small, friendly 'Marindian' (Marin and Indian, get it?)" Sausalito "charmer" "looks like an old-style counter restaurant coffee shop", it serves the "oddest sounding" Eclectic "amalgam of cuisines" (Punjab, Mexican and a "wonderful touch of healthy Californian"); it's like nothing you've "experienced" before, but somehow the "marvelous array of flavors and textures" "work spectacularly well", plus there's an "excellent wine and beer selection" to boot.

Barndiva ⓜ *American* 18 | 23 | 15 | $43

Healdsburg | 231 Center St. (Matheson St.) | 707-431-0100 | www.barndiva.com

"To call it a 'Barn' is to call the Louvre a 'museum'" muse admirers who dosey-do over to this "chic, urban-style" Healdsburg boîte serving "innovative" Modern American country fare made from sustainable ingredients; the "lively" environment makes it "good for a late-night bite" while the garden is "delightful" for "lingering outside" over a "relaxing Sunday brunch"; still, nitpickers grumble it's "great" for "'farm-hip' tourists" but it's got a "little too much attitude for the real winery crowd" who gather "after work in our boots."

Barney's Gourmet Hamburgers *Hamburgers* 19 | 12 | 14 | $15

San Rafael | 1020 Court St. (4th St.) | 415-454-4594 | www.barneyshamburgers.com

See review in City of San Francisco Directory.

Betty's Fish & Chips ⊠ⓜ *Seafood* ▽ 20 | 9 | 17 | $18

Santa Rosa | 4046 Sonoma Hwy. (Streamside Dr.) | 707-539-0899

"Why wait until Lent when the fish is this good?" joke "Londoners" and Santa Rosa blokes and birds who satisfy "hankerings" for "hearty old-fashioned fish 'n' chips" washed down with a "good selection of beer" at this "funky" hang on Highway 12; still, the less-chipper carp that the cod's "kind of expensive" considering it's a "hole-in-the-wall."

NEW Bistro des Copains *French* ▽ 27 | 20 | 24 | $41

Occidental | 3782 Bohemian Hwy. (bet. Coleman Valley & Graton Rds.) | 707-874-2436 | www.bistrodescopains.com

"Hidden beneath the neon bulk of big Italian restaurants" that dominate "bucolic Occidental", this *très* "charming" yet "urbane" bistro set in a wooden house is quickly making friends and winning influence with West County locals who're impressed by the "splendid" Provençal offerings, "intelligent" French-Sonoma wine list and "welcoming" service; the claw-feet tables covered in white butcher paper, "bustling atmosphere" and "awesome" cuisine "lovingly prepared" with farm ingredients make you feel like you've just "popped your head into the South of France."

Bistro Don Giovanni *Italian* 23 | 22 | 21 | $46

Napa | 4110 Howard Ln. (bet. Oak Knoll & Salvador Aves.) | 707-224-3300 | www.bistrodongiovanni.com

"Forget the hype of the area", "foodie tourists" who "mingle on the patio" with "the more moneyed locals" know this "happening" haunt is "the place to be" ("and has been since the moment it opened"); it's "one of the few" spots "where you can enjoy vineyard views", "soulful, unvarnished Italian" *cucina* and "take advantage of Napa's (and Italia's) fine wine offerings"; "considering the quality", prices are "reasonable", plus even when the "big, boisterous" villalike interior gets "excruciatingly busy", "grand host Giovanni" "takes great care of you."

☑ Bistro Jeanty *French*   25 | 21 | 22 | $50

Yountville | 6510 Washington St. (Mulberry St.) | 707-944-0103 | www.bistrojeanty.com

"Another winner" "in the middle of fine-dining central", Philippe Jeanty's convivial Yountville bistro "induces easy spirits" where regulars indulge in "soul food" "like *grand-mère* use to make" in a "*très* authentic", "get-to-know-your-neighbors" setting (plus a pooch-friendly patio); best of all, this bargain boîte is open all day (should "you lose yourself in the wineries") and "walk-ins" can "wait for seating at the bar", where vintners and other locals often "linger" over "their own wines."

Bistro Ralph ☒ *Californian/French*   21 | 17 | 22 | $44

Healdsburg | 109 Plaza St. (Healdsburg Ave.) | 707-433-1380

A "longtime player in the Healdsburg restaurant scene", this "simple, fun" "local hangout" "overlooking the town square" remains a "comfortable" lunch or dinner spot to "kick back"; while the "wonderful" "but not fancy" Cal-French menu "hasn't changed this century" and there's "not much decor", the "energetic staff" (including "Ralph, who comes in to say hello"), "hard-to-find" Sonoma-only vintages and "great martini menu" (particularly welcoming "after lots of wine") "encourages good conversations and enjoyable evenings."

Bistro V *French/Italian*   ▽ 22 | 17 | 19 | $37

Sebastopol | 2295 Gravenstein Hwy. (Bloomfield Rd.) | 707-823-1262 | www.bistro-v.com

There's "nothing in Sonoma County" quite like this "creative" Sebastopol bistro set in a converted "house in the countryside" and run by a husband-and-wife team preparing a "wide range of different tastes" from "fresh local ingredients"; the "servers can get overwhelmed", but his "tantalizing" French-Italian dishes (with Peruvian and Mediterranean influences) and her "wonderful" "housemade breads, pastas and desserts" are "worth the wait" – plus sometimes the "hospitable chef" "comes out to talk to you" after the meal.

Boca *Argentinean/Steak*   20 | 22 | 19 | $44

Novato | 340 Ignacio Blvd. (Rte. 101) | 415-883-0901 | www.bocasteak.com

George Morrone's "popular" steakhouse with its "trendy, upbeat" "Tahoe lodge meets Novato" "cowhide decor" and "oversized flatware" enlivens the "foodie desert" of Marin; the "limited menu" of "oak-fired" "grass- or grain"-fed beef prepared Argentinean-style with a "sauce to complement any meat", "great homemade pickles" and "fries cooked in duck fat" pleases the "blue-rinse brigade" of carnivores, but detractors dis the "spotty service" and pronounce it "overpriced" (except for "good midweek deals" on South American wines).

Boon Fly Café *Californian*   - | - | - | M

Napa | Carneros Inn | 4048 Sonoma Hwy. (Los Carneros Ave.) | 707-299-4900 | www.thecarnerosinn.com

"Forget those expensive, celebrity chef, P.R. company–driven spots in the Valley", the Carneros Inn's casual, tractor-red, rustic-chic Napa roadhouse serving Californian comfort food is "the real thing" – and a "favorite stop coming back" – or en route – to wine country; locals, day-trippers and hotel guests drop in for coffee and housemade mini doughnuts in the morning, Kobe beef burgers on brioche at lunch or "belly up to the bar" come evening for an impromptu dinner and regional wine priced just over retail.

Boonville Hotel *Californian*   ▽ 21 | 18 | 19 | $39

Boonville | Boonville Hotel | 14050 Hwy. 128 (Lambert Ln.) | 707-895-2210 | www.boonvillehotel.com

"The apple doesn't fall far from the tree" josh fans of this "funky" Boonville roadhouse, "run by the son of the founders" of the nearby Apple Farm, serving "satisfying", "simple" seasonal Californian cuisine with Anderson Valley vintages; on Thursdays, locals bring their own wine (sans corkage), settling into the "rustic" Shaker-style dining room for the "excellent" prix fixe, while daydreaming day-trippers "long to be back" "on a lovely summer day" because "nothing's more enjoyable than dinner in the garden."

☑ Bouchon ● *French*   25 | 23 | 22 | $54

Yountville | 6534 Washington St. (Yount St.) | 707-944-8037 | www.frenchlaundry.com

Thomas Keller's "lively", "delightful" and, *oui,* "superlative" Yountville sibling to the French Laundry "nails the bistro concept" so accurately it almost feels like it was "airlifted over" from Paris concur scores of Francophiles who applaud its "panache", "perfectly crafted" cuisine, "exceptional" vino list and "caring service"; "definitely do not pass on the famous raw bar", the "awesome fries" or "scrumptious" "light, fresh" "takes on the classics" – this is "as good as it gets without a six week wait" – and after all these years it still "remains unique."

Bounty Hunter *BBQ*   17 | 17 | 18 | $31

Napa | 975 First St. (Main St.) | 707-255-0622

Located near the Napa River, this "neat" Wild West wine bar/retail shop is "entertaining" "before a show at the Opera House" or after "recovering from a day of tastings"; though primarily an oenophile's outlet – the "large assortment" of 400 vins and "dozens by the glass" is "fun to play in" – and the servers "really know" their stuff, the "microscopic kitchen" also delivers "the best beer-can chicken" and "satisfying" BBQ ribs; P.S. it sometimes gets "packed with the meat-market crowd."

Bovolo *Italian*   22 | 12 | 16 | $25

Healdsburg | Plaza Farms | 106 Matheson St. (Healdsburg Ave.) | 707-431-2962 | www.bovolorestaurant.com

"Best slow food in Healdsburg if you want a quick bite" divulge "guinea pigs" ("emphasis on the 'pig' part") who go hog wild, spending "big money" for "small" though "terrific pizzas, sandwiches and gelato" scoops at this zazu offshoot, an Italian cafe and bellini bar in the Plaza Farms market hall; still, most eschew the "grade-school-cafeteria" interior, preferring to gobble "artisanal salumi" on the "nice" pooch-and-kid-friendly patio; N.B. open for dinner Friday–Sunday, plus it has monthly family-style 'Big Night Out' prix fixe menus.

Brannan's Grill *American/French* 19 | 20 | 20 | $41

Calistoga | 1374 Lincoln Ave. (Washington St.) | 707-942-2233 |
www.brannansgrill.com

"After a long day of wine tasting, a martini and well-prepared steak
sound nice" agree admirers who also indulge in "solid" American-
French "comfort food" at this "consistent Calistoga favorite" with a
"lively", "historic vibe"; whether you snag a table by the accordion
windows for "great people-watching" or chow down at the "fabulous
old bar" you're in for a "memorable" meal, especially when the "great"
live jazz kicks in on weekends.

BRIX Restaurant & Wine Shop *Californian* 22 | 21 | 21 | $49

Yountville | 7377 St. Helena Hwy./Hwy. 29 (bet. Washington St. &
Yount Mill Rd.) | 707-944-2749 | www.brix.com

"Time seems to stand still" when you "do nothing more than enjoy
wonderful" Californian fare "paired with excellent wine choices" in a
"pleasing environment" while soaking up "stunning views of the vineyards, Mayacamas Mountains" and olive groves from this Yountville
standby's "delightful" patio; the "bucolic" garden made for "roaming"
"shows why the veggies taste fresh" plus there's even an on-site vino
shop if you want to "splurge" – "isn't that what it's all about?".

☒ Buckeye Roadhouse *American/BBQ* 23 | 23 | 21 | $43

Mill Valley | 15 Shoreline Hwy. (west of Hwy. 101) | 415-331-2600 |
www.buckeyeroadhouse.com

Truly "a roadhouse in the classic sense of the word", albeit "perfectly
rendered" for the "Marin ladies" and hungry hiker set, this Mill Valley
"favorite" dishes out "delicious", "dressed-up" Cal-American fare and
"excellent BBQ" in a "comfy Old West" "hunting-lodge" dining room
replete with a "huge fireplace"; reservations are a must, unless you
"wrestle your way" to the "pickup bar" that "packs 'em in" with "beautiful people angling to meet other beautiful people" over 'Oysters
Bingo' and "ice cold martinis."

Bungalow 44 *American* 21 | 18 | 19 | $41

Mill Valley | 44 E. Blithedale Ave. (Sunnyside Ave.) | 415-381-2500 |
www.Bungalow44.com

It's no Bungalow 8, but this Downtown "local hang" (from the Buckeye
boys) serving "wonderful" American chow and buzzing with "LA
types", "toned moms" and "couples with kids" may be the "hippest
viewing place in Mill Valley"; enjoy a "civilized dinner" on the "enclosed patio with a romantic fireplace" – it's a "real treat" and "worth
waiting for" as the "happening" Arts and Crafts–styled main room gets
"way too noisy" and service too "spotty", especially when the "bar
scene is hopping."

Cafe Beaujolais *Californian/French* 25 | 21 | 23 | $50

Mendocino | 961 Ukiah St. (School St.) | 707-937-5614 |
www.cafebeaujolais.com

A change of hands has "restored the magic" to this "homey" Mendocino
grand-mère of Cal-French North Coast cuisine", a "romantic" Victorian
house with a "lovely, understated New Englandy decor" and "professional service"; "breads baked on-site in a brick oven are rightfully legendary", the wine list is "outstanding" and locals "rejoice at the return

of lunch" as "reservations are a must" for dinner when those making the "gorgeous drive" on Highway 28 arrive.

Cafe Citti *Italian*

22 | 12 | 15 | $25

Kenwood | 9049 Sonoma Hwy./Hwy. 12 (Shaw Ave.) | 707-833-2690
"Sonoma locals" hail the "great Caesar" and other "garlicky" Tuscan goodies like the "simple but flavorful" pasta and roast chicken at this "roadside spot" in Kenwood that's "noisy and cramped" but "fun" and "friendly", like a "trattoria should be"; if Citti-slickers scoff at the "casual wine country counter service" and an "uninspiring" vino list, admirers retort that the "value" prices make it "good for a quickie" between "winery hopping", particularly if you "bring your own" bottle.

Café Gratitude *Vegan*
19 | 16 | 18 | $21

NEW **San Rafael** | 2200 Fourth St. (bet. Alexander Ave. & Santa Margarita Dr.) | 415-824-4652 | www.cafegratitude.com
See review in City of San Francisco Directory.

☒ Cafe La Haye ☒Ⓜ *American/Californian*
26 | 18 | 24 | $50

Sonoma | 140 E. Napa St. (bet. E. 1st & E. 2nd Sts.) | 707-935-5994 | www.cafelahaye.com
"Extraordinary food" "does come in small packages" – so say the Sonomans who "literally squeeze into" this "delightful spot" off the square for "dynamite" Cal–New American cuisine served with a "small" selection of "interesting wines"; while the kitchen gets props for "surviving the change" from the original chef "without missing a beat", the "happy" front-of-house staffers also get "credit for not colliding into each other" in the 35-seat dining room (which "showcases local art as well").

Caprice, The *American*
▽ 21 | 25 | 20 | $54

Tiburon | 2000 Paradise Dr. (Mar West St.) | 415-435-3400 | www.thecaprice.com
It's "with good reason" this "unique", "upscale" Tiburon aerie has been "an institution in the North Bay" since 1964: the views of "San Francisco Bay and Angel Island" afforded from its "cliffside" "perch over the water" are "magnificent"; as not to compete with what's outside, the interior is appropriately demure (though bedecked with fireplaces), while the "wonderfully" "revitalized" New American menu complements the surroundings – which "you pay much for."

Carneros Bistro & Wine Bar *Californian*
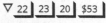
▽ 22 | 23 | 20 | $53

Sonoma | The Lodge at Sonoma | 1325 Broadway (bet. Clay St. & Leveroni Rd.) | 707-931-2042 | www.thelodgeatsonoma.com
If you want to preview some of the "herbs used in the kitchen", look to the "garden outside the dining-room windows" at this "beautiful" Californian hotel eatery; guests get off to a "healthy" start with "great breakfasts", while "even the locals come" for "relaxed" lunches and dinners of "wood-fired pizzas", pasta and salads accompanied by "interesting" wines amassed exclusively from Sonoma and Carneros vintners.

Celadon American *Eclectic*
23 | 21 | 22 | $49

Napa | The Historic Napa Mill | 500 Main St. (5th St.) | 707-254-9690 | www.celadonnapa.com
The "riverfront gem" in the Historic Napa Mill that started the area's "restaurant boom" "still manages to impress" with "elegant", "innova-

tive" Eclectic–New American comfort food served in "generous portions" by a "skilled" staff gloats the green team; the "minimalist"
environment showcases the "original stone" and brick indoors, while
the "glorious" patio is warmed by a fireplace during "cool weather"
and the bar now has a full-liquor license.

Central Market   *Californian/Mediterranean*   ▽ 23 | 19 | 19 | $37

Petaluma | 42 Petaluma Blvd. N. (Petaluma Blvd. S.) | 707-778-9900 |
www.centralmarketpetaluma.com

Members of the "Clean Plate Club" can "often be seen licking their
dishes to glean every morsel" of the "rich" Cal-Med cuisine served at
this "casual" bistro, which is set in a restored turn-of-the-century
building on Petaluma's "main drag"; likewise, the "personable" chef-
owner (whose "creative" menu makes "occasional nods" to his "New
Orleans roots") can frequently be spotted making "tableside visits" to
his "satisfied" patrons.

Chapter and Moon ⓜ *American*   ▽ 21 | 13 | 15 | $29

Fort Bragg | 32150 N. Harbor Dr. (Shoreline Hwy.) | 707-962-1643

"Don't judge this book by its cover" caution Fort Braggers, because despite "teetering on the edge" of the "rough-and-tumble harbor area",
the "fabulously fresh seafood", "organic salads" and "refreshingly
imaginative" American "comfort food" served at the "unassuming",
"moderately priced" breakfast, lunch and dinner joint is "delightful";
the service is "occasionally grumpy", but "the view of the fishing boats
going and coming" is a "classic Mendo Coast experience."

Charcuterie   *French*   22 | 15 | 21 | $36

Healdsburg | Healdsburg Plaza | 335 Healdsburg Ave. (Plaza St.) |
707-431-7213

"Pig out in Downtown Healdsburg" at this "charming" shrine to swine,
which serves a "traditional" French-bistro "blackboard" menu; the "laid-
back" vibe and "fair prices" on both the food (including "some of the best
pork products outside of France") and the Sonoma-centric wines make it
"a favorite among locals and winemakers" alike; N.B. a recent remodel
from porcine-themed to modern may impact the Decor score.

Christophe   *French*   ▽ 20 | 18 | 21 | $32

Sausalito | 1919 Bridgeway (Spring St.) | 415-332-9244 |
www.french-restaurant-marin.com

"It's like being in Montmartre, except for the cigarette smoke" fawn
fans of this long-running, "minuscule" "romantic" Gallic bistro in
Sausalito, noting the "French music playing", occasional cabaret acts
and seating so "squished" you can "hear other patrons sigh over the
delicious roasted rabbit or juicy escargot"; if the less-enthralled feel
the fare is "stuck in the '80s", even they concede you "save a bundle"
on the prix fixe dinners and "unbeatable" early-bird menus.

Cindy's
Backstreet Kitchen   *American/Californian*   24 | 20 | 22 | $41

St. Helena | 1327 Railroad Ave. (bet. Adams St. & Hunt Ave.) |
707-963-1200 | www.cindysbackstreetkitchen.com

You're "likely to run into a winemaker or two" and "comfort-food
queen" Cindy Pawlcyn herself at "Mustards' little sister", a "bright",
"welcoming" "cozy charmer" serving "amazing", "creative" Cal–New

American chow as varied as mole, "meatloaf and duck burgers"; whether you sit among the "happy crowd" in the dining room, "on the patio while wood-fired delights bake in the outdoor grill" or "hang out" at the "well-stocked bar" "watching the pros" "craft" "imaginative" drinks, you'll find it's the "funnest" "backstreet" in St. Helena.

☑ Cole's Chop House *Steak*
25 | 22 | 23 | $59

Napa | 1122 Main St. (bet. 1st & Pearl Sts.) | 707-224-6328 | www.coleschophouse.com

Having proven his chops at Celadon, Greg Cole continues to beef it up, offering "wonderful, dry-aged" choice cuts at this "cool, historic" stone building near Napa Creek that's considered "the place for steak" and a "mean martini" in the South Valley; what a "carnival of flavors" – the porterhouse is "tender", the hash browns "crispy and fluffy", the wine list "solid" and it's all delivered by a "super-friendly staff that helps you along this meat-packed journey"; still, a few grumble it's "pricey" and "inconsistent."

Cook St. Helena *Italian*
24 | 15 | 23 | $39

St. Helena | 1310 Main St. (Hunt Ave.) | 707-963-7088

A "favorite place in the Valley", this "worst-kept secret" "in the heart of St. Helena" lures regulars with "excellent, creative" Northern Italian specialties, "simple", "delicious" pasta and "panna cotta to kill for", all "so satisfying" "you're happy every time" you dine in the "cozy" quarters; we're "fortunate" to have such a "friendly", "comfortable place" where "everyone knows your name" muse admirers – it's "small" enough to "keep the locals in and scare the tourists away."

Cork *Italian*
∇ 19 | 16 | 20 | $28

Sausalito | 317 Johnson St. (Bridgeway) | 415-332-2975 | www.corksf.com

"Tiny with a big heart" and set "away from tourist throng", this "wonderful enoteca" is Sausalito's "wine bar version of *Cheers*": a "comfortable spot to catch up with friends" and enjoy some vino and a "light bite"; from the "inventive" Italian nibbles to the frequently changing "international collection" of "by-the-glass and tasting flights" featuring "little-known varietals and "boutique makers", "quality rules"; still a few hungry for more find the offerings "microscopic", "pricey" and "limited."

Cucina Paradiso ☒ *Italian*
∇ 26 | 15 | 24 | $34

Petaluma | Golden Eagle Shopping Ctr. | 56 E. Washington St. (Petaluma Blvd.) | 707-782-1130 | www.cucinaparadisopetaluma.com

Sure, the "decor is not the greatest" and it's set in an "unlikely" strip-mall location in Petaluma, but don't let that "deter you", because this "unpretentious" "piece of Italy" with "spirited service" is a "real find"; the "wonderfully authentic trattoria fare" is *magnifico* with "attention devoted to the quality of each dish", be it "great" homemade pasta or "sublime" daily specials; little wonder it's "always packed" (didn't mom always say "it's what's on the inside that counts"?).

Cucina Restaurant & Wine Bar Ⓜ *Italian*
24 | 17 | 21 | $35

San Anselmo | 510 San Anselmo Ave. (Tunstead Ave.) | 415-454-2942

San Anselmo-ites not hip to this "tiny" trattoria bustling with the "energy of locals" just don't know Jack – yup, he's the chef/co-owner/"wine guru" overseeing the "fresh yet simple" "rustic Italian" fare (including the "delectable wood-fired pizza" served weekdays) while "sharing stories" and recommending vino pairings that are "always right on"; the "exciting" eats also "never falter", but much like at his city venture, Jackson Fillmore, the "agreeable" staff treats you "better if it knows you."

Cuvée *American*

| 20 | 22 | 20 | $50 |

Napa | 1650 Soscol Ave. (Vallejo St.) | 707-224-2330 | www.cuveenapa.com
Sporting "an attractive interior" and "great courtyard" for soaking up the "nice" Napa weather, this "oasis on Soscol Avenue" from the owners of now-defunct Restaurant Budo conjures up "clean, classic" "beautifully presented" American fare and an interesting bar program featuring "wines from the barrel" that "won't break the bank"; but the less-bubbly cite "uneven pacing" and "inconsistent service" and believe it may still be "too upmarket for locals."

☑ Cyrus *French*

| 28 | 27 | 28 | $110 |

Healdsburg | Les Mars Hotel | 29 North St. (Healdsburg Ave.) | 707-433-3311 | www.cyrusrestaurant.com
"Who needs Napa?" quip fans "blown away" by this "pull-out-the-stops" lair of "luxury", a "gorgeous" "budget-breaker" in Healdsburg's Les Mars Hotel; "no detail is overlooked", from the "caviar cart where the pricey eggs are weighed on a scale with a real gold bullion" to the "decadent" New French "mix-and-match" prix fixe menus "beautifully presented" by staffers that move like a "well-choreographed ballet"; there are no "absurd reservation hoops" to jump through, plus "everyone is treated" "like the leader of a small country" – what a "memorable experience."

Della Fattoria
Downtown Café Ⓜ *Bakery/Eclectic*

| ▽ 26 | 18 | 18 | $23 |

Petaluma | 141 Petaluma Blvd. N. (bet. Washington St. & Western Ave.) | 707-763-0161 | www.dellafattoria.com
Carb-happy habitués clamor for the "excellent housemade" loaves ("used by many local restaurants"), "marvelous European-style breakfast sandwiches" and "better-than-Paris" pastries "tantalizing you in the shiny cases" at Petaluma's "friendly", "wonderful, little" (mostly) daytime Eclectic cafe/bakery; the brick-oven goodies may be the bread and butter of this "hands-down favorite", but devotees declare that the "luscious lunches", including "creative salads", and Friday night dinners with "superb" wine pairings also "rival the best in the city."

Della Santina's *Italian*

| 21 | 18 | 20 | $37 |

Sonoma | 133 E. Napa St. (1st St. E.) | 707-935-0576 | www.dellasantinas.com
The "height of comfort food, Lucca-style" exclaim enthusiasts who "return regularly" to this Sonoma "keeper" to get their Tuscan "carb fix" (try the "heavenly gnocchi") and "consistently delicious grilled meats" accompanied by a "bountiful wine selection"; the "delightful" "courtyard feels like Italy" while the atmosphere is "super friendly" thanks to a "well-intentioned" staff and an owner who has a "real passion for the business."

Deuce *American*

| ▽ 20 | 17 | 20 | $41 |

Sonoma | 691 Broadway (Andrieux St.) | 707-933-3823 | www.dine-at-deuce.com
It "feels like you're going to someone's house for dinner" confide guests who tuck into "inviting", "dependable" New American fare at

this "very pleasant" "local favorite" with a "lovely garden" off Sonoma Square; it's owned by the "nicest couple", plus the "low-key" farmhouse setting "belies a sophisticated kitchen"; add in a "wonderful" wine list that showcases "options from small wineries you won't find" elsewhere and it's easy to see why it's "worth a visit."

Dipsea Cafe, The *American*

17 | 14 | 17 | $20

Mill Valley | 200 Shoreline Hwy./Hwy. 1 (Tennessee Valley Rd.) | 415-381-0298 | www.dipseacafe.com

"Breakfasts rock" at this "homey", "kid-friendly" Mill Valley "crowd-pleaser", a "charming country kitchen" with a "pretty view" of the creek, a "bright atmosphere", an "easygoing staff" and "long waits" on weekends; it's the "perfect stopping-off place before a day of hiking or biking" at nearby Mt. Tam – and now they serve "satisfying", "straightforward" American dinners too; but others are at sea as to why "it's so popular", deeming it "overpriced" and "ordinary."

Downtown Bakery & Creamery ⊘ *Bakery*

24 | 10 | 15 | $14

Healdsburg | 308A Center St. (Matheson St.) | 707-431-2719 | www.downtownbakery.net

"I d'éclair, theirs are the best" swear surveyors sweet on the "awesome sticky buns", "homemade ice creams", pizzas and other goodies produced by this beloved bakery "on the Square" in Healdsburg; created by "a Chez Panisse alum", it also serves "divine" breakfasts and "hearty lunches", so grab a seat in the enlarged cafe, "forget your diet" and dig in.

Drake's Beach Café *Californian*

∇ 19 | 16 | 17 | $24

Inverness | Point Reyes National Seashore | 1 Drake's Beach Rd. | 415-669-1297

It's "fun to grab a table outside and watch the surf" and unobstructed views of Drake's Bay at this funky seaside Inverness cafe located next door to the Visitor's Center; drop in during the day for affordable Californian fare like burgers and sandwiches, made with ingredients sourced from local and sustainable Marin farmers and ranchers, or reserve a 6 or 8 PM seating for the Friday and Saturday night prix fixe menu; N.B. now under new management.

Dry Creek Kitchen *American*

24 | 24 | 22 | $65

Healdsburg | Hotel Healdsburg | 317 Healdsburg Ave. (Matheson St.) | 707-431-0330 | www.charliepalmer.com

"It isn't Aureole", but Charlie Palmer's "fashionable" New American, which "opened the door for fine dining in Healdsburg", proves he can "work his magic on both coasts"; what an "inventive" tasting menu – "it's amazing what they come up with" using locally sourced ingredients – "this is what wine country cuisine is all about" declare denizens who also give a "big cheer for no-corkage charge on Sonoma County" vino brought in; still, parched patrons pout about "inconsistent service" and "minuscule portions" – given the "lovely" "surroundings and celebrity status, we wanted more."

Duck Club, The *American*

20 | 21 | 20 | $48

Bodega | Bodega Bay Lodge & Spa | 103 S. Hwy. 1 (Doran Park Rd.) | 707-875-3525 | www.bodegabaylodge.com

See review in South of San Francisco Directory.

	FOOD	DECOR	SERVICE	COST

E&O Trading Company *SE Asian*   19 | 20 | 18 | $36

Larkspur | 2231 Larkspur Landing Circle (Old Quarry Rd.) | 415-925-0303 | www.eotrading.com

See review in City of San Francisco Directory.

El Dorado Kitchen *Californian/Mediterranean*   23 | 23 | 21 | $47

Sonoma | El Dorado Hotel | 405 First St. W. (W. Spain St.) | 707-996-3030 | www.eldoradosonoma.com

Offering a "perfect blend of casual wine-country unpretentiousness" and "sophisticated" Cal-Med food, this "chichi" "favorite", partly owned by an "alumni of Auberge" in the El Dorado Hotel on the Sonoma plaza, also boasts a "great atmosphere inside" and on the "wonderful patio"; the fare's so "inventive" you can "point to the menu and order anything", and to go-with: a "real sleeper" from the vino list or a "potent" cocktail; still, some snap service is "not up to par" with the "beautiful setting."

El Paseo Ⓜ *French*   23 | 25 | 23 | $62

Mill Valley | 17 Throckmorton Ave. (bet. Blithedale & Sunnyside Aves.) | 415-388-0741 | www.elpaseorestaurant.com

"Bring your lover" or your intended on the day you "ask her to marry you" to this "ultimate date destination" in Mill Valley that's "all about the ambiance", "romance" and "superb" French fare with Japanese and "international influences"; the "new chef is wonderful", and the "terrific" prix fixe menus are "such an adventure" – what a "breath of fresh air"; if a few el pass-o, citing "smug" service, most retort it's "superlative."

Emporio Rulli *Dessert/Italian*   20 | 20 | 15 | $23

Larkspur | 464 Magnolia Ave. (bet. Cane & Ward Sts.) | 415-924-7478 | www.rulli.com

"You feel *molto Italiano*" savoring a "double espresso" in the "European atmosphere" "under the ceiling fresco" or outside on *la strada* while watching the "passing scene" at this "real *pasticceria*" in Larkspur (with Marina and Union Square branches); "replenish your energy with a panini" and wine but hey, "life is short", so opt for "heavenly pastries" from the "well-positioned dessert case" – but don't count on pronto service – the staff "would have to be moving backwards to move any slower."

Étoile *Californian*   25 | 26 | 25 | $71
(fka Domaine Chandon)

Yountville | Domaine Chandon Winery | 1 California Dr. (Solano Ave.) | 707-944-2892 | www.chandon.com

Restored to "its former glory", this "impressive" Californian at Yountville's Domaine Chandon Winery boasts a "spectacular setting" "fit for a champagne baron" "overlooking the immaculate grounds and ponds"; a "tie and coat are commonplace", the staff "makes you feel like a star" and the prix fixe menus are "amazing"; "unwind" with a selection from the "overlooked wine list" or a "glass of bubbly" at the "beautiful bar before dinner" or on the patio after the tour and enjoy an "exquisite evening"; prices are a "bit steep", but it's "worth it for special occasions."

Ⓩ NEW Farm *American*   23 | 27 | 20 | $62

Napa | Carneros Inn | 4048 Sonoma Hwy. (Old Sonoma Hwy.) | 707-299-4882 | www.thecarnerosinn.com

Boasting "a wow setting" overlooking the Carneros Inn's town square, this "stunning", "country-meets-city" Napa newcomer feels like the

	FOOD	DECOR	SERVICE	COST

"gateway to the real wine country"; the kitchen pays "homage to all that's good in season" with "delicious" New American farm fare offset, in PlumpJack-fashion, by a "killer" area-centric vino list at "bargain prices"; don't forget to "leave time on cold nights to have a drink outside by the fire"; still, scoffers sigh service is "earnest but amateurish"; N.B. a new chef took over, which may impact the Food score.

⛾ Farmhouse Inn & Restaurant, The *Californian*

27	25	25	$64

Forestville | Farmhouse Inn | 7871 River Rd. (bet. Trenton & Wohler Rds.) | 707-887-3300 | www.farmhouseinn.com

"Put on your best duds", grab "your most significant other" and "hop over" to this "charming" "old" clapboard farmhouse in "lovely" Forestville hidden "away from the Napa crowds" for the "fabulous" signature rabbit dish; add in a "cheese course that would tempt a Frenchman" and other "wonderfully prepared" Californian fare made with bounty from the family ranch and an "extensive wine list", all "served with a deft hand", and it's plain to see why this "sparkling gem" is on a par with the "biggies."

fig cafe & winebar *French*
(fka the girl & the gaucho)

23	19	22	$37

Glen Ellen | 13690 Arnold Dr. (bet. Horn Ave. & Odonnell Ln.) | 707-938-2130 | www.thefigcafe.com

A "friendly", "casual" "drop-in" option to "cap off" a day of vino tasting, this "lively", "comfy" "stripped-down version of its Sonoma big sister", girl & the fig, is "home away from home" for the "local winemakers" and "loaded" with "Glen Ellen-ites"; the "tantalizing" menu of "reasonably priced", "simple but delicious" country French "treats" made with "only the freshest ingredients" "delivers", plus "there's no corking fee – ever!"

Fish ⛾ *Seafood*

24	13	13	$31

Sausalito | 350 Harbor Dr. (Clipper Yacht Harbor) | 415-331-3474 | www.331fish.com

It's a "must-stop for ultra-fresh, sustainable" Pacific Northwest–style seafood – yes, this "low-key", cash-only counter-service "joint" set "on a dock off the beaten path" in Sausalito may be "tough to find, but worth the effort"; it's "neither cheap, nor leisurely, nor luxurious" – in fact, it feels like a "rustic" "shack on Martha's Vineyard" – but the "fabulously prepared" "just-off-the-boat" fin fare is "delectable" and the view from your picnic table "can't be beat", making it an "outstanding foodie" destination.

Flavor ⛾ *Californian/Eclectic*

20	17	18	$30

Santa Rosa | 96 Old Courthouse Sq. (bet. 3rd & 4th Sts.) | 707-573-9600 | www.flavorbistro.com

There's "something for everyone at this well-priced, always-packed" "family-friendly" "favorite" in Santa Rosa serving an "extensive" Cal-Eclectic menu incorporating Pacific Rim, Med and European cuisines; "grab a seat near the fireplace and people-watch while sipping" the region's "wines at bargain" prices and "noshing" on "tasty" "comfort food"; sure, the "noise level can get out of control", but that's what "gives it a fun atmosphere" (read: "not for a quiet, romantic dinner").

	FOOD	DECOR	SERVICE	COST

Foothill Grille 🅜 *American* (fka Foothill Café)

| | - | - | - | M |

Napa | J & P Shopping Ctr. | 2766 Old Sonoma Rd. (Foothill Blvd.) | 707-257-2270

Back in business after a short hiatus, this casual 42-seat Traditional American joint, hidden in Napa's J & P Shopping Center, is once again filled with locals who come round for original founder Jerry Shaffer's (formerly of Masa's) legendary babyback ribs, crispy calamari and oak-roasted prime rib (served only on Fridays and Saturdays), plus new dinner fare like Baha-style tacos with tortillas handmade next door; the vino list is short, but the no-corkage fee still lures in the wine industry crowd.

Fork 🅜 *Californian/French*

| | 24 | 18 | 22 | $49 |

San Anselmo | 198 Sir Francis Drake Blvd. (bet. Bank St. & Tunstead Ave.) | 415-453-9898 | www.marinfork.com

Although the "chefs keep changing" as frequently as the seasonal Cal-French menu at San Anselmo's "small restaurant with a big heart", the "intense", "interesting plates" of various sizes still "wow" and you can sip "some unusual wines not often seen"; "when we want to pretend we're eating in SF", we head to this "foodie sampler spot", especially for the early-bird prix fixe – "you can dine like royalty without handing over all of your jewels."

Frantoio *Italian*

| | 21 | 19 | 20 | $41 |

Mill Valley | 152 Shoreline Hwy. (west of Hwy. 101) | 415-289-5777 | www.frantoio.com

Starting with "super-fresh ingredients" and "housemade olive oil", this "cavernous" Mill Valley "surprise hidden" in a "funky location" alongside a Holiday Inn Express cooks up "imaginative" Northern Italian dishes that leave you feeling "light yet satisfied", along with "heavenly" pasta and wood-fired pizzas, all delivered by a "devoted" staff; little wonder the "sleek" "contemporary space" is usually "packed with knowing locals"; P.S. from October–December you can watch the "great mill wheels" crush the "newly harvested olives" "behind the glass wall."

⧮ French Laundry, The *American/French*

| | 29 | 26 | 28 | $291 |

Yountville | 6640 Washington St. (Creek St.) | 707-944-2380 | www.frenchlaundry.com

"Thomas Keller's magnum opus" in Yountville may be "famous for being famous but consider yourself royalty if you land a table" at this "haute" French–New American "gastronomic experience" that's "expensive" enough "for three-lifetimes" and "fantastic" enough to "halt all conversation"; "foodies with four hours on their hands" know the drill: "stroll through the gardens", then let the "gracious", "mind-reading" staff handle the "spot-on wine pairings" and "prepare for orbit" as each "wildly imaginative" course in the tasting menus arrives; P.S. it's "better than ever" with new chef de cuisine Corey Lee onboard.

Fumé Bistro & Bar *American*

| | ▽ 19 | 17 | 20 | $39 |

Napa | 4050 Byway E. (Wine Country Ave.) | 707-257-1999 | www.fumebistro.com

"Small" and "intimate", this American bistro in Napa is a "local favorite" thanks to its "happy staff", "high-quality ingredients at fair prices",

	FOOD	DECOR	SERVICE	COST

mix of "comfort foods and more upscale choices" and "bar-only specials"; however, this "tucked-away" joint is so "noisy" and the acoustics so "terrible", the noise-sensitive suggest "eat there, converse later."

Gary Chu's Ⓜ Chinese
22 | 19 | 20 | $28

Santa Rosa | 611 Fifth St. (bet. D St. & Mendocino Ave.) | 707-526-5840 | www.garychus.com

"Consistently pleasurable", local chef Gary Chu's "creative" Chinese spot is "one of the busiest restaurants in Santa Rosa" serving a "small", "up-to-date" menu studded with "favorites" like the "delightful" whole fish and "especially well-liked" tea-smoked duck; still, choosier types tut the decor is "outdated" and the fare "unexceptional."

Gaylord India Indian
18 | 17 | 18 | $36

Sausalito | 201 Bridgeway (bet. Princess & Richardson Sts.) | 415-339-0172 | www.gaylords.com

See review in City of San Francisco Directory.

General's Daughter, The Ⓜ American
- | - | - | M

Sonoma | 400 W. Spain St. (W. 4th St.) | 707-938-4004 | www.thegeneralsdaughter.com

"Chef Preston Dishman takes California-inspired, Low-Country cooking to new heights" at this converted "Civil War–era Victorian" house-cum-restaurant serving "reasonably priced" New American fare along with a top-brass wine pairing program; it's stationed near Sonoma Square, which has been experiencing a semi-renaissance since entering a partnership with Benziger Family Winery, and, in fact, it's their biodynamic, organic gardens (and nearby farms) that supply the produce.

girl & the fig, the French
23 | 21 | 21 | $44

Sonoma | Sonoma Hotel | 110 W. Spain St. (1st St.) | 707-938-3634 | www.thegirlandthefig.com

"Who knew a fig could be the object of such creativity" gush guests at this "delightful" all-day cafe famous for its "rustic" farm-fresh Provençal fare featuring you-know-what and a "cheese plate that would leave a Frenchman speechless"; the "relaxing" setup provides "the perfect Sonoma experience", particularly in the "adorable outdoor garden" or at the bar "where winemakers" "mingle" over the "Rhône-specific" list.

NEW Go Fish Eclectic/Seafood
24 | 22 | 20 | $52

St. Helena | 641 Main St. (Mills Ln.) | 707-963-0700 | www.gofishrestaurant.net

Cindy Pawlcyn's Eclectic seafooder is a "wholesome" addition to her wine-country stable (Mustards Grill and Cindy's Backstreet Kitchen), featuring "super sandwiches" and "exceptionally tasty", "fresh", fish, plus a "magnificent sushi" bar masterminded by Hana's Ken Tominaga; the "gorgeous redo" of St. Helena's Pinot Blanc space has resulted in a "barnlike" yet "somehow very comfortable" setting, swimming with servers who have "movie-star" looks, though fin-icky sorts warn that the staff is "still getting their sea legs."

Guaymas Mexican
17 | 19 | 15 | $34

Tiburon | 5 Main St. (Tiburon Blvd.) | 415-435-6300

Located "steps off the ferry", the deck of this Tiburon watersider presents a "spectacular" vista of San Francisco as well as "rockin'" 'ritas and a menu that offers a "different take" on Mexican fare, which despite having "a real flair" for fish, is just "ok"; indeed, "if only the food" and the service (which seems "hurried and disorganized") "were as good as the view", then this might really be "the happiest place on earth."

Hana Japanese Restaurant Ⓜ *Japanese*   25 | 15 | 19 | $42

Rohnert Park | Doubletree Plaza | 101 Golf Course Dr. (Roberts Lake Rd.) | 707-586-0270 | www.hanajapanese.com

"There is a reason why chefs come" to this Rohnert Park sushi spot "on their days off" – the "dive" "strip-mall location" "hides" some of the "best Japanese food north of the bay"; Ken Tominaga (the "Samurai of Sonoma") "surprises" diners with "creative", "pristine" meals comprised of "exotic" fish ("much of which is flown in from Japan"); P.S. "sit at the bar to get a flavor of what's possible beyond the printed menu."

Heritage House *Californian*   - | - | - | E

Little River | The Heritage House | 5200 N. Hwy. 1 (bet. Andiron & Frog Pond Rds.) | 707-937-5885 | www.heritagehouseinn.com

Perched on cliffs overlooking the craggy Mendocino coastline, this Little River inn made famous in the 1970s film *Same Time, Next Year* is now under new management and has been retooled to look like an English country house; recently installed Aussie chef Nancy Kinchela crafts "classically inspired" Californian "dishes with a lighter twist using fresh, local ingredients" offset by an "outstanding wine list that is made up of small producers" including a special Heritage Collection from Anderson Valley.

Hurley's Restaurant   20 | 19 | 20 | $46
& Bar *Californian/Mediterranean*

Yountville | 6518 Washington St. (Yount St.) | 707-944-2345 | www.hurleysrestaurant.com

Chef "Bob Hurley has really pegged his style" of "creative", "fun" and "powerful" Cal-Med flavors (he also "does a great job with game"), and the "lively crowd" of "locals" that frequents this "solid" Yountville grill is hooked; snag a spot "on the fountain-clad patio" "on a warm evening", order a bottle from the "intriguing", local-vintner-heavy wine list and "stare at the French Laundry–goers" while digging into your "relatively cheap" meal.

Il Davide Ⓜ *Italian*   21 | 18 | 20 | $36

San Rafael | 901 A St. (bet. 3rd & 4th Sts.) | 415-454-8080 | www.ildavide.net

San Rafael "locals continue to flock" to this "neighborhood" Italian ristorante, declaring the "fairly large menu" displays "flair" and the wine list is "excellent"; the "well-prepared" dishes "handled with care" "can't be beat" – they even "exceed" "expectations", plus the outdoor area "brings a hint of Italy to Northern California" in the summertime, making it the "perfect" choice "after the movies on a Saturday night"; still, doubters pout the fare has lost that "inventive feeling."

⛝ Il Fornaio *Italian*   19 | 20 | 18 | $37

Corte Madera | Corte Madera | 223 Corte Madera Town Ctr. (Madera Blvd.) | 415-927-4400 | www.ilfornaio.com

See review in City of San Francisco Directory.

	FOOD	DECOR	SERVICE	COST

Z In-N-Out Burger ⦿ *Hamburgers* | 22 | 10 | 17 | $8 |

Mill Valley | 798 Redwood Hwy. (Belvedere Dr.) | 800-786-1000
Napa | 820 Imola Ave./Hwy. 121 (Napa Valley Hwy.) |
800-786-1000
www.in-n-out.com
See review in City of San Francisco Directory.

Insalata's *Mediterranean* | 24 | 22 | 22 | $41 |

San Anselmo | 120 Sir Francis Drake Blvd. (Barber Ave.) | 415-457-7700 |
www.insalatas.com

The "addictively flavorful", "seasonally inspired" Mediterranean cuisine "goes way beyond salads" at this San Anselmo "scene" assert regulars who saluta the "beautiful", "spacious" dining room hung with canvasses of "fruits and vegetables"; "little-known boutique wines" and "friendly" servers who "know the list well" further elevate the experience - little wonder why It's "earned its reputation as one of Marin's best" for "biz lunches", "special occasions, date night" or simply takeout.

Izzy's Steaks & Chops *Steak* | 19 | 16 | 18 | $40 |

Corte Madera | 55 Tamal Vista Blvd. (Madera Blvd.) | 415-924-3366 |
www.izzysmarin.com
See review in City of San Francisco Directory.

Jimtown Store *Deli* | 19 | 16 | 14 | $19 |

Healdsburg | 6706 Hwy. 128 (1 mi. east of Russian River) | 707-433-1212 |
www.jimtown.com

"Way off the beaten path" in Healdsburg, this "kitschy" country kitchen and general store looks like a "throwback" to a "bygone era", with "delicious" "high-end" breakfasts and sandwiches you can enjoy with a "good glass of wine" on the "funky" patio or take out for a picnic "among the vineyards"; just "don't stop if you're in a big hurry", as it's "impossible to get in and out without buying an odd trinket or toy."

Joe's Taco Lounge & Salsaria *Mexican* | 18 | 16 | 16 | $17 |

Mill Valley | 382 Miller Ave. (Montford Ave.) | 415-383-8164

A "religious experience if you like fish tacos" – and don't forget to "ask for the homemade chipotle salsa" confide worshipers who patronize this "lively" Mexican taqueria, a "Mill Valley standard" "packed" "morning, noon and night" with "soccer families, locals" and "people of all ages"; the "funky", "kitschy decor" evocative of a "Baja roadhouse" adds to its "charm" – "it's a 'joint' in the best sense of the word", plus prices are "reasonable."

John Ash & Co. *Californian* | 23 | 25 | 23 | $57 |

Santa Rosa | 4330 Barnes Rd. (River Rd.) | 707-527-7687 |
www.johnashrestaurant.com

"Nestled in the vineyards next to the Vintner's Inn", this Santa Rosa "mainstay" pleases loyalists with a "beautiful soothing atmosphere", "wonderful" "farm-fresh" Californian fare (the very "definition of 'wine country cuisine'"), an "outstanding" vino list and a "hospitable" staff; it's "lovely for special occasions", plus you can also "request the patio for an even more romantic experience" capped with a drink in the "big cozy cave" of a bar; still, faultfinders feel the "food doesn't match up to the ambiance" – or "its reputation."

| | FOOD | DECOR | SERVICE | COST |

Julia's Kitchen *Californian/French* | 23 | 19 | 21 | $50 |

Napa | COPIA | 500 First St. (bet. Silverado Trail & Soscol Ave.) |
707-265-5700 | www.copia.org

It's a "fabulous" way to "complement a tour" of COPIA's food museum
agree admirers who head to Napa's "bright", "modern" "must-visit"
"monument to Julia" Child (boasting her famed copper pot collection)
for "creative" Cal-French fare that the "legend would approve of"; the
"beautiful" fruits and vegetables are "absolutely the freshest" – most
are "grown outside the door in their own gardens", plus the "kitchen
aims high – and hits the mark"; P.S. the local's prix fixe Thursday dinner is a "steal."

Kabab & Curry House *Indian* | ▽ 21 | 20 | 20 | $32 |

Santa Rosa | 507 Fourth St. (B St.) | 707-523-7780 |
www.kababandcurryhouse.com

Truly a "surprise in Downtown Santa Rosa!" enthuse devotees who
consider the "tasty" Indian fare at this "lovely", "well-decorated"
subcontinental spot a "step above the usual"; the "charming" owner is
"always gracious", the ambiance is "pleasant" and the fare is redolent
of "wonderful spices"; still, cynics skewer the chow as "so-so" and
"nothing really special."

K&L Bistro 🅱 *French* | 25 | 17 | 22 | $42 |

Sebastopol | 119 S. Main St. (Bodega Hwy./Hwy. 12) |
707-823-6614

"What a find!" – it's like "Boul' Mich on the Boul' Main" marvel
Francophiles who fall for this "terrific" bit of "Paris in Sebastopol";
"unpretentious excellence" is the "hallmark" of this "cozy, bustling"
bistro, turning out "cooked to perfection" French fare with "flair" and
"always tempting specials" from the "chalkboard menu", all "impec-
cably" served by a "pleasant" staff; P.S. the prix fixe lunch and dinner
menus are a "steal."

Kenwood 🅼 *American/French* | 22 | 19 | 22 | $47 |

Kenwood | 9900 Sonoma Hwy./Hwy. 12 (Warm Springs Rd.) |
707-833-6326 | www.kenwoodrestaurant.com

Nothing "epitomizes" "casual wine country dining" like this "bright,
cheerful" "oldie but goodie" roadhouse in Kenwood; the "midpriced"
New American–French fare and "terrific wine" offerings "rarely
change", but they're "always outstanding" and "served all day" by a
"cheerful" crew; sure, the digs are "charming" and the "chatty bar" alluring, but loyalists insist that "nothing's better" than a meal on the
"beautiful patio" overlooking the vineyards.

Kitchen at 868 Grant 🅼 *Californian* | ▽ 25 | 18 | 21 | $44 |

Novato | 868 Grant Ave. (Sherman Ave.) | 415-892-6100 |
www.kitchen868.com

In the "wilds of Novato" this "cozy" "neighborhood gem" "fills the vac-
uum" "for fine food", serving a "limited" Californian menu of "complex, but focused" seasonal fare that "changes fairly often"; the
"moody, dark" ambiance and service that's "friendly", not "cloying"
make it "great for a date – or several" – and, in fact, the food "makes
you want to come back time after time"; P.S. check out the "early-bird
prix fixe" menu.

	FOOD	DECOR	SERVICE	COST

La Boulange at Strawberry *Bakery* | 22 | 15 | 16 | $15 |

NEW **Mill Valley** | 800 Redwood Hwy. #125 (off Tiburon Blvd.) | 415-381-1260 | www.baybread.com
See Boulange do Cole review in City of San Francisco Directory.

La Ginestra Ⓜ *Italian* | ▽ 18 | 13 | 19 | $30 |

Mill Valley | 127 Throckmorton Ave. (Miller Ave.) | 415-388-0224
"Maybe it isn't Gary Danko", but loyalists "love the predictable comfort" of this "sweet, little" "old-time favorite in Downtown Mill Valley" that's "ideal for family dinners out" and a "cheap and easy" "red-sauce Italian meal"; the "noisy, happy", "diner ambiance", "hearty portions", "crispy thin-crust pizzas" and no-reservations policy ensure the booths are "solidly packed", though a few whisper the "bar is fairly wide open."

Lark Creek Inn, The *American* | 23 | 25 | 22 | $55 |

Larkspur | 234 Magnolia Ave. (Madrone Ave.) | 415-924-7766 | www.larkcreek.com
Bradley Ogden's "enchanted hideaway" located in a "beautiful Victorian next to a creek" in an "idyllic" Larkspur locale is "still Marin's most romantic", "grand old friend"; even with a "revolving door" of chefs, it's a "consistently memorable" "special-occasion splurge" thanks to the "hearty, high-end" Traditional American comfort food", "elegantly spacious dining room" replete with a "lovely view" of the redwoods and "outdoor dining in the back garden in the summer."

LaSalette *Portuguese* | 23 | 18 | 21 | $42 |

Sonoma | Mercado Center | 452 First St. E., Suite H (bet. Napa & Spain Sts.) | 707-938-1927 | www.lasalette-restaurant.com
"Step off the plaza" and into this slice of "small-town Portugal" for "superb", "authentic homestyle" seafood specialties; it's a "rare opportunity" to partake of "wonderful rustic" dishes prepared in the open wood-burning oven "from mama's recipes" "with the special freshness" of ingredients "Sonoma is famous for" – what a "shot in the arm" to the wine country scene; P.S. sail over for Sunday "breakfast before hitting the wineries."

Las Camelias *Mexican* | 20 | 14 | 20 | $25 |

San Rafael | 912 Lincoln Ave. (bet. 3rd & 4th Sts.) | 415-453-5850 | www.lascameliasrestaurant.com
There are "more than tacos" and "mere burritos" to be had at this "charming" San Rafael spot that "graciously" serves up a "taste of Mexico for those on a budget" in a "remarkably consistent manner"; don't expect a "shallow taqueria" menu – this standby was one of the "first places to elevate" south-of-the-border fare "to gourmet" and it still offers "real" "solid" cooking; N.B. no hard liquor means no margaritas.

❷ La Toque Ⓜ *French* | 26 | 23 | 26 | $105 |

Rutherford | 1140 Rutherford Rd. (east of Hwy. 29) | 707-963-9770 | www.latoque.com
"Toques off" to "incredible" chef Ken Frank – he "continues to wow" purr patrons "impressed by" the "attention to detail" from the "superior" service to the "rustic setting" in Rutherford; "sit by the fire and swoon" over the "always-evolving", "over-the-top" French prix fixe menu – you feel so "pampered" – and "for an extra treat", get the "superb" wine pairings as "excellent" sommelier Scott Tracy's "insights"

may be the "best part of the night"; "yes, you need a special occasion to justify the expense, but that's what celebrating is for, right?"

Ledford House ▨ *Californian/Mediterranean* ▽ 23 | 23 | 22 | $46

Albion | 3000 N. Hwy. 1 (Spring Grove Rd.) | 707-937-0282 | www.ledfordhouse.com

"Spectacular ocean" vistas, a "welcoming atmosphere", "attentive owners" "directly involved in preparing" the "ultrafresh", "hearty un-pretentious" Cal-Med fare and "solid wine choices" make this "un-beatable location" on a bluff in the Albion headlands a "definite must for a fogless sunset dinner on the Mendocino coast"; music aficiona-dos suggest "skip dinner" (served Wednesday–Sunday only) and head to the bar for nightly jazz and the same "view that won't quit."

Left Bank *French* 18 | 20 | 17 | $38

Larkspur | Blue Rock Inn | 507 Magnolia Ave. (Ward St.) | 415-927-3331 | www.leftbank.com

Watch for "sore throats after trying to carry on a conversation" at this "jam-packed", "ear-shatteringly" "noisy" "Lyon-style" Larkspur bras-serie with a "lively bar scene" (and branches South and East of SF); the "happy", "inviting atmosphere" and "satisfying" French fare make it suitable for a "pleasurable" lunch with "local gentry, high-tech deal makers or soccer moms" – or even a "night out with the kids"; P.S. "try the patio on a warm day – if you squint you might think" you're abroad.

Little River Inn *Californian/Seafood* 20 | 20 | 21 | $43

Little River | Little River Inn | 7901 N. Hwy. 1 (Little River Airport Rd.) | 707-937-5942 | www.littleriverinn.com

After dining on new chef Marc Dym's "tasty, well-prepared" Cal sea-food in the main restaurant, "you must have a drink in Ole's Whale Watch Bar" – it's such "fun" and the views of the Mendocino coast are "priceless"; come brunchtime, order the "to-die-for Swedish pancakes" – that's what helps to "build wonderful memories" muse admirers of this "homey" Little River "favorite"; still, a few "can't wait" for the fare to "sing", shrugging it's "still not innovative" enough.

Lotus Cuisine of India *Indian* 22 | 16 | 20 | $25

San Rafael | 704 Fourth St. (bet. Lincoln & Tamalpais Aves.) | 415-456-5808 | www.lotusrestaurant.com

A "jewel in the North" that's been "rolling since it opened", this "wel-coming" standby with a "totally charming open-air ceiling in the sum-mer" "sets the standard for gourmet Indian cuisine" in the San Rafael area; the "wide variety of choices" ensure "you can't go wrong", plus the dishes are "just spicy enough and very flavorful" and the "value"-priced lunch buffet is "one of the better ones around."

MacCallum House *Californian* 24 | 23 | 22 | $48

Mendocino | MacCallum House Inn | 45020 Albion St. (bet. Kasten & Lansing Sts.) | 707-937-5763 | www.maccallumhouse.com

The "charming ambiance" of this "quaint" restaurant/inn occupying a "historic" Mendocino Victorian makes "you feel like you've stepped back in time" but the seasonal, organic Californian cuisine is thor-oughly "modern"; "tourists" flock to "breakfast on the deck" while lo-cals prefer the less "spendy" "casual fare" in the Gray Whale Bar with its "roaring fire, slouchy couches" and "great ocean views."

FOOD | DECOR | SERVICE | COST

☒ Madrona Manor Ⓜ *American/French* 25 | 27 | 25 | $65

Healdsburg | Madrona Manor | 1001 Westside Rd. (W. Dry Creek Rd.) | 707-433-4231 | www.madronamanor.com

Boasting a "setting to make Jane Austen jealous", this Healdsburg Victorian inn/restaurant with "splendid decor" and "lush grounds" is "one of the most beautiful spots in wine country" – and the "nouvelle" American-French fare (much of it "fresh" from its gardens) is "every bit as good" as the atmosphere; add "nonrushed" service and it's a prime spot for anything from "celebrating" to simply enjoying drinks "on the veranda"; P.S. in "chilly" weather, nab a seat "near a fireplace."

Manzanita ☒Ⓜ *Californian/Mediterranean* 20 | 19 | 19 | $45

Healdsburg | 336 Healdsburg Ave. (North St.) | 707-433-8111 | www.manzanita336.com

For "another reason to get to know Healdsburg" head to this Cal-Med kitchen that supporters call one of the "best values on the Square", especially for "wood-fired pizzas" and when it offers its "local's night" prix fixe; the "rustic", "cozy" setting and "attentive" but "not overly friendly" service also satisfy most; still, a handful feel it's "nothing memorable."

Marché aux Fleurs ☒Ⓜ *French* 25 | 20 | 23 | $48

Ross | 23 Ross Common (off Lagunitas Rd.) | 415-925-9200 | www.marcheauxfleursrestaurant.com

Reminiscent of a "country inn in France", this "cozy" "gem" run by a "husband-and-wife" team in "small-town Ross" continues to blossom, offering a Gallic-style "touch of the Mediterranean" via "seasonal" menus showcasing "local products" and a "superb selection" of vins from "boutique wineries"; service is "caring" and the patio's a "delight" in summer; N.B. the owners recently opened AVA in San Anselmo.

Maria Manso World Cuisine ☒Ⓜ *Eclectic* ▽ 20 | 16 | 20 | $43

San Rafael | 1613 Fourth St. (F St.) | 415-453-7877 | www.mariamanso.com

Chef-owner Maria Manso dishes up "interesting" "post–Asia de Cuba" crosscultural fare backed up by "excellent wines" and Korean soju cocktails at this Eclectic "sleeper" in West San Rafael; while some quibble that dinner prices are "out of sync" with the "downscale neighborhood", lunch is deemed "fairly priced" and it's the only place around to grab a Cuban sandwich to go.

Market *American* 22 | 19 | 22 | $37

St. Helena | 1347 Main St. (bet. Adam & Spring Sts.) | 707-963-3799 | www.marketsthelena.com

"After a hard day making world-famous" vinos, "winemakers and their friends" "come in their jeans" to this "cute", "everyday"-people St. Helena "hangout", aka "Cyrus' affordable sibling", concur keen observers of co-owner/chef Douglas Keane's "friendly" enterprise set in an 1800s building; "love the casual attitude" – "why go anywhere else" for "tasty, hearty" "reasonably priced" American eats with "imagination" – plus now there's a "nice" oyster bar too.

Martini House *American* 25 | 25 | 23 | $62

St. Helena | 1245 Spring St. (bet. Main & Oak Sts.) | 707-963-2233 | www.martinihouse.com

Although this "gorgeous" St. Helena "Craftsman home meets Montana hunting lodge" is hidden in a "residential neighborhood", "celebs and regulars" who crave "fine dining without the stuffiness" proclaim it's "in the running with the big dogs of Napa Valley"; the "jolly", "clubby" atmosphere inside and the "romantic" garden patio set the stage for "mushroom freak" chef Todd Humphries' "superb", "light-as-a-cloud" New American fare, but some suggest the "real star" is the "Prohibition-style" "underground (literally) bar" where locals sip selections from the "witty wine list" and cocktails made with the "best ingredients."

Max's *Deli*

16 | 14 | 16 | $25

Corte Madera | 60 Madera Blvd. (Hwy. 101) | 415-924-6297 | www.maxsworld.com
See review in City of San Francisco Directory.

Meadowood Grill *Californian*

20 | 22 | 22 | $49

St. Helena | Meadowood Napa Valley | 900 Meadowood Ln. (Meadowood Rd., off Silverado Trail) | 707-963-3646 | www.meadowood.com
"No wonder" President "Bush chose to stay" at the Meadowood in St. Helena on a recent visit – with its "lovely surroundings" and "resort atmosphere", it feels like a "hidden gem in Napa Valley"; the "casual" Californian grill on-site boasts a "top-notch" setting "overlooking the golf course" and a "beautiful" terrace just made for an "unrushed" breakfast or lunch; stop by for a "relaxing" dinner too "after wine tasting all day" and "you won't want to leave."

Mendo Bistro *American*

25 | 18 | 23 | $35

Fort Bragg | The Company Store | 301 N. Main St., 2nd fl. (Redwood Ave.) | 707-964-4974 | www.mendobistro.com
Chef Nicholas Petti "continues his amazing track record" at this Fort Bragg "labor of love" where he and his "gracious" wife, Jaimi, "act like they've known you forever", "providing creative" New American "cuisine at prices even locals can afford"; "it doesn't have to be a special occasion" to "indulge" in some of the "best crab cakes on the coast" – or to order one of the "excellent" protein entrees cooked as you like it, and to go-with, an "innovative" sauce – but "whenever you do, it always is."

Mendocino Hotel *Californian*

▽ 17 | 22 | 18 | $39

Mendocino | Mendocino Hotel | 45080 Main St. (off Rte. 1) | 707-937-0511 | www.mendocinohotel.com
The "new chef brings a new zest to the Californian menu" agree admirers who find it a "joy to sit" in the Mendocino Hotel's supposedly haunted Victorian dining room with "dark" but "charming period decor" or the more casual garden room and nosh on "traditional and unusual dishes"; "check out" the "beautiful wood bar" in the lobby and sip a drink under the "stained-glass dome" – it's quite the "local gathering spot"; still, ghostbusters sigh this "location deserves better."

ⓩ Mirepoix Ⓜ *French*

26 | 21 | 26 | $50

Windsor | 275 Windsor River Rd. (Honsa Ave.) | 707-838-0162 | www.restaurantmirepoix.com
There's "major creative skill in the kitchen" affirm aficionados agog over the "extraordinary execution" of French "bistro favorites" for "relatively low prices" accompanied by an "amazing" wine list at this "homey", "small beauty in Windsor"; what an "incredible find" – it's "worth the drive from the city" to dine on "dynamite specials" de-

livered by "attentive, accommodating" servers and to soak up the "*très romantique*" atmosphere.

Model Bakery ▣ *Bakery* ▽ 21 | 10 | 13 | $14

St. Helena | 1357 Main St. (bet. Adams & Spring Sts.) | 707-963-8192 | www.themodelbakery.com

"Perfect for breakfast" – try the "rich pastries" with a side of "local gossip" – and a "good stopover for a sandwich" on "amazing fresh-baked bread" or a "sweet snack", this art deco bakery in "beautiful St. Helena" "feels like France"; still, a few loafers who meet their "buddies for coffee" caution that surrounding diners may "eavesdrop", and lament that the "Gen Next" servers are in another "cosmos"; N.B. a branch is slated to open in the New Oxbow Public Market fall 2007.

Monti's Rotisserie & Bar *Mediterranean* 19 | 19 | 18 | $37

Santa Rosa | Montgomery Village Shopping Ctr. | 714 Village Ct. (Farmers Ln.) | 707-568-4404 | www.montisroti.net

"Don't let the mall location fool you" – this Santa Rosa outpost of the Willi's enterprise is a "welcome choice" to "drop after you shop"; it's "packed for a reason" – the "inventive" Med small plates are a "pleasure to share" ("love" how they "mix things up"), the "open fire creates a cozy" feel and there's a "lively bar scene" too; but some skewer the "spotty" service and say it's "not as good" as its "seafood counterparts."

Moosse Café *Californian* 23 | 19 | 22 | $40

Mendocino | 390 Kasten St. (Albion St.) | 707-937-4323 | www.theblueheron.com

Insiders make tracks to this "sweet" "Mendo sleeper" in a "quaint" New Englandy cottage for "wonderful" Californian coastal cuisine, "exciting" specials and on Mondays, an "out-of-this-world" prix fixe menu, all accompanied by "superb local wines"; the "sophisticated but unpretentious" vibe, "pretty patio" and "welcoming staff" make it all the more en-deering – and a "lovely" retreat for lunch or dinner; N.B. closed Tuesdays and Wednesdays during the winter.

Mosaic Restaurant ▣ *Californian* ▽ 25 | 22 | 22 | $47

Forestville | 6675 Front St. (2nd St.) | 707-887-7503

"Fabulous food in Forestville? for real!" marvel early adopters of this "extraordinary" "surprise" that's "even more so for being in such a tiny town"; the chef-owner's "creativity and enthusiasm spills over" into the "friendly service" while the "cozy" room boasting a "super cocktail lounge", a fireplace and a peekaboo view of the kitchen offers a "warm, hospitable setting" for dining on a mosaic of "outstanding" Californian dishes, all "artfully presented"; N.B. there's also a garden patio out back.

Mustards Grill *American/Californian* 24 | 19 | 22 | $47

Yountville | 7399 St. Helena Hwy./Hwy. 29 (bet. Oakville Grade Rd. & Washington St.) | 707-944-2424 | www.mustardsgrill.com

Cindy Pawlcyn's "original" "foodie road stop" in Yountville – the "one that started it all" – still has that "electricity"– even "after all these years" concur groupies who pronounce it a "perennial favorite"; what "wonderful" fare "for the soul" – every Cal-New American "dish is a delight" (check out the "blackboard for the daily menu") and a "perfect complement to a weekend of wine tasting", plus the "skilled" staff "makes you comfortable", whether you're a "winemaker" at the bar or a member of the "rental car set."

Napa General Store Café *Californian/Eclectic* ▽ 20 | 16 | 15 | $23

Napa | Napa General Store | 540 Main St. (5th St.) | 707-259-0762

"Surprisingly damn good" Cal-Eclectic fare with "Asian touches" – "don't miss it" (just get there before 6 PM closing) suggest Downtown Napa visitors who descend on the daytime cafe counterpart of a local gourmet food/craft store, all set in a historic former mill; sit on the "wonderful" pooch-friendly terrace overlooking the Napa River and nosh on stone-oven pizzas and rotisserie meats or tote away a picnic basket; N.B. the Decor score may not reflect a recent renovation.

Napa Valley Grille *Californian* 20 | 19 | 20 | $43

Yountville | Washington Sq. | 6795 Washington St. (off Hwy. 29) | 707-944-8686 | www.napavalleygrille.com

"What a pleasant discovery" in "gorgeous" Yountville agree acolytes of this "inviting", "always dependable" chainlet "standby" offering "beautiful views of the vineyards" and the exhibition kitchen; "go at an off time" and "enjoy" the "interesting" Californian fare and "excellent" wine list in a "leisurely way" in the rustic environs or out on the patio; but the less-enthused find the fare "solid", "not remarkable."

Napa Valley Wine Train *Californian* 15 | 23 | 19 | $69

Napa | 1275 McKinstry St. (bet. 1st St. & Soscol Ave.) | 707-253-2111 | www.winetrain.com

Hop aboard one of the "historic" train cars, "wave to the cars stopped at the crossing gates", "chat with winemakers" and enjoy the "unique" "moving feast" of Californian fare served by a "nimble staff" while making tracks through "Napa's countryside"; it's a "must-do" experience "worth at least one trip" – and a "wonderful way" to "soak in" the "serene beauty" of the "endless vineyards"; but "derailed" detractors rumble "you can't eat the view", deeming the fare "plain and inconsistent."

NEW **Nick's Cove** 🏻Ⓜ *Californian* - | - | - | M

Marshall | 23240 Hwy. 1 (near Miller Park) | 415-723-1071 | www.nickscove.com

Nestled on the shores of Tomales Bay off Highway 1, this lovingly restored oyster bar and roadhouse presents a seafood-centric menu under the direction of Farallon chef Mark Franz, who incorporates local ingredients into the Californian cuisine; its lodgelike dining room boasts a 30-ft. marble bar for shucking, walls made of recycled original-growth redwood and sweeping pier-side views.

955 Ukiah Ⓜ *American/French* ▽ 22 | 18 | 20 | $42

Mendocino | 955 Ukiah St. (School St.) | 707-937-1955 | www.955restaurant.com

"A true Mendo experience awaits" at this "unpretentious" local "favorite", once a "delightful old art studio" and now a "homey" country cabin with "high ceilings and an upstairs loft" "tucked away" off the street in a "gardenlike setting"; if a handful find the fare "hit-or-miss", most applaud the "hard-working" chef-owner's "witty" New American-French menu showcasing "fantastic fresh ingredients" and wines from the North Coast, agreeing it "never disappoints" N.B. open for dinner only Thursday–Sunday.

n.v. Restaurant & Lounge ⓈⓂ *Californian* ▽ 22 | 22 | 21 | $53

Napa | 1106 First St. (Main St.) | 707 265-6400 |
www.nvrestaurantandlounge.com

One of the "best food-and-nightlife combos" to "burst onto the Downtown Napa scene" declare devotees who rave about the "cool bar", "arty" setting and Californian dishes that are "creative without being bizarre"; bring four friends, squeeze into the "intimate" 'love booth' and "play with" "interesting food and wine pairings" while watching the "beautiful people"; but a few carp the fare "sometimes overreaches" adding it's "hard to get excited about a location next to Mervyn's."

Olema Inn *Californian/Mediterranean* ▽ 22 | 23 | 22 | $49

Olema | Olema Inn | 10000 Sir Francis Drake Blvd. (Hwy. 1) | 415-663-9559 |
www.theolemainn.com

Though now under new ownership, it's still "worth the trip" to this "out-of-the-way", "beautifully restored" historic farmhouse and "romantic country inn" near the Pt. Reyes National Seashore agree admirers who settle in for "innovative but not outré" Cal-Med fare made with "local, often organic" ingredients; whether you "sit near the garden before sunset" or relax over a "lovely" lunch or brunch, it's such a "civilized" place – and the "best game in town" for "fine dining."

Ora *Pan-Asian* 21 | 18 | 18 | $42

Mill Valley | 24 Sunnyside Ave. (Blithedale Ave.) | 415-381-7500 |
www.oramv.com

"After many failed attempts", this Mill Valley spot "finally has a real winner" rave admirers who come for a "night of new tastes", sampling "unusual" Pan-Asian plates "attractively served" with "wonderful" flights of sake; but while diehards insist it "keeps getting better", a few grumblers grouch the "too small" portions come up short and suggest trying it when you're "not in a hurry" as service is "unpredictable."

Osake Ⓢ *Californian/Japanese* 22 | 17 | 20 | $35

Santa Rosa | 2446 Patio Ct. (Farmers Ln.) | 707-542-8282

Sake 'O Ⓜ *Californian/Japanese*

Healdsburg | 505 Healdsburg Ave. (Piper St.) | 707-433-2669 |
www.garychus.com

Osaka-trained chef-owner "Gary Chu is everywhere" – and the faithful are "thankful for it", "satisfying cravings" for "creative" Cal-Japanese combinations ("could eat the martini prawns every day!") and "inventive" sushi at the strip-mall Santa Rosa site and "larger", "delightful" Healdsburg sibling; fans keep "coming back" to try the "unique" variations suggesting "sit at the bar" if you want "dinner and a show"; still, a few quibble about "crowded" quarters and sometimes "slow" service.

Pacific Catch *Seafood* 21 | 12 | 16 | $20

Corte Madera | 133 Corte Madera Town Ctr. (off Hwy. 101) | 415-927-3474 |
www.pacificcatch.com

See review in City of San Francisco Directory.

Pangaea Ⓜ *Californian/French* ▽ 25 | 18 | 21 | $53

Gualala | 39165 S. Hwy. 1 (east side of the Hwy.) | 707-884-9669 |
www.pangaeacafe.com

"What a find!" marvel Mendocino-bound travelers who stumble upon this "cozy" North Coast cottage that's "much better than one would expect" in a "seaside town" like Gualala; inside the colorful dining room, a "well-informed staff" ferries out "excellent" but oh-"so-eclectic" (hence, Pangaea), mostly organic Californian-French fare along with "unusual" biodynamic wines; N.B. only open Wednesday–Sunday nights.

Pearl ☒Ⓜ *Californian* ▽ 22 | 17 | 22 | $35
Napa | 1339 Pearl St. (bet. Franklin & Polk Sts.) | 707-224-9161 | www.therestaurantpearl.com

The proprietors of this "tucked-away" Napa jewel "know how to make everyone feel welcome" as they dish out "generous portions" of California "comfort food at its finest" (and oysters, natch) complemented by local wines; the "very small" interior is "spare" but there's "great patio seating on warmer days" and it's a "real bargain in an otherwise pricey town."

Piatti *Italian* 19 | 19 | 19 | $36
Mill Valley | 625 Redwood Hwy. (Hwy. 101) | 415-380-2525 | www.piatti.com
See review in East of San Francisco Directory.

Piazza D'Angelo *Italian* 19 | 19 | 19 | $38
Mill Valley | 22 Miller Ave. (bet. Sunnyside & Throckmorton Aves.) | 415-388-2000 | www.piazzadangelo.com

"Beautiful Marin-ites" gather at this Mill Valley Italian institution where the "people-watching" and "middle-age pickup scene at the bar" – "the weekend watering place" for local "glitterati" – are as notable as the "fresh", "solid" food; the "gracious and welcoming" owners keep things "lively", but grouches groan that it's "noisy" and advise "try for a table in the back" or the quieter upstairs.

Picco *Italian* 24 | 21 | 20 | $45
Larkspur | 320 Magnolia Ave. (King St.) | 415-924-0300 | www.restaurantpicco.com

A "can't-miss evening every time" concur acolytes who alight at this "always packed", "super-popular" Larkspur haunt serving "excellent" Italian "small plates to fit any appetite or craving" and "fairly priced" wines "from all over the world"; chef-owner Bruce Hill "shines" – he has a true "knack" for pairing "unique and wonderful flavors", plus it's delivered by "gorgeous modellike servers"; P.S. if you "don't want to spend a week's paycheck", join the "folks gobbling" "sublime" pies from the adjacent Pizzeria Picco.

Pilar ☒Ⓜ *Californian* 25 | 18 | 25 | $49
Napa | 807 Main St. (3rd St.) | 707-252-4474 | www.pilarnapa.com
"Don't let the simple menu fool you" – "some of the freshest ideas" come out of the open kitchen of this "hospitable" "little jewel in Downtown Napa" where the husband-and-wife chef-owners prepare "true Californian cuisine"; "everything is perfect", even "extraordinary", from the "inventive" fare and "homey atmosphere" to the "passionate service" – "what a grand way to end" a day of wine tasting; if a few find the digs "spartan", even they admit "we're not there to eat the furniture."

Pine Cone Diner ⌽ *Diner* ▽ 19 | 10 | 11 | $27
Point Reyes Station | 60 Fourth St. (bet. 3rd & 5th Sts.) | 415-663-1536
"Colorful" and "funky" with green vinyl-covered tables, round stools and a "1950ish" feel reminiscent of its roots as a former truck stop,

this "gourmet" daytime diner in Point Reyes Station lures locals with "unexpectedly good" New American fare that branches into "inventive" terrain; tuck into the "ample portions" made from local, organic ingredients but leave room – the "pies alone are worth the trip"; N.B. closes around 4 PM.

Pizza Antica *Pizza*

21 | 16 | 17 | $25

Mill Valley | Strawberry Village | 800 Redwood Hwy., Suite 705 (Belvedere Dr.) | 415-383-0600 | www.pizzaantica.com
See review in South of San Francisco Directory.

Pizza Azzurro 🅰 *Pizza*

▽ 22 | 10 | 16 | $19

Napa | 1400 Second St. (Franklin St.) | 707-255-5552
"Always our steady favorite for lunch or a casual dinner", this "simple", "nondescript" Napa storefront "on the corner" backed by a "delightful staff" serves up "seasonal", "delicious thin-crust" pies that are a "real treat" along with a "good little beer and wine selection"; when you're not "in a pizza mood", opt for the "solid salad and pasta choices"; N.B. plans are underway to relocate to Main Street in early 2008.

🅩 Pizzeria Picco *Pizza*

25 | 15 | 19 | $22

Larkspur | 316 Magnolia Ave. (King St.) | 415-945-8900 | www.pizzeriapicco.com
There's "nothing better than kicking back with a good glass of wine", "amazing" wood-fired pizzas with "delicate thin crusts" and "topnotch salads" seemingly "picked that morning" marvel Marinites who carboload at this bite-sized Larkspur offshoot of Picco; also "not to be missed": the soft-serve vanilla ice cream with olive oil and salt (it "changed my life!"); P.S. nab a table outside and "look at Mt. Tam" as there's "very little inside seating" at the counter.

Pizzeria Tra Vigne *Pizza*

21 | 16 | 17 | $27

St. Helena | Inn at Southbridge | 1016 Main St. (Pope St.) | 707-967-9999 | www.travignerestaurant.com
"Perfect" "when you want a break from oh-so-rich food on a wine country weekend" – and "just about the only place to take kids" without spending loads of "dough" declare St. Helenans who congregate at the Inn at Southbridge's pizzeria; service can be "frustrating", but few mind because the Neapolitan crusts and salads are topped with "what the good earth in Napa has to offer", while the "big-screen TV, pool table" and patio ensure there's "never a dull moment"; P.S. "no-corkage makes it a steal."

Poggio Ristorante *Italian*

21 | 23 | 20 | $45

Sausalito | Casa Madrona | 777 Bridgeway (Bay St.) | 415-332-7771 | www.poggiotrattoria.com
"Grab a sidewalk seat" and "people-watch when it's warm" at this "lovely", "bustling" waterfront "favorite" that's "worthy" of the "beautiful" Sausalito setting; it "feels like you're in a seaside Italian town" rejoice locals who heap "praise" – a "rare" thing in this "serene" nexus of "tourist traps" – on the "deep dark wood" decor, "extensive" Tuscan menu spotlighting "seasonal specialties" and veggies plucked from the on-site garden, and the "excellent" wine list; still, a handful huff it's a "tad pricey."

Press *American/Steak*

23 | 25 | 22 | $73

St. Helena | 587 St. Helena Hwy. (White Ln.) | 707-967-0550 | www.presssthelena.com

"Urbane splendor on Napa Valley's main drag" – "what a room!" gasp aesthetes agog over the "chic, citylike decor" at this "dynamite" "modern" American farmhouse-meatery in "sleepy St. Helena; "tuck into" the "unbelievable steak", "homestyle portions" of "simply prepared", "delightful" seafood, poultry and chops, peruse the "fun" to read vino list, and you'll soon "forget all those wine-sotted drivers whizzing past"; but while some quip "bring opm (other people's money)", those pressed for Benjamins opine the "only thing exceptional" are the "high prices."

Ravenous Cafe *Californian/Eclectic*

23 | 18 | 19 | $41

Healdsburg | 420 Center St. (North St.) | 707-431-1302

"Repeat sensualists" and locals "in vineyard boots" "stick with this tried-and-true" Healdsburg "hideaway" with a "hometown feel" serving "creative" Cal-Eclectic cuisine with "zero attitude"; despite "acidorange walls" and a "crazy layout", the "back porch with a neato tiki lounge–type bar" is "the perfect" "wine country fantasy" perch "to hang out on summer nights" or days; still, a handful quip we "might be a little more ravenous" if service weren't "so slow."

Ravens Restaurant, The *Vegan*

▽ 23 | 23 | 22 | $45

Mendocino | Stanford Inn & Spa | Coast Hwy. & Comptche Ukiah Rd. (Hwy. 1) | 707-937-5615 | www.stanfordinn.com

"Start the day" or end it by drinking in "gorgeous views of Mendo Bay" at this standby in the "lovely" Stanford Inn while dining on "beautifully prepared", "innovative" vegan fare made from "flawless organic" ingredients "grown on-site"; "packed with flavor and texture", it's a meal to "remember" especially when matched with biodynamic wines; still, a few find the menu "too rigid", lamenting "it's just not my particular cup of tea"; N.B. breakfast and dinner only.

Z Redd Restaurant *Californian*

26 | 22 | 23 | $70

Yountville | 6480 Washington St. (California Dr.) | 707-944-2222 | www.reddnapavalley.com

"We're always 'reddy' for our next visit" to chef Richard Reddington's "astonishingly good", "much-heralded" Californian "gem" in "glorious", "foodie-filled Yountville"; "prices soar" but so do the "dazzling" à la carte and tasting menus "starring" "fabulous" ingredients "gathered from local farms" and served by an "attentive" staff in "modern, minimalist" digs with a "pretty patio" ("think Finland meets Amish Country") that dispense with that "tired rustic-wine-country cliché"; N.B. the bar has its own "unique menu."

Rendezvous Inn & Restaurant *French*

▽ 27 | 20 | 22 | $49

Fort Bragg | 647 N. Main St. (Bush St.) | 707-964-8142 | www.rendezvousinn.com

Although this "wonderful find" is a "little way out of Mendocino" it's "definitely worth" a rendezvous to "down-to-earth Fort Bragg"; Kim Badenbop was "trained in France and it shows" in his "carefully" crafted, seasonally driven New French fare "cooked to perfection", all "at Laundromat prices"; dining in the "turn-of-the-century" Craftsmanstyle B&B with redwood paneling and a fireplace is "like eating in someone's very gracious home" – the staff is "attentive" and the chef even "visits each table, ensuring that guests enjoy their meals."

Restaurant, The *American/Eclectic* ▽ 23 | 16 | 24 | $43

Fort Bragg | 418 N. Main St. (W. Laurel St.) | 707-964-9800 | www.therestaurantfortbragg.com

Chef-owner Jim Larsen "has been working miracles for decades" at this "charming", "low-key" "locals' favorite" set in a Fort Bragg storefront; fans champion the "innovative" New American–Eclectic fare employing "the freshest seafood available", and "warm, friendly atmosphere that makes up for the lack of fancy" decor, noting that the "fascinating collectibles" and largest collection of "Olaf Palm paintings" "keep the eyes busy"; N.B. dinner served Thursday–Monday only.

Restaurant at Meadowood 🅴 *Californian* ▽ 23 | 24 | 24 | $77

St. Helena | Meadowood Napa Valley | 900 Meadowood Ln. (Meadowood Rd., off Silverado Trail) | 707-967-1205 | www.meadowood.com

"It was well worth the long wait" agree admirers who applaud the "revival" of this "beautifully redesigned" fine-dining Meadowood flagship restaurant in St. Helena serving "innovative" Californian fare in a "unique setting tucked" "among tree-lined fairways"; chef Joseph Humphrey (ex Michael Mina) "leads an all-star cast", conjuring up "superb" flexible prix fixe menus featuring "scintillating" seasonal Napa Valley-sourced ingredients, all designed to complement "one of the greatest wine lists anywhere" (optional pairings available); gilding the lily: a "remarkable" staff.

Restaurant at Stevenswood, The *Mediterranean* ▽ 20 | 20 | 23 | $58

Little River | Stevenswood Lodge | 8211 Shoreline Hwy./Hwy. 1 (1.5 minutes south of Mendocino) | 707-937-2810 | www.stevenswood.com

Changes are afoot at the Stevenswood Lodge, a Little River resort with a "beautiful setting" on the Mendocino coast that's been overhauled by a new owner; the "main glory" is "walking the beaches and headlands", and with chef Randy Lewis (also of SF Mecca) now in place, there may be others too; indeed, diners who noted a "drop-off from earlier brilliance" may want to revisit the "quiet", 28-seat dining room where you can now create Cal-Med tasting menus from globally inspired, locally sourced dishes.

Ristorante Fabrizio 🅴 *Italian* 19 | 15 | 19 | $33

Larkspur | 455 Magnolia Ave. (Cane St.) | 415-924-3332

"Fabrizio [Martinelli] and his mom" treat everyone "like a regular" aver admirers of this "mellow" "family favorite" in Larkspur specializing in "reliable" "Italian home cooking", particularly "delicious" pasta; it's "not pretentious and they don't try to do too much" – instead, the chef "sticks to the basics", pleasing locals with "solid simple" dishes; hit the "wonderful patio in the summer" – but enjoy the "cheerful" vibe anytime.

Robata Grill & Sushi *Japanese* 20 | 15 | 16 | $33

Mill Valley | 591 Redwood Hwy./Hwy. 101 (Seminary Dr.) | 415-381-8400 | www.robatagrill.com

What an "enjoyable way to get your weekly intake of raw fish" muse fin fans who get in the sushi swim at this "quiet, lovely" Mill Valley "crowd-pleaser" that makes you feel "welcome"; "you can't beat" the "creative daily specials" and "excellent appetizer"-size robata dishes, and the tempura is a "treat"; but the less-impressed shrug it's "way too expensive and nothing to jump up and down about."

Royal Thai Thai
22 | 17 | 19 | $26

San Rafael | 610 Third St. (Irwin St.) | 415-485-1074 | www.royalthaisanrafael.com

"You could throw darts at the menu and still be sure" of an "excellent" meal at this "longtime local hot spot" in San Rafael that's served "up-scale" Thai food "for ages"; the "warren of rooms is filled with delectable aromas" and "loyal" subjects are "warmly welcomed" by the "very professional" staff – what a "consistently good dining experience."

Rutherford Grill American
23 | 20 | 22 | $37

Rutherford | 1180 Rutherford Rd. (Hwy. 29) | 707-963-1792 | www.houstons.com

Chainster "Houston's sister" is the "perfect restaurant to enjoy the bottle of wine" that "you just picked up at the winery down the road" agree admirers who, if they have their druthers, choose this "enjoyable" Rutherford "favorite" serving "hearty" American fare; it's "comfortable and relaxed" inside and the patio is "welcoming" (and dog-friendly) – in short, it "lacks the pretension" of some other Napa Valleyites nearby – plus "who can beat the no-corkage" policy?

Sabor of Spain Ⓜ Spanish
18 | 17 | 17 | $38

San Rafael | 1301 Fourth St. (C St.) | 415-457-8466 | www.saborofspain.com

"*Viva Espagne!*" – the "unusual and mostly outstanding" small and large dishes are "the reason to go" to this "comfortable" San Rafaelite, but you'll also "love" the "excellent list of Spanish wines" and "prompt, smooth" service; still, a few carp that tapas portions are "tiny" and "pricey for what you get"; P.S. "you can purchase bottles to take home" along with cookware and ingredients from the retail store next door.

Santé Californian
▽ 24 | 23 | 23 | $61

Sonoma | Fairmont Sonoma Mission Inn & Spa | 100 Boyes Blvd. (Sonoma Hwy.) | 707-939-2415 | www.fairmont.com

"My favorite place to drive to – wish I had a mistress to take along" jest habitués who make tracks to this "wonderful" Californian that's "def-initely up to the quality" of the "elegant, but not stuffy" Fairmont Sonoma Mission Inn; the "well-thought-out" fare is "nicely executed", the wine list "excellent", the "engaging" "staff makes dining enjoy-able" and with the resort right there, there's "no need to leave"; still a handful huff it's "not as memorable as the bill would have me believe."

Santi Italian
23 | 20 | 22 | $46

Geyserville | 21047 Geyserville Ave. (Hwy. 128) | 707-857-1790 | www.tavernasanti.com

This "authentic taverna" "makes its own salumi", sausages and pastas from "local ingredients" – it's "as close" as you "can get to being in Italy" in the "tiny backwater town of Geyserville"; "you simply can't order badly" given the "great Tuscan peasant specialties" and "fabulous" vino list – it's always "worth seeking out", whether you sit by the fireplace on a "chilly wine country night" or on the patio in warm weather; P.S. "drive up during daylight hours" and "appreciate the breathtaking views."

Scoma's *Italian/Seafood*   21 | 17 | 20 | $43

Sausalito | 588 Bridgeway (Princess St.) | 415-332-9551 |
www.scomassausalito.com

See review in City of San Francisco Directory.

Seaweed Café Ⓜ *Californian/French*   24 | 19 | 21 | $45

Bodega Bay | 1580 Eastshore Rd. (Hwy. 1) | 707-875-2700 |
www.seaweedcafe.com

"The sign at the door says it all": "if you want fast food, go somewhere else" – so "don't be in a hurry" advise admirers who celebrate the "West County spirit of Slow Food" at this "hard to find, harder to forget" Cal-French "oasis for hungry travelers" a "few yards from the Pacific"; the "talented team" "puts heart" into the "handcrafted" fare – the "only fresher seafood is still swimming" in Bodega Bay – while the "helpful" service makes you feel "pampered"; N.B. dinner Thursday–Sunday.

Sharon's By the Sea *Italian/Seafood*   ∇ 20 | 14 | 19 | $32

Fort Bragg | Noyo Harbor | 32096 N. Harbor Dr. (Hwy. 1) | 707-962-0680 |
www.sharonsbythesea.com

For "always satisfying" Italian seafood accompanied by Mendo wines, locals pronounce this "wonderful find" right on "the Fort Bragg wharf" by the Noyo Bridge "the place to go"; "scarf down" "standout dishes" like crab Louie made with crustaceans plucked "straight from waters outside the door" of the "cozy", "kitschy" "tight" quarters or sit outside and "watch the Coastguard tugs enter the harbor" and "sea otters leaping."

Sol Food *Puerto Rican*   22 | 16 | 15 | $17

San Rafael | 732 4th St. (Lincoln Ave.) | 415-902-7816
NEW **San Rafael** | 901 Lincoln Ave. (3rd St.) | 415-451-4765
www.solfoodrestaurant.com

When seeking a "touch of Puerto Rico in San Rafael", Sol sisters and brothers "drop in" to this "lively", "bright green" "idyllic roadside hut" and its "newer, more spacious" brother and "fill up" on "jaw-droppingly good" food "at bargain-basement prices" washed down with "cooling iced tea"; sure, "jockeying" for a seat "can be anxiety producing", but the "communal tables turn the meal into a party" – the only thing missing is the "cold beer"; N.B. no BYO accepted.

Sonoma Meritage &   ∇ 19 | 19 | 20 | $43
Oyster Bar *French/Italian*

Sonoma | 165 W. Napa St. (bet. 1st & 2nd Sts.) | 707-938-9430 |
www.sonomameritage.com

Yes, the chef has a "special way with fish" confirm fans of this "festive" French-Italian standby in Sonoma that's "bustling on weekends"; "tables of six are not uncommon – it's the "place to schmooze" thanks to "comfortable" digs, a "beautiful bar" and "friendly" staffers who shake and pour "great martinis"; but while admirers agree the "sometimes memorable meals" merit mention, others grumble it's just "serviceable."

Sooze Wine Bar Café Ⓜ *Californian*   ∇ 18 | 11 | 15 | $37

Petaluma | Great Petaluma Mall | 6 Petaluma Blvd. N. (B St.) | 707-762-3743 |
www.soozewine.com

Although this "hidden gem" in an "unusual setting in an old feed mill" in the Great Petaluma Mall flies under the radar, locals report it's "gaining ground"; "friendly" proprietor Soo Young Kim is everywhere in the "intimate" 24-seat dining room, assisting patrons in pairing the "eclectic" Californian food with the 61-strong wine list; the vinos are described in detail, available by the taste and sold at "half price by the glass during happy hour."

Station House Cafe, The *Californian*   17 | 15 | 15 | $29
Point Reyes Station | 11180 State Rte. 1 (4th St.) | 415-663-1515 | www.stationhousecafe.com
"Aging hippies", "weekend cyclists" and "out-of-town San Franciscans" convene to eat "hearty", "homestyle" Californian fare in the "spacious" garden at this "laid-back" "unexpected find" in "rural" Point Reyes Station; the "tasty" dishes are made with "fresh, organic and local sustainable ingredients", and the vibe is "family-friendly"; still, the Station-impatient grumble "if you've got lots of time" to endure the "slow" service, "this is the place for you."

St. Orres *Californian*   ▽ 24 | 26 | 22 | $59
Gualala | 36601 S. Hwy. 1 (2 mi. north of Gualala) | 707-884-3303 | www.saintorres.com
"Still a treasure" after 30-plus years muse admirers who stop into this "charming" onion-domed restaurant with "Russian decor" on the grounds of St. Orres Bed & Breakfast north of Gualala "after a long days' activity" "along the coast" to indulge in "rich" Californian fare; "genius" chef-owner "Rosemary Campiformio and her kitchen staff" can be "counted on" to offer "something 'wild'" on the "exotic" prix fixe menus – if only you didn't have to go such a "long way" for it.

⏣ Sushi Ran *Japanese*   28 | 20 | 22 | $50
Sausalito | 107 Caledonia St. (bet. Pine & Turney Sts.) | 415-332-3620 | www.sushiran.com
"If there's a better" place to shed your "disposable income" than Sausalito's fin-fare "mecca" that "takes Japanese food to a totally different solar system", "I haven't found it" report gaga "gaijins" and "true aficionados"; whether you "splurge" on rolls that "rival sushi temples in Tokyo" or "innovative", "top-notch cooked entrees", "every meal here" ends with "a sigh of profound pleasure"; P.S. it's "hard to hook a reservation", but remember the adjacent "sake bar has blossomed with its own identity"

Syrah *Californian/French*   25 | 19 | 23 | $49
Santa Rosa | 205 Fifth St. (Davis St.) | 707-568-4002 | www.syrahbistro.com
A "taste of the big city" that lights up "sleepy Santa Rosa's "black hole of dining" scene declare devotees who keep "coming back for more" of chef Josh Silver's "whimsical" Cal-French creations; watch his "amazing touch" at work in the open kitchen (a "great conversation starter if on a date") and remember, the "lusty" tasting menu is an "experience worth paying for" especially when accompanied by the "innovative wine" list; P.S. "in spite of the sort of industrial decor, it always has a warm, friendly feel."

Table Café ⓩ *Californian*   ▽ 24 | 10 | 18 | $21
(fka Tabla)
Larkspur | 1167 Magnolia Ave. (Estrelle Rd.) | 415-461-6787
The name may have changed following a "trademark" dispute with NYC's Tabla, but disciples still beat the drum for this "tiny", "casual"

 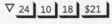

spot in Larkspur known for its "creative" Californian dosas made with "fresh, organic ingredients"; whether you "grab" a "quick lunch", early dinner or "order to-go" "picnic fare" it's always a pleasure" – plus, you leave feeling "full, not fattened" up; N.B. closes at 7 PM.

Taylor's Automatic Refresher *Diner* | 21 | 12 | 14 | $17 |

St. Helena | 933 Main St. (bet. Charter Oak Ave. & Pope St.) | 707-963-3486 | www.taylorsrefresher.com

After "froufrou wine tastings", this "red-picnic table" "oasis in a sea of highfalutin'" St. Helena restaurants (and its Ferry Building sidekick) is the perfect "joint" to "enjoy the sun" and a "pricey" blue cheese or ahi burger with some "Turley Zin" and a "chocolate shake on the side"; "the only improvement would be girls on roller skates" carting food carside and "perhaps some walls" at the Main Street location; N.B. a branch is slated to open fall 2007 in Napa's new Oxbow Public Market.

☑ Terra *American* | 26 | 24 | 25 | $68 |

St. Helena | 1345 Railroad Ave. (bet. Adams St. & Hunt Ave.) | 707-963-8931 | www.terrarestaurant.com

Hiro Sone's "quiet" St. Helena "oasis" of "fine dining", proffering "re-strained service", "excellent wines, of course", and "innovative", "eclectic" New American fare that "blends" "classic European country food with an exotic Asian touch" "looks and feels like a grown-up res-taurant, not a trendy, flash-in-the-pan spot du jour"; the "amazing" dishes aren't "overdone" and the "intimate", "romantic", century-old fieldstone foundry is just the place "to enjoy it all"; little wonder "local foodies" maintain it's "impeccable in every way."

Tra Vigne *Italian* | 23 | 24 | 22 | $54 |

St. Helena | 1050 Charter Oak Ave. (Hwy. 29) | 707-963-4444 | www.travignerestaurant.com

"Still a transporting" experience, this "long-established" St. Helena Italian with a "Tuscan villa" feel boasts an "amazing courtyard", a "pe-rennial favorite" for "sitting out among the breezes" and "unwinding af-ter a day of wine tasting" while nibbling on "subtle but lushly flavored" fare (including "made-to-order mozzarella"); thanks to the new chef, many cheer "the old standards are back and better than ever" – happily, the "well-informed" staffers who "make you feel wanted" never change.

🆕 Ubuntu *Californian/Vegan* | - | - | - | M |

Napa | 1140 Main St. (Pearl St.) | 707-251-5656 | www.ubuntunapa.com

The doors haven't opened yet at this all-day cafe, expected to debut in Downtown Napa in late August 2007, but its name, which means 'hu-manity towards others' in Zulu, already signals its intent; former Manresa chef Jeremy Fox's daily changing sophisticated Cal, vegetarian and vegan cuisine, inspired by ingredients plucked from the restaurant's own biodynamic gardens, will be matched with sustainably farmed wines, to be served in the green dining room, made with recycled wood, and on the garden patio; a yoga studio will operate on the mezzanine.

Underwood Bar & Bistro Ⓜ *Mediterranean* | 22 | 21 | 19 | $43 |

Graton | 9113 Graton Rd. (Edison St.) | 707-823-7023 | www.underwoodgraton.com

Perhaps "closest thing" to a "happening San Francisco scene" in "Podunk" Graton, this "country-yuppie" place is "worth seeking out" for "excellent" Mediterranean tapas, "oysters and special entrees" "after a day of vino tasting"; dark wood and frosted glass create an "urban feel", as do the "noisy" "crowds-beyond-belief for dinner" – so either "bring a megaphone" or just "give your table to someone else and stay at the bar" to revel in "spectacular cocktails and knowledgeable wine service."

Uva Trattoria & Bar Ⓜ *Italian*
21 | **17** | **21** | **$37**

Napa | 1040 Clinton St. (bet. Brown & Main Sts.) | 707-255-6646 | www.uvatrattoria.com

Everyone from "young" "singles" "hanging out" at the "jumping bar" to "winery geezers swapping stories and drinking from the great wine selection" takes "pride" in this "cozy" Napa "hot spot", which cranks out a "reasonably priced", "unexpectedly good" roster of "ever-changing" pizzas, pastas and "old-style Italian standbys with a twist"; "enjoyable live jazz" "five nights a week" further ensures it remains "insanely popular."

Wappo Bar Bistro *Eclectic*
22 | **18** | **19** | **$40**

Calistoga | 1226 Washington St. (Lincoln Ave.) | 707-942-4712 | www.wappobar.com

"In a town where restaurants come and go, it's no wonder" this "Calistoga standby" has "been here for so long", as the "ambitious", often "ingenious", "very Eclectic" "creations", augmented by "delicious local wines you don't see everywhere", continue to "surprise"; although the atmosphere in the redwood-bedecked interior is "quite good", the "delightfully landscaped patio", "blazing with colors" and topped by a grapevine covered arbor, is "too inviting not to eat on."

Water Street Bistro ⊄ *French*
▽ **24** | **14** | **17** | **$23**

Petaluma | 100 Petaluma Blvd. N. (Western Ave.) | 707-763-9563

"Nothing's better than sitting outside on a sunny day" and enjoying the "consistently excellent, interesting" "homemade" breakfasts and lunches offered for "almost sandwich-shop prices" at this "lovely", newly "expanded" French bistro "on the Petaluma waterfront"; "service can be slow", but chef-owner "Stephanie Rastetter makes sure everyone leaves feeling well taken care of", particularly in warm weather, when she stays opens for dinner on Friday and Saturday and creates "wonderful" monthly prix fixes – "a real treat!"

NEW West County Grill *Californian/Italian*
- | **-** | **-** | **M**

Sebastopol | 6948 Sebastopol Ave. (off Hwy. 116, on the Plaza) | 707-829-9500 | www.westcountygrill.com

This midpriced Cal-Italian grill, set in a sprawling, industrial-chic warehouse space just off the main plaza of Sebastopol, has put this sleepy wine country town on the culinary map; its all-star team – including chefs Jonathan Waxman (NYC's Barbuto) and right-hand man Darren McRonald (ex Chez Panisse) – pulls out all the stops, from the de rigueur raw bar to the globe-trotting wine list that still manages to include selections from vineyards just down the road.

Willi's Seafood & Raw Bar *Seafood*
23 | **19** | **19** | **$43**

Healdsburg | 403 Healdsburg Ave. (North St.) | 707-433-9191 | www.willisseafood.net

"Like its counterpart in Santa Rosa", Healdsburg's "seafood-oriented" Willi's "serves a Western version of dim sum" that "charms the socks off you" with "predictably pricey" "amazing raw bar options, equally outstanding drinks" and 40 wines by the glass; not everyone is in "on board" with the "Planet Hollywood"–"steamboat" digs, plus it's really "jumping" on weekends, which "affects service" – nevertheless, it's "relaxing" to "sit outside when the weather is nice and watch the tasting room junkies stumble by."

Willi's Wine Bar *Eclectic*   24 | 18 | 21 | $45

Santa Rosa | Orchard Inn | 4404 Old Redwood Hwy. (Ursuline Rd.) | 707-526-3096 | www.williswinebar.net

"Willi ever quit talking about" the "really clever", "memorable" Eclectic small plates and "small pour" vinos that "tempt you to overspend" wonder loquacious sorts of this "stylish", "funky" Santa Rosa roadhouse; this "gem" in the "empire" is perfect "after a day of wine tasting" or before a "Luther Burbank performance", with an "outdoor patio for warm" days, and a "neighborhood-bar-feeling" interior, filled with the "young and randy" along with "Sonoma's great chefs on their night off."

☒ Willow Wood Market   25 | 18 | 17 | $30
Cafe *Eclectic/Mediterranean*

Graton | 9020 Graton Rd. (Brush St.) | 707-823-0233 | www.willowwoodgraton.com

"Wine biz folks" and tourists alike "drive quite a way" on Russian River "expeditions" to this "consistently charming", "quirky cafe" in the "middle-of-nowhere, no-stoplight town" of Graton for the "ultimate" Eclectic-Med "comfort food"; brunch is "worth getting out of bed for", though afterwards, you "feel like the big fat bumblebees who buzz languidly on the back porch"; "service is often slower than molasses", so check out the "doodads" in the General Store "while waiting for a table."

Wine Spectator Greystone *Californian*   22 | 23 | 22 | $52

St. Helena | Culinary Institute of America | 2555 Main St. (Deer Park Rd.) | 707-967-1010 | www.ciachef.edu

Although it's within the "prestigious culinary institute" in St. Helena's "historic" Christian Brothers Winery, this "real treat" with a "buzzzing" atomosphere isn't "training" ground for "America's future chefs", rather it's run by a professional staff "on top of their game"; "foodies" feast on "well-executed" Californian fare with a "wine list that lives up to the region" while "curious eyes" watch the "culinary show" in the open kitchen and the terrace-inclined take in the "spectacular view overlooking the Valley"; still, some shrug the food "should be better given its pedigree."

Wolf House ☒ *Californian*   ▽ 20 | 19 | 18 | $40

Glen Ellen | 13740 Arnold Dr. (London Ranch Rd.) | 707-996-4401 | www.jacklondonlodge.com

"Belly up to the bar" with "your favorite local winemaker" at this "historic" old "reliable" in "quaint" Glen Ellen ("don't blink or you'll miss it"); the "cozy" "ambiance harkens back to its days as a haunt of writer Jack London", while the "tasty" Californian fare and "well-priced" county-centric wines are the "icing on the cake"; wolf it down in a "window seat" or nab a spot on one of the two decks in the spring and summer – it'll "put you on top of the Sonoma Creek."

Yankee Pier *New England/Seafood*

| 17 | 15 | 17 | $33 |

Larkspur | 286 Magnolia Ave. (bet. King St. & William Ave.) | 415-924-7676 | www.yankeepier.com

Bradley Ogden's "kitschy" "New England clam shacks" in Larkspur and Santana Row feel like "Martha's Vineyard with the Atlantic Ocean outside the door"; chowda and "chatter abound" with "kids getting good and dirty in the sandbox" while "parents tuck into a glass of wine" and "that fabulous butterscotch pudding"; however, crabs cry it's "overpriced beach" fare and bemoan "babysitter-type" staffers; P.S. the SFO branch "makes it fun to get to the airport early."

zazu Ⓜ *American/Italian*

| 25 | 18 | 22 | $47 |

Santa Rosa | 3535 Guerneville Rd. (Willowside Rd.) | 707-523-4814 | www.zazurestaurant.com

A "hidden gem" "if you can find it", this "funky" Santa Rosan from the "hip, young chefs" behind Healdsburg's Bovolo is a "restorative experience"; the vibe is "homey", the atmosphere "relaxing" – it's like "roadside dining ratcheted up a notch or three" – plus the "brilliant", "inspired" New American–Northern Italian fare" and "stunning wine list" "capitalizes" on Sonoma County's "bounty"; "zazu! is what you'll scream when you see the bill" – though perhaps not on midweek 'Pizza & Pinot' nights; N.B. dinner served Wednesday–Sunday.

Zin *American*

| 22 | 18 | 21 | $42 |

Healdsburg | 344 Center St. (North St.) | 707-473-0946 | www.zinrestaurant.com

"It would be a zin not to take advantage of the fairly priced" Zinfandels and other varietals at this "popular pit stop" for tasting-room junkies near Healdsburg Square that also delivers "homespun" New American "comfort food with a Sonoma twist" using "incredible" produce from the owners' garden; add in an "unpretentious" vibe and "blue-plate specials" and it's little wonder why locals "keep coming back week after week"; still, a few zap the "industrial" feel and lament it's too "loud."

Zinsvalley Ⓢ *American*

| ▽ 20 | 16 | 19 | $36 |

Napa | Browns Valley Shopping Ctr. | 3253 Browns Valley Rd. (bet. Austin & Larkin Sts.) | 707-224-0695 | www.zinsvalley.com

"Loved by locals and visitors lucky enough to have found it", this "haunt" with a "friendly" vibe and two fireplaces "tucked away in a Napa strip mall" well off Highway 29 serves up "simple but tasty" New American fare in "lovely surroundings"; "peek in the door and you'll be drawn into" the "cozy" digs with a "patio next to the creek" and fountain – what a "nice place" to "enjoy some Zin"; N.B. there's never any corkage.

Ⓩ Zuzu *Spanish*

| 24 | 18 | 21 | $37 |

Napa | 829 Main St. (bet. 2nd & 3rd Sts.) | 707-224-8555 | www.zuzunapa.com

"Anyone who dines in Napa" without going to this "hip little" Spanish tapas "joint" is "missing out" on a "charming" "experience" reveal locals; the "music, lighting and ambiance are most agreeable", the vibe is "vibrant" and the menu is "constantly changing"; "nibble" on the "unique", "delicious" dishes whipped up by "cooks who care", sip a "fantastic" selection from the "carefully thought out" wine list and you too may become an "instant fan."

SOUTH OF SAN FRANCISCO

Top Food Ratings

Ratings are to the left of names. Lists exclude places with low votes.

28	Kaygetsu		Evvia	
27	Le Papillon		Village Pub	
	Manresa		Bouchée	
	L'Auberge Carmel	25	Cafe Gibraltar	
26	Marinus		Alexander's Steak	
	Sierra Mar		Chez TJ	
	Marché		John Bentley's	
	Navio		Passionfish	
	O'mei		Pacific's Edge	
	Tamarine		Amber India	

BY CUISINE

AMERICAN
27 Manresa
26 Navio
    Village Pub
25 Pacific's Edge
23 231 Ellsworth

ASIAN
26 Tamarine
24 Flying Fish Grill
23 Krung Thai
    Three Seasons
20 Straits Cafe

CALIFORNIAN
27 L'Auberge Carmel
26 Sierra Mar
    Bouchée
25 John Bentley's
    Passionfish

CHINESE
26 O'mei
23 Koi Palace
22 Hunan Home/Garden
20 Fook Yuen Seafood
    Chef Chu's

CONTINENTAL
24 Fresh Cream
23 Anton & Michel
22 Bella Vista
21 Ecco
    Maddalena's

FRENCH
27 Le Papillon
26 Marinus

    Marché
25 Chez TJ
24 Bistro Elan

INDIAN
25 Amber India
23 Roti Indian Bistro
22 Shalimar
    Junnoon
20 Udupi Palace

ITALIAN
23 Osteria
    Casanova
22 Quattro Restaurant
    Pasta Moon
21 Pizza Antica

JAPANESE
28 Kaygetsu
25 Alexander's Steak
23 Fuki Sushi
22 Hotaru
21 Blowfish Sushi

MED./GREEK
26 Evvia
25 Cafe Gibraltar
24 Café Marcella
23 Stokes
    Fandango

SEAFOOD
25 Passionfish
24 Flying Fish Grill
23 Koi Palace
21 Old Port Lobster
20 Fook Yuen Seafood

BY SPECIAL FEATURE

BREAKFAST/BRUNCH

26 Navio
25 Roy's
   Gayle's Bakery
23 Koi Palace
22 Flea St. Café

OUTDOOR SEATING

25 Chez TJ
   Roy's
24 Bistro Elan
23 Anton & Michel
15 Sam's Chowder Hse.

PEOPLE-WATCHING

26 Tamarine
   Evvia
   Village Pub
20 Sino
   Zibibbo

ROMANCE

27 Le Papillon
   L'Auberge Carmel
26 Sierra Mar
25 Chez TJ
   Pacific's Edge

SINGLES SCENES

20 Sino
   Zibibbo
19 E&O Trading Co.
   Nectar Wine Lounge
17 Kingfish

SMALL PLATES

26 Tamarine
23 Stokes
   Three Seasons
20 Cascal
   Straits Cafe

TASTING MENUS

28 Kaygetsu
27 Le Papillon
   Manresa
   L'Auberge Carmel
26 Marinus

WINNING WINE LISTS

27 Le Papillon
   Manresa
   L'Auberge Carmel
26 Marinus
   Bouchée

BY LOCATION

CARMEL/MONTEREY

27 L'Auberge Carmel
26 Marinus
   Bouchée
25 Pacific's Edge
24 Flying Fish Grill

HALF MOON BAY/ COAST

26 Navio
25 Cafe Gibraltar
22 Pasta Moon
   Cetrella Bistro
18 Taqueria 3 Amigos

PALO ALTO/ MENLO PARK

28 Kaygetsu
26 Marché
   Tamarine
   Evvia
24 Bistro Elan

PENINSULA

26 Village Pub
25 John Bentley's
24 Viognier
23 231 Ellsworth
   Koi Palace

SANTA CRUZ/ CAPITOLA

26 O'mei
25 Gayle's Bakery
23 Shadowbrook

SILICON VALLEY

27 Le Papillon
   Manresa
25 Alexander's Steak
   Chez TJ
   Amber India

Top Decor Ratings

Ratings are to the left of names.

28 Pacific's Edge	Anton & Michel
27 Shadowbrook	Tamarine
Navio	L'Auberge Carmel
Marinus	Le Papillon
Sierra Mar	Sino
25 Roy's	**23** Fresh Cream
24 Nepenthe	Village Pub
Manresa	Junnoon
Quattro Restaurant	Tanglewood
Cetrella Bistro	Mantra

Top Service Ratings

Ratings are to the left of names.

27 Marinus	John Bentley's
Le Papillon	Village Pub
26 Navio	Anton & Michel
Sierra Mar	**23** Roy's
25 Manresa	Pacific's Edge
Chez TJ	Maddalena's
Marché	Sent Sovi*
L'Auberge Carmel	Flying Fish Grill
Kaygetsu	Viognier
24 Fresh Cream	Alexander's Steak

Best Buys

In order of Bang for the Buck rating.

1. In-N-Out Burger	11. North Beach Pizza
2. La Cumbre Taqueria	12. Patxi's Chicago Pizza
3. La Taqueria	13. Amici's Pizzeria
4. Taqueria 3 Amigos	14. Dish Dash
5. Burger Joint	15. Krung Thai
6. Pancho Villa	16. Hotaru
7. Gayle's Bakery	17. Shalimar
8. Udupi Palace	18. Zao Noodle
9. Asqew Grill	19. Pasta Pomodoro
10. jZcool	20. Pizza Antica

OTHER GOOD VALUES

Butterfly Bistro	Osteria
Fishwife	St. Michael's
Flying Fish Grill	Taqueria Tlaquepaque
Gator's Neo-Soul	Tarpy's Roadhouse
La Victoria Taqueria	Thea Mediterranean
Mezza Luna	Three Seasons
Old Port Lobster	Zucca

South of San Francisco

Z Alexander's Steakhouse *Japanese/Steak*   25 | 22 | 23 | $69
Cupertino | Vallco Shopping Ctr. | 10330 N. Wolfe Rd. (Wolfe Rd.) |
408-446-2222 | www.alexanderssteakhouse.com
"For expense-account diners with a yen (indeed, unlimited yen) for
a Japanese-style take on the classic steakhouse", this "big barn" of a
meatery in Cupertino's Vallco Shopping Center offers plenty of options "beyond monster hunks of well-marbled cow"; still, die-hard carnivores steer clear of the "killer crustacean" and "Asian-flair
appetizers" and "head straight for the luscious", "life-changing"
"must-try Kobe beef tasting menu" and leave "happily satiated";
P.S. the complimentary "whimsical cotton candy" makes the bill
"sweeter to swallow."

Z Amber Café *Indian*   25 | 18 | 18 | $31
Mountain View | 600 W. El Camino Real (View St.) | 650-968-1751
Z Amber India *Indian*
Mountain View | Olive Tree Shopping Ctr. | 2290 W. El Camino Real
(S. Rengstorff Ave.) | 650-968-7511
San Jose | 377 Santana Row (bet. Olin Ave. & Olsen Dr.) |
408-248-5400
www.amber-india.com
"For the best Indian food" "this side of Hyderabad", "Silicon Valley
high-techies" (many of them expatriates) head to these purveyors of
"the highest quality" "modern" subcontinental fare "as hot as you'll
have it"; at the original "nondescript shopping center" site and young-
est sibling in Mountain View and the "fancy-shmancy outpost in
Santana Row", "the lunch buffet is a good way to sample" the "un-
touchable butter chicken" "at a better price", just "don't be in a rush"
as the waiters "definitely aren't."

Amici's East Coast Pizzeria *Pizza*   20 | 12 | 16 | $19
Mountain View | 790 Castro St. (Yosmite Ave.) | 650-961-6666
Redwood Shores | 226 Redwood Shores Pkwy. (bet. Shoreline &
Twin Dolphin Drs.) | 650-654-3333
NEW **San Jose** | 225 W. Santa Clara St. (bet. N. Almaden &
Notre Dame Aves.) | 408-289-9000
San Mateo | 69 Third Ave. (bet. Dartmouth Rd. & S. El Camino Real) |
650-342-9392
www.amicis.com
See review in City of San Francisco Directory.

Anton & Michel Restaurant *Continental*   23 | 24 | 24 | $56
Carmel | Mission St. (bet. Ocean & 7th Aves.) | 831-624-2406 |
www.carmelsbest.com
"One of Carmel's long-standing" "special-occasion" destinations,
this "warm, welcoming" "classic Continental", with fireplaces and
a "European garden setting" replete with reflecting pools and
fountains, exudes a "romantic" "old-world feel" that makes it a
"must to repeat every visit"; devotees appreciate the "wonderful oil
paintings", "attentive" service and exhaustive wine list; still, a handful
are "not that impressed" given its "exalted reputation" – it feels "a bit
out of the 1960s."

	FOOD	DECOR	SERVICE	COST

A.P. Stump's Chop House *Steak*   21 | 21 | 22 | $47

San Jose | 163 W. Santa Clara St. (bet. Almaden Blvd. & San Pedro St.) | 408-292-9928 | www.apstumps.com

A "Silicon Valley expense-account" set makes for some "swanky scenery" at Jim Stump's "sophisticated" Downtown San Jose steakhouse that can get "super busy during conventions", or "before a concert or Sharks game"; regulars rally for the "hobnobber happy hour", "succulent" beef and entrees with a "gourmet twist", plus the "excellent" cult Cabernet wine list; if a few grumble that it's "unfathomly pricey" ("miss the original menu") even they admit that this incarnation "still delivers."

Arcadia *American*   23 | 21 | 22 | $59

San Jose | San Jose Marriott | 100 W. San Carlos St. (Market St.) | 408-278-4555 | www.michaelmina.net

"It's nice to see the best of the old menu left" at Michael Mina's "friendly" San Jose outpost, which recently morphed into a New American steakhouse but still features "stellar" "signature dishes" that "show whimsy" like lobster corn dogs and a "luxurious whole chicken"; if a few aesthetes find the ambiance too "businessy" (they "need to shake" that "'hotel' feeling"), fans feel it's "surprisingly hip for a Marriott" marquee and a "fine choice" for "entertaining VIP clients" or that "special occasion."

Asqew Grill *Californian*   18 | 11 | 15 | $15

NEW **San Jose** | 200 S. First St. (bet. San Carlos & San Fernando Sts.) | 408-275-1962 | www.asqewgrill.com

See review in City of San Francisco Directory.

Barbara's Fishtrap ⊘ *Seafood*   19 | 12 | 17 | $23

Princeton by the Sea | 281 Capistrano Rd. (Hwy. 1) | 650-728-7049

Nothing "satisfies your fried seafood fix" better than the "fresh-as-it-gets" fish 'n' chips "served with a smile" and a brew at this "funky", "authentic seaside shack"; nosh on "simple" fare as the water practically "laps at your toes" surrounded by "nets hanging from the ceiling" and "lovely views" of Princeton harbor; "the catch": the "'fishing line' is out the door", but you can get it to go and sit at the picnic tables.

Barracuda *Brazilian/Japanese*   ▽ 17 | 18 | 17 | $36

Burlingame | 347 Primrose Rd. (Burlingame Ave.) | 650-548-0300
NEW **Daly City** | Serramonte Mall | 98 Serramonte Ctr., Suite 127H (Gellert Ave.) | 650-757-6833
www.barracudasushi.com

See review in City of San Francisco Directory.

Basin, The *American*   ▽ 19 | 18 | 21 | $43

Saratoga | 14572 Big Basin Way (5th St.) | 408-867-1906 | www.thebasin.com

"Comfortable" and "convivial", this "homey" Downtown Saratoga neighborhood bar and restaurant is a "safe bet" for a "casual" night out; the "sophisticated", "satisfying" seasonal New American food (with Spanish and Italian influences) is "spot on", the martini bar is a "highlight" and the garden seating under a 200-year-old oak tree is "especially nice", but what keeps locals "going back" is the staff and owner's "incredible" "hospitality."

	FOOD	DECOR	SERVICE	COST

Basque Cultural Center *Spanish* | 20 | 13 | 17 | $30 |

South San Francisco | 599 Railroad Ave. (bet. Orange & Spruce Aves.) | 650-583-8091 | www.basqueculturalcenter.com

Although "no one would mistake" this South San Francisco Basque "community center" boasting a "high volume of seniors" and "old-world charm" for a "fine-dining" destination, it's "worth going out of your way for"; expect "hearty service" and food that's "delicious without the fuss" – "like someone's mom made" – served in "generous" family-style portions", plus "cocktails for a song" ($5 martinis); still, critics scoff "don't bother" – it's "like dining in a large school cafeteria."

Bella Vista *Continental* | 22 | 22 | 22 | $54 |

Woodside | 13451 Skyline Blvd. (5 mi. south of Rte. 92) | 650-851-1229 | www.bvrestaurant.com

Come for the "stunning mountaintop views of the South Bay and the ocean" – the drive up Skyline is a "treat" – but stay for the "romantic setting", "handsomely prepared" Continental dishes and "flaming desserts"; add in tuxedoed waiters who make you "genuinely feel pampered" and a wine list "devoted to the classic California Cab", and it's little wonder Casanovas looking to "get 'lucky'" "take their dates" to this "lodgelike" Woodside stalwart; still, critics counter the "tired" food and decor "suffer from the same malaise" as the staff.

Bistro Elan ⓈⓂ *Californian/French* | 24 | 18 | 21 | $46 |

Palo Alto | 448 S. California Ave. (bet. Birch St. & El Camino Real) | 650-327-0284

"Come on down to California Avenue and check out the real Palo Alto" suggest admirers of this "tiny" "hidden gem", a "local's pleaser" that's "worth squeezing into", especially on those "special occasions" when you "don't want to go into the City"; "love the intimacy" – it's a "class act from start to finish", proffering "delicious, creative" seasonal "French comfort food à la California" in a "quaint", "real Parisian" atmosphere; P.S. "if you want to hear and be heard", head to the "lovely" garden.

Bistro Vida *French* | 18 | 18 | 18 | $36 |

Menlo Park | 641 Santa Cruz Ave. (bet. Curtis St. & El Camino Real) | 650-462-1686

For *"la bonne franquette"* (informal meal) "in the suburbs", Downtown Menlo Park patrons "walk through the red velvet curtains" and into this neighborhood boîte where the "blackboard menu of bistro food done right" is served in an "authentic noisy" setting; it's "much more French in overall execution" than that other Gallic standby a "few doors down" insist a few *amis* who "keep going back", both for the "friendly soccer-loving owner" and some of the "best weekend brunches."

Blowfish Sushi To Die For *Japanese* | 21 | 20 | 16 | $41 |

San Jose | 335 Santana Row (bet. Stevens Creek Blvd. & Tatum Ln.) | 408-345-3848 | www.blowfishsushi.com

See review in City of San Francisco Directory.

Bouchée *Californian/French* | 26 | 22 | 22 | $64 |

Carmel | Mission St. (bet. Ocean & 7th Aves.) | 831-626-7880 | www.boucheecarmel.com

This "cozy" restaurant/enoteca continues to be "one of the very best in Carmel" thanks to its "country character", "esoteric", "excellent selection" of regional vinos (courtesy of the adjacent Bouchée Wine Merchants shop) and staff that "makes you feel like you're its most important guest"; new chef Christopher Dettmer (ex Campton Place) is now manning the recently remodeled exhibition kitchen, preparing "enticing" new French dishes fashioned from Monterey coast ingredients, which may outdate the Food and Decor scores.

Buca di Beppo *Italian*   14 | 15 | 16 | $25

Campbell | Pruneyard Shopping Ctr. | 1875 S. Bascom Ave. (Campbell Ave.) | 408-377-7722
Palo Alto | 643 Emerson St. (bet. Forest & Hamilton Aves.) | 650-329-0665
San Jose | Oakridge Mall | 925 Blossom Hill Rd. (Santa Teresa Blvd.) | 408-226-1444
www.bucadibeppo.com

"No one leaves without leftovers" at this "kitschy" Italian "crowd-pleaser" with a "*Tony and Tina*-like atmosphere"; yeah, the "monstrous", "hearty" family-style portions are "plenty good, but not great", but they still hit the spot "if you're not expecting gourmet", and besides, this "gaudy" "party place" that's suitable for kids, "great for groups" and inexpensive enough for "undergrads, or those who wish they still were", is more about the "fun", "festive atmosphere" than anything else.

Burger Joint ● *Hamburgers*   18 | 12 | 14 | $13

South San Francisco | San Francisco Int'l Airport | Int'l Terminal, Boarding Area A | 650-583-5863
See review in City of San Francisco Directory.

⊞⊞⊞ Butterfly Bistro *Vietnamese*   - | - | - | I

San Bruno | The Shops at Tanforan | 1150 El Camino Real (Sneath Ln.) | 650-553-5151 | www.butterflybistro.com

A more mainstream spin-off of chef Robert Lam's Butterfly on the Embarcadero's Pier 33, this upbeat family-friendly Vietnamese bistro provides a pleasant yet affordable dining option in the recently renovated Shops at the Tanforan Mall in San Bruno; the kitchen prepares a wide range of regional standards, all served in a sleek bamboo-and-lantern-accented dining room or the adjacent cocktail lounge; N.B. heated, outdoor seating on the patio is in the works.

Cafe Gibraltar Ⓜ *Mediterranean/Vegan*   25 | 21 | 22 | $41

El Granada | 425 Avenue Alhambra (Palma St.) | 650-560-9039 | www.cafegibraltar.com

"Just off the beach" in El Granada, this "destination" showcases "imaginative" Mediterranean and vegan meze and meals in an "intimate" Moroccan-style setting; whether you "sit cross-legged on comfortable pillows" at the "floor-level" booths in back or grab a traditional table to become "mesmerized by the action" in the open kitchen in front, "you won't forget the magical aromas" and flavors of the "wizard" chef-owner's "seasonal menu", made with "fresh ingredients" from his "on-site garden" and "lots of heart."

Café Marcella Ⓜ *French/Mediterranean* 24 | 19 | 22 | $43

Los Gatos | 368 Village Ln. (bet. N. Santa Cruz & University Aves.) | 408-354-8006 | www.cafemarcella.com

"Consistently delicious" French-Med cuisine with "pizzazz" coupled with an "excellent range" of *vins* are the hallmarks of this "absolute gem" of a "boutique restaurant" in Los Gatos; it may be "hard to carry on a conversation when its full", but if you "come early to beat the crowd and the noise", you'll find it "great for a date" or a "special" "dinner with the family"; N.B. there's also an attached wine shop.

Café Rustica Ⓜ Californian
▽ 23 | 20 | 22 | $37

Carmel Valley | 10 Del Fino Pl. (Carmel Valley Rd.) | 831-659-4444 | www.caferusticacarmelvalley.com

It's understandably "crowded with locals", but carloads from the coast declare it's "worth the drive inland to laid-back Carmel Valley" for the "friendly hospitality" and "reasonably priced" "variety of hearty", "creative" Californian dishes (with shout-outs to the "delicious" "thin-crust", wood-fired pizzas and "enormous salads") proffered at this "terrific" cottage; inside can get "a little cramped and noisy", but on a "hot, dry day or a starlit night", the "gorgeous patio" "feels like Tuscany."

Cantankerous Fish, The Seafood
18 | 17 | 18 | $34

Mountain View | 420 Castro St. (bet. California & Mercy Sts.) | 650-966-8124 | www.thecantankerousfish.com

"Close to the Mountain View Center for the Performing Arts", this fish house draws "pre-theater" parties for "reliable, fresh seafood" served in "not-flashy" preparations, while non-ticket-holders enjoy "live jazz" on Wednesday and Sunday evenings; "business-lunchers" are reeled in for "casual meals" on the patio, but a few seeking something more than just "nice-ish" gripe it's "not worth going back" for "middle-of-the-road" fin fare.

Cantinetta Luca Italian
▽ 22 | 21 | 20 | $47

Carmel | Dolores St. (bet. Ocean & 7th Aves.) | 831-625-6500 | www.cantinettaluca.com

Restaurateur David Fink's "wonderful addition" brings "well-done" pastas, pizzas, whole-roasted fish and other Italian staples (not to mention an all-Boot wine cellar and a variety of "great" cured meats, much of which is dried on the premises) to the "fairy-tale setting of Downtown Carmel"; for being so "family-friendly" and "high-energy", the dining room, with beamed ceilings and brick walls encircling an open kitchen, is surprisingly "gorgeous."

Casanova French/Italian
23 | 23 | 21 | $54

Carmel | Fifth Ave. (Mission St.) | 831-625-0501 | www.casanovarestaurant.com

If you're feeling amorous in Carmel, breeze into this "gloriously romantic" "old-timer" where "rich", "filling" Northern Italian–French selections are served in "cozy" candlelit rooms and a "charming", pooch-friendly "semi-enclosed terrace"; some, though, feel the mostly prix fixe menu is "too expensive" ("you'll need a price-be-damned attitude to plunge too far into the huge wine list" as well), and the servers, though "enthusiastic", can be "disorganized" (there are also reports they're "not very nice to travelers").

Cascal Pan-Latin
20 | 22 | 17 | $34

Mountain View | 400 Castro St. (California St.) | 650-940-9500 | www.cascalrestaurant.com

"Go with a large group" and "share" the "delicious small plates" with "imaginative" Pan-Latin "twists" to have "a real taste experience" at this "bright", "trendy" spot in Downtown Mountain View, where "creative cocktails" and "refreshing sangria", not to mention "fun live music on weekends", add to the "party atmosphere"; however, "sometimes shoddy service", "long waits, even with reservations", and "noise levels" that can "induce tinnitus" have some sniffing they "shall not return."

Cetrella Bistro & Café *Mediterranean*   22 | 24 | 20 | $48
Half Moon Bay | 845 Main St. (Monte Vista Ln.) | 650-726-4090 | www.cetrella.com

"Like a beacon calling to you" from "tiny" Half Moon Bay, this "upscale" "mainstay" entices with "creative" Mediterranean meals and a "high-profile wine list" served in an "elegant" setting reminiscent of an "old farm" and warmed by a "beautiful" central fireplace; if some locals lament it's "priced for tourists that frequent the Ritz-Carlton" nearby, they still hit the "smart bar" to soak up the "excellent" live jazz; N.B. the recent departure of the chef and owner may impact the scores.

Chantilly ☒ *Continental*   ▽ 25 | 23 | 26 | $62
Redwood City | 3001 El Camino Real (Selby Ln.) | 650-321-4080 | www.chantillyrestaurant.com

Catering to "the old-money crowd from nearby Atherton", this "elegant", "genteel" Redwood City "charmer" provides Continental cuisine and service that are as "superb" as they are "old-fashioned"; some non-"AARP card"-carriers think it's as "stuffy" as "eating in your grandmother's dining room", but even they're won over by co-owner Gus, the "ultimate host."

Cheesecake Factory, The *American*   16 | 16 | 16 | $28
San Jose | 925 Blossom Hill Rd. (bet. Oakridge Mall & Winfield Blvd.) | 408-225-6948
Santa Clara | Westfield Shoppingtown Valley Fair | 3041 Stevens Creek Blvd. (Santana Row) | 408-246-0092 ●
www.thecheesecakefactory.com
See review in City of San Francisco Directory.

Chef Chu's *Chinese*   20 | 13 | 19 | $26
Los Altos | 1067 N. San Antonio Rd. (El Camino Real) | 650-948-2696 | www.chefchu.com

For more than three decades this "pace-setting gourmet Chinese" "staple" in Los Altos has remained "always packed" with "loyal customers" "enjoying" its "well-prepared and seasoned" Mandarin meals; while sightings of "Chef Chu or his son" "overseeing it all" thrill as much as "looking at photos of celebrities that have eaten there", some decry the food's "not spectacular" – and neither is decor that, despite a recent refresh, looks like it's "from the Yuan Dynasty."

NEW Chef Wai *Chinese*   ▽ 20 | 15 | 19 | $31
San Mateo | 111 E. Fourth Ave. (S. San Mateo Dr.) | 650-342-8388

"Once you dine" at this "high-end" newcomer, a Cantonese banquet hall in Downtown San Mateo that's the "closest you can get to a traditional Hong Kong–style restaurant on the Peninsula", "you know Wai" "it's the perfect place to take the family for an upscale" Chinese feast; "try the Shanghainese dumplings", "fresh"-from-the-tank seafood and "delicate" "meatless but not heartless" options – or just ask chef Andy himself (of SF's "defunct Harbor Village") to "stir up" a "treat."

Chez Shea *Eclectic*

▽ 22 | 17 | 19 | $19

Half Moon Bay | 408 Main St. (Mill St.) | 650-560-9234 | www.chez-shea.com

Nicknamed "Chez Squared", this "relaxed" Half Moon Bay "favorite" "named for the daughter" of the "amazing chef" who also co-owns Cafe Gibraltar is "quicker, more homey" and "cheaper" than its "big sister", but still serves up "complex, delightful" Eclectic dishes "from Mexico to the Middle East" made with organic ingredients; there's "no better place for lunch" (even if it is counter service during the day), and the fare is "never boring", no matter the meal.

Chez TJ 🅂🅼 *French*

25 | 22 | 25 | $94

Mountain View | 938 Villa St. (bet. Castro St. & Shoreline Blvd.) | 650-964-7466 | www.cheztj.com

Mountain View's "most romantic" "gem" has "got fine dining figured out" agree admirers who settle into the "intimate rooms" of this "converted 1890 Victorian for "exceptionally well put-together" New French prix fixe menus "prettily presented" with "outstanding pacing" by a "top-shelf" staff; "nothing beats a cocktail on the front porch on a cool Valley evening" before the "varied", "complex dishes roll out of the kitchen" – "the attention to detail is worth every calorie"; still, a few feel it's "oh-so-pricey" for "minuscule" portions.

Club XIX *Californian/French*

▽ 25 | 25 | 25 | $75

Pebble Beach | The Lodge at Pebble Beach | 1500 Cypress Dr. (Palmero Way) | 831-625-8519 | www.pebblebeach.com

"Every golfer should dine overlooking the 18th at Pebble Beach" – what a "spectacular view" reveal well-heeled links-lovers who "rehash the rounds" over the "fantastic" weekend brunch or dinner at this Lodge hotel restaurant sporting an "upscale ambiance" "with prices to match"; even if you're not a player, "go after dark and pay attention to the food" – old-school French-Californian classics like "delicious whole Dover sole" – matched by an exhaustive wine and cognac selection.

Dasaprakash *Indian*

▽ 21 | 18 | 19 | $20

Santa Clara | 2636 Homestead Rd. (bet. Kiely Blvd. & San Tomas Expwy.) | 408-246-8292 | www.dasaprakash.com

Skip the cheaper curry couriers and head to this "eclectic", "funky", "quietly hushed" Southern" subcontinental spot in Downtown Santa Clara (with branches in Delhi and Southern California) for "refined" vegetarian "delicacies" including "true dosas" ("not your garden variety") and Thali plates; it's "filled with Indians, a true testament" to the kitchen's "expertise at layering spices and depth of flavor", and customers are "welcomed as treasured, old friends."

Deetjen's Big Sur Restaurant *Californian*

▽ 22 | 21 | 21 | $40

Big Sur | Deetjen's Big Sur Inn | 48865 Hwy. 1 (30 mi. south of Carmel) | 831-667-2377 | www.deetjens.com

Whether or not you bunk in the "rustic" rooms and cottages on the grounds, a "magical" meal of Californian fare at this "wonderfully atmospheric", "fairy-tale" inn with "rough-hewn wood walls and funky exterior" feels like a "slice of tranquility" – it's a "must during a Big Sur stay"; the "lovely" alfresco breakfasts and fireside dinners boasting "delicious, freshly picked local" ingredients and a "very well-chosen wine list", navigated by a "cheerful" staff, complete the "cozy", "romantic" picture; N.B. no lunch.

NEW Dio Deka *Greek*

| - | - | - | E |

Los Gatos | Hotel Los Gatos | 210 E. Main St. (Los Gatos Blvd.) | 408-354-7700 | www.diodeka.com

Perhaps the "best new restaurant in the South Bay" declare disciples who descend on Hotel Los Gatos' "spectacular" estatoria for "divine" Greek and Mediterranean cuisine fit for a god and an "extensive wine list" worthy of Dionysus; five of the partners behind this group effort (including key folks from Evvia and Kokkari) work the floor, ensuring "incredible, personal service" that reflects *filoxenia,* the art of hospitality; whether you start with an ouzu cocktail or finish with coffee brewed over hot sand, expect a big fat night out on the town.

Z Dish Dash ⑤ *Mideastern*

| 23 | 16 | 17 | $23 |

Sunnyvale | 190 S. Murphy Ave. (Washington Ave.) | 408-774-1889 | www.dishdash.net

"If it wasn't for the noise level" and the lunch crowds "spilling over on to the sidewalk" ("even after the expansion next door"), this "frenzied" falafel ferrier in Sunnyvale churning out "fresh" "Nuevo Arabic" meals would easily be "Silicon Valley's premier Middle Eastern" "oasis"; still, "with food like this, who's listening" to all the "chatting and dishes clanging" marvel mavens content to sop up the "tender" signature lamb *mansaf* stew with "endless warm pita."

Don Pico's Original Mexican Bistro *Mexican*

| ▽ 20 | 14 | 19 | $24 |

San Bruno | 461 El Camino Real (Jenevein Ave.) | 650-589-1163

As the name suggests, this San Bruno standby with a funky bordello feel and a "congenial atmosphere" is "not your typical" south of the border–style cantina; amigos "wax rhapsodic" about the "unique twists" on "tasty" seafood and "creative" specialties accompanied by pitchers of sangria and tequila margaritas and pack in on "absurdly" crowded, "fun" live music nights to see the likes of Mexican Frank Sinatra and Patsy Cline take the mike.

Duarte's Tavern *American*

| 21 | 12 | 19 | $28 |

Pescadero | 202 Stage Rd. (Pescadero Rd.) | 650-879-0464 | www.duartestavern.com

This "all-time favorite" "historic roadhouse" "in the boondocks" of Pescadero "reeks of the Old West, where horses were as welcome as people" – yes, siree, it's an American "dive worth the drive" just to hear the "delightful" staff "call you 'hon'"; "don't give away your tourist status by ordering the artichoke soup" – instead, order it "half 'n' half", mixed into a green chile "combo", and "repeat this mantra": "fresh fish and olallieberry pie"; yup, "simple is sometimes better."

Duck Club, The *American*

| 20 | 21 | 20 | $48 |

Monterey | Monterey Plaza Hotel & Spa | 400 Cannery Row (Wave St.) | 831-646-1700 | www.woodsidehotels.com
Menlo Park | Stanford Park Hotel | 100 El Camino Real (Sand Hill Rd.) | 650-330-2790 | www.stanfordparkhotel.com

"Don't overlook" this "charming" "favorite" quartet for an "intimate dinner" or a "very special" Sunday brunch confide insiders who

	FOOD	DECOR	SERVICE	COST

paddle over for the "wonderful view" (in Bodega and Monterey) and "delicious", "heartwarming" New American standards served in "casual yet elegant" clubby digs; but squawkers quack that "for the setting and price, you'd expect more" – "nothing strikes you as unusual or even real tasty."

E&O Trading Company *SE Asian*   19 | 20 | 18 | $36

San Jose | 96 S. First St. (San Fernando St.) | 408-938-4100 | www.eotrading.com
See review in City of San Francisco Directory.

Ecco Restaurant 🖫 *Californian/Continental*   21 | 19 | 19 | $50

Burlingame | 322 Lorton Ave. (Burlingame Ave.) | 650-342-7355 | www.eccorestaurant.com
"You can walk right by" this "traditional" ("not trendy") Continental-Californian "favorite" in Burlingame and "not know there's a restaurant here, but once you "discover" the "rose-painted room" "quiet" enough for "conversation with friends" you'll follow the lead of the "older crowd" and become a "return patron"; a "sure hand in the kitchen" makes the "delicious" "food shine" and the "wine list is broad", but a few feel service is "inconsistent" (sometimes "cordial", sometimes "snotty").

Eulipia Restaurant & Bar Ⓜ *American*   ▽ 20 | 18 | 19 | $37

San Jose | 374 S. First St. (bet. E. San Carlos & San Salvador Sts.) | 408-280-6161 | www.eulipia.com
"Come enjoy" a "good variety" of New American dishes at this "consistently pleasant", "relatively sophisticated" "favorite" "conveniently located" in Downtown San Jose "near the opera, symphony and theater" with "excellent pre-concert service"; they "try to be creative, and sometimes they pull it off", nevertheless the less-enthused feel it's "lost its edge", declaring it's "dependable, but uninspired."

�Z Evvia *Greek*   26 | 23 | 22 | $47

Palo Alto | 420 Emerson St. (bet. Lytton & University Aves.) | 650-326-0983 | www.evvia.net
Palo Alto locals "hate to spread the word" about this "hip" yet "homey" Hellenic sister of SF's Kokkari, which "never fails to deliver" "ambrosial" "countryside cooking like Yaya" used to make, but "updated" with a modern Mediterranean "flair"; it's forever "jampacked" – "but who cares" – it's "always a joy" to indulge in "incredible" Greek dishes fashioned from the "finest fresh ingredients" straight from the "charming wood-fired oven" (you won't "leave a speck on your plate"), plus the "genuinely warm service makes the experience quite special."

Fandango *Mediterranean*   23 | 21 | 22 | $44

Pacific Grove | 223 17th St. (bet. Laurel & Lighthouse Aves.) | 831-372-3456 | www.fandangorestaurant.com
Everyone "from 12-year-old granddaughters to 97-year-old fathers" "come away feeling special" after dining at this "delightful spot" in Pacific Grove; the "cozy and warm" "Mediterranean villa" feel, "delicious" dishes like "super-rich lamb", an "amazing" wine list and "wonderful service" help ensure that meals here are "always an enjoyable occasion"; still, a few killjoys counter it's "caught in a time warp" and "in urgent need of an update."

Fishwife at Asilomar Beach *Caribbean/Seafood*   23 | 14 | 20 | $32

Pacific Grove | 1996 1/2 Sunset Dr. (Asilomar Ave.) | 831-375-7101 |
www.fishwife.com

"Far more charming" than most places on the Wharf, this "laid-back",
"everyday" "family-friendly" "locals' favorite" in Pacific Grove
serves up "excellent" "fresh" sustainable seafood with an "interesting" Cal-Caribbean accent; it may not be "fine dining", but the "funky
decor is just right for the beachy area" and it feels like a "welcome
break from the overt affluence of the Pebble Beach/Spanish Bay" area,
plus "Madame Fishwife" "greets you" and "makes you feel like her
long-lost" pal.

Flea St. Café Ⓜ *American*   22 | 18 | 21 | $44

Menlo Park | 3607 Alameda de las Pulgas (Avy Ave.) | 650-854-1226 |
www.cooleatz.com

You "feel good, like you're doing your small part", dining at this "all-
organic, all the time" trailblazer, the "pinnacle" of Jesse Ziff Cool's
"empire" (aka "the Alice Waters of Menlo Park") crow "localvores",
"vegetarians and meat eaters" who "commune" over "straight-up"
"homey" Cal–New American dishes boasting sustainable, seasonal ingredients; the staff "takes care of the little things that make the big effect" serving "without pretension" in one of Silicon Valley's "most
inviting settings"; still, a handful feel it "needs a boost."

Flying Fish Grill *Californian/Seafood*   24 | 19 | 23 | $43

Carmel | Carmel Plaza | Mission St. (bet. Ocean & 7th Aves.) | 831-625-1962

"Atmosphere is king" at this "unassuming" "underground gem", an
"absolute Carmel favorite" with "'70s"-style "warm boxwood"-paneled
walls and a "distinctive" "dungeon/ski-cabin feel" tucked away in a
Downtown shopping center; "personable" chef-owner Kenny
Fukomoto "makes you feel at home", preparing "excellent" Cal-Asian
seafood with "clean, bright flavors" that "always interest your taste
buds" – and "consistently fly above other local choices" – ensuring
a "satisfying" experience.

Flying Fish Grill Ⓜ *Californian/Seafood*   ▽ 21 | 10 | 16 | $18

Half Moon Bay | 99 San Mateo Rd. (bet. Main St. & Rte. 92) | 650-712-1125 |
www.flyingfishgrill.net

An "idyllic seaside shack without the sea (it's not within view)", this
"modest" Half Moon Bay "hole-in-the-wall" cranks out "excellent"
Californian seafood including some of the "best fish tacos on the
Coast" at "value" prices; "blink and you'll miss" it as you head toward
Highway 1, but "once you try it, you'll be hooked"; P.S. on a "sunny
day, sit out on the tiny patio."

Fook Yuen Seafood *Chinese/Seafood*   20 | 10 | 13 | $28

Millbrae | 195 El Camino Real (Victoria Ave.) | 650-692-8600

Even "Chinese food snobs" say this Sino seafooder is "worth a trip to
Millbrae" for "fresh", "authentic" dim sum and banquet food where,
after you "stop giggling at the name", you "take a number", get in
line and "wait to be processed" while watching everything "go by
on trays"; the "not-so-flashy" "atmosphere could use some spiffing
up", but most just "ignore the decor" and concentrate on the "solid"
"well-priced" fare.

	FOOD	DECOR	SERVICE	COST

Forbes Mill Steakhouse *Steak*   23 | 21 | 21 | $60

Los Gatos | 206 N. Santa Cruz Ave. (Royce St.) | 408-395-6434 |
www.forbesmillsteakhouse.com

"Meat, meat and more meat" including "Kobe, Kobe, Kobe" and "big
cuts" of Angus too – yes, this "rustic" Los Gatos steakhouse (with a
Danville branch) brimming with "lots of character" and a "festive environment" and a staff that's "polite, not pushy", is the "one to write
home about"; "every last thing" on the "impressive menu" is "delicious, including the side dishes" – but since you're in "expense-
account territory", you may need a "pound of $20s for the bill."

☒ Fresh Cream *French*   24 | 23 | 24 | $66

Monterey | Heritage Harbor | 99 Pacific St. (bet. Artillery & Scott Sts.) |
831-375-9798 | www.freshcream.com

A "delightful" "way to spend the evening" in Monterey, this French
spot serves up "consistent" "old-fashioned" fare featuring "the
finest fresh local seafood" topped with traditional "heavy sauces";
you "can't beat the locale", especially the "fabulous" view overlooking the old Wharf and Bay, and "no detail is forgotten" by the
"gracious" servers, making this "romantic" "time warp" "first class
all the way."

Fuki Sushi *Japanese*   23 | 18 | 18 | $40

Palo Alto | 4119 El Camino Real (bet. Arastradero & Page Mill Rds.) |
650-494-9383 | www.fukisushi.com

Japanophile's looking for "authentic" eats go wild for the "excellent"
fish and shabu-shabu at this pricey Palo Altan where the "professional", "cheerful" (yet often "slow") service shuttles out "homestyle"
Japanese fare alongside the "wonderful" sushi and sashimi that's
among "the best in Palo Alto"; the "chef's choice" is a real treat for
"epicurean explorers" or Tokyo businessmen with "Japanese expense
accounts", and the private tatami rooms are great for both "business
meetings" and "boisterous" gatherings.

Gabriella Café *Californian/Italian*   ▽ 22 | 17 | 20 | $37

Santa Cruz | 910 Cedar St. (bet. Church & Locust Sts.) | 831-457-1677 |
www.gabriellacafe.com

"Innovative" "Cal-Italian comfort food" lovingly prepared from "organic and sustainable ingredients", complemented by locally leaning
wine make this "tiny" "hot spot" in Downtown Santa Cruz "the best for
miles around"; with "great" service, prices that "won't break the bank"
and a "fantastically" "charming" setting, it's the ideal lair for "a romantic dinner" (or alfresco lunch), as long as you "don't mind sitting
on top of your neighbor."

NEW Gator's Neo-Soul Café Ⓜ *Southern*   - | - | - | I

San Mateo | 129 S. B St. (bet. 1st & 2nd Aves.) | 650-685-8100 |
www.gatorsneosoul.com

At his casual cafe in Downtown San Mateo, chef Glenn 'Gator'
Thompson (of the shuttered Alcatraces) reinterprets Southern classics for health-conscious California diners – think organic, pan-fried
chicken and black-eyed peas over wild brown rice; plans are in the
works to open Gator's Back Porch BBQ, an eco-friendly, take-out
smokehouse and deli, behind the premises in winter 2007.

	FOOD	DECOR	SERVICE	COST

Gayle's Bakery & Rosticceria *Bakery*   `25` `12` `18` `$17`

Capitola | 504 Bay Ave. (Capitola Ave.) | 831-462-1200 |
www.gaylesbakery.com

"Take a number and start drooling" over the "dreamy" pastries "in the
display case" and "mouthwatering smells emanating from the rotisserie" at this "incredible" Capitola bakery/cafe that's "a lovely stop-
ping point" off Highway 1 between "the Bay Area and Monterey"; with
a mix of "blue-plate specials", "barbecue", sandwiches and salads,
"you could eat every meal here and be quite content", but "cafeteria-
style" service prompts most patrons to tote their picnic provisions
"to the beach."

Grasing's Coastal Cuisine *Californian*   `23` `19` `19` `$48`

Carmel | Jordan Ctr. | Sixth St. (Mission St.) | 831-624-6562 |
www.grasings.com

"Delightful" Californian cuisine that's "creative" but "not too far out"
keeps chef Kurt Grasing's "quiet", "warm and welcoming" "hideaway"
"on a backstreet" on Carmelites' radars; the prix fixe menu options
(paired with wines culled from a 1,000-bottle cellar) are "great values", but local pet-owners really appreciate that it "allows dogs" on
the patio – "they'll even bring treats" for them!

Happy Cafe Restaurant ⊉ *Chinese*   ▽ `22` `5` `12` `$15`

San Mateo | 250 S. B St. (bet. 2nd & 3rd Aves.) | 650-340-7138

There's "not much ambiance" – "think paper place mats and plastic
tablecloths" – but this "fantastic" San Mateo Shanghainese spot is
"worth the drive for city folk" for "authentic" lunches and dim-sum
brunches starring "melt-in-your-mouth" dumplings (dinner served
Wednesday only); sure, service is "not too cordial", but with "great food"
for "hardly any cash" "everyone should patronize" this "hidden gem."

Hotaru *Japanese*   `22` `11` `15` `$21`

San Mateo | 33 E 3rd Ave. (bet. S. El Camino Real & S. San Mateo Dr.) |
650-343-1152 | www.hotarurestaurant.com

"Generous portions" of "consistently delicious" "Japanese staples" "at
reasonable prices" ensure the line to get into this "tiny" San Mateo
spot is "always" "out the door" – but it's "well worth the wait" for the
"fresh rolls" and "well-prepared" bento boxes "for non-sushi-eaters";
the service can feel "rushed" and the dining room can get "noisy", but
if you "just eat and get outta there", you'll feel "satisfied."

Hunan Garden *Chinese*   `22` `11` `18` `$24`

Palo Alto | 3345 El Camino Real (bet. Fernando & Lambert Aves.) |
650-565-8868

Hunan Home's Restaurant *Chinese*

Los Altos | 4880 El Camino Real (Showers Dr.) | 650-965-8888
See Hunan Home's Restaurant review in City of San Francisco Directory.

Iberia *Spanish*   `21` `21` `16` `$45`

Menlo Park | 1026 Alma St. (bet. Oak Grove & Ravenswood Aves.) |
650-325-8981 | www.iberiarestaurant.com

"Just steps from Downtown Menlo Park", this "secluded" Spaniard is
"just like being in Barcelona" with "housemade sangria" and a "whole
page" of "stunning tapas" to share in the "romantic bar" (the only
place they are served during dinner), while heartier options are of-

fered in the dining room; however, after alleging that the "waiters and owner are arrogant" and "brusque" at times, many find the mandatory 19-percent service charge to be "out-of-line" and "will never go again."

☑ Il Fornaio *Italian*   19 | 20 | 18 | $37

Burlingame | 327 Lorton Ave. (bet. Burlingame Ave. & California Dr.) | 650-375-8000

Carmel | The Pine Inn | Ocean Ave. (Monte Verde St.) | 831-622-5100

Palo Alto | Garden Court Hotel | 520 Cowper St. (bet. Hamilton & University Aves.) | 650-853-3888

San Jose | Sainte Claire | 302 S. Market St. (San Carlos St.) | 408-271-3366
www.ilfornaio.com

See review in City of San Francisco Directory.

Il Postale *Italian*   20 | 16 | 18 | $31

Sunnyvale | 127 W. Washington Ave. (bet. Frances St. & S. Murphy Ave.) | 408-733-9600 | www.ilpostale.com

"The smell of garlic hits you" the moment you step into this Sunnyvale post office–turned–Italian bistro, "which leads to grumbling stomachs" that the "friendly owner" and his staff sate with "large portions" of both "traditional" and "inventive" eats, washed down with "fun martinis" and "decent wines"; the "lovely outdoor garden" trumps the "small, packed" interior, but the "solid values" prove "perfect for underdressed professionals" and couples all around.

☑ In-N-Out Burger ● *Hamburgers*   22 | 10 | 17 | $8

Millbrae | 11 Rollins Rd. (Millbrae Ave.) | 800-786-1000

Mountain View | 1159 N. Rengstorff Ave. (Amphitheatre Pkwy) | 800-786-1000

Mountain View | 53 W. El Camino Real (bet. Bay St. & Grant Rd.) | 800-786-1000

San Jose | 5611 Santa Teresa Blvd. (bet. Blossom Hill Rd. & Summerbrook Ln.) | 800-786-1000

Daly City | 260 Washington St. (Sullivan Ave.) | 800-786-1000
www.in-n-out.com

See review in City of San Francisco Directory.

Izzy's Steaks & Chops *Steak*   19 | 16 | 18 | $40

San Carlos | 525 Skyway Rd. (off Hwy. 101) | 650-654-2822

See review in City of San Francisco Directory.

☑ John Bentley's Ⓢ *Californian*   25 | 21 | 24 | $54

Redwood City | 2915 El Camino Real (bet. Dumberton Ave. & Selby Ln.) | 650-365-7777

Woodside | 2991 Woodside Rd. (bet. Cañada & Whiskey Hill Rds.) | 650-851-4988 Ⓜ
www.johnbentleys.com

The recently renovated Woodside location is "charming" with a "clubby feel" and "better suited for romantic dinners and small group entertaining" while the Redwood City site's "peaceful", "almost hip" "interior belies the fact that it's on El Camino Real" yet both "always make us feel at home"; the "fantastic" Californian cuisine is "adventurous enough to be fun" plus the "attentive" but "not intrusive" servers know the "creative wine list" (a "rarity") making it an "excellent" place for a "splurge."

Juban *Japanese*   17 | 15 | 16 | $33

Burlingame | 1204 Broadway (Laguna Ave.) | 650-347-2300
Menlo Park | 712 Santa Cruz Ave. (2 blocks west of El Camino Real) |
650-473-6458
www.jubanrestaurant.com

"Forget the all-you-can-eat BBQ posers – this is *yakiniku* done right, in
proud Japanese form" confide insiders who dig the "tasty marinated
meats" and "do-it-yourself" concept at this outfit in Burlingame,
Menlo Park (and Japantown too); it's a "favorite with the kids – they
love cooking on the in-table grills", and it's all "presented simply and
neatly"; still, kvetchers quibble that it's "overpriced" and you leave
"smelling" like "tender beef."

Junnoon *Indian*   22 | 23 | 19 | $45

Palo Alto | 150 University Ave. (High St.) | 650-329-9644 |
www.junnoon.com

"Wonderfully light yet rich" offerings are given "glamorous names"
and served in "snazzy SF-esque" surroundings at this "amazingly
modern" Indian akin to "Mumbai" eateries or even "Tabla, NYC" and
London's Cinnamon Club, from whence the on-site and consulting
chefs come; the "delectable" edibles are "expensive but rewarding",
suited for "power lunches" or a "special night on the town" in Palo
Alto – and a "far cry from neighborhood curry houses"; still, fence-
sitters deem it a "roller coaster of imaginative" dishes – some "work
marvelously", some "come up short on tastiness."

jZcool *Californian*   20 | 12 | 12 | $16

Menlo Park | 827 Santa Cruz Ave. (bet. Crane St. & University Dr.) |
650-325-3665 | www.cooleatz.com

How "cool that all the food" at Flea St.'s recently reconceptualized
Menlo Park sibling is "organic, local, sustainable" – and more "impor-
tantly", "delicious", marvels the green team that's long turned up for
"quick lunches" and now returns for dinner Tuesday–Saturday; the deli
cases are history and the "bare-bones" digs have been revamped, but
the "tasty salads", panini, Californian tapas and large plates still make
you "feel like you're doing your body a favor"; N.B. the revamp may
impact the scores.

Kabul Afghan Cuisine *Afghan*   22 | 15 | 19 | $28

San Carlos | San Carlos Plaza | 135 El Camino Real (bet. Hull Dr. & Oak St.) |
650-594-2840

"Don't let the strip-mall location dissuade you" from trying this
"perennial neighborhood favorite in San Carlos" that's "nicer on the
inside" – especially if "you've never enjoyed Afghan cuisine" before,
find yourself "in the mood for something different" or just "have a
hearty appetite"; "can't go without" the "very tasty shish kebab grilled
to your liking" or the "authentic", "absolutely delicious" stews – "we're
lucky to have this place on the Peninsula."

NEW Kanpai 🅢🅜 *Japanese*   ∇ 24 | 19 | 16 | $37

Palo Alto | 330 Lytton Ave. (bet. Bryant & Florence Sts.) |
650-325-2696

Sushi-seekers raise a toast and shout '*kanpai*' to this "tiny", "nicely designed" "upscale cousin of Menlo Park's Naomi"; what a "wonderful

addition to the Palo Alto dining" scene assert admirers who applaud the "passionate" "real-deal" sushi chef tapped "from New York's famous Nobu 57" who prepares omakase menus boasting "unique, upscale combinations" of "consistently fresh fish" and "presents it as art" from behind the 15-seat Japanese wood bar.

Ⓩ Kaygetsu Ⓜ *Japanese*　　28 | 18 | 25 | $80

Menlo Park | Sharon Heights Shopping Ctr. | 325 Sharon Park Dr. (Sand Hill Rd.) | 650-234-1084 | www.kaygetsu.com

"You'll be hard-pressed to find Japanese food made with more care and flair" without "getting on a jet to Tokyo" attest admirers who say get thee to this "spartan" yet "transcendent" "power dining spot for VCs" in a Menlo Park strip mall; the fish is "über-fresh" and the seasonal kaiseki dinners are "extraordinary", from the "beautiful presentation" that's like "art on a plate" to the "melt-in-your-mouth creations" that taste like "heaven"; the "drawback: you must offer your paycheck to the sushi gods" ("genius chef"/owner Toshi) but it's "worth every penny."

Kingfish　*American/Cajun*　　17 | 19 | 16 | $37

San Mateo | 201 S. B St. (2nd Ave.) | 650-343-1226 | www.kingfish.net

"I wouldn't call it elegant, but you don't always want daintiness" confer San Mateo anglers hooked on the "vibrant social scene", "expansive setting" and "New Orleans–inspired" Cajun–New American menu offering "something for everyone"; it's "loud and jazzy" and the "beautiful" art deco "interior measures up" too, with "stained glass and lots of windows on the first floor" offset by "plush" upper levels; if few spout it's "pedestrian", most declare it's "definitely a return situation."

Koi Palace　*Chinese*　　23 | 15 | 11 | $33

Daly City | Serramonte Plaza | 365 Gellert Blvd. (bet. Hickey & Serramonte Blvds.) | 650-992-9000 | www.koipalace.com

For "divine" dim sum, "delicious" Hong Kong–style dishes and "unusual seafood" specialties, press on to this "palatial" Daly City "emperor"; experienced enthusiasts exult in the "truly inventive" "exotic" creations, but there are also plenty of "high-quality, high-flavor" "basics" for neophytes too; just remember that "standard warnings apply: go early", "check your patience in the parking lot", then "endure a line to China" on weekends – and "do not expect solicitous service."

Krung Thai　*Thai*　　23 | 13 | 16 | $22

San Jose | 642 S. Winchester Blvd. (Moorpark Ave.) | 408-260-8224

"Judging by the crowd that often congregates" in the "humble surroundings" of this San Jose "favorite", "everyone and their mother agrees" that the "awesome Thai grub" is "economical", "excellent" and some of the "hottest in town"; still, the less-exuberant confide they'd "come more often" if the "service were better", kvetching "you might feel rushed", plus the "long wait" is "annoying."

Kuleto's　*Italian*　　20 | 19 | 19 | $42

Burlingame | 1095 Rollins Rd. (Broadway) | 650-342-4922 | www.kuletostrattoria.com
See review in City of San Francisco Directory.

	FOOD	DECOR	SERVICE	COST

Kurt's Carmel Chop House *Steak* ▽ 23 | 19 | 22 | $51

Carmel | Fifth Ave. & San Carlos St. | 831-625-1199 |
www.carmelchophouse.com

Years after establishing Grasing's, his eponymous Californian up the
street, "Kurt found a way to fit a steakhouse into cozy Carmel", culti-
vating a following with "delicious" chops, Kobe beef burgers, weekend
prime rib platters and sides made with "fresh ingredients", capped
with an "incredible wine selection"; the "personable staff" " treats you
well here" – you'll have a "meal that won't disappoint"; still, a handful
huff it's "nothing out of the ordinary."

La Cumbre Taqueria *Mexican* 22 | 8 | 15 | $11

San Mateo | 28 N. B St. (bet. 1st & Tilton Aves.) | 650-344-8989
See review in City of San Francisco Directory.

La Forêt Ⓜ *French* ▽ 27 | 24 | 27 | $65

San Jose | 21747 Bertram Rd. (Almaden Rd.) | 408-997-3458 |
www.laforetrestaurant.com

"Use your GPS to find" this "jaw-droppingly beautiful" French restaurant with a "woodsy setting" and "great creekside view" in the hills
near San Jose; persevere and you'll be "highly rewarded" with a "dining experience you want to allow time" for, replete with "superb", "innovative" prix fixe and à la carte menus (and "wonderful" wild game
specials for the "adventurous"), a "romantic" ambiance just right for a
"quiet evening" or if you're "celebrating an event" and "impeccable"
yet "not pretentious" service.

La Strada *Italian* 21 | 20 | 18 | $38

Palo Alto | 335 University Ave. (bet. Bryant & Florence Sts.) | 650-324-8300 |
www.lastradapaloalto.com

"Better" than most "Italians on Italian-stocked University Avenue",
this "always bustling" "favorite" in Palo Alto with an "inviting" atmosphere entices with "excellent, imaginative" fare, including
"wonderful homemade pasta"; "sit at the bar and watch the food
preparation – it's inspiring and you'll often get a little taste treat" – or
head to the "great front patio" and indulge in "people-watching"; still,
a handful shrug "nothing wows" you, deeming the menu somewhat
"odd" and "very limited."

ⓩ La Taqueria Ⓢ🍴 *Mexican* 24 | 7 | 12 | $11

San Jose | 15 S. First St. (Santa Clara Ave.) | 408-287-1542
See review in City of San Francisco Directory.

ⓩ L'Auberge Carmel *Californian* 27 | 24 | 25 | $102

Carmel | L'Auberge Carmel | Monte Verde St. (7th Ave.) | 831-624-8578 |
www.laubergecarmel.com

"Every morsel" of "fabulous" Californian fare is an "imaginative adventure in taste and texture" concur admirers of this "little slice of
heaven" in the "quaint" L'Aubere Carmel inn in this "sleepy" town; "if
you have the time" to "savor" a "culinary journey" and can "snag a
reservation" at one of the 12 tables, "do it – you won't be disappointed"; the staff operates like a "well-oiled machine", the tasting
menu is "inventive yet approachable", plus the bistro offerings in the
lobby's salon are a "great deal"; N.B. chef Timothy Mosblech recently
took the reins.

	FOOD	DECOR	SERVICE	COST

Lavanda *Mediterranean* | 19 | 19 | 19 | $44 |

Palo Alto | 185 University Ave. (bet. Emerson & High Sts.) | 650-321-3514 | www.lavandarestaurant.com

"Prepare to be pleasantly surprised" at this "attractive" Palo Alto establishment that delivers a "regularly updated" menu of Mediterranean fare "done with care"; the "delicious" small plates are definitely the way to go – "paired with winning, uncommon wines by the glass" it's an "excellent" choice for "date night"; still, the less-convinced quibble that the nibbles can range from "exquisite" to "huh?" and find it "a bit disappointing for all the fanciness."

La Victoria Taqueria ● *Mexican* | ▽ 20 | 6 | 11 | $13 |

San Jose | 140 W. San Carlos St. (Almaden Blvd.) | 408-298-5335

Cute Victorian-style digs aside, this Downtown taqueria "doesn't pretend to be anything it isn't" – in other words, it's just a "plain good" cheap and cheery Mexican dive that plies its trade from dawn till "after the bars close" serving starving San Jose State students breakfast burritos, tortas and tacos; "don't miss the special sauce" that's orange in color but derives its fiery flavor from red chiles.

Left Bank *French* | 18 | 20 | 17 | $38 |

Menlo Park | 635 Santa Cruz Ave. (Doyle St.) | 650-473-6543
San Jose | 377 Santana Row (S. Winchester Blvd.) | 408-984-3500
San Mateo | Whole Foods Shopping Center | 1100 Park Pl. (Saratoga Dr.) | 650-345-2250
www.leftbank.com

See review in North of San Francisco Directory.

☑ Le Papillon *French* | 27 | 24 | 27 | $67 |

San Jose | 410 Saratoga Ave. (Kiely Blvd.) | 408-296-3730 | www.lepapillon.com

Escape the "hustle and bustle of Silicon Valley" at this "hidden gem" in San Jose that feels like a "little bit of France"; the "classy" environment means you can "speak quietly to your tablemates" – it's enough to make you "stand and cheer", the staff that's "second to none" extends the "elegant treatment" and the "over-the-top", "outstanding" wine and food pairings on the New French tasting menu offer "interesting twists" that "leave you floating like the proverbial butterfly."

Lion & Compass ☒ *American* | 19 | 16 | 21 | $41 |

Sunnyvale | 1023 N. Fair Oaks Ave. (Weddell Dr.) | 408-745-1260 | www.lionandcompass.com

After 25 years, this Silicon Valley "staple" is "still the home of power brokers" and the "senior" Sand Hill set who wheel and deal over "tasty", "pricey" New American expense-account lunches, after-work drinks and "relaxing dinners"; still, the less-impressed roar that someone "should redo" the "dated" colonial Caribbean setting and "make it shine" as it seems to "resonate with the ghosts of diners past."

Lure ☒Ⓜ *Seafood* | ▽ 23 | 19 | 21 | $49 |

San Mateo | 204A Second Ave. (S. Ellsworth Ave.) | 650-340-9040 | www.lurerestaurant.com

"San Francisco chic comes to the Peninsula" – how "refreshing" applaud San Mateo locals who consider this Californian seafooder "surprise" quite a "catch"; the digs – a "narrow building with a small window front – are easy to miss", but the seasonal fin fare "bursting with flavor" and prepared by the "very clever" Malaysian-born chef with "progressive culinary flair" is "hard to forget"; what an "enjoyable" "place to escape to."

MacArthur Park *American*

16 | 17 | 17 | $37

Palo Alto | 27 University Ave. (El Camino Real) | 650-321-9990 | www.spectrumfoods.com

The Palo Alto "standby" set in a "lovely, historic building" may be the last "old-timer" standing since its SF brother recently closed – but it still "delivers what it promises" pledge patrons who slip into this "standard spot" where "Stanford parents take their kids" when "hankering for ribs" and other "no-fuss" Traditional "American classics"; but critics cry "there are no surprises, no triumphs" at this "flashback to the '80s"– it's "running on empty."

Maddalena's & Café Fino 🔏 *Continental*

21 | 22 | 23 | $41

Palo Alto | 544 Emerson St. (bet. Hamilton & University Aves.) | 650-326-6082 | www.maddalenasrestaurant.com

"They don't make this kind of place any more" declare devotees of this Palo Alto "throwback" that's "been there forever", delivering "old-fashioned" Continental standards including "cherries jubilee" made "tableside"; for a more swinging time, head to the "lively" adjacent art deco jazz bar, Café Fino, where "gracious host" Freddy may "make you dance with him" and "octogenarian bartender-poet Maurice" shakes "top-notch martinis."

NEW Mandaloun *Californian/Mediterranean*

- | - | - | M

Redwood City | 2021 Broadway (Main St.) | 650-367-7974 | www.mandaloun.biz

"Word is out" about this stylish newcomer that's fast become a "definite do-not-miss spot" "in, of all places, Redwood City" thanks to its "excellent", seasonal Mediterranean-Californian fare; the gracious layout, dominated by a wood-fired grill and rotisserie inside and a 45-seat heated, trellis-shaded patio, is perfect for grazing on small and large plates "before going to the Fox Theater" – or ending the evening with a wine-cap, choosing from a list of 20 by-the-glass options.

🄩 Manresa 🄜 *American*

27 | 24 | 25 | $108

Los Gatos | 320 Village Ln. (bet. N. Santa Cruz & University Aves.) | 408-354-4330 | www.manresarestaurant.com

"Worth the detour" to Los Gatos, David Kinch's "celestial" New American "foodie paradise" serves meals so wildly "inventive" that some wonder if the chef's "creative genius" is tinged with "a touch of insanity"; for best results, "bring an open mind" (and wallet) and splurge on the "three-hour long" tasting menu, which "surprises with every course"; sure, a few find the service and "casually elegant" setting less wow-worthy than the food, but overall most predict this "will easily be your dinner of the year."

Mantra *Californian/Indian*

20 | 23 | 18 | $45

Palo Alto | 632-636 Emerson St. (bet. Forest & Hamilton Aves.) | 650-322-3500 | www.mantrapaloalto.com

Under a new chef (ex Amber India and NYC's Bouley), this "upscale" Palo Alto–meets–"Bollywood" hot spot is injecting "imagination" into the "boring" Silicon Valley subcontinental dining scene with California "riffs" on traditional Indian dishes, yielding what fans call "mélanges that sound crazy but taste great"; "cool red decor" and a "happening bar scene" are further assets, though faultfinders cite "sloppy" service and say sometimes "the fusion doesn't fuse."

Z Marché ⓈⓂ *Californian/French*   26 | 23 | 25 | $68

Menlo Park | 898 Santa Cruz Ave. (University Dr.) | 650-324-9092 | www.restaurantmarche.com

This "special-occasion" New French in Menlo Park "rivals the best of the big city up north" thanks to its "ambitious" menu of "fresh", "seasonal" fare "pulled off with flair"; a "very urban", "low-key" setting and "efficient" servers who seem to "read your mind" add to what most consider a "top-notch experience", but since it's "très expensive" you may need "a second job" to afford frequent visits.

Z Marinus *French*   26 | 27 | 27 | $86

Carmel Valley | Bernardus Lodge | 415 Carmel Valley Rd. (Laureles Grade Rd.) | 831-658-3500 | www.bernardus.com

Another "reason for traveling to Carmel", this "old-world"-"elegant" Bernardus Lodge standout wins acclaim for Cal Stamenov's "beyond reproach" New French menus (prix fixe only), served by a staff that knows how to "pamper" and made all the better by a "treasure" of a wine list and "beautiful" grounds ("allow time to wander"); dining here is "a mini-vacation", especially if you "really splurge and spend the night" – it's "worth the kids' tuition."

Max's *Deli*   16 | 14 | 16 | $25

Burlingame | 1250 Old Bayshore Hwy. (Broadway) | 650-342-6297
Palo Alto | Stanford Shopping Ctr. | 711 Stanford Shopping Ctr. (Sand Hill Rd.) | 650-323-6297
Redwood City | Sequoia Station | 1001 El Camino Real (James Ave.) | 650-365-6297
www.maxsworld.com

See review in City of San Francisco Directory.

Mezza Luna *Italian*   21 | 18 | 20 | $34

Princeton by the Sea | 459 Prospect Way (Capistrano Rd.) | 650-728-8108 | www.mezzalunabythesea.com

A "lovely spot to dine with friends", this "charming" "seaside delight" in Princeton by the Sea, near Half Moon Bay, feels like a "slice of Italy"; while locals proclaim it's an "everyday place I come back to over and over", others view it as a "wonderful destination restaurant for a date" that gives you reason to "dress up"; either way it's "nice to be" by the Pacific dining on "well-crafted", "simple, but always homemade" Southern Italian fare.

Mistral Ⓢ *French/Italian*   19 | 20 | 18 | $39

Redwood Shores | 370-6 Bridge Pkwy. (Marine World Pkwy.) | 650-802-9222 | www.mistraldining.com

"Always ask for patio seating" with an "amazing lagoon view" or idle by the "lovely" outdoor fireplace and "sip a drink with the Oracle crowd" and other "corporate types" at this "longtime Redwood Shores favorite"; wherever you land, the atmosphere is "soothing" "all year round" while the French-Italian fare is "reliable", with a "wide array of choices"; still, a few hiss about service "blunders" and feel the food "isn't up to par."

Montrio Bistro *Californian*

23 | 21 | 23 | $44

Monterey | 414 Calle Principal (Franklin St.) | 831-648-8880 | www.montrio.com

Feels like a "big-city bistro" bellow boosters who praise the "lusty", "out-of-this-world" Californian cuisine, "well-chosen" wine list and "quasi-industrial feel" of this converted firehouse in "sleepy" Downtown Monterey; the "decidedly hip" digs make it a "favorite" spot to "unwind after work with a cocktail" or for a "leisurely dinner" or a "business meeting", plus the "atmosphere is lively after 8 PM" – a "godsend" in these parts; still, noise-sensitive sorts suggest "bring your earplugs for the din."

Morton's, The Steakhouse *Steak*

23 | 21 | 22 | $67

NEW **San Jose** | 177 Park Ave. (bet. Alamden Blvd. & Market St.) | 408-947-7000 | www.mortons.com

See review in City of San Francisco Directory.

Naomi Sushi *Japanese*

▽ 21 | 11 | 15 | $40

Menlo Park | 1328 El Camino Real (bet. Glenwood & Oak Grove Aves.) | 650-321-6902 | www.naomisushi.com

"By the end of the night, the chefs were calling us by our first name" report regulars and card-carrying "sake club" members who frequent this Japanese "favorite" in Menlo Park, the lower-priced "sister to Kanpai"; ask "what's good today – you won't be disappointed" – or just join the "serious sushi-eaters" indulging in omakase dinners; sure it's "loud", the "decor leaves something to be desired" and staffers move at a "glacial pace", but you "forget about that" once the "trustworthy" food arrives.

☑ Navio *American*

26 | 27 | 26 | $71

Half Moon Bay | Ritz-Carlton Half Moon Bay | 1 Miramontes Point Rd. (Hwy. 1) | 650-712-7000 | www.ritzcarlton.com

"Perched high on the cliffs" at "the tip of Half Moon Bay" with a "jaw-dropping view of the Pacific", a "posh" interior modeled after an upside-down ship and "outstanding" service, this oceanside "stunner" boasts "all the glitz of the Ritz"; the "top-notch" New American cuisine is "superb in every way", from the "spectacular" Sunday brunch offering "endless selections" to the "fabulous" tasting menu with wine pairings for the "adventurous"; natch, it's a "special-occasion splurge", but it's "worth indulging just to rub shoulders with the Rolls-Royce and Bentley crowd."

Nectar Wine Lounge *Californian*

19 | 23 | 20 | $35

NEW **Burlingame** | 270 Lorton Ave. (bet. Burlingame & Howard Aves.) | 650-558-9200 | www.nectarwinelounge.com

See review in City of San Francisco Directory.

Nepenthe *American*

16 | 24 | 16 | $36

Big Sur | 48510 Hwy. 1 (¼ mi. south of Ventana Inn & Spa) | 831-667-2345 | www.nepenthebigsur.com

It's "no longer the love nest Orson Welles built for Rita Hayworth", but there's "still magic" at this "funky" "Big Sur icon", a "coastal hideaway" perched high "above the Pacific"; the "to-die-for" burgers, American chow and "strong pours" are best enjoyed outside with your "feet hanging off the end of the world"; if gripers rail against "bored surfer" servers and "uninspired" eats, vistameisters shrug with a "drop-dead view" "like this, who needs food"?

North Beach Pizza ● *Pizza* | 18 | 9 | 14 | $16 |

San Mateo | 240 E. Third Ave. (B St.) | 650-344-5000 | www.northbeachpizza.com
See review in City of San Francisco Directory.

Oak City Bar & Grill *American* | 18 | 17 | 16 | $39 |

Menlo Park | 1029 El Camino Real (Menlo Ave.) | 650-321-6882 | www.oakcitybarandgrill.com
The "all-around tasty" New American fare with a "gourmet twist" is "prepared with care and always very fresh" – and you "can't beat the prix fixe lunch special" concur followers of this "convivial" Menlo Park standby; but knockers bark that "service is all over the place" and the fare "nothing special" suggesting "stick with a drink at the slick-looking bar."

Old Port Lobster Shack *Seafood* | 21 | 11 | 14 | $28 |

Redwood City | 851 Veteran's Blvd. (bet. Jefferson Ave. & Middlefield Rd.) | 650-366-2400 | www.oplobster.com
"Who figured" you could "relive New England coastal" joints in Redwood City – you can "almost hear the Boston" accents "marvel" mavens who hightail it to this "cute pseudo" "wharf in a strip mall" – and now its new City branch, North Beach Lobster Shack, too; never mind the "vacationland" shack decor – "it's all about the lobster roll" ("simple, fresh" "just lightly kissed with mayo"), and, yeah, it's "pretty spendy", but hey, it's an "exotic treat" in these parts.

☑ O'mei Ⓜ *Chinese* | 26 | 14 | 17 | $31 |

Santa Cruz | 2316 Mission St. (King St.) | 831-425-8458 | www.omeifood.com
You don't "expect to find such a treasure on the way out of Santa Cruz" assert addicts agog over the "unique" Chinese fare "fit for the gods" served at this beach town "experience"; the "amazingly fresh", "creative" dishes are so "exceptional" you just "overlook other factors" like "indifferent service" and "low-rent location"; neither aspect "detracts from the meal", which is "worth every penny" – including the service charge that's added to every check.

Original Joe's ● *American/Italian* | 18 | 14 | 18 | $29 |
(aka Joe's, OJ's)

San Jose | 301 S. First St. (San Carlos St.) | 408-292-7030 | www.originaljoes.com
See review in City of San Francisco Directory.

Osteria ⓩ *Italian* | 23 | 14 | 19 | $33 |

Palo Alto | 247 Hamilton Ave. (Ramona St.) | 650-328-5700
"Firmly in our list of favorites" agree *amici* who descend on this "old-fashioned gem" "without the glitz" in Palo Alto for "delicious" Italian fare at "reasonable prices", delighting in the "divine" homemade pasta, "classic" dishes that offer "more than sauce" and salads that "shine"; "sometimes it's a little too cramped" (you'll "get to know your neighbors"), service can be "brusque" and the "menu seldom changes but who cares – once you taste the food" you "won't be disappointed."

	FOOD	DECOR	SERVICE	COST

☒ Pacific's Edge *American/French* | 25 | 28 | 23 | $76 |

Carmel | Hyatt Highlands Inn | 120 Highlands Dr. (Hwy. 1) | 831-620-1234 | www.pacificsedge.com

Given the "drop-dead California-beautiful" views "overlooking Carmel Bay" and "unbeatable setting", it's no wonder the awestruck vote this Hyatt Highlands Inn "idyll" No. 1 for Decor in this Survey; "get there in time for sunset – it's a real treat" – and so is the "over-the-top" French-New American cuisine (try the "prix fixe menu with the wine pairings"), the Sunday brunch that's akin to a "spiritual experience" and the "magical service"; this is one "real dining experience" "you'll remember" "long after you leave."

Pancho Villa Taqueria *Mexican* | 20 | 8 | 13 | $12 |

San Mateo | 365 S. B St. (bet. 3rd & 4th Aves.) | 650-343-4123

See review in City of San Francisco Directory.

Parcel 104 *Californian* | 23 | 22 | 23 | $59 |

Santa Clara | Santa Clara Marriott | 2700 Mission College Blvd. (Great America Pkwy.) | 408-970-6104 | www.parcel104.com

South Bay "suits" "bring their best customers and wallet" to this "classy" Santa Clara "hot spot", which, despite its locale, is "not your mother's Marriott hotel restaurant"; Bradley Ogden's Californian kitchen is "fanatical about fresh, local ingredients", and feasters rave about the "unique desserts" and "expensive" but "delightful wine list" (including a "good selection of half bottles"), proffered by the "very attentive staff."

Passage to India *Indian*   ▽ | 19 | 14 | 15 | $20 |

Mountain View | 1991 W. El Camino Real (Clark Ave.) | 650-969-9990 | www.passagetoindia.net

Though it looks "like a former Denny's", this Northern Indian in Mountain View is "packed with throngs" who find it "worth the few extra bucks" for the buffet (Tuesday, Friday and weekend nights) and à la carte offerings, including Chinese-subcontinental hybrids and "unusual chaat items" as well as more "typical fare"; a few locals warn, though, that the "quality" of the food has "declined" and the service has "deteriorated."

Passionfish *Californian/Seafood* | 25 | 17 | 22 | $43 |

Pacific Grove | 701 Lighthouse Ave. (Congress Ave.) | 831-655-3311 | www.passionfish.net

Aquarium visitors "who crave fish after staring at them all day" leave pricey "Carmel, Monterey and Pebble Beach behind" for this "unpretentious", "environmentally friendly" Cal seafooder in Pacific Grove serving "super-fresh" sustainable finfare in Pacific Grove; "attentive" service and an "extensive" list of vinos priced "essentially at cost" help compensate for the "cramped quarters" and "former pancake house" decor.

Pasta Moon *Italian* | 22 | 19 | 21 | $38 |

Half Moon Bay | 315 Main St. (Mills St.) | 650-726-5125 | www.pastamoon.com

"Amazing housemade pastas", "locally grown produce" and an "excellent Italian wine list" keep locals "returning" to this "charming" Half Moon Bay trattoria where there is "always a personal greeting at the door" and the "owner makes every customer feel like the center of attention"; to dissenters who grumble about the "close tables" and "overpriced" menu, regulars retort that the "food is the thing."

	FOOD	DECOR	SERVICE	COST

Pasta Pomodoro *Italian*
16 | 13 | 16 | $20

San Jose | Evergreen Mkt. | 4898 San Felipe Rd. (Yerba Buena Blvd.) | 408-532-0271 | www.pastapomodoro.com
See review in City of San Francisco Directory.

Patxi's Chicago Pizza Ⓜ *Pizza*
20 | 12 | 16 | $20

Palo Alto | 441 Emerson St. (bet. Lytton & University Aves.) | 650-473-9999 | www.patxispizza.com

You'll "swear you just heard the L rumble by" posit "stuffed" surveyors who head to this Palo Alto pizzeria and Hayes Valley offshoot (pronounced PAH-cheese) sporting a "college dining hall" look for a taste of the "Windy City"; gorge on "gigantic", "deep-dish delights", perhaps the most "real" pies, if not the "best", this "side of The Loop"; sure the waits can be "long", but it's "totally worth it", and the "good" beer selection helps compensate.

Pearl Alley Bistro *French/Italian*
▽ 22 | 17 | 19 | $36

Santa Cruz | 110 Pearl Alley, 2nd fl. (bet. Lincoln St. & Walnut Ave.) | 831-429-8070 | www.pearlalley.com

"Warm owners" and "creative food" keep Santa Cruz diners hooked on this thirtysomething, "intimate" "second-floor" gem where the Italian-French menu "changes often", making it "a fun place to try new things"; be "sure you have a reservation on the weekend", though, or "you may have to eat at the bar" – which isn't so bad, given the "sensational wine list."

Piatti *Italian*
19 | 19 | 19 | $36

Carmel | Sixth Ave. (Junipero St.) | 831-625-1766
Santa Clara | 3905 Rivermark Plaza (Montague Expwy.) | 408-330-9212
www.piatti.com
See review in East of San Francisco Directory.

Pizza Antica *Pizza*
21 | 16 | 17 | $25

San Jose | 334 Santana Row, Suite 1065 (Stevens Creek Blvd.) | 408-557-8373 | www.pizzaantica.com

"Families galore" "jonesing" for Neapolitan-style "designer" pies descend on this "upscale", "child-packed" Bay Area outfit churning out "legendary", "super-crispy", "blistered"-crust versions that "give a fresh face to an old favorite", "proving that pizza can be thin, innovative and delicious"; the "frosting" on top: "creative", "unusual" add-ons, "unique starters" and "interesting" wine choices; still, gripers grumble that the "young" staff is "dazed and confused" and shout it's "100 db inside", suggesting "eat outside to escape" the "din."

Plumed Horse Ⓧ *Californian*
- | - | - | E

Saratoga | 14555 Big Basin Way (4th St.) | 408-867-4711 | www.plumedhorse.com

Saratoga's veteran fine-dining thoroughbred is expected to be back in the saddle again come fall 2007 when it reopens under new ownership; leading the charge: new executive chef/co-owner Peter Armellino (former chef de cuisine at Aqua) who will oversee the upscale, contemporary Californian menu; the completely remodeled, three-story dining room, featuring a new fireplace-lit lounge, chef's table and dramatic wine display housing its exhaustive cellar offerings, will no doubt lure a well-heeled stable of South Bay diners.

	FOOD	DECOR	SERVICE	COST

Quattro Restaurant & Bar *Italian*　　22 | 24 | 22 | $54

East Palo Alto | Four Seasons Hotel | 2050 University Ave. (Woodland Ave.) | 650-470-2889 | www.quattrorestaurant.com

"Upscale Italian in East Palo Alto – who would've thought?" – then again, this "lovely jewel box" is in a "Four Seasons, so it's precisely what you should expect"; the "modern interior" works for "special dinners" "while the "hip bar" is a "wonderful place to have a glass of wine after a terrific massage" – "you can't believe the 101 is just over the wall" – plus the patio is "pretty" for brunch; still, a handful lament this "chichi hotel" "deserves more creative food."

Rio Grill *Californian*　　22 | 19 | 20 | $39

Carmel | Crossroads Shopping Ctr. | 101 Crossroads Blvd. (Rio Rd.) | 831-625-5436 | www.riogrill.com

"Go often and try everything" – you won't walk "away hungry" declare diehards who descend on this "festive" "favorite" "old standby" in a Carmel strip mall that's been "turning out reliable chow" since the 1980s; "sit back with a margarita and enjoy" "hearty portions" of "lusty", "imaginative" Cal fare with a "Southwestern flair" delivered by "service that's eager to please", and remember, "there's no better place to catch up on the local gossip than the bar."

Ristorante Capellini *Italian*　　19 | 19 | 18 | $38

San Mateo | 310 Baldwin Ave. (B St.) | 650-348-2296 | www.capellinis.com

You can "always count" on the "tasty, well-thought-out" fare at this "cornerstone Italian" "favorite" in San Mateo agree admirers who delight in the "European atmosphere" and "interesting people"; the "dark, rich" Pat Kuleto–designed three-story space is a "great complement to the delicious food" making it a "solid standby for business and personal meetings" but wears thin for others who shrug it's "tired" and service is "slow."

Robert's Whitehouse Ⓜ *French*　　▽ 25 | 24 | 25 | $48

Pacific Grove | 649 Lighthouse Ave. (19th St.) | 831-375-9626 | www.robertswhitehouse.com

"As romantic as it gets in a restored Victorian in Pacific Grove" attest voters who congregate in the "gracious dining environment" for chef-owner Robert Kincaid's "very inventive", "tasty and nicely plated" French "soup-to-nuts dinners"; the "small-town atmosphere" with a "touch of casual elegance" is what this "charming whiteboard" mansion "excels in", plus the "servers are knowledgeable and on top of things without being intrusive"; P.S. save room for the "killer" desserts.

Rogue Chefs Ⓢ Ⓜ *Californian*　　▽ 21 | 17 | 15 | $55

Half Moon Bay | 730 Main St. (Correas St.) | 650-712-2000 | www.roguechefs.com

Rogue indeed, this "small-town-quaint" yet "sophisticatedly urban" Half Moon Bay hybrid – part cooking school/part "sit-down restaurant" – requires a certain customer "flexibility" given that the prix fixe "menu changes constantly" and hours "can be erratic"; chef-owner Kevin Koebel is "instructive entertainment", "chatting up guests" while cooking "outstanding" Californian fare in his exhibition kitchen; however, the less-maverick wisecrack it's a "lot of falderal" and dough for "variable food"; N.B. currently open Friday–Saturday nights only.

	FOOD	DECOR	SERVICE	COST

Roti Indian Bistro *Indian*   23 19 19 $32

Burlingame | 209 Park Rd. (Howard Ave.) | 650-340-7684 |
www.rotibistro.com

There's nothing rote about the "nouvelle" subcontinental fare with a "hip
California flair" at this "noisy" "upmarket" duo in Burlingame and SF's
West Portal; the "true bistro setup" is "such a step-up" from "your father's dive" it "even has a good wine" list, and prices are only "mildly
expensive" – just "beware": the kitchen's "spicy-scale" is "authentic";
still, cynics sniff the only Indians you see are in the "pictures on the wall."

Roy's at Pebble Beach *Hawaiian*   25 25 23 $58

Pebble Beach | The Inn at Spanish Bay | 2700 17 Mile Dr. (Congress Rd.) |
831-647-7423 | www.pebblebeach.com

"Cocktails on the patio at sunset, bagpipers in the distance", Maui-like
"vistas" and Hawaiian Regional seafood "that's leaps above" other Roy's
adds up to a "memorable dining experience" at the Inn at Spanish
Bay – especially after the "17 Mile Drive"; "if you can get past the
Golden Girls Florida–style decor and chummy laughter of men whose
golf day has run" long, it's the place to "live it up" in Pebble Beach – plus,
the staff "doesn't rush you" so you can savor your "glorious meal."

NEW Sam's Chowder House *Seafood*   15 22 14 $34

Half Moon Bay | 4210 N. Cabrillo Hwy. (Capistrano Rd.) | 650-712-0245 |
www.samschowderhouse.com

Half Moon Bay's seafooder and fish market hovering "on a cliffside overlooking miles of beach" offers "stunning ocean vistas that make virtually
anything served palatable if not delicious"; soak up the "spectacular"
view from the "wonderful" heated patio or inside the "large dining
room" with "food that's perfect for the setting"; if others carp about the
"inexperienced staff" and "mediocre" fare, the more optimistic muse
"given their pedigree (ex Cetrella owners), we "hope it will improve.""

Sardine Factory *American/Seafood*   20 20 21 $53

Monterey | 701 Wave St. (Prescott Ave.) | 831-373-3775 |
www.sardinefactory.com

"Sure the tourists pile in" to Monterey's Cannery Row seafood "standby"
after visiting the aquarium, but even locals "make time for the Factory"
claiming it's "worth a stop" to dive into "fresh-caught fish" and American
standards; you're always "treated like kings and queens" and the
building broken up into "quirky" "quaint rooms" feels "impressive";
but others no-can-do, citing "lackluster dishes" and "tired" digs.

Scott's of Palo Alto *Seafood*   19 18 18 $40

Palo Alto | #1 Town & Country Vill. (Embarcadero Rd.) | 650-323-1555 |
www.scottsseafood.com

Scott's of San Jose *Seafood*

San Jose | 185 Park Ave. (Almaden Blvd.) | 408-971-1700 |
www.scottsseafoodsj.com

See Scott's Seafood review in East of San Francisco Directory.

Sent Sovi Ⓜ *Californian*   24 21 23 $68

Saratoga | 14583 Big Basin Way (5th St.) | 408-867-3110 | www.sentsovi.com

"At only 29 years old", "passionate" chef-owner Josiah Stone is definitely "coming out of Kinch's shadow nicely", staging "fun wine
events" and creating "delicious" French-influenced Californian prix

fixe menus declare devotees who descend on this "very charming", "must-go" Saratoga spot in the Santa Cruz mountain foothills; the "cozy" brushed copper and wood-lined dining room, coupled with service that's "not overbearing", is heaven sent for "a casual business dinner, a relaxing evening out" or a "special-occasional celebration."

Seven Restaurant & Lounge 🅱 *American/French*
▽ 21 | 21 | 19 | $41

San Jose | 754 The Alameda (Bush St.) | 408-280-1644 | www.7restaurant.us

It "really belongs in SF or NY" assert sophisticates who join the "hip crowd" at this "trendy" "metro cosmopolitan" San Jose spot with "eclectic" industrial decor for "creative" French–New American eats; it's the "loungiest" "place to see and be seen", plus it's "excellent for business lunches"; but it doesn't always add up for others who shrug the "food fluctuates" – if it "consistently delivered, it would be fantastic."

71 Saint Peter 🅱 *Californian/Mediterranean*
22 | 18 | 21 | $39

San Jose | San Pedro Square | 71 N. San Pedro St. (bet. W. Santa Clara & W. St. John Sts.) | 408-971-8523 | www.71saintpeter.com

It's so "intimate", "cozy and conversation-friendly", perhaps they should consider renaming this "lovely" Cal-Med bistro "hidden" at the end of Downtown San Jose's San Pedro Square "Quaint" Peter quip worshipers who "always come away satisfied"; whether you "eat, drink and visit with friends" at lunch on the outdoor patio, grab a "pre-Sharks game" meal or settle in for the "excellent" tasting menu, the "inventive" fare provides a "great change of pace."

🆉 Shadowbrook *American/Californian*
22 | 27 | 22 | $48

Capitola | 1750 Wharf Rd. (Capitola Rd.) | 831-475-1511 | www.shadowbrook-capitola.com

The ride down in the funicular through the "amazing hillside" "cascading in green" to Capitola's five-level seven-room "nature-laden getaway" is "just the beginning" of a "unique, romantic" "fabulous dining experience"; take in the "lovely view" of "lush gardens" and "twilight twinkling" on Soquel Creek or canoodle by the "cozy fireplace" in the Swiss chaletlike setting while enjoying an "elegant" Cal–New American repast – it's "like dining in a treehouse in the middle of a forest, yet not as kitschy as you might expect."

Shalimar *Indian/Pakistani*
22 | 3 | 9 | $15

Sunnyvale | 1146 W. El Camino Real (bet. S. Bernardo & Grape Aves.) | 408-530-0300 | www.shalimarsf.com

See review in City of San Francisco Directory.

🆉 Sierra Mar *Californian/Eclectic*
26 | 27 | 26 | $79

Big Sur | Post Ranch Inn | Post Ranch/Hwy. 1 (30 mi. south of Carmel) | 831-667-2800 | www.postranchinn.com

Now that this "high-end resort" restaurant is back in its original glassed-in cliffside location, "stunned" visitors can't say "which is more impressive", the "breathtaking views" over Big Sur that almost make you feel like you're "looking from the cockpit of an airplane out over the ocean" or the "exceptional" Cal-Eclectic food that "complements" the coastal "scenery perfectly"; completing the "otherworldly experience": a "spectacular" 1,200-bottle wine list and an "awesome" staff – it's such a "special treat" that the "astronomical prices seem down-to-earth."

Sino *Chinese*

| 20 | 24 | 17 | $37 |

San Jose | Santana Row | 377 Santana Row (Olin Ave.) | 408-247-8880 |
www.sinorestaurant.com

"Fun . . . fun . . . fun – and delicious – describe both the food and atmosphere" at Straits' sibling on San Jose's "trendy Santana Row" that's
"part hip bar, part Chinese restaurant" serving "traditional and newer
dishes"; although the "sexy" lounge "captures the young singles' bar
dollar", desperately seeking dumpling diners suggest "go early in the
week when the meat market isn't in full swing" and you don't have to
"hail down" servers with "more fervor than a taxi cab" at "midnight" to
"satisfy" dim sum "cravings."

Stacks *American*

| - | - | - | I |

Burlingame | 361 California Dr. (Lorton Ave.) | 650-579-1384
Menlo Park | 600 Santa Cruz Ave. (El Camino Real) | 650-838-0066
www.stacksrestaurant.com

Join the "long lines on weekends" and "stack up on lumberjack pancakes" at this all-day, "all-American breakfast and lunch" chainlet
with branches in Burlingame, Menlo Park and now Hayes Valley too;
"from the name, you might guess what their specialty is", but insiders
wink "if it's not on the menu (which is large to start with), just ask" –
the "wonderful staff including the cooks" is happy to oblige special re-
quests; N.B. open 7 AM–2:30 PM

St. Michael's Alley ⓜ *Californian*

| 22 | 20 | 22 | $38 |

Palo Alto | 806 Emerson St. (Homer Ave.) | 650-326-2530 |
www.stmikes.com

This "romantic" "gem" "tucked away" in Palo Alto may be "off the
beaten path", but it's not so "hidden as time goes on", especially since it
was a "Clinton favorite" when "daughter Chelsea attended Stanford";
squeeze into the "intimate" quarters for "delicious" Californian fare
with an "accent on local ingredients and wine" or enjoy a "delightful"
"Sunday brunch on the sidewalk", all "topped with" "enthusiastic service"; N.B. a move is pending to 140 Homer Avenue nearby.

Stokes Restaurant & Bar *Californian/Mediterranean*

| 23 | 20 | 21 | $45 |

Monterey | 500 Hartnell St. (bet. Madison & Polk Sts.) | 831-373-1110 |
www.stokesrestaurant.com

"What a treat to dine" in this circa-1833 "cozy adobe" in the "historic
old Monterey district" agree admirers who also get stoked about the
"truly inspired" Cal-Med small and large plates imbued with "sunny
European flavors" and "personable" service; "if you're looking for energy, this isn't your place", but if you want an "informal, comfortable"
spot without that "tourist feeling" where you can "reconnect with your
special someone" you'll "enjoy" this locals' "favorite."

Straits Cafe *Singaporean*

| 20 | 19 | 17 | $37 |

Burlingame | 1100 Burlingame Ave. (Highland Ave.) |
650-373-7883
Palo Alto | 3295 El Camino Real (Lambert Ave.) | 650-494-7168
San Jose | 333 Santana Row, Suite 1100 (bet. Olin Ave. & Tatum Ln.) |
408-246-6320
www.straitsrestaurants.com
See review in City of San Francisco Directory.

Tai Pan *Chinese* ▽ 23 | 25 | 21 | $36

Palo Alto | 560 Waverly St. (Hammilton St. & University Ave.) |
650-329-9168 | www.taipanpaloalto.com

"Hong Kong delivered to Downtown Palo Alto!" exclaim enthusiasts
who "dress up" to chow down at this "lovely", "white-tablecloth"
Chinese "favorite" "beautifully decorated" with "gorgeous furnishings
and artifacts"; the "excellent", "elegantly prepared" dishes "really deliver" and so does the "pleasant" staff; still, a handful feel the fare's
"pricey" for such "small portions"

☑ Tamarine *Vietnamese* 26 | 24 | 22 | $47

Palo Alto | 546 University Ave. (Tasso St.) | 650-325-8500 |
www.tamarinerestaurant.com

The "superbly prepared", "delectable" Vietnamese small and large plates
"bursting with flavor" and "expertly served" reach a "whole new level of
taste and texture" at Bong Su's "amazing" older sister in Palo Alto; the
fare is so "terrific" "you could choose dishes by throwing a dart at the
menu" – "go with a crowd so you can taste everything" – plus the "elegant", "Zen-like" ambiance replete with "rotating art" and the "super-
chic", "hip, affluent crowd" adds to the "remarkable" experience.

NEW Tanglewood *American* 21 | 23 | 17 | $49

San Jose | Santana Row | 334 Santana Row, Suite 1000 (Stevens Creek Blvd.) |
408-244-0464 | www.tanglewood.com

Co-owner Roland Passot of La Folie and his chef "put a lot of thought into
the whole experience" at this "softly lit, intimate" Santana Row newcomer agree admirers who sing the praises of the "handsome", "elegant" rough-hewn furnishings with a Berkshires feel; the presentation
is "excellent" and so are the "intriguing, updated twists on American
classics" made with local ingredients, and the "great value" wines;
still, detractors bark the "green" service is a "tangled mess" for a
"place with ambition" and pout that portions are "tiny."

Taqueria 3 Amigos *Mexican* 18 | 10 | 14 | $12

Half Moon Bay | 200 S. Cabrillo Hwy. (Kelly Ave.) | 650-347-4513
San Mateo | 243 S. B St. (bet. 2nd & E. 3rd Aves.) | 650-347-4513

It's "worth the drive" to this "coastside favorite" in a "funky old gas
station" in Half Moon Bay for "cheap, quick, tasty" Mexican; it's "always fresh and never tastes greasy" – "if only I could bring myself to
order anything but a burrito"; still, nitpickers pout that "things don't
quite taste as zingy" "since the remodel" – "some of the oomph" got
"lost in the transition"; N.B. there's also a branch in San Mateo.

Taqueria Tlaquepaque *Mexican* ▽ 23 | 12 | 17 | $16

San Jose | 2222 Lincoln Ave. (bet. Curtner & Franquette Aves.) |
408-978-3665
San Jose | 699 Curnter Ave. (Canoas Garden Ave.) | 408-448-1230
San Jose | 721 Willow St. (Delmas Ave.) | 408-287-9777 Ⓜ

"Always a wait for a table – for a reason" rave fans of this taqueria trio
in San Jose offering "big" and "small eaters" a "large variety" of "fast,
good and cheap" Mexican dishes; "get there early" and indulge in
"great homemade tortillas" "washed down" with a "must-be-tried"
"Chevelas cocktail – light or dark beer with juice and an optional shot
of tequila"; still, a handful huff the "decor and service are atrocious."

	FOOD	DECOR	SERVICE	COST

Tarpy's Roadhouse *American*

22 | 21 | 20 | $40

Monterey | 2999 Monterey-Salinas Hwy. (Canyon Del Rey Blvd.) |
831-647-1444 | www.tarpys.com

"Quirky" and "festive" this "off-the-beaten-path" old stone abode
with "true roadhouse atmosphere" is well suited for lunch or dinner or
just "sampling local wines on your arrival into Monterey"; "sit on the
patio in the sun", where you (and your dog) can "almost reach up and
grab the planes as they land" and chow down on "hearty", "excellent-
value" Traditional American eats; sure, it gets "noisy" and service
"varies", but mostly it's just "great fun."

Thea Mediterranean

21 | 21 | 18 | $37

Cuisine *Greek/Mediterranean*

San Jose | Santana Row | 3090 Olsen Dr. (S. Winchester Blvd.) |
408-260-1444 | www.thearestaurant.com

"You feel like you've entered Greece" – dining at this "buzzy", "light,
airy" Santana Row "favorite" is "like taking a mini-vacation" vow
habitués who also put the "absolutely delicious", "Greek-inflected"
"Mediterranean specialties", including "top-notch" fish, on a pedes-
tal; the "open space and decor make it pleasant to dwell" for a spell,
and the staffers are "some of the friendliest" fans have "encountered";
still, a handful take leave citing "bland", "uninspired" fare.

Theo's 🌊Ⓜ *Californian/French*

▽ 24 | 20 | 24 | $52

Soquel | 3101 N. Main St. (Soquel Dr.) | 831-462-3657 |
www.theosrestaurant.com

"Imaginative chef" Nicci Tripp "constantly outdoes himself", presenting "superb", "inspired seasonal" Californian-French cuisine
(featuring "amazing housemade cheeses") in a "beautiful" converted stucco home; sure, it's a safe bet you'll "blow your allow-
ance", but it's to be expected from someplace that's not only "as
formal as it gets" in small-town Soquel outside of Santa Cruz, but "as
delightful" as well.

Three Seasons *Vietnamese*

23 | 20 | 18 | $35

Palo Alto | 518 Bryant St. (University Ave.) | 650-838-0353 |
www.threeseasonsrestaurant.com
See review in City of San Francisco Directory.

Trader Vic's *Polynesian*

16 | 21 | 18 | $45

Palo Alto | Dina's Garden Hotel | 4269 El Camino Real
(bet. Charleston & San Antonio Rds.) | 650-849-9800 |
www.tradervicspaloalto.com
See review in East of San Francisco Directory.

Turmeric *Indian*

▽ 21 | 18 | 17 | $27

Sunnyvale | 141 S. Murphy St. (bet. Evelyn & Washington Aves.) |
408-617-9100 | www.turmericrestaurant.com

At this Sunnyvale "spice" spot, an "inspired chef" creates "lavish",
"high-quality" Indian buffets that aren't meant for "timid palates",
filled with "distinctively flavored" "atypical offerings" for lunch
and dinner, plus an à la carte menu; the midday spread is "one of the
best – and most popular – deals in town" while the decor is a "cut
above" – "what a pleasant change of pace" to eat subcontinental fare
in a "more lush environment."

231 Ellsworth ⧈ *American* | 23 | 20 | 21 | $58 |

San Mateo | 231 S. Ellsworth Ave. (bet. 2nd & E. 3rd Aves.) | 650-347-7231 | www.231ellsworth.com

Spend a "special evening" "among the foodies" at this South Bay "classic" that feels like a "quiet formal island in the midst of Downtown San Mateo"; the "wonderful New American" cuisine, including a prix fixe menu, and the "very extensive wine list" are "elegantly presented" in "delightfully sedate", "spacious" chandeliered digs by an "attentive" staff that "takes good care of you"; still, a "disappointed" few huff that the setting is "drab" and the fare "overpriced and uninspiring."

Udupi Palace *Indian/Vegetarian* | 20 | 8 | 12 | $13 |

Sunnyvale | 976 E. El Camino Real (Poplar Ave.) | 408-830-9600 | www.udupipalaceca.com

See review in East of San Francisco Directory.

Uncle Frank's at Francesca's ⧈ *BBQ* | ∇ 22 | 4 | 11 | $18 |

Mountain View | 2135 Old Middlefield Way (Rengstorff Ave.) | 650-964-4476 | www.unclefranksbbq.com

"Hidden in the back" of a "slumlike" bar, this Mountain View "dive" smokes with "slow-cooked-to-perfection" "Louisiana-style BBQ the way it should be served: messy and on cheap tables with silverware that doesn't match"; "just get there early" for "killer" sides of cornbread, Cajun corn, collared greens, etc. – they're "made fresh daily" and "when they run out, there ain't no more"; N.B. under-21s are only allowed on the patio.

Village Pub, The *American* | 26 | 23 | 24 | $58 |

Woodside | 2967 Woodside Rd. (Whiskey Hill Rd.) | 650-851-9888 | www.thevillagepub.net

Just look around at the "wealthy" Woodside "movers and shakers" – "power brokers", "wives of venture capitalists", "49ers", etc. – and you'll suspect this is "not a pub at all", but rather a "sophisticated" "fine-dining establishment"; if "magician" chef Mark Sullivan's "superb", "innovative New American cuisine" or the "snazzy" "Pottery Barn"–meets-"country inn" design don't clue you in, then the "outrageous" tabs (especially on the "extensive" though "inflated" wine list) certainly will.

Viognier *French* | 24 | 22 | 23 | $55 |

San Mateo | Draeger's Mktpl. | 222 E. Fourth Ave. (bet. B St. & Ellsworth Ave.) | 650-685-3727 | www.viognierrestaurant.com

"Don't let the fact that it's on top of" a "deluxe grocery" "dissuade you", because this French "destination" never fails to "blow the socks off" San Mateo "foodies" – and it's evident that the "new chef" "takes advantage" of the market's proximity, as "salads glisten with freshness", meats taste like they came "directly up the stairs" from the butcher and the menu itself is "ever-changing"; the "crisp", "caring" staff includes an "excellent sommelier" adept at "stellar wine" pairings.

NEW Vittoria Ristorante Italiano *Italian* | ∇ 20 | 17 | 16 | $38 |

Los Gatos | 27 N. Santa Cruz Ave. (W. Main St.) | 408-395-6000 | www.vittorialosgatos.com

"Several worthy dishes" help elevate this "safe bet" for "simple", "casual", "reasonably priced" Italian fare in the "chops, ravioli and Chianti" vein; the big windows that open "right onto Los Gatos' main street" are *molto bene* for a "summer evening", but the "earsplitting noise through-out" the faux finished yellow room cries out for "sound absorption" – at least the "fun" "scene at the bar is better" and helps you "forgive the inconsistent" service.

Yankee Pier *American/Seafood*

| 17 | 15 | 17 | $33 |

San Jose | 378 Santana Row (S. Winchester Ave.) | 408-244-1244
South San Francisco | San Francisco Int'l Airport |
United Domestic Departure Terminal 3 | 650-821-8938
www.yankeepier.com
See review in North of San Francisco Directory.

Zao Noodle Bar *Pan-Asian*

| 14 | 12 | 14 | $17 |

Palo Alto | 261 University Ave. (bet. Bryant & Ramona Sts.) | 650-328-1988 |
www.zao.com
See review in City of San Francisco Directory.

Zibibbo *Mediterranean*

| 20 | 20 | 19 | $41 |

Palo Alto | 430 Kipling St. (bet. Lytton & University Aves.) | 650-328-6722 |
www.zibibborestaurant.com
The "liveliest thing in the dot-com era is still going strong" – in fact, Restaurant LuLu's "very social" Palo Alto sibling is the "place to see Silicon Valley VC's cut deals over small-plate Mediterranean" food; it's "huge", with a "greenhouse feel" – but it "still feels inviting", "classy and welcoming" – and the "delicious, not pretentious" dishes and "excellent" wine flights are a "definite plus"; still, "bring a flare gun" to get servers' attention, because it's "jammed on weekends."

Zucca Ristorante *Mediterranean*

| 19 | 17 | 18 | $33 |

Mountain View | 186 Castro St. (bet. Central & Villa Sts.) | 650-864-9940 |
www.zuccaristorante.com
A "perennial favorite" for "solid Mediterranean fare" confirm aficiona-dos who congregate at this "welcoming" "gem" in the "heart of lovely" Mountain View; "we like the bar" (the "drink menu is really fun") and the "small plates, but the large plates are wonderful too" ("anything with lamb is a winner"), plus the owners "make sure every little detail is covered"; sit "outside in the spring or summer" – that's the place to be with a "date in the evenings."

INDEXES

LOCATION MAPS

All places are in San Francisco unless otherwise noted (East of San Francisco=E; North of San Francisco=N; South of San Francisco=S).

Cuisines

Includes restaurant names, locations and Food ratings. ☑ indicates places with the highest ratings, popularity and importance.

AFGHAN

Kabul Afghan | **San Carlos/S** — 22

AMERICAN

Enrico's | **N Beach** — -
NEW Salt House | **SoMa** — 21

AMERICAN (NEW)

☑ Ame | **SoMa** — 26
Arcadia | **San Jose/S** — 23
NEW AVA | **San Anselmo/N** — -
Basin | **Saratoga/S** — 19
Beach Chalet | **Outer Sunset** — 13
Belden Taverna | **Downtown** — 20
Big 4 | **Nob Hill** — 22
Bing Crosby's | **Walnut Creek/E** — 18
Blue Plate | **Mission** — 23
Boulette's Larder | **Embarcadero** — 25
☑ Boulevard | **Embarcadero** — 27
Brick | **Tenderloin** — 20
Bungalow 44 | **Mill Valley/N** — 21
Cafe Esin | **San Ramon/E** — 25
☑ Cafe La Haye | **Sonoma/N** — 26
Campton Place | **Downtown** — 25
Caprice | **Tiburon/N** — 21
Celadon | **Napa/N** — 23
☑ Chenery Park | **Glen Pk** — 22
☑ Chow/Park Chow | **multi. loc.** — 20
Cindy's | **St. Helena/N** — 24
NEW Circa | **Marina** — 18
Cosmopolitan | **SoMa** — 20
Deuce | **Sonoma/N** — 20
Dottie's | **Tenderloin** — 25
Dry Creek | **Healdsburg/N** — 24
Duck Club | **multi. loc.** — 20
Eulipia | **San Jose/S** — 20
NEW Eureka | **Castro** — 21
Evan's | **S Lake Tahoe/E** — 27
NEW ☑ Farm | **Napa/N** — 23
Flea St. Café | **Menlo Pk/S** — 22
Fog City Diner | **Embarcadero** — 19
☑ French Laundry | **Yountville/N** — 29
Frisson | **Downtown** — 20
Fumé Bistro | **Napa/N** — 19
Gar Woods | **Carnelian Bay/E** — 19

☑ Gary Danko | **Fish. Wharf** — 29
General's | **Sonoma/N** — -
Indigo | **Civic Ctr** — 20
Jodie's Rest. | **Albany/E** — 20
Kenwood | **Kenwood/N** — 22
Kingfish | **San Mateo/S** — 17
Lion & Compass | **Sunnyvale/S** — 19
Luna Park | **Mission** — 19
☑ Madrona Manor | **Healdsburg/N** — 25
☑ Manresa | **Los Gatos/S** — 27
Martini House | **St. Helena/N** — 25
Mecca | **Castro** — 20
Mendo Bistro | **Ft Bragg/N** — 25
☑ Michael Mina | **Downtown** — 28
MoMo's | **S Beach** — 17
Monti's | **Santa Rosa/N** — 19
Moose's | **N Beach** — 20
Mustards Grill | **Yountville/N** — 24
☑ Myth | **Downtown** — 26
☑ Navio | **Half Moon Bay/S** — 26
955 Ukiah | **Mendocino/N** — 22
Oak City B&G | **Menlo Pk/S** — 18
One Market | **Embarcadero** — 22
☑ Pacific's Edge | **Carmel/S** — 25
Park Chalet | **Outer Sunset** — 15
Park Grill | **Downtown** — 20
Pine Cone Diner | **Pt Reyes/N** — 19
☑ Postrio | **Downtown** — 24
NEW Presidio Social | **Presidio** — 18
Public | **SoMa** — 18
☑ Range | **Mission** — 26
Restaurant | **Ft Bragg/N** — 23
rnm rest. | **Lower Haight** — 25
Rotunda | **Downtown** — 20
Seven | **San Jose/S** — 21
☑ Shadowbrook | **Capitola/S** — 22
Slow Club | **Mission** — 22
Soule Domain | **Kings Bch/E** — 23
NEW Spork | **Mission** — -
NEW Spruce | **Presidio Hts** — -
Street | **Russian Hill** — 21
Tablespoon | **Russian Hill** — 22
NEW Tanglewood | **San Jose/S** — 21

ⓩ Terra | **St. Helena/N**	26
Town Hall | **SoMa**	23
Town's End | **Embarcadero**	19
2223 | **Castro**	21
NEW TWO | **SoMa**	21
231 Ellsworth | **San Mateo/S**	23
Universal Cafe | **Mission**	23
Village Pub | **Woodside/S**	26
NEW Vitrine | **SoMa**	–
Washington Sq. B&G | **N Beach**	19
Woodward's Gdn. | **Mission**	25
XYZ | **SoMa**	20
zazu | **Santa Rosa/N**	25
Zin | **Healdsburg/N**	22
Zinsvalley | **Napa/N**	20

AMERICAN (TRADITIONAL)

ⓩ ad hoc | **Yountville/N**	26
ⓩ Ahwahnee | **Yosemite/E**	19
Balboa Cafe | **Cow Hollow**	19
Barndiva | **Healdsburg/N**	18
ⓩ BIX | **Downtown**	23
Brannan's Grill | **Calistoga/N**	19
Brazen Head | **Cow Hollow**	20
ⓩ Buckeye | **Mill Valley/N**	23
Chapter & Moon | **Ft Bragg/N**	21
Cheesecake | **multi. loc.**	16
Chloe's Cafe | **Noe Valley**	21
Cuvée | **Napa/N**	20
Dipsea Cafe | **Mill Valley/N**	17
Duarte's Tavern | **Pescadero/S**	21
Ella's | **Presidio Hts**	20
Foothill Grille | **Napa/N**	–
Hard Rock | **Fish. Wharf**	13
Home | **Castro**	18
ⓩ In-N-Out | **multi. loc.**	22
NEW Jones Rest. | **Marina**	–
Lark Creek | **Walnut Creek/E**	22
Lark Creek Inn | **Larkspur/N**	23
Liberty Cafe | **Bernal Hts**	22
MacArthur Park | **Palo Alto/S**	16
ⓩ Mama's Wash. Sq. | **N Beach**	25
Mama's Royal | **Oakland/E**	20
Market | **St. Helena/N**	22
Maverick | **Mission**	22
Mo's | **multi. loc.**	20
Nepenthe | **Big Sur/S**	16
Original Joe's | **multi. loc.**	18

Pluto's Fresh | **multi. loc.**	19
Pork Store | **multi. loc.**	21
Press | **St. Helena/N**	23
Q | **Inner Rich**	20
Red Hut | **multi. loc.**	25
Rick & Ann's | **Berkeley/E**	21
Rutherford Grill | **Rutherford/N**	23
Sardine Factory | **Monterey/S**	20
Sauce | **Hayes Valley**	18
Scott's | **multi. loc.**	19
Sears Fine Food | **Downtown**	18
Somerset | **Oakland/E**	–
Stacks | **multi. loc.**	–
Tarpy's | **Monterey/S**	22
Taylor's Auto | **Embarcadero**	21
NEW Toast | **Noe Valley**	18

ARGENTINEAN

Boca | **Novato/N**	20
El Raigon | **N Beach**	21

ASIAN

AsiaSF | **SoMa**	17
Bridges | **Danville/E**	20
Butterfly | **Embarcadero**	19
Circolo | **Mission**	19
Dragonfly | **Truckee/E**	23
Eos Rest./Wine | **Cole Valley**	23
Sparrow | **Nob Hill**	20
SUMI | **Castro**	23

ASIAN FUSION

Asia de Cuba | **Downtown**	21
Azie | **SoMa**	19
CAFÉ KATi | **Japantown**	23
Flying Fish | **Carmel/S**	24
ⓩ House, The | **N Beach**	26
Koo | **Inner Sunset**	24
NEW Sudachi | **Polk Gulch**	–
NEW Sutra | **SoMa**	19

BAKERIES

Alexis Baking Co. | **Napa/N**	22
Boulange | **multi. loc.**	22
Citizen Cake | **Hayes Valley**	20
Della Fattoria | **Petaluma/N**	26
Downtown Bakery | **Healdsburg/N**	24
Gayle's Bakery | **Capitola/S**	25
Liberty Cafe | **Bernal Hts**	22

☑ Mama's Wash. Sq. | **N Beach**	25
Model Bakery | **St. Helena/N**	21
☑ Tartine | **Mission**	26
Town's End | **Embarcadero**	19

BARBECUE

☑ Bo's Barbecue | **Lafayette/E**	23
Bounty Hunter | **Napa/N**	17
☑ Buckeye | **Mill Valley/N**	23
Everett & Jones | **multi. loc.**	20
Memphis Minnie | **Lower Haight**	20
Q | **Inner Rich**	20
NEW Roadside BBQ | **Inner Rich**	19
T Rex Barbecue | **Berkeley/E**	17
Uncle Frank's | **Mtn View/S**	22
Zeitgeist | **Mission**	16

BELGIAN

Frjtz Fries | **multi. loc.**	19

BRAZILIAN

Barracuda | **multi. loc.**	17
Espetus | **Hayes Valley**	21
Mangarosa | **N Beach**	19

BRITISH

Betty's Fish | **Santa Rosa/N**	20
Lovejoy's Tea | **Noe Valley**	20

BURMESE

Burma Superstar | **Inner Rich**	24
Mandalay | **Inner Rich**	21
Nan Yang | **Oakland/E**	22

CAJUN

☑ Chenery Park | **Glen Pk**	22
Elite Cafe | **Upper Fillmore**	19
Kingfish | **San Mateo/S**	17

CALIFORNIAN

Adagia | **Berkeley/E**	19
☑ Ahwahnee | **Yosemite/E**	19
Albion River Inn | **Albion/N**	24
All Season's | **Calistoga/N**	21
Amber Bistro | **Danville/E**	20
Americano | **Embarcadero**	17
Applewood Inn | **Guerneville/N**	24
☑ Aqua | **Downtown**	26
A. Sabella's | **Fish. Wharf**	18
AsiaSF | **SoMa**	17
Asqew Grill | **multi. loc.**	18
☑ Auberge du Sol. | **Rutherford/N**	25

bacar | **SoMa**	22
Bar Tartine | **Mission**	22
☑ Bay Wolf | **Oakland/E**	25
Bistro Aix | **Marina**	22
Bistro Boudin | **Fish. Wharf**	20
Bistro Elan | **Palo Alto/S**	24
Bistro Ralph | **Healdsburg/N**	21
Blackhawk Grille | **Danville/E**	19
Boon Fly Café | **Napa/N**	-
Boonville Hotel | **Boonville/N**	21
Bouchée | **Carmel/S**	26
Bridges | **Danville/E**	20
BRIX | **Yountville/N**	22
Bucci's | **Emeryville/E**	20
Butterfly | **Embarcadero**	19
Cafe Beaujolais | **Mendocino/N**	25
Café Cacao | **Berkeley/E**	20
☑ Cafe La Haye | **Sonoma/N**	26
Café Majestic | **Pacific Hts**	-
Café Rustica | **Carmel Valley/S**	23
Caffè Verbena | **Oakland/E**	19
Canteen | **Downtown**	25
Carnelian Room | **Downtown**	17
Carneros Bistro | **Sonoma/N**	22
Central Market | **Petaluma/N**	23
☑ Chez Panisse | **Berkeley/E**	27
☑ Chez Panisse Café | **Berkeley/E**	27
Christy Hill | **Tahoe City/E**	25
Cindy's | **St. Helena/N**	24
Citizen Cake | **multi. loc.**	20
Citron | **Oakland/E**	24
Cliff House Bistro | **Outer Rich**	18
Club XIX | **Pebble Bch/S**	25
Coco 500 | **SoMa**	22
Coi | **N Beach**	25
Deetjen's | **Big Sur/S**	22
downtown | **Berkeley/E**	20
Dragonfly | **Truckee/E**	23
Drake's | **Inverness/N**	19
Ecco | **Burlingame/S**	21
El Dorado | **Sonoma/N**	23
Eos Rest./Wine | **Cole Valley**	23
☑ Erna's Elderberry | **Oakhurst/E**	28
Étoile | **Yountville/N**	25
☑ Farmhouse | **Forestville/N**	27
1550 Hyde | **Russian Hill**	22
Fifth Floor | **SoMa**	25
Firecracker | **Mission**	19

Fishwife | **Pacific Grove/S**	23
Flavor | **Santa Rosa/N**	20
Flea St. Café | **Menlo Pk/S**	22
☑ Fleur de Lys | **Nob Hill**	28
Flying Fish | **Half Moon Bay/S**	21
Foreign Cinema | **Mission**	21
Fork | **San Anselmo/N**	24
Fournou's | **Nob Hill**	22
☑ Frascati | **Russian Hill**	26
Gabriella Café | **Santa Cruz/S**	22
☑ Garden Court | **Downtown**	19
Garibaldis | **multi. loc.**	21
Globe | **Downtown**	21
Grasing's Coastal | **Carmel/S**	23
Heritage House | **Little River/N**	–
Hurley's | **Yountville/N**	20
Jack Falstaff | **SoMa**	20
Jake's/Lake | **Tahoe City/E**	16
☑ Jardinière | **Hayes Valley**	26
Jimmy Bean's | **Berkeley/E**	20
John Ash & Co. | **Santa Rosa/N**	23
☑ John Bentley's | **multi. loc.**	25
Jordan's | **Berkeley/E**	18
Julia's | **Napa/N**	23
jZcool | **Menlo Pk/S**	20
Kitchen at 868 | **Novato/N**	25
Lalime's | **Berkeley/E**	26
La Scene | **Downtown**	17
☑ L'Auberge | **Carmel/S**	27
Ledford Hse. | **Albion/N**	23
Little River Inn | **Little River/N**	20
Luella | **Russian Hill**	22
Luka's Taproom | **Oakland/E**	20
Lure | **San Mateo/S**	23
MacCallum Hse. | **Mendocino/N**	24
NEW Mandaloun | **Redwood City/S**	–
Mantra | **Palo Alto/S**	20
Manzanita | **Healdsburg/N**	20
Meadowood | **St. Helena/N**	20
Mendocino Hotel | **Mendocino/N**	17
Mezze | **Oakland/E**	23
Modern Tea | **Hayes Valley**	20
Montrio Bistro | **Monterey/S**	23
Moody's Bistro | **Truckee/E**	25
Moosse Café | **Mendocino/N**	23
Mosaic Rest. | **Forestville/N**	25
Mustards Grill | **Yountville/N**	24

Napa General | **Napa/N**	20
Napa Valley Grille | **Yountville/N**	20
Napa Wine Train | **Napa/N**	15
Nectar Wine | **multl. loc.**	19
NEW Nick's Cove | **Marshall/N**	–
NoPa | **W Addition**	23
n.v. Rest. | **Napa/N**	22
Olema Inn | **Olema/N**	22
Oola | **SoMa**	20
Osake/Sake 'O | **Santa Rosa/N**	22
Pangaea | **Gualala/N**	25
Pappo | **Alameda/E**	23
Parcel 104 | **Santa Clara/S**	23
Passionfish | **Pacific Grove/S**	25
Pearl | **Napa/N**	22
NEW Piccino | **Dogpatch**	19
Pilar | **Napa/N**	25
Plumed Horse | **Saratoga/S**	–
PlumpJack | **multi. loc.**	24
Ravenous Cafe | **Healdsburg/N**	23
☑ Redd Rest. | **Yountville/N**	26
Rest. at Meadowood | **St. Helena/N**	23
Richmond Rest. | **Inner Rich**	22
Rio Grill | **Carmel/S**	22
River Ranch | **Tahoe City/E**	17
☑ Rivoli | **Berkeley/E**	27
Rogue Chefs | **Half Moon Bay/S**	21
Rubicon | **Downtown**	24
Saha | **Tenderloin**	24
Santé | **Sonoma/N**	24
Scott Howard | **Downtown**	23
Seaweed Café | **Bodega Bay/N**	24
Sent Sovi | **Saratoga/S**	24
71 Saint Peter | **San Jose/S**	22
☑ Shadowbrook | **Capitola/S**	22
☑ Sierra Mar | **Big Sur/S**	26
Soizic | **Oakland/E**	22
Sooze Wine | **Petaluma/N**	18
Spettro | **Oakland/E**	20
Station House | **Pt Reyes/N**	17
St. Michael's | **Palo Alto/S**	22
Stokes | **Monterey/S**	23
St. Orres | **Gualala/N**	24
Sushi Groove | **Walnut Creek/E**	23
Sutro's | **Outer Rich**	19
Syrah | **Santa Rosa/N**	25
Table Café | **Larkspur/N**	24

Theo's | **Soquel/S**	24
Townhouse B&G | **Emeryville/E**	21
2223 | **Castro**	21
NEW TWO | **SoMa**	21
NEW Ubuntu | **Napa/N**	-
Venus | **Berkeley/E**	19
Waterfront | **Embarcadero**	18
Wente Vineyards | **Livermore/E**	23
NEW West Co. Grill | **Sebastopol/N**	-
Wine Spectator | **St. Helena/N**	22
Wolfdale's | **Tahoe City/E**	25
Wolf House | **Glen Ellen/N**	20
NEW Wood Tav. | **Oakland/E**	23
Woodward's Gdn. | **Mission**	25
XYZ | **SoMa**	20

CAMBODIAN

Angkor Borei | **Mission**	20
Battambang | **Oakland/E**	22

CARIBBEAN

Cha Cha Cha | **multi. loc.**	19
Fishwife | **Pacific Grove/S**	23
NEW Front Porch | **N Beach**	20

CAVIAR

Tsar Nicoulai | **Embarcadero**	22

CHEESE STEAKS

Jake's Steaks | **Cow Hollow**	20
Jay's | **multi. loc.**	17

CHINESE

(* dim sum specialist)

Alice's | **Noe Valley**	19
Bow Hon 4 | **Chinatown**	22
Brandy Ho's | **multi. loc.**	20
Chef Chu's | **Los Altos/S**	20
NEW Chef Wai | **San Mateo/S**	20
Dragon Well | **Marina**	20
Eliza's | **multi. loc.**	22
Eric's | **Noe Valley**	20
Firecracker | **Mission**	19
Fook Yuen* | **Millbrae/S**	20
Gary Chu's | **Santa Rosa/N**	22
Gold Mountain* | **Chinatown**	20
Good Luck* | **Inner Rich**	22
Great China | **Berkeley/E**	23
Great Eastern* | **Chinatown**	22
Happy Cafe* | **San Mateo/S**	22

Henry's Hunan | **multi. loc.**	21
House of Nanking | **Chinatown**	21
Hunan | **multi. loc.**	22
Imperial/Berkeley | **multi. loc.**	17
Jai Yun | **Chinatown**	23
Koi Palace* | **Daly City/S**	23
Mayflower* | **Outer Rich**	22
New Asia | **Chinatown**	18
Z O'mei | **Santa Cruz/S**	26
Oriental Pearl | **Chinatown**	22
R & G Lounge | **Chinatown**	23
Rest. Peony* | **Oakland/E**	20
San Tung | **Inner Sunset**	23
Shanghai Dumpling | **Outer Rich**	22
Shanghai 1930 | **Embarcadero**	20
Shen Hua | **Berkeley/E**	20
Sino* | **San Jose/S**	20
Tai Pan | **Palo Alto/S**	23
Tommy Toy's | **Downtown**	24
Z Ton Kiang* | **Outer Rich**	25
Z Yank Sing* | **multi. loc.**	25
Yuet Lee | **Chinatown**	21

COFFEEHOUSES

Café Cacao | **Berkeley/E**	20

COFFEE SHOPS/DINERS

Bette's Oceanview | **Berkeley/E**	21
FatApple's | **multi. loc.**	17
Jimmy Bean's | **Berkeley/E**	20
Mel's Drive-In | **multi. loc.**	13
Pine Cone Diner | **Pt Reyes/N**	19
Sears Fine Food | **Downtown**	18
St. Francis | **Mission**	19
Taylor's Auto | **multi. loc.**	21

CONTINENTAL

Anton & Michel | **Carmel/S**	23
Bella Vista | **Woodside/S**	22
Chantilly | **Redwood City/S**	25
Ecco | **Burlingame/S**	21
Z Fresh Cream | **Monterey/S**	24
Maddalena/Fino | **Palo Alto/S**	21
O'Reilly's | **Polk Gulch**	18

CREOLE

Elite Cafe | **Upper Fillmore**	19
PJ's Oyster | **Inner Sunset**	19

CUBAN

Asia de Cuba | **Downtown**	21

DELIS

Jimtown Store	**Healdsburg/N**	19
Max's	**multi. loc.**	16
Moishe's Pippic	**Hayes Valley**	19
Saul's Rest./Deli	**Berkeley/E**	18

DESSERT

Café Cacao	**Berkeley/E**	20
Cheesecake	**multi. loc.**	16
Downtown Bakery	**Healdsburg/N**	24
Emporio Rulli	**multi. loc.**	20
⚡ Tartine	**Mission**	26
Town Hall	**SoMa**	23

ECLECTIC

NEW Alembic	**Haight-Ashbury**	22
Andalu	**Mission**	20
Avatars	**Sausalito/N**	22
Celadon	**Napa/N**	23
Chez Shea	**Half Moon Bay/S**	22
Cottonwood	**Truckee/E**	20
Delancey St.	**Embarcadero**	18
Della Fattoria	**Petaluma/N**	26
NEW District	**SoMa**	17
⚡ Firefly	**Noe Valley**	25
Flavor	**Santa Rosa/N**	20
NEW Go Fish	**St. Helena/N**	24
Jodie's Rest.	**Albany/E**	20
NEW Jovino	**Cow Hollow**	-
Levende	**multi. loc.**	20
Lime	**Castro**	18
Maria Manso	**San Rafael/N**	20
Napa General	**Napa/N**	20
Pomelo	**multi. loc.**	22
NEW Pres a Vi	**Presidio**	21
Ravenous Cafe	**Healdsburg/N**	23
Red Door	**Nob Hill**	20
Restaurant	**Ft Bragg/N**	23
⚡ Sierra Mar	**Big Sur/S**	26
supperclub	**SoMa**	17
Va de Vi	**Walnut Creek/E**	24
Wappo Bar	**Calistoga/N**	22
Willi's Wine	**Santa Rosa/N**	24
⚡ Willow Wood	**Graton/N**	25

ETHIOPIAN

Axum Cafe	**Lower Haight**	20
Massawa	**Haight-Ashbury**	21

FRENCH

À Côté	**Oakland/E**	24
⚡ Ana Mandara	**Fish. Wharf**	23
Angèle	**Napa/N**	22
⚡ Aqua	**Downtown**	26
⚡ Auberge du Sol.	**Rutherford/N**	25
Baraka	**Potrero Hill**	21
NEW Bistro/Copains	**Occidental/N**	27
Bistro V	**Sebastopol/N**	22
⚡ BIX	**Downtown**	23
Boulange	**multi. loc.**	22
Brannan's Grill	**Calistoga/N**	19
Cafe Beaujolais	**Mendocino/N**	25
Café Fanny	**Berkeley/E**	22
Cafe Jacqueline	**N Beach**	26
Café Majestic	**Pacific Hts**	-
Café Marcella	**Los Gatos/S**	24
Casanova	**Carmel/S**	23
Chez Spencer	**Mission**	24
Club XIX	**Pebble Bch/S**	25
Coi	**N Beach**	25
Couleur Café	**Potrero Hill**	16
El Paseo	**Mill Valley/N**	23
fig cafe	**Glen Ellen/N**	23
Fork	**San Anselmo/N**	24
⚡ French Laundry	**Yountville/N**	29
Gregoire	**multi. loc.**	24
Isa	**Marina**	24
⚡ Jardinière	**Hayes Valley**	26
Jordan's	**Berkeley/E**	18
Julia's	**Napa/N**	23
Kenwood	**Kenwood/N**	22
⚡ La Folie	**Russian Hill**	27
La Forêt	**San Jose/S**	27
La Provence	**Mission**	18
⚡ La Toque	**Rutherford/N**	26
Luna Park	**Mission**	19
⚡ Madrona Manor	**Healdsburg/N**	25
Mistral	**Redwood Shores/S**	19
Nizza La Bella	**Albany/E**	19
Olivia	**Berkeley/E**	23
⚡ Pacific's Edge	**Carmel/S**	25
Pangaea	**Gualala/N**	25
NEW Rest. Cassis	**Pacific Hts**	-
Rest. LuLu/Petite	**SoMa**	20
rnm rest.	**Lower Haight**	25

CUISINES

Robert's | **Pacific Grove/S**	25
NEW Rouge/Blanc | **Downtown**	–
Scala's Bistro | **Downtown**	22
Scott Howard | **Downtown**	23
Seaweed Café | **Bodega Bay/N**	24
Seven | **San Jose/S**	21
Soizic | **Oakland/E**	22
Sonoma Meritage | **Sonoma/N**	19
Sparrow | **Nob Hill**	20
Theo's | **Soquel/S**	24
Viognier | **San Mateo/S**	24

FRENCH (BISTRO)

Alamo Sq. | **W Addition**	21
Anjou | **Downtown**	23
Baker St. Bistro | **Marina**	20
Bistro Aix | **Marina**	22
Bistro Clovis | **Hayes Valley**	19
Bistro Elan | **Palo Alto/S**	24
Z Bistro Jeanty | **Yountville/N**	25
Bistro Liaison | **Berkeley/E**	22
Bistro Ralph | **Healdsburg/N**	21
Bistro Vida | **Menlo Pk/S**	18
Z Bouchon | **Yountville/N**	25
Butler & The Chef | **SoMa**	20
Cafe Bastille | **Downtown**	18
Café Claude | **Downtown**	20
Café de la Presse | **Downtown**	16
Café Rouge | **Berkeley/E**	21
Z Chapeau! | **Outer Rich**	27
Charcuterie | **Healdsburg/N**	22
Chez Maman | **multi. loc.**	21
Chez Papa Bistrot | **Potrero Hill**	23
Chouchou | **Forest Hills**	21
Christophe | **Sausalito/N**	20
Clémentine | **Inner Rich**	24
Côté Sud | **Castro**	20
Florio | **Pacific Hts**	19
Z Fringale | **SoMa**	24
girl & the fig | **Sonoma/N**	23
Grand Cafe | **Downtown**	20
Hyde St. Bistro | **Russian Hill**	21
Jeanty at Jack's | **Downtown**	23
Jojo | **Oakland/E**	25
K&L Bistro | **Sebastopol/N**	25
La Note | **Berkeley/E**	22
NEW La Terrasse | **Presidio**	19
Le Central Bistro | **Downtown**	19

Le Charm Bistro | **SoMa**	21
Le Petit Robert | **Russian Hill**	19
NEW Le P'tit Laurent | **Glen Pk**	–
Le Zinc | **Noe Valley**	18
Z Mirepoix | **Windsor/N**	26
Pearl Alley | **Santa Cruz/S**	22
Plouf | **Downtown**	22
South Park | **SoMa**	22
Syrah | **Santa Rosa/N**	25
Ti Couz | **Mission**	22
Water St. Bistro | **Petaluma/N**	24
Zazie | **Cole Valley**	22

FRENCH (BRASSERIE)

Absinthe | **Hayes Valley**	20
Left Bank | **multi. loc.**	18
Luka's Taproom | **Oakland/E**	20

FRENCH (NEW)

Bouchée | **Carmel/S**	26
Chaya Brasserie | **Embarcadero**	21
Chez TJ | **Mtn View/S**	25
Citron | **Oakland/E**	24
Z Cyrus | **Healdsburg/N**	28
Z Erna's Elderberry | **Oakhurst/E**	28
Fifth Floor | **SoMa**	25
Z Fleur de Lys | **Nob Hill**	28
Le Colonial | **Downtown**	21
Z Le Papillon | **San Jose/S**	27
Les Amis | **Downtown**	22
Z Marché | **Menlo Pk/S**	26
Marché aux Fleurs | **Ross/N**	25
Z Marinus | **Carmel Valley/S**	26
Z Masa's | **Downtown**	27
955 Ukiah | **Mendocino/N**	22
Z Quince | **Pacific Hts**	26
Rendezvous Inn | **Ft Bragg/N**	27
Rigolo | **Presidio Hts**	18
Z Ritz-Carlton Din. Rm. | **Nob Hill**	27
SUMI | **Castro**	23

GERMAN

Rosamunde Grill | **Lower Haight**	25
Suppenküche | **Hayes Valley**	21
Walzwerk | **Mission**	20

GREEK

NEW Dio Deka | **Los Gatos/S**	–
Z Evvia | **Palo Alto/S**	26
Z Kokkari | **Downtown**	26
Thea Med. | **San Jose/S**	21

HAMBURGERS

Balboa Cafe	**Cow Hollow**	19
Barney's	**multi. loc.**	19
Burger Joint	**multi. loc.**	18
FatApple's	**multi. loc.**	17
☑ In-N-Out	**multi. loc.**	22
☑ Joe's Cable Car	**Excelsior**	24
Mel's Drive-In	**multi. loc.**	13
Mo's	**multi. loc.**	20
Red's Java	**Embarcadero**	14
Taylor's Auto	**multi. loc.**	21

HAWAIIAN

Roy's	**SoMa**	22
Roy's	**Pebble Bch/S**	25

HEALTH FOOD

jZcool	**Menlo Pk/S**	20
Lettus	**Marina**	20
Mixt Greens	**Downtown**	22

HOT DOGS

Caspers Hot Dogs	**multi. loc.**	18
NEW Underdog	**Inner Sunset**	-

ICE CREAM PARLORS

Fentons Creamery	**Oakland/E**	18

INDIAN

☑ Ajanta	**Berkeley/E**	24
☑ Amber India	**multi. loc.**	25
Breads of India	**multi. loc.**	21
Dasaprakash	**Santa Clara/S**	21
Dosa	**Mission**	20
Gaylord India	**multi. loc.**	18
Indian Oven	**Lower Haight**	23
Junnoon	**Palo Alto/S**	22
Kabab & Curry	**Santa Rosa/N**	21
Lotus of India	**San Rafael/N**	22
Mantra	**Palo Alto/S**	20
Naan/Curry	**multi. loc.**	18
Passage to India	**Mtn View/S**	19
Rotee	**Lower Haight**	18
Roti Indian	**multi. loc.**	23
Shalimar	**multi. loc.**	22
Turmeric	**Sunnyvale/S**	21
Udupi Palace	**multi. loc.**	20
Vik's Chaat	**Berkeley/E**	23
Zante	**Bernal Hts**	18

ITALIAN

(N=Northern; S=Southern)

☑ Acquerello	**Polk Gulch**	27
Albona Rist.	N	**N Beach**	24
Alioto's	S	**Fish. Wharf**	19
Antica Trattoria	**Russian Hill**	23
Aperto	**Potrero Hill**	20
☑ A 16	S	**Marina**	23
NEW Bar Bambino	**Mission**	-
Bella Trattoria	S	**Inner Rich**	21
Bistro Don Giovanni	**Napa/N**	23
Bistro V	**Sebastopol/N**	22
Bovolo	**Healdsburg/N**	22
Brindisi	S	**Downtown**	18
Buca di Beppo	**multi. loc.**	14
Bucci's	**Emeryville/E**	20
Cafe Citti	N	**Kenwood/N**	22
Café Fiore	N	**S Lake Tahoe/E**	24
Café Tiramisu	N	**Downtown**	21
Caffe Delle Stelle	N	**Hayes Valley**	16
Caffè Macaroni	S	**N Beach**	20
Caffè Museo	**SoMa**	16
Caffè Verbena	**Oakland/E**	19
Cantinetta Luca	**Carmel/S**	22
Casanova	N	**Carmel/S**	23
Casa Orinda	**Orinda/E**	17
NEW Chiaroscuro	S	**Downtown**	-
Cook St. Helena	N	**St. Helena/N**	24
Cork	**Sausalito/N**	19
Cucina Paradiso	S	**Petaluma/N**	26
Cucina Rest.	**San Anselmo/N**	24
☑ Delfina	N	**Mission**	26
Della Santina's	N	**Sonoma/N**	21
Dopo	**Oakland/E**	25
NEW Ducca	N	**SoMa**	-
E'Angelo	**Marina**	20
Eccolo	N	**Berkeley/E**	20
Emmy's Spaghetti	**Bernal Hts**	19
Emporio Rulli	**multi. loc.**	20
NEW Farina	**Mission**	-
Fior d'Italia	N	**N Beach**	19
Florio	**Pacific Hts**	19
Frantoio	N	**Mill Valley/N**	21
Gabriella Café	**Santa Cruz/S**	22
NEW Gialina	**Glen Pk**	24
Globe	**Downtown**	21
Il Davide	N	**San Rafael/N**	21

🅉 Il Fornaio | **multi. loc.**	19
Il Postale | **Sunnyvale/S**	20
Incanto | N | **Noe Valley**	24
Jackson Fillmore | **Upper Fillmore**	21
Joe DiMaggio's | **N Beach**	20
Julius Castle | **Telegraph Hill**	–
Kuleto's | N | **multi. loc.**	20
La Ciccia | **Noe Valley**	22
La Ginestra | S | **Mill Valley/N**	18
La Strada | **Palo Alto/S**	21
Last Supper | S | **Mission**	19
Lo Coco's | S | **multi. loc.**	21
L'Osteria | N | **N Beach**	24
Mangarosa | **N Beach**	19
Mario's Bohemian | N | **N Beach**	18
Mescolanza | N | **Outer Rich**	22
Mezza Luna | S | **Princeton Sea/S**	21
Mistral | **Redwood Shores/S**	19
Nizza La Bella | **Albany/E**	19
Nob Hill Café | N | **Nob Hill**	20
North Beach Rest. | N | **N Beach**	21
Oliveto Cafe | **Oakland/E**	23
Oliveto Restaurant | **Oakland/E**	25
Original Joe's | **multi. loc.**	18
Osteria | **Palo Alto/S**	23
Ottimista | **Cow Hollow**	20
Palio d'Asti | **Downtown**	19
Pane e Vino | N | **Cow Hollow**	22
Pasta Moon | **Half Moon Bay/S**	22
Pasta Pomodoro | **multi. loc.**	16
Pazzia | **SoMa**	22
🆕 Perbacco | **Downtown**	24
Pesce | N | **Russian Hill**	22
Pianeta | N | **Truckee/E**	23
Piatti | **multi. loc.**	19
Piazza D'Angelo | **Mill Valley/N**	19
🆕 Piccino | **Dogpatch**	19
Picco | **Larkspur/N**	24
Pizza Antica | **multi. loc.**	21
Pizza Azzurro | **Napa/N**	22
Pizzaiolo | S | **Oakland/E**	24
🅉 Pizzeria Picco | S | **Larkspur/N**	25
Pizzeria Tra Vigne | **St. Helena/N**	21
Poggio | N | **Sausalito/N**	21
🅉 Postino | **Lafayette/E**	24
Prima | N | **Walnut Creek/E**	24
Quattro | **E Palo Alto/S**	22

🅉 Quince | **Pacific Hts**	26
Rist. Bacco | **Noe Valley**	23
Rist. Capellini | **San Mateo/S**	19
Rist. Fabrizio | N | **Larkspur/N**	19
Rist. Ideale | S | **N Beach**	24
Rist. Milano | N | **Russian Hill**	24
Ristorante Parma | **Marina**	22
Rist. Umbria | N | **SoMa**	20
Rose Pistola | N | **N Beach**	21
Rose's Cafe | N | **Cow Hollow**	21
Salute E Rist. | **Richmond/E**	19
Santi | N | **Geyserville/N**	23
Scoma's | **Sausalito/N**	21
Sharon's | **Ft Bragg/N**	20
Sociale | N | **Presidio Hts**	23
Sonoma Meritage | N | **Sonoma/N**	19
Spettro | **Oakland/E**	20
Tommaso's | S | **N Beach**	25
Tratt. Contadina | **N Beach**	23
Tratt. La Siciliana | S | **Berkeley/E**	23
Tra Vigne | N | **St. Helena/N**	23
Uva Trattoria | **Napa/N**	21
Venezia | **Berkeley/E**	20
Venticello | N | **Nob Hill**	23
🆕 Vittoria | **Los Gatos/S**	20
Vivande | S | **Pacific Hts**	23
Washington Sq. B&G | **N Beach**	19
🆕 West Co. Grill | **Sebastopol/N**	–
zazu | N | **Santa Rosa/N**	25
Zuppa | S | **SoMa**	19

JAPANESE

(* sushi specialist)

Ace Wasabi's* | **Marina**	20
🅉 Alexander's | **Cupertino/S**	25
ANZU* | **Downtown**	21
Ariake | **Outer Rich**	26
Barracuda | **multi. loc.**	17
Blowfish Sushi* | **multi. loc.**	21
Bushi-tei | **Japantown**	24
Chaya Brasserie | **Embarcadero**	21
Cha-Ya Veg.* | **multi. loc.**	24
Daimaru* | **Castro**	24
Deep Sushi* | **Noe Valley**	21
Ebisu* | **Inner Sunset**	23
Fuki Sushi* | **Palo Alto/S**	23
Godzila Sushi* | **Pacific Hts**	17

Grandeho Kamekyo* | multi. loc.	23
Hamano Sushi* | Noe Valley	20
Hana Japanese* | Rohnert Pk/N	25
NEW Hime* | Marina	22
Hotaru | San Mateo/S	22
Hotei* | Inner Sunset	18
Isobune* | Japantown	17
Juban | multi. loc.	17
Kabuto* | Outer Rich	25
NEW Kanpai* | Palo Alto/S	24
☑ Kaygetsu* | Menlo Pk/S	28
Kiji Sushi Bar* | Mission	24
Kirala* | Berkeley/E	25
Kiss Sushi | Japantown	27
Koo* | Inner Sunset	24
Kyo-Ya* | Downtown	23
Maki | Japantown	23
Medicine | Downtown	18
Mifune | Japantown	18
Moki's Sushi* | Bernal Hts	21
Naked Fish* | S Lake Tahoe/E	22
Naomi Sushi* | Menlo Pk/S	21
Nihon | Mission	21
O Chamé | Berkeley/E	24
Osake/Sake 'O' | multi. loc.	22
Oyaji | Outer Rich	23
Ozumo | Embarcadero	24
Robata Grill* | Mill Valley/N	20
Ryoko's* | Tenderloin	23
Sanraku* | multi. loc.	23
Sebo* | Hayes Valley	25
Shabu-Sen | Japantown	18
NEW Sudachi* | Polk Gulch	–
Sushi Groove* | multi. loc.	23
☑ Sushi Ran* | Sausalito/N	28
Sushi Zone* | Castro	26
Takara* | Japantown	22
Ten-Ichi* | Upper Fillmore	21
Tokyo Go Go* | Mission	22
Tsunami* | W Addition	23
NEW Umami | Cow Hollow	20
Uzen* | Oakland/E	24
Yoshi's* | Oakland/E	18
Yuzu* | Marina	19
Zushi Puzzle* | Marina	26

JEWISH

Saul's Rest./Deli | Berkeley/E	18

KOREAN

(* barbecue specialist)

Brother's Korean* | Inner Rich	22
Koryo BBQ* | Oakland/E	21
My Tofu* | Inner Rich	20
RoHan Lounge | Inner Rich	18
San Tung | Inner Sunset	23
So | Outer Sunset	21

MEDITERRANEAN

Absinthe | Hayes Valley	20
À Côté | Oakland/E	24
bacar | SoMa	22
Bar Tartine | Mission	22
☑ Bay Wolf | Oakland/E	25
Belden Taverna | Downtown	20
Bursa Kebab | W Portal	19
Cafe Gibraltar | El Granada/S	25
Café Marcella | Los Gatos/S	24
Café Rouge | Berkeley/E	21
Caffè Museo | SoMa	16
Campton Place | Downtown	25
Cav Wine Bar | Hayes Valley	22
Central Market | Petaluma/N	23
Cetrella | Half Moon Bay/S	22
☑ Chez Panisse | Berkeley/E	27
☑ Chez Panisse Café | Berkeley/E	27
Coco 500 | SoMa	22
Cortez | Downtown	23
Couleur Café | Potrero Hill	16
NEW Dio Deka | Los Gatos/S	–
downtown | Berkeley/E	20
El Dorado | Sonoma/N	23
Enrico's | N Beach	–
Fandango | Pacific Grove/S	23
1550 Hyde | Russian Hill	22
Foreign Cinema | Mission	21
Fournou's | Nob Hill	22
☑ Frascati | Russian Hill	26
Garibaldis | multi. loc.	21
Gar Woods | Carnelian Bay/E	19
Hurley's | Yountville/N	20
Insalata's | San Anselmo/N	24
Lalime's | Berkeley/E	26
La Méditerranée | multi. loc.	19
La Scene | Downtown	17
Lavanda | Palo Alto/S	19
Ledford Hse. | Albion/N	23
Luella | Russian Hill	22

NEW Mandaloun | **Redwood City/S**	–
Manzanita | **Healdsburg/N**	20
MarketBar | **Embarcadero**	17
Medjool | **Mission**	18
Mezze | **Oakland/E**	23
Monti's | **Santa Rosa/N**	19
NEW Nua Rest. | **N Beach**	–
Olema Inn | **Olema/N**	22
Ottimista | **Cow Hollow**	20
NEW Palmetto | **Cow Hollow**	–
Pappo | **Alameda/E**	23
paul k | **Hayes Valley**	21
PlumpJack | **multi. loc.**	24
Rest. at Stevenswood | **Little River/N**	20
Rest. LuLu/Petite | **SoMa**	20
⚡ Ritz-Carlton Terr. | **Nob Hill**	24
⚡ Rivoli | **Berkeley/E**	27
Savor | **Noe Valley**	18
71 Saint Peter | **San Jose/S**	22
Stokes | **Monterey/S**	23
Terzo | **Cow Hollow**	22
Thea Med. | **San Jose/S**	21
⚡ Truly Med. | **Mission**	23
Underwood Bar | **Graton/N**	22
Wente Vineyards | **Livermore/E**	23
⚡ Willow Wood | **Graton/N**	25
Zatar | **Berkeley/E**	21
Zibibbo | **Palo Alto/S**	20
Zucca | **Mtn View/S**	19
⚡ Zuni Café | **Hayes Valley**	25

MEXICAN

Cactus Taqueria | **multi. loc.**	20
Colibrí Mexican | **Downtown**	20
Doña Tomás | **Oakland/E**	24
Don Pico's | **San Bruno/S**	20
El Balazo | **Haight-Ashbury**	18
El Metate | **Mission**	23
Green Chile | **W Addition**	19
Guaymas | **Tiburon/N**	17
Joe's Taco | **Mill Valley/N**	18
Juan's | **Berkeley/E**	16
La Cumbre | **multi. loc.**	22
Las Camelias | **San Rafael/N**	20
⚡ La Taqueria | **multi. loc.**	24
La Victoria | **San Jose/S**	20
Mamacita | **Marina**	22

Maya | **SoMa**	22
NEW Mexico DF | **Embarcadero**	–
Mijita | **Embarcadero**	20
Nick's Tacos | **Russian Hill**	20
Pancho Villa | **multi. loc.**	20
Papalote | **multi. loc.**	21
Picante Cocina | **Berkeley/E**	21
Puerto Alegre | **Mission**	18
Tacubaya | **Berkeley/E**	22
⚡ Tamarindo | **Oakland/E**	24
Taqueria Can-Cun | **multi. loc.**	21
Taqueria 3 Amigos | **multi. loc.**	18
Taqueria Tlaquepaque | **San Jose/S**	23
Tres Agaves | **S Beach**	18
NEW Zazil Coastal | **Downtown**	19

MIDDLE EASTERN

⚡ Dish Dash | **Sunnyvale/S**	23
Goood Frikin' Chicken | **Mission**	19
Kan Zaman | **Haight-Ashbury**	17
La Méditerranée | **multi. loc.**	19
Saha | **Tenderloin**	24
⚡ Truly Med. | **Mission**	23
Yumma's | **Inner Sunset**	20

MOROCCAN

Aziza | **Outer Rich**	24
Tajine | **Polk Gulch**	23

NEPALESE

Little Nepal | **Bernal Hts**	21

NEW ENGLAND

Old Port/N. Bch. Lobster | **multi. loc.**	21
Woodhse. | **Castro**	19
Yankee Pier | **multi. loc.**	17

NOODLE SHOPS

Citizen Thai | **N Beach**	20
Citrus Club | **Haight-Ashbury**	19
Hotei | **Inner Sunset**	18
Mifune | **Japantown**	18
Osha Thai | **multi. loc.**	22
San Tung | **Inner Sunset**	23
So | **Outer Sunset**	21
Zao Noodle | **multi. loc.**	14

NUEVO LATINO

Circolo | **Mission**	19
Sol y Lago | **Tahoe City/E**	17

PACIFIC RIM

Pacific Catch	**multi. loc.**	21
Z Silks	**Downtown**	24
Tonga	**Nob Hill**	13

PAKISTANI

Naan/Curry	**multi. loc.**	18
Pakwan	**multi. loc.**	21
Rotee	**Lower Haight**	18
Shalimar	**multi. loc.**	22

PAN-ASIAN

Betelnut Pejiu	**Cow Hollow**	23
NEW B Star Bar	**Inner Rich**	–
Bushi-tei	**Japantown**	24
Citrus Club	**Haight-Ashbury**	19
NEW Mercury	**Marina**	–
Ora	**Mill Valley/N**	21
Poleng	**W Addition**	22
Ponzu	**Downtown**	21
RoHan Lounge	**Inner Rich**	18
Straits Cafe	**multi. loc.**	20
Tonga	**Nob Hill**	13
Zao Noodle	**multi. loc.**	14

PAN-LATIN

Cascal	**Mtn View/S**	20
Charanga	**Mission**	21
Z Fonda Solana	**Albany/E**	24

PERSIAN

Maykadeh	**N Beach**	23

PERUVIAN

Destino	**Castro**	22
NEW Essencia	**Hayes Valley**	–
Fresca	**multi. loc.**	22
Z Limón	**Mission**	22
Mochica	**SoMa**	23
NEW Piqueo's	**Bernal Hts**	–

PIZZA

Amici's	**multi. loc.**	20
Arinell Pizza	**multi. loc.**	22
NEW Gialina	**Glen Pk**	24
Gioia Pizzeria	**Berkeley/E**	24
Giorgio's Pizzeria	**Inner Rich**	20
Goat Hill Pizza	**multi. loc.**	19
La Ginestra	**Mill Valley/N**	18
Lanesplitter Pub	**multi. loc.**	18
Z Little Star Pizza	**multi. loc.**	25

Lo Coco's	**multi. loc.**	21
North Beach Pizza	**multi. loc.**	18
Palio d'Asti	**Downtown**	19
Patxi's Pizza	**multi. loc.**	20
Pauline's Pizza	**Mission**	22
Pizza Antica	**multi. loc.**	21
Pizza Azzurro	**Napa/N**	22
Pizzaiolo	**Oakland/E**	24
Pizza Rustica	**Oakland/E**	19
Pizzeria Delfina	**Mission**	24
Z Pizzeria Picco	**Larkspur/N**	25
Pizzeria Tra Vigne	**St. Helena/N**	21
Pizzetta 211	**Outer Rich**	25
Z Postrio	**Downtown**	24
Rigolo	**Presidio Hts**	18
Tommaso's	**N Beach**	25
Zachary's Pizza	**multi. loc.**	24
Zante	**Bernal Hts**	18

POLYNESIAN

Trader Vic's	**multi. loc.**	16

PORTUGUESE

LaSalette	**Sonoma/N**	23

PUB FOOD

Bridgetender	**Tahoe City/E**	16

RUSSIAN

Katia's Tea	**Inner Rich**	19

SANDWICHES

Downtown Bakery	**Healdsburg/N**	24
Gayle's Bakery	**Capitola/S**	25
Giordano	**N Beach**	21
Jimtown Store	**Healdsburg/N**	19
Boulange	**Mill Valley/N**	22
Mario's Bohemian	**N Beach**	18
Max's	**multi. loc.**	16
Model Bakery	**St. Helena/N**	21
Pluto's Fresh	**multi. loc.**	19
Rest. LuLu/Petite	**Embarcadero**	20
Saigon Sandwiches	**Tenderloin**	23
'wichcraft	**Downtown**	17

SEAFOOD

Alamo Sq.	**W Addition**	21
Alioto's	**Fish. Wharf**	19
Anchor Oyster	**Castro**	23
Z Aqua	**Downtown**	26

A. Sabella's | **Fish. Wharf**	18
Barbara Fish | **Princeton Sea/S**	19
Bar Crudo | **Downtown**	25
Brindisi | **Downtown**	18
Cantankerous | **Mtn View/S**	18
Catch | **Castro**	19
☑ Farallon | **Downtown**	24
Fish | **Sausalito/N**	24
Flying Fish | **Carmel/S**	24
Flying Fish | **Half Moon Bay/S**	21
Fook Yuen | **Millbrae/S**	20
NEW Go Fish | **St. Helena/N**	24
Great Eastern | **Chinatown**	22
Guaymas | **Tiburon/N**	17
Hayes St. Grill | **Hayes Valley**	22
Hog Island Oyster | **Embarcadero**	25
Koi Palace | **Daly City/S**	23
Little River Inn | **Little River/N**	20
Lure | **San Mateo/S**	23
Marica | **Oakland/E**	22
Mayflower | **Outer Rich**	22
McCormick/Kuleto | **Fish. Wharf**	19
Old Port/N. Bch. Lobster | **Redwood City/S**	21
O'Reilly's | **Polk Gulch**	18
Pacific Café | **Outer Rich**	22
Pacific Catch | **multi. loc.**	21
Passionfish | **Pacific Grove/S**	25
Pearl Oyster | **Oakland/E**	24
Pesce | **Russian Hill**	22
NEW Pescheria | **Noe Valley**	21
PJ's Oyster | **Inner Sunset**	19
NEW Sam's Chowder | **Half Moon Bay/S**	15
Sam's Grill | **Downtown**	20
Sardine Factory | **Monterey/S**	20
Scoma's | **multi. loc.**	21
Scott's | **multi. loc.**	19
Sea Salt | **Berkeley/E**	22
Sharon's | **Ft Bragg/N**	20
Sonoma Meritage | **Sonoma/N**	19
Sunnyside | **Tahoe City/E**	18
☑ Swan Oyster | **Polk Gulch**	26
☑ Tadich Grill | **Downtown**	22
Tsar Nicoulai | **Embarcadero**	22
Waterfront | **Embarcadero**	18
NEW Weird Fish | **Mission**	18
Willi's Seafood | **Healdsburg/N**	23

Woodhse. | **Castro**	19
Yabbies Coastal | **Russian Hill**	22
Yankee Pier | **multi. loc.**	17
NEW Zazil Coastal | **Downtown**	19

SINGAPOREAN

Straits Cafe | **multi. loc.**	20

SMALL PLATES

(See also Spanish tapas specialist)

À Côté | **French/Med.** | **Oakland/E**	24
NEW Alembic | **Eclectic** | **Haight-Ashbury**	22
Andalu | **Eclectic** | **Mission**	20
AsiaSF | **Calif./Asian** | **SoMa**	17
Baraka | **French/Med.** | **Potrero Hill**	21
Cascal | **Pan-Latin** | **Mtn View/S**	20
Cha Cha Cha | **Carib.** | **multi. loc.**	19
Charanga | **Pan-Latin** | **Mission**	21
Cortez | **Med.** | **Downtown**	23
NEW District | **Eclectic** | **SoMa**	17
E&O Trading | **SE Asian** | **Downtown**	19
Eos Rest./Wine | **Asian/Calif.** | **Cole Valley**	23
☑ Fonda Solana | **Latin Amer.** | **Albany/E**	24
Fork | **Calif./French** | **San Anselmo/N**	24
Isa | **French** | **Marina**	24
jZcool | **Calif.** | **Menlo Pk/S**	20
Lavanda | **Med.** | **Palo Alto/S**	19
Levende | **Eclectic** | **Mission**	20
Lime | **Eclectic** | **Castro**	18
Medjool | **Med.** | **Mission**	18
NEW Mercury | **Pan-Asian** | **Marina**	-
Mezze | **Calif./Med.** | **Oakland/E**	23
Monti's | **Med.** | **Santa Rosa/N**	19
Ora | **Pan-Asian** | **Mill Valley/N**	21
Ottimista | **Italian/Med.** | **Cow Hollow**	20
Pearl Oyster | **Seafood** | **Oakland/E**	24
Pesce | **Italian/Seafood** | **Russian Hill**	22
Picco | **Italian** | **Larkspur/N**	24
NEW Piqueo's | **Peruvian** | **Bernal Hts**	-

Poleng | Pan-Asian | **W Addition** 22

Ponzu | Pan-Asian | **Downtown** 21

NEW Pres a Vi | Eclectic | **Presidio** 21

rnm rest. | Amer./French | 25
  Lower Haight

RoHan Lounge | Pan-Asian | 18
  Inner Rich

NEW Rouge/Blanc | French | -
  Downtown

Sol y Lago | Nuevo Latino | 17
  Tahoe City/E

Stokes | Calif./Med. | **Monterey/S** 23

Straits Cafe | Singapor. | **multi. loc.** 20

NEW Sudachi | Asian Fusion | -
  Polk Gulch

Z Tamarine | Viet. | **Palo Alto/S** 26

Terzo | Med. | **Cow Hollow** 22

Three Seasons | Viet. | **multi. loc.** 23

Underwood Bar | Med. | **Graton/N** 22

Va de Vi | Eclectic | 24
  Walnut Creek/E

Willi's Seafood | Seafood | 23
  Healdsburg/N

Willi's Wine | Eclectic | 24
  Santa Rosa/N

Zibibbo | Med. | **Palo Alto/S** 20

Zucca | Med. | **Mtn View/S** 19

SOUL FOOD

farmerbrown | **Tenderloin** 19

Home of Chicken | **Oakland/E** 15

SOUTHEAST ASIAN

E&O Trading | **multi. loc.** 19

Z Tamarine | **Palo Alto/S** 26

SOUTHERN

Blackberry Bistro | **Oakland/E** 21

Blue Jay | **W Addition** 15

Everett & Jones | **multi. loc.** 20

NEW Gator's | **San Mateo/S** -

Home of Chicken | **Oakland/E** 15

Z Kate's Kitchen | **Lower Haight** 22

Powell's | **W Addition** 18

SOUTHWESTERN

Boogaloos | **Mission** 17

SPANISH

(* tapas specialist)

Alegrias* | **Marina** 20

Basque Cultural | 20
  S San Francisco/S

B44 | **Downtown** 21

Z Bocadillos* | **N Beach** 22

César* | **multi. loc.** 22

Esperpento* | **Mission** 21

Iberia* | **Menlo Pk/S** 21

Iluna Basque* | **N Beach** 17

NEW Laïola | **Marina** -

Z Piperade | **Downtown** 25

Ramblas* | **Mission** 20

Sabor of Spain* | **San Rafael/N** 18

Zarzuela* | **Russian Hill** 22

Z Zuzu* | **Napa/N** 24

STEAKHOUSES

Acme Chophouse | **S Beach** 19

Z Alexander's | **Cupertino/S** 25

Alfred's Steak | **Downtown** 21

A.P. Stump's | **San Jose/S** 21

Arcadia | **San Jose/S** 23

Boca | **Novato/N** 20

Casa Orinda | **Orinda/E** 17

Z Cole's Chop Hse. | **Napa/N** 25

El Raigon | **N Beach** 21

Espetus | **Hayes Valley** 21

Forbes Mill Steak | **multi. loc.** 23

Harris' | **Polk Gulch** 25

House of Prime | **Polk Gulch** 24

Izzy's Steak | **multi. loc.** 19

Joe DiMaggio's | **N Beach** 20

Kurt's Carmel | **Carmel/S** 23

NEW Lark Creek Steak | 22
  Downtown

Morton's | **multi. loc.** 23

Press | **St. Helena/N** 23

Ruth's Chris | **Polk Gulch** 24

Sunnyside | **Tahoe City/E** 18

Vic Stewart's | **Walnut Creek/E** 21

SWISS

Matterhorn Swiss | **Russian Hill** 21

TEAROOMS

Imperial/Berkeley | **multi. loc.** 17

Lovejoy's Tea | **Noe Valley** 20

Modern Tea | **Hayes Valley** 20

Poleng | **W Addition** 22

THAI

Basil Thai | **SoMa** 22

Cha Am Thai | **multi. loc.** 19

Citizen Thai | **N Beach** 20

Khan Toke | **Outer Rich** 23

King of Thai | **multi. loc.** 19

Koh Samui | **SoMa** 21

Krung Thai | **San Jose/S** 23

Z Manora's Thai | **SoMa** 23

Marnee Thai | **multi. loc.** 22

Osha Thai | **multi. loc.** 22

Plearn Thai | **multi. loc.** 19

Royal Thai | **San Rafael/N** 22

Soi Four | **Oakland/E** 23

Suriya Thai | **Mission** 23

Thai Buddhist | **Berkeley/E** 20

Thai House | **multi. loc.** 20

Z Thep Phanom | **Lower Haight** 24

TURKISH

A La Turca | **Tenderloin** 20

Bursa Kebab | **W Portal** 19

Ephesus | **Walnut Creek/E** 21

Troya | **Inner Rich** 22

VEGETARIAN

(* vegan)

Cafe Gibraltar* | **El Granada/S** 25

Café Gratitude* | **multi. loc.** 19

Cha-Ya Veg. | **multi. loc.** 24

Z Greens | **Marina** 24

Herbivore* | **multi. loc.** 17

Medicine | **Downtown** 18

Z Millennium* | **Downtown** 24

Ravens Rest.* | **Mendocino/N** 23

Saha | **Tenderloin** 24

NEW Ubuntu* | **Napa/N** -

Udupi Palace | **multi. loc.** 20

VIETNAMESE

Z Ana Mandara | **Fish. Wharf** 23

Annalien | **Napa/N** 24

Bodega Bistro | **Tenderloin** 23

Bong Su | **SoMa** 22

NEW Butterfly Bistro | **San Bruno/S** -

Crustacean | **Polk Gulch** 23

Le Cheval | **multi. loc.** 21

Le Colonial | **Downtown** 21

Le Soleil | **Inner Rich** 20

Mangosteen | **Tenderloin** 18

Out the Door | **multi. loc.** 22

Pho 84 | **Oakland/E** 24

Saigon Sandwiches | **Tenderloin** 23

Z Slanted Door | **Embarcadero** 26

Z Tamarine | **Palo Alto/S** 26

Tao Cafe | **Mission** 18

Thanh Long | **Outer Sunset** 24

Three Seasons | **multi. loc.** 23

Tu Lan | **SoMa** 20

NEW Xyclo | **Oakland/E** 19

NEW Zadin | **Castro** -

Locations

Includes restaurant names, cuisines, Food ratings and, for locations that are mapped, top list and map coordinates. ☑ indicates places with the highest ratings, popularity and importance.

City of San Francisco

AT&T PARK/ SOUTH BEACH

(See map on page 271)

Acme Chophouse	*Steak*	**H5**	19
Amici's	*Pizza*	**G5**	20
MoMo's	*Amer.*	**H5**	17
Tres Agaves	*Mex.*	**H5**	18

BERNAL HEIGHTS

Emmy's Spaghetti	*Italian*	19
Liberty Cafe	*Amer.*	22
Little Nepal	*Nepalese*	21
Moki's Sushi	*Jap.*	21
NEW Piqueo's	*Peruvian*	–
Zante	*Indian/Pizza*	18

CASTRO

(See map on page 272)

TOP FOOD

SUMI	*French*	**E2**	23
Anchor Oyster	*Seafood*	**E3**	23
Destino	*Nuevo Latino*	**A6**	22
2223	*Calif.*	**C4**	21
Thai House	*Thai*	**E3**	20

LISTING

Anchor Oyster	*Seafood*	**E3**	23
Asqew Grill	*Calif.*	**C3**	18
Barracuda	*Brazilian/Jap.*	**C4**	17
Brandy Ho's	*Chinese*	**E3**	20
Catch	*Seafood*	**D3**	19
☑ Chow/Park Chow	*Amer.*	**B5**	20
Côté Sud	*French*	**E2**	20
Daimaru	*Jap.*	**C4**	24
Destino	*Nuevo Latino*	**A6**	22
NEW Eureka	*Amer.*	**D3**	21
Home	*Amer.*	**B4**	18
La Méditerranée	*Med./Mideast.*	**C3**	19
Lime	*Eclectic*	**C4**	18
Mecca	*Amer.*	**B5**	20
Pasta Pomodoro	*Italian*	**C3**	16
SUMI	*French*	**E2**	23
Sushi Zone	*Jap.*	**A6**	26

Thai House	*Thai*	**E3**	20
2223	*Calif.*	**C4**	21
Woodhse.	*New Eng./Seafood*	**B5**	19
NEW Zadin	*Viet.*	**D3**	–

CHINA BASIN/ DOGPATCH

NEW Piccino	*Calif./Italian*	19

CHINATOWN

(See map on page 268)

TOP FOOD

R & G Lounge	*Chinese*	**G7**	23
Great Eastern	*Chinese*	**F6**	22
Hunan	*Chinese*	**F6**	22

LISTING

Bow Hon 4	*Chinese*	**G6**	22
Brandy Ho's	*Chinese*	**F6**	20
Gold Mountain	*Chinese*	**F6**	20
Great Eastern	*Chinese*	**F6**	22
House of Nanking	*Chinese*	**F7**	21
Henry's Hunan	*Chinese*	**F8**	21
Hunan	*Chinese*	**F6**	22
Jai Yun	*Chinese*	**F5**	23
New Asia	*Chinese*	**F6**	18
Oriental Pearl	*Chinese*	**G6**	22
R & G Lounge	*Chinese*	**G7**	23
Yuet Lee	*Chinese*	**F6**	21

COW HOLLOW

(See map on page 270)

TOP FOOD

PlumpJack	*Calif./Med.*	**F4**	24
Betelnut Pejiu	*Pan-Asian*	**G5**	23
Boulange	*Bakery*	**G5**	22

LISTING

Balboa Cafe	*Amer.*	**F4**	19
Betelnut Pejiu	*Pan-Asian*	**G5**	23
Brazen Head	*Amer.*	**G4**	20
Chez Maman	*French*	**F5**	21
Jake's Steaks	*Cheese Stks.*	**G4**	20
NEW Jovino	*Coffee/Eclectic*	**F5**	–
Boulange	*Bakery*	**G5**	22
Osha Thai	*Thai*	**G5**	22
Ottimista	*Italian/Med.*	**H5**	20

DOWNTOWN
(See map on page 268)

TOP FOOD

LISTING

EMBARCADERO

Americano	*Calif.*	17
Boulette's Larder	*Amer.*	25
Z Boulevard	*Amer.*	27
Butterfly	*Asian/Calif.*	19
Chaya Brasserie	*French/Jap.*	21
Delancey St.	*Eclectic*	18
Fog City Diner	*Amer.*	19
Hog Island Oyster	*Seafood*	25
Imperial/Berkeley	*Tea*	17
MarketBar	*Med.*	17
NEW Mexico DF	*Mex.*	-
Mijita	*Mex.*	20
One Market	*Amer.*	22
Out the Door	*Viet.*	22
Ozumo	*Jap.*	24
Pancho Villa	*Mex.*	20
Red's Java	*Hamburgers*	14
Rest. LuLu/Petite	*Sandwiches*	20
Shanghai 1930	*Chinese*	20
Z Slanted Door	*Viet.*	26
Taylor's Auto	*Diner*	21
Town's End	*Amer./Bakery*	19
Tsar Nicoulai	*Caviar/Seafood*	22
Waterfront	*Calif./Seafood*	18

EXCELSIOR

Z Joe's Cable Car	*Hamburgers*	24
North Beach Pizza	*Pizza*	18

FISHERMAN'S WHARF

(See map on page 268)

TOP FOOD

Gary Danko	*Amer.*	**B3**	29
Grandeho Kamekyo	*Jap.*	**B3**	23
Ana Mandara	*Viet.*	**B2**	23

LISTING

Alioto's	*Italian*	**A4**	19
Z Ana Mandara	*Viet.*	**B2**	23
A. Sabella's	*Seafood*	**A4**	18
Bistro Boudin	*Calif.*	**A4**	20
Z Gary Danko	*Amer.*	**B3**	29
Grandeho Kamekyo	*Jap.*	**B3**	23
Hard Rock	*Amer.*	**B6**	13
Z In-N-Out	*Hamburgers*	**A4**	22
McCormick/Kuleto	*Seafood*	**B2**	19
North Beach Pizza	*Pizza*	**B6**	18
Scoma's	*Seafood*	**A6**	21

FOREST HILLS/ WEST PORTAL

Bursa Kebab	*Mideast.*	19
Chouchou	*French*	21
Fresca	*Peruvian*	22
Roti Indian	*Indian*	23

GLEN PARK

Z Chenery Park	*Amer.*	22
NEW Gialina	*Pizza*	24
NEW Le P'tit Laurent	*French*	-

HAIGHT-ASHBURY/ COLE VALLEY

NEW Alembic	*Eclectic*	22
Asqew Grill	*Calif.*	18
Boulange	*Bakery*	22
Cha Cha Cha	*Carib.*	19
Citrus Club	*Pan-Asian*	19
El Balazo	*Mex.*	18
Eos Rest./Wine	*Asian/Calif.*	23
Grandeho Kamekyo	*Jap.*	23
Kan Zaman	*Mideast.*	17
Massawa	*African*	21
North Beach Pizza	*Pizza*	18
Pork Store	*Amer.*	21
Zazie	*French*	22

HAYES VALLEY/ CIVIC CENTER

Absinthe	*French/Med.*	20
Bistro Clovis	*French*	19
Caffe Delle Stelle	*Italian*	16
Cav Wine Bar	*Med.*	22
Citizen Cake	*Bakery/Calif.*	20
Espetus	*Brazilian*	21
NEW Essencia	*Peruvian*	-
Frjtz Fries	*Belgian*	19
Hayes St. Grill	*Seafood*	22
Indigo	*Amer.*	20
Z Jardinière	*Calif./French*	26
Max's	*Deli*	16
Mel's Drive-In	*Diner*	13
Modern Tea	*Calif./Tea*	20
Moishe's Pippic	*Deli*	19
Patxi's Pizza	*Pizza*	20
paul k	*Med.*	21
Sauce	*Amer.*	18
Sebo	*Jap.*	25
Stacks	*Amer.*	-

LOCATIONS

| Suppenküche | *German* | 21 |
| Zuni Café | *Med.* | 25 |

INNER RICHMOND

Bella Trattoria	*Italian*	21
Brother's Korean	*Korean*	22
NEW B Star Bar	*Pan-Asian*	-
Burma Superstar	*Burmese*	24
Clémentine	*French*	24
Giorgio's Pizzeria	*Pizza*	20
Good Luck	*Chinese*	22
Katia's Tea	*Russian*	19
King of Thai	*Thai*	19
Le Soleil	*Viet.*	20
Mandalay	*Burmese*	21
Mel's Drive-In	*Diner*	13
My Tofu	*Korean*	20
Q	*Amer.*	20
Richmond Rest.	*Calif.*	22
NEW Roadside BBQ	*BBQ*	19
RoHan Lounge	*Pan-Asian*	18
Troya	*Turkish*	22

INNER SUNSET

Café Gratitude	*Vegan*	19
Chow/Park Chow	*Amer.*	20
Ebisu	*Jap.*	23
Hotei	*Jap.*	18
Koo	*Asian Fusion*	24
Marnee Thai	*Thai*	22
Naan/Curry	*Indian/Pakistani*	18
Pasta Pomodoro	*Italian*	16
PJ's Oyster	*Creole/Seafood*	19
Pluto's Fresh	*Amer.*	19
Pomelo	*Eclectic*	22
San Tung	*Chinese/Korean*	23
NEW Underdog	*Hot Dogs*	-
Yumma's	*Med./Mideast.*	20

JAPANTOWN

Bushi-tei	*Pan-Asian*	24
CAFÉ KATi	*Asian Fusion*	23
Isobune	*Jap.*	17
Juban	*Jap.*	17
Kiss Sushi	*Jap.*	27
Maki	*Jap.*	23
Mifune	*Jap.*	18
Shabu-Sen	*Jap.*	18
Takara	*Jap.*	22

LAUREL HEIGHTS/ PRESIDIO HEIGHTS

Asqew Grill	*Calif.*	18
Ella's	*Amer.*	20
Garibaldis	*Calif./Med.*	21
Pasta Pomodoro	*Italian*	16
Rigolo	*French*	18
Sociale	*Italian*	23
NEW Spruce	*Amer.*	-

LOWER HAIGHT

Axum Cafe	*Ethiopian*	20
Burger Joint	*Hamburgers*	18
Indian Oven	*Indian*	23
Kate's Kitchen	*Southern*	22
Memphis Minnie	*BBQ*	20
rnm rest.	*Amer./French*	25
Rosamunde Grill	*German*	25
Rotee	*Indian/Pakistani*	18
Thep Phanom	*Thai*	24

MARINA

(See map on page 270)

TOP FOOD

Zushi Puzzle	*Jap.*	**G4**	26
Isa	*French*	**F4**	24
Greens	*Veg.*	**H2**	24
A 16	*Italian*	**E3**	23
Three Seasons	*Viet.*	**F4**	23

LISTING

Ace Wasabi's	*Jap.*	**F4**	20
Alegrias	*Spanish*	**F4**	20
Amici's	*Pizza*	**F4**	20
A 16	*Italian*	**E3**	23
Asqew Grill	*Calif.*	**F4**	18
Baker St. Bistro	*French*	**D4**	20
Barney's	*Hamburgers*	**F4**	19
Bistro Aix	*Calif./French*	**F4**	22
NEW Circa	*Amer.*	**F3**	18
Dragon Well	*Chinese*	**E3**	20
E'Angelo	*Italian*	**E3**	20
Emporio Rulli	*Dessert/Italian*	**E3**	20
Greens	*Veg.*	**H2**	24
NEW Hime	*Jap.*	**E4**	22
Isa	*French*	**F4**	24
Izzy's Steak	*Steak*	**F4**	19
NEW Jones Rest.	*Amer.*	**E4**	-
NEW Laïola	*Spanish*	**F3**	-
Lettus	*Health*	**F4**	20

Mamacita | *Mex.* | **E3** 22
Mel's Drive-In | *Diner* | **F4** 13
🆕 Mercury | *Pan-Asian* | **I4** –
Nectar Wine | *Calif.* | **F4** 19
Pacific Catch | *Seafood* | **F3** 21
Pluto's Fresh | *Amer.* | **E4** 19
Ristorante Parma | *Italian* | **F4** 22
Three Seasons | *Viet.* | **F4** 23
Yuzu | *Jap.* | **F4** 19
Zushi Puzzle | *Jap.* | **G4** 26

MISSION

(See map on page 272)

TOP FOOD
Tartine | *Bakery* | **D6** 26
Delfina | *Italian* | **D6** 26
Range | *Amer.* | **E6** 26
Little Star Pizza | *Pizza* | **C6** 25
Woodward's Gdn. | 25
   Amer./Calif. | **B7**

LISTING
Andalu | *Eclectic* | **C6** 20
Angkor Borei | *Cambodian* 20
Arinell Pizza | *Pizza* | **C6** 22
🆕 Bar Bambino | *Italian* | **C7** –
Bar Tartine | *Med.* | **D6** 22
Blowfish Sushi | *Jap.* | **E9** 21
Blue Plate | *Amer.* | **J7** 23
Boogaloos | *Southwestern* | **F6** 17
Burger Joint | *Hamburgers* | **E6** 18
Café Gratitude | *Vegan* | **E9** 19
Cha Cha Cha | *Carib.* | **E7** 19
Charanga | *Pan-Latin* | **E7** 21
Cha-Ya Veg. | *Jap./Vegan* | **E6** 24
Chez Spencer | *French* | **B8** 24
Circolo | *Asian/Nuevo Latino* | **D9** 19
🆝 Delfina | *Italian* | **D6** 26
Dosa | *Indian* | **F6** 20
El Metate | *Mex.* | **F9** 23
Esperpento | *Spanish* | **F6** 21
🆕 Farina | *Italian* | **D6** –
Firecracker | *Calif./Chinese* | **F6** 19
Foreign Cinema | *Calif./Med.* | **F7** 21
Frjtz Fries | *Belgian* | **D6** 19
Goood Frikin' Chicken | 19
   Mideast. | **J6**
Herbivore | *Vegan* | **F6** 17
Jay's | *Cheese Stks.* | **F6** 17
Kiji Sushi Bar | *Jap.* | **F6** 24

La Cumbre | *Mex.* | **C6** 22
La Provence | *French* | **F6** 18
Last Supper | *Italian* | **G6** 19
🆝 La Taqueria | *Mex.* | **H7** 24
Levende | *Eclectic* | **B7** 20
🆝 Limón | *Peruvian* | **C6** 22
🆝 Little Star Pizza | *Pizza* | **C6** 25
Luna Park | *Amer./French* | **D6** 19
Maverick | *Amer.* | **D7** 22
Medjool | *Med.* | **F7** 18
Nihon | *Jap.* | **B8** 21
Osha Thai | *Thai* | **E6** 22
Pakwan | *Pakistani* | **C6** 21
Pancho Villa | *Mex.* | **C6** 20
Papalote | *Mex.* | **G6** 21
Pauline's Pizza | *Pizza* | **B6** 22
Pizzeria Delfina | *Pizza* | **D6** 24
Pork Store | *Amer.* | **C6** 21
Puerto Alegre | *Mex.* | **C6** 18
Ramblas | *Spanish* | **D6** 20
🆝 Range | *Amer.* | **E6** 26
Slow Club | *Amer.* | **D10** 22
🆕 Spork | *Amer.* | **F6** –
St. Francis | *Diner* | **G10** 19
Suriya Thai | *Thai* | **H6** 23
Tao Cafe | *Viet.* | **F6** 18
Taqueria Can-Cun | *Mex.* | **E7** 21
🆝 Tartine | *Bakery* | **D6** 26
Ti Couz | *French* | **C6** 22
Tokyo Go Go | *Jap.* | **C6** 22
🆝 Truly Med. | *Med.* | **C6** 23
Universal Cafe | *Amer.* | **E9** 23
Walzwerk | *German* | **C7** 20
🆕 Weird Fish | *Seafood* | **D7** 18
Woodward's Gdn. | 25
   Amer./Calif. | **B7**
Zeitgeist | *BBQ* | **B6** 16

NOB HILL

(See map on page 268)

TOP FOOD
Fleur de Lys | *Calif./French* | **I4** 28
Ritz-Carlton Din. Rm. | *French* | **H6** 27
Ritz-Carlton Terr. | *Med.* | **H6** 24

LISTING
Big 4 | *Amer.* | **H4** 22
🆝 Fleur de Lys | *Calif./French* | **I4** 28
Fournou's | *Calif./Med.* | **H5** 22

Nob Hill Café	*Italian*	**G4**	20
Red Door	*Eclectic*	**H2**	20
🅉 Ritz-Carlton Din. Rm.	*French*	**H6**	27
🅉 Ritz-Carlton Terr.	*Med.*	**H6**	24
Sparrow	*Asian/French*	**H4**	20
Tonga	*Pan-Asian/Pac. Rim*	**H5**	13
Venticello	*Italian*	**G4**	23

NOE VALLEY

(See map on page 272)

TOP FOOD
Firefly	*Eclectic*	**H2**	25
Incanto	*Italian*	**I5**	24
Rist. Bacco	*Italian*	**H2**	23
La Ciccia	*Italian*	**K5**	22
Fresca	*Peruvian*	**H4**	22

LISTING
Alice's	*Chinese*	**J5**	19
Barney's	*Hamburgers*	**H3**	19
Chloe's Cafe	*Amer.*	**H5**	21
Deep Sushi	*Jap.*	**J5**	21
Eric's	*Chinese*	**I5**	20
🅉 Firefly	*Eclectic*	**H2**	25
Fresca	*Peruvian*	**H4**	22
Hamano Sushi	*Jap.*	**H3**	20
Incanto	*Italian*	**I5**	24
La Ciccia	*Italian*	**K5**	22
Le Zinc	*French*	**H3**	18
Lovejoy's Tea	*Tea*	**H5**	20
Pasta Pomodoro	*Italian*	**H4**	16
🆕 Pescheria	*Seafood*	**J5**	21
Pomelo	*Eclectic*	**K5**	22
Rist. Bacco	*Italian*	**H2**	23
Savor	*Med.*	**H4**	18
🆕 Toast	*Amer.*	**J5**	18

NORTH BEACH

(See map on page 268)

TOP FOOD
House, The	*Asian Fusion*	**E6**	26
Cafe Jacqueline	*French*	**E6**	26
Coi	*Calif./French*	**F7**	25
Mama's Wash. Sq.	*Amer.*	**D6**	25
Tommaso's	*Italian*	**F7**	25

LISTING
Albona Rist.	*Italian*	**C5**	24
🅉 Bocadillos	*Spanish*	**G7**	22
Cafe Jacqueline	*French*	**E6**	26

Caffè Macaroni	*Italian*	**F7**	20
Citizen Thai	*Thai*	**F6**	20
Coi	*Calif./French*	**F7**	25
El Raigon	*Argent.*	**E6**	21
Enrico's	*Amer./Med.*	**F7**	–
Fior d'Italia	*Italian*	**C5**	19
🆕 Front Porch	*Carib.*	**J6**	20
Giordano	*Sandwiches*	**F6**	21
🅉 House, The	*Asian Fusion*	**E6**	26
Iluna Basque	*Spanish*	**E5**	17
Joe DiMaggio's	*Italian/Steak*	**E6**	20
Boulange	*Bakery*	**E6**	22
L'Osteria	*Italian*	**E6**	24
🅉 Mama's Wash. Sq.	*Amer.*	**D6**	25
Mangarosa	*Brazilian/Italian*	**E6**	19
Mario's Bohemian	*Italian*	**E6**	18
Maykadeh	*Persian*	**E6**	23
Moose's	*Amer.*	**D6**	20
Mo's	*Amer.*	**E6**	20
Naan/Curry	*Indian/Pakistani*	**F7**	18
Old Port/N. Bch. Lobster	*Seafood*	**E6**	21
North Beach Pizza	*Pizza*	**E6**	18
North Beach Rest.	*Italian*	**E6**	21
🆕 Nua Rest.	*Med.*	**E6**	–
Pasta Pomodoro	*Italian*	**E5**	16
Rist. Ideale	*Italian*	**E6**	24
Rose Pistola	*Italian*	**E6**	21
Tommaso's	*Italian*	**F7**	25
Tratt. Contadina	*Italian*	**E5**	23
Washington Sq. B&G	*Amer./Italian*	**E5**	19

OUTER RICHMOND
Ariake	*Jap.*	26
Aziza	*Moroccan*	24
🅉 Chapeau!	*French*	27
Cliff House Bistro	*Calif.*	18
Kabuto	*Jap.*	25
Khan Toke	*Thai*	23
Mayflower	*Chinese*	22
Mescolanza	*Italian*	22
Oyaji	*Jap.*	23
Pacific Café	*Seafood*	22
Pizzetta 211	*Pizza*	25
Shanghai Dumpling	*Chinese*	22
Sutro's	*Calif.*	19
🅉 Ton Kiang	*Chinese*	25

OUTER SUNSET

Beach Chalet | *Amer.*	13
King of Thai | *Thai*	19
Marnee Thai | *Thai*	22
Park Chalet | *Amer.*	15
So | *Korean/Noodles*	21
Thanh Long | *Viet.*	24

PACIFIC HEIGHTS

Café Majestic | *Calif./French*	-
Eliza's | *Chinese*	22
Florio | *French/Italian*	19
Godzila Sushi | *Jap.*	17
Boulange | *Bakery*	22
Z Quince | *French/Italian*	26
NEW Rest. Cassis | *French*	-
Vivande | *Italian*	23

POLK GULCH

(See map on page 268)

TOP FOOD

Acquerello | *Italian* | **G1**	27
Swan Oyster | *Seafood* | **H1**	26
Harris' | *Steak* | **F1**	25

LISTING

Z Acquerello | *Italian* | **G1**	27
Crustacean | *Viet.* | **H1**	23
Harris' | *Steak* | **F1**	25
House of Prime | *Steak* | **G1**	24
O'Reilly's | *Continental/Seafood* | **I1**	18
Ruth's Chris | *Steak* | **H1**	24
Shalimar | *Indian/Pakistani* | **H1**	22
NEW Sudachi | *Asian Fusion* | **I1**	-
Z Swan Oyster | *Seafood* | **H1**	26
Tajine | *Moroccan* | **H1**	23

POTRERO HILL

Aperto | *Italian*	20
Baraka | *French/Med.*	21
Chez Maman | *French*	21
Chez Papa Bistrot | *French*	23
Couleur Café | *French/Med.*	16
Eliza's | *Chinese*	22
Goat Hill Pizza | *Pizza*	19

PRESIDIO

NEW La Terrasse | *French*	19
NEW Pres a Vi | *Eclectic*	21
NEW Presidio Social | *Amer.*	18

RUSSIAN HILL

(See map on page 268)

TOP FOOD

La Folie | *French* | **E1**	27
Frascati | *Calif./Med.* | **E3**	26
Rist. Milano | *Italian* | **F2**	24
Sushi Groove | *Jap.* | **E3**	23

LISTING

Antica Trattoria | *Italian* | **E1**	23
Boulange | *Bakery* | **E1**	22
1550 Hyde | *Calif./Med.* | **F3**	22
Z Frascati | *Calif./Med.* | **E3**	26
Hyde St. Bistro | *French* | **F3**	21
Z La Folie | *French* | **E1**	27
Le Petit Robert | *French* | **E1**	19
Luella | *Calif./Med.* | **E3**	22
Matterhorn Swiss | *Swiss* | **E1**	21
Nick's Tacos | *Mex.* | **F1**	20
Pesce | *Italian/Seafood* | **E1**	22
Rist. Milano | *Italian* | **F2**	24
Street | *Amer.* | **F1**	21
Sushi Groove | *Jap.* | **E3**	23
Tablespoon | *Calif.* | **E1**	22
Yabbies Coastal | *Seafood* | **E1**	22
Zarzuela | *Spanish* | **E3**	22

SOMA

(See map on page 271)

TOP FOOD

Ame | *Amer.* | **H1**	26
Yank Sing | *Chinese* | **J2**	25
Fifth Floor | *Cal./French* | **F1**	25
Fringale | *French* | **G4**	24
Manora's Thai | *Thai* | **B3**	23

LISTING

Z Ame | *Amer.* | **H1**	26
AsiaSF | *Calif./Asian* | **C2**	17
Azie | *Asian Fusion* | **F3**	19
bacar | *Calif./Med.* | **G4**	22
Basil Thai | *Thai* | **D3**	22
Bong Su | *Viet.* | **G3**	22
Buca di Beppo | *Italian* | **F2**	14
Butler & The Chef | *French* | **H4**	20
Caffè Museo | *Italian/Med.* | **G2**	16
Cha Am Thai | *Thai* | **G3**	19
Coco 500 | *Calif./Med.* | **G4**	22
Cosmopolitan | *Amer.* | **J2**	20
NEW District | *Eclectic* | **G5**	17

LOCATIONS

NEW Ducca	Italian	**G1**	–
Fifth Floor	Cal./French	**F1**	25
Z Fringale	French	**G4**	24
Goat Hill Pizza	Pizza	**G3**	19
Henry's Hunan	Chinese	**C4** | **H2**	21
Jack Falstaff	Calif.	**H4**	20
Koh Samui	Thai	**G4**	21
Le Charm Bistro	French	**F3**	21
Z Manora's Thai	Thai	**B3**	23
Maya	Mex.	**H3**	22
Mel's Drive-In	Diner	**G1**	13
Mochica	Peruvian	**F3**	23
Mo's	Amer.	**G3**	20
Oola	Calif.	**F3**	20
Osha Thai	Thai	**H2**	22
Pazzia	Italian	**G3**	22
Public	Amer.	**B3**	18
Rest. LuLu/Petite	French/Med.	**F3**	20
Rist. Umbria	Italian	**H2**	20
Roy's	Hawaiian	**H1**	22
NEW Salt House	Amer.	**I1**	21
Sanraku	Jap.	**G1**	23
South Park	French	**H4**	22
supperclub	Eclectic	**H3**	17
Sushi Groove	Jap.	**B3**	23
NEW Sutra	Asian Fusion	**I4**	19
Town Hall	Amer.	**I2**	23
Tu Lan	Viet.	**E1**	20
NEW TWO	Calif.	**H2**	21
NEW Vitrine	Amer.	**G2**	–
XYZ	Amer./Calif.	**G2**	20
Z Yank Sing	Chinese	**J2**	25
Zuppa	Italian	**G4**	19

TELEGRAPH HILL

| Julius Castle | Italian | – |

TENDERLOIN

(See map on page 268)

TOP FOOD
Dottie's	Diner	**J4**	25
Bodega Bistro	Viet.	**K2**	23
Saigon Sandwiches	Sandwiches/Viet.	**K2**	23

LISTING
A La Turca	Turkish	**J2**	20
Bodega Bistro	Viet.	**K2**	23
Brick	Amer.	**I2**	20

Dottie's	Diner	**J4**	25
farmerbrown	Soul	**K5**	19
Mangosteen	Viet.	**K2**	18
Naan/Curry	Indian/Pakistani	**K3**	18
Original Joe's	Amer./Italian	**K4**	18
Osha Thai	Thai	**J3**	22
Pakwan	Pakistani	**J4**	21
Ryoko's	Jap.	**I4**	23
Saha	Mideast.	**I2**	24
Saigon Sandwiches	Sandwiches/Viet.	**K2**	23
Shalimar	Indian/Pakistani	**J4**	22
Thai House	Thai	**J2**	20

UPPER FILLMORE

Elite Cafe	Cajun/Creole	19
Fresca	Peruvian	22
Jackson Fillmore	Italian	21
La Méditerranée	Med./Mideast.	19
Ten-Ichi	Jap.	21
Zao Noodle	Pan-Asian	14

WESTERN ADDITION

Alamo Sq.	French/Seafood	21
Blue Jay	Southern	15
Green Chile	Mex.	19
Herbivore	Vegan	17
Jay's	Cheese Stks.	17
Z Little Star Pizza	Pizza	25
NoPa	Calif.	23
Papalote	Mex.	21
Poleng	Pan-Asian	22
Powell's	Southern	18
Tsunami	Jap.	23

East of San Francisco

ALAMEDA
| Pappo | Calif./Med. | 23 |

ALBANY
Caspers Hot Dogs	Hot Dogs	18
Z Fonda Solana	Latin Amer.	24
Jodie's Rest.	Amer./Eclectic	20
Nizza La Bella	French/Italian	19

BERKELEY
Adagia	Calif.	19
Z Ajanta	Indian	24
Arinell Pizza	Pizza	22
Barney's	Hamburgers	19

Bette's Oceanview | *Diner* 21
Bistro Liaison | *French* 22
Breads of India | *Indian* 21
Cactus Taqueria | *Mex.* 20
Café Cacao | *Calif./Coffee* 20
Café Fanny | *French* 22
Café Gratitude | *Vegan* 19
Café Rouge | *French/Med.* 21
César | *Spanish* 22
Cha Am Thai | *Thai* 19
Cha-Ya Veg. | *Jap./Vegan* 24
🛛 Chez Panisse | *Calif./Med.* 27
🛛 Chez Panisse Café | *Calif./Med.* 27
downtown | *Calif./Med.* 20
Eccolo | *Italian* 20
FatApple's | *Diner* 17
Gioia Pizzeria | *Pizza* 24
Great China | *Chinese* 23
Gregoire | *French* 24
Imperial/Berkeley | *Tea* 17
Jimmy Bean's | *Diner* 20
Jordan's | *Calif./French* 18
Juan's | *Mex.* 16
Kirala | *Jap.* 25
Lalime's | *Calif./Med.* 26
La Méditerranée | *Med./Mideast.* 19
Lanesplitter Pub | *Pizza* 18
La Note | *French* 22
Le Cheval | *Viet.* 21
Lo Coco's | *Italian* 21
Naan/Curry | *Indian/Pakistani* 18
North Beach Pizza | *Pizza* 18
O Chamé | *Jap.* 24
Olivia | *French* 23
Picante Cocina | *Mex.* 21
Plearn Thai | *Thai* 19
Rick & Ann's | *Amer.* 21
🛛 Rivoli | *Calif./Med.* 27
Saul's Rest./Deli | *Deli* 18
Sea Salt | *Seafood* 22
Shen Hua | *Chinese* 20
Tacubaya | *Mex.* 22
Thai Buddhist | *Thai* 20
Tratt. La Siciliana | *Italian* 23
T Rex Barbecue | *BBQ* 17
Udupi Palace | *Indian/Veg.* 20
Venezia | *Italian* 20
Venus | *Calif.* 19

Vik's Chaat | *Indian* 23
Zachary's Pizza | *Pizza* 24
Zatar | *Med.* 21

CARNELIAN BAY

Gar Woods | *Amer./Med.* 19

DANVILLE

Amber Bistro | *Calif.* 20
Blackhawk Grille | *Calif.* 19
Bridges | *Calif./Asian* 20
Forbes Mill Steak | *Steak* 23
Piatti | *Italian* 19

DUBLIN

Amici's | *Pizza* 20
Caspers Hot Dogs | *Hot Dogs* 18

EL CERRITO

FatApple's | *Diner* 17

EMERYVILLE

Asqew Grill | *Calif.* 18
Bucci's | *Calif./Italian* 20
Pasta Pomodoro | *Italian* 16
Townhouse B&G | *Calif.* 21
Trader Vic's | *Polynesian* 16
Zao Noodle | *Pan-Asian* 14

FREMONT

Shalimar | *Indian/Pakistani* 22

HAYWARD

Caspers Hot Dogs | *Hot Dogs* 18
Everett & Jones | *BBQ* 20
Pakwan | *Pakistani* 21

KINGS BEACH

Soule Domain | *Amer.* 23

LAFAYETTE

🛛 Bo's Barbecue | *BBQ* 23
🛛 Chow/Park Chow | *Amer.* 20
Duck Club | *Amer.* 20
Pizza Antica | *Pizza* 21
🛛 Postino | *Italian* 24

LIVERMORE

Wente Vineyards | *Calif./Med.* 23

OAKLAND

À Côté | *French/Med.* 24
Barney's | *Hamburgers* 19
Battambang | *Cambodian* 22

LOCATIONS

Z Bay Wolf | *Calif./Med.* — 25

Blackberry Bistro | *Southern* — 21

Breads of India | *Indian* — 21

Cactus Taqueria | *Mex.* — 20

Caffè Verbena | *Calif./Italian* — 19

Caspers Hot Dogs | *Hot Dogs* — 18

César | *Spanish* — 22

Citron | *Calif./French* — 24

Doña Tomás | *Mex.* — 24

Dopo | *Italian* — 25

Everett & Jones | *BBQ* — 20

Fentons Creamery | *Ice Cream* — 18

Garibaldis | *Calif./Med.* — 21

Gregoire | *French* — 24

Home of Chicken | *Southern* — 15

Z In-N-Out | *Hamburgers* — 22

Jade Villa | *Chinese* — 17

Jojo | *Calif./French* — 25

Koryo BBQ | *Korean* — 21

Lanesplitter Pub | *Pizza* — 18

Le Cheval | *Viet.* — 21

Levende | *Eclectic* — 20

Lo Coco's | *Italian* — 21

Luka's Taproom | *Calif./French* — 20

Mama's Royal | *Amer.* — 20

Marica | *Seafood* — 22

Max's | *Deli* — 16

Mezze | *Calif./Med.* — 23

Nan Yang | *Burmese* — 22

Oliveto Cafe | *Italian* — 23

Oliveto Restaurant | *Italian* — 25

Pasta Pomodoro | *Italian* — 16

Pearl Oyster | *Seafood* — 24

Pho 84 | *Viet.* — 24

Pizzaiolo | *Pizza* — 24

Pizza Rustica | *Pizza* — 19

Rest. Peony | *Chinese* — 20

Scott's | *Seafood* — 19

Soi Four | *Thai* — 23

Soizic | *Calif./French* — 22

Somerset | *Amer.* — -

Spettro | *Calif./Italian* — 20

Z Tamarindo | *Mex.* — 24

Uzen | *Jap.* — 24

NEW Wood Tav. | *Calif.* — 23

NEW Xyclo | *Viet.* — 19

Yoshi's | *Jap.* — 18

Zachary's Pizza | *Pizza* — 24

OLYMPIC VALLEY

PlumpJack | *Calif./Med.* — 24

ORINDA

Casa Orinda | *Italian/Steak* — 17

PLEASANT HILL

Caspers Hot Dogs | *Hot Dogs* — 18

Left Bank | *French* — 18

RICHMOND

Caspers Hot Dogs | *Hot Dogs* — 18

Salute E Rist. | *Italian* — 19

SAN RAMON

Cafe Esin | *Amer.* — 25

Zachary's Pizza | *Pizza* — 24

SOUTH LAKE TAHOE/STATELINE

Café Fiore | *Italian* — 24

Evan's | *Amer.* — 27

Fresh Ketch | *Seafood* — 18

Naked Fish | *Jap.* — 22

Red Hut | *Amer.* — 25

TAHOE CITY

Bridgetender | *Pub* — 16

Christy Hill | *Calif.* — 25

Jake's/Lake | *Calif.* — 16

River Ranch | *Calif.* — 17

Sol y Lago | *Nuevo Latino* — 17

Sunnyside | *Seafood/Steak* — 18

Wolfdale's | *Calif.* — 25

TRUCKEE

Cottonwood | *Eclectic* — 20

Dragonfly | *Asian/Calif.* — 23

Moody's Bistro | *Calif.* — 25

Pianeta | *Italian* — 23

WALNUT CREEK

Bing Crosby's | *Amer.* — 18

Breads of India | *Indian* — 21

Caspers Hot Dogs | *Hot Dogs* — 18

Ephesus | *Mideast.* — 21

Z Il Fornaio | *Italian* — 19

Lark Creek | *Amer.* — 22

Plearn Thai | *Thai* — 19

Prima | *Italian* — 24

Scott's | *Seafood* — 19

Sushi Groove | *Jap.* — 23

Va de Vi | *Eclectic* 24
Vic Stewart's | *Steak* 21

YOSEMITE/OAKHURST

Ⓩ Ahwahnee | *Amer./Calif.* 19
Ⓩ Erna's Elderberry | *Calif./French* 28

North of San Francisco

BODEGA/BODEGA BAY

Duck Club | *Amer.* 20
Seaweed Café | *Calif./French* 24

CALISTOGA

All Season's | *Calif.* 21
Brannan's Grill | *Amer./French* 19
Wappo Bar | *Eclectic* 22

CORTE MADERA

Ⓩ Il Fornaio | *Italian* 19
Izzy's Steak | *Steak* 19
Max's | *Deli* 16
Pacific Catch | *Seafood* 21

FORESTVILLE

Ⓩ Farmhouse | *Calif.* 27
Mosaic Rest. | *Calif.* 25

GEYSERVILLE

Santi | *Italian* 23

GLEN ELLEN/KENWOOD

Cafe Citti | *Italian* 22
fig cafe | *French* 23
Kenwood | *Amer./French* 22
Wolf House | *Calif.* 20

GUERNEVILLE

Applewood Inn | *Calif.* 24

HEALDSBURG/WINDSOR

Barndiva | *Amer.* 18
Bistro Ralph | *Calif./French* 21
Bovolo | *Italian* 22
Charcuterie | *French* 22
Ⓩ Cyrus | *French* 28
Downtown Bakery | *Bakery* 24
Dry Creek | *Amer.* 24
Jimtown Store | *Deli* 19
Ⓩ Madrona Manor | 25
    Amer./French
Manzanita | *Calif./Med.* 20
Ⓩ Mirepoix | *French* 26

Ravenous Cafe | *Calif./Eclectic* 23
Osake/Sake 'O | *Calif./Jap.* 22
Willi's Seafood | *Seafood* 23
Zin | *Amer.* 22

LARKSPUR

E&O Trading | *SE Asian* 19
Emporio Rulli | *Dessert/Italian* 20
Lark Creek Inn | *Amer.* 23
Left Bank | *French* 18
Picco | *Italian* 24
Ⓩ Pizzeria Picco | *Pizza* 25
Rist. Fabrizio | *Italian* 19
Table Café | *Calif.* 24
Yankee Pier | *New Eng./Seafood* 17

MENDOCINO COUNTY

Albion River Inn | *Calif.* 24
Boonville Hotel | *Calif.* 21
Cafe Beaujolais | *Calif./French* 25
Chapter & Moon | *Amer.* 21
Heritage House | *Calif.* -
Ledford Hse. | *Calif./Med.* 23
Little River Inn | *Calif./Seafood* 20
MacCallum Hse. | *Calif.* 24
Mendo Bistro | *Amer.* 25
Mendocino Hotel | *Calif.* 17
Moosse Café | *Calif.* 23
955 Ukiah | *Amer./French* 22
Pangaea | *Calif./French* 25
Ravens Rest. | *Vegan* 23
Rendezvous Inn | *French* 27
Restaurant | *Amer./Eclectic* 23
Rest. at Stevenswood | *Med.* 20
Sharon's | *Italian/Seafood* 20
St. Orres | *Calif.* 24

MILL VALLEY

Ⓩ Buckeye | *Amer./BBQ* 23
Bungalow 44 | *Amer.* 21
Dipsea Cafe | *Amer.* 17
El Paseo | *French* 23
Frantoio | *Italian* 21
Ⓩ In-N-Out | *Hamburgers* 22
Joe's Taco | *Mex.* 18
Boulange | *Bakery* 22
La Ginestra | *Italian* 18
Ora | *Pan-Asian* 21
Piatti | *Italian* 19

Piazza D'Angelo	*Italian*	19
Pizza Antica	*Pizza*	21
Robata Grill	*Jap.*	20

NAPA

Alexis Baking Co.	*Bakery*	22
Angèle	*French*	22
Annalien	*Viet.*	24
Bistro Don Giovanni	*Italian*	23
Boon Fly Café	*Calif.*	-
Bounty Hunter	*BBQ*	17
Celadon	*Amer./Eclectic*	23
☑ Cole's Chop Hse.	*Steak*	25
Cuvée	*Amer.*	20
NEW ☑ Farm	*Amer.*	23
Foothill Grille	*Amer.*	-
Fumé Bistro	*Amer.*	19
☑ In-N-Out	*Hamburgers*	22
Julia's	*Calif./French*	23
Napa General	*Calif./Eclectic*	20
Napa Wine Train	*Calif.*	15
n.v. Rest.	*Calif.*	22
Pearl	*Calif.*	22
Pilar	*Calif.*	25
Pizza Azzurro	*Pizza*	22
NEW Ubuntu	*Calif./Vegan*	-
Uva Trattoria	*Italian*	21
Zinsvalley	*Amer.*	20
☑ Zuzu	*Spanish*	24

NOVATO

Boca	*Argent./Steak*	20
Kitchen at 868	*Calif.*	25

OCCIDENTAL

NEW Bistro/Copains	*French*	27

PETALUMA

Central Market	*Calif./Med.*	23
Cucina Paradiso	*Italian*	26
Della Fattoria	*Bakery/Eclectic*	26
Sooze Wine	*Calif.*	18
Water St. Bistro	*French*	24

ROSS

Marché aux Fleurs	*French*	25

RUTHERFORD

☑ Auberge du Sol.	*Calif./French*	25
☑ La Toque	*French*	26
Rutherford Grill	*Amer.*	23

SAN ANSELMO

NEW AVA	*Amer.*	-
Cucina Rest.	*Italian*	24
Fork	*Calif./French*	24
Insalata's	*Med.*	24

SAN RAFAEL

Amici's	*Pizza*	20
Barney's	*Hamburgers*	19
Café Gratitude	*Vegan*	19
Il Davide	*Italian*	21
Las Camelias	*Mex.*	20
Lotus of India	*Indian*	22
Maria Manso	*Eclectic*	20
Royal Thai	*Thai*	22
Sabor of Spain	*Spanish*	18
Sol Food	*Puerto Rican*	22

SANTA ROSA/ ROHNERT PARK

Betty's Fish	*Seafood*	20
Flavor	*Calif./Eclectic*	20
Gary Chu's	*Chinese*	22
Hana Japanese	*Jap.*	25
John Ash & Co.	*Calif.*	23
Kabab & Curry	*Indian*	21
Monti's	*Med.*	19
Osake/Sake 'O	*Calif./Jap.*	22
Syrah	*Calif./French*	25
Willi's Wine	*Eclectic*	24
zazu	*Amer./Italian*	25

SAUSALITO

Avatars	*Eclectic*	22
Christophe	*French*	20
Cork	*Italian*	19
Fish	*Seafood*	24
Gaylord India	*Indian*	18
Poggio	*Italian*	21
Scoma's	*Italian/Seafood*	21
☑ Sushi Ran	*Jap.*	28

SEBASTOPOL/GRATON

Bistro V	*French/Italian*	22
K&L Bistro	*French*	25
Underwood Bar	*Med.*	22
NEW West Co. Grill	*Calif./Italian*	-
☑ Willow Wood	*Eclectic/Med.*	25

SONOMA

☑ Cafe La Haye | *Amer./Calif.* 26
Carneros Bistro | *Calif.* 22
Della Santina's | *Italian* 21
Deuce | *Amer.* 20
El Dorado | *Calif./Med.* 23
General's | *Amer.* -
girl & the fig | *French* 23
LaSalette | *Portug.* 23
Santé | *Calif.* 24
Sonoma Meritage | *French/Italian* 19

ST. HELENA

Cindy's | *Amer./Calif.* 24
Cook St. Helena | *Italian* 24
NEW Go Fish | *Eclectic/Seafood* 24
Market | *Amer.* 22
Martini House | *Amer.* 25
Meadowood | *Calif.* 20
Model Bakery | *Bakery* 21
Pizzeria Tra Vigne | *Pizza* 21
Press | *Amer./Steak* 23
Rest. at Meadowood | *Calif.* 23
Taylor's Auto | *Diner* 21
☑ Terra | *Amer.* 26
Tra Vigne | *Italian* 23
Wine Spectator | *Calif.* 22

TIBURON

Caprice | *Amer.* 21
Guaymas | *Mex.* 17

WEST MARIN/OLEMA

Drake's | *Calif.* 19
NEW Nick's Cove | *Calif.* -
Olema Inn | *Calif./Med.* 22
Pine Cone Diner | *Diner* 19
Station House | *Calif.* 17

YOUNTVILLE

☑ ad hoc | *Amer.* 26
☑ Bistro Jeanty | *French* 25
☑ Bouchon | *French* 25
BRIX | *Calif.* 22
Étoile | *Calif.* 25
☑ French Laundry | *Amer./French* 29
Hurley's | *Calif./Med.* 20
Mustards Grill | *Amer./Calif.* 24
Napa Valley Grille | *Calif.* 20
☑ Redd Rest. | *Calif.* 26

South of San Francisco

BIG SUR

Deetjen's | *Calif.* 22
Nepenthe | *Amer.* 16
☑ Sierra Mar | *Calif./Eclectic* 26

BURLINGAME

Barracuda | *Brazilian/Jap.* 17
Ecco | *Calif./Continental* 21
☑ Il Fornaio | *Italian* 19
Juban | *Jap.* 17
Kuleto's | *Italian* 20
Max's | *Deli* 16
Nectar Wine | *Calif.* 19
Roti Indian | *Indian* 23
Stacks | *Amer.* -
Straits Cafe | *Singapor.* 20

CAMPBELL

Buca di Beppo | *Italian* 14

CARMEL/ MONTEREY PENINSULA

Anton & Michel | *Continental* 23
Bouchée | *Calif./French* 26
Cantinetta Luca | *Italian* 22
Casanova | *French/Italian* 23
Club XIX | *Calif./French* 25
Duck Club | *Amer.* 20
Fandango | *Med.* 23
Fishwife | *Carib./Seafood* 23
Flying Fish | *Calif./Seafood* 24
☑ Fresh Cream | *French* 24
Grasing's Coastal | *Calif.* 23
☑ Il Fornaio | *Italian* 19
Kurt's Carmel | *Steak* 23
☑ L'Auberge | *Calif.* 27
Montrio Bistro | *Calif.* 23
☑ Pacific's Edge | *Amer./French* 25
Passionfish | *Calif./Seafood* 25
Piatti | *Italian* 19
Rio Grill | *Calif.* 22
Robert's | *French* 25
Roy's | *Hawaiian* 25
Sardine Factory | *Amer./Seafood* 20
Stokes | *Calif./Med.* 23
Tarpy's | *Amer.* 22

CARMEL VALLEY

Café Rustica | *Calif.* 23
☑ Marinus | *French* 26

CUPERTINO

Z Alexander's | *Jap./Steak* 25

EAST PALO ALTO

Quattro | *Italian* 22

HALF MOON BAY/COAST

Barbara Fish | *Seafood* 19
Cafe Gibraltar | *Med./Vegan* 25
Cetrella | *Med.* 22
Chez Shea | *Eclectic* 22
Duarte's Tavern | *Amer.* 21
Flying Fish | *Calif./Seafood* 21
Mezza Luna | *Italian* 21
Z Navio | *Amer.* 26
Pasta Moon | *Italian* 22
Rogue Chefs | *Calif.* 21
NEW Sam's Chowder | *Seafood* 15
Taqueria 3 Amigos | *Mex.* 18

LOS ALTOS

Chef Chu's | *Chinese* 20
Hunan | *Chinese* 22

LOS GATOS

Café Marcella | *French/Med.* 24
NEW Dio Deka | *Greek* -
Forbes Mill Steak | *Steak* 23
Z Manresa | *Amer.* 27
NEW Vittoria | *Italian* 20

MENLO PARK

Bistro Vida | *French* 18
Duck Club | *Amer.* 20
Flea St. Café | *Amer.* 22
Iberia | *Spanish* 21
Juban | *Jap.* 17
jZcool | *Calif.* 20
Z Kaygetsu | *Jap.* 28
Left Bank | *French* 18
Z Marché | *French* 26
Naomi Sushi | *Jap.* 21
Oak City B&G | *Amer.* 18
Stacks | *Amer.* -

MILLBRAE

Fook Yuen | *Chinese/Seafood* 20
Z In-N-Out | *Hamburgers* 22

MOUNTAIN VIEW

Z Amber India | *Indian* 25
Amici's | *Pizza* 20
Cantankerous | *Seafood* 18

Cascal | *Pan-Latin* 20
Chez TJ | *French* 25
Z In-N-Out | *Hamburgers* 22
Passage to India | *Indian* 19
Uncle Frank's | *BBQ* 22
Zucca | *Med.* 19

PALO ALTO

Bistro Elan | *Calif./French* 24
Buca di Beppo | *Italian* 14
Z Evvia | *Greek* 26
Fuki Sushi | *Jap.* 23
Hunan | *Chinese* 22
Z Il Fornaio | *Italian* 19
Junnoon | *Indian* 22
NEW Kanpai | *Jap.* 24
La Strada | *Italian* 21
Lavanda | *Med.* 19
MacArthur Park | *Amer.* 16
Maddalena/Fino | *Continental* 21
Mantra | *Calif./Indian* 20
Max's | *Deli* 16
Osteria | *Italian* 23
Patxi's Pizza | *Pizza* 20
Scott's | *Seafood* 19
St. Michael's | *Calif.* 22
Straits Cafe | *Singapor.* 20
Tai Pan | *Chinese* 23
Z Tamarine | *Viet.* 26
Three Seasons | *Viet.* 23
Trader Vic's | *Polynesian* 16
Zao Noodle | *Pan-Asian* 14
Zibibbo | *Med.* 20

REDWOOD CITY

Chantilly | *Continental* 25
Z John Bentley's | *Calif.* 25
NEW Mandaloun | *Calif./Med.* -
Max's | *Deli* 16
Old Port/N. Bch. Lobster | *Seafood* 21

REDWOOD SHORES

Amici's | *Pizza* 20
Mistral | *French/Italian* 19

SAN BRUNO

NEW Butterfly Bistro | *Viet.* -
Don Pico's | *Mex.* 20

SAN CARLOS

Izzy's Steak | *Steak* 19
Kabul Afghan | *Afghan* 22

SAN JOSE

Ⓩ Amber India | *Indian*	25
Amici's | *Pizza*	20
A.P. Stump's | *Steak*	21
Arcadia | *Amer.*	23
Asqew Grill | *Calif.*	18
Blowfish Sushi | *Jap.*	21
Buca di Beppo | *Italian*	14
Cheesecake | *Amer.*	16
E&O Trading | *SE Asian*	19
Eulipia | *Amer.*	20
Ⓩ Il Fornaio | *Italian*	19
Ⓩ In-N-Out | *Hamburgers*	22
Krung Thai | *Thai*	23
La Forêt | *French*	27
Ⓩ La Taqueria | *Mex.*	24
La Victoria | *Mex.*	20
Left Bank | *French*	18
Ⓩ Le Papillon | *French*	27
Morton's | *Steak*	23
Original Joe's | *Amer./Italian*	18
Pasta Pomodoro | *Italian*	16
Pizza Antica | *Pizza*	21
Scott's | *Seafood*	19
Seven | *Amer./French*	21
71 Saint Peter | *Calif./Med.*	22
Sino | *Chinese*	20
Straits Cafe | *Singapor.*	20
ᴺᴱᵂ Tanglewood | *Amer.*	21
Taqueria Tlaquepaque | *Mex.*	23
Thea Med. | *Greek/Med.*	21
Yankee Pier | *New Eng./Seafood*	17

SAN MATEO

Amici's | *Pizza*	20
ᴺᴱᵂ Chef Wai | *Chinese*	20
ᴺᴱᵂ Gator's | *Southern*	-
Happy Cafe | *Chinese*	22
Hotaru | *Jap.*	22
Kingfish | *Amer./Cajun*	17
La Cumbre | *Mex.*	22
Left Bank | *French*	18
Lure | *Seafood*	23
North Beach Pizza | *Pizza*	18

Pancho Villa | *Mex.*	20
Rist. Capellini | *Italian*	19
Taqueria 3 Amigos | *Mex.*	18
231 Ellsworth | *Amer.*	23
Viognier | *French*	24

SANTA CLARA

Cheesecake | *Amer.*	16
Dasaprakash | *Indian*	21
Parcel 104 | *Calif.*	23
Piatti | *Italian*	19

SANTA CRUZ/APTOS/ CAPITOLA/SOQUEL

Gabriella Café | *Calif./Italian*	22
Gayle's Bakery | *Bakery*	25
Ⓩ O'mei | *Chinese*	26
Pearl Alley | *French/Italian*	22
Ⓩ Shadowbrook | *Amer./Calif.*	22
Theo's | *Calif./French*	24

SARATOGA

Basin | *Amer.*	19
Plumed Horse | *Calif.*	-
Sent Sovi | *Calif.*	24

SOUTH SAN FRANCISCO/ DALY CITY

Barracuda | *Brazilian/Jap.*	17
Basque Cultural | *Spanish*	20
Burger Joint | *Hamburgers*	18
Ⓩ In-N-Out | *Hamburgers*	22
Koi Palace | *Chinese*	23
Yankee Pier | *New Eng./Seafood*	17

SUNNYVALE

Ⓩ Dish Dash | *Mideast.*	23
Il Postale | *Italian*	20
Lion & Compass | *Amer.*	19
Shalimar | *Indian/Pakistani*	22
Turmeric | *Indian*	21
Udupi Palace | *Indian/Veg.*	20

WOODSIDE

Bella Vista | *Continental*	22
Ⓩ John Bentley's | *Calif.*	25
Village Pub | *Amer.*	26

LOCATIONS

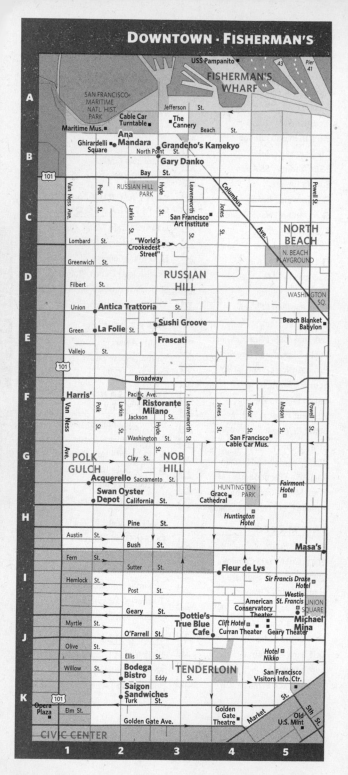

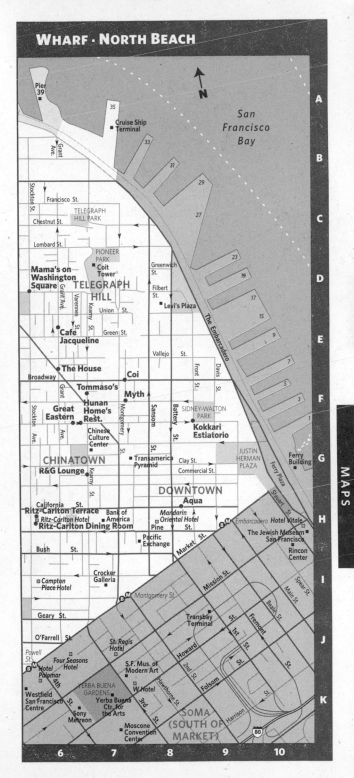

A

B

C

D

E

F

G

H

I

J

K

San Francisco Bay

Pier 39

35

Cruise Ship Terminal

33

31

29

27

Grant Ave.

Stockton St.

Francisco St.

TELEGRAPH HILL PARK

Chestnut St.

Lombard St.

PIONEER PARK

Mama's on Washington Square

Coit Tower

Greenwich St.

23

19

TELEGRAPH HILL

Filbert St.

Levi's Plaza

17

Varennes St.

Grant Ave.

Kearny St.

Union St.

15

Cafe Jacqueline

Green St.

9

Vallejo St.

Front St.

Davis St.

The Embarcadero

7

The House

Broadway

Coi

5

Grant Ave.

Tommaso's

Myth

3

Great Eastern

Hunan Home's Rest.

Montgomery St.

Sansom St.

Battery St.

SIDNEY-WALTON PARK

1

Stockton Ave.

Chinese Culture Center

Kokkari Estiatorio

CHINATOWN

Kearny St.

Transamerica Pyramid

Clay St.

JUSTIN HERMAN PLAZA

Ferry Plaza

Ferry Building

R&G Lounge

Commercial St.

DOWNTOWN

Aqua

California St.

Ritz-Carlton Terrace

Ritz-Carlton Hotel

Bank of America

Mandarin Oriental Hotel

Pine St.

Stewart St.

Embarcadero **Hotel Vitale**

Ritz-Carlton Dining Room

Pacific Exchange

Market St.

The Jewish Museum San Francisco

Bush St.

Mission St.

Rincon Center

Crocker Galleria

Spear St.

Main St.

Campton Place Hotel

Montgomery St.

Beale St.

Geary St.

Transbay Terminal

Fremont St.

O'Farrell St.

St. Regis Hotel

Howard St.

1st St.

Powell St.

Four Seasons Hotel

S.F. Mus. of Modern Art

2nd St.

Folsom St.

Hotel Palomar

4th St.

YERBA BUENA GARDENS

W Hotel

Hawthorne St.

Harrison St.

Westfield San Francisco Centre

Yerba Buena Ctr. for the Arts

3rd St.

SOMA (SOUTH OF MARKET)

Sony Metreon

Moscone Convention Center

80

6 7 8 9 10

MAPS

COW HOLLOW · MARINA

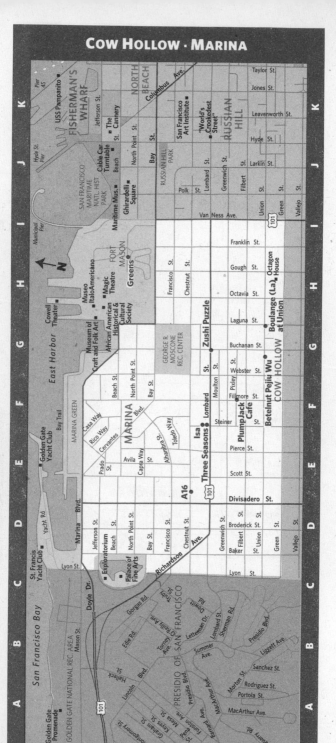

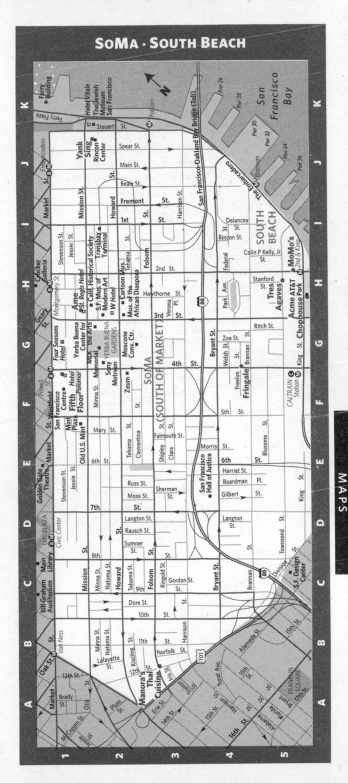

SoMa · South Beach

San Francisco Bay

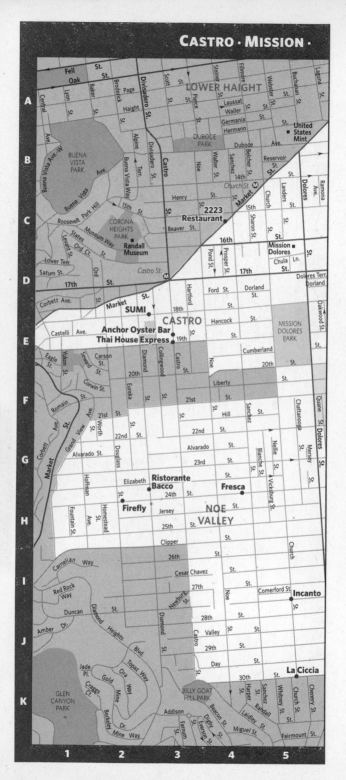

CASTRO · MISSION ·

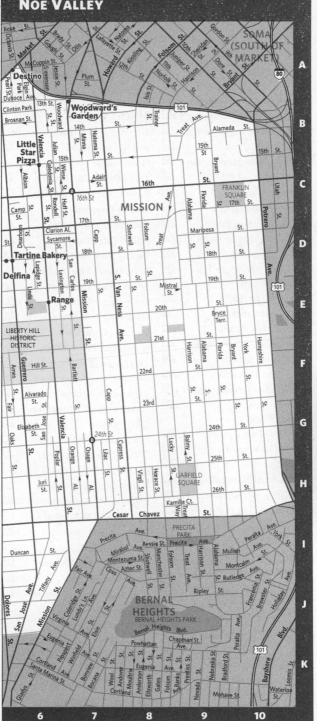

NOE VALLEY

SOMA (SOUTH OF MARKET)

80

Rose St.
Octavia St.
Market St.
Brady St.
Gough St.
Otis
Lafayette St.
Natoma St.
St.
Howard St.
Folsom St.
Gordon St.
10th
Sheridan
9th
St.
McCoppin St.
Stevenson
Jessie St.
Plum St.
12th St.
Kissling
Juniper St.
Fifth St.
Isis
Dore St.
Bryant St.
Harrison
Norfolk St.

Destino
Elgin Park
Pearl St.
Duboce Ave.
13th St.
Woodward
Woodward's Garden
14th St.
Trainor St.
101
Treat Ave.
Alameda St.

Clinton Park
Brosnan St.
Minna St.
Natoma St.
15th St
Bryant St.
15th St.

Little Star Pizza
Valencia St.
Julian
Caledonia St.
Wiese St.
15th St.
Adair St.
16th St.
Mission Ave.
Alabama St.
Florida St.
FRANKLIN SQUARE
17th St.
Utah St.

Albion
Camp St.
Hoff St.
Rondell St.
16th St
17th St.
Capp St.
Shotwell St.
Folsom St.
Treat
Mariposa St.
Potrero Ave.

Dearborn St.
Clarion Al.
Sycamore St.
Tartine Bakery
Lapidge St.
18th St.
San Carlos St.
St.
18th St.
101

Delfina
Lexington St.
19th St.
Mistral St.
19th St.

Linda St.
Range
Mission St.
S. Van Ness Ave.
20th St.
Bryce Terr.

LIBERTY HILL HISTORIC DISTRICT
21st St.
Harrison St.
Alabama St.
Florida St.
Bryant St.
York St.
Hampshire St.

Ames St.
Guerrero St.
Hill St.
Bartlett
22nd St.
S. St.

Fair St.
Alvarado St.
San Jose
Capp St.
23rd St.

Oaks St.
Elizabeth St.
Valencia St.
24th St.
Lucky
Balmy
24th St.

Juri St.
24th St
Poplar St.
Orange St.
Osage Al.
Lilac St.
Cypress St.
Virgil St.
Horace St.
GARFIELD SQUARE
25th St.
26th St.

Kamille Ct.
Treat Way
Cesar Chavez St.

Duncan St.
PRECITA PARK
Precita Ave.
Ressie St.
Precita Ave.
Peralta Ave.
York St.
Alabama St.
Mullen Ave.

Tiffany Ave.
Mission St.
Fair Ave.
Mirabel Ave.
Montezuma St.
Coso Ave.
Aztec St.
Shotwell St.
Manchester St.
Folsom St.
Treat Ave.
Harrison St.
Montcalm
Rutledge Ave.
Franconia St.
Brewster Ave.
Holladay Ave.
Ripley St.

Dolores St.
San Jose Ave.
Virginia
Coleridge St.
Lundys Ln.
Elsie St.
BERNAL HEIGHTS
BERNAL HEIGHTS PARK
Bernal Heights Blvd.
Peralta Ave.
Bayshore Blvd.
101

Eugenia Ave.
Prospect Ave.
Winfield St.
Elsie St.
Powhattan Ave.
Chapman St. Ave.

Glady St.
San Jose St.
Mission St.
Cortland Ave.
Santa Marina St.
Bonview St.
Bocana St.
Wool St.
Andover St.
Moultrie St.
Anderson St.
Ellsworth St.
Gates St.
Folsom St.
Eugenia Ave.
Banks St.
Prentiss St.
Nevada St.
Nebraska St.
Bradford St.
Mohave St.
Waterloo St.
Loomis St.

A B C D E F G H I J K

6 7 8 9 10

MAPS

Special Features

Listings cover the best in each category and include restaurant names, locations and Food ratings. Multi-location restaurants' features may vary by branch.
Z indicates places with the highest ratings, popularity and importance.

BREAKFAST

(See also Hotel Dining)

Alexis Baking Co.	**Napa/N**	22
Bette's Oceanview	**Berkeley/E**	21
Blackberry Bistro	**Oakland/E**	21
Boulange	**multi. loc.**	22
Boulette's Larder	**Embarcadero**	25
Butler & The Chef	**SoMa**	20
Café Cacao	**Berkeley/E**	20
Café Fanny	**Berkeley/E**	22
Chloe's Cafe	**Noe Valley**	21
Dipsea Cafe	**Mill Valley/N**	17
Dottie's	**Tenderloin**	25
Downtown Bakery	**Healdsburg/N**	24
Ella's	**Presidio Hts**	20
Emporio Rulli	**multi. loc.**	20
FatApple's	**multi. loc.**	17
Gayle's Bakery	**Capitola/S**	25
Z Il Fornaio	**multi. loc.**	19
Jimmy Bean's	**Berkeley/E**	20
Jimtown Store	**Healdsburg/N**	19
Z Kate's Kitchen	**Lower Haight**	22
Koi Palace	**Daly City/S**	23
La Note	**Berkeley/E**	22
Z Mama's Wash. Sq.	**N Beach**	25
Mama's Royal	**Oakland/E**	20
Mel's Drive-In	**multi. loc.**	13
Model Bakery	**St. Helena/N**	21
Mo's	**multi. loc.**	20
Napa General	**Napa/N**	20
Oliveto Cafe	**Oakland/E**	23
Pork Store	**multi. loc.**	21
Red's Java	**Embarcadero**	14
Rick & Ann's	**Berkeley/E**	21
Rigolo	**Presidio Hts**	18
Rose's Cafe	**Cow Hollow**	21
Savor	**Noe Valley**	18
Sears Fine Food	**Downtown**	18
Z Tartine	**Mission**	26
Town's End	**Embarcadero**	19
Venus	**Berkeley/E**	19
Water St. Bistro	**Petaluma/N**	24

Z Willow Wood	**Graton/N**	25
Zazie	**Cole Valley**	22

BRUNCH

Absinthe	**Hayes Valley**	20
Adagia	**Berkeley/E**	19
Z Ahwahnee	**Yosemite/E**	19
Alexis Baking Co.	**Napa/N**	22
Americano	**Embarcadero**	17
ANZU	**Downtown**	21
Baker St. Bistro	**Marina**	20
Balboa Cafe	**Cow Hollow**	19
Beach Chalet	**Outer Sunset**	13
Bistro Liaison	**Berkeley/E**	22
Bistro V	**Sebastopol/N**	22
Bistro Vida	**Menlo Pk/S**	18
Blackhawk Grille	**Danville/E**	19
Blue Jay	**W Addition**	15
Z Buckeye	**Mill Valley/N**	23
Café Cacao	**Berkeley/E**	20
Campton Place	**Downtown**	25
Canteen	**Downtown**	25
Carnelian Room	**Downtown**	17
Catch	**Castro**	19
Chez Maman	**Potrero Hill**	21
Chloe's Cafe	**Noe Valley**	21
Z Chow/Park Chow	**multi. loc.**	20
Citizen Cake	**Hayes Valley**	20
Delancey St.	**Embarcadero**	18
Dipsea Cafe	**Mill Valley/N**	17
Dottie's	**Tenderloin**	25
Duck Club	**multi. loc.**	20
Elite Cafe	**Upper Fillmore**	19
Ella's	**Presidio Hts**	20
Z Erna's Elderberry	**Oakhurst/E**	28
Fandango	**Pacific Grove/S**	23
fig cafe	**Glen Ellen/N**	23
Flea St. Café	**Menlo Pk/S**	22
Foreign Cinema	**Mission**	21
Gabriella Café	**Santa Cruz/S**	22
Z Garden Court	**Downtown**	19
Garibaldis	**Oakland/E**	21
Gayle's Bakery	**Capitola/S**	25

girl & the fig | **Sonoma/N**	23
Grand Cafe | **Downtown**	20
☑ Greens | **Marina**	24
Home | **Castro**	18
Insalata's | **San Anselmo/N**	24
John Ash & Co. | **Santa Rosa/N**	23
Jordan's | **Berkeley/E**	18
☑ Kate's Kitchen | **Lower Haight**	22
La Forêt | **San Jose/S**	27
La Note | **Berkeley/E**	22
Lark Creek | **Walnut Creek/E**	22
Lark Creek Inn | **Larkspur/N**	23
Last Supper | **Mission**	19
Le Petit Robert | **Russian Hill**	19
Levende | **Mission**	20
Le Zinc | **Noe Valley**	18
Liberty Cafe | **Bernal Hts**	22
Luna Park | **Mission**	19
MoMo's | **S Beach**	17
Moose's | **N Beach**	20
☑ Navio | **Half Moon Bay/S**	26
Nob Hill Café | **Nob Hill**	20
Park Chalet | **Outer Sunset**	15
Piazza D'Angelo | **Mill Valley/N**	19
Picante Cocina | **Berkeley/E**	21
Q | **Inner Rich**	20
Rest. LuLu/Petite | **SoMa**	20
Rick & Ann's | **Berkeley/E**	21
Rio Grill | **Carmel/S**	22
☑ Ritz-Carlton Terr. | **Nob Hill**	24
Rose's Cafe | **Cow Hollow**	21
Savor | **Noe Valley**	18
Scott's | **multi. loc.**	19
Seasons | **Downtown**	24
Seaweed Café | **Bodega Bay/N**	24
☑ Shadowbrook | **Capitola/S**	22
Slow Club | **Mission**	22
St. Michael's | **Palo Alto/S**	22
Tarpy's | **Monterey/S**	22
Town's End | **Embarcadero**	19
Trader Vic's | **Emeryville/E**	16
2223 | **Castro**	21
Universal Cafe | **Mission**	23
Venus | **Berkeley/E**	19
Viognier | **San Mateo/S**	24
Washington Sq. B&G | **N Beach**	19
Wente Vineyards | **Livermore/E**	23
☑ Willow Wood | **Graton/N**	25

Zazie | **Cole Valley**	22
Zibibbo | **Palo Alto/S**	20
Zucca | **Mtn View/S**	19
☑ Zuni Café | **Hayes Valley**	25

BUSINESS DINING

Acme Chophouse | **S Beach**	19
☑ Alexander's | **Cupertino/S**	25
Alfred's Steak | **Downtown**	21
☑ Amber India | **Mtn View/S**	25
☑ Ame | **SoMa**	26
Americano | **Embarcadero**	17
ANZU | **Downtown**	21
A.P. Stump's | **San Jose/S**	21
☑ Aqua | **Downtown**	26
Azie | **SoMa**	19
bacar | **SoMa**	22
Basin | **Saratoga/S**	19
Belden Taverna | **Downtown**	20
Big 4 | **Nob Hill**	22
Bing Crosby's | **Walnut Creek/E**	18
Bistro V | **Sebastopol/N**	22
Boca | **Novato/N**	20
Bong Su | **SoMa**	22
☑ Boulevard | **Embarcadero**	27
Bushi-tei | **Japantown**	24
Café de la Presse | **Downtown**	16
Caffè Verbena | **Oakland/E**	19
Campton Place | **Downtown**	25
Cantankerous | **Mtn View/S**	18
Carnelian Room | **Downtown**	17
Cha Am Thai | **SoMa**	19
Chantilly | **Redwood City/S**	25
Chaya Brasserie | **Embarcadero**	21
Chef Chu's | **Los Altos/S**	20
NEW Chef Wai | **San Mateo/S**	20
NEW Chiaroscuro | **Downtown**	–
Coco 500 | **SoMa**	22
☑ Cole's Chop Hse. | **Napa/N**	25
Colibrí Mexican | **Downtown**	20
Cosmopolitan | **SoMa**	20
NEW Dio Deka | **Los Gatos/S**	–
NEW District | **SoMa**	17
NEW Ducca | **SoMa**	–
Duck Club | **Menlo Pk/S**	20
E&O Trading | **San Jose/S**	19
☑ Evvia | **Palo Alto/S**	26
☑ Farallon | **Downtown**	24

Flea St. Café	**Menlo Pk/S**	22	Park Grill	**Downtown**	20
Fournou's	**Nob Hill**	22	Pazzia	**SoMa**	22
Z Fresh Cream	**Monterey/S**	24	**NEW** Perbacco	**Downtown**	24
Fuki Sushi	**Palo Alto/S**	23	Picco	**Larkspur/N**	24
Gaylord India	**Downtown**	18	**Z** Piperade	**Downtown**	25
Grand Cafe	**Downtown**	20	Poggio	**Sausalito/N**	21
Harris'	**Polk Gulch**	25	Ponzu	**Downtown**	21
House of Prime	**Polk Gulch**	24	**Z** Postrio	**Downtown**	24
Iberia	**Menlo Pk/S**	21	**NEW** Presidio Social	**Presidio**	18
Z Il Fornaio	**multi. loc.**	19	Press	**St. Helena/N**	23
Izzy's Steak	**Marina**	19	Quattro	**E Palo Alto/S**	22
Jack Falstaff	**SoMa**	20	Rest. LuLu/Petite	**SoMa**	20
Jeanty at Jack's	**Downtown**	23	Rist. Umbria	**SoMa**	20
Joe DiMaggio's	**N Beach**	20	**Z** Ritz-Carlton Din. Rm.	**Nob Hill**	27
Junnoon	**Palo Alto/S**	22	Roy's	**SoMa**	22
NEW Kanpai	**Palo Alto/S**	24	Rubicon	**Downtown**	24
Z Kaygetsu	**Menlo Pk/S**	28	Ruth's Chris	**Polk Gulch**	24
Z Kokkari	**Downtown**	26	**NEW** Salt House	**SoMa**	21
Kuleto's	**multi. loc.**	20	Sam's Grill	**Downtown**	20
Kyo-Ya	**Downtown**	23	Sanraku	**multi. loc.**	23
La Forêt	**San Jose/S**	27	Scott Howard	**Downtown**	23
NEW Lark Creek Steak	**Downtown**	22	Seasons	**Downtown**	24
	71 Saint Peter	**San Jose/S**	22
NEW La Terrasse	**Presidio**	19	Shanghai 1930	**Embarcadero**	20
Lavanda	**Palo Alto/S**	19	**Z** Silks	**Downtown**	24
Le Central Bistro	**Downtown**	19	Sino	**San Jose/S**	20
Z Le Papillon	**San Jose/S**	27	South Park	**SoMa**	22
Les Amis	**Downtown**	22	St. Michael's	**Palo Alto/S**	22
Lion & Compass	**Sunnyvale/S**	19	**Z** Tadich Grill	**Downtown**	22
MacArthur Park	**Palo Alto/S**	16	Tommy Toy's	**Downtown**	24
Z Marinus	**Carmel Valley/S**	26	Townhouse B&G	**Emeryville/E**	21
MarketBar	**Embarcadero**	17	231 Ellsworth	**San Mateo/S**	23
Z Masa's	**Downtown**	27	Viognier	**San Mateo/S**	24
Max's	**Oakland/E**	16	Waterfront	**Embarcadero**	18
Meadowood	**St. Helena/N**	20	**Z** Yank Sing	**multi. loc.**	25
NEW Mexico DF	**Embarcadero**	–	Zibibbo	**Palo Alto/S**	20
Mijita	**Embarcadero**	20	**Z** Zuni Café	**Hayes Valley**	25
Mistral	**Redwood Shores/S**	19	Zuppa	**SoMa**	19
Mixt Greens	**Downtown**	22		
MoMo's	**S Beach**	17	**CATERING**	
Moose's	**N Beach**	20	**Z** Acquerello	**Polk Gulch**	27
Morton's	**multi. loc.**	23	Adagia	**Berkeley/E**	19
Z Myth	**Downtown**	26	Alexis Baking Co.	**Napa/N**	22
Oak City B&G	**Menlo Pk/S**	18	All Season's	**Calistoga/N**	21
One Market	**Embarcadero**	22	Americano	**Embarcadero**	17
Osteria	**Palo Alto/S**	23	Asqew Grill	**multi. loc.**	18
Ozumo	**Embarcadero**	24	Azie	**SoMa**	19
Palio d'Asti	**Downtown**	19	Barndiva	**Healdsburg/N**	18

Betelnut Pejiu | **Cow Hollow**	23	La Strada | **Palo Alto/S**	21
Bistro Lialson | **Berkeley/E**	22	Lavanda | **Palo Alto/S**	19
Bistro V | **Sebastopol/N**	22	Left Bank | **multi. loc.**	18
☑ BIX | **Downtown**	23	Manzanita | **Healdsburg/N**	20
Blowfish Sushi | **multi. loc.**	21	☑ Marché | **Menlo Pk/S**	26
☑ Bocadillos | **N Beach**	22	☑ Marinus | **Carmel Valley/S**	26
Boonville Hotel | **Boonville/N**	21	Max's | **Downtown**	16
☑ Buckeye | **Mill Valley/N**	23	Memphis Minnie | **Lower Haight**	20
Cafe Esin | **San Ramon/E**	25	Mochica | **SoMa**	23
CAFÉ KATi | **Japantown**	23	Moki's Sushi | **Bernal Hts**	21
Caffè Verbena | **Oakland/E**	19	Monti's | **Santa Rosa/N**	19
César | **Berkeley/E**	22	Napa General | **Napa/N**	20
Cha Cha Cha | **multi. loc.**	19	Nick's Tacos | **Russian Hill**	20
Charanga | **Mission**	21	Ozumo | **Embarcadero**	24
Chef Chu's | **Los Altos/S**	20	Pangaea | **Gualala/N**	25
☑ Chenery Park | **Glen Pk**	22	Piatti | **multi. loc.**	19
Chez Papa Bistrot | **Potrero Hill**	23	Piazza D'Angelo | **Mill Valley/N**	19
Chez Spencer | **Mission**	24	Picante Cocina | **Berkeley/E**	21
Citron | **Oakland/E**	24	Pilar | **Napa/N**	25
Coco 500 | **SoMa**	22	Pizza Antica | **Lafayette/E**	21
Cucina Paradiso | **Petaluma/N**	26	Pizza Rustica | **Oakland/E**	19
Della Santina's | **Sonoma/N**	21	PJ's Oyster | **Inner Sunset**	19
Destino | **Castro**	22	Pomelo | **Inner Sunset**	22
downtown | **Berkeley/E**	20	Q | **Inner Rich**	20
Ebisu | **Inner Sunset**	23	Rest. LuLu/Petite | **SoMa**	20
Emporio Rulli | **Larkspur/N**	20	Rick & Ann's | **Berkeley/E**	21
Eos Rest./Wine | **Cole Valley**	23	Rose's Cafe | **Cow Hollow**	21
☑ Evvia | **Palo Alto/S**	26	Roy's | **SoMa**	22
fig cafe | **Glen Ellen/N**	23	Sabor of Spain | **San Rafael/N**	18
☑ Frascati | **Russian Hill**	26	Santi | **Geyserville/N**	23
Fresca | **multi. loc.**	22	Saul's Rest./Deli | **Berkeley/E**	18
☑ Fringale | **SoMa**	24	Seaweed Café | **Bodega Bay/N**	24
Gabriella Café | **Santa Cruz/S**	22	Shalimar | **multi. loc.**	22
Gayle's Bakery | **Capitola/S**	25	☑ Slanted Door | **Embarcadero**	26
Globe | **Downtown**	21	Sociale | **Presidio Hts**	23
Grasing's Coastal | **Carmel/S**	23	St. Michael's | **Palo Alto/S**	22
☑ Greens | **Marina**	24	Stokes | **Monterey/S**	23
Hana Japanese | **Rohnert Pk/N**	25	Straits Cafe | **multi. loc.**	20
Iberia | **Menlo Pk/S**	21	Tacubaya | **Berkeley/E**	22
Il Davide | **San Rafael/N**	21	Town's End | **Embarcadero**	19
☑ Il Fornaio | **San Jose/S**	19	Tratt. La Siciliana | **Berkeley/E**	23
Insalata's | **San Anselmo/N**	24	Tra Vigne | **St. Helena/N**	23
Jack Falstaff | **SoMa**	20	☑ Truly Med. | **Mission**	23
Jimtown Store | **Healdsburg/N**	19	Village Pub | **Woodside/S**	26
Julia's | **Napa/N**	23	Vivande | **Pacific Hts**	23
jZcool | **Menlo Pk/S**	20	Wappo Bar | **Calistoga/N**	22
☑ Kokkari | **Downtown**	26	Washington Sq. B&G | **N Beach**	19
La Méditerranée | **multi. loc.**	19	Wente Vineyards | **Livermore/E**	23

Willi's Seafood | **Healdsburg/N** 23

Willi's Wine | **Santa Rosa/N** 24

Yabbies Coastal | **Russian Hill** 22

⚡ Yank Sing | **multi. loc.** 25

Yumma's | **Inner Sunset** 20

Zao Noodle | **multi. loc.** 14

Zatar | **Berkeley/E** 21

zazu | **Santa Rosa/N** 25

Zibibbo | **Palo Alto/S** 20

Zin | **Healdsburg/N** 22

Zuppa | **SoMa** 19

CELEBRITY CHEFS

Acme Chophouse | 19
Traci Des Jardins | **S Beach**

⚡ Ame | *Hiro Sone* | **SoMa** 26

⚡ Aqua | *Laurent Manrique* | 26
Downtown

Arcadia | *Michael Mina* | 23
San Jose/S

⚡ Bistro Jeanty | *Philippe Jeanty* | 25
Yountville/N

Boca | *George Morrone* | **Novato/N** 20

⚡ Bocadillos | *Gerald Hirigoyen* | 22
N Beach

⚡ Bouchon | *Thomas Keller* | 25
Yountville/N

⚡ Boulevard | *Nancy Oakes* | 27
Embarcadero

Bushi-tei | 24
Seiji "Waka" Wakabayashi |
Japantown

Chef Chu's | *Lawrence Chu* | 20
Los Altos/S

NEW Chef Wai | *Andy Wai* | 20
San Mateo/S

⚡ Chez Panisse | *Alice Waters* | 27
Berkeley/E

Cindy's | *Cindy Pawlcyn* | 24
St. Helena/N

Citizen Cake | *Elizabeth Falkner* | 20
Hayes Valley

Coco 500 | *Loretta Keller* | **SoMa** 22

Coi | *Daniel Patterson* | **N Beach** 25

⚡ Cyrus | *Douglas Keane* | 28
Healdsburg/N

⚡ Delfina | *Craig Stoll* | **Mission** 26

Dry Creek | *Charles Palmer* | 24
Healdsburg/N

NEW Essencia | —
Anne Gingrass Paik |
Hayes Valley

⚡ Farallon | *Mark Franz* | 24
Downtown

Fifth Floor | *Melissa Perello* | 25
SoMa

Flea St. Café | *Jesse Cool* | 22
Menlo Pk/S

⚡ Fleur de Lys | *Hubert Keller* | 28
Nob Hill

⚡ French Laundry | *Thomas Keller* | 29
Yountville/N

⚡ Gary Danko | *Gary Danko* | 29
Fish. Wharf

NEW Go Fish | *Cindy Pawlcyn* | 24
St. Helena/N

⚡ Jardinière | *Traci Des Jardins* | 26
Hayes Valley

Jeanty at Jack's | *Philippe Jeanty* | 23
Downtown

⚡ La Folie | *Roland Passot* | 27
Russian Hill

Lark Creek Inn | *Bradley Ogden* | 23
Larkspur/N

NEW Lark Creek Steak | 22
Bradley Ogden | **Downtown**

⚡ La Toque | *Ken Frank* | 26
Rutherford/N

Left Bank | *Roland Passot* | 18
multi. loc.

Market | *Douglas Keane* | 22
St. Helena/N

Martini House | *Todd Humphries* | 25
St. Helena/N

⚡ Masa's | *Gregory Short* | 27
Downtown

⚡ Michael Mina | *Michael Mina* | 28
Downtown

Mijita | *Traci Des Jardins* | 20
Embarcadero

Mustards Grill | *Cindy Pawlcyn* | 24
Yountville/N

NEW Nick's Cove | *Mark Franz* | —
Marshall/N

NoPa | *Laurence Jossel* | 23
W Addition

Oliveto Restaurant | *Paul Bertolli* | 25
Oakland/E

Out the Door | *Charles Phan* | 22
Embarcadero

Parcel 104 | *Bradley Ogden* | 23
Santa Clara/S

Picco | *Bruce Hill* | **Larkspur/N** 24

Pilar | *Pilar Sanchez* | **Napa/N** 25

Piperade | *Gerald Hirigoyen* | 25
Downtown

Pizzeria Delfina | *Craig Stoll* | 24
Mission

🗹 Pizzeria Picco | *Bruce Hill* | 25
Larkspur/N

🗹 Postrio | *Wolfgang Puck* | 24
Downtown

🗹 Redd Rest. | *Richard Reddington* | 26
Yountville/N

🗹 Ritz-Carlton Din. Rm. | 27
Ron Siegel | **Nob Hill**

Roy's | *Roy Yamaguchi* | **SoMa** 22

Roy's | *Roy Yamaguchi* | 25
Pebble Bch/S

Rubicon | *Stuart Brioza* | 24
Downtown

NEW Salt House | *Mitchell and* 21
Steven Rosenthal | **SoMa**

Scott Howard | *Scott Howard* | 23
Downtown

Sino | *Chris Yeo* | **San Jose/S** 20

🗹 Slanted Door | *Charles Phan* | 26
Embarcadero

Straits Cafe | *Chris Yeo* | **multi. loc.** 20

🗹 Terra | *Hiro Sone* | **St. Helena/N** 26

Town Hall | *Steven and* 23
Mitchell Rosenthal | **SoMa**

NEW TWO | *David Gingrass and* 21
Bridget Batson | **SoMa**

NEW West Co. Grill | –
Jonathon Waxman |
Sebastopol/N

'wichcraft | *Tom Colicchio* | 17
Downtown

Yankee Pier | *Bradley Ogden* | 17
S San Francisco/S

🗹 Zuni Café | *Judy Rodgers* | 25
Hayes Valley

CHILD-FRIENDLY

(Alternatives to the usual fast-food
places; * children's menu available)

Acme Chophouse | **S Beach** 19

🗹 Ahwahnee* | **Yosemite/E** 19

Alexis Baking Co. | **Napa/N** 22

Alice's | **Noe Valley** 19

Alioto's* | **Fish. Wharf** 19

Amici's* | **multi. loc.** 20

Aperto* | **Potrero Hill** 20

Arcadia* | **San Jose/S** 23

A. Sabella's* | **Fish. Wharf** 18

Asqew Grill* | **multi. loc.** 18

Barbara Fish* | **Princeton Sea/S** 19

Barney's* | **multi. loc.** 19

Basque Cultural* | 20
S San Francisco/S

Beach Chalet* | **Outer Sunset** 13

Bette's Oceanview | **Berkeley/E** 21

Bistro Boudin* | **Fish. Wharf** 20

Boulange | **multi. loc.** 22

Brandy Ho's | **Chinatown** 20

Brannan's Grill | **Calistoga/N** 19

Buca di Beppo* | **multi. loc.** 14

Bucci's | **Emeryville/E** 20

🗹 Buckeye* | **Mill Valley/N** 23

Bungalow 44* | **Mill Valley/N** 21

Burger Joint | **multi. loc.** 18

Burma Superstar | **Inner Rich** 24

Cactus Taqueria* | **multi. loc.** 20

Café Cacao | **Berkeley/E** 20

Cafe Citti | **Kenwood/N** 22

Caffe Delle Stelle | **Hayes Valley** 16

Caffè Macaroni | **N Beach** 20

Caffè Museo | **SoMa** 16

Caspers Hot Dogs | **multi. loc.** 18

Cetrella* | **Half Moon Bay/S** 22

Cha Am Thai | **multi. loc.** 19

Cheesecake | **multi. loc.** 16

🗹 Chenery Park* | **Glen Pk** 22

Chez Spencer | **Mission** 24

🗹 Chow/Park Chow* | **multi. loc.** 20

Cindy's | **St. Helena/N** 24

Citrus Club | **Haight-Ashbury** 19

Cliff House Bistro | **Outer Rich** 18

Cook St. Helena | **St. Helena/N** 24

Delancey St. | **Embarcadero** 18

Dipsea Cafe* | **Mill Valley/N** 17

Dottie's | **Tenderloin** 25

Downtown Bakery | 24
Healdsburg/N

Duarte's Tavern* | **Pescadero/S** 21

El Balazo* | **Haight-Ashbury** 18

Eliza's | **multi. loc.** 22

Ella's* | **Presidio Hts** 20

Emmy's Spaghetti* | **Bernal Hts** 19

Emporio Rulli | **multi. loc.** 20

Enrico's | **N Beach** –

Eric's | **Noe Valley** 20

Everett & Jones | **Oakland/E** 20

FatApple's* | multi. loc.	17
Fentons Creamery* | Oakland/E	18
Fish | Sausalito/N	24
Flavor* | Santa Rosa/N	20
Fog City Diner* | Embarcadero	19
Fook Yuen | Millbrae/S	20
Forbes Mill Steak* | Danville/E	23
Fournou's* | Nob Hill	22
Garibaldis* | Oakland/E	21
Gar Woods* | Carnelian Bay/E	19
Giordano | N Beach	21
Giorgio's Pizzeria | Inner Rich	20
Goat Hill Pizza | Potrero Hill	19
Goood Frikin' Chicken | Mission	19
Great China | Berkeley/E	23
Great Eastern | Chinatown	22
Guaymas* | Tiburon/N	17
Hard Rock* | Fish. Wharf	13
Henry's Hunan | multi. loc.	21
Hunan | multi. loc.	22
Hurley's* | Yountville/N	20
Z Il Fornaio* | multi. loc.	19
Insalata's* | San Anselmo/N	24
Jade Villa | Oakland/E	17
Jay's | multi. loc.	17
Jimmy Bean's* | Berkeley/E	20
Jimtown Store* | Healdsburg/N	19
Z Joe's Cable Car | Excelsior	24
Joe's Taco | Mill Valley/N	18
Juan's | Berkeley/E	16
Juban | multi. loc.	17
jZcool* | Menlo Pk/S	20
King of Thai | multi. loc.	19
Koi Palace | Daly City/S	23
Koryo BBQ | Oakland/E	21
Kuleto's* | multi. loc.	20
La Cumbre | Mission	22
La Méditerranée* | multi. loc.	19
Lark Creek* | Walnut Creek/E	22
Left Bank* | multi. loc.	18
Lo Coco's | Berkeley/E	21
Lovejoy's Tea* | Noe Valley	20
Z Mama's Wash. Sq. | N Beach	25
Market | St. Helena/N	22
Max's* | multi. loc.	16
Mel's Drive-In* | multi. loc.	13
Memphis Minnie | Lower Haight	20
Mifune | Japantown	18
Model Bakery | St. Helena/N	21
Mo's* | SoMa	20
Napa General | Napa/N	20
Napa Valley Grille* | Yountville/N	20
Nepenthe* | Big Sur/S	16
Nick's Tacos | Russian Hill	20
North Beach Pizza | multi. loc.	18
North Beach Rest. | N Beach	21
Z O'mei | Santa Cruz/S	26
Original Joe's* | multi. loc.	18
Pacific Catch* | multi. loc.	21
Pancho Villa | multi. loc.	20
Parcel 104* | Santa Clara/S	23
Park Chalet* | Outer Sunset	15
Pasta Pomodoro* | multi. loc.	16
Pauline's Pizza | Mission	22
Piatti* | multi. loc.	19
Picante Cocina* | Berkeley/E	21
Pizza Antica* | multi. loc.	21
Pizza Azzurro | Napa/N	22
Pizza Rustica | Oakland/E	19
Z Pizzeria Picco | Larkspur/N	25
Pizzeria Tra Vigne* | St. Helena/N	21
Pork Store | multi. loc.	21
Powell's* | W Addition	18
Q | Inner Rich	20
R & G Lounge | Chinatown	23
Rest. Peony | Oakland/E	20
Rick & Ann's* | Berkeley/E	21
Rigolo* | Presidio Hts	18
Robata Grill | Mill Valley/N	20
Saul's Rest./Deli* | Berkeley/E	18
Savor* | Noe Valley	18
Scoma's* | multi. loc.	21
Sears Fine Food | Downtown	18
Sharon's* | Ft Bragg/N	20
Shen Hua | Berkeley/E	20
Taqueria Can-Cun | multi. loc.	21
Tarpy's* | Monterey/S	22
Taylor's Auto | multi. loc.	21
Tommaso's | N Beach	25
Z Ton Kiang | Outer Rich	25
Venezia* | Berkeley/E	20
Waterfront* | Embarcadero	18
Z Willow Wood | Graton/N	25
Yankee Pier* | multi. loc.	17
Z Yank Sing | multi. loc.	25
Yumma's | Inner Sunset	20

| Zachary's Pizza | multi. loc. | 24 |
| Zao Noodle* | multi. loc. | 14 |

CRITIC-PROOF

(Gets lots of business despite so-so food)

Beach Chalet	Outer Sunset	13
Buca di Beppo	multi. loc.	14
Mel's Drive-In	multi. loc.	13
Zao Noodle	multi. loc.	14

DANCING

AsiaSF	SoMa	17
Jordan's	Berkeley/E	18
Kan Zaman	Haight-Ashbury	17
Le Colonial	Downtown	21
Levende	Mission	20
Luka's Taproom	Oakland/E	20
Maddalena/Fino	Palo Alto/S	21
Medjool	Mission	18
Plumed Horse	Saratoga/S	-
Shanghai 1930	Embarcadero	20
Straits Cafe	San Jose/S	20
Tonga	Nob Hill	13
XYZ	SoMa	20

DELIVERY

Alexis Baking Co.	Napa/N	22
Amici's	multi. loc.	20
Angkor Borei	Mission	20
Basil Thai	SoMa	22
Brandy Ho's	Chinatown	20
☑ Dish Dash	Sunnyvale/S	23
Gary Chu's	Santa Rosa/N	22
Goat Hill Pizza	SoMa	19
Henry's Hunan	SoMa	21
Insalata's	San Anselmo/N	24
Jimtown Store	Healdsburg/N	19
La Méditerranée	Castro	19
Max's	multi. loc.	16
North Beach Pizza	multi. loc.	18
Pakwan	Hayward/E	21
Piatti	Carmel/S	19
Pizza Antica	San Jose/S	21
Pizza Rustica	Oakland/E	19
Pork Store	Mission	21
Powell's	W Addition	18
Rio Grill	Carmel/S	22
Seven	San Jose/S	21
☑ Swan Oyster	Polk Gulch	26

☑ Ton Kiang	Outer Rich	25
Vivande	Pacific Hts	23
Zante	Bernal Hts	18

DINING ALONE

(Other than hotels and places with counter service)

Absinthe	Hayes Valley	20
Ace Wasabi's	Marina	20
Acme Chophouse	S Beach	19
☑ Amber India	Mtn View/S	25
Andalu	Mission	20
Ariake	Outer Rich	26
Arinell Pizza	multi. loc.	22
Asqew Grill	multi. loc.	18
Avatars	Sausalito/N	22
bacar	SoMa	22
Bar Crudo	Downtown	25
Barney's	San Rafael/N	19
Bar Tartine	Mission	22
Bette's Oceanview	Berkeley/E	21
☑ Bistro Jeanty	Yountville/N	25
Bistro Ralph	Healdsburg/N	21
Blowfish Sushi	multi. loc.	21
Blue Jay	W Addition	15
☑ Bocadillos	N Beach	22
Bodega Bistro	Tenderloin	23
Bong Su	SoMa	22
☑ Bouchon	Yountville/N	25
☑ Boulevard	Embarcadero	27
Bovolo	Healdsburg/N	22
Breads of India	multi. loc.	21
☑ Buckeye	Mill Valley/N	23
Bungalow 44	Mill Valley/N	21
Burger Joint	multi. loc.	18
NEW Butterfly Bistro	San Bruno/S	-
Cafe Bastille	Downtown	18
Cafe Citti	Kenwood/N	22
Café Claude	Downtown	20
Café de la Presse	Downtown	16
Café Gratitude	multi. loc.	19
Café Rouge	Berkeley/E	21
Cascal	Mtn View/S	20
Cav Wine Bar	Hayes Valley	22
César	Berkeley/E	22
Cetrella	Half Moon Bay/S	22
Cha Cha Cha	multi. loc.	19
Cha-Ya Veg.	multi. loc.	24

SPECIAL FEATURES

Chez Maman	**multi. loc.**	21
Chez Papa Bistrot	**Potrero Hill**	23
Chouchou	**Forest Hills**	21
Citizen Cake	**Hayes Valley**	20
Coco 500	**SoMa**	22
Coi	**N Beach**	25
Cook St. Helena	**St. Helena/N**	24
Cork	**Sausalito/N**	19
Couleur Café	**Potrero Hill**	16
Cuvée	**Napa/N**	20
Daimaru	**Castro**	24
Della Fattoria	**Petaluma/N**	26
Z Dish Dash	**Sunnyvale/S**	23
Dosa	**Mission**	20
Duarte's Tavern	**Pescadero/S**	21
E&O Trading	**San Jose/S**	19
Ebisu	**Inner Sunset**	23
Emporio Rulli	**Larkspur/N**	20
Enrico's	**N Beach**	–
Eos Rest./Wine	**Cole Valley**	23
Z Evvia	**Palo Alto/S**	26
farmerbrown	**Tenderloin**	19
FatApple's	**multi. loc.**	17
1550 Hyde	**Russian Hill**	22
Z Firefly	**Noe Valley**	25
Fog City Diner	**Embarcadero**	19
Z Fringale	**SoMa**	24
Frjtz Fries	**multi. loc.**	19
Gioia Pizzeria	**Berkeley/E**	24
Godzila Sushi	**Pacific Hts**	17
Good Luck	**Inner Rich**	22
Grandeho Kamekyo	**multi. loc.**	23
Green Chile	**W Addition**	19
Gregoire	**Oakland/E**	24
Hamano Sushi	**Noe Valley**	20
NEW Hime	**Marina**	22
Hog Island Oyster	**Embarcadero**	25
Home of Chicken	**Oakland/E**	15
Hurley's	**Yountville/N**	20
Jack Falstaff	**SoMa**	20
Jodie's Rest.	**Albany/E**	20
Kabuto	**Outer Rich**	25
NEW Kanpai	**Palo Alto/S**	24
Z Kaygetsu	**Menlo Pk/S**	28
King of Thai	**multi. loc.**	19
Kirala	**Berkeley/E**	25
Kiss Sushi	**Japantown**	27
Koo	**Inner Sunset**	24

Krung Thai	**San Jose/S**	23
Boulange	**multi. loc.**	22
Lanesplitter Pub	**multi. loc.**	18
La Note	**Berkeley/E**	22
Last Supper	**Mission**	19
La Victoria	**San Jose/S**	20
Left Bank	**multi. loc.**	18
Le Petit Robert	**Russian Hill**	19
Lettus	**Marina**	20
Le Zinc	**Noe Valley**	18
Mario's Bohemian	**N Beach**	18
MarketBar	**Embarcadero**	17
Matterhorn Swiss	**Russian Hill**	21
Maverick	**Mission**	22
Medicine	**Downtown**	18
Medjool	**Mission**	18
Mel's Drive-In	**Inner Rich**	13
Mixt Greens	**Downtown**	22
Modern Tea	**Hayes Valley**	20
Mustards Grill	**Yountville/N**	24
Z Myth	**Downtown**	26
My Tofu	**Inner Rich**	20
Naan/Curry	**Downtown**	18
Naked Fish	**S Lake Tahoe/E**	22
Naomi Sushi	**Menlo Pk/S**	21
Napa General	**Napa/N**	20
Nectar Wine	**Burlingame/S**	19
Nizza La Bella	**Albany/E**	19
NEW Nua Rest.	**N Beach**	–
n.v. Rest.	**Napa/N**	22
Old Port/N. Bch. Lobster		21
Redwood City/S	
Oliveto Cafe	**Oakland/E**	23
Ora	**Mill Valley/N**	21
O'Reilly's	**Polk Gulch**	18
Ottimista	**Cow Hollow**	20
Out the Door	**multi. loc.**	22
Oyaji	**Outer Rich**	23
Pacific Catch	**Corte Madera/N**	21
Pancho Villa	**Embarcadero**	20
Papalote	**multi. loc.**	21
Pasta Pomodoro	**multi. loc.**	16
Patxi's Pizza	**multi. loc.**	20
Pearl Oyster	**Oakland/E**	24
NEW Piccino	**Dogpatch**	19
Pine Cone Diner	**Pt Reyes/N**	19
Z Piperade	**Downtown**	25
Pizza Antica	**multi. loc.**	21

subscribe to zagat.com

Pluto's Fresh | **multi. loc.** 19

Powell's | **W Addition** 18

Red Door | **Nob Hill** 20

Z Redd Rest. | **Yountville/N** 26

Red Hut | **S Lake Tahoe/E** 25

rnm rest. | **Lower Haight** 25

Robata Grill | **Mill Valley/N** 20

NEW Rouge/Blanc | **Downtown** -

Ryoko's | **Tenderloin** 23

Osake/Sake 'O | **Healdsburg/N** 22

Sebo | **Hayes Valley** 25

Shabu-Sen | **Japantown** 18

Shanghai Dumpling | **Outer Rich** 22

Sino | **San Jose/S** 20

So | **Outer Sunset** 21

Sonoma Meritage | **Sonoma/N** 19

NEW Spork | **Mission** -

Suppenküche | **Hayes Valley** 21

Z Sushi Ran | **Sausalito/N** 28

Sushi Zone | **Castro** 26

Z Swan Oyster | **Polk Gulch** 26

Table Café | **Larkspur/N** 24

Tablespoon | **Russian Hill** 22

Taqueria Can-Cun | **multi. loc.** 21

Taqueria 3 Amigos | **multi. loc.** 18

Taqueria Tlaquepaque | **San Jose/S** 23

Terzo | **Cow Hollow** 22

Thai House | **multi. loc.** 20

Ti Couz | **Mission** 22

Tokyo Go Go | **Mission** 22

Tommaso's | **N Beach** 25

Town Hall | **SoMa** 23

Tra Vigne | **St. Helena/N** 23

Tres Agaves | **S Beach** 18

T Rex Barbecue | **Berkeley/E** 17

Tsunami | **W Addition** 23

Uncle Frank's | **Mtn View/S** 22

NEW Underdog | **Inner Sunset** -

Viognier | **San Mateo/S** 24

Vivande | **Pacific Hts** 23

Willi's Seafood | **Healdsburg/N** 23

Woodhse. | **Castro** 19

NEW Xyclo | **Oakland/E** 19

Z Yank Sing | **SoMa** 25

Yoshi's | **Oakland/E** 18

Zachary's Pizza | **San Ramon/E** 24

Zatar | **Berkeley/E** 21

Zazie | **Cole Valley** 22

Zeitgeist | **Mission** 16

Zibibbo | **Palo Alto/S** 20

Z Zuni Café | **Hayes Valley** 25

Zushi Puzzle | **Marina** 26

ENTERTAINMENT

(Call for days and times of performances)

Z Ahwahnee | piano | **Yosemite/E** 19

Albion River | piano | **Albion/N** 24

Z Ana Mandara | jazz | **Fish. Wharf** 23

ANZU | jazz | **Downtown** 21

AsiaSF | gender illusionists | **SoMa** 17

bacar | jazz | **SoMa** 22

Beach Chalet | jazz | **Outer Sunset** 13

Big 4 | piano | **Nob Hill** 22

Bing Crosby's | piano | **Walnut Creek/E** 18

Z BIX | jazz | **Downtown** 23

Blowfish Sushi | DJ | **San Jose/S** 21

Blue Jay | jazz | **W Addition** 15

Butterfly | DJ | **Embarcadero** 19

Cafe Bastille | jazz | **Downtown** 18

Café Claude | jazz | **Downtown** 20

Cascal | Spanish band | **Mtn View/S** 20

Catch | jazz/piano | **Castro** 19

Cetrella | jazz | **Half Moon Bay/S** 22

Chaya Brasserie | jazz | **Embarcadero** 21

Circolo | DJ | **Mission** 19

Cosmopolitan | piano/vocals | **SoMa** 20

Deep Sushi | DJ | **Noe Valley** 21

downtown | jazz | **Berkeley/E** 20

Emmy's Spaghetti | DJ | **Bernal Hts** 19

Enrico's | jazz | **N Beach** -

Everett & Jones | varies | **Oakland/E** 20

Foreign Cinema | movies | **Mission** 21

Frisson | DJ | **Downtown** 20

Frjtz Fries | DJ | **Hayes Valley** 19

Z Garden Court | harp/jazz | **Downtown** 19

Giordano | varies | **N Beach** 21

Harris' | jazz/piano | **Polk Gulch** 25

Jordan's | jazz | **Berkeley/E** 18

Kan Zaman | belly dancers | **Haight-Ashbury** 17

Katia's Tea | accordion | **Inner Rich** 19

La Note | accordion | **Berkeley/E** 22

Ledford Hse. | jazz | **Albion/N** 23

Left Bank | jazz/vocals | **Larkspur/N** 18

Levende | DJ | **Mission** 20

Lime | DJ | **Castro** 18

Maddalena/Fino | jazz | **Palo Alto/S** 21

🆉 Marinus | jazz | **Carmel Valley/S** 26

Max's | singing waiters | **multi. loc.** 16

Mecca | DJ/jazz | **Castro** 20

Moose's | jazz | **N Beach** 20

🆉 Navio | jazz | **Half Moon Bay/S** 26

Olema Inn | varies | **Olema/N** 22

Plumed Horse | jazz/piano | **Saratoga/S** –

Powell's | gospel | **W Addition** 18

Prima | jazz | **Walnut Creek/E** 24

Puerto Alegre | mariachi trio | **Mission** 18

Ravenous Cafe | varies | **Healdsburg/N** 23

RoHan Lounge | DJ | **Inner Rich** 18

Rose Pistola | jazz | **N Beach** 21

Rose's | guitar | **Cow Hollow** 21

Santé | piano | **Sonoma/N** 24

Sardine Factory | piano | **Monterey/S** 20

Scott's | jazz/piano | **multi. loc.** 19

Seasons | piano | **Downtown** 24

Shanghai 1930 | jazz | **Embarcadero** 20

🆉 Slanted Door | DJ | **Embarcadero** 26

Straits Cafe | DJ/jazz | **multi. loc.** 20

Sushi Groove | DJ | **SoMa** 23

Tonga | live music | **Nob Hill** 13

Townhouse | jazz | **Emeryville/E** 21

Uva Trattoria | jazz | **Napa/N** 21

Vic Stewart's | piano | **Walnut Creek/E** 21

Wappo Bar | jazz | **Calistoga/N** 22

Washington Sq. B&G | piano | **N Beach** 19

XYZ | DJ | **SoMa** 20

Yoshi's | jazz | **Oakland/E** 18

🆉 Zuni Café | piano | **Hayes Valley** 25

FIREPLACES

Adagia | **Berkeley/E** 19

Albion River Inn | **Albion/N** 24

🆉 Alexander's | **Cupertino/S** 25

🆉 Ame | **SoMa** 26

Anton & Michel | **Carmel/S** 23

Applewood Inn | **Guerneville/N** 24

A. Sabella's | **Fish. Wharf** 18

Asia de Cuba | **Downtown** 21

🆉 Auberge du Sol. | **Rutherford/N** 25

Barney's | **Berkeley/E** 19

Bella Vista | **Woodside/S** 22

Betelnut Pejiu | **Cow Hollow** 23

Big 4 | **Nob Hill** 22

Bing Crosby's | **Walnut Creek/E** 18

Bistro Don Giovanni | **Napa/N** 23

🆉 Bistro Jeanty | **Yountville/N** 25

Boca | **Novato/N** 20

Boonville Hotel | **Boonville/N** 21

Bouchée | **Carmel/S** 26

Boulette's Larder | **Embarcadero** 25

Brannan's Grill | **Calistoga/N** 19

BRIX | **Yountville/N** 22

🆉 Buckeye | **Mill Valley/N** 23

Cafe Citti | **Kenwood/N** 22

Café Gratitude | **Berkeley/E** 19

Caprice | **Tiburon/N** 21

Casanova | **Carmel/S** 23

Casa Orinda | **Orinda/E** 17

Cetrella | **Half Moon Bay/S** 22

Chantilly | **Redwood City/S** 25

Chapter & Moon | **Ft Bragg/N** 21

Chez Spencer | **Mission** 24

Chez TJ | **Mtn View/S** 25

🆉 Chow/Park Chow | **multi. loc.** 20

Christy Hill | **Tahoe City/E** 25

Cottonwood | **Truckee/E** 20

Cuvée | **Napa/N** 20

Deetjen's | **Big Sur/S** 22

Della Santina's | **Sonoma/N** 21

Dipsea Cafe | **Mill Valley/N** 17

Duck Club | **multi. loc.** 20

E&O Trading | **Larkspur/N** 19

El Dorado | **Sonoma/N** 23

El Paseo | **Mill Valley/N** 23

Erna's Elderberry | Oakhurst/E 28
Étoile | Yountville/N 25
NEW Eureka | Castro 21
Z Evvia | Palo Alto/S 26
Fandango | Pacific Grove/S 23
NEW Z Farm | Napa/N 23
Z Farmhouse | Forestville/N 27
Flavor | Santa Rosa/N 20
Z Fleur de Lys | Nob Hill 28
Flying Fish | Carmel/S 24
Forbes Mill Steak | Los Gatos/S 23
Foreign Cinema | Mission 21
Z French Laundry | Yountville/N 29
Z Fresh Cream | Monterey/S 24
Fresh Ketch | S Lake Tahoe/E 18
Garibaldis | Oakland/E 21
Gar Woods | Carnelian Bay/E 19
Guaymas | Tiburon/N 17
Harris' | Polk Gulch 25
Heritage House | Little River/N –
Home | Castro 18
House of Prime | Polk Gulch 24
Iberia | Menlo Pk/S 21
Z Il Fornaio | multi. loc. 19
Jake's/Lake | Tahoe City/E 16
John Ash & Co. | Santa Rosa/N 23
Z John Bentley's | Woodside/S 25
Julius Castle | Telegraph Hill –
Kenwood | Kenwood/N 22
Kingfish | San Mateo/S 17
Z Kokkari | Downtown 26
Lark Creek Inn | Larkspur/N 23
Z La Toque | Rutherford/N 26
Ledford Hse. | Albion/N 23
Left Bank | Larkspur/N 18
Le Soleil | Inner Rich 20
MacArthur Park | Palo Alto/S 16
MacCallum Hse. | Mendocino/N 24
Z Madrona Manor | 25
Healdsburg/N
NEW Mandaloun | –
Redwood City/S
Z Marinus | Carmel Valley/S 26
Martini House | St. Helena/N 25
Mendocino Hotel | Mendocino/N 17
Mezza Luna | Princeton Sea/S 21
Moosse Café | Mendocino/N 23
Mosaic Rest. | Forestville/N 25

Napa General | Napa/N 20
Z Navio | Half Moon Bay/S 26
Nepenthe | Big Sur/S 16
NEW Nick's Cove | Marshall/N –
n.v. Rest. | Napa/N 22
Oak City B&G | Menlo Pk/S 18
Olivia | Berkeley/E 23
Ora | Mill Valley/N 21
Z Pacific's Edge | Carmel/S 25
Parcel 104 | Santa Clara/S 23
Park Chalet | Outer Sunset 15
Piatti | multi. loc. 19
Piazza D'Angelo | Mill Valley/N 19
Plouf | Downtown 22
Plumed Horse | Saratoga/S –
PlumpJack | Olympic Valley/E 24
Poleng | W Addition 22
Z Postino | Lafayette/E 24
Press | St. Helena/N 23
Prima | Walnut Creek/E 24
Ravenous Cafe | Healdsburg/N 23
Ravens Rest. | Mendocino/N 23
Rendezvous Inn | Ft Bragg/N 27
Rest. at Meadowood | 23
St. Helena/N
Rest. at Stevenswood | 20
Little River/N
Rest. LuLu/Petite | SoMa 20
Rio Grill | Carmel/S 22
River Ranch | Tahoe City/E 17
Robert's | Pacific Grove/S 25
Rutherford Grill | Rutherford/N 23
Salute E Rist. | Richmond/E 19
Santé | Sonoma/N 24
Santi | Geyserville/N 23
Sardine Factory | Monterey/S 20
Seasons | Downtown 24
Seaweed Café | Bodega Bay/N 24
Z Shadowbrook | Capitola/S 22
Shanghai 1930 | Embarcadero 20
Z Sierra Mar | Big Sur/S 26
Sol y Lago | Tahoe City/E 17
Soule Domain | Kings Bch/E 23
Stokes | Monterey/S 23
St. Orres | Gualala/N 24
NEW Tanglewood | San Jose/S 21
Tarpy's | Monterey/S 22
Terzo | Cow Hollow 22

SPECIAL FEATURES

Theo's | **Soquel/S**	24
Townhouse B&G | **Emeryville/E**	21
Troya | **Inner Rich**	22
Vic Stewart's | **Walnut Creek/E**	21
Village Pub | **Woodside/S**	26
Viognier | **San Mateo/S**	24
Wine Spectator | **St. Helena/N**	22
Wolf House | **Glen Ellen/N**	20
Zibibbo | **Palo Alto/S**	20
Zinsvalley | **Napa/N**	20

HISTORIC PLACES

(Year opened; * building)

1800 | Côté Sud* | **Castro**	20
1800 | Market* | **St. Helena/N**	22
1829 | Cindy's* | **St. Helena/N**	24
1844 | Celadon* | **Napa/N**	23
1848 | La Forêt* | **San Jose/S**	27
1849 | Tadich Grill | **Downtown**	22
1856 | Garden Ct.* | **Downtown**	19
1857 | Little River Inn* | **Little River/N**	20
1860 | Pizza Antica* | **Lafayette/E**	21
1863 | Cliff House Bistro | **Outer Rich**	18
1864 | Boonville Hotel* | **Boonville/N**	21
1864 | Jeanty at Jack's* | **Downtown**	23
1865 | O'Reilly's* | **Polk Gulch**	18
1867 | Sam's Grill | **Downtown**	20
1875 | La Note* | **Berkeley/E**	22
1876 | Olema Inn* | **Olema/N**	22
1877 | Heritage House* | **Little River/N**	-
1878 | A.P. Stump's* | **San Jose/S**	21
1878 | Mendocino Hotel* | **Mendocino/N**	17
1880 | Deuce* | **Sonoma/N**	20
1880 | Pianeta* | **Truckee/E**	23
1881 | Il Fornaio* | **Carmel/S**	19
1881 | Madrona Manor* | **Healdsburg/N**	25
1882 | MacCallum Hse.* | **Mendocino/N**	24
1884 | Napa General* | **Napa/N**	20
1884 | Terra* | **St. Helena/N**	26
1886 | Cole's Chop* | **Napa/N**	25
1886 | Fior d'Italia | **N Beach**	19
1886 | Mendo Bistro* | **Ft Bragg/N**	25
1886 | Willi's Wine* | **Santa Rosa/N**	24
1888 | Bounty Hunter* | **Napa/N**	17
1889 | Boulevard* | **Embarcadero**	27
1889 | Lark Creek Inn* | **Larkspur/N**	23
1889 | Pacific Café* | **Outer Rich**	22
1890 | Chez TJ* | **Mtn View/S**	25
1890 | Eureka* | **Castro**	21
1890 | Scoma's* | **Sausalito/N**	21
1893 | Cafe Beaujolais* | **Mendocino/N**	25
1893 | Jimtown Store* | **Healdsburg/N**	19
1894 | Duarte's Tavern* | **Pescadero/S**	21
1894 | Fentons Creamery | **Oakland/E**	18
1894 | Robert's* | **Pacific Grove/S**	25
1895 | Restaurant* | **Ft Bragg/N**	23
1897 | Rendezvous Inn* | **Ft Bragg/N**	27
1897 | Rogue Chefs* | **Half Moon Bay/S**	21
1900 | Axum* | **Lower Haight**	20
1900 | Central Market* | **Petaluma/N**	23
1900 | Cha Cha Cha* | **Mission**	19
1900 | French Laundry* | **Yountville/N**	29
1900 | La Ginestra* | **Mill Valley/N**	18
1900 | Pauline's Pizza* | **Mission**	22
1900 | Salute E Rist.* | **Richmond/E**	19
1902 | Café Majestic | **Pacific Hts**	-
1902 | Santi* | **Geyserville/N**	23
1904 | Moosse Café* | **Mendocino/N**	23
1904 | paul k* | **Hayes Valley**	21
1905 | Model Bakery* | **St. Helena/N**	21
1905 | Postino* | **Lafayette/E**	24
1905 | Public* | **SoMa**	18
1906 | Coco 500* | **SoMa**	22
1906 | Imperial/Berkeley* | **Embarcadero**	17
1906 | Pork Store* | **Haight-Ashbury**	21
1907 | Town Hall* | **SoMa**	23

1909 | Campton Place* | **Downtown** _25_

1910 | Catch* | **Castro** _19_

1910 | Harris'* | **Polk Gulch** _25_

1910 | Poleng* | **W Addition** _22_

1910 | Rest. LuLu/Petite* | **SoMa** _20_

1912 | Swan Oyster | **Polk Gulch** _26_

1913 | Balboa Cafe | **Cow Hollow** _19_

1913 | Zuni* | **Hayes Valley** _25_

1914 | Red's Java* | **Embarcadero** _14_

1915 | Jordan's* | **Berkeley/E** _18_

1915 | MacArthur Park* | **Palo Alto/S** _16_

1915 | Napa Wine Train* | **Napa/N** _15_

1917 | Original Joe's* | **Tenderloin** _18_

1917 | Pacific's Edge* | **Carmel/S** _25_

1917 | Tarpy's* | **Monterey/S** _22_

1918 | Olivia* | **Berkeley/E** _23_

1918 | St. Francis | **Mission** _19_

1919 | Albion River Inn* | **Albion/N** _24_

1919 | Ana Mandara* | **Fish. Wharf** _23_

1919 | Sauce* | **Hayes Valley** _18_

1920 | Acquerello* | **Polk Gulch** _27_

1920 | Albona Rist.* | **N Beach** _24_

1920 | A. Sabella's | **Fish. Wharf** _18_

1920 | Bistro Vida* | **Menlo Pk/S** _18_

1920 | Boogaloos* | **Mission** _17_

1920 | Kingfish* | **San Mateo/S** _17_

1922 | Julius Castle* | **Telegraph Hill** _–_

1923 | Martini House* | **St. Helena/N** _25_

1925 | Adagia* | **Berkeley/E** _19_

1925 | Alioto's | **Fish. Wharf** _19_

1925 | John Bentley's* | **Redwood City/S** _25_

1925 | Rist. Capellini* | **San Mateo/S** _19_

1927 | Ahwahnee | **Yosemite/E** _19_

1927 | Bella Vista* | **Woodside/S** _22_

1927 | Townhouse B&G* | **Emeryville/E** _21_

1928 | Alfred's Steak | **Downtown** _21_

1928 | Elite Cafe* | **Upper Fillmore** _19_

1929 | L'Auberge* | **Carmel/S** _27_

1930 | Big 4* | **Nob Hill** _22_

1930 | Caprice* | **Tiburon/N** _21_

1930 | Evan's* | **S Lake Tahoe/E** _27_

1930 | Foreign Cinema* | **Mission** _21_

1930 | Lalime's* | **Berkeley/E** _26_

1930 | Lo Coco's* | **Oakland/E** _21_

1930 | Ravenous Cafe* | **Healdsburg/N** _23_

1930 | Theo's* | **Soquel/S** _24_

1932 | Casa Orinda* | **Orinda/E** _17_

1933 | Luka's Taproom* | **Oakland/E** _20_

1934 | Caspers | **multi. loc.** _18_

1935 | Tommaso's | **N Beach** _25_

1936 | Gabriella Café* | **Santa Cruz/S** _22_

1937 | Buckeye | **Mill Valley/N** _23_

1937 | 231 Ellsworth* | **San Mateo/S** _23_

1938 | Deetjen's* | **Big Sur/S** _22_

1938 | Sears | **Downtown** _18_

1945 | Tonga | **Nob Hill** _13_

1947 | Shadowbrook | **Capitola/S** _22_

1949 | House of Prime | **Polk Gulch** _24_

1949 | Nepenthe | **Big Sur/S** _16_

1949 | Taylor's Auto | **St. Helena/N** _21_

1950 | Alexis Baking Co.* | **Napa/N** _22_

1950 | Red Hut* | **S Lake Tahoe/E** _25_

1952 | Plumed Horse | **Saratoga/S** _–_

1953 | Mel's Drive-In* | **Inner Rich** _13_

1955 | Breads of India* | **Berkeley/E** _21_

1956 | Original Joe's | **San Jose/S** _18_

HOTEL DINING

Adagio Hotel
Cortez | **Downtown** _23_

Ahwahnee Hotel
☒ Ahwahnee | **Yosemite/E** _19_

Auberge du Soleil
☒ Auberge du Sol. | **Rutherford/N** _25_

Bernardus Lodge
☒ Marinus | **Carmel Valley/S** _26_

Blue Rock Inn
Left Bank | **Larkspur/N** _18_

Boonville Hotel
Boonville Hotel | **Boonville/N** _21_

SPECIAL FEATURES

California, Hotel
  Z Millennium | **Downtown**   24

Campton Place Hotel
  Campton Place | **Downtown**   25

Carlton Hotel
  Saha | **Tenderloin**   24

Carneros Inn
  Boon Fly Café | **Napa/N**   -
  NEW Z Farm | **Napa/N**   23

Casa Madrona
  Poggio | **Sausalito/N**   21

Château du Sureau
  Z Erna's Elderberry | 28
  Oakhurst/E

Claremont Resort & Spa
  Jordan's | **Berkeley/E**   18

Clift Hotel
  Asia de Cuba | **Downtown**   21

Commodore Hotel
  Canteen | **Downtown**   25

Dina's Garden Hotel
  Trader Vic's | **Palo Alto/S**   16

Doubletree Plaza
  Hana Japanese | **Rohnert Pk/N**   25

El Dorado Hotel
  El Dorado | **Sonoma/N**   23

Fairmont Hotel
  Tonga | **Nob Hill**   13

Fairmont Sonoma Mission
  Santé | **Sonoma/N**   24

Farmhouse Inn
  Z Farmhouse | **Forestville/N**   27

Four Seasons Hotel
  Quattro | **E Palo Alto/S**   22
  Seasons | **Downtown**   24

Garden Court Hotel
  Z Il Fornaio | **Palo Alto/S**   19

Healdsburg, Hotel
  Dry Creek | **Healdsburg/N**   24

Heritage House
  Heritage House | -
  Little River/N

Hilltop Lodge
  Cottonwood | **Truckee/E**   20

Huntington Hotel
  Big 4 | **Nob Hill**   22

Hyatt Highlands Inn
  Z Pacific's Edge | **Carmel/S**   25

Inn at Southbridge
  Pizzeria Tra Vigne | 21
  St. Helena/N

Inn at Spanish Bay
  Roy's | **Pebble Bch/S**   25

Lafayette Park Hotel & Spa
  Duck Club | **Lafayette/E**   20

L'Auberge Carmel
  Z L'Auberge | **Carmel/S**   27

Les Mars Hotel
  Z Cyrus | **Healdsburg/N**   28

Little River Inn
  Little River Inn | **Little River/N**   20

Lodge at Pebble Beach
  Club XIX | **Pebble Bch/S**   25

Lodge at Sonoma
  Carneros Bistro | **Sonoma/N**   22

Los Gatos, Hotel
  NEW Dio Deka | **Los Gatos/S**   -

MacCallum House Inn
  MacCallum Hse. | 24
  Mendocino/N

Madrona Manor
  Z Madrona Manor | 25
  Healdsburg/N

Majestic, Hotel
  Café Majestic | **Pacific Hts**   -

Mandarin Oriental Hotel
  Z Silks | **Downtown**   24

Maxwell Hotel
  Max's | **Downtown**   16

Meadowood Napa Valley
  Meadowood | **St. Helena/N**   20
  Rest. at Meadowood | 23
  St. Helena/N

Mendocino Hotel
  Mendocino Hotel | 17
  Mendocino/N

Monaco, Hotel
  Grand Cafe | **Downtown**   20

Monterey Plaza Hotel & Spa
  Duck Club | **Monterey/S**   20

Nikko, Hotel
  ANZU | **Downtown**   21

Olema Inn
  Olema Inn | **Olema/N**   22

Palace Hotel
  Z Garden Court | **Downtown**   19
  Kyo-Ya | **Downtown**   23

subscribe to zagat.com

Palomar, Hotel
Fifth Floor | **SoMa** 25

Park Hyatt Hotel
Park Grill | **Downtown** 20

Pine Inn, The
Z Il Fornaio | **Carmel/S** 19

PlumpJack Squaw Valley Inn
PlumpJack | 24
Olympic Valley/E

Post Ranch Inn
Z Sierra Mar | **Big Sur/S** 26

Prescott Hotel
Z Postrio | **Downtown** 24

Renaissance Stanford Ct.
Fournou's | **Nob Hill** 22

Ritz-Carlton Half Moon Bay
Z Navio | **Half Moon Bay/S** 26

Ritz-Carlton Hotel
Z Ritz-Carlton Din. Rm. | 27
Nob Hill

Z Ritz-Carlton Terr. | 24
Nob Hill

Sainte Claire
Z Il Fornaio | **San Jose/S** 19

San Jose Marriott
Arcadia | **San Jose/S** 23

San Remo Hotel
Fior d'Italia | **N Beach** 19

Santa Clara Marriott
Parcel 104 | **Santa Clara/S** 23

Serrano Hotel
Ponzu | **Downtown** 21

Sir Francis Drake Hotel
Scala's Bistro | **Downtown** 22

Sonoma Hotel
girl & the fig | **Sonoma/N** 23

Stanford Inn & Spa
Ravens Rest. | **Mendocino/N** 23

Stanford Park Hotel
Duck Club | **Menlo Pk/S** 20

Stevenswood Lodge
Rest. at Stevenswood | 20
Little River/N

St. Regis
NEW Vitrine | **SoMa** –

St. Regis Hotel
Z Ame | **SoMa** 26

Truckee Hotel
Moody's Bistro | **Truckee/E** 25

Villa Florence Hotel
Kuleto's | **Downtown** 20

Vintage Ct., Hotel
Z Masa's | **Downtown** 27

Vitale, Hotel
Americano | **Embarcadero** 17

Warwick Regis
La Scene | **Downtown** 17

Westin San Francisco
NEW Ducca | **SoMa** –

Westin St. Francis
Z Michael Mina | **Downtown** 28

W Hotel
XYZ | **SoMa** 20

JACKET REQUIRED
(* Tie also required)

Z Ahwahnee | **Yosemite/E** 19

Z Erna's Elderberry* | 28
Oakhurst/E

Z French Laundry | **Yountville/N** 29

Z Masa's | **Downtown** 27

Z Ritz-Carlton Din. Rm. | **Nob Hill** 27

Tommy Toy's | **Downtown** 24

LATE DINING
(Weekday closing hour)

Absinthe | 12 AM | **Hayes Valley** 20

NEW Alembic | 12 AM | 22
Haight-Ashbury

Z Bouchon | 12:30 AM | 25
Yountville/N

Brazen Head | 1 AM | **Cow Hollow** 20

Brick | 12 AM | **Tenderloin** 20

Burger Joint | 12 AM | 18
S San Francisco/S

Caspers Hot Dogs | 11:30 PM | 18
multi. loc.

NEW District | 1 AM | **SoMa** 17

Z Fonda Solana | 12:30 AM | 24
Albany/E

Globe | 1 AM | **Downtown** 21

Great Eastern | 1 AM | **Chinatown** 22

Home of Chicken | varies | 15
Oakland/E

Z In-N-Out | 1 AM | **multi. loc.** 22

King of Thai | varies | **multi. loc.** 19

Koryo BBQ | 12 AM | **Oakland/E** 21

Lanesplitter Pub | varies | 18
multi. loc.

La Victoria | 2:00 AM | **San Jose/S** 20

SPECIAL FEATURES

Lime | varies | **Castro** 18

Mel's Drive-In | varies | **multi. loc.** 13

🆕 Mercury | 12 AM | **Marina** –

🆕 Mexico DF | 1 AM | **Embarcadero** –

Naan/Curry | varies | **multi. loc.** 18

Nihon | 12 AM | **Mission** 21

NoPa | 1 AM | **W Addition** 23

North Beach Pizza | varies | **multi. loc.** 18

Oola | 1 AM | **SoMa** 20

Original Joe's | varies | **San Jose/S** 18

Osha Thai | varies | **multi. loc.** 22

Pancho Villa | varies | **Mission** 20

Ryoko's | 2 AM | **Tenderloin** 23

🆕 Salt House | 12 AM | **SoMa** 21

Sauce | 12 AM | **Hayes Valley** 18

Scala's Bistro | 12 AM | **Downtown** 22

Taqueria Can-Cun | varies | **Mission** 21

Thai House | varies | **Tenderloin** 20

Tsunami | 12 AM | **W Addition** 23

Zeitgeist | 2 AM | **Mission** 16

🅩 Zuni Café | 12 AM | **Hayes Valley** 25

MEET FOR A DRINK

Absinthe | **Hayes Valley** 20

🆕 Alembic | **Haight-Ashbury** 22

🅩 Alexander's | **Cupertino/S** 25

Amber Bistro | **Danville/E** 20

Americano | **Embarcadero** 17

🅩 Ana Mandara | **Fish. Wharf** 23

Andalu | **Mission** 20

AsiaSF | **SoMa** 17

Azie | **SoMa** 19

bacar | **SoMa** 22

Balboa Cafe | **Cow Hollow** 19

🆕 Bar Bambino | **Mission** –

Barndiva | **Healdsburg/N** 18

Barracuda | **Castro** 17

Bar Tartine | **Mission** 22

Beach Chalet | **Outer Sunset** 13

Belden Taverna | **Downtown** 20

Betelnut Pejiu | **Cow Hollow** 23

Big 4 | **Nob Hill** 22

Bing Crosby's | **Walnut Creek/E** 18

Bistro Clovis | **Hayes Valley** 19

🆕 Bistro/Copains | **Occidental/N** 27

Bistro Don Giovanni | **Napa/N** 23

Bistro V | **Sebastopol/N** 22

Bistro Vida | **Menlo Pk/S** 18

🅩 BIX | **Downtown** 23

Blowfish Sushi | **Mission** 21

Bong Su | **SoMa** 22

Boogaloos | **Mission** 17

🅩 Bouchon | **Yountville/N** 25

🅩 Boulevard | **Embarcadero** 27

Brazen Head | **Cow Hollow** 20

Brick | **Tenderloin** 20

Bridgetender | **Tahoe City/E** 16

🅩 Buckeye | **Mill Valley/N** 23

Bungalow 44 | **Mill Valley/N** 21

Butterfly | **Embarcadero** 19

Cafe Bastille | **Downtown** 18

Café Claude | **Downtown** 20

Café de la Presse | **Downtown** 16

Café Rouge | **Berkeley/E** 21

Carnelian Room | **Downtown** 17

Cascal | **Mtn View/S** 20

Catch | **Castro** 19

Cav Wine Bar | **Hayes Valley** 22

Celadon | **Napa/N** 23

Central Market | **Petaluma/N** 23

César | **Berkeley/E** 22

Cetrella | **Half Moon Bay/S** 22

Cha Cha Cha | **Mission** 19

Chaya Brasserie | **Embarcadero** 21

🆕 Circa | **Marina** 18

Citizen Thai | **N Beach** 20

Cliff House Bistro | **Outer Rich** 18

Coi | **N Beach** 25

Colibrí Mexican | **Downtown** 20

Cork | **Sausalito/N** 19

Cortez | **Downtown** 23

Cosmopolitan | **SoMa** 20

Cottonwood | **Truckee/E** 20

Cuvée | **Napa/N** 20

🅩 Cyrus | **Healdsburg/N** 28

🅩 Delfina | **Mission** 26

🆕 Dio Deka | **Los Gatos/S** –

🆕 District | **SoMa** 17

Doña Tomás | **Oakland/E** 24

Don Pico's | **San Bruno/S** 20

Dragonfly | **Truckee/E** 23

🆕 Ducca | **SoMa** –

E&O Trading | **multi. loc.** 19

Elite Cafe | **Upper Fillmore**	19
Enrico's | **N Beach**	–
Eos Rest./Wine | **Cole Valley**	23
NEW Eureka | **Castro**	21
Z Farallon | **Downtown**	24
NEW Z Farm | **Napa/N**	23
farmerbrown | **Tenderloin**	19
1550 Hyde | **Russian Hill**	22
fig cafe | **Glen Ellen/N**	23
Florio | **Pacific Hts**	19
Z Fonda Solana | **Albany/E**	24
Foreign Cinema | **Mission**	21
Fresh Ketch | **S Lake Tahoe/E**	18
Frisson | **Downtown**	20
Fritz Fries | **multi. loc.**	19
Garibaldis | **multi. loc.**	21
Gar Woods | **Carnelian Bay/E**	19
NEW Go Fish | **St. Helena/N**	24
Guaymas | **Tiburon/N**	17
NEW Hime | **Marina**	22
Home | **Castro**	18
Hurley's | **Yountville/N**	20
Iberia | **Menlo Pk/S**	21
Incanto | **Noe Valley**	24
Jack Falstaff | **SoMa**	20
Jake's/Lake | **Tahoe City/E**	16
Jake's Steaks | **Cow Hollow**	20
Z Jardinière | **Hayes Valley**	26
Joe DiMaggio's | **N Beach**	20
NEW Jones Rest. | **Marina**	–
NEW Jovino | **Cow Hollow**	–
Junnoon | **Palo Alto/S**	22
Kan Zaman | **Haight-Ashbury**	17
Kingfish | **San Mateo/S**	17
Z Kokkari | **Downtown**	26
NEW Laïola | **Marina**	–
Lanesplitter Pub | **multi. loc.**	18
NEW Lark Creek Steak | **Downtown**	22
Last Supper | **Mission**	19
NEW La Terrasse | **Presidio**	19
Lavanda | **Palo Alto/S**	19
Le Colonial | **Downtown**	21
Left Bank | **multi. loc.**	18
Le Petit Robert | **Russian Hill**	19
Levende | **Mission**	20
Le Zinc | **Noe Valley**	18
Lime | **Castro**	18
Luka's Taproom | **Oakland/E**	20
Luna Park | **Mission**	19
Lure | **San Mateo/S**	23
MacArthur Park | **Palo Alto/S**	16
Maddalena/Fino | **Palo Alto/S**	21
Mamacita | **Marina**	22
Mantra | **Palo Alto/S**	20
Manzanita | **Healdsburg/N**	20
MarketBar | **Embarcadero**	17
Martini House | **St. Helena/N**	25
Maverick | **Mission**	22
Mecca | **Castro**	20
Medjool | **Mission**	18
Mendocino Hotel | **Mendocino/N**	17
NEW Mercury | **Marina**	–
NEW Mexico DF | **Embarcadero**	–
Z Michael Mina | **Downtown**	28
Modern Tea | **Hayes Valley**	20
MoMo's | **S Beach**	17
Montrio Bistro | **Monterey/S**	23
Moody's Bistro | **Truckee/E**	25
Moose's | **N Beach**	20
Mosaic Rest. | **Forestville/N**	25
Mustards Grill | **Yountville/N**	24
Z Myth | **Downtown**	26
Naomi Sushi | **Menlo Pk/S**	21
Nectar Wine | **Burlingame/S**	19
Nepenthe | **Big Sur/S**	16
Nihon | **Mission**	21
Nizza La Bella | **Albany/E**	19
NoPa | **W Addition**	23
NEW Nua Rest. | **N Beach**	–
n.v. Rest. | **Napa/N**	22
Oliveto Cafe | **Oakland/E**	23
Oliveto Restaurant | **Oakland/E**	25
One Market | **Embarcadero**	22
Ora | **Mill Valley/N**	21
O'Reilly's | **Polk Gulch**	18
Ottimista | **Cow Hollow**	20
Oyaji | **Outer Rich**	23
Ozumo | **Embarcadero**	24
Palio d'Asti | **Downtown**	19
NEW Palmetto | **Cow Hollow**	–
Pangaea | **Gualala/N**	25
Park Chalet | **Outer Sunset**	15
paul k | **Hayes Valley**	21
Pearl Alley | **Santa Cruz/S**	22

SPECIAL FEATURES

NEW Perbacco | **Downtown** 24
Pianeta | **Truckee/E** 23
NEW Piccino | **Dogpatch** 19
Picco | **Larkspur/N** 24
Plouf | **Downtown** 22
Plumed Horse | **Saratoga/S** –
Poleng | **W Addition** 22
Ponzu | **Downtown** 21
NEW Presidio Social | **Presidio** 18
Prima | **Walnut Creek/E** 24
Public | **SoMa** 18
Puerto Alegre | **Mission** 18
Ramblas | **Mission** 20
Z Range | **Mission** 26
Z Redd Rest. | **Yountville/N** 26
NEW Rest. Cassis | **Pacific Hts** –
Rest. LuLu/Petite | **SoMa** 20
River Ranch | **Tahoe City/E** 17
Rogue Chefs | **Half Moon Bay/S** 21
RoHan Lounge | **Inner Rich** 18
Rose Pistola | **N Beach** 21
Rose's Cafe | **Cow Hollow** 21
NEW Rouge/Blanc | **Downtown** –
Roy's | **SoMa** 22
NEW Sam's Chowder | 15
  Half Moon Bay/S
Sardine Factory | **Monterey/S** 20
Scott Howard | **Downtown** 23
Sea Salt | **Berkeley/E** 22
Shanghai 1930 | **Embarcadero** 20
Sino | **San Jose/S** 20
Slow Club | **Mission** 22
Sol y Lago | **Tahoe City/E** 17
Sonoma Meritage | **Sonoma/N** 19
Soule Domain | **Kings Bch/E** 23
Sparrow | **Nob Hill** 20
NEW Spork | **Mission** –
NEW Sudachi | **Polk Gulch** –
Sunnyside | **Tahoe City/E** 18
Suppenküche | **Hayes Valley** 21
Sushi Groove | **Russian Hill** 23
Tablespoon | **Russian Hill** 22
Z Tamarine | **Palo Alto/S** 26
Terzo | **Cow Hollow** 22
Tokyo Go Go | **Mission** 22
Tonga | **Nob Hill** 13
Town Hall | **SoMa** 23
Townhouse B&G | **Emeryville/E** 21

Trader Vic's | **Emeryville/E** 16
Tra Vigne | **St. Helena/N** 23
Tres Agaves | **S Beach** 18
2223 | **Castro** 21
NEW TWO | **SoMa** 21
NEW Umami | **Cow Hollow** 20
Underwood Bar | **Graton/N** 22
Va de Vi | **Walnut Creek/E** 24
Washington Sq. B&G | **N Beach** 19
Waterfront | **Embarcadero** 18
NEW West Co. Grill | –
  Sebastopol/N
Willi's Seafood | **Healdsburg/N** 23
Wine Spectator | **St. Helena/N** 22
NEW Wood Tav. | **Oakland/E** 23
NEW Xyclo | **Oakland/E** 19
Zachary's Pizza | **San Ramon/E** 24
Zibibbo | **Palo Alto/S** 20
Zin | **Healdsburg/N** 22
Z Zuni Café | **Hayes Valley** 25
Zuppa | **SoMa** 19
Z Zuzu | **Napa/N** 24

NATURAL/ORGANIC

(These restaurants often or always
use organic, local ingredients)

Absinthe | **Hayes Valley** 20
Acme Chophouse | **S Beach** 19
Adagia | **Berkeley/E** 19
Z ad hoc | **Yountville/N** 26
Albion River Inn | **Albion/N** 24
Antica Trattoria | **Russian Hill** 23
Aperto | **Potrero Hill** 20
A. Sabella's | **Fish. Wharf** 18
NEW AVA | **San Anselmo/N** –
Balboa Cafe | **Cow Hollow** 19
Barndiva | **Healdsburg/N** 18
Basin | **Saratoga/S** 19
Bistro Aix | **Marina** 22
NEW Bistro/Copains | 27
  Occidental/N
Bistro Don Giovanni | **Napa/N** 23
Bistro V | **Sebastopol/N** 22
Blue Plate | **Mission** 23
Z Bo's Barbecue | **Lafayette/E** 23
Boulange | **multi. loc.** 22
Boulette's Larder | **Embarcadero** 25
Bovolo | **Healdsburg/N** 22
Breads of India | **multi. loc.** 21

☑ Buckeye | **Mill Valley/N**	23
Butler & The Chef | **SoMa**	20
Cactus Taqueria | **multi. loc.**	20
Cafe Beaujolais | **Mendocino/N**	25
Cafe Gibraltar | **El Granada/S**	25
Café Gratitude | **multi. loc.**	19
☑ Cafe La Haye | **Sonoma/N**	26
Café Majestic | **Pacific Hts**	–
Caffè Museo | **SoMa**	16
Caffè Verbena | **Oakland/E**	19
Caprice | **Tiburon/N**	21
Carneros Bistro | **Sonoma/N**	22
☑ Chez Panisse | **Berkeley/E**	27
Chez Shea | **Half Moon Bay/S**	22
☑ Chow/Park Chow | **multi. loc.**	22
Coi | **N Beach**	25
Cork | **Sausalito/N**	19
Cortez | **Downtown**	23
Côté Sud | **Castro**	20
Deetjen's | **Big Sur/S**	22
Delancey St. | **Embarcadero**	18
☑ Delfina | **Mission**	26
Della Fattoria | **Petaluma/N**	26
Doña Tomás | **Oakland/E**	24
Don Pico's | **San Bruno/S**	20
Drake's | **Inverness/N**	19
Eccolo | **Berkeley/E**	20
☑ Erna's Elderberry | **Oakhurst/E**	28
NEW Essencia | **Hayes Valley**	–
NEW Farina | **Mission**	–
NEW ☑ Farm | **Napa/N**	23
farmerbrown | **Tenderloin**	19
☑ Farmhouse | **Forestville/N**	27
1550 Hyde | **Russian Hill**	22
Firecracker | **Mission**	19
☑ Firefly | **Noe Valley**	25
Fish | **Sausalito/N**	24
Flavor | **Santa Rosa/N**	20
Flea St. Café | **Menlo Pk/S**	22
☑ Fleur de Lys | **Nob Hill**	28
☑ Fonda Solana | **Albany/E**	24
Foothill Grille | **Napa/N**	–
Foreign Cinema | **Mission**	21
Frantoio | **Mill Valley/N**	21
General's | **Sonoma/N**	–
Grasing's Coastal | **Carmel/S**	23
Green Chile | **W Addition**	19
Hayes St. Grill | **Hayes Valley**	22

Heritage House | **Little River/N**	–
Hog Island Oyster | **Embarcadero**	25
Home | **Castro**	18
Imperial/Berkeley | **Berkeley/E**	17
Indigo | **Civic Ctr**	20
Insalata's | **San Anselmo/N**	24
Jack Falstaff | **SoMa**	20
☑ Jardinière | **Hayes Valley**	26
Jeanty at Jack's | **Downtown**	23
John Ash & Co. | **Santa Rosa/N**	23
☑ John Bentley's | **multi. loc.**	25
Jojo | **Oakland/E**	25
NEW Jones Rest. | **Marina**	–
Julia's | **Napa/N**	23
jZcool | **Menlo Pk/S**	20
Kitchen at 868 | **Novato/N**	25
La Ciccia | **Noe Valley**	22
La Forêt | **San Jose/S**	27
NEW Laïola | **Marina**	–
Lalime's | **Berkeley/E**	26
Lark Creek | **Walnut Creek/E**	22
Lark Creek Inn | **Larkspur/N**	23
Las Camelias | **San Rafael/N**	20
Last Supper | **Mission**	19
NEW La Terrasse | **Presidio**	19
☑ La Toque | **Rutherford/N**	26
☑ L'Auberge | **Carmel/S**	27
Ledford Hse. | **Albion/N**	23
Lettus | **Marina**	20
Lion & Compass | **Sunnyvale/S**	19
Lotus of India | **San Rafael/N**	22
Luna Park | **Mission**	19
MacCallum Hse. | **Mendocino/N**	24
Maddalena/Fino | **Palo Alto/S**	21
☑ Madrona Manor | **Healdsburg/N**	25
Mandalay | **Inner Rich**	21
NEW Mandaloun | **Redwood City/S**	–
☑ Manresa | **Los Gatos/S**	27
Manzanita | **Healdsburg/N**	20
☑ Marché | **Menlo Pk/S**	26
Marché aux Fleurs | **Ross/N**	25
☑ Marinus | **Carmel Valley/S**	26
Market | **St. Helena/N**	22
MarketBar | **Embarcadero**	17
Martini House | **St. Helena/N**	25
☑ Masa's | **Downtown**	27

Meadowood	**St. Helena/N**	20
Medicine	**Downtown**	18
Mendo Bistro	**Ft Bragg/N**	25
Mendocino Hotel	**Mendocino/N**	17
Z Millennium	**Downtown**	24
Mixt Greens	**Downtown**	22
Model Bakery	**St. Helena/N**	21
Moki's Sushi	**Bernal Hts**	21
Moody's Bistro	**Truckee/E**	25
Moose's	**N Beach**	20
Moosse Café	**Mendocino/N**	23
Morton's	**San Jose/S**	23
Mosaic Rest.	**Forestville/N**	25
Z Navio	**Half Moon Bay/S**	26
Nectar Wine	**multi. loc.**	19
Nepenthe	**Big Sur/S**	16
Nick's Tacos	**Russian Hill**	20
Nizza La Bella	**Albany/E**	19
NoPa	**W Addition**	23
North Beach Rest.	**N Beach**	21
NEW Nua Rest.	**N Beach**	–
n.v. Rest.	**Napa/N**	22
Oak City B&G	**Menlo Pk/S**	18
O Chamé	**Berkeley/E**	24
Olema Inn	**Olema/N**	22
Oliveto Cafe	**Oakland/E**	23
Oliveto Restaurant	**Oakland/E**	25
One Market	**Embarcadero**	22
Oola	**SoMa**	20
Original Joe's	**Tenderloin**	18
Osake/Sake 'O	**multi. loc.**	22
Osteria	**Palo Alto/S**	23
Ozumo	**Embarcadero**	24
Pacific Catch	**Marina**	21
Z Pacific's Edge	**Carmel/S**	25
NEW Palmetto	**Cow Hollow**	–
Pangaea	**Gualala/N**	25
Pappo	**Alameda/E**	23
Parcel 104	**Santa Clara/S**	23
Park Grill	**Downtown**	20
Passionfish	**Pacific Grove/S**	25
Pasta Moon	**Half Moon Bay/S**	22
Pauline's Pizza	**Mission**	22
paul k	**Hayes Valley**	21
Pearl	**Napa/N**	22
Pearl Alley	**Santa Cruz/S**	22
Pearl Oyster	**Oakland/E**	24
Pesce	**Russian Hill**	22

Pianeta	**Truckee/E**	23
Piatti	**multi. loc.**	19
NEW Piccino	**Dogpatch**	19
Picco	**Larkspur/N**	24
Pilar	**Napa/N**	25
Pine Cone Diner	**Pt Reyes/N**	19
Pizza Antica	**Lafayette/E**	21
Pizzaiolo	**Oakland/E**	24
Z Pizzeria Picco	**Larkspur/N**	25
Pizzeria Tra Vigne	**St. Helena/N**	21
Pizzetta 211	**Outer Rich**	25
PJ's Oyster	**Inner Sunset**	19
PlumpJack	**multi. loc.**	24
Z Postrio	**Downtown**	24
Press	**St. Helena/N**	23
Prima	**Walnut Creek/E**	24
Z Quince	**Pacific Hts**	26
Ramblas	**Mission**	20
Z Range	**Mission**	26
Ravenous Cafe	**Healdsburg/N**	23
Ravens Rest.	**Mendocino/N**	23
Rendezvous Inn	**Ft Bragg/N**	27
Restaurant	**Ft Bragg/N**	23
Rest. at Meadowood	**St. Helena/N**	23
Rest. at Stevenswood	**Little River/N**	20
Rest. LuLu/Petite	**SoMa**	20
Richmond Rest.	**Inner Rich**	22
Rio Grill	**Carmel/S**	22
Rist. Fabrizio	**Larkspur/N**	19
Rist. Ideale	**N Beach**	24
Rist. Milano	**Russian Hill**	24
Z Ritz-Carlton Din. Rm.	**Nob Hill**	27
Z Ritz-Carlton Terr.	**Nob Hill**	24
River Ranch	**Tahoe City/E**	17
Z Rivoli	**Berkeley/E**	27
rnm rest.	**Lower Haight**	25
Rogue Chefs	**Half Moon Bay/S**	21
RoHan Lounge	**Inner Rich**	18
Rosamunde Grill	**Lower Haight**	25
Rose Pistola	**N Beach**	21
Rose's Cafe	**Cow Hollow**	21
Roti Indian	**W Portal**	23
Rotunda	**Downtown**	20
Royal Thai	**San Rafael/N**	22
Rubicon	**Downtown**	24
Ryoko's	**Tenderloin**	23

Sabor of Spain | **San Rafael/N**	18
Sanraku | **SoMa**	23
Santi | **Geyserville/N**	23
Sardine Factory | **Monterey/S**	20
Saul's Rest./Deli | **Berkeley/E**	18
Savor | **Noe Valley**	18
Scala's Bistro | **Downtown**	22
Scoma's | **multi. loc.**	21
Seaweed Café | **Bodega Bay/N**	24
Sent Sovi | **Saratoga/S**	24
Seven | **San Jose/S**	21
Z Shadowbrook | **Capitola/S**	22
Shanghai 1930 | **Embarcadero**	20
Sharon's | **Ft Bragg/N**	20
Z Sierra Mar | **Big Sur/S**	26
Z Silks | **Downtown**	24
Z Slanted Door | **Embarcadero**	26
Slow Club | **Mission**	22
Sociale | **Presidio Hts**	23
Soi Four | **Oakland/E**	23
Soizic | **Oakland/E**	22
Sol Food | **San Rafael/N**	22
Sol y Lago | **Tahoe City/E**	17
Sonoma Meritage | **Sonoma/N**	19
Sooze Wine | **Petaluma/N**	18
Soule Domain | **Kings Bch/E**	23
Sparrow | **Nob Hill**	20
NEW Spork | **Mission**	-
NEW Spruce | **Presidio Hts**	-
St. Michael's | **Palo Alto/S**	22
Stokes | **Monterey/S**	23
St. Orres | **Gualala/N**	24
Straits Cafe | **multi. loc.**	20
Street | **Russian Hill**	21
NEW Sudachi | **Polk Gulch**	-
SUMI | **Castro**	23
Sushi Groove | **SoMa**	23
Z Sushi Ran | **Sausalito/N**	28
Sutro's | **Outer Rich**	19
Syrah | **Santa Rosa/N**	25
Table Café | **Larkspur/N**	24
Tablespoon | **Russian Hill**	22
Tacubaya | **Berkeley/E**	22
Z Tadich Grill | **Downtown**	22
Z Tamarindo | **Oakland/E**	24
Z Tamarine | **Palo Alto/S**	26
Z Tartine | **Mission**	26
Theo's | **Soquel/S**	24

Three Seasons | **multi. loc.**	23
Town Hall | **SoMa**	23
Town's End | **Embarcadero**	19
Trader Vic's | **Emeryville/E**	16
Tratt. La Siciliana | **Berkeley/E**	23
Tra Vigne | **St. Helena/N**	23
Tsunami | **W Addition**	23
2223 | **Castro**	21
NEW Ubuntu | **Napa/N**	-
NEW Umami | **Cow Hollow**	20
NEW Underdog | **Inner Sunset**	-
Underwood Bar | **Graton/N**	22
Universal Cafe | **Mission**	23
Va de Vi | **Walnut Creek/E**	24
Venus | **Berkeley/E**	19
Viognier | **San Mateo/S**	24
NEW Vitrine | **SoMa**	-
NEW Vittoria | **Los Gatos/S**	20
Waterfront | **Embarcadero**	18
Water St. Bistro | **Petaluma/N**	24
NEW Weird Fish | **Mission**	18
'wichcraft | **Downtown**	17
Willi's Seafood | **Healdsburg/N**	23
Willi's Wine | **Santa Rosa/N**	24
Z Willow Wood | **Graton/N**	25
Wolfdale's | **Tahoe City/E**	25
Wolf House | **Glen Ellen/N**	20
Woodward's Gdn. | **Mission**	25
XYZ | **SoMa**	20
Yabbies Coastal | **Russian Hill**	22
Yankee Pier | **San Jose/S**	17
Yoshi's | **Oakland/E**	18
Yumma's | **Inner Sunset**	20
Zante | **Bernal Hts**	18
Zatar | **Berkeley/E**	21
Zazie | **Cole Valley**	22
zazu | **Santa Rosa/N**	25
Zibibbo | **Palo Alto/S**	20
Zin | **Healdsburg/N**	22
Zinsvalley | **Napa/N**	20
Z Zuni Café | **Hayes Valley**	25
Z Zuzu | **Napa/N**	24

NOTEWORTHY
NEWCOMERS

Alembic | **Haight-Ashbury**	22
AVA | **San Anselmo/N**	-
Bar Bambino | **Mission**	-
Bistro/Copains | **Occidental/N**	27

SPECIAL FEATURES

3 Star Bar | **Inner Rich**	-]
Butterfly Bistro | **San Bruno/S**	-]
Chef Wai | **San Mateo/S**	20]
Chiaroscuro | **Downtown**	-]
Circa | **Marina**	18]
Dio Deka | **Los Gatos/S**	-]
District | **SoMa**	17]
Ducca | **SoMa**	-]
Essencia | **Hayes Valley**	-]
Eureka | **Castro**	21]
Farina | **Mission**	-]
☑ Farm | **Napa/N**	23]
Front Porch | **N Beach**	20]
Gator's | **San Mateo/S**	-]
Gialina | **Glen Pk**	24]
Go Fish | **St. Helena/N**	24]
Hime | **Marina**	22]
Jones Rest. | **Marina**	-]
Jovino | **Cow Hollow**	-]
Kanpai | **Palo Alto/S**	24]
Laïola | **Marina**	-]
Lark Creek Steak | **Downtown**	22]
La Terrasse | **Presidio**	19]
Le P'tit Laurent | **Glen Pk**	-]
Mandaloun | **Redwood City/S**	-]
Mercury | **Marina**	-]
Mexico DF | **Embarcadero**	-]
Nick's Cove | **Marshall/N**	-]
Nua Rest. | **N Beach**	-]
Palmetto | **Cow Hollow**	-]
Perbacco | **Downtown**	24]
Pescheria | **Noe Valley**	21]
Piccino | **Dogpatch**	19]
Piqueo's | **Bernal Hts**	-]
Pres a Vi | **Presidio**	21]
Presidio Social | **Presidio**	18]
Rest. Cassis | **Pacific Hts**	-]
Roadside BBQ | **Inner Rich**	19]
Rouge/Blanc | **Downtown**	-]
Salt House | **SoMa**	21]
Sam's Chowder | **Half Moon Bay/S**	15]
Spork | **Mission**	-]
Spruce | **Presidio Hts**	-]
Sudachi | **Polk Gulch**	-]
Sutra | **SoMa**	19]
Tanglewood | **San Jose/S**	21]
Toast | **Noe Valley**	18]

TWO | **SoMa**	21]
Ubuntu | **Napa/N**	-]
Umami | **Cow Hollow**	20]
Underdog | **Inner Sunset**	-]
Vitrine | **SoMa**	-]
Vittoria | **Los Gatos/S**	20]
Weird Fish | **Mission**	18]
West Co. Grill | **Sebastopol/N**	-]
Wood Tav. | **Oakland/E**	23]
Xyclo | **Oakland/E**	19]
Zadin | **Castro**	-]
Zazil Coastal | **Downtown**	19]

OFFBEAT

Ace Wasabi's | **Marina**	20]
Albona Rist. | **N Beach**	24]
AsiaSF | **SoMa**	17]
Avatars | **Sausalito/N**	22]
Aziza | **Outer Rich**	24]
Barndiva | **Healdsburg/N**	18]
Basque Cultural | **S San Francisco/S**	20]
Blowfish Sushi | **Mission**	21]
Boogaloos | **Mission**	17]
Buca di Beppo | **multi. loc.**	14]
☑ Buckeye | **Mill Valley/N**	23]
Café Gratitude | **multi. loc.**	19]
Caffè Macaroni | **N Beach**	20]
Casa Orinda | **Orinda/E**	17]
Caspers Hot Dogs | **multi. loc.**	18]
Cha Cha Cha | **multi. loc.**	19]
Cha-Ya Veg. | **multi. loc.**	24]
Destino | **Castro**	22]
Don Pico's | **San Bruno/S**	20]
Duarte's Tavern | **Pescadero/S**	21]
E&O Trading | **Larkspur/N**	19]
Fish | **Sausalito/N**	24]
Flying Fish | **Carmel/S**	24]
Frjtz Fries | **multi. loc.**	19]
Home of Chicken | **Oakland/E**	15]
Jimtown Store | **Healdsburg/N**	19]
Jodie's Rest. | **Albany/E**	20]
☑ Joe's Cable Car | **Excelsior**	24]
Kan Zaman | **Haight-Ashbury**	17]
Katia's Tea | **Inner Rich**	19]
Khan Toke | **Outer Rich**	23]
Lovejoy's Tea | **Noe Valley**	20]
Martini House | **St. Helena/N**	25]

Matterhorn Swiss | **Russian Hill**	21
Maykadeh | **N Beach**	23
☑ Millennium | **Downtown**	24
Nick's Tacos | **Russian Hill**	20
Oyaji | **Outer Rich**	23
Puerto Alegre | **Mission**	18
Ravens Rest. | **Mendocino/N**	23
Red's Java | **Embarcadero**	14
RoHan Lounge | **Inner Rich**	18
Sino | **San Jose/S**	20
Sol Food | **San Rafael/N**	22
Spettro | **Oakland/E**	20
NEW Spork | **Mission**	-
St. Orres | **Gualala/N**	24
supperclub | **SoMa**	17
Thai Buddhist | **Berkeley/E**	20
Tonga | **Nob Hill**	13
Trader Vic's | **Emeryville/E**	16
Uncle Frank's | **Mtn View/S**	22
NEW Underdog | **Inner Sunset**	-
Venezia | **Berkeley/E**	20
Yoshi's | **Oakland/E**	18
Zante | **Bernal Hts**	18

OUTDOOR DINING

(G=garden; P=patio; S=sidewalk; T=terrace; W=waterside)

Absinthe | S | **Hayes Valley**	20
À Côté | P | **Oakland/E**	24
Adagia | P | **Berkeley/E**	19
Alexis Baking Co. | S | **Napa/N**	22
Angèle | P, W | **Napa/N**	22
Anton & Michel | G, P | **Carmel/S**	23
Aperto | S | **Potrero Hill**	20
Applewood Inn | G, T | **Guerneville/N**	24
A.P. Stump's | P | **San Jose/S**	21
☑ Auberge du Sol. | T | **Rutherford/N**	25
Baker St. Bistro | S | **Marina**	20
Barbara Fish | P, S, W | **Princeton Sea/S**	19
Barndiva | G, P | **Healdsburg/N**	18
Barney's | P | **multi. loc.**	19
Basin | P | **Saratoga/S**	19
Beach Chalet | W | **Outer Sunset**	13
Betelnut Pejiu | S | **Cow Hollow**	23
B44 | S | **Downtown**	21
Bistro Aix | P | **Marina**	22
Bistro Boudin | P | **Fish. Wharf**	20

Bistro Don Giovanni | P, T | **Napa/N**	2
Bistro Elan | P | **Palo Alto/S**	24
☑ Bistro Jeanty | P | **Yountville/N**	25
Bistro Liaison | P | **Berkeley/E**	22
Bistro Vida | S | **Menlo Pk/S**	18
Blackhawk Grille | P, T, W | **Danville/E**	19
Blue Plate | G, P | **Mission**	23
Boca | P | **Novato/N**	20
☑ Bo's Barbecue | T | **Lafayette/E**	23
☑ Bouchon | P | **Yountville/N**	25
Boulange | S | **multi. loc.**	22
Bridges | P | **Danville/E**	20
Brindisi | S | **Downtown**	18
BRIX | P | **Yountville/N**	22
Bucci's | P | **Emeryville/E**	20
☑ Buckeye | P | **Mill Valley/N**	23
Bungalow 44 | P | **Mill Valley/N**	21
Cactus Taqueria | S | **Oakland/E**	20
Cafe Bastille | S, T | **Downtown**	18
Cafe Citti | P | **Kenwood/N**	22
Café Claude | S | **Downtown**	20
Café Fanny | P | **Berkeley/E**	22
Café Rouge | P | **Berkeley/E**	21
Café Tiramisu | S | **Downtown**	21
Caffè Museo | S | **SoMa**	16
Casanova | P | **Carmel/S**	23
Cascal | P | **Mtn View/S**	20
Catch | P, S | **Castro**	19
Celadon | P | **Napa/N**	23
César | P | **Berkeley/E**	22
Charanga | P | **Mission**	21
Chaya Brasserie | P, S | **Embarcadero**	21
Cheesecake | P, T | **Downtown**	16
Chez Maman | S | **Potrero Hill**	21
Chez Papa Bistrot | S | **Potrero Hill**	23
Chez Spencer | G, P | **Mission**	24
Chez TJ | T | **Mtn View/S**	25
Chloe's Cafe | S | **Noe Valley**	21
☑ Chow/Park Chow | P, S, T | **multi. loc.**	20
Cindy's | P | **St. Helena/N**	24
Citron | P | **Oakland/E**	24
Club XIX | P, W | **Pebble Bch/S**	25
☑ Cole's Chop Hse. | T, W | **Napa/N**	25
Cork | P | **Sausalito/N**	19

...té Sud | P | **Castro** 20

...ucina Paradiso | P, W | 26
Petaluma/N

Delancey St. | P, S | **Embarcadero** 18

Ⓩ Delfina | P | **Mission** 26

Della Santina's | G, P | **Sonoma/N** 21

Deuce | G, P | **Sonoma/N** 20

Doña Tomás | G, P | **Oakland/E** 24

Dopo | S | **Oakland/E** 25

Dry Creek | S | **Healdsburg/N** 24

NEW Ducca | P | **SoMa** -

Duck Club | P | **Menlo Pk/S** 20

Eccolo | P | **Berkeley/E** 20

El Dorado | P, W | **Sonoma/N** 23

El Paseo | P | **Mill Valley/N** 23

Emporio Rulli | P, S | **multi. loc.** 20

Enrico's | P | **N Beach** -

Étoile | P, T, W | **Yountville/N** 25

Everett & Jones | P, S | **multi. loc.** 20

Fentons Creamery | P | **Oakland/E** 18

Fish | T, W | **Sausalito/N** 24

Flavor | P | **Santa Rosa/N** 20

Flea St. Café | P | **Menlo Pk/S** 22

Fog City Diner | S | **Embarcadero** 19

Ⓩ Fonda Solana | S | **Albany/E** 24

Foreign Cinema | P | **Mission** 21

Frantoio | G, P | **Mill Valley/N** 21

Fritz Fries | P | **Hayes Valley** 19

Fumé Bistro | P | **Napa/N** 19

Gabriella Café | P | **Santa Cruz/S** 22

Gayle's Bakery | P | **Capitola/S** 25

girl & the fig | P | **Sonoma/N** 23

Grasing's Coastal | P | **Carmel/S** 23

Gregoire | S | **Berkeley/E** 24

Guaymas | P, T, W | **Tiburon/N** 17

Hog Island Oyster | P, W | 25
Embarcadero

Home | P | **Castro** 18

Hurley's | P | **Yountville/N** 20

Hyde St. Bistro | S | **Russian Hill** 21

Iberia | P | **Menlo Pk/S** 21

Il Davide | P | **San Rafael/N** 21

Ⓩ Il Fornaio | P | **multi. loc.** 19

Isa | P | **Marina** 24

Jack Falstaff | P | **SoMa** 20

Jimmy Bean's | S | **Berkeley/E** 20

Jimtown Store | P | **Healdsburg/N** 19

John Ash & Co. | P | **Santa Rosa/N** 23

Kenwood | G | **Kenwood/N** 22

La Note | P | **Berkeley/E** 22

Lark Creek | P | **Walnut Creek/E** 22

Lark Creek Inn | P | **Larkspur/N** 23

LaSalette | P | **Sonoma/N** 23

La Strada | T | **Palo Alto/S** 21

Le Charm Bistro | P | **SoMa** 21

Le Colonial | P | **Downtown** 21

Left Bank | P, S | **multi. loc.** 18

Le Zinc | G | **Noe Valley** 18

Lion & Compass | P | **Sunnyvale/S** 19

MacCallum Hse. | T | 24
Mendocino/N

Ⓩ Madrona Manor | T | 25
Healdsburg/N

Marché aux Fleurs | P | **Ross/N** 25

Maria Manso | P | **San Rafael/N** 20

MarketBar | P | **Embarcadero** 17

Martini House | P | **St. Helena/N** 25

Meadowood | T | **St. Helena/N** 20

Medjool | P | **Mission** 18

Mezze | S | **Oakland/E** 23

Mistral | P, W | 19
Redwood Shores/S

MoMo's | T | **S Beach** 17

Monti's | P | **Santa Rosa/N** 19

Moosse Café | T, W | 23
Mendocino/N

Mo's | P | **SoMa** 20

Napa General | T, W | **Napa/N** 20

Napa Valley Grille | P | 20
Yountville/N

Nepenthe | P, W | **Big Sur/S** 16

Nizza La Bella | S | **Albany/E** 19

O Chamé | P | **Berkeley/E** 24

Olema Inn | G | **Olema/N** 22

Oliveto Cafe | S | **Oakland/E** 23

Pangaea | T | **Gualala/N** 25

Parcel 104 | P | **Santa Clara/S** 23

Park Chalet | G, W | **Outer Sunset** 15

Pasta Moon | P | **Half Moon Bay/S** 22

Pazzia | P | **SoMa** 22

Piatti | P, W | **multi. loc.** 19

Piazza D'Angelo | P | **Mill Valley/N** 19

Picante Cocina | P | **Berkeley/E** 21

Ⓩ Piperade | P | **Downtown** 25

Pizza Antica | P | **multi. loc.** 21

Pizzeria Tra Vigne | P | 21
St. Helena/N

Pizzetta 211 | S | **Outer Rich** 25
Plouf | S, T | **Downtown** 22
PlumpJack | P | **Olympic Valley/E** 24
Poggio | S | **Sausalito/N** 21
☑ Postino | P | **Lafayette/E** 24
🆕 Pres a Vi | P | **Presidio** 21
Press | P | **St. Helena/N** 23
Prima | P | **Walnut Creek/E** 24
Ravenous Cafe | P | **Healdsburg/N** 23
Red's Java | P, W | **Embarcadero** 14
Rest. at Meadowood | T | 23
    St. Helena/N
Rick & Ann's | P | **Berkeley/E** 21
☑ Ritz-Carlton Terr. | T | **Nob Hill** 24
Rose Pistola | S | **N Beach** 21
Rose's Cafe | S | **Cow Hollow** 21
Roy's | P | **Pebble Bch/S** 25
Rutherford Grill | P | **Rutherford/N** 23
🆕 Sam's Chowder | P | 15
    Half Moon Bay/S
Santi | P | **Geyserville/N** 23
Savor | G, P | **Noe Valley** 18
Scoma's | P, W | **Sausalito/N** 21
Sea Salt | P | **Berkeley/E** 22
Seaweed Café | P, S | 24
    Bodega Bay/N
71 Saint Peter | P | **San Jose/S** 22
Sharon's | P, W | **Ft Bragg/N** 20
☑ Sierra Mar | T, W | **Big Sur/S** 26
Slow Club | S | **Mission** 22
Sociale | G, P | **Presidio Hts** 23
Sonoma Meritage | G, P | 19
    Sonoma/N
South Park | S | **SoMa** 22
St. Michael's | S | **Palo Alto/S** 22
Straits Cafe | P | **multi. loc.** 20
☑ Sushi Ran | P | **Sausalito/N** 28
Tarpy's | P | **Monterey/S** 22
☑ Tartine | S | **Mission** 26
Taylor's Auto | G, P | **multi. loc.** 21
Ti Couz | S | **Mission** 22
Townhouse B&G | P | **Emeryville/E** 21
Town's End | P | **Embarcadero** 19
Trader Vic's | T | **Palo Alto/S** 16
Tra Vigne | G | **St. Helena/N** 23
Underwood Bar | P | **Graton/N** 22
Universal Cafe | P | **Mission** 23
Va de Vi | S, T | **Walnut Creek/E** 24
Wappo Bar | P | **Calistoga/N** 22

Waterfront | P, W | **Embarcadero** 18
Water St. Bistro | P, W | 24
    Petaluma/N
Wente Vineyards | P | 23
    Livermore/E
Willi's Seafood | P | **Healdsburg/N** 23
Willi's Wine | P | **Santa Rosa/N** 24
Wine Spectator | T | **St. Helena/N** 22
Yankee Pier | P | **multi. loc.** 17
Yumma's | G | **Inner Sunset** 20
Zazie | G | **Cole Valley** 22
Zibibbo | G, P | **Palo Alto/S** 20
Zinsvalley | P | **Napa/N** 20
Zucca | S | **Mtn View/S** 19
☑ Zuni Café | S | **Hayes Valley** 25

PEOPLE-WATCHING

Absinthe | **Hayes Valley** 20
Ace Wasabi's | **Marina** 20
À Côté | **Oakland/E** 24
☑ Ana Mandara | **Fish. Wharf** 23
Asia de Cuba | **Downtown** 21
AsiaSF | **SoMa** 17
Balboa Cafe | **Cow Hollow** 19
Barndiva | **Healdsburg/N** 18
Barracuda | **Castro** 17
Bar Tartine | **Mission** 22
Belden Taverna | **Downtown** 20
Betelnut Pejiu | **Cow Hollow** 23
Bing Crosby's | **Walnut Creek/E** 18
Bistro Don Giovanni | **Napa/N** 23
☑ Bistro Jeanty | **Yountville/N** 25
☑ BIX | **Downtown** 23
Blowfish Sushi | **Mission** 21
Bong Su | **SoMa** 22
Boogaloos | **Mission** 17
☑ Bouchon | **Yountville/N** 25
☑ Boulevard | **Embarcadero** 27
Brick | **Tenderloin** 20
Bridgetender | **Tahoe City/E** 16
Bungalow 44 | **Mill Valley/N** 21
Cafe Bastille | **Downtown** 18
Café Claude | **Downtown** 20
Café de la Presse | **Downtown** 16
Cascal | **Mtn View/S** 20
Catch | **Castro** 19
Cav Wine Bar | **Hayes Valley** 22
Central Market | **Petaluma/N** 23
César | **Berkeley/E** 22

Cha Cha Cha | **multi. loc.**	19
Chaya Brasserie | **Embarcadero**	21
Z Chez Panisse Café | **Berkeley/E**	27
NEW Circa | **Marina**	18
Circolo | **Mission**	19
Cottonwood | **Truckee/E**	20
NEW Dio Deka | **Los Gatos/S**	-
NEW District | **SoMa**	17
Dosa | **Mission**	20
downtown | **Berkeley/E**	20
Downtown Bakery | Healdsburg/N	24
Dragonfly | **Truckee/E**	23
NEW Ducca | **SoMa**	-
E&O Trading | **Larkspur/N**	19
Enrico's | **N Beach**	-
Z Evvia | **Palo Alto/S**	26
NEW Farina | **Mission**	-
Flea St. Café | **Menlo Pk/S**	22
Foreign Cinema | **Mission**	21
Fresh Ketch | **S Lake Tahoe/E**	18
Frisson | **Downtown**	20
Frjtz Fries | **multi. loc.**	19
NEW Front Porch | **N Beach**	20
Gar Woods | **Carnelian Bay/E**	19
Jack Falstaff | **SoMa**	20
Jake's/Lake | **Tahoe City/E**	16
Z Jardinière | **Hayes Valley**	26
NEW Jovino | **Cow Hollow**	-
Julia's | **Napa/N**	23
Junnoon | **Palo Alto/S**	22
NEW Laïola | **Marina**	-
Last Supper | **Mission**	19
Left Bank | **Larkspur/N**	18
Levende | **Mission**	20
Lime | **Castro**	18
Lure | **San Mateo/S**	23
Mamacita | **Marina**	22
Mario's Bohemian | **N Beach**	18
MarketBar | **Embarcadero**	17
Martini House | **St. Helena/N**	25
Maverick | **Mission**	22
Mecca | **Castro**	20
Medjool | **Mission**	18
NEW Mexico DF | **Embarcadero**	-
Mijita | **Embarcadero**	20
Moody's Bistro | **Truckee/E**	25
Moose's | **N Beach**	20

Mustards Grill | **Yountville/N**	24
Z Myth | **Downtown**	26
Nectar Wine | **multi. loc.**	19
Nihon | **Mission**	21
NoPa | **W Addition**	23
NEW Nua Rest. | **N Beach**	-
Oliveto Cafe | **Oakland/E**	23
Ottimista | **Cow Hollow**	20
NEW Palmetto | **Cow Hollow**	-
Pasta Pomodoro | **Castro**	16
Picco | **Larkspur/N**	24
Poggio | **Sausalito/N**	21
Z Postino | **Lafayette/E**	24
Z Postrio | **Downtown**	24
NEW Presidio Social | **Presidio**	18
Public | **SoMa**	18
Z Redd Rest. | **Yountville/N**	26
Rest. LuLu/Petite | **SoMa**	20
River Ranch | **Tahoe City/E**	17
Rose Pistola | **N Beach**	21
Rose's Cafe | **Cow Hollow**	21
Scala's Bistro | **Downtown**	22
Scott Howard | **Downtown**	23
Sino | **San Jose/S**	20
NEW Sudachi | **Polk Gulch**	-
Sunnyside | **Tahoe City/E**	18
supperclub | **SoMa**	17
Sushi Groove | **multi. loc.**	23
Z Tamarine | **Palo Alto/S**	26
Tokyo Go Go | **Mission**	22
Town Hall | **SoMa**	23
Tra Vigne | **St. Helena/N**	23
Tres Agaves | **S Beach**	18
Tsunami | **W Addition**	23
2223 | **Castro**	21
NEW Umami | **Cow Hollow**	20
Village Pub | **Woodside/S**	26
Viognier | **San Mateo/S**	24
NEW West Co. Grill | Sebastopol/N	-
NEW Wood Tav. | **Oakland/E**	23
Zibibbo | **Palo Alto/S**	20
Z Zuni Café | **Hayes Valley**	25
Zuppa | **SoMa**	19

POWER SCENES

Z Alexander's | **Cupertino/S**	25
Z Ana Mandara | **Fish. Wharf**	23
Z Aqua | **Downtown**	26

Arcadia | **San Jose/S**	23
Asia de Cuba | **Downtown**	21
Z Auberge du Sol. | **Rutherford/N**	25
bacar | **SoMa**	22
Big 4 | **Nob Hill**	22
Blackhawk Grille | **Danville/E**	19
Z Bouchon | **Yountville/N**	25
Z Boulevard | **Embarcadero**	27
Chaya Brasserie | **Embarcadero**	21
Chef Chu's | **Los Altos/S**	20
NEW Chef Wai | **San Mateo/S**	20
NEW Dio Deka | **Los Gatos/S**	-
downtown | **Berkeley/E**	20
Z Evvia | **Palo Alto/S**	26
Fifth Floor | **SoMa**	25
Z Fleur de Lys | **Nob Hill**	28
Forbes Mill Steak | **multi. loc.**	23
Z Gary Danko | **Fish. Wharf**	29
Z Il Fornaio | **Palo Alto/S**	19
Jack Falstaff | **SoMa**	20
Z Jardinière | **Hayes Valley**	26
Jeanty at Jack's | **Downtown**	23
Z Kokkari | **Downtown**	26
Le Central Bistro | **Downtown**	19
Le Colonial | **Downtown**	21
Lion & Compass | **Sunnyvale/S**	19
Martini House | **St. Helena/N**	25
Z Masa's | **Downtown**	27
Z Michael Mina | **Downtown**	28
Mistral | **Redwood Shores/S**	19
Moose's | **N Beach**	20
Morton's | **San Jose/S**	23
Z Myth | **Downtown**	26
One Market | **Embarcadero**	22
Ottimista | **Cow Hollow**	20
Ozumo | **Embarcadero**	24
Parcel 104 | **Santa Clara/S**	23
Park Grill | **Downtown**	20
Plumed Horse | **Saratoga/S**	-
Z Postrio | **Downtown**	24
Press | **St. Helena/N**	23
Quattro | **E Palo Alto/S**	22
Z Redd Rest. | **Yountville/N**	26
Z Ritz-Carlton Din. Rm. | **Nob Hill**	27
Rubicon | **Downtown**	24
Sam's Grill | **Downtown**	20
Sanraku | **multi. loc.**	23
Z Silks | **Downtown**	24

Z Tadich Grill | **Downtown**	22
Tommy Toy's | **Downtown**	24
Town Hall | **SoMa**	23
Village Pub | **Woodside/S**	26
Viognier | **San Mateo/S**	24
Z Zuni Café | **Hayes Valley**	25

PRE-THEATER DINING

(Call for prices and times)

Z Chapeau! | **Outer Rich**	27
Clémentine | **Inner Rich**	24
Colibrí Mexican | **Downtown**	20
Hayes St. Grill | **Hayes Valley**	22
Hyde St. Bistro | **Russian Hill**	21
Indigo | **Civic Ctr**	20
La Scene | **Downtown**	17
paul k | **Hayes Valley**	21
Z Postrio | **Downtown**	24
Venus | **Berkeley/E**	19

PRIVATE ROOMS

(Restaurants charge less at off times; call for capacity)

Absinthe | **Hayes Valley**	20
Acme Chophouse | **S Beach**	19
À Côté | **Oakland/E**	24
Z Acquerello | **Polk Gulch**	27
Adagia | **Berkeley/E**	19
Z Ahwahnee | **Yosemite/E**	19
Alegrias | **Marina**	20
Z Alexander's | **Cupertino/S**	25
Alfred's Steak | **Downtown**	21
Z Ana Mandara | **Fish. Wharf**	23
Andalu | **Mission**	20
Angèle | **Napa/N**	22
Anton & Michel | **Carmel/S**	23
A.P. Stump's | **San Jose/S**	21
Arcadia | **San Jose/S**	23
Z Auberge du Sol. | **Rutherford/N**	25
Aziza | **Outer Rich**	24
bacar | **SoMa**	22
Baraka | **Potrero Hill**	21
Barndiva | **Healdsburg/N**	18
Basin | **Saratoga/S**	19
Z Bay Wolf | **Oakland/E**	25
Bella Vista | **Woodside/S**	22
Betelnut Pejiu | **Cow Hollow**	23
Big 4 | **Nob Hill**	22
Bing Crosby's | **Walnut Creek/E**	18
Bistro Aix | **Marina**	22

SPECIAL FEATURES

Bistro Liaison	**Berkeley/E**	22
Blackhawk Grille	**Danville/E**	19
Blue Plate	**Mission**	23
Boca	**Novato/N**	20
Boonville Hotel	**Boonville/N**	21
⚡ Boulevard	**Embarcadero**	27
Bridges	**Danville/E**	20
BRIX	**Yountville/N**	22
Buca di Beppo	**multi. loc.**	14
⚡ Buckeye	**Mill Valley/N**	23
Butterfly	**Embarcadero**	19
CAFÉ KATi	**Japantown**	23
Café Rouge	**Berkeley/E**	21
Campton Place	**Downtown**	25
Caprice	**Tiburon/N**	21
Carnelian Room	**Downtown**	17
Carneros Bistro	**Sonoma/N**	22
Casanova	**Carmel/S**	23
Cetrella	**Half Moon Bay/S**	22
Cha Cha Cha	**Mission**	19
Chantilly	**Redwood City/S**	25
Chaya Brasserie	**Embarcadero**	21
Chez TJ	**Mtn View/S**	25
Cindy's	**St. Helena/N**	24
Citizen Thai	**N Beach**	20
Citron	**Oakland/E**	24
Cliff House Bistro	**Outer Rich**	18
Club XIX	**Pebble Bch/S**	25
Cortez	**Downtown**	23
Cosmopolitan	**SoMa**	20
⚡ Cyrus	**Healdsburg/N**	28
downtown	**Berkeley/E**	20
Dry Creek	**Healdsburg/N**	24
El Paseo	**Mill Valley/N**	23
Eos Rest./Wine	**Cole Valley**	23
⚡ Erna's Elderberry	**Oakhurst/E**	28
Eulipia	**San Jose/S**	20
Fandango	**Pacific Grove/S**	23
⚡ Farallon	**Downtown**	24
Fifth Floor	**SoMa**	25
Flea St. Café	**Menlo Pk/S**	22
⚡ Fleur de Lys	**Nob Hill**	28
Florio	**Pacific Hts**	19
Foreign Cinema	**Mission**	21
Frantoio	**Mill Valley/N**	21
⚡ French Laundry	**Yountville/N**	29
Frisson	**Downtown**	20
Garibaldis	**Oakland/E**	21
Gary Chu's	**Santa Rosa/N**	22
⚡ Gary Danko	**Fish. Wharf**	29
girl & the fig	**Sonoma/N**	23
Grand Cafe	**Downtown**	20
Grasing's Coastal	**Carmel/S**	23
Harris'	**Polk Gulch**	25
Hurley's	**Yountville/N**	20
Iberia	**Menlo Pk/S**	21
Il Davide	**San Rafael/N**	21
⚡ Il Fornaio	**multi. loc.**	19
Incanto	**Noe Valley**	24
Indigo	**Civic Ctr**	20
Insalata's	**San Anselmo/N**	24
⚡ Jardinière	**Hayes Valley**	26
Jeanty at Jack's	**Downtown**	23
John Ash & Co.	**Santa Rosa/N**	23
⚡ John Bentley's	**multi. loc.**	25
Kenwood	**Kenwood/N**	22
Khan Toke	**Outer Rich**	23
⚡ Kokkari	**Downtown**	26
Kurt's Carmel	**Carmel/S**	23
⚡ La Folie	**Russian Hill**	27
La Forêt	**San Jose/S**	27
Lalime's	**Berkeley/E**	26
Lark Creek Inn	**Larkspur/N**	23
La Strada	**Palo Alto/S**	21
Last Supper	**Mission**	19
⚡ La Toque	**Rutherford/N**	26
⚡ L'Auberge	**Carmel/S**	27
Lavanda	**Palo Alto/S**	19
Le Colonial	**Downtown**	21
Ledford Hse.	**Albion/N**	23
Left Bank	**multi. loc.**	18
⚡ Le Papillon	**San Jose/S**	27
Lion & Compass	**Sunnyvale/S**	19
Little River Inn	**Little River/N**	20
MacCallum Hse.	**Mendocino/N**	24
Maddalena/Fino	**Palo Alto/S**	21
⚡ Madrona Manor	**Healdsburg/N**	25
⚡ Manresa	**Los Gatos/S**	27
Manzanita	**Healdsburg/N**	20
⚡ Marché	**Menlo Pk/S**	26
⚡ Marinus	**Carmel Valley/S**	26
Martini House	**St. Helena/N**	25
⚡ Masa's	**Downtown**	27
Maya	**SoMa**	22
⚡ Millennium	**Downtown**	24

Montrio Bistro | **Monterey/S** 23
Moose's | **N Beach** 20
Morton's | **Downtown** 23
Ⓩ Myth | **Downtown** 26
Ⓩ Navio | **Half Moon Bay/S** 26
North Beach Rest. | **N Beach** 21
Olema Inn | **Olema/N** 22
Oliveto Restaurant | **Oakland/E** 25
One Market | **Embarcadero** 22
Ozumo | **Embarcadero** 24
Ⓩ Pacific's Edge | **Carmel/S** 25
Palio d'Asti | **Downtown** 19
Parcel 104 | **Santa Clara/S** 23
Passionfish | **Pacific Grove/S** 25
Pauline's Pizza | **Mission** 22
Pesce | **Russian Hill** 22
Piatti | **multi. loc.** 19
Piazza D'Angelo | **Mill Valley/N** 19
Plumed Horse | **Saratoga/S** ⁻
PlumpJack | **multi. loc.** 24
Poggio | **Sausalito/N** 21
Ponzu | **Downtown** 21
Ⓩ Postino | **Lafayette/E** 24
Ⓩ Postrio | **Downtown** 24
Press | **St. Helena/N** 23
Prima | **Walnut Creek/E** 24
R & G Lounge | **Chinatown** 23
Rest. LuLu/Petite | **SoMa** 20
Rio Grill | **Carmel/S** 22
Ⓩ Ritz-Carlton Din. Rm. | **Nob Hill** 27
Robert's | **Pacific Grove/S** 25
Rose Pistola | **N Beach** 21
Roy's | **SoMa** 22
Rubicon | **Downtown** 24
Ruth's Chris | **Polk Gulch** 24
Santi | **Geyserville/N** 23
Sardine Factory | **Monterey/S** 20
Sauce | **Hayes Valley** 18
Scala's Bistro | **Downtown** 22
Scott's | **multi. loc.** 19
Seasons | **Downtown** 24
71 Saint Peter | **San Jose/S** 22
Ⓩ Shadowbrook | **Capitola/S** 22
Shanghai 1930 | **Embarcadero** 20
Ⓩ Silks | **Downtown** 24
Ⓩ Slanted Door | **Embarcadero** 26
Soi Four | **Oakland/E** 23
Soizic | **Oakland/E** 22

St. Orres | **Gualala/N** 24
Straits Cafe | **San Jose/S** 20
Syrah | **Santa Rosa/N** 25
Ⓩ Tamarine | **Palo Alto/S** 26
Tarpy's | **Monterey/S** 22
Ⓩ Terra | **St. Helena/N** 26
Ti Couz | **Mission** 22
Tommy Toy's | **Downtown** 24
Town Hall | **SoMa** 23
Townhouse B&G | **Emeryville/E** 21
Trader Vic's | **multi. loc.** 16
Tratt. La Siciliana | **Berkeley/E** 23
Tra Vigne | **St. Helena/N** 23
2223 | **Castro** 21
231 Ellsworth | **San Mateo/S** 23
Underwood Bar | **Graton/N** 22
Vic Stewart's | **Walnut Creek/E** 21
Village Pub | **Woodside/S** 26
Viognier | **San Mateo/S** 24
Wappo Bar | **Calistoga/N** 22
Wente Vineyards | **Livermore/E** 23
Ⓩ Yank Sing | **SoMa** 25
Zarzuela | **Russian Hill** 22
Zibibbo | **Palo Alto/S** 20
Zinsvalley | **Napa/N** 20
Zuppa | **SoMa** 19

PRIX FIXE MENUS

(Call for prices and times)

Absinthe | **Hayes Valley** 20
Ⓩ Acquerello | **Polk Gulch** 27
Ⓩ Ajanta | **Berkeley/E** 24
Alamo Sq. | **W Addition** 21
Anjou | **Downtown** 23
Ⓩ Aqua | **Downtown** 26
Ⓩ Auberge du Sol. | **Rutherford/N** 25
Aziza | **Outer Rich** 24
Baker St. Bistro | **Marina** 20
Bistro Liaison | **Berkeley/E** 22
Ⓩ BIX | **Downtown** 23
Boonville Hotel | **Boonville/N** 21
Bouchée | **Carmel/S** 26
Café Marcella | **Los Gatos/S** 24
Carnelian Room | **Downtown** 17
Casanova | **Carmel/S** 23
Chantilly | **Redwood City/S** 25
Ⓩ Chapeau! | **Outer Rich** 27
Ⓩ Chez Panisse | **Berkeley/E** 27
Ⓩ Chez Panisse Café | **Berkeley/E** 27

hez Spencer | **Mission**	24
Chez TJ | **Mtn View/S**	25
Christophe | **Sausalito/N**	20
Citron | **Oakland/E**	24
Côté Sud | **Castro**	20
🔲 Cyrus | **Healdsburg/N**	28
Dry Creek | **Healdsburg/N**	24
Duck Club | **Lafayette/E**	20
Ecco | **Burlingame/S**	21
🔲 Erna's Elderberry | **Oakhurst/E**	28
Espetus | **Hayes Valley**	21
Étoile | **Yountville/N**	25
🔲 Farallon | **Downtown**	24
🔲 Firefly | **Noe Valley**	25
🔲 Fleur de Lys | **Nob Hill**	28
Fork | **San Anselmo/N**	24
Fournou's | **Nob Hill**	22
🔲 French Laundry | **Yountville/N**	29
🔲 Gary Danko | **Fish. Wharf**	29
girl & the fig | **Sonoma/N**	23
Grasing's Coastal | **Carmel/S**	23
🔲 Greens | **Marina**	24
Hana Japanese | **Rohnert Pk/N**	25
Hurley's | **Yountville/N**	20
Indigo | **Civic Ctr**	20
🔲 Jardinière | **Hayes Valley**	26
Julia's | **Napa/N**	23
Kyo-Ya | **Downtown**	23
🔲 La Folie | **Russian Hill**	27
La Forêt | **San Jose/S**	27
Lark Creek Inn | **Larkspur/N**	23
La Strada | **Palo Alto/S**	21
🔲 La Toque | **Rutherford/N**	26
Le Charm Bistro | **SoMa**	21
Ledford Hse. | **Albion/N**	23
🔲 Le Papillon | **San Jose/S**	27
Le Zinc | **Noe Valley**	18
MacCallum Hse. | **Mendocino/N**	24
🔲 Madrona Manor | **Healdsburg/N**	25
🔲 Manresa | **Los Gatos/S**	27
🔲 Marinus | **Carmel Valley/S**	26
Market | **St. Helena/N**	22
Martini House | **St. Helena/N**	25
🔲 Masa's | **Downtown**	27
Maya | **SoMa**	22
🔲 Michael Mina | **Downtown**	28
🔲 Millennium | **Downtown**	24

🔲 Navio | **Half Moon Bay/S**	26
🔲 Pacific's Edge | **Carmel/S**	25
Ponzu | **Downtown**	21
🔲 Postrio | **Downtown**	24
🔲 Ritz-Carlton Din. Rm. | **Nob Hill**	27
rnm rest. | **Lower Haight**	25
Robert's | **Pacific Grove/S**	25
Roy's | **SoMa**	22
Sanraku | **multi. loc.**	23
Santé | **Sonoma/N**	24
Seasons | **Downtown**	24
Sent Sovi | **Saratoga/S**	24
Shanghai 1930 | **Embarcadero**	20
🔲 Sierra Mar | **Big Sur/S**	26
🔲 Silks | **Downtown**	24
🔲 Slanted Door | **Embarcadero**	26
South Park | **SoMa**	22
St. Orres | **Gualala/N**	24
Syrah | **Santa Rosa/N**	25
Tao Cafe | **Mission**	18
Tommy Toy's | **Downtown**	24
🔲 Ton Kiang | **Outer Rich**	25
Town's End | **Embarcadero**	19
Tratt. La Siciliana | **Berkeley/E**	23
231 Ellsworth | **San Mateo/S**	23
Viognier | **San Mateo/S**	24

QUIET CONVERSATION

🔲 Acquerello | **Polk Gulch**	27
🔲 Alexander's | **Cupertino/S**	25
Applewood Inn | **Guerneville/N**	24
🔲 Auberge du Sol. | **Rutherford/N**	25
🔲 Bay Wolf | **Oakland/E**	25
Bella Vista | **Woodside/S**	22
Bushi-tei | **Japantown**	24
Cafe Jacqueline | **N Beach**	26
Campton Place | **Downtown**	25
Casanova | **Carmel/S**	23
Chantilly | **Redwood City/S**	25
🔲 Chez Panisse | **Berkeley/E**	27
Chez TJ | **Mtn View/S**	25
🔲 Cyrus | **Healdsburg/N**	28
Duck Club | **multi. loc.**	20
El Paseo | **Mill Valley/N**	23
🔲 Farmhouse | **Forestville/N**	27
Fifth Floor | **SoMa**	25
🔲 Fleur de Lys | **Nob Hill**	28
Forbes Mill Steak | **multi. loc.**	23

Fournou's | **Nob Hill** 22

Z Gary Danko | **Fish. Wharf** 29

NEW Hime | **Marina** 22

Lalime's | **Berkeley/E** 26

Z La Toque | **Rutherford/N** 26

Z L'Auberge | **Carmel/S** 27

Lovejoy's Tea | **Noe Valley** 20

Z Madrona Manor | 25
  Healdsburg/N

Z Manresa | **Los Gatos/S** 27

Marché aux Fleurs | **Ross/N** 25

Z Masa's | **Downtown** 27

Morton's | **San Jose/S** 23

O Chamé | **Berkeley/E** 24

Z Pacific's Edge | **Carmel/S** 25

Park Grill | **Downtown** 20

Z Postino | **Lafayette/E** 24

Quattro | **E Palo Alto/S** 22

Z Quince | **Pacific Hts** 26

Rest. at Meadowood | 23
  St. Helena/N

NEW Rouge/Blanc | **Downtown** –

Seasons | **Downtown** 24

Z Silks | **Downtown** 24

Soule Domaine | **Kings Bch/E** 23

Sparrow | **Nob Hill** 20

St. Orres | **Gualala/N** 24

SUMI | **Castro** 23

Terzo | **Cow Hollow** 22

RAW BARS

Absinthe | **Hayes Valley** 20

Acme Chophouse | **S Beach** 19

Anchor Oyster | **Castro** 23

Angèle | **Napa/N** 22

A.P. Stump's | **San Jose/S** 21

Z Aqua | **Downtown** 26

Bar Crudo | **Downtown** 25

Bistro Vida | **Menlo Pk/S** 18

Z Bouchon | **Yountville/N** 25

Café Rouge | **Berkeley/E** 21

Central Market | **Petaluma/N** 23

Cetrella | **Half Moon Bay/S** 22

Z Farallon | **Downtown** 24

Fish | **Sausalito/N** 24

Fog City Diner | **Embarcadero** 19

Foreign Cinema | **Mission** 21

Fresca | **Upper Fillmore** 22

Godzila Sushi | **Pacific Hts** 17

NEW Go Fish | **St. Helena/N** 24

Hog Island Oyster | **Embarcadero** 25

Kingfish | **San Mateo/S** 17

Market | **St. Helena/N** 22

O'Reilly's | **Polk Gulch** 18

Pearl Oyster | **Oakland/E** 24

Pesce | **Russian Hill** 22

Quattro | **E Palo Alto/S** 22

Rest. LuLu/Petite | **SoMa** 20

Scott Howard | **Downtown** 23

Seasons | **Downtown** 24

Sonoma Meritage | **Sonoma/N** 19

Station House | **Pt Reyes/N** 17

Z Sushi Ran | **Sausalito/N** 28

Z Swan Oyster | **Polk Gulch** 26

Willi's Seafood | **Healdsburg/N** 23

Woodhse. | **Castro** 19

Yabbies Coastal | **Russian Hill** 22

Yankee Pier | **multi. loc.** 17

Zibibbo | **Palo Alto/S** 20

Z Zuni Café | **Hayes Valley** 25

ROMANTIC PLACES

Z Acquerello | **Polk Gulch** 27

Z Ahwahnee | **Yosemite/N** 19

Albion River Inn | **Albion/N** 24

Z Alexander's | **Cupertino/S** 25

Z Ana Mandara | **Fish. Wharf** 23

Anton & Michel | **Carmel/S** 23

Applewood Inn | **Guerneville/N** 24

Z Auberge du Sol. | **Rutherford/N** 25

Aziza | **Outer Rich** 24

Barndiva | **Healdsburg/N** 18

Bella Vista | **Woodside/S** 22

Big 4 | **Nob Hill** 22

Bing Crosby's | **Walnut Creek/E** 18

Bistro Clovis | **Hayes Valley** 19

NEW Bistro/Copains | 27
  Occidental/N

Bistro Elan | **Palo Alto/S** 24

Bistro Vida | **Menlo Pk/S** 18

Z Boulevard | **Embarcadero** 27

Bushi-tei | **Japantown** 24

Cafe Beaujolais | **Mendocino/N** 25

Cafe Jacqueline | **N Beach** 26

Caprice | **Tiburon/N** 21

Carnelian Room | **Downtown** 17

Casanova | **Carmel/S** 23

Cav Wine Bar | **Hayes Valley** 22

Chantilly | **Redwood City/S**	25
🛂 Chapeau! | **Outer Rich**	27
🛂 Chez Panisse | **Berkeley/E**	27
Chez Spencer | **Mission**	24
Chez TJ | **Mtn View/S**	25
Christophe | **Sausalito/N**	20
Christy Hill | **Tahoe City/E**	25
Citron | **Oakland/E**	24
Coi | **N Beach**	25
🛂 Cyrus | **Healdsburg/N**	28
Deetjen's | **Big Sur/S**	22
🆕 Ducca | **SoMa**	–
Duck Club | **multi. loc.**	20
El Paseo | **Mill Valley/N**	23
🛂 Erna's Elderberry | **Oakhurst/E**	28
Étoile | **Yountville/N**	25
🛂 Farmhouse | **Forestville/N**	27
Fifth Floor | **SoMa**	25
Flea St. Café | **Menlo Pk/S**	22
🛂 Fleur de Lys | **Nob Hill**	28
🛂 French Laundry | **Yountville/N**	29
🛂 Fresh Cream | **Monterey/S**	24
Gabriella Café | **Santa Cruz/S**	22
🛂 Garden Court | **Downtown**	19
🛂 Gary Danko | **Fish. Wharf**	29
General's | **Sonoma/N**	–
🆕 Hime | **Marina**	22
Incanto | **Noe Valley**	24
Indigo | **Civic Ctr**	20
🛂 Jardinière | **Hayes Valley**	26
John Ash & Co. | **Santa Rosa/N**	23
🛂 John Bentley's | **Woodside/S**	25
Katia's Tea | **Inner Rich**	19
Khan Toke | **Outer Rich**	23
🛂 La Folie | **Russian Hill**	27
La Forêt | **San Jose/S**	27
Lalime's | **Berkeley/E**	26
La Note | **Berkeley/E**	22
Lark Creek Inn | **Larkspur/N**	23
🛂 La Toque | **Rutherford/N**	26
🛂 L'Auberge | **Carmel/S**	27
🛂 Le Papillon | **San Jose/S**	27
Les Amis | **Downtown**	22
Little River Inn | **Little River/N**	20
MacCallum Hse. | **Mendocino/N**	24
Maddalena/Fino | **Palo Alto/S**	21
🛂 Madrona Manor | **Healdsburg/N**	25

Mantra | **Palo Alto/S**	20
Marché aux Fleurs | **Ross/N**	25
🛂 Marinus | **Carmel Valley/S**	26
Martini House | **St. Helena/N**	25
🛂 Masa's | **Downtown**	27
Matterhorn Swiss | **Russian Hill**	21
Medjool | **Mission**	18
🛂 Michael Mina | **Downtown**	28
Moosse Café | **Mendocino/N**	23
Napa Wine Train | **Napa/N**	15
🆕 Nick's Cove | **Marshall/N**	–
O Chamé | **Berkeley/E**	24
Olema Inn | **Olema/N**	22
🛂 Pacific's Edge | **Carmel/S**	25
Pianeta | **Truckee/E**	23
Picco | **Larkspur/N**	24
🛂 Quince | **Pacific Hts**	26
Rest. at Meadowood | **St. Helena/N**	23
Rest. at Stevenswood | **Little River/N**	20
🛂 Ritz-Carlton Din. Rm. | **Nob Hill**	27
🛂 Ritz-Carlton Terr. | **Nob Hill**	24
River Ranch | **Tahoe City/E**	17
Robert's | **Pacific Grove/S**	25
🆕 Rouge/Blanc | **Downtown**	–
Roy's | **Pebble Bch/S**	25
Salute E Rist. | **Richmond/E**	19
Sea Salt | **Berkeley/E**	22
Sent Sovi | **Saratoga/S**	24
71 Saint Peter | **San Jose/S**	22
🛂 Shadowbrook | **Capitola/S**	22
🛂 Sierra Mar | **Big Sur/S**	26
🛂 Silks | **Downtown**	24
Slow Club | **Mission**	22
Soizic | **Oakland/E**	22
Sol y Lago | **Tahoe City/E**	17
Soule Domain | **Kings Bch/E**	23
St. Michael's | **Palo Alto/S**	22
Stokes | **Monterey/S**	23
St. Orres | **Gualala/N**	24
Sunnyside | **Tahoe City/E**	18
supperclub | **SoMa**	17
🛂 Terra | **St. Helena/N**	26
Terzo | **Cow Hollow**	22
Venticello | **Nob Hill**	23
Viognier | **San Mateo/S**	24

Wente Vineyards | **Livermore/E**	23
Wolfdale's | **Tahoe City/E**	25
Wolf House | **Glen Ellen/N**	20
Woodward's Gdn. | **Mission**	25
Zarzuela | **Russian Hill**	22

SENIOR APPEAL

Acme Chophouse | **S Beach**	19
☑ Acquerello | **Polk Gulch**	27
Alfred's Steak | **Downtown**	21
Alioto's | **Fish. Wharf**	19
Anton & Michel | **Carmel/S**	23
Bella Vista | **Woodside/S**	22
Big 4 | **Nob Hill**	22
Bing Crosby's | **Walnut Creek/E**	18
Cantankerous | **Mtn View/S**	18
Caprice | **Tiburon/N**	21
Chantilly | **Redwood City/S**	25
Christophe | **Sausalito/N**	20
Christy Hill | **Tahoe City/E**	25
☑ Cole's Chop Hse. | **Napa/N**	25
Cook St. Helena | **St. Helena/N**	24
☑ Cyrus | **Healdsburg/N**	28
Duck Club | **multi. loc.**	20
Eulipia | **San Jose/S**	20
Fior d'Italia | **N Beach**	19
☑ Fleur de Lys | **Nob Hill**	28
Forbes Mill Steak | **multi. loc.**	23
Fournou's | **Nob Hill**	22
☑ Garden Court | **Downtown**	19
Harris' | **Polk Gulch**	25
Hayes St. Grill | **Hayes Valley**	22
House of Prime | **Polk Gulch**	24
Izzy's Steak | **Marina**	19
Joe DiMaggio's | **N Beach**	20
La Ginestra | **Mill Valley/N**	18
Lalime's | **Berkeley/E**	26
Le Central Bistro | **Downtown**	19
☑ Masa's | **Downtown**	27
Morton's | **multi. loc.**	23
North Beach Rest. | **N Beach**	21
Plumed Horse | **Saratoga/S**	-
Rest. at Meadowood | **St. Helena/N**	23
Robert's | **Pacific Grove/S**	25
Rotunda | **Downtown**	20
Sardine Factory | **Monterey/S**	20
Scoma's | **Fish. Wharf**	21
Soule Domain | **Kings Bch/E**	23

☑ Tadich Grill | **Downtown**	22
Vic Stewart's | **Walnut Creek/E**	21

SINGLES SCENES

Ace Wasabi's | **Marina**	20
Andalu | **Mission**	20
Asia de Cuba | **Downtown**	21
Balboa Cafe | **Cow Hollow**	19
Barndiva | **Healdsburg/N**	18
Beach Chalet | **Outer Sunset**	13
Betelnut Pejiu | **Cow Hollow**	23
☑ BIX | **Downtown**	23
Blowfish Sushi | **Mission**	21
Blue Plate | **Mission**	23
Butterfly | **Embarcadero**	19
Cafe Bastille | **Downtown**	18
Café Claude | **Downtown**	20
Cascal | **Mtn View/S**	20
Catch | **Castro**	19
Cha Cha Cha | **multi. loc.**	19
Circolo | **Mission**	19
Cosmopolitan | **SoMa**	20
Cottonwood | **Truckee/E**	20
NEW District | **SoMa**	17
Dragonfly | **Truckee/E**	23
E&O Trading | **multi. loc.**	19
Elite Cafe | **Upper Fillmore**	19
Emmy's Spaghetti | **Bernal Hts**	19
Firecracker | **Mission**	19
Foreign Cinema | **Mission**	21
Frisson | **Downtown**	20
Fritz Fries | **multi. loc.**	19
Gar Woods | **Carnelian Bay/E**	19
Guaymas | **Tiburon/N**	17
Home | **Castro**	18
Jack Falstaff | **SoMa**	20
Jake's/Lake | **Tahoe City/E**	16
Kan Zaman | **Haight-Ashbury**	17
Kingfish | **San Mateo/S**	17
NEW Laïola | **Marina**	-
Levende | **Mission**	20
Lime | **Castro**	18
Luna Park | **Mission**	19
Mecca | **Castro**	20
Medjool | **Mission**	18
NEW Mercury | **Marina**	-
MoMo's | **S Beach**	17
Moody's Bistro | **Truckee/E**	25

Nectar Wine | multi. loc. 19
Nihon | **Mission** 21
NEW Nua Rest. | **N Beach** -
Ottimista | **Cow Hollow** 20
Ozumo | **Embarcadero** 24
NEW Palmetto | **Cow Hollow** -
Pearl Alley | **Santa Cruz/S** 22
PJ's Oyster | **Inner Sunset** 19
Poleng | **W Addition** 22
Public | **SoMa** 18
Puerto Alegre | **Mission** 18
Quattro | **E Palo Alto/S** 22
Ramblas | **Mission** 20
River Ranch | **Tahoe City/E** 17
rnm rest. | **Lower Haight** 25
RoHan Lounge | **Inner Rich** 18
Rose Pistola | **N Beach** 21
Seven | **San Jose/S** 21
Sino | **San Jose/S** 20
Slow Club | **Mission** 22
NEW Sudachi | **Polk Gulch** -
Sunnyside | **Tahoe City/E** 18
Sushi Groove | multi. loc. 23
Ti Couz | **Mission** 22
Tokyo Go Go | **Mission** 22
Tres Agaves | **S Beach** 18
Tsunami | **W Addition** 23
2223 | **Castro** 21
NEW Umami | **Cow Hollow** 20
Universal Cafe | **Mission** 23
Zibibbo | **Palo Alto/S** 20
Z Zuni Café | **Hayes Valley** 25

SLEEPERS

(Good to excellent food, but little
known)
NEW Alembic | **Haight-Ashbury** 22
Annalien | **Napa/N** 24
Applewood Inn | **Guerneville/N** 24
Ariake | **Outer Rich** 26
Avatars | **Sausalito/N** 22
Battambang | **Oakland/E** 22
Bella Vista | **Woodside/S** 22
NEW Bistro/Copains |
   Occidental/N 27
Bistro V | **Sebastopol/N** 22
Bodega Bistro | **Tenderloin** 23
Bow Hon 4 | **Chinatown** 22
Cafe Citti | **Kenwood/N** 22

Café Fiore | **S Lake Tahoe/E** 24
Café Rustica | **Carmel Valley/S** 23
Cantinetta Luca | **Carmel/S** 22
Carneros Bistro | **Sonoma/N** 22
Central Market | **Petaluma/N** 23
Chantilly | **Redwood City/S** 25
Chez Shea | **Half Moon Bay/S** 22
Christy Hill | **Tahoe City/E** 25
Club XIX | **Pebble Bch/S** 25
Cucina Paradiso | **Petaluma/N** 26
Cucina Rest. | **San Anselmo/N** 24
Daimaru | **Castro** 24
Deetjen's | **Big Sur/S** 22
Della Fattoria | **Petaluma/N** 26
Dragonfly | **Truckee/E** 23
El Metate | **Mission** 23
Evan's | **S Lake Tahoe/E** 27
Gabriella Café | **Santa Cruz/S** 22
NEW Gialina | **Glen Pk** 24
Happy Cafe | **San Mateo/S** 22
Jai Yun | **Chinatown** 23
Z Joe's Cable Car | **Excelsior** 24
NEW Kanpai | **Palo Alto/S** 24
Kiji Sushi Bar | **Mission** 24
Kiss Sushi | **Japantown** 27
Kitchen at 868 | **Novato/N** 25
Kurt's Carmel | **Carmel/S** 23
La Forêt | **San Jose/S** 27
LaSalette | **Sonoma/N** 23
Ledford Hse. | **Albion/N** 23
Lure | **San Mateo/S** 23
Maykadeh | **N Beach** 23
Mendo Bistro | **Ft Bragg/N** 25
Mochica | **SoMa** 23
Moody's Bistro | **Truckee/E** 25
Moosse Café | **Mendocino/N** 23
Mosaic Rest. | **Forestville/N** 25
Naked Fish | **S Lake Tahoe/E** 22
955 Ukiah | **Mendocino/N** 22
n.v. Rest. | **Napa/N** 22
Olema Inn | **Olema/N** 22
Z O'mei | **Santa Cruz/S** 26
Oyaji | **Outer Rich** 23
Pangaea | **Gualala/N** 25
Pappo | **Alameda/E** 23
Pearl | **Napa/N** 22
Pearl Alley | **Santa Cruz/S** 22
Pianeta | **Truckee/E** 23

Pizza Azzurro | **Napa/N**	22
❷ Pizzeria Picco | **Larkspur/N**	25
Ravens Rest. | **Mendocino/N**	23
Red Hut | **multi. loc.**	25
Rendezvous Inn | **Ft Bragg/N**	27
Restaurant | **Ft Bragg/N**	23
Rest. at Meadowood | **St. Helena/N**	23
Richmond Rest. | **Inner Rich**	22
Robert's | **Pacific Grove/S**	25
Ryoko's | **Tenderloin**	23
Saha | **Tenderloin**	24
Santé | **Sonoma/N**	24
Seaweed Café | **Bodega Bay/N**	24
Sebo | **Hayes Valley**	25
Sent Sovi | **Saratoga/S**	24
Soule Domain | **Kings Bch/E**	23
Stokes | **Monterey/S**	23
St. Orres | **Gualala/N**	24
Suriya Thai | **Mission**	23
Sushi Zone | **Castro**	26
Table Café | **Larkspur/N**	24
Tai Pan | **Palo Alto/S**	23
Tajine | **Polk Gulch**	23
Taqueria Tlaquepaque | **San Jose/S**	23
Theo's | **Soquel/S**	24
Tokyo Go Go | **Mission**	22
Troya | **Inner Rich**	22
❷ Truly Med. | **Mission**	23
Tsar Nicoulai | **Embarcadero**	22
Tsunami | **W Addition**	23
Uncle Frank's | **Mtn View/S**	22
Water St. Bistro | **Petaluma/N**	24
Wolfdale's | **Tahoe City/E**	25
NEW Wood Tav. | **Oakland/E**	23

TASTING MENUS

❷ Acquerello | **Polk Gulch**	27
All Season's | **Calistoga/N**	21
❷ Ame | **SoMa**	26
Applewood Inn | **Guerneville/N**	24
❷ Aqua | **Downtown**	26
❷ Auberge du Sol. | **Rutherford/N**	25
Aziza | **Outer Rich**	24
Bistro V | **Sebastopol/N**	22
Bouchée | **Carmel/S**	26
Bushi-tei | **Japantown**	24
Cafe Gibraltar | **El Granada/S**	25

Campton Place | **Downtown**	25
Chantilly | **Redwood City/S**	25
❷ Chapeau! | **Outer Rich**	27
Chez Spencer | **Mission**	24
Chez TJ | **Mtn View/S**	25
Citron | **Oakland/E**	24
Coi | **N Beach**	25
Côté Sud | **Castro**	20
❷ Cyrus | **Healdsburg/N**	28
Dry Creek | **Healdsburg/N**	24
Duck Club | **Lafayette/E**	20
Ecco | **Burlingame/S**	21
El Dorado | **Sonoma/N**	23
El Paseo | **Mill Valley/N**	23
Étoile | **Yountville/N**	25
Fifth Floor | **SoMa**	25
Fior d'Italia | **N Beach**	19
Fork | **San Anselmo/N**	24
❷ French Laundry | **Yountville/N**	29
❷ Gary Danko | **Fish. Wharf**	29
Hana Japanese | **Rohnert Pk/N**	25
NEW Hime | **Marina**	22
❷ Jardinière | **Hayes Valley**	26
Jordan's | **Berkeley/E**	18
Julia's | **Napa/N**	23
NEW Kanpai | **Palo Alto/S**	24
❷ Kaygetsu | **Menlo Pk/S**	28
Kiss Sushi | **Japantown**	27
Koi Palace | **Daly City/S**	23
Kyo-Ya | **Downtown**	23
❷ La Folie | **Russian Hill**	27
La Forêt | **San Jose/S**	27
❷ La Toque | **Rutherford/N**	26
❷ L'Auberge | **Carmel/S**	27
❷ Le Papillon | **San Jose/S**	27
Les Amis | **Downtown**	22
MacCallum Hse. | **Mendocino/N**	24
❷ Madrona Manor | **Healdsburg/N**	25
❷ Manresa | **Los Gatos/S**	27
❷ Marinus | **Carmel Valley/S**	26
Martini House | **St. Helena/N**	25
❷ Masa's | **Downtown**	27
Medicine | **Downtown**	18
❷ Michael Mina | **Downtown**	28
❷ Millennium | **Downtown**	24
❷ Navio | **Half Moon Bay/S**	26
❷ Pacific's Edge | **Carmel/S**	25

☑ Postrio | **Downtown**	24	☑ Pizzeria Picco | **Larkspur/N**	25
Prima | **Walnut Creek/E**	24	Rutherford Grill | **Rutherford/N**	23
☑ Redd Rest. | **Yountville/N**	26	Sardine Factory | **Monterey/S**	20
Rest. at Meadowood | **St. Helena/N**	23	Shen Hua | **Berkeley/E**	20
☑ Ritz-Carlton Din. Rm. | **Nob Hill**	27	Sunnyside | **Tahoe City/E**	18
Sanraku | **Downtown**	23	Taylor's Auto | **St. Helena/N**	21
Santé | **Sonoma/N**	24	Tonga | **Nob Hill**	13
Seasons | **Downtown**	24		

THEME RESTAURANTS

Sent Sovi | **Saratoga/S**	24	Bing Crosby's | **Walnut Creek/E**	18
71 Saint Peter | **San Jose/S**	22	Buca di Beppo | **multi. loc.**	14
Shanghai 1930 | **Embarcadero**	20	Hard Rock | **Fish. Wharf**	13
☑ Silks | **Downtown**	24	Joe DiMaggio's | **N Beach**	20
Sonoma Meritage | **Sonoma/N**	19	Max's | **multi. loc.**	16
Sparrow | **Nob Hill**	20	Napa Wine Train | **Napa/N**	15
NEW Sudachi | **Polk Gulch**	–	supperclub | **SoMa**	17
supperclub | **SoMa**	17		

TRENDY

Syrah | **Santa Rosa/N**	25	Ace Wasabi's | **Marina**	20
Theo's | **Soquel/S**	24	À Côté | **Oakland/E**	24
Tommy Toy's | **Downtown**	24	Amber Bistro | **Danville/E**	20
231 Ellsworth | **San Mateo/S**	23	☑ Ame | **SoMa**	26
Wolf House | **Glen Ellen/N**	20	☑ Aqua | **Downtown**	26
		Asia de Cuba | **Downtown**	21

TEEN APPEAL

		☑ A 16 | **Marina**	23
Asqew Grill | **multi. loc.**	18	Azie | **SoMa**	19
Barney's | **multi. loc.**	19	Balboa Cafe | **Cow Hollow**	19
Beach Chalet | **Outer Sunset**	13	Barndiva | **Healdsburg/N**	18
Buca di Beppo | **multi. loc.**	14	Bar Tartine | **Mission**	22
Burger Joint | **multi. loc.**	18	Betelnut Pejiu | **Cow Hollow**	23
Cactus Taqueria | **multi. loc.**	20	Bing Crosby's | **Walnut Creek/E**	18
Cheesecake | **multi. loc.**	16	Bistro Don Giovanni | **Napa/N**	23
FatApple's | **multi. loc.**	17	☑ BIX | **Downtown**	23
Fentons Creamery | **Oakland/E**	18	Blowfish Sushi | **Mission**	21
Fog City Diner | **Embarcadero**	19	Blue Jay | **W Addition**	15
Gar Woods | **Carnelian Bay/E**	19	Blue Plate | **Mission**	23
Goat Hill Pizza | **Potrero Hill**	19	☑ Bocadillos | **N Beach**	22
Hard Rock | **Fish. Wharf**	13	Bong Su | **SoMa**	22
Jake's/Lake | **Tahoe City/E**	16	Boogaloos | **Mission**	17
Jake's Steaks | **Cow Hollow**	20	☑ Bouchon | **Yountville/N**	25
☑ Joe's Cable Car | **Excelsior**	24	☑ Boulevard | **Embarcadero**	27
Lettus | **Marina**	20	Brick | **Tenderloin**	20
MacArthur Park | **Palo Alto/S**	16	☑ Buckeye | **Mill Valley/N**	23
Max's | **multi. loc.**	16	Bungalow 44 | **Mill Valley/N**	21
Mel's Drive-In | **multi. loc.**	13	Café Fanny | **Berkeley/E**	22
Mo's | **multi. loc.**	20	Café Rouge | **Berkeley/E**	21
Park Chalet | **Outer Sunset**	15	Cascal | **Mtn View/S**	20
Pauline's Pizza | **Mission**	22	Cav Wine Bar | **Hayes Valley**	22
Picante Cocina | **Berkeley/E**	21	César | **Berkeley/E**	22
Pizza Antica | **Lafayette/E**	21		

Cetrella | **Half Moon Bay/S**	22
Cha Cha Cha | **multi. loc.**	19
Charanga | **Mission**	21
🔁 Chez Panisse Café | **Berkeley/E**	27
Chez Papa Bistrot | **Potrero Hill**	23
Cindy's | **St. Helena/N**	24
Circolo | **Mission**	19
Coco 500 | **SoMa**	22
Deep Sushi | **Noe Valley**	21
🔁 Delfina | **Mission**	26
Doña Tomás | **Oakland/E**	24
Dosa | **Mission**	20
downtown | **Berkeley/E**	20
Dry Creek | **Healdsburg/N**	24
NEW Ducca | **SoMa**	–
E&O Trading | **Larkspur/N**	19
Ebisu | **Inner Sunset**	23
Emmy's Spaghetti | **Bernal Hts**	19
Enrico's | **N Beach**	–
Eos Rest./Wine | **Cole Valley**	23
🔁 Evvia | **Palo Alto/S**	26
🔁 Farallon | **Downtown**	24
NEW Farina | **Mission**	–
farmerbrown | **Tenderloin**	19
Flea St. Café | **Menlo Pk/S**	22
🔁 Fonda Solana | **Albany/E**	24
Foreign Cinema | **Mission**	21
🔁 Fringale | **SoMa**	24
Frisson | **Downtown**	20
Fritz Fries | **multi. loc.**	19
NEW Front Porch | **N Beach**	20
Garibaldis | **Oakland/E**	21
girl & the fig | **Sonoma/N**	23
Globe | **Downtown**	21
NEW Go Fish | **St. Helena/N**	24
NEW Hime | **Marina**	22
Iluna Basque | **N Beach**	17
Isa | **Marina**	24
Jack Falstaff | **SoMa**	20
Jake's/Lake | **Tahoe City/E**	16
🔁 Jardinière | **Hayes Valley**	26
Junnoon | **Palo Alto/S**	22
NEW Laïola | **Marina**	–
Last Supper | **Mission**	19
Levende | **Mission**	20
Lime | **Castro**	18
🔁 Limón | **Mission**	22
Luna Park | **Mission**	19
Mamacita | **Marina**	–
Martini House | **St. Helena/N**	25
Maverick | **Mission**	22
Mecca | **Castro**	20
Medjool | **Mission**	18
NEW Mercury | **Marina**	–
NEW Mexico DF | **Embarcadero**	–
Moose's | **N Beach**	20
Mustards Grill | **Yountville/N**	24
🔁 Myth | **Downtown**	26
Naked Fish | **S Lake Tahoe/E**	22
Nectar Wine | **Burlingame/S**	19
Nihon | **Mission**	21
NoPa | **W Addition**	23
Osha Thai | **SoMa**	22
Ottimista | **Cow Hollow**	20
Ozumo | **Embarcadero**	24
NEW Palmetto | **Cow Hollow**	–
Pearl Oyster | **Oakland/E**	24
Piazza D'Angelo | **Mill Valley/N**	19
Picco | **Larkspur/N**	24
🔁 Piperade | **Downtown**	25
Pizza Antica | **San Jose/S**	21
Pizzeria Delfina | **Mission**	24
🔁 Pizzeria Picco | **Larkspur/N**	25
Plouf | **Downtown**	22
PlumpJack | **Cow Hollow**	24
Poggio | **Sausalito/N**	21
Poleng | **W Addition**	22
🔁 Postino | **Lafayette/E**	24
🔁 Postrio | **Downtown**	24
Press | **St. Helena/N**	23
Public | **SoMa**	18
Rest. LuLu/Petite | **SoMa**	20
rnm rest. | **Lower Haight**	25
Rose Pistola | **N Beach**	21
Rose's Cafe | **Cow Hollow**	21
NEW Salt House | **SoMa**	21
Santi | **Geyserville/N**	23
Scott Howard | **Downtown**	23
Sebo | **Hayes Valley**	25
Sino | **San Jose/S**	20
🔁 Slanted Door | **Embarcadero**	26
Slow Club | **Mission**	22
NEW Spork | **Mission**	–
NEW Sudachi | **Polk Gulch**	–
supperclub | **SoMa**	17
Sushi Groove | **multi. loc.**	23

Tamarine	Palo Alto/S	26
...erzo	Cow Hollow	22
Ti Couz	Mission	22
Tokyo Go Go	Mission	22
Town Hall	SoMa	23
Trader Vic's	multi. loc.	16
Tres Agaves	S Beach	18
Tsunami	W Addition	23
2223	Castro	21
NEW TWO	SoMa	21
NEW Umami	Cow Hollow	20
Universal Cafe	Mission	23
Village Pub	Woodside/S	26
NEW West Co. Grill	Sebastopol/N	–
Willi's Seafood	Healdsburg/N	23
NEW Wood Tav.	Oakland/E	23
NEW Xyclo	Oakland/E	19
XYZ	SoMa	20
Zibibbo	Palo Alto/S	20
Z Zuni Café	Hayes Valley	25
Zuppa	SoMa	19
Z Zuzu	Napa/N	24

VALET PARKING

Absinthe	Hayes Valley	20
Acme Chophouse	S Beach	19
Z Ahwahnee	Yosemite/E	19
Albona Rist.	N Beach	24
Amber Bistro	Danville/E	20
Z Ame	SoMa	26
Americano	Embarcadero	17
Z Ana Mandara	Fish. Wharf	23
Andalu	Mission	20
ANZU	Downtown	21
Z Aqua	Downtown	26
Arcadia	San Jose/S	23
Asia de Cuba	Downtown	21
Z Auberge du Sol.	Rutherford/N	25
Azie	SoMa	19
Aziza	Outer Rich	24
bacar	SoMa	22
Balboa Cafe	Cow Hollow	19
Big 4	Nob Hill	22
Bing Crosby's	Walnut Creek/E	18
Z BIX	Downtown	23
Blowfish Sushi	San Jose/S	21
Bong Su	SoMa	22
Boulette's Larder	Embarcadero	25

Z Boulevard	Embarcadero	27
Bridges	Danville/E	20
Z Buckeye	Mill Valley/N	23
Butterfly	Embarcadero	19
Café Majestic	Pacific Hts	–
Campton Place	Downtown	25
Caprice	Tiburon/N	21
Casa Orinda	Orinda/E	17
Catch	Castro	19
Cha Am Thai	SoMa	19
Chantilly	Redwood City/S	25
Chaya Brasserie	Embarcadero	21
Cheesecake	Santa Clara/S	16
NEW Circa	Marina	18
Citizen Cake	Hayes Valley	20
Club XIX	Pebble Bch/S	25
Coi	N Beach	25
Z Cole's Chop Hse.	Napa/N	25
Crustacean	Polk Gulch	23
Delancey St.	Embarcadero	18
Destino	Castro	22
NEW Dio Deka	Los Gatos/S	–
NEW Ducca	SoMa	–
Duck Club	Lafayette/E	20
Ecco	Burlingame/S	21
Elite Cafe	Upper Fillmore	19
El Raigon	N Beach	21
Enrico's	N Beach	–
NEW Essencia	Hayes Valley	–
Z Evvia	Palo Alto/S	26
Z Farallon	Downtown	24
NEW Farina	Mission	–
Fifth Floor	SoMa	25
Fior d'Italia	N Beach	19
Z Fleur de Lys	Nob Hill	28
Florio	Pacific Hts	19
Foreign Cinema	Mission	21
Fournou's	Nob Hill	22
Frisson	Downtown	20
Garibaldis	multi. loc.	21
Z Gary Danko	Fish. Wharf	29
Gaylord India	Sausalito/N	18
Grand Cafe	Downtown	20
Harris'	Polk Gulch	25
Hayes St. Grill	Hayes Valley	22
NEW Hime	Marina	22
Home	Castro	18
House of Prime	Polk Gulch	24

Il Fornaio	**multi. loc.**	19
Insalata's	**San Anselmo/N**	24
Jack Falstaff	**SoMa**	20
Jardinière	**Hayes Valley**	26
Joe DiMaggio's	**N Beach**	20
Jordan's	**Berkeley/E**	18
Julius Castle	**Telegraph Hill**	–
Kingfish	**San Mateo/S**	17
Kokkari	**Downtown**	26
Kuleto's	**multi. loc.**	20
Kyo-Ya	**Downtown**	23
La Folie	**Russian Hill**	27
Lark Creek Inn	**Larkspur/N**	23
La Scene	**Downtown**	17
L'Auberge	**Carmel/S**	27
Lavanda	**Palo Alto/S**	19
Left Bank	**multi. loc.**	18
Le Petit Robert	**Russian Hill**	19
Levende	**Mission**	20
Lion & Compass	**Sunnyvale/S**	19
MacArthur Park	**Palo Alto/S**	16
Mangarosa	**N Beach**	19
Marinus	**Carmel Valley/S**	26
Masa's	**Downtown**	27
Matterhorn Swiss	**Russian Hill**	21
Max's	**Civic Ctr**	16
Maykadeh	**N Beach**	23
Mecca	**Castro**	20
Medjool	**Mission**	18
NEW Mexico DF	**Embarcadero**	–
Michael Mina	**Downtown**	28
Millennium	**Downtown**	24
MoMo's	**S Beach**	17
Moose's	**N Beach**	20
Morton's	**Downtown**	23
Myth	**Downtown**	26
Navio	**Half Moon Bay/S**	26
Nob Hill Café	**Nob Hill**	20
North Beach Rest.	**N Beach**	21
NEW Nua Rest.	**N Beach**	–
n.v. Rest.	**Napa/N**	22
One Market	**Embarcadero**	22
Oola	**SoMa**	20
Ozumo	**Embarcadero**	24
Pacific's Edge	**Carmel/S**	25
Parcel 104	**Santa Clara/S**	23
NEW Perbacco	**Downtown**	24
Piazza D'Angelo	**Mill Valley/N**	19

Picco	**Larkspur/N**	24
Pizzeria Picco	**Larkspur/N**	25
Plumed Horse	**Saratoga/S**	–
PlumpJack	**Cow Hollow**	24
Poggio	**Sausalito/N**	21
Ponzu	**Downtown**	21
Postino	**Lafayette/E**	24
Postrio	**Downtown**	24
Prima	**Walnut Creek/E**	24
Quince	**Pacific Hts**	26
Rest. LuLu/Petite	**multi. loc.**	20
Rist. Capellini	**San Mateo/S**	19
Ritz-Carlton Din. Rm.	**Nob Hill**	27
Ritz-Carlton Terr.	**Nob Hill**	24
rnm rest.	**Lower Haight**	25
Rose Pistola	**N Beach**	21
Roy's	**Pebble Bch/S**	25
Rubicon	**Downtown**	24
Ruth's Chris	**Polk Gulch**	24
Santé	**Sonoma/N**	24
Scoma's	**Fish. Wharf**	21
Scott Howard	**Downtown**	23
Scott's	**Walnut Creek/E**	19
Seasons	**Downtown**	24
Shanghai 1930	**Embarcadero**	20
Sierra Mar	**Big Sur/S**	26
Silks	**Downtown**	24
Slanted Door	**Embarcadero**	26
Straits Cafe	**Downtown**	20
Suppenküche	**Hayes Valley**	21
supperclub	**SoMa**	17
Terzo	**Cow Hollow**	22
Thanh Long	**Outer Sunset**	24
Tokyo Go Go	**Mission**	22
Tommy Toy's	**Downtown**	24
Townhouse B&G	**Emeryville/E**	21
Trader Vic's	**multi. loc.**	16
NEW TWO	**SoMa**	21
231 Ellsworth	**San Mateo/S**	23
NEW Ubuntu	**Napa/N**	–
Venticello	**Nob Hill**	23
NEW Vitrine	**SoMa**	–
NEW Vittoria	**Los Gatos/S**	20
Waterfront	**Embarcadero**	18
Wente Vineyards	**Livermore/E**	23
Wine Spectator	**St. Helena/N**	22
XYZ	**SoMa**	20
Yankee Pier	**Larkspur/N**	17

NEW Zazil Coastal	Downtown	19
Zibibbo	Palo Alto/S	20
Z Zuni Café	Hayes Valley	25

VIEWS

Z Ahwahnee	Yosemite/E	19
Albion River Inn	Albion/N	24
Alioto's	Fish. Wharf	19
Americano	Embarcadero	17
Angèle	Napa/N	22
Applewood Inn	Guerneville/N	24
A.P. Stump's	San Jose/S	21
A. Sabella's	Fish. Wharf	18
Z Auberge du Sol.	Rutherford/N	25
Barbara Fish	Princeton Sea/S	19
Barndiva	Healdsburg/N	18
Beach Chalet	Outer Sunset	13
Bella Vista	Woodside/S	22
Bistro Boudin	Fish. Wharf	20
Bistro Don Giovanni	Napa/N	23
Blackhawk Grille	Danville/E	19
Boulette's Larder	Embarcadero	25
Bridgetender	Tahoe City/E	16
BRIX	Yountville/N	22
Cafe Beaujolais	Mendocino/N	25
Cafe Gibraltar	El Granada/S	25
Caprice	Tiburon/N	21
Carnelian Room	Downtown	17
Chaya Brasserie	Embarcadero	21
Cheesecake	Downtown	16
Chez TJ	Mtn View/S	25
Christy Hill	Tahoe City/E	25
Cliff House Bistro	Outer Rich	18
Club XIX	Pebble Bch/S	25
Cottonwood	Truckee/E	20
Cucina Paradiso	Petaluma/N	26
Delancey St.	Embarcadero	18
Dragonfly	Truckee/E	23
Dry Creek	Healdsburg/N	24
Duck Club	multi. loc.	20
Enrico's	N Beach	–
Eos Rest./Wine	Cole Valley	23
Z Erna's Elderberry	Oakhurst/E	28
Étoile	Yountville/N	25
Z Farmhouse	Forestville/N	27
Fish	Sausalito/N	24
Z Frascati	Russian Hill	26
Z Fresh Cream	Monterey/S	24
Gar Woods	Carnelian Bay/E	19

Gaylord India	Sausalito/N	18
Z Greens	Marina	24
Guaymas	Tiburon/N	17
Heritage House	Little River/N	–
Hog Island Oyster	Embarcadero	25
Z Il Fornaio	Carmel/S	19
Imperial/Berkeley	Berkeley/E	17
Jake's/Lake	Tahoe City/E	16
John Ash & Co.	Santa Rosa/N	23
Jordan's	Berkeley/E	18
Julia's	Napa/N	23
Julius Castle	Telegraph Hill	–
Kenwood	Kenwood/N	22
La Forêt	San Jose/S	27
Lark Creek Inn	Larkspur/N	23
NEW La Terrasse	Presidio	19
Ledford Hse.	Albion/N	23
Lion & Compass	Sunnyvale/S	19
Little River Inn	Little River/N	20
Z Mama's Wash. Sq.	N Beach	25
Z Marinus	Carmel Valley/S	26
MarketBar	Embarcadero	17
McCormick/Kuleto	Fish. Wharf	19
Meadowood	St. Helena/N	20
Medjool	Mission	18
Mendocino Hotel	Mendocino/N	17
Mezza Luna	Princeton Sea/S	21
Mijita	Embarcadero	20
Mistral	Redwood Shores/S	19
MoMo's	S Beach	17
Moosse Café	Mendocino/N	23
Mo's	SoMa	20
Napa General	Napa/N	20
Napa Valley Grille	Yountville/N	20
Napa Wine Train	Napa/N	15
Z Navio	Half Moon Bay/S	26
Nepenthe	Big Sur/S	16
One Market	Embarcadero	22
Ora	Mill Valley/N	21
Ozumo	Embarcadero	24
Z Pacific's Edge	Carmel/S	25
Park Chalet	Outer Sunset	15
Piatti	multi. loc.	19
Picco	Larkspur/N	24
Z Pizzeria Picco	Larkspur/N	25
Poggio	Sausalito/N	21
Press	St. Helena/N	23
Ravens Rest.	Mendocino/N	23

Red's Java | **Embarcadero** 14

Rest. at Meadowood | 23
St. Helena/N

Rest. at Stevenswood | 20
Little River/N

River Ranch | **Tahoe City/E** 17

Z Rivoli | **Berkeley/E** 27

Rogue Chefs | **Half Moon Bay/S** 21

Rotunda | **Downtown** 20

Roy's | **Pebble Bch/S** 25

Salute E Rist. | **Richmond/E** 19

Scoma's | **multi. loc.** 21

Scott's | **Oakland/E** 19

Z Shadowbrook | **Capitola/S** 22

Sharon's | **Ft Bragg/N** 20

Z Sierra Mar | **Big Sur/S** 26

Z Slanted Door | **Embarcadero** 26

Sol y Lago | **Tahoe City/E** 17

St. Orres | **Gualala/N** 24

Sutro's | **Outer Rich** 19

Trader Vic's | **multi. loc.** 16

Venticello | **Nob Hill** 23

Waterfront | **Embarcadero** 18

Wente Vineyards | **Livermore/E** 23

Wine Spectator | **St. Helena/N** 22

Wolfdale's | **Tahoe City/E** 25

zazu | **Santa Rosa/N** 25

VISITORS ON EXPENSE ACCOUNT

Z Acquerello | **Polk Gulch** 27

Z Alexander's | **Cupertino/S** 25

Z Aqua | **Downtown** 26

Z Auberge du Sol. | **Rutherford/N** 25

Azie | **SoMa** 19

Z Boulevard | **Embarcadero** 27

Campton Place | **Downtown** 25

Carnelian Room | **Downtown** 17

Z Chez Panisse | **Berkeley/E** 27

Chez TJ | **Mtn View/S** 25

Club XIX | **Pebble Bch/S** 25

Z Cyrus | **Healdsburg/N** 28

Deetjen's | **Big Sur/S** 22

Dry Creek | **Healdsburg/N** 24

Z Erna's Elderberry | **Oakhurst/E** 28

Eulipia | **San Jose/S** 20

Z Evvia | **Palo Alto/S** 26

Fifth Floor | **SoMa** 25

Flea St. Café | **Menlo Pk/S** 22

Z Fleur de Lys | **Nob Hill** 28

Forbes Mill Steak | **Los Gatos/S** 23

Z French Laundry | **Yountville/N** 29

Z Fresh Cream | **Monterey/S** 24

Z Gary Danko | **Fish. Wharf** 29

Z Greens | **Marina** 24

Harris' | **Polk Gulch** 25

Jack Falstaff | **SoMa** 20

Z Jardinière | **Hayes Valley** 26

John Ash & Co. | **Santa Rosa/N** 23

Z Kaygetsu | **Menlo Pk/S** 28

Z Kokkari | **Downtown** 26

Kyo-Ya | **Downtown** 23

Z La Folie | **Russian Hill** 27

La Forêt | **San Jose/S** 27

Lark Creek Inn | **Larkspur/N** 23

Z La Toque | **Rutherford/N** 26

Z L'Auberge | **Carmel/S** 27

Z Manresa | **Los Gatos/S** 27

Z Marinus | **Carmel Valley/S** 26

Z Masa's | **Downtown** 27

McCormick/Kuleto | **Fish. Wharf** 19

Z Michael Mina | **Downtown** 28

Morton's | **Downtown** 23

Napa Wine Train | **Napa/N** 15

Oliveto Restaurant | **Oakland/E** 25

Z Pacific's Edge | **Carmel/S** 25

Park Grill | **Downtown** 20

Plumed Horse | **Saratoga/S** -

Press | **St. Helena/N** 23

Rest. at Meadowood | 23
St. Helena/N

Z Ritz-Carlton Din. Rm. | **Nob Hill** 27

Z Ritz-Carlton Terr. | **Nob Hill** 24

Roy's | **SoMa** 22

Roy's | **Pebble Bch/S** 25

Santé | **Sonoma/N** 24

Seasons | **Downtown** 24

Sent Sovi | **Saratoga/S** 24

71 Saint Peter | **San Jose/S** 22

Shanghai 1930 | **Embarcadero** 20

Z Sierra Mar | **Big Sur/S** 26

Z Silks | **Downtown** 24

Sino | **San Jose/S** 20

Tommy Toy's | **Downtown** 24

Village Pub | **Woodside/S** 26

NEW West Co. Grill | -
Sebastopol/N

WINE BARS

All Season's | **Calistoga/N**	21
🔢 A 16 | **Marina**	23
bacar | **SoMa**	22
NEW Bar Bambino | **Mission**	–
Bar Tartine | **Mission**	22
Bouchée | **Carmel/S**	26
Bounty Hunter | **Napa/N**	17
Café Marcella | **Los Gatos/S**	24
Cantinetta Luca | **Carmel/S**	22
Carneros Bistro | **Sonoma/N**	22
Cav Wine Bar | **Hayes Valley**	22
Cork | **Sausalito/N**	19
Cucina Paradiso | **Petaluma/N**	26
Cucina Rest. | **San Anselmo/N**	24
NEW District | **SoMa**	17
El Paseo | **Mill Valley/N**	23
Eos Rest./Wine | **Cole Valley**	23
1550 Hyde | **Russian Hill**	22
fig cafe | **Glen Ellen/N**	23
🔢 Frascati | **Russian Hill**	26
girl & the fig | **Sonoma/N**	23
Incanto | **Noe Valley**	24
NEW Jovino | **Cow Hollow**	–
Kuleto's | **Downtown**	20
🔢 La Toque | **Rutherford/N**	26
Le Zinc | **Noe Valley**	18
Liberty Cafe | **Bernal Hts**	22
Martini House | **St. Helena/N**	25
Maverick | **Mission**	22
🔢 Millennium | **Downtown**	24
Napa General | **Napa/N**	20
Napa Wine Train | **Napa/N**	15
Nectar Wine | **multi. loc.**	19
NEW Nua Rest. | **N Beach**	–
Ottimista | **Cow Hollow**	20
Pearl Alley | **Santa Cruz/S**	22
Picco | **Larkspur/N**	24
Prima | **Walnut Creek/E**	24
Rest. LuLu/Petite | **SoMa**	20
Richmond Rest. | **Inner Rich**	22
Rogue Chefs | **Half Moon Bay/S**	21
Sabor of Spain | **San Rafael/N**	18
Sociale | **Presidio Hts**	23
🔢 Sushi Ran | **Sausalito/N**	28
🔢 Tartine | **Mission**	26
Va de Vi | **Walnut Creek/E**	24
Vivande | **Pacific Hts**	23

Wente Vineyards | **Livermore/E**	23
Willi's Seafood | **Healdsburg/N**	23
Willi's Wine | **Santa Rosa/N**	24
Yabbies Coastal | **Russian Hill**	22
Zibibbo | **Palo Alto/S**	20
Zin | **Healdsburg/N**	22

WINNING WINE LISTS

Absinthe | **Hayes Valley**	20
Acme Chophouse | **S Beach**	19
À Côté | **Oakland/E**	24
🔢 Acquerello | **Polk Gulch**	27
Albion River Inn | **Albion/N**	24
NEW Alembic | **Haight-Ashbury**	22
🔢 Alexander's | **Cupertino/S**	25
Alioto's | **Fish. Wharf**	19
All Season's | **Calistoga/N**	21
🔢 Ame | **SoMa**	26
Angèle | **Napa/N**	22
Anton & Michel | **Carmel/S**	23
A.P. Stump's | **San Jose/S**	21
🔢 Aqua | **Downtown**	26
🔢 A 16 | **Marina**	23
🔢 Auberge du Sol. | **Rutherford/N**	25
Azie | **SoMa**	19
bacar | **SoMa**	22
NEW Bar Bambino | **Mission**	–
Bar Tartine | **Mission**	22
🔢 Bay Wolf | **Oakland/E**	25
Bella Vista | **Woodside/S**	22
Bistro Aix | **Marina**	22
Bistro Clovis | **Hayes Valley**	19
Bistro Don Giovanni | **Napa/N**	23
Bistro Ralph | **Healdsburg/N**	21
Blackhawk Grille | **Danville/E**	19
🔢 Bocadillos | **N Beach**	22
Bouchée | **Carmel/S**	26
🔢 Bouchon | **Yountville/N**	25
🔢 Boulevard | **Embarcadero**	27
Bridges | **Danville/E**	20
BRIX | **Yountville/N**	22
CAFÉ KATi | **Japantown**	23
🔢 Cafe La Haye | **Sonoma/N**	26
Campton Place | **Downtown**	25
Cantinetta Luca | **Carmel/S**	22
Carnelian Room | **Downtown**	17
Carneros Bistro | **Sonoma/N**	22
Casanova | **Carmel/S**	23
Cav Wine Bar | **Hayes Valley**	22

Celadon | **Napa/N**	23
Central Market | **Petaluma/N**	23
César | **Berkeley/E**	22
Cetrella | **Half Moon Bay/S**	22
Z Chapeau! | **Outer Rich**	27
Z Chez Panisse | **Berkeley/E**	27
Z Chez Panisse Café | **Berkeley/E**	27
Chez TJ | **Mtn View/S**	25
Citron | **Oakland/E**	24
Club XIX | **Pebble Bch/S**	25
Z Cole's Chop Hse. | **Napa/N**	25
Cork | **Sausalito/N**	19
Côté Sud | **Castro**	20
Cuvée | **Napa/N**	20
Z Cyrus | **Healdsburg/N**	28
Deuce | **Sonoma/N**	20
NEW Dio Deka | **Los Gatos/S**	-
NEW District | **SoMa**	17
downtown | **Berkeley/E**	20
Dry Creek | **Healdsburg/N**	24
El Paseo | **Mill Valley/N**	23
Eos Rest./Wine | **Cole Valley**	23
Z Erna's Elderberry | **Oakhurst/E**	28
Étoile | **Yountville/N**	25
Fandango | **Pacific Grove/S**	23
Z Farallon | **Downtown**	24
NEW Z Farm | **Napa/N**	23
Z Farmhouse | **Forestville/N**	27
1550 Hyde | **Russian Hill**	22
Fifth Floor | **SoMa**	25
fig cafe | **Glen Ellen/N**	23
Flea St. Café | **Menlo Pk/S**	22
Z Fleur de Lys | **Nob Hill**	28
Forbes Mill Steak | **multi. loc.**	23
Fournou's | **Nob Hill**	22
Z French Laundry | **Yountville/N**	29
Frisson | **Downtown**	20
Gabriella Café | **Santa Cruz/S**	22
Z Gary Danko | **Fish. Wharf**	29
General's | **Sonoma/N**	-
girl & the fig | **Sonoma/N**	23
Grasing's Coastal | **Carmel/S**	23
Z Greens | **Marina**	24
NEW Hime | **Marina**	22
Incanto | **Noe Valley**	24
Indigo | **Civic Ctr**	20
Jack Falstaff | **SoMa**	20
Z Jardinière | **Hayes Valley**	26

Jeanty at Jack's | **Downtown**	2.
John Ash & Co. | **Santa Rosa/N**	23
Julia's | **Napa/N**	23
Kenwood | **Kenwood/N**	22
Z Kokkari | **Downtown**	26
Kuleto's | **multi. loc.**	20
Kurt's Carmel | **Carmel/S**	23
Z La Folie | **Russian Hill**	27
La Forêt | **San Jose/S**	27
NEW Laïola | **Marina**	-
Lark Creek Inn | **Larkspur/N**	23
NEW Lark Creek Steak | **Downtown**	22
LaSalette | **Sonoma/N**	23
Z La Toque | **Rutherford/N**	26
Z L'Auberge | **Carmel/S**	27
Lavanda | **Palo Alto/S**	19
Ledford Hse. | **Albion/N**	23
Z Le Papillon | **San Jose/S**	27
Liberty Cafe | **Bernal Hts**	22
Luella | **Russian Hill**	22
Z Madrona Manor | **Healdsburg/N**	25
Z Manresa | **Los Gatos/S**	27
Manzanita | **Healdsburg/N**	20
Z Marché | **Menlo Pk/S**	26
Z Marinus | **Carmel Valley/S**	26
Martini House | **St. Helena/N**	25
Z Masa's | **Downtown**	27
Meadowood | **St. Helena/N**	20
Mecca | **Castro**	20
Mendo Bistro | **Ft Bragg/N**	25
Z Michael Mina | **Downtown**	28
Z Millennium | **Downtown**	24
Monti's | **Santa Rosa/N**	19
Montrio Bistro | **Monterey/S**	23
Moose's | **N Beach**	20
Mosaic Rest. | **Forestville/N**	25
Mustards Grill | **Yountville/N**	24
Z Myth | **Downtown**	26
Naomi Sushi | **Menlo Pk/S**	21
Napa Valley Grille | **Yountville/N**	20
Napa Wine Train | **Napa/N**	15
Z Navio | **Half Moon Bay/S**	26
Nectar Wine | **Burlingame/S**	19
NEW Nick's Cove | **Marshall/N**	-
955 Ukiah | **Mendocino/N**	22
North Beach Rest. | **N Beach**	21

NEW Nua Rest. | N Beach	-
Lv. Rest. | Napa/N	22
Oliveto Cafe | Oakland/E	23
Oliveto Restaurant | Oakland/E	25
One Market | Embarcadero	22
Ottimista | Cow Hollow	20
Z Pacific's Edge | Carmel/S	25
Palio d'Asti | Downtown	19
Pangaea | Gualala/N	25
Park Grill | Downtown	20
Passionfish | Pacific Grove/S	25
Pearl Alley | Santa Cruz/S	22
Picco | Larkspur/N	24
Pilar | Napa/N	25
Z Piperade | Downtown	25
Plumed Horse | Saratoga/S	-
PlumpJack | multi. loc.	24
Poggio | Sausalito/N	21
Z Postrio | Downtown	24
Prima | Walnut Creek/E	24
Z Quince | Pacific Hts	26
Z Redd Rest. | Yountville/N	26
Rest. at Meadowood | St. Helena/N	23
Rest. LuLu/Petite | SoMa	20
Rio Grill | Carmel/S	22
Z Ritz-Carlton Din. Rm. | Nob Hill	27
Z Rivoli | Berkeley/E	27
Rose Pistola | N Beach	21
NEW Rouge/Blanc | Downtown	-
Roy's | SoMa	22
Roy's | Pebble Bch/S	25
Rubicon | Downtown	24
Sabor of Spain | San Rafael/N	18
Santé | Sonoma/N	24
Santi | Geyserville/N	23
Sardine Factory | Monterey/S	20
Scala's Bistro | Downtown	22
Seasons | Downtown	24
Sent Sovi | Saratoga/S	24
Z Sierra Mar | Big Sur/S	26
Z Silks | Downtown	24
Z Slanted Door | Embarcadero	25
Sol y Lago | Tahoe City/E	17
St. Michael's | Palo Alto/S	22
St. Orres | Gualala/N	24
Sushi Groove | multi. loc.	23
Z Sushi Ran | Sausalito/N	28

Syrah | Santa Rosa/N	25
Z Terra | St. Helena/N	26
Terzo | Cow Hollow	22
Theo's | Soquel/S	24
Town Hall | SoMa	23
Tra Vigne | St. Helena/N	23
NEW TWO | SoMa	21
231 Ellsworth | San Mateo/S	23
Va de Vi | Walnut Creek/E	24
Vic Stewart's | Walnut Creek/E	21
Village Pub | Woodside/S	26
Viognier | San Mateo/S	24
Wappo Bar | Calistoga/N	22
Wente Vineyards | Livermore/E	23
NEW West Co. Grill | Sebastopol/N	-
Willi's Seafood | Healdsburg/N	23
Wine Spectator | St. Helena/N	22
Yabbies Coastal | Russian Hill	22
Zibibbo | Palo Alto/S	20
Zin | Healdsburg/N	22
Zinsvalley | Napa/N	20
Z Zuni Café | Hayes Valley	25

WORTH A TRIP

Albion
Albion River Inn	24
Ledford Hse.	23

Berkeley
César	22
Z Chez Panisse	27
Z Chez Panisse Café	27
Lalime's	26
Z Rivoli	27
Zachary's Pizza	24

Big Sur
Deetjen's	22
Z Sierra Mar	26

Carmel
Bouchée	26
Cantinetta Luca	22
Z L'Auberge	27
Z Marinus	26
Z Pacific's Edge	25

El Granada
Cafe Gibraltar	25

Forestville
Z Farmhouse	27
Mosaic Rest.	25

subscribe to zagat.com

SPECIAL FEATURES

subscribe to zagat.com

ALPHABETICAL
PAGE INDEX

All places are in San Francisco unless otherwise noted (East of San
Francisco=E; North of San Francisco=N; South of San Francisco=S).

e at zagat.com   321

Wine Vintage Chart

This chart, based on our 0 to 30 scale, is designed to help you select wine. The ratings (by **Howard Stravitz,** a law professor at the University of South Carolina) reflect the vintage quality and the wine's readiness to drink. We exclude the 1987, 1991–1993 vintages because they are not that good. A dash indicates the wine is either past its peak or too young to rate.

Whites	86	88	89	90	94	95	96	97	98	99	00	01	02	03	04	05
French:																
Alsace	–	–	26	26	25	24	24	23	26	24	26	27	25	22	24	25
Burgundy	25	–	23	22	–	28	27	24	23	26	25	24	27	23	25	26
Loire Valley	–	–	–	–	–	–	–	–	–	24	25	26	23	24	25
Champagne	25	24	26	29	–	26	27	24	23	24	24	22	26	–	–	–
Sauternes	28	29	25	28	–	21	23	25	23	24	24	28	25	26	21	26
California:																
Chardonnay	–	–	–	–	–	–	–	–	24	23	26	26	27	28	29	
Sauvignon Blanc	–	–	–	–	–	–	–	–	–	–	27	28	26	27	26	
Austrian:																
Grüner Velt./ Riesling	–	–	–	–	–	25	21	28	28	27	22	23	24	26	26	26
German:	–	25	26	27	24	23	26	25	26	23	21	29	27	25	26	26

Reds	86	88	89	90	94	95	96	97	98	99	00	01	02	03	04	05
French:																
Bordeaux	25	23	25	29	22	26	25	23	25	24	29	26	24	25	23	27
Burgundy	–	–	24	26	–	26	27	26	22	27	22	24	27	24	24	25
Rhône	–	26	28	28	24	26	22	24	27	26	27	26	–	25	24	–
Beaujolais	–	–	–	–	–	–	–	–	–	–	24	–	23	27	23	28
California:																
Cab./Merlot	–	–	–	28	29	27	25	28	23	26	22	27	26	25	24	24
Pinot Noir	–	–	–	–	–	–	–	24	23	24	23	27	28	26	23	–
Zinfandel	–	–	–	–	–	–	–	–	–	–	–	25	23	27	22	–
Oregon:																
Pinot Noir	–	–	–	–	–	–	–	–	–	–	–	26	27	24	25	–
Italian:																
Tuscany	–	–	–	25	22	24	20	29	24	27	24	26	20	–	–	–
Piedmont	–	–	27	27	–	23	26	27	26	25	28	27	20	–	–	–
Spanish:																
Rioja	–	–	–	–	26	26	24	25	22	25	24	27	20	24	25	–
Ribera del Duero/Priorat	–	–	–	–	26	26	27	25	24	25	24	27	20	24	26	–
Australian:																
Shiraz/Cab.	–	–	–	–	24	26	23	26	28	24	24	27	27	25	26	–